D1810736

THE
ELDER DEMPSTER
FLEET HISTORY
1852–1985

JAMES E. COWDEN

JOHN O. C. DUFFY

Also by J. E. Cowden

The Course I Steered 1939–1948 (Published privately)

The Price of Peace—Elder Dempster 1939–1945

ISBN 0 9509453 1 5

© 1986 James E. Cowden and John O. C. Duffy

All rights reserved. No part of this publication may be
reproduced or transmitted in any form or by any means,
electronic or mechanical, including photocopy, recording, or any
information storage and retrieval system, without permission
in writing from the publisher and copyright holders.

 Computer typeset and printed by Page Bros (Norwich) Ltd

Bound by Dorstel Press Ltd, Harlow

FOREWORD

I am very pleased to commend this history of the Elder Dempster Lines fleet to readers. The preparation of the book has been a labour of love for James Cowden and John Duffy, both of whom are former seafarers. Now, after 8 years of research and writing, they have produced what I believe is probably the most comprehensive history of a major British liner shipping fleet. The company is indebted to them for their dedication in setting out a unique record which complements splendidly *The Trade Makers*, a book on the company's commercial history, written by Dr P. N. Davies 12 years ago.

Since the Elder Dempster story began in 1852 with the sailing of *Forerunner*, the company has made significant contribution to the development of trade between West Africa and the rest of the world. Containerisation and other factors have meant that the size of our fleet has been sharply reduced in recent years. Elder Dempster Lines, however, is still a leader in shipping to West Africa, working in close cooperation with the National Lines of the various West African countries.

It is a particular pleasure to write this Foreword, since I served in various Elder Dempster ships between 1951 and 1965. Thus I have personal knowledge of our seafarers' professionalism and devotion to duty, without which there might not be a fleet history to write about. The contribution made by our seafarers was never greater than in two world wars, when so many officers and ratings gave their lives in the service of their country.

The following pages form a fine reference book, a collector's item for those interested in Britain's maritime history, but the book is more than that—it is a monument to the work of staff, afloat and ashore, who have served Elder Dempster down the years. It will also be an inspiration for all those serving the company today and in the future.

Kenneth H. Birch
Managing Director, Elder Dempster Lines Ltd

This photograph, taken aboard **ABINSI** around 1922, was presented to J. E. Cowden by Captain Wise in 1981. Captain Wise is one of the two apprentices seated on the deck. The photograph bears the autographs of Captain J. B. Wright, of Chief Officer W. Minns, who lost his life when **SEAFORTH** was sunk in World War II, and Second Officer C. H. Sweeny, whose career culminated in his appointment as Commodore of Elder Dempster Lines Ltd

CONTENTS

LAKE MANITOBA (*ship No. 464*), *in late 1902 as Boer War Transport No. 23* (Photo Ship Society of South Africa, Leendertz Collection)

ROYAL CHARTER GRANTED TO THE AFRICAN STEAMSHIP COMPANY—1852

VICTORIA, by the Grace of God, of the United Kingdom of Great Britain and Ireland Queen, Defender of the Faith, To ALL TO WHOM THESE PRESENTS SHALL COME, GREETING:— Whereas it has been represented to Us that the persons hereinafter named, and others, have agreed to form a Company in copartnership, for the purpose of establishing and maintaining a postal and other communication, by means of steam navigation, between Great Britain and Ireland and the West Coast of Africa, and elsewhere, and have already expended and invested, or agreed to pay, the sum of £83,800 and upwards, in acquiring certain steam vessels and other effects, and for the purpose of fulfilling a contract made for the conveyance of Government Mails: And that the said parties propose to raise a capital, as hereinafter mentioned, for the purpose of carrying on the business of the said undertaking, and have humbly besought Us to grant to them, and the other subscribers of such capital, Our Charter of Incorporation, which We are minded to do on the conditions hereinafter mentioned: Now know ye that as well upon the prayer of the said persons, as also of Our special grace, certain knowledge, and mere motion, We by these presents for Us, Our heirs and successors, do give, grant, make, ordain, constitute, declare and appoint, that Macgregor Laird, of Fenchurch Street, ship owner, John Forster, of New City Chambers, merchant, and William Law Ogilby, of Ingram Court, ship and insurance broker, together with such and so many other persons or bodies, politic or corporate, as have become, or from time to time hereafter shall become, members of the said Copartnership or Company so agreed to be formed, and shall take and hold shares therein of not less than £20 each in the capital of the said Company, shall be one body politic or corporate in deed and in name, by the name of "The African Steam Ship Company," for the purposes hereinafter named, and by that name shall and may sue and be sued, implead and be impleaded, in all courts, whether of law or equity, as well in Our United Kingdom of Great Britain and Ireland as in Our Colonial possessions or elsewhere, and shall have perpetual succession, with a common seal, which may be by them changed and varied at their pleasure, but subject to the directions and provisions in this Our Royal Charter contained: And We do declare that the said Company shall be established for the purpose of purchasing, providing, hiring, and employing ships or vessels, to be impelled by steam power or other motive power, with all engines, machinery, articles, matters, and things necessary for the same, and for the purposes of conveying goods and passengers, and for the carriage of mails, and for establishing communication with the West Coast of Africa, and also of establishing a communication between such West Coast and the British West Indies, with power on any outward or homeward voyage from the West Coast of Africa to call at any port of Portugal, or at any port of France or Spain not eastward of the Straits of Gibraltar, and for the purpose of carrying on all such businesses as is usually carried on by owners of ships employed in carrying goods, mails, and passengers, with power to the said Company to carry on any business for the purpose of land transit connected with the said businesses as aforesaid: And We do further declare and ordain that the capital of the said Company shall consist, in the first instance, of the sum of £250,000, including the amount already expended and invested in acquiring the aforesaid ships and effects as aforesaid, and in obtaining the said contract with the Government, to be subscribed in 12,500 shares of £20 each, and that such capital may be increased under the circumstances and in manner hereinafter mentioned: And further We do declare and ordain that the Board of Directors of the said Company, to be constituted and provided by the deed hereinafter directed to be executed, shall have full power and authority to enter into all contracts on behalf of the said Company, and to make and execute all purchases, sales, assurances, and other acts to which the corporate seal shall be required to be affixed, and generally to do all acts which they shall consider necessary for the well ordering the affairs of the said Company, and to execute all the powers in relation to the said Company, and to bind the said Company as if the same were done with the assent of the whole body, so as the same be done in conformity with the provisions of these presents and of the deed hereinafter mentioned: And We further will and ordain that the said Board of Directors shall have power to order and dispose of the custody of the common seal of the said Company: And We do further ordain and grant that it shall be lawful for the said Company to purchase, take, hold, and enjoy to them and their successors, as well in Our United Kingdom as in Our Colonial possessions and other places beyond the seas such wharfs, docks, houses, offices, buildings, lands, and other hereditaments as shall from time to time be necessary or proper for the purpose of managing, conducting, and carrying on the affairs, concerns, and business of the said Company, but not for any other purposes, and particularly not for the purpose of reselling the same, nor so as to be in any manner made instrumental for the purposes of speculation, but nevertheless with power to sell, convey, and dispose of the same respectively when not wanted for the purposes of the said business, but this as between the Crown and the Company is not to enlarge their powers: Provided always that the yearly value of such wharfs, docks, houses, offices, buildings, lands, and other hereditaments within the United Kingdom of Great Britain and Ireland at the time when the said Company shall enter into possession thereof, shall not exceed in the whole the sum of £1000, unless the said Company shall have the special license of Ourselves, Our heirs or successors, to purchase or hold any lands, tenements, or hereditaments of a greater yearly value: And We do hereby grant unto all and every person and persons and bodies politic or corporate, who are or shall be otherwise competent, Our special license and authority to grant, sell, demise, assign, alien, and convey in Mortmain, unto and to the use of the said Company and their successors, any such wharfs, docks, houses, offices, buildings, lands and other hereditaments and property whatsoever as aforesaid accordingly, hereby nevertheless declaring that it shall not be necessary for such persons or bodies or any purchasers from the said Company to enquire as to the amount of the income of the property which may have been previously acquired by the said Company: And We do hereby direct that the members for the time being of the said Company shall within one year from the date of these presents enter into and execute a proper deed of copartnership and settlement, whereby the capital of the said Company, including the amount so expended and invested as aforesaid, shall be divided into the aforesaid number of shares, to be numbered in regular succession, beginning from one upwards, and whereby all the members for the time being of the said Company shall enter into proper covenants for the payment of such portion of the said Capital as shall remain unpaid for the time being, and as and when the same shall be called for by the Directors having the management of the affairs of the said Company, and whereby provision shall be made for the registration of the names of all the members from time to time in proper books to be provided for that purpose, and for the management of the affairs of the said Company by a Board of Directors, such Directors in the first instance appointed in the said deed, and afterwards to be elected by the shareholders in general meeting assembled, and wherein shall also be inserted provision for the election by the shareholders of two Auditors of the accounts of the said Company, and also such other clauses and provisions as may be usual and expedient in the like cases: And We do further direct that in the said deed shall be contained a provision for the producing at the ordinary meetings of the said Company a true and correct balance sheet, such as is usual in mercantile accounts, and also an absolute provision for the dissolution of the said Company when and as it shall appear in the opinion of the Board of Directors or of the Auditors that three-fourths of the subscribed capital or joint stock of the said Company shall have been lost in the course of trade or otherwise, and for the winding up the affairs of the said Company, and also for the furnishing annually to the President of the Committee of Our Privy Council appointed for the consideration of all matters relating to trade and foreign plantations (commonly and hereinafter called the Board of Trade), copies of such balance sheet and also such other accounts as may from time to time be required by the President of the Board of Trade: And We do hereby further direct that such deed of settlement shall be prepared to the satisfaction of the President of the Board of Trade, and that a copy of such deed shall within the aforesaid period of one year be lodged with the said Board of Trade, and that a certificate to that effect, indorsed on this Our Royal Charter, under the hand of one of the Secretaries of the said Board of Trade, or under the hand of such other person as shall be empowered in that behalf by the President of the said Board for the time being, shall be conclusive evidence that the said deed of settlement has been duly prepared, and a copy thereof deposited in accordance with Our directions in that behalf above contained, but such certificate shall not be given until it has been made to appear to the President of the Board of Trade, either by the certificate of at least three of the Directors of the said Company or otherwise as he shall require, that all the Directors for the time being, and at least two-thirds of the number of the members for the time being, of the said Company, holding at least half the capital of the said Company, and each of such shareholders holding at least three shares have executed the same: And We do hereby further declare that it shall be lawful for the shareholders of the said Company, present at two successive general or extraordinary general meetings duly convened with the sanction of five at least of the Directors, for the purpose under the provisions to be contained in the aforesaid deed, and with an interval not exceeding one calendar month from time to time, to make all or any by-laws for regulating and conducting the affairs of the Company, except so far as the same may be repugnant to the provisions of this Our Royal Charter, or the laws of Our Realm or of any of Our Colonial possessions or dependencies where the operations of the said Company may be carried on: Provided nevertheless that no by-law that may be made shall have any force or effect until the same shall have been approved of by the President of the Board of Trade, and notice of such approval shall have been given under his hand or under the hand of one of the Secretaries of the said Board: And We do hereby further direct that the said Company shall not carry on the said business until it shall have been made to appear to the President of the Board of Trade, either by the certificate of at least three of the Directors of the said Company or otherwise as he shall direct, that at least one-half of the said Capital of £250,000 has been subscribed for under hand and seal by parties, each of whom shall hold at least three of the said £20 shares in the said capital, and that at least £50,000 has been paid up or has been expended and is then invested in the said steam vessels and other effects which shall at that time have become the property of the said Company, and the certificate of the President of the Board of Trade endorsed on this Our Royal Charter shall be sufficient evidence that the above provisions have been complied with: And We do hereby further declare that after it shall have been certified or shown to the President of the Board of Trade in like manner as last aforesaid, that the whole of the said capital of £250,000 has been subscribed for, and that at least one-half of the said capital has been paid up, it shall be lawful for the said Company by a resolution or resolutions of the shareholders in general meeting assembled, according to the provisions to be in that behalf contained in such deed as aforesaid, either at one time or from time to time, to determine that the capital of the said Company shall be increased to the sum of £500,000, and to any sum beyond the said sum of £500,000 not exceeding £1,000,000 sterling, but so as no increase beyond the said sum of £500,000 shall be made except with the consent in writing of the said President of the Board of Trade first had and obtained: Provided always, and We do hereby will and declare, that in case the said Company shall fail to enter into and execute such deed of settlement as aforesaid, and to deposit a copy thereof within the period before limited in that behalf and subject as aforesaid, or in case the said Company shall not comply with any other the directions and conditions of this Our Royal Charter contained, or if the said Company, after they shall have begun to run vessels to some part of the West Coast of Africa, shall, for the space of one whole year, cease to run any vessel to the West Coast of Africa for the purposes aforesaid, it shall be lawful for Us, Our heirs and successors, by any writing under the Great Seal of Us, Our heirs or successors, to revoke and make void this Our Royal Charter, and every clause, matter and thing herein contained, either absolutely or under such terms and conditions as We or they shall think fit: Provided also, that notwithstanding anything herein contained, it shall be lawful for Us, Our heirs and successors, either under the Great Seal of Us, Our heirs or successors, at any period after the expiration of thirty-one years from the date of these presents, to revoke and make void this Our Royal Charter and every clause, matter and thing therein contained, or to add such modifications, conditions or provisions thereto as We, Our heirs or successors shall think fit: And We do hereby declare, that when the said Company shall have been dissolved, in pursuance of the provisions hereinbefore contained, or if the said Company shall, for two years consecutively, cease to carry on the aforesaid trade, and when the affairs of the Company shall have been completely wound up and its debts and obligations fully discharged, this Our Royal Charter shall be absolutely void: And we do hereby direct, that the aforesaid deed so directed to be prepared shall, within six calendar months from the date thereof, be enrolled in Our High Court of Chancery, and that any by-laws to be made by the said Company shall be, from time to time, enrolled in like manner within six calendar months from the making thereof: And We for Ourselves, Our heirs and successors do grant and declare that these Our Letters Patent or the enrolment thereof shall be in all things valid and effectual in the law, according to the true intent and meaning of the same, and shall be so recognized by all Our courts and judges in Our United Kingdom of Great Britain and Ireland, and in all Our colonies, possessions or dependencies, and elsewhere, and by the governors, consuls, and all other officers in any of the colonies, territories, dominions, or dependencies belonging to Us, Our heirs or successors, or upon the high seas or elsewhere, and all other officers, bodies politic or corporate whom it doth, shall or may concern, and that the same shall be taken, construed and adjudged in the most favourable and beneficial sense, and for the best advantage of the said Corporation, as well in Our several courts of record in Our United Kingdom of Great Britain and Ireland or elsewhere, notwithstanding any non-recital, mis-recital, uncertainty, or imperfection in these Our Letters Patent: And lastly, We do hereby require and enjoin all governors, consuls and other officers and persons for the time being, in Our colonial possessions or elsewhere, whom it may concern, to give full force and effect to these Our Letters Patent, and to be in all things aiding and abetting to the said Company and their successors: In witness whereof We have caused these Our Letters to be made Patent.

Witness Ourself at Our Palace at Westminster, this Seventh day of August, in the Sixteenth Year of Our Reign.

By Her Majesty's Command,
EDMUNDS.

An African Steam Ship Company vegetable dish, bearing the Company's crest

CHRONOLOGY OF COMPANIES FEATURED
IN THIS HISTORY

AFRICAN STEAMSHIP COMPANY	1852–1932	Shipowners. Managed by Elder Dempster from 1891.
BRITISH AND AFRICAN STEAM NAVIGATION COMPANY	1868–1883	Shipowners.
BRITISH AND AFRICAN STEAM NAVIGATION COMPANY LIMITED	1883–1932	Shipowners. In 1900 the Company was re-organised and retitled with the addition of (1900) before Limited but this minor detail was not generally used and has been disregarded.
ELDER, DEMPSTER AND COMPANY	1887–1910	Shipowners and Managers.
ELDER DEMPSTER SHIPPING LIMITED	1889–1910	Shipowners.
COMPANIA DE VAPORES CORREOS INTERINSULARES CANARIOS (Interinsular Mail Steamship Company Limited)	1892–1912	Shipowners. Las Palmas.
SIERRA LEONE COALING COMPANY LIMITED	1892–1932	Shipowners.
OCEAN TRANSPORT COMPANY LIMITED	1894–1903	Shipowners. Company owned by Harland & Wolff Limited and managed by Elder Dempster.
DOMINION LINE	1894	Bristol–Canada service only
BEAVER LINE	1898–1903	Shipowners.
IMPERIAL DIRECT WEST INDIA MAIL SERVICE COMPANY LIMITED	1901–1911	Shipowners. Jamaica Service.
BRISTOL LIGHTERAGE COMPANY LIMITED	1901–1903	Shipowners.
MERSEY TOWAGE AND LIGHTERAGE CO	1901–1903	Shipowners.
NIGERIAN DRYDOCK AND ENGINEERING COMPANY LIMITED	1905–date	Ship repairers.
ELDER, DEMPSTER AND COMPANY LIMITED	1910–1932	Shipowners and Managers.
ELDER LINE LIMITED	1910–1936	Shipowners.
IMPERIAL DIRECT LINE LIMITED	1911–1932	Shipowners. Successors to the IDWIMS but not involved in that trade.
NIGERIAN TRANSPORT COMPANY LIMITED	1928–1934	Shipowners.
WEST AFRICAN LIGHTERAGE AND TRANSPORT COMPANY LIMITED	1928–date	Shipowners.
ELDER DEMPSTER LINES LIMITED	1932–date	Shipowners. Formed to acquire fleets of the above named companies operating at that time.
ELDER DEMPSTER LINES (HOLDINGS) LIMITED	1936–1952	Holding Company for Elder Dempster Lines Ltd.
ELDER DEMPSTER LINES (CANADA) LIMITED	1946–1962	Shipowners. Canada–Cape Trade.
BRITISH AND BURMESE STEAM NAVIGATION COMPANY LIMITED (Henderson Line)	1952–date	Shipowners. Acquired by EDLHL in 1952. Ships variously employed on Burma or West African routes.
LINER HOLDINGS COMPANY LIMITED	1953–date	Holding Company. Successor to EDL(H)L.
GUINEA GULF LINE LIMITED	1965–date	Shipowners. Acquired by Liner Holdings Limited in 1965.
SEAWAY CAR TRANSPORTERS LIMITED	1967–1972	Shipowners. Acquired by Liner Holdings Limited in 1967.
OCEAN STEAMSHIP COMPANY LIMITED (incorporating Blue Funnel Line Ltd, China Mutual Steam Navigation Co Ltd, Glen Line Ltd, Nederlandsche Stoomvaart Maatschappij Oceaan)	1968–1973	Shipowners. Acquired Liner Holdings Limited and subsidiary companies in 1968.
SEAWAY FERRIES LIMITED	1972–date	Shipowners.
OCEAN TRANSPORT AND TRADING LIMITED	1973–1982	Shipowners and Holding Company.
OCEAN TRANSPORT AND TRADING PLC	1982–date	Shipowners and Holding Company.
PALM LINE LIMITED	1985–date	Shipowners. Acquired by Ocean Transport & Trading plc in 1985.

Note—The Compagnie Maritime Belge du Congo was founded on 24 January 1895, with 4150 of the original 4200 shares held by the African Steamship Company, whose Chairman P. W. Bond became the first President of the new concern. Other prominent founders included Alfred Lewis Jones, W. J. Pirrie of Harland & Wolff Ltd, and Sir Francis de Winton, a former Governor-General of The Congo Free State. On the Belgian side the founders included three shipbrokers, G. de Baerdemaecker, of Ghent, and P. Walford and J. Pickard, both of Antwerp.

FUNNEL COLOURS AND FLAG DESIGNS

	Funnel	Flag
AFRICAN STEAMSHIP COMPANY ELDER, DEMPSTER AND COMPANY ELDER, DEMPSTER AND COMPANY LIMITED ELDER DEMPSTER SHIPPING COMPANY ELDER LINE LIMITED NIGERIAN DRY DOCK AND ENGINEERING COMPANY LIMITED NIGERIAN TRANSPORT COMPANY LIMITED ELDER DEMPSTER LINES LIMITED ELDER DEMPSTER LINES (CANADA) LIMITED IMPERIAL DIRECT WEST INDIA MAIL STEAMSHIP COMPANY LIMITED IMPERIAL DIRECT LINE LIMITED OCEAN TRANSPORT COMPANY LIMITED COMPANIA DE VAPORES CORREOS INTERINSULAR CANARIOS WEST AFRICAN LIGHTERAGE AND TRANSPORT COMPANY LIMITED SEAWAY CAR TRANSPORTERS LIMITED SEAWAY FERRIES LIMITED	Buff	White swallowtail, red cross, gold crown in centre
BRITISH AND AFRICAN STEAM NAVIGATION COMPANY	Black	Blue swallowtail, white cross
BRITISH AND AFRICAN STEAM NAVIGATION COMPANY LIMITED	Originally black, but by 1920's generally buff	As above
BRISTOL LIGHTERAGE COMPANY LIMITED	Red, black top	Not traced
MERSEY TOWAGE AND LIGHTERAGE CO	Not traced	Not traced
BEAVER LINE SERVICE	Black with two white bands or black	Beaver emblem on pennant and square flag
BRITISH AND BURMESE STEAM NAVIGATION COMPANY LIMITED	Black	French tricolour with Union flag in centre
GUINEA GULF LINE LIMITED	Red, black top	Blue with five-pointed white star and black GG in centre
DOMINION LINE SERVICE (Bristol–Canada only)	Red, black top, white band on red	As Elder Dempster and Company
PALM LINE LIMITED	Green, black top, white band central with white circle bearing green palm tree	Green background with white St Andrew's cross, white circle in centre with green palm tree

FLEET LIST NOTES

1 The Fleet List is arranged as follows:

Part 1   Sea-going vessels engaged in the West African and Canada–Cape trades, The Canary Isles inter-island service, and, from 1968 onwards vessels owned or part owned by Elder Dempster Lines Ltd and operated on other routes served by lines within the Ocean Transport and Trading Group and vice versa, also vessels of the British and Burmese Steam Navigation Company Ltd operated on that line's Far Eastern routes, the Guinea Gulf Line Ltd and Palm Line Ltd. *Ship Nos 1 to 419.*

Part 2   Vessels engaged primarily in the transatlantic trade, including those sold to Canadian Pacific Railway Co in 1903. *Ship Nos 420 to 468.*

Elder, Dempster & Co's interest in the North Atlantic trade commenced in April 1890, and for the next few years was carried on in close liaison with Atlantic Transport Line Ltd. In 1894 the business was further expanded when Elder, Dempster were appointed Managers of Ocean Transport Co Ltd which had acquired two ships built for D. & C. MacIver's City of Liverpool Steam Navigation Co Ltd. Also, certain West African service vessels were chartered to Mississippi & Dominion Line Co Ltd (Dominion Line) for their Bristol–Quebec service, acquired by Elder, Dempster late in 1895, although operated under the Dominion Line name until 1897.

In December 1898 Elder, Dempster & Co acquired the Beaver Line service, founded in 1875 by the Canada Shipping Co Ltd. In 1894 H. E. Murray and J. Hyde of Montreal and R. W. Roberts of Liverpool were appointed liquidators of the company, management of which was passed by the Canadian debenture holders to D. & C. MacIver, who operated a 'Beaver Line Associated Steamers'. This proved no more successful, and, following a Court Order, Elder, Dempster & Co intervened, settled outstanding claims, and acquired the service and ships, operating under the old name. During the Boer War many of the North Atlantic ships were chartered for Government service, and in 1903 Elder, Dempster & Co accepted an offer of £1.4 million for the 'Beaver Line' goodwill, service, and 15 ships, the remainder being re-assigned to other Elder, Dempster services. The management arrangement with Ocean Transport Co Ltd had previously terminated, and thus the North Atlantic services ended.

Part 3   Vessels operated on the Jamaica service. *Ship Nos 469 to 473.*

This service arose from Alfred L. Jones' efforts to promote the banana in the United Kingdom. Unlike the North Atlantic trade, a separate company was formed for this service, which was fortnightly for an annual subsidy of £40,000. The relevant contract for the carriage of HM Mails was not renewed in 1910 and the service ceased and the ships were sold.

Part 4   Vessels operated in sheltered waters on the West African coast and rivers. *Ship Nos 474 to 526.*

Part 5   Vessels managed by Elder Dempster companies during the two World Wars on behalf of His Majesty's Government. *Ship Nos 527 to 562.*

Part 6   Vessels acquired for service as hulks, and vessels nominally owned by Elder Dempster companies but (other than in Part 1) not in their service. *Ship Nos 563 to 581.*

Addenda   *Ship Nos 582 to 585.*
Stop Press   *Ship No 586.*

2 Vessels are numbered from 1 to 586, allocated as above.

3 Details of vessels are extracted from *Lloyd's Registers*, from the Mercantile Navy Lists, from builders' records and the Ships' Certificates held at the Public Record Office, and by the Registrar General of Shipping. Certain details prior to 1855 are not always wholly reliable.

4 Vessels are listed in order of acquisition within the various parts of the Fleet List, except that vessels of a particular class are listed consecutively.

5 The notation (I), (II) etc in brackets after the ship's name indicates the first, second, etc ship of that name in the Fleet. No numeral is shown where a name is used only once. In certain cases a ship may have served under two names and both such names are included in the headings.

6 Arrangement of data:
Identifying Number and name of ship.
Official Number and date of service.
Class if one of a group of broadly similar ships.
Brief description.
Length×beam×depth, tonnages net (n), gross (g), deadweight (d).
Builders, original owners and name. Port of Registry.
Engine particulars.
Career details.
List of vessels of the same class (only shown in the first ship of a class).
Origin of name (only shown on the first ship of any name).

7 For vessels acquired up to 1943 dimensions are registered dimensions, thereafter overall length, beam, and maximum draught. Dimensions are stated in feet and tenths of feet, except in the case of new buildings after 1972 when metric measurements are used. The abbreviations TMK refers to the alternative tonnages introduced in 1967.

Engine particulars include a brief description of the engines; for reciprocators engines abbreviations used are, C = compound, T = triple expansion, Q = quadruple expansion. Then follow number of cylinders, diameter and stroke. Horse powers are shown as hp (per register), nhp (nominal) or ihp (indicated). Speed in knots.

In the case of Steam Turbines the abbreviations SR or DR are used to indicate Single or Double Reduction gearing, LP indicates low pressure, nhp (nominal horse power), or shp (shaft horse power). Speed in knots.

In the case of motor vessels, engine type is followed by 2SC or 4SC, indicating 2- or 4-stroke cycle, SA or DA, meaning single or double acting, the number of cylinders, diameter and stroke, nhp (nominal horse power), bhp (brake horse power), or Kw (kilowatts). Speed in knots.

8 Particulars are shown as when the ship was completed, unless specifically indicated to the contrary, and where no change of any particulars are shown, eg after a change of ownership it indicates that those particulars were unchanged.

In instances where confusion or ambiguity may otherwise arise the flag under which the ship sailed is indicated after the port of registry.

9 Throughout, the name or names of the ship within its own section is shown in bold capitals, and the name of any other ship which forms part of this history and appears in the index is shown in italic capitals.

10 During the period of this study the style of certain of the owning companies changed from time to time. The title as shown is that which applied at the time and it is not considered necessary to itemise subsequent alterations within each ship's history. This mainly concerns the British & African Steam Navigation Co (Ltd from 1883) which was also re-organised in 1900 when that date, in brackets, was added to the title. This refinement, which soon lapsed into desuetude has been disregarded.

11 Details are correct to 31 August 1985 or later if specifically stated.

NEW BROOKLYN (ship No. 254) in dry-dock, 11 April 1947 (Photo J. H. Cleet)

xv

MYRMIDON *(ship No. 416) photographed in January 1982 with a record cargo of 22,248 tonnes*

PART 1

Vessels engaged in the West African and Canada–Cape trades, the Canary Isles inter-island service, and in sea-going service on the West African coast

Ship Nos 1–419

ANGOLA (ship No. 80), *ready to depart from the Mersey* (McRoberts collection)

2

1 FORERUNNER

O.N. Not traced   1852–1854

Iron screw schooner
161.5′×22.0′×11.4′   174 n   381 g
Built by John Laird, Birkenhead, Yard No 88, for African Steamship Co. Registered London. 50 hp by Fawcett, Preston & Co, Liverpool.
Limited passenger accommodation.

1852   3 July, launched. 24 September, commenced maiden voyage from London. 30 September, arrived Madeira (called at Plymouth). 1 October, arrived Tenerife. 8 October, arrived Bathurst. 12 October, arrived Sierra Leone. 16 October, depart Sierra Leone homeward bound. Ran into bad weather, lost fore and main masts during severe gales, funnel also carried away. Put into Gibraltar for repairs. 21 November, arrived Plymouth.

FORERUNNER

1854   25 October, wrecked on east end of Fora on voyage from West Africa to United Kingdom (voyage 8), having left Madeira in the afternoon, and struck before nightfall. Fourteen lives lost, 25 survived. The resultant enquiry read as follows:

An enquiry having been instituted into the circumstances attending the loss of the African mail steamer FORERUNNER (Captain Thomas Johnstone) off the coast of Madeira on 25 October last, and into the question whether the Master and other Officers of that vessel had shown themselves, by reason of incompetency or misconduct, unfit to discharge their duties—Rear Admiral F. W. Berchey and Captain W. H. Walker HCS assisted according to the Mercantile Marine Act, by Mr. Edward Yardley, the Thames Police-Court Magistrate, examined the witnesses, and having heard Captain Johnstone's defence, presented the following report to the Lords Commissioners of the Committee of the Privy Council for Trade:

"We are of the opinion that the loss of the FORERUNNER was occasioned by her being negligently run upon a well-known rock, situated about 200 yards from the cliff of Fora, forming the eastern extremity of the island of Madeira, the land being at the time distinctly visible and there being no necessity whatever for the vessel being so near that spot.

"That, previous to this, the vessel was kept unnecessarily, and sometimes dangerously, near the shore.

"That, by the direction of the Master, she was taken out of her direct route, where he had a channel open before him of nearly 10 miles in width, apparently for the purpose of skirting the coast.

"That, this unnecessarily close proximity to the rocks was such that Captain Gregory remarked to the Captain on the danger of passing so near, that afterwards the vessel struck and was found to be fast filling with water. The Master then quitted his post, and went below to the cabin and occupied himself in saving the chronometers and money of the ship, instead of providing for the safety of his passengers and crew, and endeavouring to maintain the discipline of the ship, which especially became him as Captain of this vessel at this, a moment of imminent peril.

"Previous to the occurrence at Madeira it appears, from the evidence, that the vessel under his command struck upon the bar of the Bonny, after he was cautioned by Captain Gregory, a seafaring person, well acquainted with the navigation of the river, that he was going too wide

Wreck of **FORERUNNER**

3

of the buoy moored for the purpose of marking the channel and that after this, on 19th October, the FORERUNNER was greatly endangered by being run into shallow water upon Arguin Bank, the bearing of the route of that vessel being very improperly continued too far to the eastward, and by the soundings not being attended to sufficiently early, by which the position of the vessel would have been known, and this ominous danger been avoided. That after the vessel was reported to him to be in shallow water, he nevertheless continued the course at full speed upon the bank, until she came round in very shallow water and passed over 2½ fathoms of water only, and very narrowly escaped destruction.

"That had it been night instead of day, when the discolouration of the water could not have been observed, the consequences probably would have been the loss of the vessel and the imminent danger of the lives of the passengers.

"Putting these several circumstances together, and considering how frequently he has, by his misconduct, perilled the vessel and the lives of the several persons embarked in her, and being impressed, most forcibly, with his culpable abandonment of his post and of his authority, as Captain of the vessel, in the hour of danger and at a moment when the preservation of discipline and order was especially required, we are of the opinion that he is, from incompetency, unfit to discharge the duties of a Master of any British merchant vessel.

"On coming to this conclusion, we have to state that it has been formed wholly from the evidence which has been brought before us in the case under investigation. But we cannot withhold from your Lordships that that opinion has been strengthened on reading the documents which have been placed in our hands by Mr. Johnstone himself in support of his character. By one of these documents it appears that Mr. Johnstone last year commanded a vessel called the ARGENTINA, belonging to the South American General Steam Navigation Co, and lost her upon a rock between Monte Video and Buenos Aires; and we find the loss thus accounted for by the agent of the company while testifying to the zeal and ability of Mr. Johnstone; he says that he was at his post aboard the vessel when she struck; but there is no doubt, and no one more sensible of it than himself, that he was doing wrong in shaving so close to a rocky shore.

F. W. Berchey
W. H. Walker"

Admiral Berchey, at the close of the investigation, (addressing Mr. Johnstone) said: "This report having been delivered to their Lordships, together with the evidence and what you have stated in your defence, their Lordships have been pleased to determine that your certificate shall be cancelled, which has been done accordingly. But, before dismissing the case, I would observe that the loss of the FORERUNNER has added one more to the list of those distressing occurrences at sea which have, of late, been so frequently attended, in many cases, with lamentable loss of life. I do not stop to inquire into the question of those casualties, whether they have arisen from neglect of lead or compass, or reckless speed, or any acts such as those of which you have been convicted; it is sufficient to observe that if those fatal occurrences continue, they cannot fail to diminish that confidence of the public in steam-vessels, to which they are justly entitled when prudently and properly navigated. This observation, I hope, will go forth through the length and breadth of the land, and the sentence of the court which has been passed upon you will have the intended effect and influence on Masters of all British vessels in general, and especially to you, should you be placed ever again in a situation of responsibility in your profession."

Note—Dimensions shown are taken from the builder's records. The certificate shows 156.5′×21.5′×11.0′.

2 FAITH

O.N. Not traced 1853–1855

Iron screw schooner
204.9′×30.0′×15.0′ 564 n 894 g
Built by John Laird, Birkenhead, Yard No 89, for African Steamship Co. Registered London. 110 hp, 9 K.
Limited passenger accommodation.

1852 October, launched.
1853 27 January, commenced maiden voyage from London.
1855 28 September, returned to owners after Crimean War trooping service and sold to Government of Turkey. 30 December, foundered off Isle of Wight on passage to Constantinople.

Note—Dimensions shown are taken from the builder's records. The certificate shows 197.2′×28.8′×15.0′.

FAITH

John Laird's Yard, Birkenhead, c 1840

John Laird's yard, Birkenhead, c 1860

S.S. "FAITH"

London to Africa and back calling at

Madeira
Teneriffe
Goree
Bathurst
Sierra Leone
Monrovia Liberia
Cape Coast Castle
Accra
Whydah   Cameroons River
Badagry   Calabar   ---
Lagos   Bonny   ---
Fernando Po.

Memoranda-
John Whitford.

Contents.

Steam Ship "Faith", James Parsons, Commander
January

Date	Lat.	Long.	Distance Run	Course	Wind	Bar.	Ther.	No. of Fires	Steam Gauge	Revol. per minute
Thursday, Jan.y 27 1853	12.30 noon slipped moorings. 6.15 anchored									
Friday, — 28	5.15 a.m. got under way. 11 a.m. off Deal. 12 noon									
Saturday — 29	1 p.m. arrived at Plymouth. 10.35 p.m. stood									
Sunday — 30	9 a.m. Lat 49° 9' N. Long. 5° 23' W. Broke air pump									
Monday — 31	Lying at anchor in Falmouth Roads.									
Tuesday, Feb 1	7 p.m. weighed anchor and stood out to sea.									

from London towards Africa.
1853.

Coals	Tallow	Oil		Remarks.

at the Nore.

off Dover Castle, wind N.N.E., sail set, going 10 knots.

out to sea.

rod and cap of Larboard Engine so put about for Falmouth, at time No. of fires lighted. 8. Steam 11 lbs per sq. in., Revs. per minute, 55. 5 p.m. anchored in Falmouth Roads.

8 p.m. Pilot left the Ship.

Steam Ship "Faith," James Parsons, Commander

Date		Lat. N.	Long. W.	Distance Run	Course	Wind	Bar. per Thermometer in Saloon	Ther.	No. of Fires	Steam Gauge	Revs per minute
Tuesday Feb. 1853	1			Miles							
Wednesday —	2	48°7'	6°5'	140	S 2½ W	V'ble.			8	11	50 & 54
Thursday —	3	45.26	8.27	218	S S W	N.W.	30.10	58°	4 & 8	8 & 11	45 & 52
Friday —	4	41.51	11.48	253	S 25° W	N.W. & N.N.E	30.30	60	4	8	45
Saturday —	5	38.23	14.24	245	S 33° W	N.E	30.36	62	4	6 & 7	45
Sunday —	6	34.21	16.32	270	S 21 W	& N N E	30.30	68	4 & 8	8 & 11	45 & 52
Monday —	7		Madeira				30.35	68	---	---	---
Tuesday —	8		Teneriffe				30.36	68	---	---	---
Wednesday —	9	27.1		87	S 5° W	Variable	30.40	68	---	---	---
Thursday —	10	24.5	17.09	185	S 1¼ W	with light airs	30.42	68	---	---	---
Friday —	11	20.50	18.30	208	S 20° W	—	30.20	65	---	---	---
Saturday —	12	16.56	18.19	236	S ¾ E.	—	30.05	69	4	4 to 5 12 hours & 7 to 9	42 45 & 48
Sunday —	13		Goree.				30.30	72	---	---	---
Monday —	14		Bathurst				30.30	78			
Tuesday —	15		—do—				30.30	75	8	10 & 11	55
Wednesday —	16	10.4	16.54	197	S 3° W	Variable light airs	30.30	78	8 & 4	7 & 12	45 & 55
Thursday —	17	8.42	13.55	202	S 69° E	—	30.30	75	---	---	---
Friday —	18		Sierra Leone				30.30	78			
Saturday —	19						30.10	90	8	12 & 13	55 & 58
Sunday —	20	6.54	12.31			Light & Variable	30.10	79	---	---	---
Monday —	21		Monrovia				30.10	85			
Tuesday —	22	4.41				Calm	30.10	80	---	---	---
Wednesday —	23	4.24				—	30.10	84	---	---	---
Thursday —	24	4.41	2°7'	200	N 82° E	Variable	30.20	85	---	---	---
Friday —	25		Cape Coast Castle			—	30.-	85			

Forward

from London towards Africa

Coals	Tallow	Oil	No. hours with 1 Boiler	Stoppages	Remarks
Tons.	lbs.	Galls.			at 7 p.m. left Falmouth
15	10	6			
18	10	4½	4		
10	15	4½	24		
10	15	4½	24		
10	12	2	16	hours 8	laying off Funchal durg night
9	10	2½	12	6	At Madeira { 6 a.m. arrived / 12 noon left for Teneriffe
12 Pat Fuel	10	2½	9	9·30	At Teneriffe { 3 p.m. arrived —"— / 12·30 midnight left for Goree
12	15	3	14		
13	10½	3	10		
16	15	3	9	0·50	Stopped Engines to disconnect but wind fell off
10½	15	3	24		
12	10	3	4	2·30	Stopped at Goree { a.m. 7·30 arrived at Goree / 10·0. left Goree for Gambia
				10·	Anchored off Gambia { p.m. 7·15 anchored off Gambia / a.m. 5·30 weighed anchor
9	5	1½		25·40	{ Bathurst { Gambia River } 6.— Pilot came on board / 8.— arrived at Bathurst / 15th 9.40 a.m. left Bathurst.
3	5	1½			
15	15	3	18		
12	10	3	7		
3	5	Chiefly for Lamps 3 Getting fuel on board		50.—	At Sierra Leone { Arrived at Sierra Leone Feb. 17th at 4 p.m. / Left Feb. 19th — 6 / 50 hours.
16	10	3		5.—	Lying to off Monrovia.
12	10	2½		7.—	At Monrovia { Arrived Monrovia 7 a.m. / Landed Consul and baggage & mails & left } 2 p.m.
18	15	3			
18	15	2½			
18	10	2			
6	5	qts 0·3		25·40	At Cape Coast { arrived 24th 8·20 p.m. / Left 25th 10.— —"—
277½	252½	67	175	150·10	

Steam Ship "Faith", James Parsons, Commander.

Date		Lat	Long	Distance Run	Course	Wind	Bar	Ther	No of Fires	Steam Gauge	Revs per minute
							NBrought forward				
Saturday, Feb.	26		Accra				29.30	85	8	12&13	55&58
Sunday --	27	6.21	E 2.16	Whydah					3p.m. 6	8&9	49&52
									6	8&9	49&52
(9 p.m. arrived off Lagos)				Badagry			29.24	85			
Monday Feb.	28			Lagos			29.30	85	8	11&12	55&58
Tuesday, Mch	1	N. 4.51	E 5.21	155	S54°E	Vble	29.50	86	--	--	--
Wednesday --	2			Fernando Po			29.50	85	--	--	--

from London towards Africa.

Coals	Tallow	Oil.	No. hours with 1 Boiler.	Stoppages.	Remarks.
277½	252½	galls. 67	175	150·10	
9	–	1		3·20	At Accra {Arrived 6·40 a.m. / Left 10·– a.m
14	10	1½		5·45	Anchored near Whydah {Anchored 26th 11·45 p.m. / Weighed 27th 9·30 a.m.
				1·–	Off Whydah {Arrived 9 a.m / Left 10 ––
		galls. –·3		1·–	Off Badagry {Arrived 3·30 p.m / Left 4·30 ––
5 ret fuel				21·0	Off Lagos {Arrived 27th 9 p.m / Left 28th 6 ––
15	10	3 galls			6 fires only for 30 hours before arrival at Lagos.
18	15	3 ––			
1·10		galls. –·3			Arrived at Fernando Po. Wednesday, March 2nd at 3.p.m.
	16 in Boiler				
340	303½	77	175	182·15	

—— Abstract ——

		days. hours.	hours.
Left Falmouth, Feb. 1 at 7 p.m			
Arrived Fernando Po, Mch. 2 at 3 p.m		28·20	= 692
Less Stoppages		7·14	= 182
Actual Time under Way.		21·6	= 510
Distance.		4855 miles {taken from Coy's Maps distance to Fernando Po from Plymouth.	
Average Speed.		228 miles per day	9½ Knots per. hour.

A trifling deduction to be made for proceeding from Lagos direct to Fernando Po. not calling at Bonny Calabar & Cameroons – the distance being computed for that

Stayed at Fernando Po. days hours 3. 7

Discharged Cargo. Took water 2000 galls.

Shifted Coals from Holds into Bunkers – a very slow process detaining

Cargo coming on board. Took on board 151 casks Palm Oil.

Kroomen could not be had to work all night.

Steam Ship "Faith." James Parsons, Commander.

Date		Lat.	Long.	Distance Run	Course	Wind	Bar.	Ther.	No. of Fires	Steam Gauge	Revs. per minute
	1853										
Saturday Mch.	5		Fernando Po.				29.45	87°			
Sunday ---	6		Cameroons R.				29.50	85	12 hours 4 8	5 & 7 11 & 12	30 57 & 59
Monday ---	7		Calabar R.				29.50	85	---	---	---
Tuesday ---	8	4.7					29.54	85	---	13	---
Wednesday ---	9	N. E.	Bonny				29.54	86	---	---	---
Thursday --	10	4.2	5.18				29.50	86	---	---	---
Friday ---	11		Lagos.				29.50	85	---	---	---
Saturday ---	12	6.12	Badagry and Whydah.				29.30	86	---	---	---
Sunday ---	13		Accra				29.50	85	---	---	---
Monday ---	14		Cape Coast Castle				29.50	85	---	---	---
Tuesday ---	15	4.57	W 1.35	25	S 64° W	S.S.W.	29.48	83	---	---	---
Wednesday --	16	4.14	4.59	183	S 80° W	V'ble	29.48	84	---	---	59 & 60
Thursday ---	17	4.09	7.59	196	W.	light	30.00	81	---	---	---
Friday ---	18	6.11	Monrovia				30.09	79½	---	---	59 & 61
Saturday --	19						30.10	80	---	---	---
Sunday ---	20		Sierra Leone				30.10	87			
Monday ---	21		-do-				30.10	87			
Tuesday ---	22		-do-				30.00	86			
Wednesday ---	23		-do-				30.00	85			
Thursday --	24	9°28'	W 14°48	111	N. 56 W.	West strong head wind	29.42	77	---	---	---
Friday ---	25	10.45	17.3	177	N. 60 W.	N.W. strong head wind	29.42	73	---	---	---
Saturday --	26	13.24	17.2	165	N.	-do-	28.42	71	---	---	---

Forward.

from Fernando Po towards London.

Coals	Tallow	Oil	No of hours with 1 Boiler	Stoppages	Remarks
Tons	lbs.	galls.		hours. min.	10 p.m. left Fernando Po
13	10	2½	12	1·20	Cameroons River {stopped 9.30 a.m. started 10.50}
Ince Hall Coal 13	5	1½		9·30	Anchored off Calabar River {Anchored 6th 7.30 p.m. weighed a. 7th 5.- a.m.}
				2·30	Off Dukestown Old Calabar {arrived --- 1.- p.m left --- 3.30 ---}
				11·-	Anchored off Calabar River near mouth {Anchored --- 6.45 --- left 8th 5.40 a.m.}
8	10	2		16·45	Anchored off Bonny River {Anchored --- 6.15 p.m weighed a. 9th, 11.- a.m.}
7	10	1½		2·45	Bonny town {arrived --- 12.45 noon left --- 3.30 p.m.}
16	10	2¼			
18	10	2½		10·30	Off Lagos {arrived 11th 10.15 a.m left --- 8.45 p.m.}
12	5	1½		-·30	Off Badagry {arrived 12th 1.30 a.m. left --- 2.- ---}
				-·45	Off Whydah {arrived --- 10.- --- left --- 10.45 --}
16	10	1½		4·-	Off Accra {arrived 8 a.m left noon}
6				37·45	Off Cape Coast {arrived 13th 8 p.m left 15th 9.45 a.m.}
3	served out at noon former supply not out				
18	10	2¼			Maintopmast housed.
18	10	2¼			
Ince Hall & Pat fuel 18	10	3		5·40	At Monrovia {arrived 18th 1.35 p.m left --- 7.15 ---}
17	10	2¼			
9	10	1½		94·00	At Sierra Leone {arrived Midnight 19th/20th left 23rd 10 p.m.}
Pat fuel 14	5	qts. -·3			
18	15	galls. 3			
18	10	3		17·30	At Bathurst {arrived 26th 5 p.m Left 27th 10.30 a.m.}
242	150	33	12	214·30	

Steam Ship "Faith," James Parsons, Commander.

Date		Lat.	Long.	Distance Run.	Course	Wind	Bar.	Ther.	No. of Fires	Steam Gauge	Revs per minute
					Brought forward.						
Sunday, Mch	27		Bathurst Goree				29.30	68	8	13	59 & 61
Monday —	28	N. 15.45	W. 17.47	61 from Cape de Verd	N. 11° W.	strong head wind	29.42	71	---	---	---
Tuesday —	29	17.57	18.-	137	N. 9° W.	very strong head wind almost a gale	29.50	71	---	---	---
Wednesday —	30	20°.2	19.7	144	N. 25 W.	N.N.E. strong gale heavy sea	29.42	68	---	11 & 13	45 & 55
Thursday —	31	22.38	19.41	158	N. 9 W.	-do-	29.54	70	---	---	55 & 57
Friday, April	1	25.30	19.40	178	N. 1 W.	strong head wind	29.50	69	---	---	---
Saturday —	2	27.2	17.25	169	N. 46 E.	-do-	30.06	67½	---	---	---
Sunday —	3		Teneriffe				29.54	68	---	---	---
Monday —	4	29.55	15.48	89	N. 9 E.	V'ble	29.54	67	---	---	57 & 59
Tuesday —	5		Madeira				29.42	67	---	---	---
Wednesday —	6	35.11	15.34	168	N 19.45 E.	V'ble	29.42	66	---	---	---
Thursday —	7	37.57	13.29	203	N. 34 E.	E. b N.	29.42	65	---	---	---
Friday —	8	40.37	12.19	175	N. 20 E	Blowing hard gale from N.E. to E.N.E.	29.42	63	---	---	---
Saturday —	9	42.11 Unable to get observation		105		-do-	29.42	63	6 working expansively.	5	48 & 54 35
Sunday —	10	44.0	11.57	106	N. b E. & E.	---	29.54	64	---	---	---
Monday —	11	46.24	9.33	183	N. 34 E.	strong breeze E. & E.S.E.	30.12	63	8	11 & 13	58 & 60
Tuesday —	12	48.31	5.41	218	N. 51 E.	Mod. head wind N. to N.N.E.	30.24	61	---	---	---
Wednesday —	13	4 a.m. arrived at Plymouth					30.24	60	---	---	---

from Fernando Po towards London.

Coals	Tallow	Oil	No. of hours 1 Boiler	Stoppages	Remarks.
242 Patent Fuel	150	33	12	214.30	
9	10	3			
				2.—	At Goree {Arrived 27th 11 p.m / Left 28th 1 a.m
18	10	3			
18	15	2½			
18	10	2½			Strong gale from N.N.E. with heavy sea
18	15	3¼			–do– –do– –do–
Ince Hall & P.fuel 18	15	2¼			
18	10	2¼			
14	10	1½		15.40	At Teneriffe {Arrived 7 a.m / Left 10.40 p.m.
P.fuel & Sand Coal 16	10	2¼			
14½	10	2		9.—	At Madeira {Arrived 7.30 a.m. / Left 4.30 p.m.
16	10	2			
18	10	2¼			Housed fore Maintopmasts into lowermasts. Jib boom on deck.
17	10	2			Blowing hard gale from E to E.N.E.—very heavy sea on—ship going thro' it beautifully close reefed Fore and Main trysails unable to head it out so close hauled on Starboard tack.
14	10	1½			–do—do– sea running very high increasing gale all day, passed two vessels outward bound under close reefed topsails.
14½	10	2			–do—do– gale rather moderated—out reefs and set jib
18	10	1½			Strong breeze—fore and aft sails set going 8 and 9 knots close by the wind.
18	10	2¼			Breeze ahead—steaming head to breeze 9¾ knots, smooth water.
14	8	1½			4 a.m. arrived at Plymouth
533	343	72½			

Abstract of Manifest of Cargo on board S.S. "Faith." 1st Voyage Homewards.

From	Palm Oil	Gold Dust	Gum	Ginger	Camwood	Pepper	Arrowroot	Sundries
Fernando Po	Casks 151	65 ozs.						
Cape Coast		1,085	Casks 15					
Sierra Leone	11	554	11	Bags 1,700	Billets 423 Tons 22	Bags 130 Barrels 6 Punchion 1	Boxes 217	Ivory Bales 5 Palm Nuts Bags. 80
Bathurst	.	.	.	.	.	.	.	Bees Wax 6 Bales. Ivory 5 Bales.
Teneriffe	Cochineal 111 Bags wg 150 lbs each	Wine 10 pipes 20 h hds 41 qt casks						
Madeira	76 Boxes Lemons.							

Consumption of Coals by S.S. "Faith".

1st Voyage.

England to Fernando Po and back.

Taken on board.

1853.		Tons.
Jany.	At Liverpool	585
--- 29th	-- Plymouth	44
Feb. 19th	-- Sierra Leone	201
Mch. 22nd	-- -do-	120
April 3rd	-- Teneriffe	95
--- 5th	-- Madeira	10
		1,055

Consumption

	Tons
Trial Trip	30
L'pool to London	60
London to Plymouth	36
Plyth. to Falmouth 12 tons	
Plymouth to F.Po.	352
Fernando Po to Plymouth 533	
	1011

Coals nearly all used, so what was taken abroad must have been short weight

---

South Wales Coal for 8 fires	Consumption pr hour	13 cwt.
Ince Hall Coal	-do-	-do-	-do-	15 --
Patent Fuel	-do-	-do-	-do-	15 --

South Wales & Ince Hall burn freely and to ashes & do not choke the tubes. Patent fuel leaves large caked cinders which will not burn.
Ince Hall emits thick black smoke and although it does not choke tubes, yet soot accumulates in funnels.
Patent fuel taken on return out of "Mariner" of a very bad quality containing sand & foreign matter. Bricks run 160 to the ton a little over 14 lbs. each.

Madeira.

Coal Depôt.

Messr. Blandy & Son's have two sheds capable of containing 7000 tons of Coal.

The Sheds are substantial stone buildings with air holes, and tile roofs — one situated on the Beach and the other a little higher up.

Vessels discharge coals into barges alongside — the coal is put into bags, each bag containing about 50 lbs, these bags of coal are stowed in the barge — the barge is hauled up the beach and the coal carried to the Sheds and there emptied and piled up.

When Steamers are expected Messr. Blandy have some 4 to 500 bags of Coal ready on the beach to put into Barges at a moment's notice ready to ship from 120 to 180 tons per day.

Good Anchorage near the Beach Shed, in from 10 to 14 fathoms.

Price of South Wales Coal from ´31/- to ´35/- per ton, according to the market — delivered alongside the Steamer — ´1/- per ton extra is charged for putting into Bunkers or Hold.

In transhipping the coal they take great care not to break it, and it looks very well.

Madeira.

Landing of Goods.

No wharf, — goods are landed on beach which is stony — round stones — the streets of Funchal are paved with small sized round stones from the beach, closely set, and very compact — and goods are conveyed from the Beach along the streets on wooden sleighs drawn by Bullocks — one yoke to each sleigh.

Port Charges.

Portuguese Bill of Health to free ship at Teneriffe.

Teneriffe.

Coal Depôt.

Owned by Messr. Bruce Hamilton & Co., the system of coaling Steamers here, is the best and quickest on the Coast.

Coal Store is at head of Wharf, coal is conveyed in bags by Barges, from 'Wharf' to Steamer, anchored off; each Barge holds 200 bags each weighing 1 cwt.

<u>Teneriffe.</u>

<u>Landing of Goods.</u>

Goods are landed from Steamers in Barges - the Barges land at the Pier at Mole - the streets of Santa Cruz are paved with small round stones closely set as at Funchal, and the mode of Conveying goods is similar, one yoke of oxen drawing a wooden sleigh, the wooden sleighs or trucks are about two inches thick, and when we were there, it being rainy and wet, in many places water was above trucks, and the Bales got wet; the goods were hauled from Wharf at Mole to Mess. Bruce Hamilton & Co's store; Captain Parsons pointed this out to Mr. Hamilton, who was present.

<u>Port Charges.</u>

Outwards { Spanish Bill of Health
French -do- -do- to free ship at Goree

Homewards, Portuguese -do- -do- -do- Madeira.

Goree.

Coal Depôt.

The French Government have a depôt on this Island for their steamers - on 13th February there were 6 war steamers anchored in the Roads. The Commandant would supply coals in an emergency.

Wharf.

There is a good wooden wharf at Goree built on piles for landing goods from Boats and Barges.

Sandy streets.

The Agent does not speak English, but is very obliging and attentive to the interests of the Company.

The Portuguese Bill of Health got at Madeira requires to be endorsed by the French Consul at Teneriffe to free the ship at Goree.

Very little trade between this and other ports of coast with the exception of the Senegal.

Bathurst. River Gambia.

Wharf.

14 feet water - a very poor wharf - a new one run a little farther out on piles, is much wanted - so as to allow large sized steamers to come alongside - but when the wind sets on shore raising a heavy swell and surf it would not answer.

Goods.

Passengers Luggage should not be entered on the manifest, as a permit will be required for landing same, and some difficulty and annoyance about paying 4% duty.

The Governor appears inclined to give every assistance to the steamers - but the others in authority - Collector of Customs, &c are very exacting.

Ground nuts very abundant at Bathurst. The oil prepared by the natives sold in the town.

There appears to be considerable travelling between this port and Sierra Leone chiefly deck passengers.

Baron de Schorter - passenger p. "Faith"
from Bathurst to Sierra Leone - returns to
England this spring, and intends coming
out again in the Fall, so as to start from
Sierra Leone in the month of November 1853,
on an expedition to Timbo - territory of
Fonta Djallon - up the Rio Grande - he will
start from Sierra Leone in company with
traders from Timbo overland.

 Strongly recommends The African Steam
Ship Company to run small steamers up the
various rivers, especially up the Gambia - the
Steamers to have a rudder at each end.

 Recommends Establishments to be formed
at Timbo and also at the junction of the
Tchad and the Niger.

<u>Timbo</u>.

 States that Coal is found in the District
around - it would have to be conveyed some
distance to the Rio Grande and thence in
barges.

 The Country around Timbo is mountainous
and healthy - the Timbo native traders fear
the unhealthiness of the coast as much as
white men do.

<u>Junction of Tchad and Niger</u>.

 States that this region is likewise mountainous and healthy, and contains valuable
products unknown in England.

 States that on the Eastward side of
the mountains, gold is found in large pieces,

while on this side it is fine and small.

Indigo grows in great abundance all over the country from the Senegal South. The Natives make it up in cakes, paint themselves with it and also sell it in the market at Bathurst in small quantities.

States that many of the Merchants in Bathurst have been in business there some 20 to 30 years and have never penetrated farther than 8 or 10 miles into the interior - and are entirely ignorant of the products of the Country, and are the worst people to apply to for any information respecting the interior or its products.

The Sshea Nut

grows in great abundance near the coast as well as in interior, and is not yet an article of trade except among the Natives - it yields a very fine oil used by the natives like butter - it does not get rancid - and would suit well for Engine oil or any other purpose - Can be obtained in great quantities.

Palm Oil in the Gambia district very scarce and only used by the natives in small quantities, they boil the nuts in water in a kettle, and skim off the oil.

Dye woods of various kinds very plentiful.

Ground Nuts very plentiful in the
Gambia district – exported from Bathurst in
large quantities to France, and also the
United States – contracts on hand at present
for 4000 tons.

A Barrel of Shea Nut oil was brought to
England and left neglected in a warehouse in
Liverpool – after laying for 7 years it was opened
and found to be perfectly fresh.

The natives use it to anoint their bodies
and as an article of food in various ways.

Sierra Leone.

Ground Nut Oil

Excellent ground nut oil suitable for Engines, prepared at Sierra Leone and sold at Mr. Oldfields store for 3/6 per gallon.

As Consignees at this place are scattered about, considerable difficulty and delay is experienced in landing goods - did the steamers always go alongside "Satira" the goods could easily be put on board - but as they will seldom do this on account of double transhipment of coal - it would be well for the Agent to have a barge to take goods ashore or to "Satira", store them and charge consignees on delivery for so doing so as to give despatch to steamers.

Captr Mackintosh of the "Satira" in loading "Faith" outward with Patent fuel from "Aurora" a vessel lying off Sierra Leone, used every despatch by having 2 gangs of Kroomen passing the coal on board - night and day.

The Government have a large coal store capable of containing 7 or 8000 tons, ashore near wharf. If the African Coy had such a coal shed, with an agent to have 2 to 3 or 400 tons coal always ready for shipment - say in bags of from 50 to 60 lbs. each - piled in two or four barges, to go alongside steamer on arrival - four gangs of men could be kept at work (two on each side of vessel) and from 2 to 300 tons taken on board in 24 hours easily.

If the African Steam Ship Company decide upon Sierra Leone as the <u>chief depôt</u> for their Steamers to coal at - as the Government have done with theirs - it would perhaps be mutually advantageous to run a wharf out, so that Steamers could come alongside - discharge their goods and take in coals with little trouble.

The present wharf at Sierra Leone is only suitable for small boats and barges - by running it out say 20 to 50 yards - large vessels could come alongside.

With a <u>Coal Shed</u> and <u>Wharf</u> - steamers could always depend upon a supply from the coal shed - while in most cases - when laying at wharf dis- charging her cargo - the vessel laden with coal could come and discharge into Steamer on other side - saving transhipment - and if necessary for great despatch, receive coals from shed as well.

The inconvenience of Hulk appears to be, - double transhipment and only being able at most to work two gangs of men on one side steamer.

It is very likely that small traders from this place will come to England in fore Cabin - buy their goods and return, and make a practice of doing so.

Sierra Leone to Bathurst

A very large trade is carried on by small native traders from Sierra Leone to Bathurst — which by accommodation of Steamers can be developed to a large extent. A small trader pays $8 for his passage on deck, and takes 20 to 30 Bags of Colars, Rice or Arrowroot at $1 each Bag to Bathurst. Bags can be stowed on deck at risk of the owners.

Returning — Sierra Leone to Bathurst "Faith" took 12 of these native traders as Deck passengers with

131	Bags	Colars	
7	—"—	Yams	
4	—"—	Rice	
2	—"—	Cocos	at $1 each Bag.
2	—"—	Arrowroot	
1	—"—	Ginger	
1	—"—	Pepper	
3	Cans	Palm Oil	

also shipped by Merchants at S. Leone 20 tons Rice at £1 pr. ton.

Sierra Leone pilots charge 5/- pr. foot in
and 5/- pr. foot out.
—do— Light dues £7 for "Faith" in and out outwards — none charged Homewards. —— ——
Spanish and French Bills of Health 10/- each

Liberia!

Price in Monrovia of a Building lot of Land $200 to $500 - the latter choice lots - River St. Pauls settled on both banks for 15 and 20 miles up - several brick houses - Brick kilns - 400 farms and 1000 settlers - several Steam Saw Mills erected in various parts of Liberia.

One portion of Liberia called Maryland is about to declare itself independent = great jealousy exists between the President and some leading Citizens.

The Country wants more Settlers to till the soil. Several fine rivers navigable 15 and 20 miles run out on the Coast of Liberia between Monrovia and Cape Palmas - which are at the present time being explored as well as the interior by the United States Government.

The opinion of many parties is that if the affairs of Liberia are not properly managed, the Republic will be broken up and fall through.

An Episcopal Am. Mission Station, is in operation near Cape Palmas - they educate young native girls, and go on the principle of marrying them to converted niggers.

It is the opinion of the Commander of U.S. Exploring party from actual observation, that the high lands of Sierra Leone, Cape Verde, Monrovia and so on to Cape Palmas are off-shoots of a mountain range in the interior

Monrovia - Liberia.
Landing of Goods.

Consignees of goods send out barges or large boats alongside Steamer as soon as they receive advice of having goods on board - the barges go inside the bar (8 to 9 feet water in bar) and land their goods on banks of river at foot of town of Monrovia, it costs them 1/6 to 4/- per ton according to quantity.

The President of the Republic of Liberia appears desirous of affording facilities for trade with England, as no anchorage or light dues are charged African Steam Ship Co's Steamers - the only charge is a fee to Collector of Customs for entering and clearing ship - optional.

The Light House on Cape Mensurado (the headland at Monrovia) is very imperfect, everyone complains of its being badly kept, and insufficient for the purpose.

Mr. Warner (Coloured Merchant) has been in Monrovia for 30 years - Came originally from Baltimore, U.S. - states population of Monrovia is 2,500 - of the Republic 4 to 5000 - believes that considerable trade will be done by African Steam Ship Co's Steamers - states that the Emigration for last 4 years into the Republic from U.S. has doubled the population - the last arrival of Emigrants was in December 1852 when two vessels brought over 300 Emigrants.

St. Pauls River runs out at Monrovia — for 20 or 30 miles up, it is thickly settled by farmers, who raise a little Coffee — sugar Cane and great quantities of ginger, arrowroot and Cam wood — there is no trading establishment up the river, and the natives have great quantities of Ivory and Cam wood to dispose of — the President would afford every facility to any English Merchant who would start a trading Establishment up the river — the goods best suited for natives are, —

Manchester printed Calico (Called satin stripe)
Blue cotton cloth.
Brass Kettles so
Muskets (flint and steel.)
Powder. (Coarse)
Machets (or Cutlasses)
Tobacco (but this can be bought at Monrovia 18 cts. p. lb,
The natives would trade for Camwood & Ivory.
The settlers for Ginger & Arrowroot.

_____

The above is a first-rate chance for trade for English Merchant as none of the Monrovians have any Capital to start with. — Palm oil scarce and dear in this district, sell for 50 cents per gallon up river.

Cape Coast Castle.

Landing of Goods.

Goods are landed through the surf, in large Canoes – the Canoes carry about 1 ton freight, and are propelled by 13 natives – Charge $1 per trip – one dollar –

When there is a heavy surf goods cannot land, and without the natives are humoured a little with a bottle of rum – they may take it into their heads to capsize the Canoe and give their passengers a ducking – this happened with a large canoe that left "Faith" on her arrival

Live stock and provisions are expensive at this place.

Uccra.

Landing of Goods

Heavy surf - goods landed in large Canoes in same manner as at Cape Coast - large Canoes propelled by 13 natives able to carry 1 ton freight - 1 dollar p. trip, - smaller Canoes propelled by 7 natives not used for goods.

Live stock and provisions Can be had, -

Ducks.	two dollars p. dozen.
Fowls.	one dollar —do—
Sheep	two to 4 dollars each.
Pigs.	two to ten dollars.
Bullocks.	fourteen to sixteen dollars.
Eggs	one dollar p. 100.
Yams.	three dollars p. 100.

Sat. Feb. 26th 6. p. m. - Cape St. Pauls. W. b. N. ½ N. 4 miles - rounded Cape and found three vessels at anchor off Quitta - spoke the outside one while passing her, a French Brig.

Whydah.

Landing of Goods.

Landing of Goods must be difficult on account of tremendous Surf.

"Faith" arrived off Whydah on Sunday 27th Feb. at 9 a.m. – fired a gun and immediately a canoe came off which took Mails and passengers.

Barque "Foam" of Bristol anchored off Whydah.

The mails were delivered to a cabin passenger who came out from London, Mr. Cawley.

Very heavy surf running all along this coast.

Sunday.

Mr. Beecroft of Fernando Po suggests that the mails for Whydah and Badagry should be landed at Quitta, and taken down the Lagoons to those places – as at Quitta the surf is not so heavy as at Whydah and Badagry – he said he waited once for 10 days at Whydah for easy surf to go out in a canoe on board a vessel, but could not do so, and finally was obliged to proceed up the Lagoons to Quitta.

Homewards – arrived off Whydah at 10 a.m. March 12, got two passengers – received an enquiry from the merchants of Whydah to know if Steamers would take Palm Oil.

Several fine houses in town of Whydah – apparently fine looking from sea Barracons for slaves.

Badagry

Outwards arrived off Badagry at 4 p.m. Sunday 27th Feb. No canoes in sight ashore - and very heavy surf running - A Brig was lying at anchor the "Harriet" small trader - manned entirely by natives - the Mail Agent and Purser went on board in Dingey and delivered Her Majesty's Mails (one bag containing one newspaper, one bag containing two or three small letters) to Bill Williams - Krooman - one of the crew - he stated that his Captain & Mate (both coloured men) were ashore, and that the Missionaries did not allow Canoes to be launched on Sundays.

Homewards - arrived off Badagry at 1.30 a.m. March 12 - fired a Gun and Blue Light - stayed ½ an hour - useless for Mails to land at Badagry.

Mr. Sanderman the only white man of Badagry returns p. "Faith", being obliged to leave on a/c of disputes with Natives & Missionaries - he complains in strong terms of the interference of Missionaries in matters of war &c with the Natives -

Mails (if any) for Badagry could be landed at Lagos, Care Mr. Fraser, who would send them up Lagoons - or else at Whydah.

Homewards, between Badagry and Whydah saw a slaver unshipping slaves in haste as a man of war the "Alecto" was coming down.

Lagos.

Outwards, arrived off Lagos at 9 p.m. Sunday 27th Feby found lying at Anchor Her Majesty's Ships of War

"Penelope", steamer - flagship.

"Alecto"   --.—

Brig "Cygnet"

"Ferret"

"Britomart"

Mails for Squadron deld on board "Penelope" Lagos Mails sent up river at 6 a.m. the next morning.

Monday - Cargo for Lagos lying on Ship's deck all day, but no one came or sent for it - although the Consignees received advices and mails early and had notes despatched as well, so at 6 p.m stowed Lagos cargo in Hold and proceeded on the voyage.

Signallized the shore but no reply.

Homewards - arrived off Lagos at 10 a.m. 11th March. Mail Agent with Mails and Purser went in Gig across the Bar and up Lagos River to the Town - 7 miles from anchorage - on returning and crossing Bar at dark, Boat got swamped - water shipped knee deep - baled her out with hats, &c. no baler on board.

The Consignees live in the town and have no canoes of their own to discharge cargo and were it not for the kindness of Mr Lorenzi Diederichein, Hamburg Merchant at this place, the goods would not have been discharged, Mr Diederichein took them in his canoes and put them on board his brig, the "Africa" lying at anchor in the Roads.

Mr D. is almost the only merchant here, has 12 vessels running with Palm Oil and gets vessel loads of Cowries direct from the East Indies to Lagos - he would ship home 50 tons Palm Oil by every steamer, did they cross the Bar to Lagos, to save him the trouble of bringing down in Canoes. Has been in Lagos 14 years - 12 years ago there was no trade in Palm Oil until he commenced it - now there is 7000 Puncheons oil shipped annually which might be increased to 14 or 15,000. He has at this time in his Stores on Beach 90000 gallons Palm oil waiting for shipment.

There is only 7 feet water on Bar of Lagos at Low Water - which is the only time to cross - deep water in channel up - and Lagoons (navigable for canoes) branching right and left. Lagos full of Portuguese Slave dealers.

Ashore at Lagos was introduced to the King of Lagos and stayed half an hour with his Majesty who was surrounded by a dozen young wives, and 20 or 30 native attendants touching their noses to the ground and cracking their fingers - the Prime Minister sat on his left.

Fernando Po.

Watering.

Facilities for watering very imperfect. Barrels have to be sent on shore to the watering place distant some 50 yards on the Beach - placed under the small waterfall with a funnel to catch water - there are two small waterfalls so two barrels can be filling at one time.

It took 6 Kroomen 2½ days to get on board into tanks 2000 gallons water.

A water boat with tank containing some 1,500 gallons with a pump to pump water into tanks of steamers from alongside would expedite watering.

When hulk arrives it would be advisable to have about 20 Kroomen in the employ of the Company, to discharge cargo from steamers - shift Coals from Holds to Bunkers when necessary and assist in watering vessels and loading them with Palm oil.

Palm Oil can be taken on board by two gangs of men into fore and main holds at rate of 150 Casks per day from daylight until sunset - provided casks are alongside - either floating on the water or on vessels deck.

Cameroons River.

"Faith" steamed up this river to within a few miles of the shipping, where a boat met her with mails for England on board.

Horsfall's ships in this river.

Old Calabar River.

There seems to be a great monopoly of the trade in this river— "Faith" went 50 miles up Calabar River and anchored off Dukestown— 4 vessels at Anchor— 3 English (Liverpool) and 1 Dutchman.

The "Abeona" of Liverpool was just commencing trade with the natives— went on board and found "King Eye Honesty" and 3 or 400 natives with him receiving the "Dash"— his Majesty shook hands all round, asked a few questions and drank champagne.

Wilson & Dawson's ships in this river.

Bonny River.

"Faith" arrived off Bonny River at 6.30 pr. m. 8th March — came to anchor — fired Guns for Pilot to come off at daybreak — at 8 a. m. the next morning — four Pilots came off from Fouche Point — but water being slack had to wait till 11 a. m. before going into the River — Pilots — Peter Fouche — Jack Black — Tom Fisher and Tom Dixon — paid them for Pilotage in and out 30 silver dollars, 1 bag bread, 1 doz. rum, 1 cheese and three pieces Beef. The Traders in Bonny gave false information as to paying pilotage, stating we would have to pay them £20 — they are very jealous seemingly of natives getting to know value of money.

A Spanish Schooner was loading with slaves up New Calabar River, 20 miles from Bonny Town — The Admiralty Agent got particulars to inform the Admiral at Lagos.

Tobin & Co.

Harrison & Co

& Wilson & Dawsons ships in this river.

43

General Remarks.

It being a great risk, waste of time fuel and expense for large steamers to proceed up Cameroons - Old Calabar, and Bonny Rivers, would it not be an improvement if a small swift steamer like the "Forerunner" was placed on the Station between Lagos and Fernando Po - meeting the outward steamers at Lagos and taking the Mails for Lagos, Bonny Old Calabar and Cameroons, proceeding up those rivers delivering mails - picking up any cargo and mails for Home and then joining the large steamer at Fernando Po, she would then be at liberty for some days, until close upon arrival of next outward steamer at Lagos - which time might be employed towing sailing vessels in and out of Rivers if it would pay.

This arrangement would require the time of staying at Fernando Po to be extended to seven days, which is absolutely necessary if the ships are to take any cargo - or give satisfaction to the Public, and all concerned.

It seems advisable to make Sierra Leone the principle Coal Depôt. All steamers from England taking coal sufficient to last them there, and there take sufficient to last them to Fernando Po and back.

Fernando Po need only be a secondary Coaling Depôt for the small rivers steamer - and only in cases of emergency for large

44

steamers.

And Teneriffe another Coaling Depôt for Steamers in case of short supply at Sierra Leone.

The Hulk coming out to Fernando Pō will be sufficient there for all present purposes.

But at Sierra Leone something more is required.

I would respectfully suggest that a Coal Shed capable of containing 7000 tons of coals be erected at Sierra Leone with a store for Cargo and also a wharf run out on piles if practicable adjacent to the Coal Shed so that Steamers could come alongside - vessels laden with Coal lying at time of Steamer's arrival at Sierra Leone could discharge into Steamers while lying at Wharf saving transhipment.

Or if it is not expedient to run out a wharf - a shed is necessary with barges and coal in sacks on the Beach similar to Messr Blandy's well arranged Coal Depôts at Madeira or Messr Bruce Hamilton & Co's at Teneriffe

3 HOPE

O.N. 4656   1853–1860

Iron screw schooner
194.5′ × 28.7′ × 16.5′   585 n   759 g
Built by John Laird, Birkenhead, Yard No 90, for African Steamship Co. Registered London. 110 hp 9½ K.
1853 January, launched. 19 April, completed.
1857 6 January, remeasured. Now rigged as a 3 mast barque, 206.8′ × 30.1′ × 16.5′, 737 n, 1011 g.

HOPE

MAIL STEAMERS

LIVERPOOL TO MADEIRA, TENERIFFE,
AND THE
WEST COAST OF AFRICA,
(CALLING AT PLYMOUTH.)

The African Steam-Ship Company's

POWERFUL AND FIRST-CLASS SCREW STEAM-SHIPS

ARMENIAN . . G. Corbett, Commander.		ETHIOPE . . . A. J. M. Croft, Commander.
HOPE . . . . . . A. M'Intosh, ,,		GAMBIA . . . C. Tutt, ,,
ATHENIAN . . H. Dring, ,,		RETRIEVER . J. Phillips, ,,
CANDACE . . J. H. Rolt, ,,		

LEAVE LIVERPOOL ON THE 21ST OF EVERY MONTH,

EMBARKING THE ROYAL MAILS AND PASSENGERS AT PLYMOUTH, ON THE 24TH.

These Steamers convey Goods and Passengers to the undermentioned Ports :—

Madeira, Teneriffe, Goree, Sierra Leone, Monrovia, Cape Coast Castle, Accra, Lagos, Bonny, Old Calabar, Camaroons, and Fernando Po.

And Passengers only for Bathurst (Gambia.)

THE STEAM SHIP
HOPE,
CAPTAIN A. MCINTOSH,
**WILL LEAVE LIVERPOOL ON WEDNESDAY,
THE 21st APRIL, AT 4 A.M.**

This Vessel is now ready to receive Cargo, and all Goods must be alongside by noon on the 20th. Parcels and Specie only will be received at Plymouth up to the 23rd. No Cargo can be shipped at Plymouth.

Goods forwarded by Railway to Liverpool should be sent to the Waterloo Station, to save extra Cartage.

Goods for SIERRA LEONE will be landed there at the Company's expense but Shippers' risk, and Bills of Lading must contain a clause to this effect.

Bills of Lading, according to the Company's form, are to be had of Messrs. Whitehead and Morris, 1, Philpot-lane, Feachurch-street, London, and of Messrs. Turner and Dunnett, James-street, Liverpool. The destination, in letters two inches in length, must be marked on two sides of every package.

ALL FREIGHT MUST BE PREPAID.

NOTICE IS HEREBY GIVEN, That no Goods or Property will be conveyed as Cargo in these Vessels, except under Bills of Lading, in the form adopted by the Company for the time being. And, if from any cause whatever, Goods or Property shall be shipped as Cargo, without a Bill of Lading, the Company only agrees that the same shall be conveyed and delivered on the terms of the Bill of Lading adopted by the Company, namely :— That the Company's ships have leave to touch and stay at all intermediate ports and places whatever, particularly in connexion with their employment in Her Majesty's Mail service, with liberty to tow and assist Vessels in all situations, and to sail with or without a Pilot; and that the Company are not liable for Leakage and Breakage, Contents, or Weight of Packages, nor for the incorrect delivery of Goods from insufficiency of Marks or Numbers, nor for any Accident, Loss, or Damage, arising from the Act of God, the Queen's Enemies, Pirates, Restraints of Princes, Rulers, and People, Vermin, Jettison, Barratry, and Collision, Fire on Board, in Hulk, or Craft, or on Shore, nor for any Accident, Loss, or Damage whatsoever, from Machinery, Boilers, and Steam, and steam Navigation, or for any Perils of the Seas and Rivers, nor for any Act, Neglect, or Default whatsoever of the Pilot, Master, or Mariners in Navigating the Ship, nor any consequences of the causes above stated; and the Company shall not be under any other liability whatever than the liability incurred by them by the terms of the Bills of Lading.

For further information apply in Plymouth to H. J. Waring, Octagon; or to

LAIRD, FLETCHER & CO.
23, CASTLE STREET, LIVERPOOL. AND
49, LIME STREET, LONDON.

Liverpool, 14th April, 1858.

An early African Steamship Co Advertisement

1860 10 November, sold to W. Miles Moss and others trading as James Moss & Co. Registered Liverpool.
1864 Lengthened to 280.8′ × 30.2′ × 22.5′, 1212 n, 1420 g. 10 October, renamed **LUXOR**.
1873 31 July, ownership transferred to Moss Steamship Co Ltd. 2 cyl 45″–33″ by C. & W. Earle, Hull. 120 hp.
1877 7 September, sold to H. F. Swan & H. Clapham, joint owners (H. Clapham and Co Managers), Newcastle. Registered Newcastle.
1878 Re-engined and reboilered by Wallsend Slipway Co. C 2 cyl, 29″, 56″–33″, 120 hp, 1107 n, 1451 g.
1882 Sold to H. Clapham & Co, Newcastle.
1884 22 August, sold to Clapham Steamship Co Ltd (G. E. Macarthy, Manager). 930 n.
1898 18 March, sold to T. W. Ward, Sheffield, for demolition at Walker on Tyne.

4 CHARITY

O.N. Not traced   1853

Iron screw barquentine
243.0′ × 30.6′ × 22.6′   1007 n   1240 g
Built by John Laird, Birkenhead, Yard No 92, for African Steamship Co. Registered London. 2 cyl 54″–48″ by Geo. Forrester & Co, Liverpool.
1853 23 May, launched.
1854 16 January, commenced maiden voyage from Liverpool. October, sold to Canadian Steam Navigation Co (McKean, McLarty & Lamont), Liverpool. On first voyage for new owners took 27 days from Liverpool to Quebec. Later engaged on Crimean War transport duties.
1855 Sold to Fabre Line. Renamed **PICTAVIA**. Registered France.
1856 Sold to Spanish interests. Renamed **LA CUBANA**. Registered Spain.
1865 Sold to Lamport and Holt, Liverpool. Renamed **HERSCHEL**.
1874 Sold to R. M. Sloman, Hamburg. Converted to sail. Iron ship, four masts. Renamed **PALMERSTON**. Registered Hamburg. 246.0′ × 30.0′ × 22.0′, 1116 n, 1250 g.
1890 Sold to Bruckner and Albers, Hamburg. 1136 n, 1175 g.
1894 Sold to A. Princeti, Genoa. Renamed **FREDERICO**. Iron barque, four masts. Registered Genoa.
1899 Broken up.

CHARITY

5 NORTHERN LIGHT
O.N. 9157 Not in service

Iron screw barquentine, clipper stem and bow-sprit
238.8′×29.2′×23.8′ 814 n 1275 g

Laid down 1853 by John Laird, Birkenhead, Yard No 95, for African Steamship Co. Purchased by Canadian Steam Navigation Co (McKean McLarty & Lamont) and launched 3 November as **OTTAWA**. 2 cyl 54″–48″ by Fawcett, Preston & Co, Liverpool. 700 ihp, 10 K.
Accommodation 100 passengers.

1853 4 November, launched.
1854 3 March, commenced maiden voyage from Liverpool to Portland, Maine. Placed on Liverpool–Quebec–Montreal service.
1854 5 September, commenced last voyage to Quebec before being requisitioned as a Crimean War transport. Florence Nightingale was a frequent passenger between Scutari and Balaclava.
1857 26 January, sold for £21,000 to Peninsular & Oriental Steam Navigation Co. Employed on Bombay, Hong Kong or Suez routes.
1868 Abyssinian War trooping.
1872 Registered Hong Kong.
1873 6 November, sold for £9526 to Captain Hutchinson. Renamed **GENERAL VAN SWIETEN**. Dutch flag.
1881 29 April, sprang leak off coast of Atjeh, towed into deep water and sunk by gunfire.

6 CANDACE
O.N. 23169 1854–1858

'Candace' class
Iron screw schooner, one funnel, three masts
206.0′×25.5′×13.4′ 496 n 660 g

Built by John Laird, Birkenhead, Yard No 107, for African Steamship Co. Registered London. 120 hp.

1854 27 May, launched.
1858 4 May, in collision with Dutch barque YDA ELIZABETH when homeward bound. Sank within 15 minutes. Two passengers, the Master and four crew members lost their lives.
Ships of the 'Candace' class: CANDACE (6), ETHIOPE (7).
Candace was the name of several Queens of Ethiopia.

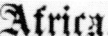
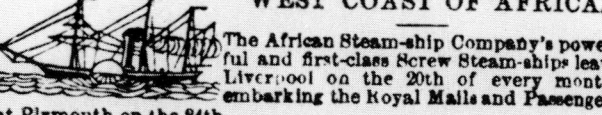

Africa.
MAIL STEAMERS FROM LIVERPOOL TO MADEIRA, TENERIFFE, AND THE WEST COAST OF AFRICA.

The African Steam-ship Company's powerful and first-class Screw Steam-ships leave Liverpool on the 20th of every month, embarking the Royal Mails and Passengers at Plymouth on the 24th.

These Steamers convey goods and passengers to the undermentioned ports:—Madeira, Teneriffe, Goree, Bathurst, Sierra Leone, Monrovia, Cape Coast Castle, Accra, Lagos, Bonny, Old Calabar, Cameroons, and Fernando Po.

The CANDACE, Captain HAWKESLEY, will be the steamer of the 20th January.

Sailing bills and all further information may be had on application in London to Messrs. Ogilby, Moore, and Co., 3, Ingram-court, Fenchurch-street; in Plymouth, to H. J. Waring, Octagon; and Liverpool to
WILLIAM LAIRD and CO., 23, Castle-street. ee154

CANDACE features on this advertisement

7 ETHIOPE (I)
O.N. 23176 1854–1867

'Candace' class
Iron screw schooner, one funnel, three masts
206.0′×25.6′×13.4′ 496 n 660 g

Built by John Laird, Birkenhead, Yard No 113, for African Steamship Co. Registered London. 120 hp.

1854 24 July, launched.
1867 28 November, sold together with *RETRIEVER* to Randolph, Elder in part payment of new building *BIAFRA*. After sale chartered back.
1870 Owned by Isbella Elder, Glasgow.
1871 Sold to William Pile, Sunderland. Renamed **ALFREDO EL GRANDE**.
1872 Lost.

Ethiope is the name of a river in the Niger Delta.

A model of ETHIOPE

RETRIEVER under sail and steam

8 RETRIEVER
O.N. 191   1854–1867

Iron ship. The figurehead was that of a female
155.0′×21.0′×13.0′   198 n   329 g
Built by Denny & Rankin, Dumbarton, for African Steamship
Co. Registered London. 60 hp, 9 K. Originally employed
on Liverpool–Hamburg service, later on the inter Colonial
service (Bonny to outports). Ordered as a replacement for
FORERUNNER.

1854   December, completed.
1861   June, refitted in the United Kingdom.
1866   Returned to United Kingdom—refitted as a collier and
       then used to transport coal from Welsh ports to bunker
       ships of the African Steamship Co.
1867   28 November, sold together with *ETHIOPE* to
       Randolph, Elder & Co in part payment of new building
       BIAFRA.
1877   Sold for demolition.

9 ATHENIAN
O.N. 16872   1858–1871

'Athenian' class
Iron screw barque, three masts, one funnel
241.2′×29.4′×20.0′   520 n   978 g
Built by Smith & Rodgers, Glasgow, for Potter & Co, Glasgow.
Registered Glasgow. 200 hp, 8 K.
1858   Acquired by African Steamship Co. Registered London.
       27 September, sailed from Liverpool for the West Coast
       of Africa with 48 passengers.

1871   Sold to Henry Ellis, Leamington. Renamed
       CAROLINE. Registered London.
1873   Converted into a sailing vessel. 243.3′×30.4′×19.7′,
       974 n 1042 g.
1887   Sold to W. Ross, London 984 n.
1888   Sold to A. E. Kinnear and Co, London.
1889   Sold to M. N. Fischer, Veile, Denmark. Renamed
       OLGA. Registered Veile. 981 n, 1061 g.
1895   Sold to C. P. Helm, Nordby, Denmark. Registered
       Nordby.
1896   Sold to South East African Transport Co Ltd. Novem-
       ber, reported hulked at Beira.

Ships of the 'Athenian' class: ATHENIAN (9), ARMENIAN
(10).

ATHENIAN

48

ARMENIAN, from a painting commissioned by Captain Leamon in 1864, when he was appointed to command her (Photo R. Cressey)

10 ARMENIAN

O.N. 3270   1857–1865

'Athenian' class
Iron screw barque
239.2′ × 29.3′ × 20.2′   553 n   1017 g
Built by Smith & Rodgers, Glasgow, for Potter & Co. Operated on the Mediterranean–Clyde service. Registered Glasgow. 200 hp, 8 K.

1855   Completed.
1857   Acquired by African Steamship Co. Registered London.
1858   Stranded in River Cameroon. Two weeks delay arriving Liverpool.
1863   Engine break-down entering Sierra Leone, continued voyage to United Kingdom on one engine. Passenger accommodation improved. 763 n, 1075 g.
1865   24 January, (Captain T. Leamon) left Liverpool 0930 hours for West Africa via Madeira and Tenerife with 42 passengers and 48 crew. 25 January, hit Arklow Bank in foggy weather and caught fire. Ship broke in two. Twenty-four survivors picked up by steamship MONTAGU. Master's certificate suspended for nine months.

ARMENIAN features in this advertisement

LOADING BERTH SOUTH-EAST SIDE HUSKISSON DOCK.

ROYAL MAIL STEAMERS
TO
MADEIRA, TENERIFFE,
AND THE
WEST COAST OF AFRICA.

The African Steam Ship Company's Vessels

Carrying Her Majesty's Mails, LEAVE LIVERPOOL, on the 24th of EVERY MONTH, (except when it falls on a Monday, when the Day of Sailing is the 25th,) proceeding direct to

Madeira, Teneriffe, Bathurst, Sierra Leone, Cape Palmas, Cape Coast Castle, Accra, Lagos, Benin, Nun, Brass, Bonny, Fernando Po, Cameroons, and Old Calabar.

NOTICE.—Goods for SIERRA LEONE will be delivered at Consignees' risk into the Company's Floating Depôt, from whence delivery is to be taken within seven days after arrival, otherwise they will be landed and put into Customs warehouse at Consignees' risk and expense, under stop for charges.

N.B.—All Goods must be taken from alongside at Shippers' risk and expense. Goods for Fernando Po, Brass, Nun, Cameroons, and Old Calabar, are transhipped at Bonny and forwarded by branch Steamer at Shippers' risk but Ship's expense, and all Bills of Lading for those destinations must contain this clause.

THE FAST AND POWERFUL SCREW STEAM-SHIP
"ARMENIAN,"
THOMAS LEAMON, COMMANDER,

WILL LEAVE LIVERPOOL on TUESDAY, the 25th October, at 3 p.m.

Goods and Heavy baggage must be alongside the ship at the Loading Berth, Huskisson Dock, not later than Noon on the 22nd, and a Shipping Note sent with each Cart Load of Goods, in which the contents of the packages must be described.

Passengers embark by Steam Tender, leaving the NORTH LANDING STAGE at 1.30 p.m. punctually. Goods & Parcels for Madeira cannot be shipped unless accompanied by a note of Marks & Numbers, Gross Weight of each Package, Contents, Value, and whether British or Foreign Manufacture.

NOTICE.—Parcels addressed to different consignees, and made up in one package, will be charged freight on each parcel as if shipped separately

No Goods or Parcels can be forwarded without prepayment of Freight

Parcels not exceeding 18 inches in measurement each way, will be received in Liverpool up to noon on the 24th.

Paper Parcels only will be received at the Company's Offices, 14, Leadenhall-street, London, up to noon of the 21st.

All Letters and Newspapers must go through the Post Office. Bills of Lading, according to the Company's form, can be had of Messrs. C. Skipper and East, Great Tower-street, London, and of Messrs. Turner and Dunnett, James-street, Liverpool. N.B.—Two unstamped copies are required with each set of Bills of Lading. The destination, in letters two inches in length, must be marked on two sides of every package.

NOTICE IS HEREBY GIVEN, That no Goods or Property will be conveyed as Cargo in these Vessels, except under Bills of Lading, in the form adopted by the Company for the time being. And, if from any cause whatever, Goods or Property shall be shipped as Cargo, without a Bill of Lading, the Company only agrees that the same shall be conveyed and delivered on the terms of the Bill of Lading adopted by the Company, namely:—That the Company's Ships have leave to touch and stay at all intermediate ports and places whatever, particularly in connexion with their employment in Her Majesty's Mail Service, with liberty to tow and assist Vessels in all situations, and to sail with or without a Pilot; and that the Company are not liable for Leakage and Breakage, Contents, or Weight of Packages, nor for the incorrect delivery of Goods from insufficiency of Marks or Numbers, nor for any Accident, Loss, or Damage, arising from the Act of God, the Queen's Enemies, Pirates, Restraints of Princes, Rulers, and People, Vermin, Jettison, Barratry, and Collision, Fire on Board, in Hulk or Craft, or on Shore, nor for any Accident, Loss, or Damage whatsoever, from Machinery, Boilers, and Steam, and Steam Navigation, nor for any Perils of the Seas and Rivers, nor for any Act, Neglect, or Default whatsoever of the Pilot, Master, or Mariners, in Navigating the Ship, nor any consequences of the causes above stated; and the Company shall not be under any other liability whatever than the liability incurred by them by the terms of the Bills of Lading.

For further information apply in London at the COMPANY'S OFFICES, 14, LEADENHALL-STREET, and in Liverpool to
FLETCHER & PARR, Agents,
(Late Laird, Fletcher & Co.)
23, CASTLE STREET.

WRECK OF THE ROYAL MAIL STEAMER ARMENIAN

The captain's sworn depositions, made to the receiver of the wreck, William Coghlan, Esq, is to the following effect:

"We left Liverpool on the 24th, at 11 a m; passed the Bell buoy at noon. At seven evening stopped and sounded in thirty-seven fathoms; at 11.55 pm, we sighted a revolving light; put the helm to starboard. The tide was ebbing, the weather was thick, and the wind blowing moderately from the N E. At midnight the aft part of the ship struck on a bank. Her head fell to N W, then to N N E and N E. Every effort was made with the engine to get her off. In half an hour after striking there was ten feet of water in her after compartments, and at one o'clock the water in the stokehole put out the fire, of course stopping the engines. As the ship was gradually sinking, the boats were got out. The ladies and children were put in the starboard lifeboat, which made for the lightship. The port lifeboat was stove in. At this time the sea was breaking over the ship, and the foremast had to be cut away to ease her. As many persons as the remaining boats could contain were then placed in them. This was all done in an orderly manner. As the ship was now (about five a.m.) settling down fast the remaining persons were ordered to take to the rigging, where they remained till two o'clock afternoon, when they were taken off by the steamer Montagu, and brought to Wexford where they arrived at eight o'clock. Two of the crew and two of the passengers were lost during the night from the wreck. Captain Clarke, of the Montagu, rendered valuable services in saving our lives, which, in all likelihood, would have been sacrificed but for him. Mr Johnson, third officer of ship, was invaluable in conducting the lifeboat to the lightship, and afterwards, also, in saving the lives of two boys at the risk of his own. I did not see a light from the time I left the Bell buoy at noon on the 24th, till 11.55 p.m. of same night. Cannot give any reason for the loss of the ship except that the compasses were incorrect, as every precaution was taken. The compasses were not adjusted previous to leaving Liverpool on this voyage. On Pilot leaving, I discovered three fourths of a point difference between the two compasses. I discovered that the bank the ship was on was the Arklow, when I was going in the boat from the wreck to the Montagu, and not before. I was also then told that four of the crew of the Arklow lightship, were lost by the upsetting of the boat, when coming to our assistance."

From the Irish Times 30 January 1865

11 GAMBIA (I)

O.N. 26622   1855–1859

Iron screw schooner. Figurehead was a male
193.2′ × 24.8′ × 14.0′   352 n   515 g
Built by Laurence Hill & Co, Port Glasgow, Yard No 352, for African Steamship Co. Registered London. 80 hp.

1855   17 July, launched.
1857   Sustained a broken main shaft when entering Bathurst which delayed her arrival in United Kingdom by six weeks.
1859   6 December, sold for £5701 9s 8d to B. Moss & Co.
1870   7 January, wrecked off the Dudgeon Light.
Gambia is the river and West African republic.

12 NIGER (I)

O.N. 13711   1856–1857

Iron screw barquentine, three masts, one funnel
208.6′ × 29.0′ × 17.0′   482 n   708 g
Built by Robert Napier & Sons, Govan, for African Steamship Co. Registered London. 200 hp.

1856   24 February, commenced maiden voyage.
1857   12 June, on voyage 5, wrecked at Santa Cruz, voyage Sierra Leone to Tenerife.
Name derived from the great African river.

OFFICIAL REPORT RESPECTING THE LOSS OF THE STEAMER 'NIGER'

It appears that the NIGER is a screw steamer of 482 tons register, schooner rigged, with three masts, with engines of 200 horse-power, and a crew consisting of 39, officers and men. She was a new ship, built in 1856, and sailed duly equipped from Plymouth on the 3rd April last, on her voyage to Fernando Po, on the Coast of Africa. She was commanded by Captain James Howard Rolt, who has a certificate of competency, and has been for two years and ten months in the employment of the company, as Commander on this station, during which time he has made six voyages to Fernando Po and back. He had previously been three years in the employment of the Pacific Steam Navigation Company, during part of which time he acted as Commander.

The NIGER arrived at Sierra Leone, on her homeward voyage, on the 27th May last, and after making up her supply of fuel to 176 tons—amply sufficient according to her ordinary rate of consumption—she proceeded on for Tenerife, touching Goree by the way. On her passage to Tenerife, she encountered strong head winds, by which, and also, as alleged, by some imperfection of her fuel, she was both retarded in her progress, and carried to the westward, out of her usual course. Falling short of fuel, it became necessary to make for Cristianos, at the south-western extremity of the island of Tenerife, the nearest place where she could obtain a supply of wood for fuel. Her proper station at Tenerife is Santa Cruz, about 45 miles to the north-eastward of Cristianos. Having obtained about 10 tons of wood, all that could be had, the NIGER left Cristianos at noon on the 12th of June. Under ordinary circumstances, the run of 45 miles to Santa Cruz could be made in four hours; but owing to the wind blowing strongly from the northward and eastward, and the wood fuel not supplying sufficient steam, she did not sight Santa Cruz till towards dusk—being about 10 or 12 miles off at 5 p.m. Her course up to this point was along the coast, from two to three miles from shore. It became quite dark about 6.30 p.m., at which time the lights on the Mole of Santa Cruz could be seen, but not the line of coast. From this time till 8.45, the ship had her sails all set, with light winds off the land, but little assistance from the engines, from the difficulty of getting up steam. A proper look-out was kept, and a leadsman placed in the chains. Just before the ship struck, the soundings suddenly dropped to 4½ fathoms, when the engines were ordered to be reversed, but too late to prevent the ship running aground. After remaining in her first position for a short time, she swung towards the shore, and is supposed to have surged a ship's length or so in-shore, where she filled and remained till she became a total wreck. Little was

attempted or could be done for the ship, but the passengers, mails, specie and some part of the cargo were saved, and every proper exertion made for that purpose.

The position of the ship when she struck was about half a mile to the south-westward of the Mole, and rather less than a quarter of a mile from the shore. Taking this as evidence of the course she must have held for the last two hours after dark, she must have been gradually getting much more in-shore than was perceived—an error resulting probably from the darkness, the frequent stoppages of the engines, and the little headway the ship was making.

If, as stated in the evidence, the ship was two or three miles off the land when lights on the Mole were sighted at 6.30 and when the course was said to be E.N.E., the Mole lights bearing N.N.E. ½E, the course she is described to have taken, if not disturbed, would have brought her clear of the shoal.

On being asked to give his own explanation of the loss of the ship, the Captain assigns the following causes:

1. That the light which had stood at the point of the Mole on his preceding voyage, had been removed, so that the farthest out light was 30 or 40 yards more in-shore than when he was last there.
2. That a current, of which he was not aware, was setting towards the shore after dark.
3. That the depth of water on the shoal opposite the Barrance Ravine where the ship grounded, has considerably decreased since the date of his chart, and
   Lastly, that the want of headway prevented a proper control over the ship.

None of these causes, however, seem fully to meet the facts of the case.

1. The change of 30 or 40 yards in the position of the light would not account for the ship's course so much in-shore.
2. The current (admitting its existence) is not proved either as to its strength or direction, and is likely to have been rather more in the line of the shoal than directly on shore.
3. The gradual decrease of water is not proved and would not excuse the ship being inside the line of five fathom soundings, as marked in his chart, and
   Lastly, the want of headway, unless there was some current or other cause of disturbance to the direction of the ship's course, would merely operate to delay its progress.

NIGER *ashore*

Without, however, disputing the existence of any or all of the causes of loss alleged by the Captain, it seems possible to account for the position of the ship by a very natural supposition, consistently with the facts as proved. It is to be observed, that on former occasions the Captain made Santa Cruz, passing the Grand Canary, and coming direct upon the land, from the southward and eastward. On this occasion, his course being from the southward and westward, was parallel to the line of shoal water. Being desirous of keeping in with the land in consequence of the state of his ship, and in order to pick up the fuel lighter which he was expecting to be sent out to meet him, and which he was signalling by firing guns and throwing up blue lights, it is probable that he may not have made sufficient allowance of offing to clear the point of the spit which lay in his way when approaching the Mole in that direction. The different aspect of the light on his Mole, and the current which is alleged to have been setting towards the shore, would both tend to increase the risk from keeping too close to the land. This explanation of the loss is, however, merely conjectural; and, even supposing it to be correct, it cannot, in my opinion, be considered as amounting to a "wrongful act or default".

In this view of the case, it is unnecessary for me to refer particularly to the strong testimonials produced by Captain Rolt, as to his general good character and ability, and as to the propriety of his behaviour on this occasion.

I have the honour to be, my Lords,
Your Lordships' obedient servant,
James Traill.

To the Lords Commissioners of the Privy Council for Trade.

I concur in the opinion that the loss of the NIGER was not to be attributed to the "wrongful act or default" of the Master.

13 CLEOPATRA
O.N. 10483   1859–1862

Iron screw steamer
219.0′×32.0′×18.0′   893 n   1280 g
Built by Alexander Denny and Bros, Dumbarton, Yard No 23, for McKean, McLarty & Lamont (Anglo-Brazilian Steam Navigation Co), Liverpool. 2 cyl 62″–54″ by Tulloch, Alexander Denny & Bros, Dumbarton. (Engine No 6) 9 K.
Passengers: 130 first, 120 second, 60 third class.

1852	21 April, launched.

1852   21 April, launched.
1854   Transferred to Canadian Steam Navigation Co. Placed on UK–Canada mail service. First voyage to Quebec took 45 days.
1857   Sold to Rigge, Cropper, Johnson, Carmichael & Co.
1859   8 June, acquired by African Steamship Co. October, commenced maiden voyage to West Africa.
1860   Fractured propeller shaft and came home from Sierra Leone under sail.
1862   6 August, departed Bonny homeward bound. 18 August, ran ashore in Sewa River, Sierra Leone. 22 August, passengers (10) and crew (61) abandoned ship. Chief Engineer drowned during rescue operation; he was the only casualty. All mail, cargo and passengers' baggage lost. Vessel declared a constructive total loss. Court of Enquiry found Captain Delamotte guilty in failing to take proper care, soundings or allowing for current. His certificate was suspended for six months.

Note—In 1862 John Holt made his first visit to West Africa in **CLEOPATRA**, sailing from Liverpool 23 June and arriving Fernando Po 28 July.

14 MACGREGOR LAIRD (I)
O.N. 44006   1862–1871

Iron screw steamer
250.0′×31.0′×19.0′   659 n   969 g
Built by Randolph, Elder & Co, Glasgow, for African Steamship Co. C 2 cyl by the builders. 200 hp.
1861   December, launched.
1870   Lengthened by 41′ to 291.0′, 1311 g. Assisted the refloating of *CALABAR* in Sherbro River.
1871   13 November, left Liverpool for Madeira and West Africa with 66 passengers and 51 crew (Captain Henry Clancy). 13 December, wrecked near Cape St Jean, Corisco Bay, Rio Muni (approximately 01°.00′N 09°.00′E). No loss of life. Master's certificate suspended for six months.

CLEOPATRA

The Liverpool *Daily Courier* reported the loss on 29 January 1872.

THE WRECK OF THE MACGREGOR LAIRD
The ship and crew attacked by Africans

A few days ago a brief telegram was received in Liverpool from Lloyd's agent at Lisbon announcing that the Portuguese mail steamer Dom Pedro had arrived at that port from the south coast of Africa and Madeira bringing intelligence of the total wreck of the West African Company's royal mail steamer MACGREGOR LAIRD, Commander Herbert Wharton, in Corisco Bay on south coast of Africa on the 18th December and adding that the crew, passengers, mail and specie were saved but the ship, cargo and baggage were a complete loss. On Saturday last however, a communication was received in Liverpool from Capt. Wharton which, although it modifies the telegram a little, is entirely confirmatory of the total wreck of the steamer. The letter was written on board the French gunboat 24th December 1871. Capt. Wharton says that the MACGREGOR LAIRD was totally wrecked on a rock improperly laid down in the Admiralty chart whilst she was rounding the land to the southward of Cape St. John to enter Eloby on the morning of the 15th December. He is, however, glad to say that the crew and passengers were all safe and well with the exception of the surgeon of the ship, Dr. Irvine and Mr. Morgan the assistant purser, both of whom were wounded slightly in the legs during a skirmish with the hostile natives who came off to the ship in hundreds some time after the ship struck and took complete possession of her. Captain Wharton says he was compelled to abandon the ship too, after she struck the rock, as there was only one boat to save the cargo and that belonged to Messrs Hatton Cookson, African merchants, which took one load away. The wreck, which lay about 11 miles from Eloby and completely covered at high water was sold as she lay for £500 and the stores for £146-10s. Capt. Wharton he also added, succeeded in saving the ship's papers.

MacGregor Laird was the founder of the African Steamship Co.

ALPES, *formerly* **MANDINGO** (Photo Hapag-Lloyd)

15 CALABAR (I)
O.N. 49907   1864–1873

Iron screw barque, two decks
260.5′×31.4′×19.2′   763 n   1122 g
Built by Randolph, Elder & Co, Glasgow, for African Steamship Co. C 4 cyl. 33″(2), 66″(2)–42″ by the builders. 250 hp.
1864   Completed.
1867   23 July, left Liverpool with John Holt's first shipment of goods to West Africa.
1870   Aground for seven days in Sherbro River, Sierra Leone, was assisted off by *MACGREGOR LAIRD*.
1873   29 July, sold to Thomas Royden and Son, Liverpool, in part payment of new building *ETHIOPIA*.
1874   New boiler fitted. Sold to R. W. Hutchenson Ltd.
1877   Sold to Chinese owners. Not traced after 1886.
Calabar is the old trading station 29 miles up the Calabar River and five miles above its junction with the Cross River, Eastern Nigeria.

16 MARGARET
O.N. 44679   1864–1865

Wooden barque
109.8′×25.5′×9.8′   254 g
Built by unrecorded builders at Philadelphia, USA for unknown owners. Date of building not recorded.
1862   Acquired by C. Saunders, Liverpool. Registered Liverpool.
1864   7 December, purchased by African Steamship Co. Registered London.
1865   6 December, reported to Directors of African Steamship Co that nothing had been heard of the ship for six months and that she must be presumed lost, voyage Liverpool to Lagos.

17 MANDINGO (I)

O.N. 54599   1866–1872

'Mandingo' class
Iron screw barque, two decks
262.3' × 32.4' × 19.3' 770 n 1216 g
Built by Randolph, Elder & Co, Glasgow, Yard No 44, for
African Steamship Co. Registered London. C 2 cyl 34", 52"–42"
by the builders. 275 hp.

1866   21 October, launched.
1872   Sold to Hornstedt & Garthorne. Registered Hull.
1873–74   Lengthened by 33.4' and re-engined by J. & J. Thomson, Glasgow. C 2 cyl 32", 60"–36", 180 hp, 1020 n, 1578 g.
1876   Sold to Atlas Steamship Co Ltd. Renamed **ALPS** (also referred to as **ALPES**). Registered Liverpool.
1889   Registered Kingston, Jamaica (British flag). 1117 n, 1725 g.
1890   Registered Liverpool.
1900   Sold to Hamburg Amerikanische Packetfahrt AG, Hamburg. Registered Hamburg.
1904   Sold to Dr Wilh. Kohlmann, New Orleans.
1907   Sold to S. d'Antoni (Vaccaro Bros, Steamship Co Managers), Glasgow. Registered British Flag.
1907   December, wrecked off coast of Spanish Honduras.

Ships of the 'Mandingo' class: MANDINGO (17), LAGOS (18).

Mandingo is the name of a major tribe in the Senegal area of West Africa.

18 LAGOS (I)

O.N. 54626   1866–1872

'Mandingo' class
Iron screw barque, two decks
262.2' × 32.4' × 19.3' 754 n 1199 g

ANDES**, formerly **LAGOS (Photo Hapag-Lloyd)

MANDINGO *under sail*

Built by Randolph, Elder & Co, Glasgow, Yard No 45, for
African Steamship Co. Registered London. C 2 cyl 36", 72"–42"
by the builders. 275 hp.

1866   Completed.
1872   Sold to Atlas Steamship Co Ltd.
1874   Lengthened and re-engined by J. Taylor & Co, Birkenhead. 294.0' × 32.4' × 19.3', 1216 n, 1638 g. C 2 cyl 24", 62"–36", 192 hp.
1876   Renamed **ANDES**. Registered London.
1889   Registered Liverpool. 1104 n, 1711 g.
1890   Re-boilered by J. Taylor & Co, Birkenhead. Now 220 hp, 1197 n, 1868 g.
1902   Sold to Hamburg Amerikanische Packetfahrt AG. Registered Hamburg.
1903   Sold to Dierich Gortz. Renamed **GORTZ**.
1908   Sold to Enrique Heilbut, Havana. Registered Hamburg. July, broken up at Genoa.

Lagos is the island and port, now the capital of Nigeria.

19   BIAFRA (I)

O.N. 60847   1868–1889

Iron screw barque, two decks
274.0'×32.2'×20.0'   797 n   1280 g
Built by Randolph, Elder & Co, Glasgow, for African Steamship
Co (Charles Dore, Manager), London. Registered London.
C 2 cyl 34", 66"–42" by the builders. 250 hp.

1868   August, completed.
1874   Lengthened to 312.0', 938 n, 1484 g.
1875   30 September, engine breakdown, towed into St Vincent.
1876   13 January, arrived Liverpool in tow. New engines and
       boilers by Laird Bros, Birkenhead. C 2 cyl 34", 57"–36",
       150 hp, 1133 n, 1487 g.
1884   24 July, blow-off pipe of port boiler gave way killing one
       man, in position 5 miles SSW Cape Mount, West Africa.
1889   Sold to Bossiere Freres & Cie, Havre. Renamed
       ENERGIQUE. Registered Havre.
1892   Sold to O. M. Essayan, Constantinople. Registered Con-
       stantinople. 879 n, 1513 g.
1893   Sold to Idarei Massousieh (Ottoman Steam Navigation
       Co), Constantinople. Renamed **INAYET**. Registered
       Constantinople.
1902   29 December, reported to Lloyds that vessel had recently
       run ashore off Chesmo, near Smyrna (in the Aegean
       Sea) and had become a total loss.
Name taken from the Bight of Biafra in the Gulf of Guinea.

20   BONNY (I)

O.N. 60402   1869–1890

'Bonny' class
Iron screw brig, one deck
261.2'×30.1'×23.0'   798 n   1277 g
Built by Randolph, Elder & Co, Glasgow, Yard No 97, for
British and African Steam Navigation Co. Registered Glasgow.
C 2 cyl 38", 68–33" by the builders. 250 hp.

1869   Completed.
1875   Mate of hulk KENT accused of murdering Master by
       pushing him overboard in the Bonny River, repatriated
       to England per **BONNY**.
1890   Sold to Caillol & St Pierre, Marseilles. Renamed
       JEANNE D'ARC. Registered Marseilles. 742 n, 1281 g.
1902   Sold to E. Caillol Duvillard, Marseilles.

1907   Sold to Cie Nouvelle Mediterraneenne de Navigation,
       (L. de Montravel & F. Roache, Managers), Marseilles.
       778 n, 1263 g.
1910   Sold for demolition.
Ships of the 'Bonny' class: BONNY (20), ROQUELLE (21),
CONGO (22).
Bonny is a river and port in the eastern portion of the Niger
delta. It is a corruption of Ubani, Umani & Ebinya.

BONNY

21   ROQUELLE (I)

O.N. 60408   1869–1882

'Bonny' class
Iron screw brig, one deck
261.0'×30.2'×23.0'   796 n   1289 g
Built by Randolph, Elder & Co, Glasgow, Yard No 98, for the
British & African Steam Navigation Co. Registered Glasgow.
C 2 cyl 38", 68"–33" by the builders. 200 hp, 11 K.

1869   Completed.
1882   June, sold to P. M. Tintore, Barcelona. Renamed
       TINTORE. Registered Barcelona.
1907   Sold to Linea Aenea de Vapores Tintore, Barcelona.
1914   Reboilered, 706 n, 1322 g.
1919   Sold to Cia Transmediterranea, Barcelona.
1933   Sold to Isiena Maritima SA, Barcelona. Registered
       Barcelona.
1934   Passenger certificate granted.
1936   Broken up in Spain.
Name derived from the Rokel River in Sierra Leone.

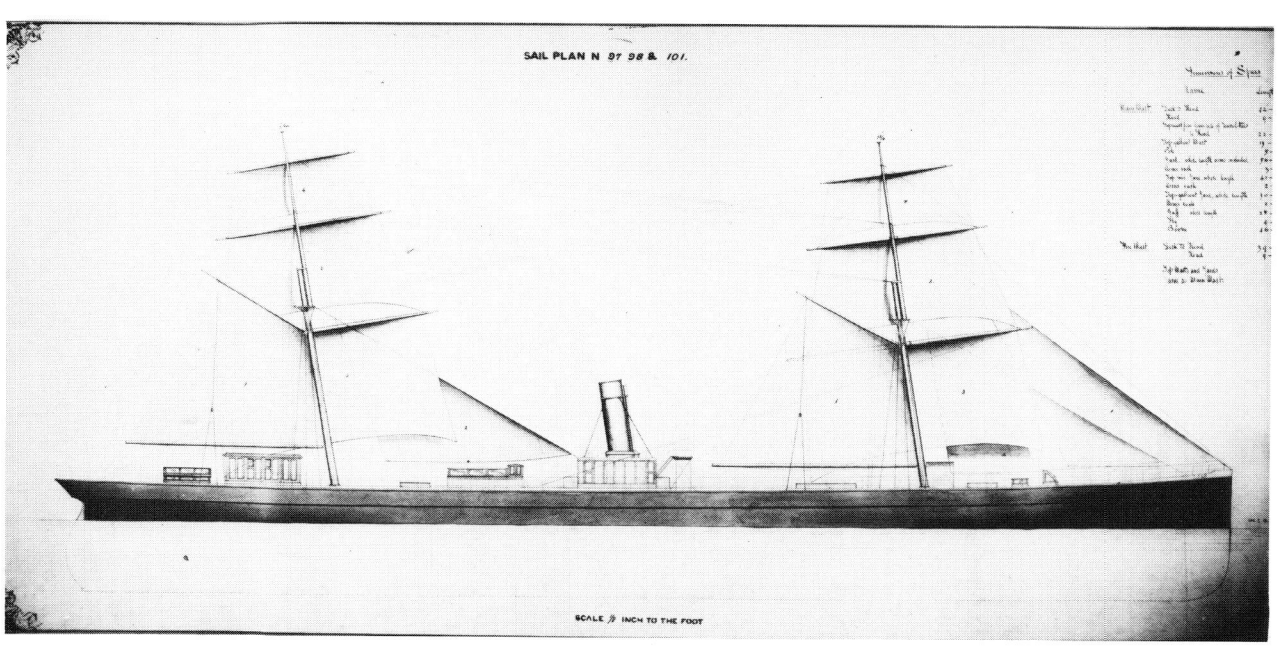

CONGO sail plan (Photo Strathclyde Regional Archives)

ROQUELLE

22 CONGO (I)
O.N. 60414   1869–1881

'Bonny' class
Iron screw brig, two decks
261.2′×30.2′×23.0′   800 n   1283 g
Built by Randolph, Elder & Co, Glasgow, Yard No 101, for
British and African Steam Navigation Co. Registered Glasgow.
C 2 cyl 38″, 68″–33″ by the builders. 200 hp, 11 K.
1869   February, completed.
1881   23 November, sold to Cie General des Bateaux a Vapeur
         a hel du Nord, Dunkirk. Registered Dunkirk.
1891   Renamed **VILLE DE MARSEILLE**. 756 n, 1277 g.
1907   April, sold for demolition at Dunkirk.
Name derived from the mighty African river.

23 BENIN (I)
O.N. 60943   1869–1881

Iron screw barque, two decks
284.3′×33.1′×23.6′   969 n   1530 g
Built by Randolph, Elder & Co, Glasgow, for British & African
Steam Navigation Co. Registered London. C 2 cyl 39¼″, 71¼″–
36″ by the builders. 200 hp, 11 K.
1869   3 July, commenced maiden voyage, (Captain Herbert
         Wharton).
1879   10 March, opened a joint service from Hamburg to West
         Africa in co-operation with the African Steamship Co.
1880   In collision with Norwegian galliot SUCCESS, which
         became a total loss.

1881   12 March, (Captain S. J. Wilkins) sunk after collision
         with DUKE OF BUCCLEUCH (3021 g/built 1874),
         Eastern Steam Ship Co Ltd, Barrow, voyage West Africa
         to Liverpool, off Start Point. No loss of life.
1954   October, salvage vessel HELP located wreck in position
         50°.53′N 03°.31′W, 18 miles SE from Start Point. Divers
         could see boilers and compound engine. Dinner plates
         bearing the Company's crest and 96 elephant tusks
         brought up.
Benin is the ancient city state of the Bini tribe of Nigeria.

The distinctive crest of the African Steamship Company can be clearly seen on this photograph of a broken plate, which was brought up from the s.s. *Benin* by the salvage vessel *Help* in October 1954, during salvage operations conducted by Messrs Risdon Beazley Limited about eighteen miles south east of Start Point, South Devon

A plate salvaged from **BENIN**

24 LIBERIA
O.N. 58336   1870–1874

'Liberia' class
Iron screw brigantine, two decks
279.0′×31.0′×23.0′   927 n   1470 g
Built by John Elder & Co, Glasgow, for British and African Steam Navigation Co. Registered Glasgow. C 2 cyl 38″, 68″–33″ by the builders. 250 hp, 11 K.
1870   Completed and chartered to Pacific Steam Navigation Co for the maiden voyage, United Kingdom–South America–United Kingdom.
1874   11 April, went missing between Liverpool and Madeira.
Ships of the 'Liberia' class: LIBERIA (24), LOANDA (25), VOLTA (26).
Liberia is a West African Republic on what was formerly known as the Grain Coast.

25 LOANDA (I)
O.N. 63776   1870–1889

'Liberia' class
Iron screw brigantine, two decks
279.1′×31.1′×23.5′   899 n   1474 g
Built by John Elder & Co, Glasgow, Yard No 111, for British & African Steam Navigation Co. Registered Glasgow. C 2 cyl. 38″, 68″–33″ by the builders. 250 hp, 11 K.
1870   May, completed.
1889   18 July, sold to David MacBrayne, Glasgow. 913 n, 1475 g. Used for some time as a coal depot.
1897   May, sold for demolition at Garston.
Name derived from port and railway terminal in Angola.

26 VOLTA
O.N. 63789   1870–1892

'Liberia' class
Iron screw brigantine, two decks
279.5′×31.1′×23.4′   931 n   1477 g

Built by John Elder & Co, Glasgow, Yard No 115, for British & African Steam Navigation Co. Registered Glasgow. C 2 cyl 38″, 68″–33″ by the builders. 250 hp, 11 K.
1870   September, completed.
1892   Sold to Alex F. Blackwater, Glasgow.
1894   December, sold for demolition.
Name derived from the major river of Ghana.

27 RIO FORMOSO
O.N. 63263   1870–1875

Iron screw steamer, one deck
120.2′×20.1′×8.3′   96 n   163 g
Built by Bowdler & Chaffner & Co Ltd, Seacombe, Yard No 163, for British & African Steam Navigation Co. Registered Liverpool. C 2 cyl 16″, 32″–18″ by J. Taylor & Co, Birkenhead. 40 hp. Designed for service on the Niger Delta.
1870   Completed.
1871   28 October, grounded in the River Niger.
1875   Sold to G. F. Fisher
1876   Sold to W. Buchanan. Registered Glasgow.
1877   Sold to G. J. Kidson. Ran aground but salved.
1879   Sold to W. Middleton, Cork. Registered Cork.
1883   Sold to W. Pollexfen & A. J. Middleton, Sligo.
1887   Sold to W. Pockett, Swansea. Registered Swansea. For coasting service Swansea–Padstow.
1890   Transferred to Pockett's Bristol Channel Steam Packet Co Ltd (T. Probert, Manager), Swansea. 100 n, 164 g.
1891   Sold to H. Flinn (T. Probert, Manager).
1902   Sold to J. Summers & Sons, Chester. 80 n, 164 g.
1904   Sold to L. du Mururi, Santander. Registered Bilbao. 75 n, 169 g.
1909   March, foundered while on voyage La Pallice to Bilbao, cargo potatoes.
Rio Formoso is the name of one of the mouths of the River Niger.

EBOE

28   EBOE (I)
O.N. 63561   1870–1875

Iron screw schooner, one deck
209.8′×27.3′×13.4′   487 n   653 g
Built by Thomas Royden, Liverpool, for African Steamship Co.
Registered London. C 2 cyl 26″, 50″–30″ by J. Jack and Co,
Liverpool. 100 hp. Designed for the West African feeder service.
1870   Completed.
1874   Returned to UK and offered for sale.
1875   Sold to Charles Tillier (Soc du Transports Figorifique).
       Renamed **FIGORIFIQUE**. Registered Rouen. Refriger-
       ating machinery and insulated cargo space installed.
1876   20 September, left Rouen with cargo of refrigerated meat
       for Buenos Aires. 25 December, arrived Buenos Aires
       with cargo in good condition. For the next five years
       Tillier unsuccessfully tried to establish the carriage of
       refrigerated meat and vegetables by steamship.
1881   Sold to Maritime Worms & Co. Refrigerating machinery
       and equipment removed, vessel reverted to general cargo
       carrier.
1884   19 March, rammed aft by British steamer RUMNEY
       in dense fog near Ile de Sein (off Pointe du Raz),
       Brittany. Crew abandoned ship but left helm hard
       over and engines running and boarded RUMNEY.
       FIGORIFIQUE then rammed the British ship on her
       starboard side and the latter began to sink. The two
       crews boarded the French ship, the engines were stopped
       but she too was sinking. Taking to the boats again all
       hands made the coast. **FIGORIFIQUE** and RUMNEY
       both sank.

Eboe (Ibo) is the name of the major tribe of Eastern Nigeria.
Figorifique is the French equivalent to 'freezer'.

29   SOUDAN (I)
O.N. 63639   1870–1875

Iron screw barque, two decks
290.3′×33.1′×23.7′   1019 n   1603 g
Built by Thomas Royden, Liverpool, for African Steamship Co
Ltd. Laid down as **SHERBRO (I)**, name change requested by
Colonial Office. Registered London. C 2 cyl 40″, 71″–36″ by J.
Jack & Co, Liverpool. 200 hp.
1870   Completed. 3 June, beached at Bonny for propeller
       repairs.
1873   Fourteen days delay at Tenerife to effect engine repairs.
1875   2 February, wrecked at Madeira. Master's certificate
       suspended for six months. All but £300 of ship value
       covered by outside insurers.

Name derived from the upper Nile territory.

SOUDAN

YORUBA

30   YORUBA (I)
O.N. 65606   1871–1873

Iron screw schooner
285.0′×33.2′×23.9′   1090 n   1705 g
Built by Laird Bros, Birkenhead, Yard No 382, for African
Steamship Co. Registered London. C 2 cyl 40″, 71″–36″ by the
builders. 200 hp, 10 K. Limited passenger accommodation.
1871   Launched 23 March.
1872   Chartered to Pacific Steam Navigation Co for a round
       voyage United Kingdom–Callao. Maintained an aver-
       age speed of 11 knots.
1873   13 May, left Liverpool for West Coast of Africa. 31 May,
       while at anchor off Cape Palmas (to deliver mail) struck
       a pinnacle of rock. Vessel beached one mile to the north
       of the cape but broke up in the heavy swell. There
       was no loss of life. Court of Enquiry acquitted Captain
       Edward Strachan Haram.

Yoruba is the name of the major tribe in Western Nigeria.

AFRICA

31   AFRICA
O.N. 65660   1872–1899

Iron screw schooner, two decks
295.3′×34.3′×23.2′   1099 n   1717 g
Built by Laird Bros, Birkenhead, Yard No 390, as **ANGOLA**,

AFRICA in a hurricane, December 1874, from a painting by Captain E. Addison

for African Steamship Co. Registered London. C 2 cyl 40″, 71″–36″ by the builders. 200 hp, 11 K.
Limited passenger accommodation.
1871   December, launched as **AFRICA**.
1872   1 March, commenced maiden voyage.
1886   Engines and boilers renewed by Harland & Wolff Ltd, Belfast. C 2 cyl 27″, 54″–36″, 146 nhp.
1899   December, sold for demolition at Hamburg.
Note—The change of name whilst vessel was on the stocks was due to the political atmosphere at the time—the Portuguese Government was about to reserve trade between Lisbon and the Portuguese settlements in West Africa for their own flag vessels.

32   SENEGAL
O.N. 67991   1872–1887

Iron screw brig
288.0′×34.0′×22.6′   1048 n   1625 g
Built by Cunliffe & Dunlop, Port Glasgow, for British and African Steam Navigation Co, Glasgow. Registered Glasgow. C 2 cyl 40″, 71″–36″ by the builders. 275 hp, 11 K.
Limited passenger accommodation.
1872   April, completed.
1880   April, resued a number of survivors from the Union liner AMERICAN, which had sunk 200 miles off Las Palmas after breaking her shaft. Then herself ran aground off Las Palmas. December, hull lengthened by 24′ to 312.0′ in course of repairs following stranding in April. 1142 n, 1793 g.
1887   2 June, wrecked near Tabou Point Guinea, when homewards towards Liverpool (Captain C. Brown).
Senegal is the republic surrounding Gambia.

33   NIGRETIA (I)
O.N. 65720   1872–1873

Iron screw steamer, two masts
299.8′×34.4′×23.0′   1168 n   1810 g
Built by Whitehaven Shipbuilding Co as **BENTINCK** for unknown owners and bought by African Steamship Co and renamed **NIGRETIA**. C 2 cyl 40″, 70″–36″ by J. Jack Rollo & Co Ltd. 200 hp.
1872   May, completed.
1873   14 June, Saturday, left Freetown 2000, ran aground on Carpenter Rock, four miles off the port, on a calm and clear night within a mile of the lighthouse. No loss of life. Mail and specie salved, also some cargo. Became a total loss.

The original owners of this vessel are unrecorded, but her dimensions are identical to those of the Union SS Co Ltd ASIATIC completed by the same builders in January 1873, and which had similarly been purchased by that company whilst on the stocks.

WRECK OF AN AFRICAN MAIL STEAMER

Sir,
The Royal Mail steamer NIGRETIA (Captain Rowlands), arrived on the morning of the 13th from England, having on board a considerable quantity of specie and a large supply of arms and material of war for Cape Coast Castle for the use of the military force now assembled there and our native allies the Fantees. She brought out some field guns of the Abyssinian pattern, a large quantity of 9 pounder rockets of the War Hall pattern and of case and shrapnel shot and among the stores were included a considerable quantity of lead and a good supply of flints. The Fantees use such antiquated weapons that it would be impossible to describe what kind of cartridge would be suitable and in many cases they are still armed with the old flintlock muskets. Among the passengers were Captain Hold one of the officers sent out to organise the new Housa force which is being raised and some Commisseriat officials for Cape Coast Castle and Dr. Gupfeldt and Lieutenant Von Hattew of the German Army, members of the expedition sent out by

the Royal Geographical Society of Berlin, to explore the Congo and to endeavour to traverse the entire breadth of Africa and to reach Abyssinia, starting from the mouth of the Congo. She left her anchorage here for Cape Coast Castle about a quarter to 8 o'clock on Saturday evening the 14th having taken on board a large number of bullocks for use down the coast where fresh meat is not procurable except when bought from here. The Nigritia was joined at Freetown by Deputy Surgeon-General Home, V.C. and C.B. the principal medical officer on the West Coast, who has been specially sent out to take charge of the troops during the impending Ashantee War and who had been engaged for the last week on a sanitary inspection of the barrack here.

Great excitement was caused in Freetown on it becoming known there about an hour and a half after the Nigritia had left that she was aground on the Carpenter Rock—a very dangerous reef at the mouth of the bay about four miles from Freetown. This rock is called the 'Carpenter' by the natives in grim allusion to the quantity of carpenters work it does in breaking up vessels that get on it. About 9 o'clock some of the residents in the Tower-hill Barracks, which are built on an eminence and have a commanding view, perceived that some vessel was on the Carpenter Rock and was firing off rockets and guns and burning blue lights. A messenger was immediately sent out to appraise the harbour officials and Mr. Shaw the Collector of Customs proceeded immediately on board the Mail Company's homeward bound steamer the Biafra, which was then at anchor in the harbour. Owing to the hill intervening between Carpenter's reef and the harbour, nothing had been seen or heard on the Biafra. Captain Stone on being informed of what had occurred, despatched with great promptitude his starboard lifeboat and a full crew to the assistance of the distressed vessel. Steam was immediately got up on board the Biafra, but this took some time as the boilers had been blown off. The anxiety was increased in Freetown by the rapidity with which the Nigritia continued to send up rockets and fire guns, especially as it was known she was very deeply laden, having over 2,700 tons of cargo on board, including a large quantity of rum in puncheons as deck cargo and that she had an unusually large number of passengers and a very full crew. The Biafra sent up rocket after rocket to show that the signals of distress were seen and about a quarter to 11 o'clock proceeded at full speed to the scene of the disaster. When about halfway, she was met by a boat from the Nigritia with a letter from the captain stating that the vessel was on the Carpenter Rock and fast filling and requesting immediate assistance. The Biafra reached the scene about half past 11 o'clock and found that the Nigritia had run full speed on the reef on its extreme westward or seaward edge and was stuck hard and fast with the rock right through her amidships. Before the Biafra reached her some assistance had come off the neighbouring village of Aberdeen and the boat thence had taken off the passengers, mail and specie and landed them on the Point Lighthouse which is three-quarters of a mile from the Carpenters reef and was mainly built to warn vessels off it. All the bullocks were thrown overboard and most of them reached the shore safely but the sharks made a meal of some of them. The specie was sent ashore in the pursers charge, in a boat manned by Kroomen of whom a large number are always taken on board by outward-bound steamers to assist the crew in loading and unloading cargo down the coast. On landing, the purser, who was armed with a revolver to protect the bullion, suddenly fired off a couple of barrels to convey to the Kroomen and the natives generally his unchangeable determination to protect the charge entrusted to him. The Kroomen believing they were about to be shot down, fled with loud cries and were not seen again. The Biafra let go her anchor close to the reef and Captain Stone went on board the Nigritia but nothing could be done for her, so Biafra returned to harbour the next morning to get lighters and men to unload the cargo.

It is feared here that this disaster may cause serious inconvenience at Cape Coast from the delay that must come in forwarding the supplies of war material, provisions and medical stores which the Nigritia contained. The loss is serious, as the Nigritia was a new steamer recently built at a cost of over £60,000 and by a strange fatality another of these newest and finest vessels, the Yoruba, 1625 tons has been lost within the last few days near Cape Palmas on the Grain Coast, about 450 miles to the south-east of this. The Yoruba was also proceeding with supplies and mails to Cape Coast when she went ashore. Thus Cape Coast Castle has been without news for the last two mails and two vessels, each laden with supplies, have failed to reach it. The Biafra on her passage up from Cape Coast lay near the Yoruba for eight days to try and get her off, but completely failed and the day Biafra left here there was a very heavy surf beating on shore. It was expected that the vessel would shortly go to pieces. This double catastrophe has caused great excitement here and it is hoped that a full and searching investigation will be made as to the loss of these two steamers, more especially into the case of the Nigritia, which has been lost on one of the best known and most clearly laid down rock on the entire coast at the mouth of the most frequented port on the West Coast of Africa, on perfectly calm and clear night within less than a mile of the lighthouse specially built to warn vessels off this rock. The pilot had left the Nigritia about a short quarter of an hour before she was run full speed on the Carpenter's. All hope of saving her has been abandoned and the crew are being sent home. Mr. Shar, the Collector of Customs has been very active since the disaster in affording any assistance to the passengers and saving cargo. It is feared that the valuable instruments brought out by the German expedition are lost or so damaged as to be useless. WEST AFRICAN EXILE, Freetown, Sierra Leone. June 18, 1873.

From *The Times* 10 July 1873

34 AMBRIZ
O.N. 65894   1873–1895

Iron screw schooner, three masts, two decks
324.6′×35.2′×25.6′   1376 n   2121 g
Built by Thomas Royden & Sons, Liverpool, Yard No 137. Purchased on the stocks by Oceanic Steam Navigation Co Ltd (White Star Line) and named **ASIATIC**. C 2 cyl 40″, 80″–36″ by Laird Bros, Birkenhead. 250 hp.
Passenger accommodation: 10.
1870   1 December, launched.
1873   25 March, commenced maiden voyage from Liverpool to Valparaiso. Offered for sale on return and acquired by African Steamship Co. Renamed **AMBRIZ**. Registered London. 12 September, commenced maiden voyage from Liverpool.
1880   18 February, grounded in River Elbe, damaged sternpost, repaired at Devonport Dockyard.
1883   December, new engines and boilers by Laird Bros. C 2 cyl 37″, 75″–36″, 281 hp.
1895   Sold to Hutton & Co, Liverpool. Registered Liverpool.
1896   Sold to Cie Francaise Charbonnage & de Batelage, Madagascar. Registered Majunga (Madagascar) (French flag). 1373 n, 2130 g.
1903   February, wrecked during coastwise voyage from Majunga.
Ambriz is a port at the mouth of the River Loje, Angola.

35 ETHIOPIA (I)
O.N. 68456   1873–1882

Iron screw schooner, one deck
293.0′×34.3′×23.2′   1125 n   1761 g
Built by Thomas Royden & Son, Liverpool, for African Steamship Co. Registered London. C 2 cyl 40″, 71″–36″ by G. Forrester & Co, Liverpool. 250 hp.
1873   Completed.
1882   28 July, wrecked off Indian Point, Loango, voyage Hamburg to West Africa with general cargo. No blame attached to the Master.

36 ELMINA (I)
O.N. 68451   1873–1878

Iron screw schooner, three masts, one deck
267.7′×31.6′×14.8′   634 n   1018 g
Built by Thomas Royden & Son, Liverpool, Yard No 149, for African Steamship Co. Registered London. C 2 cyl 35″, 70″–42″ by G. Forrester & Co, Liverpool. 150 hp, 11 K.
1873   March, completed.
1878   April, sold to J. D. Rivera, Havana. Renamed **GIBARA**. Registered Havana (Spanish flag).
1887   Ranamed **MORTERA**.
1894   Sold to Sobrenos de Herrera, Havana.

1902   Registered Havana (Cuban flag).
1907   Sold to J. de Rivera, Havana.
1909   Reported sunk.
The name is derived from the old slave port and castle in Ghana.

37   MONROVIA (I)
O.N. 68418   1873–1876
Iron screw schooner, one deck
267.7′×31.6′×14.8′   637 n   1019 g
Built by Thomas Royden & Son, Liverpool, for African Steam-ship Co Ltd. Registered London. C 2 cyl 34″, 64½″–30″ by G. Forrester & Co, Liverpool. 180 hp.
Prior to entering service there was a long outstanding dispute with the shipbuilders; alleged non-fulfilment of contract. In 1875 the case finally went to arbitration and was won by the African Steamship Co.
1873   Completed.
1874   22 December stranded at Lagos.
1875   10 January, refloated, with assistance of WHYDAH and proceeded homewards after temporary repairs. 8 April, arrived London.
1876   8 August, wrecked on Carpenter's Rock, Sierra Leone. No loss of life. Master's certificate suspended for 12 months.
Monrovia is the capital town and chief port of the Republic of Liberia.

38   WHYDAH (I)
O.N. 70645   1874–1894
Iron screw schooner, one deck
186.6′×25.9′×11.4′   241 n   418 g
Built by London and Glasgow Co Ltd, Glasgow, Yard No 178, for African Steamship Co, London. Registered London. C 2 cyl 28″, 49″–30″ by the builders. 98 hp. Designed for West African Coast feeder service.
1874   September, completed.
1877   December, returned to United Kingdom for refit.
1882   Refitted in United Kingdom. Lengthened to 202.0′. New boilers fitted. 298 n, 505 g.
1894   August, stranded on Lagos Bar, salved and hulked at Opobo.
Whydah (Ouidah) is a port on the coast of Dahomey.

39   FORCADOS (I)
O.N. 68077   1874–1904
'Forcados' class
Iron screw brig, two masts
185.6′×25.1′×11.4′   327 n   456 g
Built by Cunliffe and Dunlop, Port Glasgow, Yard No 97, for British & African Steam Navigation Co. Registered Glasgow. C 2 cyl 23″, 40″–24″ by the builders. 80 hp.
Passenger accommodation: 8 first class.
1874   Completed.
1879   Reboilered.
1900   Port of Registry Liverpool.
1904   26 April, sank after striking rock on Forcados River, 33 miles above Sapele (Captain L. Jones).
Ships of the 'Forcados' class: FORCADOS (39), FORMOSO (40).
Forcados is the name of a river and port in the Niger Delta.

FORMOSO

40   FORMOSO
O.N. 73822   1876–1893
'Forcados' class
Iron screw brig, one deck
185.4′×25.2′×11.3′   328 n   461 g
Built by Cunliffe & Dunlop, Port Glasgow, for British & African Steam Navigation Co. Registered Glasgow. C 2 cyl 23″, 40″–24″ by the builders. 80 hp.
Passenger accommodation: 8 first class.
1876   Completed.
1890   Sold to Sierra Leone Coaling Co, Liverpool.
1893   Wrecked June at Lavanna, near Sulima, when outward bound from Freetown.
Formoso was a former name of the island of Fernando Po.

41   CAMEROON
O.N. 68115   1874–1904
'Cameroon' class
Iron screw brig, two decks
302.5′×33.8′×24.0′   1185 n   1862 g
Built by John Elder & Co, Glasgow, Yard No 172, for British & African Steam Navigation Co. Registered Glasgow. C 2 cyl 40″, 71″–36″ by the builders. 280 hp, 10½ K.
Passenger accommodation: 30 first class, 8 second.
1874   May, completed.
1889   New engines and boilers by D. Rollo & Son, Liverpool. T 3 cyl 21″, 34¼″, 55¾″–36″, 157 hp.
1892   4 August, left Liverpool for West Africa. September, ran aground at Fernando Po. Captain Charles Thompson's certificate suspended for six months.
1900   Port of registry Liverpool.
1904   8 October, (Captain F. Baylis) struck submerged rock after leaving Nana Kroo, Liberia, for Sinoe, position 04°.49′N 08°.44′W on voyage Accra to Hamburg. Three passengers on board. Vessel beached to save life and property.
Ships of the 'Cameroon' class: CAMEROON (41), BENGUELA (42).
Name derived from the territory to the east of Nigeria.

42   BENGUELA (I)
O.N. 71655   1874–1905
'Cameroon' class
Iron screw brig, two decks
302.6′×33.9′×23.9′   1176 n   1860 g
Built by John Elder & Co, Glasgow, Yard No 171, for British & African Steam Navigation Co. Registered Glasgow. C 2 cyl 40″, 71″–36″ by the builders. 270 hp, 10½ K.

Passenger accommodation: 30 first class, 8 second.
1874   June, completed.
1897   New engines and boilers by Fawcett Preston & Co, Liverpool. T 3 cyl 21″, 34¼″, 55¾″–36″, 186 nhp. 1157 n, 1796 g.
1901   Port of Registry Liverpool.
1905   16 May, wrecked at Nana Kroo, Liberia, whilst on passage from Lome to Hamburg with a cargo of palm kernels, palm oil and cocoa beans. Captain M. W. Robinson and 32 crew. Three passengers. No lives lost.

A favourite ship of Miss Mary Kingsley, whose friend James Fothergill was Purser. In June 1926 the Elder Dempster House Magazine recorded his death:

The death of Mr. James Fothergill last month at the advanced age of 80 years removes from our midst a charming and interesting personality. Mr. Fothergill was born in Sussex in 1845 and joined the British & African Steam Navigation Co., in 1873, as Purser of the *Congo*. With the exception of a short interval between 1883 and 1887 when he was engaged in trade on the South-West Coast of Africa, Mr. Fothergill served continuously in our ships up to 1917. His last ship was the *Apapa* which was sunk on the voyage immediately after Mr. Fothergill left her.

Mr. Fothergill's knowledge of affairs West African was encyclopædic. He had many interesting stories to relate of early days in West Africa and could recall the troublesome times during the risings in Ashanti. He met Sir Garnet Wolseley when the General went out to the Gold Coast in 1874 as leader of one of the Ashanti expeditions. H. M. Stanley, the explorer, and Miss Mary Kingsley, the authoress, also travelled with Mr. Fothergill at different times. In one of her early books Miss Kingsley makes several complimentary references to the kindly help which she received from Mr. Fothergill during her visits to West Africa.

At the close of his service afloat, Mr. Fothergill entered the Accountant's Department of the Head Office where he remained until 1923 when he retired on pension. Almost to the last he maintained his usual robust health and with his death another link with the pioneering days in West Africa has gone.

Benguela is a port in Angola.

43   GAMBIA (II)
O.N. 73772   1875–1877

Iron screw schooner
301.1′×34.5′×23.7′   1195 n   1880 g
Built by John Elder & Co, Glasgow, for British & African Steam Navigation Co. Registered Glasgow. C 2 cyl 40″, 71″–36″ by the builders. 280 hp.
1875   Completed.
1877   18 May, stranded to the south-east of Cape Palmas, voyage Calabar to Liverpool. Subsequently broke in two.

44   CORISCO
O.N. 73855   1876–1885

'Corisco' class
Iron screw brig, one deck
300.9′×34.5′×23.6′   1182 n   1856 g
Built by John Elder & Co, Glasgow, for British and African Steam Navigation Co. Registered Glasgow. C 2 cyl 40″, 71″–36″ by the builders. 280 hp, 10½ K.
1876   Completed.
1885   23 July, grounded on rocks off River Cess, Liberia. Slipped off and sank in deep water.
Ships of the 'Corisco' class: CORISCO (44), KINSEMBO (45).
Corisco is an island and bay north of the mouth of the River Gabon.

45   KINSEMBO
O.N. 76724   1876–1893

'Corisco' class
Iron screw schooner, two decks
301.5′×34.5′×23.4′   1198 n   1868 g
Built by Cunliffe & Dunlop, Port Glasgow, Yard No 115, for British & African Steam Navigation Co. Registered Glasgow. C 2 cyl 40″, 71″–36″ by the builders. 280 hp, 10½ K.
1876   November, completed.
1893   Sold to L. Verdeau et Cie, Bordeaux. Renamed **MAROC**. Registered Bordeaux. 1137 n, 1799 g.
1898   13 January, stranded at Salins d'Hyeres. Refloated next morning.
1901   Sold to South L'Aquitaine, France. Renamed **MARIE THERESE**. Registered Bordeaux.
1903   Sold to Tonnage SA (Dykmans & van Essche, Managers), Antwerp. Registered Antwerp. 1042 n, 1923 g.
1907   15 May, foundered 60 miles off Toulon when on voyage Swansea to Sasone, cargo coal.

46   GABOON (I)
O.N. 78589   1878–1898

'Gaboon' class
Iron screw steamer, two decks
302.3′×34.2′×23.6′   1178 n   1863 g
Built by John Elder & Co, Glasgow, Yard No 219, for British & African Steam Navigation Co. Registered Glasgow. C 2 cyl 40″, 71″–36″ by the builders, 280 hp, 10½ K.
1878   March, completed.
1897   Transferred to African Steamship Co.
1898   Sold to Bank of Athens. Renamed **GALAXIDION**. Registered Piraeus. 1126 n. 1788 g.
1902   Sold to Marlas & Baltage, Piraeus.
1905   Owners now S. Baltage & Marlas, Athens.
1912   Sold for demolition in Syria.
Ships of the 'Gaboon' class: GABOON (46), LUALABA (47).
Gaboon is now Gabon.
Recollections of **GABOON** by James Deemin.

AUTOBIOGRAPHY OF JAMES DEEMIN

I signed my first Agreement in April of 1883 in the Firm's small Offices in Preesons Row, when, if I am not mistaken, the whole office staff—including the three Brothers—did not exceed 7 to 8 men. The terms of the agreement were to serve John Holt and Company on the Coast for three years with free passage out and home, food and lodgings, and such medical attention as obtainable, and Salary at the rate of £40.0.0., £50.0.0. and £60.0.0. I was instructed to sail per s.s. 'Gaboon' to Sette Camma, now forming part of the French Congo, but then unattached. My age was 19, and the only formality I had to fulfil, apart from furnishing references, was to obtain the consent of my parents, as the idea of having applicants medically examined had then not materialised.

I duly sailed as instructed and found the s.s. 'Gaboon' had a small passenger accommodation right aft, and the only promenade was on the poop over the Saloon. So far as my memory serves, the accommodation consisted of 8 small Cabins and as there were upwards of 30 passengers, most of them bound for the Congo, a number of us had to make shift on the stern sheets of the Saloon right over the prop until we got into the Bay where it was no longer possible to prevent getting rolled off on to the saloon deck so we had the beds made up in the latter as being less dangerous. The main drawback to this was we had to turn out at 5 a.m. to allow the stewards to scrub down, and the majority of us lined up on the main deck for our morning bath which was served by the Quartermaster playing the hose on us washing down decks. As there was only one small bathroom provided for passengers this served to relieve the congestion which would have been more acute had the whole of the passengers insisted on bathing in the orthodox manner.

The food provided was, to say the least, of a somewhat monotonous nature. For breakfast we usually had porridge served with water slightly coloured with condensed milk, Salt Beef curried, and Bacon, and an oily substance which was supposed to be butter. Lunch usually consisted of salt beef or pork, hot or cold, and dinner of beef or mutton (killed on board), Sweets and Cheese.

The whole question of passenger traffic to and from the Coast was then of minor importance and I have certainly no recollection of being met at the end of my voyage by Elder Dempster's Agent with an offer of a £5. note as some slight compensation for having to accept the Saloon Deck as sleeping accommodation.

Extract from *Trading in West Africa*

47 LUALABA
O.N. 78613   1878–1895

'Gaboon' class
Iron screw schooner, two decks
299.8′×34.5′×23.7′   1170 n   1850 g
Built by Cunliffe & Dunlop, Port Glasgow, Yard No 132, for British & African Steam Navigation Co. Registered Glasgow. C 2 cyl 40″, 71″–36″ by the builders. 280 hp, 10½ K.
1878   May, completed.
1888   January, took first Elder Dempster sailing from Antwerp.
1889   20 June, first vessel to negotiate passage up the Congo to Matadi (Captain John Murray).
1893   Cylinders rebored to 40⅜″ and 71¼″ diameter. 209 hp.
1895   January, sold to P. M. Tintore & Co, Barcelona. Renamed **TORDERA**. Registered Barcelona.
1915   Sold to Linea de Vapores Tintore (Liverpool agents W. L. Nickels, Son & Co).
1924   Sold to Cia Transmediterranea, Barcelona. 1014 n, 1838 g.
1934   Sold for demolition in Spain.
Lualaba is the name of the River Congo above Stanley Falls.

LUALABA

NUBIA

48 NUBIA (I)
O.N. 79660   1879–1899

Iron screw steamer, two decks
321.0′×34.7′×22.8′   1236 n   1958 g
Built by Harland & Wolff, Belfast, Yard No 121, for African Steamship Co. Registered London. C 2 cyl 36″, 66″–48″ by G. Forrester & Co, Liverpool. 188 hp, 10 K.
The first ship of the Company to have passenger accommodation amidships.
1878   9 November, launched.
1879   January, completed.
1896   October, new engines and boilers by D. Rollo & Sons, Liverpool. T 3 cyl 22″, 36″, 60″–48″, 235 nhp.
1899   Sold to Mersey Steamship Co Ltd (Leech, Harrison & Forward, Managers), Liverpool. Renamed **MOROCCO**. Registered Liverpool. 1284 n, 2042 g.
1908   December, scrapped at Alloa.
Nubia is a tract of country, with no precise limit, in North East Africa, broadly lying between Egypt and the Gezira area.

Old Ships of the Line
.... s.s. Nubia

The interesting photograph above of passengers and officers of s.s. Nubia was taken about 1890 and was sent to us by Captain W. E. Humphreys, master of R.M.V. Apapa. It includes Captain Humphreys' paternal grandfather, William Humphreys, who was a Purser on the Nubia and later became Manager of the Claims Department, and his maternal grandfather, Captain Ryan, master of the Nubia. The photograph was taken in the Canary Islands and it is believed that a number of the passengers, including perhaps the women, were probably visiting the Islands on holiday

49 COANZA
O.N. 82295   1880–1893

'Coanza' class
Steel screw schooner, one deck
290.4′×36.2′×18.0′   976 n   1518 g
Built by John Elder & Co, Glasgow, for British & African Steam Navigation Co. C 2 cyl 34″, 62″–36″ by the builders. 175 hp, 10½ K.
1880   February, completed.
1893   22 February, lost on Bayak Rock, Sinoe, outward bound from Hamburg.
Ships of the 'Coanza' class: COANZA (49), MALEMBA (50).
River Coanza (Quanza) is one of the main rivers of Angola. Length 453 miles, navigable up to the Cambambe Falls, 118 miles from the sea.

50 MALEMBA

O.N. 82307   1880–1897

'Coanza' class
Steel screw schooner, one deck
290.4′×36.2′×18.0′   980 n   1521 g
Built by John Elder & Co, Glasgow, Yard No 234, for British
& African Steam Navigation Co. Registered Glasgow. C 2 cyl
34″, 62″–36″ by the builders. 175 hp, 10½ K.

1880   May, completed.
1897   Sold to Empreza Cabotagem Nacional, Maranhao,
        Brazil. Renamed **GAURANY**. Registered Maranhao.
1902   Sold to Antwerp Mercantile & Shipping Association
        (AMASA). Renamed **BARON LAMBERMONT**.
        Registered Antwerp.
1904   Sold to SA Tonnage.
1904   11 April, wrecked off Cape Blanco.
Malemba is a port at the mouth of the Sanaga River, Cameroun.

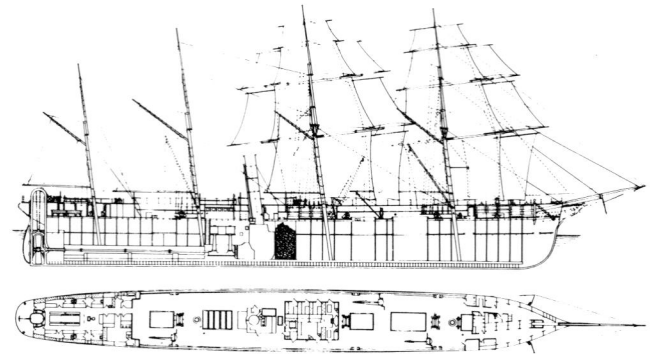

5   Powered by a two cylinder engine the *Venetian*
also had a lifting screw so that she could use her
sails to the best advantage.

A line drawing of **VENETIAN** (Photo Bibby Line)

VENETIAN, *subsequently* **LANDANA**, *from a painting by William Clark* (Photo Bibby Line)

51 LANDANA (I)

O.N. 27936   1880–1891

'Landana' class
Iron barque with lifting screw
175.4′×34.0′×22.9′   1025 n   1508 g
Built by E. J. Harland, Belfast, Yard No 1, for Bibby Sons &
Co, as **VENETIAN**. Registered Liverpool. 2 cyl 54″–39″ by the
builder. 450 ihp, 7 K.

1859   July, completed.
1872   Lengthened, barque rigged and re-engined.
        270.5′×33.7′×22.8′, 995 n, 1562 g. C 2 cyl 40″, 70″–36″
        by J. Jack, Rollo & Co, Liverpool. 200 hp.
1873   Sold to F. R. Leyland & Co, Liverpool.
1880   New engines and boilers by G. Forrester & Co, Liverpool. C 2 cyl 36″, 70″–36″, 200 hp. Acquired by African
Steamship Co, after a period on charter. Renamed
LANDANA. Registered London. 985 n, 1568 g.
1885   December, on departure from Liverpool, collided with
        and sank the pilot boat. Chief Officer's certificate sus-
        pended for a period of six months. One pilot drowned
        as a result of collision.
1891   Sold to E. Gerard, Valparaiso, Chile. Renamed
        TARAPACA. Registered Valparaiso.
1894   Transferred to ownership of E. Gerard and B. Squella.
1894   July, wrecked on Chilean coast on passage from
        Valparaiso.
Ships of the Landana class: LANDANA (51), MAYUMBA
(52).
Landana is a small port in north Angola.

52 MAYUMBA (I)
O.N. 28178   1880–1882

'Landana' class
Iron screw barque
175.4′×34.0′×22.8′   1014 n   1492 g
Built by E. J. Harland, Belfast, Yard No 2, for Bibby Sons & Co, as **SICILLIAN**. Registered Liverpool. 2 cyl 54″–38″ by the builder. 450 ihp, 7 K.
1859   November, completed.
1872   Lengthened, re-engined and re-boilered. Barque rigged. 270.5′×33.7′×22.8′, 991 n, 1569 g. C 2 cyl 40″, 70″–36″ by J. Jack, Rollo & Co, Liverpool. 200 hp.
1873   Sold to F. R. Leyland & Co, Liverpool.
1880   Acquired by African Steamship Co after a period on charter. 13 November, commenced first voyage. Renamed **MAYUMBA**. Registered Liverpool.
1881   Collided with and sank barque SEVERN (398 g built 1867) off Madeira. Second Officer held responsible.
1882   Sold to C. R. Gillchrist, Liverpool.
1883   Scuttled after fire broke out while at Arzue, Algeria, voyage Philippeville to British Caledonia.
Mayumba is a port on the coast of Gabon.

MAYUMBA

53 WINNEBAH
O.N. 82887   1881–1899

'Winnebah' class
Steel screw schooner, two decks
295.5′×30.3′×18.9′   882 n   1391 g
Built by Harland & Wolff, Belfast, Yard No 143, for African Steamship Co. Registered London. C 2 cyl 27″, 52″–36″ by the builders. 120 hp.
Passenger accommodation: 23 first class, 28 second.
1881   April, completed.
1899   February, sold to Moonlight Steamship Co Ltd (W. H. Stott & Co, Managers), Liverpool. Renamed **MOONLIGHT**. Registered Liverpool.
1909   Transferred to Stott Line Ltd. Sold for demolition in Holland.
Ships of the 'Winnebah' class: WINNEBAH (53), AKASSA (54).
Winnebah is a port in Ghana, to the west of Accra.

54 AKASSA (I)
O.N. 85042   1881–1903

'Winnebah' class
Steel screw schooner, two decks
295.5′×30.3′×18.9′   883 n   1389 g
Built by Harland & Wolff, Belfast, Yard No 144, for African Steamship Co, London. Registered London. C 2 cyl 27″, 52″–36″ by the builders. 120 hp.
Passenger accommodation: 23 first class, 28 second.
1881   June, completed.
1903   Sold to Simirotti, Ramsay & Co, Constantinople. Renamed **MINA**. Registered Piraeus. 915 n, 1466 g.
1908   Transferred to Ramsay & Co, Constantinople.
1912   Sold for demolition in Genoa.
Akassa is near the most southerly point in Nigeria. The town on the Nun entrance to the Niger River was formerly Headquarters of the Royal Niger Company.

55 MANDINGO (II)
O.N. 85144   1882–1905

Steel screw schooner, two decks
305.0′×34.2′×20.0′   1089 n   1700 g
Built by Harland & Wolff, Belfast, Yard No 149, for African Steamship Co. Registered London. C 2 cyl 32″, 64″–42″ by the builders. 221 hp, 9½ K.
Passenger accommodation: 22 first class, 28 second.
1882   March, completed. 13 May, sailed on maiden voyage.
1905   Sold to Greek Commercial Co (Stamatiadis & Riginos, Managers), Piraeus. Renamed **AVEROF**. Registered Andros.
1914   Sold to Demosthenes Delagrammatica, Constantinople. Renamed **FANNY**. Registered Piraeus.
1915   Sold to N. Michaeles, Piraeus. Renamed **MICHAEL**.
1919   Registered Ithaca.
1921   Sold to Comm. Zaccaria Oberti, Genoa. Renamed **GLAUCO**. Registered Genoa. 1579 g.
1926   Sold to Soc. Ing. D'Arrigo, Catania. Registered Catania. 950 n, 1596 g.
1927   Sold to G. D'Arrigo, Catania.
1934   Sold for demolition.

MANDINGO

CONGO

56 CONGO (II)
O.N. 85896   1882–1907

'Congo' class
Steel screw schooner, two decks
300.7′×36.2′×19.6′   1078 n   1689 g
Built by David J. Dunlop & Co, Port Glasgow, Yard No 156, for British & African Steam Navigation Co, Glasgow. Registered Glasgow. C 2 cyl 33″, 63″–36″ by the builders. 175 hp, 10 K.
Passenger accommodation: 26 first class, 4 second.
1882   January, completed.
1898   Transferred to African Steamship Co, Liverpool.
1907   4 March, sank in collision with ss LESTIS (1384 g built 1905) off Borkum, while on passage from Hamburg to Genoa.
Ships of the 'Congo' class: CONGO (56), SHERBRO (57), LAGOS (58), CALABAR (59), MADEIRA (60), TENERIFFE (61), ELMINA (62).

57 SHERBRO (I)
O.N. 85921   1882–1909

'Congo' class
Steel screw schooner, two decks
299.9′×36.2′×19.7′   1062 n   1650 g
Built by John Elder & Co, Glasgow, Yard No 256, for British & African Steam Navigation Co. Registered Glasgow.
C 2 cyl 33″, 63″–36″ by the builders. 200 hp, 10 K.
Passenger accommodation: 26 first class, 4 second.
1882   February, completed.
1891   16 July, rescued passengers and crew of *SOUDAN* when that vessel struck a rock off Tabou on the Guinea coast.
1900   Port of Registry Liverpool.
1909   February, sold for demolition at Hamburg.
Sherbro (corruption of Cerberos) Island is off the coast of Sierra Leone.

58 LAGOS (II)
O.N. 87674   1883–1902

'Congo' class
Steel screw schooner, two decks
300.3′×36.2′×20.2′   1116 n   1731 g
Built by David J. Dunlop & Co, Port Glasgow, Yard No 164, for British & African Steam Navigation Co Ltd. Registered Glasgow. C 2 cyl 33″, 63″–42″ by the builders. 220 hp, 10 K.
Passenger accommodation: 38 first class, 8 second.
1883   May, completed.
1893   August, Miss Mary Kingsley made her first voyage to the West Coast of Africa—Liverpool to Luanda—aboard this ship.
1896   Reboilered and major repairs carried out.
1900   Port of Registry Liverpool.
1902   18 January, (Captain H. Delgarno) wrecked on the Desertas, near Madeira, voyage Liverpool to West Africa.

LAGOS

59 CALABAR (II)
O.N. 87679   1883–1898

'Congo' class
Steel screw schooner, two decks
300.3′×36.2′×20.4′   1127 n   1701 g
Built by John Elder & Co, Glasgow, Yard No 276, for British
& African Steam Navigation Co Ltd. Registered Glasgow.
C 2 cyl 33″, 63″–42″ by the builders. 220 hp, 10 K.
Passenger accommodation: 26 first class, 4 second.
1883   June, completed.
1896   1111 n, 1756 g.
1898   26 October, stranded on Yellow Well Reef, Grand Bassa,
       Liberia, on voyage Sinoe (Liberia) to Liverpool, general
       cargo and specie, and became a total loss (Captain H.
       A. Yardley). No loss of life.

MADEIRA

CALABAR

60 MADEIRA
O.N. 90000   1884–1914

'Congo' class
Steel screw schooner, two decks
300.0′×36.2′×19.9′   1147 n   1773 g
Built by Barclay, Curle & Co Ltd, Glasgow, Yard No 331,
for British & African Steam Navigation Co Ltd. Registered
Glasgow. C 2 cyl 32″, 64″–42″ by the builders. 199 hp, 10 K.
Passenger accommodation: 26 first class, 4 second.
1884   December, completed.
1900   Port of Registry Liverpool.
1909   High pressure cylinder bored out to 32⅜″.
1914   17 November, foundered 35 miles west of Ushant,
       (47°.59′N 06°.28′W), after being under tow for 24 hours
       by tug MARS while on voyage West Africa to Liverpool
       with general cargo.
Name derived from the Atlantic island off West Africa.
In 1976 retired Chief Engineer Sydney Hayman recalled his
first voyage, as 4th Engineer, aboard **MADEIRA** in 1907:

Amongst my papers I found my Indentures as Engineer Apprentice
and my first Seaman's Discharge Book. In it was the reference by Mr.
G. J. Farquharson, Hamburg Superintendent, which brought back to
mind my first voyage with Elder Dempster.

On November 21st 1907, having applied for a job with E.D.'s I was
appointed 4th Engineer of the ss MADEIRA, joining her at the Afrika
Quai Hamburg on 26th November. The Master was Captain Speak-
man, the Chief Mate Riley Taylor, the second Mate M. Mehanovick
and the third Mate the late Captain E. Vaughan Davies. The Chief
Engineer was Jas. Humphreys from Liverpool and the second Mr.
Bissett of Southampton, the 3rd F. Bueck of Hamburg and myself a
Devonian as fourth.

The vessel had no double bottom tanks, the forepeak was used
entirely for domestic fresh water, and as there was no evaporator the
domestic feed was taken from the sea for the main boilers.

The main engines were two cylinder compound, and very heavily
built, 3 furnace boilers at 90 lbs per S.I. were to be operated and a
Galloway cross tube vertical boiler was in the midship house. There
was no electric light and no refrigerator. The Engineers did their
own greasing and oiling in those days. The vessel left Hamburg for
Rotterdam and when entering the Hook of Holland we passed the wreck
of the BERLIN which was lost at the entrance to the River Maas. At
Rotterdam E. Vaughan Davies was promoted 2nd Mate of the ss
SANGARA, his place on the MADEIRA being taken by Conrad
Schroller. Leaving Rotterdam on the Windward Coast Service via the
Canary Islands we spent Christmas day at Konakry. The Steam Launch
was lowered overside and steam raised. The Captain and Chief Engineer
wanted to visit old shipmates on the ss AGBERI which was lying at
that port. My job was to steam the launch and I was given strict orders
by my Chief that I was not to leave it while it was lying alongside the
AGBERI. However I was not left alone because the 3rd Mate received
the same order from the Captain. Christmas day was completed with
a dinner in the Saloon and a good time was had by all.

As it was a case of ice box storage for meat etc, plenty of salt beef
was carried in casks of brine. There were also two pigs for fattening up
during the voyage for meat. The West Indian cook was an expert in
preparing good meals under difficult circumstances.

The Mates in those days had plenty to do in their off watch periods
as it was their responsibility to check the manifests and epitome of
cargo, also to go down into the hatches to check the cargo with Kroo
labour. While the 3rd Engineer and I had our hands full when off watch
overhauling the two Dunlop Bell slewing steam cranes together with
the winches and the windlass. The steering engine was fitted on deck
abaft the Captain's quarters in teakwood housing and it was the 4th
Engineer's job to keep it oiled and in good order.

On arrival at Sinoe we saw the ss SANSU capsized and a total wreck
and farther down the Coast the ss ASCON WOERMANN wrecked at
the same time as the SANSU, which was the night before we arrived.
At Lagos we were ordered to go on the Creeks Service. Elders floating
dock and engineering works were at Forcados then. The Agent was
Captain Mills, the Engineer Superintendent Mr. Connolly who had as
his assistant Mr. Talbot. Main boilers were overhauled, cleaned and
scaled at Sapele, suitable because it was fresh water overside. We left
Forcados fully laden for Hamburg, coaling at Freetown. The Bay of
Biscay was crossed in a full gale, and while we were sailing up the
English Channel the 2nd called me and pointed to a five masted
barque—the German flyer POTOSI—which was under full sail and
moving so swiftly that she left the MADEIRA astern and arrived
Hamburg quite a time before we did.

On arrival we docked at Segel Shiffs Hafen, and there learnt of the
loss of the ss AXIM in the Biscay storm through which we passed
safely.

On April 8th Mr. Farquharson came aboard our vessel from the E.D.
tug HANSA and told me that I was the only English 4th engineer in
the Hamburg Service and he was transferring me to the ss ORON as
4th. This in my opinion was promotion and certainly promised more
comfort since my new ship was fitted with electric light and refrigeration.

At 21 years of age on July 24th 1909, I was sent on leave to sit for
my second engineer's certificate and I passed in August returning to
Hamburg later as 3rd Engineer of the ss MONROVIA. THOSE
YEARS IN THE HAMBURG SERVICE WERE VERY HAPPY
ONES INDEED.

Extract from the Elders of Elders 1976

61 TENERIFFE
O.N. 90019   1885–1919

'Congo' class
Steel screw schooner, two decks
301.0′×36.0′×19.8′   1165 n   1800 g
Built by Harland & Wolff, Belfast, Yard No 178, for British & African Steam Navigation Co Ltd. Registered Glasgow. C 2 cyl 32″, 64″–42″ by the builders. 220 hp, 10 K.
Passenger accommodation: 26 first class, 4 second.
1885   February, completed.
1895   5 March, stranded in River Congo, managed to discharge cargo into lighters.
1919   24 March, sold to The Shipping Controller (Glover Bros, Managers), London. Registered London.
1920   January, sold to Spain. Renamed **ZUGATZARTE**. 1148 n.
1921   March, wrecked near Bilbao, voyage Glasgow to Spain.
Name derived from the Canary Islands.

62 ELMINA (II)
O.N. 89698   1885–1907

'Congo' class
Steel screw schooner, two decks
300.5′×36.2′×19.8′   1143 n   1764 g
Built by Harland & Wolff, Belfast, Yard No 179, for African Steamship Co. Registered London. C 2 cyl 32″, 64″–42″ by the builders. 220 hp, 10 K.
Passenger accommodation: 26 first class, 4 second.
1885   April, completed.
1907   June, sold to H. C. Knappert, Arnhem, for demolition.

63 NIGER (II)
O.N. 87142   1883–1903

'Niger' class
Steel screw schooner, two decks
320.2′×35.6′×21.2′   1302 n   2006 g
Built by Harland & Wolff, Belfast, Yard No 161, for African Steamship Co, London. Registered London. C 2 cyl 34″, 68″–42″ by the builders. 172 hp, 9 K.
Passenger accommodation: 26 first class, 8 second.
1883   June, completed.
1900   Management transferred to Elder, Dempster & Co.
1903   June, sold for demolition at Preston.
Ships of the 'Niger' class: NIGER (63), OPOBO (64), ROQUELLE (65).

NIGER

64 OPOBO (II)
O.N. 87747   1884–1890

'Niger' class
Steel screw schooner, two decks
320.0′×36.1′×21.3′   1351 n   2078 g
Built by Barclay, Curle & Co, Glasgow, for British & African Steam Navigation Co Ltd. Registered Glasgow. C 2 cyl 34″, 68″–42″ by the builders. 225 hp, 9 K.
1884   February, completed.
1890   September, wrecked at Grand Bassam, Ivory Coast.
Wreck sold to Liverpool Steam Tug Co Ltd. Steam tug WRESTLER despatched to tow wreck to Liverpool but was unsuccessful. Part cargo salved.

65 ROQUELLE (II)
O.N. 89910   1884–1908

'Niger' class
Steel screw schooner, two decks
320.0′×36.1′×21.3′   1343 n   2070 g
Built by Barclay, Curle & Co, Glasgow, Yard No 326, for British & African Steam Navigation Co Ltd. Registered Glasgow. C 2 cyl 34″, 68″–42″ by the builders. 225 hp, 9 K.
1884   March, completed.
1901   Port of Registry Liverpool. 1305 n, 2013 g.
1905   October, in collision with *MAYUMBA* in Benin Creek.
1907   1337 n, 2082 g.
1908   Sold for demolition at Falmouth.

ROQUELLE

66 BENIN (II)
O.N. 89603   1884–1905

Steel screw steamer, two decks
330.7′×36.7′×21.7′   1437 n   2223 g
Built by Harland & Wolff, Belfast, Yard No 169, for African Steamship Co. Registered London. C 2 cyl 34″, 68″–42″ by the builders. 200 hp, 9½ K.
Passenger accommodation: 32 first class, 8 second.
1884   14 June, launched.
1889   The first vessel in the fleet to be fitted with refrigerated space.
1898   Lord Lugard travelled to Lagos.
1891   August, carried the body of King Ja Ja of Opobo from exile in Tenerife back to Nigeria.
1901   Sold to Cie de Vapores Interinsulares Canarias, Las Palmas. Renamed **ALMIRANTE DIAZ**. Registered Las Palmas.
1902   December, sold to African Steamship Co, London. Renamed **BENIN**. Registered London. 1444 n, 2262 g.

BENIN

1905 September, sold to Commercial Navigation Piraeus, (Stamatiades and Riginos, Managers). Renamed **MARASLIS**. Registered Piraeus.
1910 Sold to Lourenbzos Conbanis.
1911 May, sold for demolition at Barcelona.

COLD STORAGE IN WEST AFRICA

Old "Coasters" seeking for something to grouse about generally set about the steamship management first. They don't really mean anything, it is traditional and hereditary. All "Coasters" for generations have done it, it seems to do them good! They can cheerfully stand it all because they are virtuously conscious that they voluntarily add to the many worries of steamship managing, the comfort and well-being of the passenger, not only on board, but also after he has left the ship.

Cold storage in West Africa is one of the things the "Coaster" ought to have developed for himself many years ago. Ice was plentiful and cheap in Calcutta thirty or forty years ago, in fact all over India and the Straits Settlements and many other tropical countries which the white man has marked out for his own; refrigeration and ice in plenty, at a low cost, has been a matter of course for many years. In West Africa, it has been left to the steamship managers to accomplish, at an enormous outlay, all the pioneering and spade work.

Thirty years ago, we had no steamers fitted with refrigerating machinery. In those days, and for many years later, a "dash" of a moderate-sized block of ice was a good and efficient "cure all" for any sins of omission and commission. Did we cast envious eyes on 100 casks awaiting shipment? Try the agent with a piece of ice. Is the Collector of Customs annoyed? Give him a piece of ice and say "sorry—won't occur again." What! Thirty tins of sardines short? Give 'em a piece of ice, and ask the agent to sign a clean bill of lading; and alas! good men have died; medical skill and nursing care in vain, because "only an ice pack could save him now."

This state of affairs existed until about 1903, although in 1894 the *Cabenda* and I think also the *Benin*, had a refrigerator and used to sell fresh provisions, but not ice. These were the only two for many years, all the other ships of the fleet carried live-stock—chickens and ducks roamed about the alleyways, gaunt Jellah-Koffee turkeys looking like Xmas nightmares, got in everybody's way, thus even on the ships, the Catering Department had many problems to work out, whilst on

shore, preserved and tinned food caused West Africa to retain its evil reputation far longer than it deserved, and yet the "Coaster," neither merchant nor Government official, made any attempt at ice-making or cold storage.

The *Cabenda* was the first refrigerator steamer, that was in 1894—27 years ago. Bless me, how the years slip by! Captain W. P. Thompson, R.N.R., chief officer; Fred. Davis, purser; Percy Christian, assistant purser (and refrigerator salesman); "Tommy" Sharrock, 4th officer (and "Tommy's" room mate) the present humble writer—first voyage in the service. Fun! We were all young, and could laugh 27 years ago!

That refrigerator was a champion snowmaker, and first of all the snow had to be dug out, so we used to tell true lies by saying we had seen a foot of snow on the deck in Calabar river; the Kroo boys used to think the snow was hot! The thick snow (and the thick smell) having been dug out, operations began. There were few sales, and approaching boats kept well to windward. "Tommy" opened up by saying, with a perfectly solemn face,—"sausages, gentlemen, sausages, treat 'em kindly and gently, and they will stand up and sing all the latest pantomime songs."

Another day a big chief came on board—big canoe, fifty paddles a side, tom-toms, etc. He wanted to buy turkeys, live turkeys, and enquired if "turkey live?" "Plenty turkey live," said "Tommy," and accordingly produced one. No trade—"this turkey no live," remarked the big chief, "He die," and with a significant sniff added, "He die a long time."

That was the real beginning of cold storage in West Africa. With the advent of the *Biafa*, *Sobo*, *Fantee*, *Jebba*, and later, the *Tarquah* and *Burutu* type of ship, the fleet began to be almost entirely refrigerated—not only the express steamers, but many of the cargo boats, commencing with the *Prahsu* and *Muraji* and later, all the "E" boats of the *Eboe* type.

The West African Cold Storage Department began serious business almost by accident. In 1903, the *Tarquah* found herself short of the average number of passengers outwards and homewards. Stocks of meat, etc., were so heavy that we sold a fair quantity rather than carry it back to Liverpool. When this was reported to the late Sir Alfred Jones, he at once saw the opportunity of giving a lead in the right direction; every refrigerator steamer was turned into a floating shop, and very soon fresh provisions and ice were obtainable at frequent intervals at every port on the Coast. At that time, the steamers did not cross Lagos Bar, so to get over that difficulty, the Governor, Sir Walter

PICTAVIA,
formerly
CLARE
(Photo
G. Mercier)

Egerton, caused a cold storage and ice-making plant to be erected in Lagos, and we worked in co-operation with the Government of Southern Nigeria.

Seccondee, and the Gold Coast mining districts were more difficult to deal with. A cold store was erected in Seccondee, and an ice-house in Tarquah. These were eventually taken over by the mining companies; the plant at Lagos was taken over by the Nigerian Cold Storage Co., Ltd., who also started business at Calabar, Opobo, and Port Harcourt.

The opening of these places on shore relieved the heavy calls made upon the steamers, but the war set back the clock. Food shortage at home stopped all export. The Germans "found" many of our refrigerator ships, and so in 1919, we had to start all over again.

Now in 1922, we find the ships still supplying all the smaller ports, and many of the larger ones. Bathurst, Sierra Leone, Monrovia—all the Liberian, Ivory Coast, and Gold Coast ports, including Accra and Seccondee, still rely, to a great extent, on supplies from the steamers, but steamer supplies at irregular intervals cannot be entirely satisfactory. Ice is now made at Monrovia, Accra, and a few other places.

The contractors for the new Harbour works at Takoradi are going to have a cold store of their own, and it is interesting to note that it was one of the first details they considered. Prices are high, trade is bad, and so it seems that the steamers must, for some years to come, fill the gap in the way they have done in years gone by.

But times have altered in West Africa: not only has the European population increased enormously, but Mrs. "West-Coaster" goes out now, and often remains there a whole year.

So even at the present rate of progress, in a few years cold storage will be an absolute necessity, not only on the Coast, but at places inland, such as Coomassie and Tarquah, and those towns on the Niger which are accessible by the Nigerian Railway.

Meantime, the Department carries on, cheering people up at home, too. Whenever their friends feel a bit dull, they look in, and say, "Hullo! a brace of kippers and half a split sausage, please," and pass on to their quite unimportant duties feeling much refreshed.

From the Elder Dempster Magazine March 1922

67 BENITO (I)
O.N. 89912   1884–1894

Iron screw steamer, one deck
210.9′×28.2′×13.5′   424 n   712 g
Built by David J. Dunlop & Co, Port Glasgow, for British & African Steam Navigation Co Ltd. Registered Glasgow. C 2 cyl 24″, 46″–33″ by the builders. 90 hp.
1884   April, completed.
1894   July, sank after grounding on Lagos Bar.
Benito is the name of a river and port in Rio Muni.

68 CLARE (I)
O.N. 87899   1887–1890

Iron screw steamer, one deck
270.4′×38.4′×24.1′   1333 g   2034 n
Built by J. Blumer & Co, Sunderland, Yard No 77, for SS. Clare Ltd, (C. W. Pollexfen & Co, Managers), Liverpool. Registered Liverpool. C 2 cyl 35″, 68″–48″ by T. Clark & Co, Newcastle. 200 hp, 9½ K.
1883   June, completed.
1887   June, acquired by Alfred Lewis Jones, Esq, (Elder, Dempster & Co, Managers), Liverpool.
1890   January, sold to Cie Francaise de Navigation a Vapeur, Marseilles, (C. Fabre & Co, Managers). Renamed **PICTAVIA**. Registered Marseilles.
1899   Sold to G. B. Reforza, Genoa. Renamed **ASSUNTA**. Registered Genoa. 1363 n, 2081 g.
1904   2 February, wrecked at Bereby in Ghana, voyage Kotonou to Marseilles with a general cargo of West African produce.

69 NIGRETIA (II)
O.N. 93802   1888–1893

Steel screw steamer, one deck
295.0′×38.1′×21.5′   1632 n   2477 g
Built by Raylton Dixon & Co, Middlesbrough, Yard No 286, for Elder, Dempster & Co, Liverpool. Registered Liverpool. T 3 cyl 22″, 35″, 59″–39″ by T. Richardson & Sons, Hartlepool. 217 hp, 9 K.
1888   August, completed.
1893   March, sold to R. Cairns, Leith. Registered Leith. 1530 n, 2068 g.
1900   Sold to Nigretia Steamship Co (Samuel Morris & Co), London. Registered London.
1901   Sold to Mac Steam Ship Co (Allen & Co, Managers), Newcastle. Registered Newcastle.
1904   December, captured by Japanese warship and taken to Sasebo.
1906   Owners: Osaka Kogiyo Goshi Kaisha. Renamed **URUSAN MARU**. Registered Kobe. 1779 n, 2401 g.
1910   Sold to T. Yamamoto, Fukuyama, Oshima.
1921   Sold to Toyo Shosen Kabushiki Kaisha. Registered Tarumi. 1729 n, 2388 g.

1923	Sold to Hashiya Kabushi Kisen Kaisha, Kobe. Renamed **OBOSHI**. Registered Nishiaomiya.
1926	Renamed **DIABOSHI MARU No 3**.
1932	11 April, beached in leaking condition near Horomushiro, Murakami Bay, Chishima Archipelago. August, wrecked off Okihaya, voyage Hakodate to Murukami, cargo rice.

70 TEUTONIA
O.N. 83921   1889–1890

Iron screw schooner, two decks
290.4′×37.2′×24.5′   1490 n   2287 g
Built by Schlesinger, Davis & Co, Newcastle, Yard No 118, for Teutonia SS Co Ltd (Ward & Holzapfel, Managers), Newcastle. Registered Newcastle. C 2 cyl 35″, 65″–42″ by T. Clark & Co, Newcastle. 200 hp, 9 K.

1881	November, completed.
1887	Sold to James Hay & Sons, Glasgow.
1888	Sold to Macbeth and Grey, Glasgow.
1889	Sold to Elder, Dempster & Co. Registered Liverpool. 1550 n, 2376 g.
1890	Sold to Teutonia SS Co Ltd (T. R. Willing, Manager), Liverpool.
1899	Sold to Fratelli Cosulich, Trieste, Austria. Renamed **HERMINE**. Registered Trieste (Austro-Hungarian flag). 1431 n, 2307 g.
1900	Sold to Filli Grasso Cicerone, Genoa. Renamed **MARIA VITTORIA**. Registered Genoa. 1469 n, 2269 g.
1914	Sold to V. Bonavenain Grasso Cicerone. Renamed **CICERONE**. Registered Genoa. 1368 n, 2192 g.
1916	Reported to Lloyds that vessel had sunk as a result of enemy action.

71 LEON Y CASTILLO (I)
O.N. Not allocated   1888–1910

'Leon y Castillo' class
Steel screw schooner, one deck and part shade deck
190.2′×27.1′×12.7′   238 n   529 g
Built by David J. Dunlop & Co, Port Glasgow, Yard No 188, for Cia de Vapores Correos Interinsulares Canarios, Las Palmas. Registered Las Palmas. T 3 cyl 17″, 27″, 45″–36″ by the builders. 120 hp.

| 1888 | July, completed. |
| 1910 | October, wrecked 22 miles north of Rio Deoro, Morocco. |

Ships of the 'Leon y Castillo' class: LEON Y CASTILLO (71), VIERA Y CLAVIJO (72).

Leon y Castillo was a well known 19th century politician and Minister. In 1882 he was able to persuade the Spanish Government to provide funds for the construction of the first port installations in Las Palmas.

72 VIERA Y CLAVIJO (I)
O.N. Not allocated   1888–1911

Steel screw schooner, one deck, part shade deck
190.2′×27.1′×12.7′   236 n   529 g
Built by David J. Dunlop & Co, Port Glasgow, Yard No 189, for the Cia de Vapores Correos Interinsulares Canarios, Las Palmas. Registered Las Palmas. T 3 cyl 17″, 27″, 45″–36″ by the builders. 120 hp.

1888	August, completed, having been ordered as **ALEGRANZA** but subsequently re-named.
1911	Sold to Navigation Hellenique (John McDowell, Manager), Piraeus. Renamed **NIKI**. Registered Piraeus. 254 n, 511 g.
1917	Sold to Hellenic Co of Maritime Enterprises, Piraeus (A. Palios, Manager). Registered Piraeus.
1919	Deleted from Lloyds Register.

Viera y Clavijo was a well known 18th century historian who lived in Tenerife. He wrote the history of Tenerife which is still read widely today.

73 PEREZ GALDOS
O.N. Not allocated   1894–1907

Wood and iron screw schooner, one deck
165.3′×24.3′×11.8′   148 n   329 g
Built by Heap, Liverpool, as **TURIA** for unknown owners. Engines 80 hp built at Liverpool.

1857	Completed.
1889	Owner Nicasio Perez, Ferrol. Registered Ferrol as **MANUEL PEREZ**.
1891	Sold to A. Masias, Grand Canary. Renamed **PEREZ GALDOS**. Registered Grand Canary.
1894	Sold to Cia de Vapores Correos Interinsulares Canarios, Las Palmas. Registered Las Palmas. C 2 cyl 17½″, 36½″–24″ by J. Taylor, Birkenhead. 54 nhp.
1907/8	Deleted from Lloyds Register.

Perez Galdos, born in Las Palmas, was one of the best known 19th century Spanish writers and dramatists.

74 PALMAS
O.N. 93817   1888–1903

'Palmas' class
Steel screw steamer, two decks
312.0′×39.2′×24.7′   1560 n   2428 g
Built by Harland & Wolff Ltd, Yard No 212, for Alfred Lewis Jones Esq (Elder, Dempster & Co, Managers). Registered Liverpool. T 3 cyl 23″, 38″, 62″–42″ by McIlwaine, Lewis & Co Ltd, Belfast. 250 hp, 11 K.

1888	October, completed.
1890	Transferred to Elder, Dempster & Co.
1895	Transferred to African Steamship Co.
1903	3 January, (Captain W. G. Burton) departed Newport News for Las Palmas (via Boston), cargo of coal.
1903	March, posted missing—presumed sunk.

Ships of the 'Palmas' class: PALMAS (74), BOMA (75), MATADI (76), SOUDAN (77), COOMASSIE (78), OIL RIVERS (79), ANGOLA (80), DAHOMEY (81).

Name derived from Cape Palmas, Liberia.

75 BOMA (I)
O.N. 96090   1889–1918

'Palmas' class
Steel screw steamer, two decks
311.6′×39.2′×24.7′   1737 n   2681 g
Built by Naval Construction & Armaments Co Ltd, Barrow, Yard No 171, for British & African Steam Navigation Co Ltd. Registered Glasgow. T 3 cyl 23″, 38″, 61″–42″ by the builders. 240 hp, 11 K.

1889	15 August, launched by Mrs Elder. September, completed. Trials 1188 ihp, 12.73 K.
1892	25 November, grounded in dense fog on a sand bank near the pier at Southport. Refloated undamaged. On hearing of this grounding Mr Alexander Elder threw his top hat to the ground and jumped on it, as a mark of his displeasure.
1914	As HM Transport 4, employed during the Cameroons campaign flying the Blue Ensign. Also served as a transport in the Mediterranean.
1917	23 November, escaped undamaged from submarine torpedo attack in the English Channel.
1918	14 April, escaped undamaged from submarine torpedo attack in the Bristol Channel (U74, commanded by Oberleutnant zur See Ernst Steindorff). 11 June, torpedoed without warning and sunk in position ten miles South West ¾ West from Beer Head, Lyme Bay, Devon,

by UB80 (Kapitanleutant Max Viebeg), voyage Belfast to St Helena with general cargo.

UB80 survived the war and surrendered at Harwich on 27 November 1918. She was allocated to Italy and broken up at Spezia in 1919.

Boma is a port on the River Zaire.

76 MATADI (I)

O.N. 96100   1889–1898

'Palmas' class
Steel screw steamer, two decks
311.6′×39.2′×24.7′   1715 n   2683 g
Built by Naval Construction & Armaments Co Ltd, Barrow, Yard No 172, for British & African Steam Navigation Co Ltd. Registered Glasgow. T 3 cyl 23″, 38″, 61″–42″ by the builders. 240 hp, 11 K.
1889   8 October, launched. November, completed.
1890   Major repairs carried out.
1896   7 March, at Boma, outward from Liverpool a fire started in the forward hold and almost immediately exploded ten tons of gunpowder. Twenty-two European and 20 African crew members were killed together with three passengers (Captain H. Delgarno).

The name of the ship is taken from the port of Matadi on the Zaire River. Also, Matadi is the Zairoise name for 'Stone'—the port of Matadi being carved out of stone.

Old Congo wreck

More than 70 years after she exploded and sank, the wreck of *Matadi* (above) can still be seen by seafarers entering the Boma Roads on the River Congo.

On a fateful day in March 1896, an intruder caused a fire in the forward hold and almost immediately 10 tons of gunpowder, which was stored there, exploded. It all happened so quickly that it was impossible to evacuate the ship, and 22 European and 20 African members of the crew were killed along with three passengers.

The *Matadi* was owned by the British & African Steam Navigation Company, a line, which at that time, was managed, and later owned, by Elder Dempster. She was built by the Naval Construction & Armaments Company at Barrow in 1889 and for seven years successfully operated between Europe and West Africa.

The photograph was acquired by Dr. P. N. Davies of Liverpool University as a result of his tour of West Africa to collect information for the official history of Elder Dempster.

77 SOUDAN (II)

O.N. 96391   1889–1891

'Palmas' class
Steel screw steamer, two decks
311.6′×39.2′×24.7′   1710 n   2625 g
Built by Naval Construction & Armaments Co Ltd, Barrow, for Elder, Dempster & Co. Registered Liverpool. T 3 cyl 23″, 38″, 61″–42″ by the builders. 240 hp, 11 K.
1889   23 November, launched. December, completed. Trials 14 K.
1891   Transferred to African Steamship Co. 16 July, foundered in eight fathoms of water, one mile from beach after striking rock off Tabou, Guinea Coast. The Master (Captain Cawthorne) absolved from blame. Passengers and crew rescued by *SHERBRO*. Cargo consisted of specie and produce, from Axim for Liverpool.

Soudan (Sudan) is the West African area between Sahara and the coast.

COOMASSIE, from an old postcard

78 COOMASSIE

O.N. 97759   1890–1911

'Palmas' class
Steel screw steamer, two decks
311.6′×39.2′×24.7′   1710 n   2625 g
Built by Naval Construction & Armaments Co Ltd, Barrow, Yard No 178, for Elder, Dempster & Co. Registered Liverpool. T 3 cyl 23″, 38″, 61″–42″ by the builders. 240 hp, 11 K.
Passenger accommodation: 37 first class, 22 second.
1890   22 February, launched. March, completed. Transferred to African Steamship Co. Registered London.

COOMASSIE

1895   Transferred to Cie Maritime Belge, Antwerp. Registered Antwerp. 2354 n, 2865 g.

1896   Transferred to African Steamship Co Ltd. Registered London.

1911   Sold to Anglo-Ionian Navigation Co Ltd, London. Renamed **ASSOS**. 1841 n, 2840 g. Registered London.

1913   Sold to Navigation a Vapeur 'Ionienne' (G. Yannoulatos, Manager), Piraeus. Registered Cephalonia.

1917   4 May, torpedoed by UB38 in the English Channel off Barfleur Light, voyage Colombo to Dunkirk, cargo not stated.

Coomassie (modern spelling Kumasi) is the chief town of the Ashanti territory, Ghana.

CABENDA, *after renaming*

CABENDA ashore in 1900

79 OIL RIVERS/CABENDA
O.N. 97845   1891–1907

'Palmas' class
Steel screw steamer, two decks
312.0'×39.2'×24.6'   1792 n   2777 g
Built by Sir Raylton Dixon & Co Ltd, Middlesbrough, Yard
No 330, for Alfred Lewis Jones, Esq. Registered Liverpool. T 3
cyl 23", 38", 61"–42" by T. Richardson & Sons, Hartlepool.
240 hp, 11 K.
Passenger accommodation: 31 first class, 15 second.
1890   3 December, launched.
1891   March, completed. Transferred to Elder, Dempster &
       Co.
1892   Transferred to African Steamship Co.
1893   Renamed **CABENDA**. Registered London. Renaming
       was attributable to a high number of deaths that
       occurred on board on account of malaria and yellow
       fever.
1894   Refrigerated cargo space fitted.
1900   Grounded at Banana Point in the Zaire River.
1907   Sold to Shipping Syndicate Ltd, London. 1810 n, 2794 g.
1910   Sold to Queenstown Drydock and Shipbuilding &
       Engineering Co, County Cork. Re-named **ELMWOOD**.
       Registered London.
1912   Sold to N. Nitta, Nishinomiya. Re-named **BANYEI
       MARU**. Registered Nishinomiya. 1763 n, 2844 g.
1920   Sold to Nitta Kisen Kabushiki Kaisha. 1682 n, 2538 g.
1925   Sold to Kyoritsu Kisen Kabushiki Kaisha. Registered
       Kobe. 2020 n, 2779 g.
1930   Sold to Sugaya Kabushiki, Kobe.
1934   19 March, reported foundered in position 40°.N 132°.E
       approximately, voyage Muroran to Seikoshin, cargo
       coal.
Oil Rivers is the old name of the Niger Delta.
Cabenda is north of the River Zaire.

80 ANGOLA (II)
O.N. 97875   1891–1906

'Palmas' class
Steel screw steamer, two decks
312.0'×39.2'×24.6'   1878 n   2870 g
Built by Sir Raylton Dixon & Co Ltd, Middlesbrough, for
Alfred Lewis Jones Esq, Yard No 332. Registered London. T
3 cyl 23", 38", 61"–42" by T. Richardson & Sons, Hartlepool.
240 hp, 11 K.

ANGOLA

1891   June, completed. August, transferred to African Steam-
       ship Co.
1897   One of the ships anchored in the Mersey to com-
       memorate the Diamond Jubilee of HM Queen Victoria.
1906   Transferred to Elder Line Ltd. 1811 n, 2831 g. 10 July,
       wrecked Homicky Point near Louisburg, Cape Breton
       Island, voyage Progreso, Vera Cruz to Montreal (Cap-
       tain F. F. Thomas). Crew 40, three passengers. No lives
       lost.

81 DAHOMEY
O.N. 98996   1891–1908

'Palmas' class
Steel screw steamer, two decks
312.0'×40.0'×24.6'   1828 n   2854 g
Built by Sir Raylton Dixon & Co Ltd, Middlesbrough, Yard
No 339, for Elder, Dempster & Co. Registered Liverpool. T
3 cyl 23", 38", 61"–42" by T. Richardson & Sons, Hartlepool.
240 hp, 11 K.
1891   3 August, launched. October, completed.
1896   Transferred to African Steamship Co.
1898   6 April, (Captain J. G. Cawthorne) ran aground in thick
       fog on the Anglesey coast between Holyhead breakwater
       and the North Stack. Nine passengers, 30 crew taken off
       by **DUKE OF NORTHUMBERLAND**. This vessel
       made two further trips to salvage mail. Fire broke out, 60
       tons of explosives were removed. **DAHOMEY** refloated
       and eventually resumed her normal service.
1906   Transferred to Elder Line Ltd.
1908   13 December, (Captain F. W. Ommanney) departed
       Sydney, Cape Breton for Vera Cruz. 28 December,
       beached two miles from Nassau after being stranded at
       Abaco Island (26°.30'N 77°.11'W). Became total loss.
Dahomey is the republic to the west of Nigeria.

82 ETHIOPE (II)
O.N. 96303   1889–1891

Steel screw steamer, two decks
320.0'×40.2'×21.2'   1905 n   2893 g
Built by Sir Raylton Dixon & Co Ltd, Middlesbrough, Yard
No 295, for Elder, Dempster & Co. Registered Liverpool.
T 3 cyl 24", 38", 64"–42" by T. Richardson & Sons, Hartlepool.
250 hp, 10½ K.
1889   May, completed.
1891   June, sold to Augier Shipping Co Ltd, London. Regis-
       tered London.
1899   Sold to L. & M. Embirielos, Braila, Rumania. Renamed
       POLYXENI. Registered Andros. 1919 n, 2925 g.
1905   June, foundered after striking reef, voyage Newcastle to
       Syra.

DAHOMEY (Photo McRoberts collection)

LAURA,
formerly EBOE

83 EBOE (II)

O.N. 81388   1889–1897

'Eboe' class
Iron screw steamer, two decks
285.8′×36.1′×24.3′   1315 n   2018 g
Built by C. Mitchell & Co, Newcastle, Yard No 398, as
SIMOOM, for Bedouin Steam Navigation Co, Liverpool. Registered Liverpool. C 2 cyl 34″, 66″–42″ by Wallsend Slipway &
Engineering Co Ltd, Newcastle. 235 hp.
1880 May, launched.
1889 Acquired by African Steamship Co. Renamed **EBOE**.
      Registered London. 1346 n, 2089 g.
1895 14 September, grounded near Sherbro, Sierra Leone.
1897 Sold—owners not recorded but possibly same as those of
      No 84 *GAMBIA*. Renamed **LAURA**. Registered under
      Austria-Hungary flag.
1897 November, wrecked near Filey, Yorkshire, voyage Tyne-
      side to Trieste.
Ships of the 'Eboe' class: EBOE (83), GAMBIA (84),
YORUBA (85).

84 GAMBIA (III)

O.N. 81336   1889–1897

'Eboe' class
Iron screw steamer, two decks
286.0′×36.0′×23.0′   1283 n   1968 g
Built by C. Mitchell & Co, Newcastle, Yard No 395, as
SHEIKH, for Bedouin Steam Navigation Co, Liverpool. Registered Liverpool. C 2 cyl 34″, 66″–42″ by Wallsend Slipway &
Engineering Co Ltd, Newcastle. 235 hp.
1880 August, launched
1889 Acquired by African Steamship Co. Renamed
      GAMBIA. Registered London. 1275 n, 1915 g.
1897 July, sold to Dr A. Bing and E. Karpeles (Schenker,
      Walford & Co, Managers), London. Renamed **EMMA
      K**. Registered Trieste (Austria-Hungary flag). 1176 n,
      1963 g.
1900 Sold to M. Roca Hermanos. Renamed **CARMEN
      ROCA**. Registered Barcelona. 1519 n, 1967 g.
1904 Sold to Cia Maritime Commercial SA (J. Roca,
      Manager), Barcelona. 1352 n, 1922 g.
1913 Sold to Estefania y Dutrus, Valencia. Renamed
      VICENTE CARSI. Registered Valencia.
1916 Sold to T. Seabold (Teo Doro), Bilbao. Registered San
      Sebastian.

1918 Sold to Cia del Vapor Teodoro. Renamed **TEODORO**.
1920 Sold to J. M. Urquijo & Cia, Bilbao. Renamed
      BEGONA No 5.
1923 Transferred to Cia de Navegacion 'Begona' (J. M. de
      Urquijo, Manager), Bilbao. July, lost after collision with
      unknown vessel off Cross Sound Lightship, voyage Blyth
      to Marseille.
Note—A half model of **SHEIKH** hull is in Liverpool Museum.

GAMBIA

85 YORUBA (II)

O.N. 84061   1889–1897

'Eboe' class
Steel screw steamer, two decks
285.8′×36.0′×24.4′   1345 n   2086 g
Built by C. Mitchell & Co, Newcastle, Yard No 400, as
SIROCCO, for Bedouin Steam Navigation Co. Registered
Liverpool. C 2 cyl 34″, 66″–42″ by Wallsend Slipway & Engineering Co Ltd, Newcastle. 235 hp.
1880 November, launched.
1889 Acquired by African Steamship Co. Renamed
      YORUBA. Registered London.
1897 June, sold to Dr A. Bing and E. Karpeles (Schenker,
      Walford & Co, Managers), London. Renamed **IRENE**.
      Registered Trieste (Austria-Hungary flag). 1288 n,
      2043 g.
1900 Sold to Carlo Marigo, Padova. Renamed **VICENZA**.
      Registered Venice. 1409 n, 2163 g. High pressure cyl-
      inder re-bored to 34¾″ diameter.
1902 Sold to Banca Cattolica Vicentina.
1904 Sold for demolition at Genoa.

BIAFRA

86 BIAFRA (II)

O.N. 96295   1890–1896

Iron screw schooner, one deck
200.8′×30.1′×14.0′   562 n   846 g
Built by J. Priestman & Co, Sunderland, Yard No 53, as
ALGARVE for A. Centeno Lisbon. Registered Lisbon. C 2 cyl
24″, 48″–36″ by T. Clarke & Co, Newcastle. 95 hp.
1885   June, launched.
1889   Sold to A. Booth & Co, Liverpool. Registered Liverpool.
1890   Acquired by African Steamship Co, London. Renamed
BIAFRA. Registered London. 511 n, 808 g.
1895   19 February, stranded on Lagos Bar but later refloated.
       21 June, stranded and damaged in Forcados River later
       refloated.
1896   Sold to Rasmus F. Olsen of Bergen. Renamed **TRYG**.
       Registered Bergen. 517 n, 839 g.
1899   Now 477 n, 775 g.
1913   13 February, foundered seven miles off Iceland.

87 LOANGO

O.N. 87914   1890–1904

Steel screw schooner, two decks (one steel, one iron)
329.7′×39.2′×28.0′   1973 n, 2993 g
Built by T. Royden & Sons, Liverpool, Yard No 220, as
KNIGHT OF ST GEORGE for Knight of St George Steam
Ship Co Ltd (Greenshields, Cowie & Co, Managers), Liverpool.
Registered Liverpool. C 2 cyl 38″, 71″–48″ by G. Forrester &
Co, Liverpool. 350 hp, 11 K.

1883   October, launched.
1890   May, acquired by Elder, Dempster & Co. Renamed
       LOANGO. Registered London. 1934 n, 2935 g.
1891   Transferred to African Steamship Co.
1900   Transferred to Elder Line Ltd. 1940 n, 2993 g.
1904   Sold to H. Diederichsen, Kiel. Renamed
       NEUMUHLEN. Registered Hamburg.
1909   October, sold for demolition at Garston.
Loango is a port in Zaire, north of Point Noire.

LOANGO

MAYUMBA

88 MAYUMBA (II)
O.N. 97821   1890–1915

Steel screw steamer, one deck
297.0′×39.9′×18.8′   1649 n   2561 g
Built by Sir Raylton Dixon & Co Ltd, Middlesbrough, Yard
No 329, for Elder, Dempster & Co. Registered London. T
3 cyl 22½″, 37″, 61″–39″ by T. Richardson & Sons, Hartlepool.
250 hp.
1890   26 September, launched. October, completed.
1892   Transferred to African Steamship Co.
1905   October, in collision with *ROQUELLE* in Benin Creek.
1909   28 August, assisted the Branch steamers *ILORIN*,
       LOKOJA and *OSHOGBO* to tow *BOULAMA* off For-
       cados Bar.
1915   October, sold.
1917   Owner, Bidson Shipping Co Ltd, Liverpool (Charles M.
       Farrah, Manager).
1920/21.   Sold to the Admiralty.
1927   Used as coal hulk at Portland.
1928/9   Deleted from Lloyds Register.

89 MONROVIA (II)
O.N. 97775   1890–1914

Steel screw schooner, one deck
297.5′×40.1′×18.7′   1558 n   2402 g
Built by Sir Raylton Dixon & Co Ltd, Middlesbrough, Yard

No 313, for Elder, Dempster & Co. Registered Liverpool. T
3 cyl 22″, 35″, 59″–39″ by T. Richardson & Sons, Hartlepool.
200 hp, 9½ K.
1890   May, completed.
1892   Damage repairs carried out and part new deck fitted.
1896   Transferred to African Steamship Co. Registered
       London.
1909   Transferred to Elder, Dempster & Co.
1910   Transferred to Elder Dempster Shipping Ltd.
1914   15 June, wrecked at Black Point, Loango, voyage Liver-
       pool to West Africa, general cargo.

90 ETHIOPIA (II)
O.N. 97879   1891–1908

Steel screw schooner, one deck
297.0′×39.8′×18.8′   1657 n   2523 g
Built by Sir Raylton Dixon & Co Ltd, Middlesbrough, Yard
No 338, for African Steamship Co. Registered London. T 3 cyl
22½″, 37″, 61″–39″ by North Eastern Marine Engineering Co
Ltd. 250 hp, 9½ K.
1891   July, completed.
1900   Stranded (Captain John Davies) on Oxwich Point,
       Gower Coast, South Wales, voyage Hamburg to Port
       Talbot. Later refloated with 140 plates damaged.
1908   Sold, converted into lighter.

(No. 6023.)

"ETHIOPIA" (S.S.).

The Merchant Shipping Act, 1894.

In the matter of a formal investigation held at the Town Hall, Cardiff, on the 22nd, 24th, and 26th days of March, 1900, before Thomas William Lewis, Esquire, a Stipendiary Magistrate, assisted by Captain Kennett Hore and Captain W. H. Sinclair Loutit, as to the circumstances attending the stranding of the British steamship "Ethiopia," of London, on Oxwich Point in the British Channel, on the 23rd day of February, 1900, whereby she sustained damage.

Report of Court.

The Court having carefully inquired into the circumstances attending the above-mentioned shipping casualty, finds for the reasons stated in the Annex hereto, that the stranding of the vessel was caused by keeping her too long on a N.E. ½ E. magnetic course heading towards the land, and in the neglect to take measures to verify her position by the lead in foggy weather when according to the distance run she was in close proximity to the land. The Court finds the master, John Davies, alone to blame, and suspends his certificate for three months.

Dated this 26th day of March, 1900.

T. W. Lewis, Judge.

We concur in the above Report.

Kennett Hore,
W. H. Sinclair Loutit, } Assessors.

Annex to the Report.

This was an inquiry into the circumstances attending the stranding of the British steamship "Ethiopia" on Oxwich Point in the Bristol Channel, on the 23rd of February last, and held at the Town Hall, Cardiff, on the 22nd, 24th, and 26th days of March, 1900.

Mr. Robertson appeared for the Board of Trade, Mr. Miller represented the master, and Mr. Ingledew watched the case on behalf of the owners. The chief and second officers were not represented by counsel, and appeared in person. The "Ethiopia," official number 97,897, is a screw steamer built at Middlesbrough in 1891 by Messrs. Raylton, Dixon and Company. Her length being 297 ft., breadth 33·8 ft., and depth of hold 18·8 ft. She is a two-masted schooner-rigged vessel, fitted with triple expansion engines of 250 horse power combined. Her gross tonnage being 2,523·04 tons, and her registered tonnage 1,657·13 tons, and she is under the management of Mr. Edwin Bicker-Caarten, secretary of the owners, the African Steamship Company, of 21, Great Saint Helens, City of London, and registered under date of August 31st, 1891.

The "Ethiopia" left Hamburg on the 17th day of February, 1900, bound for Port Talbot, with a crew of 34 hands all told, in water ballast, drawing 11 ft. aft and 8 ft. forward. She was under the command of Mr. J. Davies, who held a certificate of competency, No. 018,622. She had about 520 tons of water ballast on board, and about 204 tons of bunker coal. Her consumption of coal was about 16 tons per day. They appear to have had S.W. to W. and N.W. breezes during the passage from leaving Hamburg until rounding the Longships, but no difficulty appears to have arisen on account of her being in such light ballast draught. At 10.0 a.m. on the 23rd they rounded the Longships and steered up for Lundy Island. The weather was moderate and fine but hazy. At 3.25 p.m. Trevose Head was abeam, and at 6.40 p.m. the first of a four point bearing was taken of Hartland Point and the course altered to N.E. by E. On this course there was said to be 4½ degrees of westerly deviation, but as it was then half flood this half point was allowed for the set of the tide and the course was therefore supposed to be N.E. by E. magnetic. At 7.0 p.m. the second bearing of Hartland Point was taken, and the distance found to be 3½ miles from the light. The N.E. by E. course was still continued, and the chief officer, who was then in charge of the deck, stated that at 7.50 p.m. he took the first bearing for a four point bearing of Bull Point, and the second officer who relieved him at 8.0 p.m. stated that he took the second bearing of Bull Point at 8.15 p.m., and that he allowed the distance to be 4½ miles, but as he only allowed the rate of nine miles an hour, when in point of fact the ship was, owing to the tide, going over the ground at 12 miles an hour, the distance as stated by him must therefore have been inaccurate. The bearing and distance from Bull Point at 8.15 p.m. he did not report to the master at the time, nor was the course of the ship altered after being first set N.E. by E. at 6.40 p.m. She continued on her course full speed running up with the flood tide until 9.30 p.m., when the weather came in thick with fog and drizzling rain. He therefore called the master, who came on deck and reduced the engines to half speed. It appears that the master had not been on deck up till this time. He was in the chart house suffering from an attack of African fever, but the courses were laid off by him in the chart house in consultation with the officers and given by him to the officer in charge of the deck. Although the weather was now thick and they had made some 16 miles since leaving Bull Point, no cast of the lead was taken, but the same course was continued until 10.25 p.m., when the master decided to slow and take a cast of the lead. The deep sea lead was passed forward by the boatswain and the cast taken by the second mate, but the lead and line fell on the bottom and no proper cast was taken, and the second mate immediately called out "shallow water," and hauled in the line preparatory to taking another cast. At the same time he saw breakers close ahead of the ship, and called out to the master who immediately stopped and reversed the engines, but they had only gone astern a few revolutions not sufficiently to stop her headway when she struck and remained fast on what afterwards proved to be Oxwich Point, some 12 miles N.W. of where they supposed themselves to be. The engines were kept going astern until 12.40 a.m. for the purpose of keeping the vessel's stern to the wind and thus prevent her from being blown broadside on to the rocks and breaking up. Distress signals were in the meanwhile made, but no reply was obtained, and the boats were swung out ready for lowering. The wells were sounded and No. 2 hold was found to be fast making water, so the master decided not to empty his forward water ballast tanks.

At 8.0 a.m. on the 24th the tugs "Cruiser" and "Contest" came alongside, and at 9.30 a.m. the Port Eynon life-boat came alongside to render assistance. At 11.30 a.m. the tugs got tow lines on board and commenced towing with the assistance of the steam pilot boat "Brandford," but without any effect. At 10.30 p.m. a tug from Port Talbot arrived. The weather all day was moderate and fine with a light S.E. wind and hazy. At 2.30 p.m. on the 26th the tug "Emily and Charlotte" arrived, passed hawser and commenced to tow. The ship floated but was held by a rock under No. 2 bilge. At 3.20 a.m. of the 27th the vessel was finally got off, and she was beached in Oxwich Bay for temporary repairs. On Wednesday the 28th she was towed off and taken to Port Talbot and docked in the Graving Dock, where she now is, having suffered considerable damage. It will be seen on looking at the chart that a course N.E. ½ E. from the position of the vessel at 7.0 p.m. when she was off Hartland Point would, if continued, about place her on Oxwich Point where she stranded, and as she steered N.E. by E. and there was 4½ westerly deviation on that point it is evident that the vessel made the course that was set and steered. The bearing of Bull Point at 8.15 p.m. was a correct indication to the master of the speed his vessel was making over the ground, and should have been a guide to him as to the distance run when the weather became thick and the necessity of immediately turning round and sounding when he could not see or tell where he was going. The Court, while not attaching any blame to the chief officer

79

for the stranding, considers him deserving of censure for the careless manner in keeping the log.

On the opening of the inquiry Mr. Robertson put in, and on the conclusion of the evidence submitted for the opinion of the Court, the following questions :—

1. What number of compasses had the vessel, were they in good order and sufficient for the safe navigation of the vessel, and when and by whom were they last adjusted ?

2. Did the master ascertain the deviation of his compasses by observation from time to time, were the errors correctly ascertained and the proper corrections to the courses applied ?

3. Was the vessel sufficiently ballasted ?

4. Were proper measures taken to ascertain and verify the position of the vessel at 7 p.m., and again at 8 p.m., on the 23rd February last ?

5. Was a safe and proper course set at or about 7 p.m. on the last-mentioned date, and was due and proper allowance made for tide and currents ?

6. Having regard to the fact that the vessel was light in ballast and to the direction and force of the wind, should the course have been altered at or about 8 p.m. on the last-mentioned date ?

7. When did the weather become thick with fog, and was the speed of the vessel then reduced ?

8. Was the first cast of the lead taken at 10.25 p.m., and if so should the lead have been used earlier ?

9. Was a good and proper look-out kept, and was the vessel navigated with proper and seamanlike care ?

10. What was the cause of the stranding of the vessel ?

11. Was serious damage to the vessel caused by the wrongful act or default of the master and officers or any of them ?

The Court then considered the questions and answers as follows :—

1. The " Ethiopia " had three compasses. They were in good order and sufficient for her safe navigation. There is no evidence before the Court as to when or by whom the compasses were last adjusted.

2. There were no deviation cards on board the vessel, but from a deviation book kept by the master and produced by him to the Court, it appears he ascertained the deviation of his compasses by observation from time to time, correctly ascertained their errors, and applied the proper corrections to the courses.

3. For the weather actually experienced on the voyage commencing at Hamburg on the 17th February and terminating by the stranding of the vessel on the 23rd February her ballasting appears to have been sufficient. But if instead of fine weather and smooth sea the vessel had encountered such adverse conditions of weather as might reasonably be expected for such a voyage in February the ballasting would have probably proved insufficient and a source of danger.

4. At 6.40 p.m. on the 23rd February, when the N.E. by E. course was set, making N.E. ¼ E. magnetic, proper measure, viz., a four point bearing of Hartland Point, was taken to ascertain and verify the position of the vessel. At 7.0 p.m., when the bearing was concluded, Hartland Point was abeam, and was distant 3½ miles. At 7.50 p.m. Bull Point was on the four points, and a bearing was taken by the chief officer, and again when the Point was abeam at 8.15 p.m. by the second officer. This also was a proper measure, but the distance was inaccurately calculated, for it showed Bull Point to be 4½ miles distant, and therefore must have been measured by the distance the log showed instead of the distance the vessel had travelled over the ground between Hartland Point and Bull Point. The results of these bearings were reported to the master by the Channel

pilot who was on the bridge, but not by the second officer, and when the distance of Bull Point was reported to him at 8.15 p.m. it would have been immediately obvious to him on a moment's consideration that either the distance of Bull Point was inaccurately calculated or the vessel was about two miles nearer the land than the course he had laid down. The Court is satisfied that the distance of Bull Point was inaccurately calculated, and that the vessel was on the course that had been laid down by the master at 6.40 p.m., viz. :— N.E. by E. by standard, and N.E. ¼ E. magnetic. This course was not altered, according to the master's evidence, when Bull Point was abeam, before or thereafter.

5. The course set at 6.40 p.m., as above stated, was a safe and proper course provided it was not continued too long. But although the master expected about 10 p.m. to arrive at a position about two miles to the westward of Skerweather Lightship, and, owing to the condition of the atmosphere, he failed to make the Lightship, he continued on his course for twenty-five minutes longer during which a moment's consideration of the distance he had run would have shown him he was running into danger. The master stated in evidence that he knew and made allowance for the force and direction of the flood tide, but its influence in carrying the vessel over the ground does not appear to have been a factor in the calculation of the distance of the vessel from Bull Point, nor in an estimate of her position at 10.0 p.m.

6. At 8 p.m. on the 23rd February the wind was S.S.E., light, and the sea smooth. These conditions and the weight of ballasting did not, in the opinion of the Court, render necessary any alteration in the N.E. by E. course. But for other reasons herein stated the course should have been altered about 9.30 p.m.

7. The weather became thick with fog about 9.30 p.m., and the vessel was reduced nominally to half speed.

8. The first and only cast of the lead was taken at 10.25 p.m., and before the sounding was definitely ascertained the vessel stranded. At 10 o'clock the vessel was on a course heading towards the land, the distance run showed she was not far from the land, her intended position could not, owing to fog, be verified by lights, and having regard to the result of the bearing taken of Bull Point, the master should have been specially alert. Hence the Court is of opinion that the lead should have been used earlier.

9. The evidence as to the look-out is of a conflicting character. A man was stationed in the fore part of the vessel to keep a look-out, but the Court is advised by the assessors that they are in doubt whether he kept such a good look-out as the circumstances required. The Court is therefore not prepared to find that the look-out was not good and proper.

10 and 11. The stranding of the vessel was caused by keeping her too long on a N.E. ¼ E. magnetic course heading towards the land, and in the neglect to take measures to verify her position by the lead in foggy weather when according to the distance run she was in close proximity to the land. She was therefore not navigated with proper and seamanlike care. She sustained serious damage the result of such want of care, for which the master is alone to blame. The master's certificate is suspended for three months.

T. W. LEWIS, Judge.

We concur.

KENNETT HORE,   } Assessors.
W. H. SINCLAIR LOUTIT, }

(Issued in London by the Board of Trade on the 27th day of April, 1900.)

91 KWARRA (I)
O.N. 98939   1891–1908

Steel twin screw steamer, one deck
200.3′×36.2′×12.1′   500 n   812 g
Built by Naval Construction & Armaments Co Ltd, Barrow,
Yard No 187, for African Steamship Co, London. Registered
London. 2×T 3 cyl 12½″, 20″, 31″–24″ by the builders. 120 hp.
1891   April, launched.
1902   Employed on local West African services.
1908   Sank off Forcados, December.
Kwarra is a former name of the River Niger (also known as
Joliba, Kowara and Quorra).

92 BONNY (I)
O.N. 98639   1891–1915

'Bonny' class
Steel screw steamer, two decks
327.6′×39.4′×22.0′   1713 n   2702 g
Built by Naval Construction & Armaments Co Ltd, Barrow,
Yard No 185, for British & African Steam Navigation Co Ltd,
Liverpool. Registered Glasgow. T 3 cyl 23″, 38″, 61″–42″ by the
builders. 240 hp, 10½ K.
Passenger accommodation: 44 first class, 14 second.
1891   25 April, launched by Miss Blythe. June, completed.
1900   Registered Liverpool.

BONNY

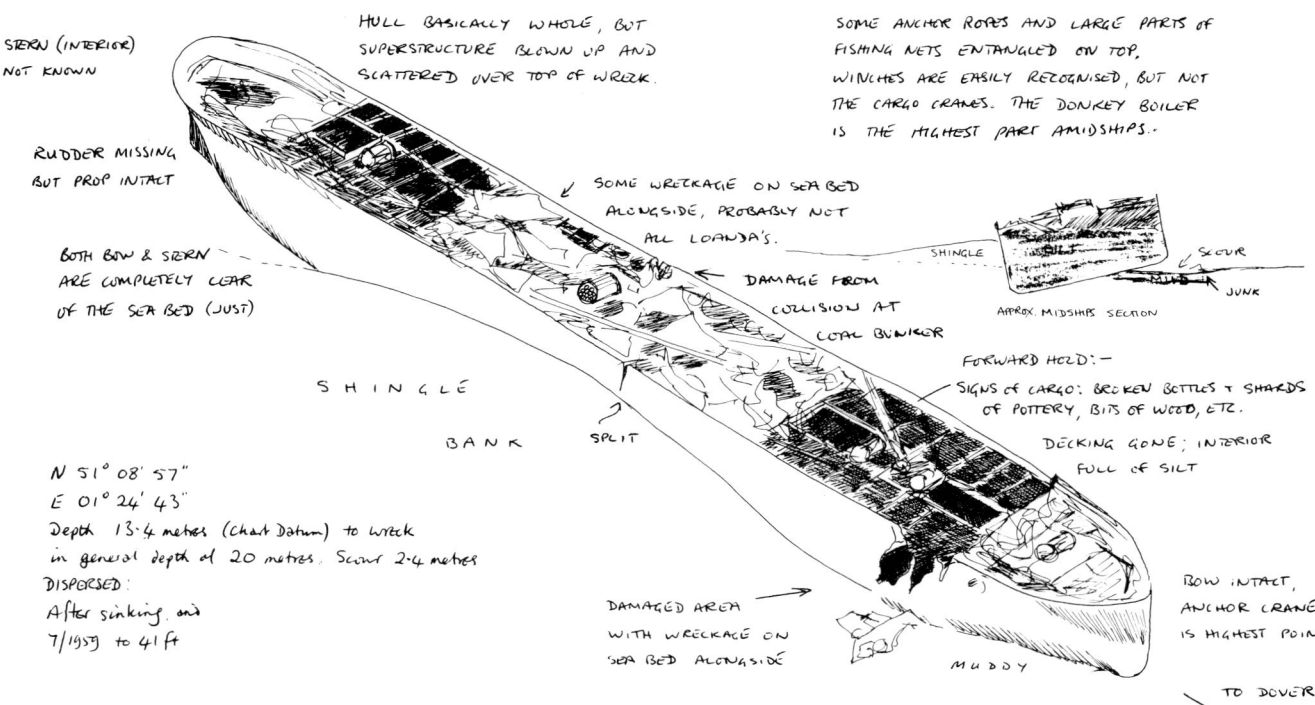

DIVER'S IMPRESSION OF SS LOANDA
Based on dives done during 1982-3

STERN (INTERIOR) NOT KNOWN

HULL BASICALLY WHOLE, BUT SUPERSTRUCTURE BLOWN UP AND SCATTERED OVER TOP OF WRECK.

SOME ANCHOR ROPES AND LARGE PARTS OF FISHING NETS ENTANGLED ON TOP. WINCHES ARE EASILY RECOGNISED, BUT NOT THE CARGO CRANES. THE DONKEY BOILER IS THE HIGHEST PART AMIDSHIPS.

RUDDER MISSING BUT PROP INTACT

SOME WRECKAGE ON SEA BED ALONGSIDE, PROBABLY NOT ALL LOANDA'S.

BOTH BOW & STERN ARE COMPLETELY CLEAR OF THE SEA BED (JUST)

DAMAGE FROM COLLISION AT COAL BUNKER

SHINGLE
SCOUR
JUNK
APPROX. MIDSHIPS SECTION

FORWARD HOLD:—

SIGNS OF CARGO: BROKEN BOTTLES & SHARDS OF POTTERY, BITS OF WOOD, ETC.

DECKING GONE; INTERIOR FULL OF SILT

SHINGLE
BANK
SPLIT

N 51° 08′ 57″
E 01° 24′ 43″
Depth 13.4 metres (Chart Datum) to wreck
in general depth of 20 metres. Scour 2.4 metres
DISPERSED:
After sinking, and
7/1959 to 41 ft

DAMAGED AREA WITH WRECKAGE ON SEA BED ALONGSIDE

MUDDY

BOW INTACT, ANCHOR CRANE IS HIGHEST POINT

TO DOVER HARBOUR

© 1984 Don Martin

LOANDA

1915 17 August, 2055, sunk by gunfire (22 rounds expended) from U38 (Kapitanleutnant Max Valentiner), 16 miles south by east from Tuskar, voyage Marseilles to Liverpool in ballast.

Ships of the 'Bonny' class: BONNY (92), LOANDA (93), VOLTA (94).

U38 surrendered at Harwich 23 February 1919 in accordance with the peace treaty.

Name derived from the river and town near its mouth in Eastern Nigeria.

93 LOANDA (II)
O.N. 98656   1891–1908

'Bonny' class
Steel screw steamer, two decks
327.6′ × 39.4′ × 22.0′   1713 n   2702 g
Built by Naval Construction & Armaments Co Ltd, Barrow, Yard No 186, for British & African Steam Navigation Co Ltd, Liverpool. Registered Glasgow. T 3 cyl 23″, 38″, 61″–42″ by the builders. 240 hp, 10½ K.
Passenger accommodation: 44 first class, 14 second.
1891 23 June, launched by Miss Blechynden. July, completed.
1900 Registered Liverpool.
1908 31 May, sank after collision with Russian ss JUNONA, (3462 g / built 1898) off South Foreland in about seven fathoms low water, voyage Hamburg to West Africa. JUNONA was on voyage Odessa to St Petersburg (Leningrad) and put into Gravesend with considerable bow damage. No loss of life.

94 VOLTA
O.N. 98668   1891–1908

Steel screw steamer, two decks
327.6′ × 39.4′ × 22.0′   1713 n   2702 g

Built by Naval Construction & Armaments Co Ltd, Barrow, Yard No 192, for British & African Steam Navigation Co Ltd, Liverpool. Registered Glasgow. T 3 cyl 23″, 38″, 61″–42″ by the builders. 240 hp, 10½ K.
Passenger accommodation: 44 first class, 14 second.
1891 8 August, launched by Miss Dempster. September, completed.
1900 Registered Liverpool.
1908 Sold to Ellerman Lines Ltd (Fred Swift, Manager), Liverpool. Renamed **VENETIAN**. Registered Liverpool. 1738 n, 2734 g.
1916 Transferred to Papayanni & Co.
1924 June, sold to Dutch shipbreakers for demolition at Alblasserdam.
Name derived from the major river in Ghana.

95 ACCRA (I)
O.N. 102608   1893–1920

'Accra' class
Steel screw steamer, two decks
336.0′ × 39.4′ × 22.3′   1788 n   2808 g
Built by Naval Construction & Armaments Co Ltd, Barrow, Yard No 219, for the British & African Steam Navigation Co Ltd. Registered Glasgow. T 3 cyl 23″, 38″, 63″–42″ by the builders. 300 hp, 10½ K.
Passenger accommodation: 44 first class, 14 second.
1893 31 May, launched. July, completed.
1900 Registered Liverpool. 1791 g, 2827 n.
1907 May, aground near Wexford, voyage Tenerife to Liverpool. Refloated, with very little damage. Vessel valued at £23,500.
1920 June, sold to Mannie Swan Shipping Co Ltd (Boulie Lagane & Co, Managers), Port Louis, Mauritius. Registered Port Louis (British flag). 1751 n, 2826 g. Employed on the pilgrim trade service.
1924 Sold to Dada Mia Khandwini, Bombay. Registered Bombay (British flag).

VOLTA

ACCRA

1925 Sold for demolition at Bombay.

Ships of the 'Accra' class: ACCRA (95), BATHURST (96), BATANGA (97), BAKANA (98), AXIM (99).

Accra is the capital city of Ghana, it stands on the Greenwich Meridian at 5°.31'N.

96 BATHURST (I)
O.N. 102614   1893–1917

'Accra' class

Steel screw steamer, two decks

336.0′×39.4′×22.3′   1788 n   2808 g

Built by Naval Construction & Armaments Co Ltd, Barrow, Yard No 220, for British & African Steam Navigation Co Ltd, Liverpool. Registered Glasgow. T 3 cyl 23″, 38″, 63″–42″ by the builders. 198 hp, 10½ K.

Passenger accommodation: 44 first class, 14 second.

1893 15 July, launched. August, completed.

1898 7 February, ashore on Opobo Bar, re-floated after part cargo jettisoned.

1900 Registered Liverpool. 1794 n, 2821 g.

1917 30 May, attacked with gunfire and torpedoed after capture by German submarine U87 (Kapitanleutnant Rudolf Schneider), position 90 miles west of Bishop Rock, voyage West Africa to Hull, cargo mahogany and palm kernels. **BATHURST** unarmed. The crew reached the Scilly Isles in boats. No loss of life.

BATHURST

U87 (then under command of Kapitanleutnant Freiherr Rudolf von Speth-Schulzburg) was rammed and sunk with all hands by HMS P56 in 52°.56′N 05°.07′W on 25 December 1917. Schneider was washed overboard from U87 and died 13 October 1917.

Bathurst (now known as Banjul) is the capital of the Gambia.

Previous to joining Elder Dempter & Company Limited I served as 2nd Mate on the only two British vessels running to the Western Ports of Sweden from England between February 1915 and July 1916. I then left to obtain my 1st Mate's Certificate. The above voyages were rather hazardous, often sighting German Men of War in the Kattegat, and being in close proximity to German vessels in Swedish ports.

My First Voyage with Elder Dempter & Company Ltd.

On obtaining My First Mate's Certificate in August 1916, I applied to E.D. & Co. Ltd. and was appointed as 2nd Officer to R.M.S. "Bathurst" at Liverpool about mid August. The "Bathurst" was built during the early years of 1890 and sailed under the British and African Steam Navigation Company Limited. She was about 2,800 tons registered and was fitted out to carry about 40 1st Class passengers, and some 2nd Class; but the latter accommodation was in disuse.

So far as I can remember, Captain "Welsh" Jones was the Master. The Officers etc. were:

Mr. ? Underwood	Chief Officer
Mr. ? McNorth	Chief Engineer
Mr. Bill Teall	Purser
Mr. Bertie Clare	Chief Steward

The ship was fitted with an Ice-Box only.

We sailed from Liverpool 2 days after my appointment, without a Third Officer (being unobtainable), and the Purser Bill Teall missed his passage on account of a mix-up with Head Office. On signing the articles, I discovered that the Chief Officer had signed on for £1 less per month than what I signed on for. We were also informed that we would receive about 2/3rds of a Third Officer's salary divided between the two of us for the voyage.

We sailed bound for Rotterdam, and during the dark watches passing through the English Channel, the Master and Chief Officer kept the 2 watches, and I was on stand by to take over any signalling that was necessary.

At Rotterdam, the lower holds were fully loaded with cases of Trade Gin, and Bales and Iron Pots in the Tween Decks. Our first port was Dakar where the Purser "Bill Teall" joined, thence to Freetown. During preparation for departure, whilst warming up the main engines, the H.P. cylinder cover cracked, so to carry on the engine was converted into compound. Cannot remember all the ports touched at, but Half Assince is remembered rowing to the s.s. "Bakana", wrecked on the beach. Our Engineers managed to board the "Bakana" in an endeavour to obtain the H.P. cover. However it was too rusted to be of any use. We finally arrived at Lagos to discharge the remainder of the cargo, having worked normally at all other ports. What impressed me was the method of discharging by surf boats, and no ports to enter. At Lagos we were informed that the "Bathurst" had been commissioned to tow the sand sucker "Quorra" or "Kworra" from Forcados to Gibraltar, from where she was intended to sail for Basra.

Discharge and loading was completed at Lagos, and a large space was left in No. 2 Hold to load all the sand sucker's pipes and gear. The "Quorra" had been occupied at Forcados in reclaiming most of the fore-shore at that port. I regret to say that when the Chief Officer saw the gear at Forcados, he was not enamoured and took to his bunk. Captain Jones gave me some advice and then just left me to do the job. The sucking tongue weighed close to 10 tons, but the "Bathurst" was equipped with a 10 ton derrick at No.2 Hatch. The tongue was too awkward and large to stow in the Lower Hold so was stood on end in the hatchway, protruding somewhat over the hatch coamings. The pipes were about 20′ long, and one foot in diameter. Half of them were stowed on the starboard side of the Hold, and then the tongue was inclined to lean against the starboard hatch coamings, the top of it clearing the underside of the hatch boards by 1 inch. The next job was to unshackle 30 fathoms of cable and drag same aft to be used as a spring for the tow. That completed, the floats for the pipes had to be loaded on top of the hatches. They were saucer shaped, seven in number and the diameter was a little in excess of the ship's beam. These were loaded two each on Nos. 1, 2 and 3 hatches, and one on No.4. The floats overlapped the port bulwark rail and just came to the starboard rail, and it required a great deal of stooping to get along the deck.

From the bridge, one could just see nicely over the floats on No.1 hatch.

BATHURST (Photo McRoberts collection)

The loading completed, came the job of coupling up the tow. The Master of the "Quorra" was very particular over this job, but was finally, after much hard work, completed to everybody that mattered, satisfaction. I cannot now remember whether the towing hawser was of wire or coir. The Chief Officer recovered his health in good time to sail. This was my first experience of working with Kru labour, and I must say that I was very much impressed by the two very efficient head-men and a grand gang of men.

Well away we went en route Freetown with the tow behaving nicely. However between Cape 3 Points and Cape Palmas, the "Quorra" hoisted a code signal one forenoon, "I am sinking". That caused a bit of a flutter, a boat was lowered and I went over to see about the trouble. It was discovered that a double bottom tank had sprung a leak, but as the "Quorra" had enough other tanks, there was nothing to worry about. On arrival at Freetown, the Authorities refused to allow the "Quorra" to proceed, owing to the danger of submarines. The "Bathurst" had to proceed to Gibraltar to discharge the gear. On arrival a few days delay was incurred, whilst the Authorities decided about the gear. We, however, then proceeded into Dock and discharged to the quay. Then a few more days delay anchored off Algeciras awaiting bunkers. When proceeding later across the bay to the coal hulks, Captain Jones was sick, the Chief Officer was in charge of the bridge and myself on the foc'sle head. During the run I noticed a vessel on our port bow proceeding to sea, and I reported same to the bridge. It appeared to me that we were on a collision course, but the other vessel kept her course. However, Mr. Underwood decided to alter and gave a blast to indicate we were turning to starboard, in an attempt to bring the two vessels beam to beam. As the blast died, I noticed someone running up the bridge ladder on the other vessel, however there was no alteration in the other vessel's direction and our port bow collided with the starboard break of the foc'sle head of the other vessel. Our port anchor had been hanging clear of the water ready for anchoring at the Coal Hulk. The impact threw me off my feet, but I managed to grab hold of a stanchion which most likely saved me an injury. However as the two vessels sheered apart, I noticed a fluke of our Bower Anchor embedded in the other vessel's side, and the crown had pierced our port bow plates. We were another two weeks at Gibraltar, repairing the damage and changing the Bower Anchor, spending Xmas Day 1916 at the port.

We arrived at Hull during January 1917 without any further incident.

The 2nd and 3rd Officers' accommodation in the poop space was occupied by other ranks, and I was accommodated in a passenger cabin, with no facilities for my gear, being fitted only with a small wash stand and a very small wardrobe. During the voyage, I was accommodated in 3 similar cabins and in each one, the deck head leaked badly. I did not feel impressed with the attitude of the Company towards its officers.

Naturally we did not receive any extra pay for the work involved with the tow, so in the circumstances I felt like resigning, but was persuaded to make another voyage.

K. Redmore, from the *Elder of Elders*

THE LAST VOYAGE OF THE "BATHURST"

By Captain K. Redmore

It was a normal coast voyage of those days, mostly Surf Ports, but I had the experience of bumping over Opobo Bar, and also getting a good old dose of malaria, otherwise no other incident that I remember. However at Freetown, homeward bound, we embarked about a dozen members of the crew of a Thos. Wilson's vessel of Hull which had been sunk by a submarine. Two of the Deck Officers I recognised as having been at the same school as myself in Hull. We left Freetown in company with another vessel fitted with a 3 pounder on her poop.

When 93 miles West of the Scilly Isles on 30th May 1917 the other vessel was torpedoed. The submarine then surfaced and commenced to shell the "BATHURST". So naturally our speed at that time being about 7 knots, we had to stop and abandon ship. We used 3 lifeboats, and Chief Officers being on the port side, from which direction we were being shelled. The Port Boat was very fortunate in getting away without sustaining any casualties. On the starboard side we could hear the scream of shells flying overhead and plumping into the port side, and the "BATHURST" was on fire before our boats got away. The 3rd Officer cast off minus his Captain, and I was pushing off when I noticed the Captain coming down the rope ladder to my boat. When clear of the ship, the Captain's boat was called alongside the submarine, where we were required to give the particulars of the "BATHURST". Whilst alongside we heard more shelling, and shells were hitting the water on our side of the submarine, but a little way off. We were cast off and

the submarine sailed away on the surface, put a torpedo into the "BATHURST", and proceeded away on the surface out of range of the armed trawler that closed us. There were no casualties on either vessel, and so that was the end of R.M.S. "BATHURST". We were all picked up by the trawler and landed at St. Mary's, Scilly Isles.

From the *Elder of Elders*

PRESENTATION TO A CAPTAIN

"Captain Norman, master of Messrs Elder, Dempster & Co's African steamer Bathurst, was presented on Monday on behalf of the officers of the Ashantee expeditionary forces which travelled to the coast in that vessel, with a pair of binocular glasses, in recognition of his kindness to the troops while on board his vessel. The glasses bear the inscription: 'Captain T. W. Norman, s.s. Bathurst. From the members of the Ashanti Expeditionary Force, 1895.' It will be remembered that amongst those on board the Bathurst were Sir Francis Scott (the commander of the expedition), Col Kempster, and HRH Prince Christian, who were feted at the Hotel Metropole, Grand Canary, by Mr A.L. Jones, on the steamer calling there. Captain Norman was the recipient of a gold watch and chain last year for having rescued the Niger Company's officials from Akassa, when that place was looted by the Brass natives in January, 1895."

Lloyds List February 1896

97 BATANGA
O.N. 102639   1893–1922

'Accra' class
Steel screw steamer, two decks
336.0′×39.4′×22.3′   1788 n   2808 g
Built by Naval Construction & Armaments Co Ltd, Barrow, Yard No 222, for British & African Steam Navigation Co Ltd, Liverpool. Registered Glasgow. T 3 cyl 23″, 38″, 63″–42″ by the builders. 198 hp, 10½ K.
Passenger accommodation: 44 first class, 14 second.
1893   12 October, launched by Miss Holt.
1900   Registered Liverpool.
1922   August, sold for £4,000 for demolition in Germany.
Note—Miss Mary Kingsley sailed aboard **BATANGA** (Captain J. Murray) from Liverpool 23 December 1894 on her second expedition, calling at Sierra Leone, Ghana and Oil Rivers. She left the ship at Calabar.
Batanga is a port on the Cameroons coast, south of Douala.

BATANGA

*The wreck of **BAKANA** photographed in February 1984*

98   BAKANA (I)
O.N. 104563   1894–1913

'Accra' class
Steel screw steamer, two decks
336.0′×39.3′×22.3′   1789 n   2793 g
Built by Naval Construction & Armaments Co Ltd, Barrow,
Yard No 232, for the British & African Steam Navigation Co
Ltd, Liverpool. Registered Glasgow. T 3 cyl 23″, 38″, 63″–42″
by the builders. 198 hp, 10½ K.
Passenger accommodation: 44 first class, 14 second.
1894   4 August, launched. September, completed.
1895   Miss Mary Kingsley, at the end of her second visit to
       the West Coast of Africa, joined **BAKANA** (Captain
       E. Porter), at Calabar for the voyage home, arriving
       Liverpool 30 November.
1900   Registered Liverpool.
1908   6 May, stranded on Opobo Bar, Eastern Spit. Refloated.
       Now 1752 n, 2802 g.
1911   Aground off Loango Point.
1913   27 August, stranded at Half Assini near the mouth of
       the Ama Azule River (the Ghana border with the Ivory
       Coast). Unsuccessful attempt to refloat made by *EBANI*.
       Became total loss.
Bakana is a Niger Delta port, nine miles through the creeks to
the west of Port Harcourt.

*Another view of the remains of **BAKANA** photographed in February 1984*

99   AXIM
O.N. 104579   1894–1910

'Accra' class
Steel screw steamer, two decks
336.0′×39.3′×22.3′   1788 n   2793 g
Built by Naval Construction & Armaments Co Ltd, Barrow,

Yard No 231, for British & African Steam Navigation Co Ltd, Liverpool. Registered Glasgow. T 3 cyl 23″, 38″, 63″–42″ by the builders. 198 hp, 10½ K.
Passenger accommodation: 44 first class, 14 second class.
1893 1 September, launched. October, completed.
1900 December, registered Liverpool.
1910 9 December, sailed from London to West Africa via Tenerife and went missing.
Axim is an open anchorage port in Ghana.

AXIM

100 SPARROW
O.N. 104810   1895

145.3′×23.1′×11.2′   188 n   395 g
Built by J. F. Meursing, Amsterdam, for General Steam Navigation Co, London. Registered London. T 3 cyl 13″, 19″, 32″–20″ by J. Stewart & Son Ltd, London. 75 hp, 10½ K.
1894 November, completed.
1895 21 June, sold to African Steamship Co 13 August, wrecked on Lagos Bar and became a total loss (Captain A. Cooper).

101 LAGOON
O.N. 104601   1895–1923

Steel screw steamer, one deck
210.0′×28.2′×13.7′   403 n   704 g
Built by Barclay, Curle & Co Ltd, Glasgow, Yard No 394, for British & African Steam Navigation Co Ltd. Registered Glasgow. T 3 cyl, 15″, 25″, 41″–33″ by the builders. 85 hp, 10½ K.
1895 Completed February.
1900 Registered Liverpool.
1908 Returned to Liverpool from West Africa for repair after being aground for ten days on Lagos Bar (Captain D. McGuire).
1923 April, beached in leaking condition and subsequently sunk off Lagos.

102 ILARO (I)
O.N. 105769   1895–1915

Steel screw steamer, one deck and spar deck
310.0′×40.6′×17.6′   1804 n   2799 g
Built by Sir Raylton Dixon & Co Ltd, Middlesbrough, Yard No 415, for African Steamship Co. Registered London. T 3 cyl 23″, 36″, 59″–42″ by North Eastern Marine Engineering Co Ltd, Sunderland. 244 nhp.
1895 19 October, launched. December, completed.

ILARO

1914 August, German crew members incited Kroo labour to an act of mutiny while discharging at Accra.
1915 23 October, mined and set on fire, four miles to the East of Dungeness, voyage West Africa to Hull, and became a total loss. One life lost.
Ilaro is a town and division in Abeokuta province, South West Nigeria.

103 BANANA
O.N. 106886   1897–1914, 1918–1919

Steel screw steamer, one deck and spar deck
310.0′×41.2′×17.6′   1801 n   2817 g
Built by J. Blumer & Co, Sunderland, Yard No 130, for Alfred Lewis Jones, Esq (Elder, Dempster & Co, Managers). Registered Liverpool. T 3 cyl 22½″, 37″, 61″–42″ by G. Clark Ltd, Sunderland. 249 nhp, 10 K.
1897 May, completed.
1899 Transferred to Elder Line Ltd.
1914–1918 **BANANA** was detained at Hamburg throughout World War I.
1919 July, sold for £83,000, to Jose Garios e Hijos, Valencia. Registered Bilbao.
1924 Sold to J. Garrigos Perez, Valencia.
1925 Sold to Antonio Menchaca, Bilbao. 1801 n, 2817 g.
1931 June, broken up at Bilbao, by A. Menchaca.
Banana is a town on Banana Creek near the mouth of River Zaire.

BANANA

BIAFRA

104 BIAFRA (III)
O.N. 108180   1896–1910

Steel screw steamer, two decks
332.0′×43.2′×23.0′   2902 n   3606 g
Built by Sir Raylton Dixon & Co Ltd, Middlesbrough, Yard
No 402, as **LEOPOLDVILLE**, for Cie Belge Maritime du
Congo. Registered Antwerp. T 3 cyl 24½″, 39″, 67″–45″ by T.
Richardson & Sons Ltd, Hartlepool. 308 nhp, 11 K.
Passenger accommodation: 88 first class, 28 second.
1894   17 September, launched.
1895   January, completed.
1896   Transferred to African Steamship Co. Renamed
       BIAFRA. Registered London. 2155 n, 3363 g.
1910   Sold to Bombay & Persia Steam Navigation Co Ltd,
       Bombay. Renamed **HOMAYUN**. 2155 n, 3363 g. Regis-
       tered Bombay (British flag).
1911   High pressure cylinder bored out to 24¹¹⁄₁₆″ diameter.
1919   Sold to HM Government.
1923   Sold for demolition in the United Kingdom.
BIAFRA was reported to be the first vessel to operate a
passenger service between Liverpool and West Africa.

105 EKURO
O.N. 106039   1896–1914

Steel screw steamer, one deck
185.6′×26.1′×11.2′   277 n   600 d   485 g
Built by C. S. Swan & Hunter Ltd, Newcastle, Yard No 211,
for British & African Steam Navigation Co Ltd. Registered
Glasgow. C 2 cyl 22″, 40″–26″ by J. P. Rennoldson & Sons,
South Shields. 70 nhp, 9½ K.
1896   October, launched.
1900   Registered Liverpool.
1914   28 May, sunk off Lagos after being dismantled.

106 IBADAN
O.N. 105822   1896–1901

Steel twin screw steamer
204.1′×35.1′×12.3′   473 n   793 g
Built by David J. Dunlop & Co, Port Glasgow, Yard No 233
for African Steamship Co. Registered London. 2×T 3 cyl 11″,
18″, 28″–24″ by the builder. 77 nhp, 9½ K.
1896   Completed.
1900   April, grounded when on passage from Forcados towards
       Lagos, refloated.
1901   Sold to P. S. Clarke, London.
1905   Sold to Mitsui Bussan Gomei Kaisha, Tokyo. Renamed
       NIREISAN MARU. Registered Kuchinotsu. 544 n,
       877 g.
1911   Sold to Kizo Hashimoto, Sasebo. Registered Osaka.
       550 n, 887 g. Low pressure cylinder bored out to 28⅛″
       diameter.
1913   Registered Nishinomiyo.
1915   Sold to Ryoto Kisen Kabushiki Kaishs, Sakata (Ryoto
       Steamship Co Ltd, Managers). Registered Hakodate.
       430 n, 806 g.
1918   August, sank after collision in the Inland Sea.
Ibadan is a large town in Oyo Province, Southern Nigeria, 119
miles north of Lagos.

107 ILORIN (I)
O.N. 105862   1896–1909

'Ilorin' class
Steel twin screw steamer, one deck
220.0′×36.1′×13.0′   565 n   946 g
Built by David J. Dunlop & Co, Port Glasgow, Yard No 234,
for African Steamship Co. Registered London. 2×T 3 cyl 13″,
21″, 34″–24″ by the builders. 128 nhp, 9½ K.

1896 Completed August.
1909 23 August, heavily strained while assisting in the towing of *BOULAMA* off Forcados Bar and as a result foundered.

Ships of the 'Ilorin' class: ILORIN (107), ASABA (108), IDDO (109), BASSA (110), OSHOGBO (111).

Ilorin is a Yoruba town, 242 miles north of Lagos.

108 ASABA (I)
O.N. 112775   1900–1917

'Ilorin' class
Steel twin screw steamer, one deck
220.0′×36.2′×13.2′   570 n   972 g
Built by Caledon Shipbuilding & Engineering Co Ltd, Dundee, Yard No 156, for African Steamship Co. Registered London. 2×C 2 cyl 18″, 36″–24″ by the builders. 114 nhp, 9½ K.
1900 November, completed.
1917 6 December, operating on Government cross-channel service. Torpedoed and sunk by German submarine U17 (Oberleutnant zur See Ulrich Pilzecker) in submerged attack in position two miles WSW of the Lizard. Captain H. Pitt and 15 crew members lost.

U17, then under the command of Oberleutnant zur See Nicolaus von Lyncker, surrendered at Harwich on 27 November 1918, and ultimately sold to Thomas W. Ward Ltd and broken up at Preston during 1919–20. Pilzecker was killed in September 1918 when U113 under his command was lost with all hands in the North Sea (probably mined).

Asaba is situated on the left bank of the Niger River almost opposite Onitsha, 205 miles above Forcados.

109 IDDO
O.N. 112791   1901–1923

'Ilorin' class
Steel twin screw steamer, one deck
219.8′×36.2′×13.1′   588 n   965 g
Built by Londonderry Shipbuilding & Engineering Co Ltd, Yard No 47, for African Steamship Co. Registered London. 2×C 2 cyl 18″, 36″–24″ by McKie & Baxter, Glasgow. 114 nhp, 9½ K.
Operated on the Lagos–Forcados branch service.
1901 January, completed.
1917 Refitted in United Kingdom.
1923 Dismantled at Lagos and scuttled.

Iddo is an environ of Lagos, Nigeria. It is an island in the lagoon connected by a causeway to the mainland. Iddo station is the terminus of the Nigerian Railway.

110 BASSA (I)
O.N. 120852   1905–1917

'Ilorin' class
Steel twin screw steamer, one deck
220.0′×36.1′×13.2′   568 n   940 g
Built by David J. Dunlop & Co, Port Glasgow, Yard No 256, for Elder, Dempster & Co. Registered Liverpool. 2×T 3 cyl 13″, 21″, 34″–24″ by the builders. 114 nhp, 9½ K.
1905 24 April, launched.
1906 Transferred to British & African Steam Navigation Co Ltd.
1909 Stranded on rock two miles from Lokoja, River Niger, in ten feet of water. No 1 hold and engine room flooded.

1910 Refloated on annual rising river. Repairs carried out at Forcados, vessel proceeded to Cammell Laird & Co Ltd, Birkenhead, for refit.
1917 Sold to San Antonio SS Co Ltd (J. S. Everden, Manager), London. Renamed **SANTA ALICIA**. Registered London.
1927 Sold to Cia Naviera del Golfo SA, Vera Cruz. Renamed **SUPERIOR**. 545 n, 1001 g. Registered Vera Cruz.
1933 Sold to Gremio Unido de Alejadores (Mexican Government), Tampico. Renamed **ALIJADORES No 2**. Registered Vera Cruz. 820 n, 1320 g.
1937 Dismantled.

Bassa is a tribal name on the lower Benue River, Nigeria.

SANTA ALICIE, formerly BASSA

OSHOGBO and AKABO (to right of picture)

111 OSHOGBO
O.N. 124013   1906–1928

'Ilorin' class
Steel twin screw steamer, one deck
220.0′×36.1′×13.2′   577 n   949 g
Built by David J. Dunlop & Co, Port Glasgow, Yard No 263, to the order of Alfred Lewis Jones and W. J. Davey (Elder, Dempster & Co, Managers). Registered Liverpool. 2×T 3 cyl 13″, 21″, 34″–24″ by the builders. 114 nhp, 9½ K.
1906 18 October, launched.
1907 Transferred to Elder Line Ltd.
1909 23 August, assisted *LOKOJA*, *MAYUMBA* and *ILORIN* in towing *BOULAMA* off Forcados Bar.
1928 12 July, ran ashore 20 miles east of Lagos—back broken, total loss.

Oshogbo is a town on the railway line between Ibadan and Ilorin, about 180 miles above Lagos.

OSHOGBO

112 LAGUNA
O.N. 106861   1897–1898

Steel screw steamer, one deck and spar deck
253.5′×33.4′×16.7′   1123 n   1620 g
Built by Nederland Stoomboot Maatschappij, Rotterdam, Yard No 160, as **KONINGIN WILHELMINA** for Nieuwe Afrikaansch Handels Vennootschap, Rotterdam. Registered Rotterdam. T 3 cyl 21″, 33″, 55″–36″ by the builders. 197 nhp.
1892   May, completed.
1897   February, acquired by African Steamship Co. Renamed **LAGUNA**. Registered Liverpool. 1085 n, 1596 g.
·1898   Sold to M. Jebson, Hamburg. Renamed **ERNA**. Registered Hamburg. 957 n, 1530 g.
1907   Sold to Cia Naviera del Pacifico SA, Mexico. Renamed **RAMON CORRAL**. Registered Guaymas.
1915   Sold to American Mexican Steam Ship & Trading Co, San Diego. Renamed **COLON**. Registered San Diego.
1916   All three cylinders rebored: 21¾″, 33½″ and 55 3⁄16″.
1917   Sold to Sugano Gomei Kaisha, Nishinada. Renamed **ANSHIN MARU**. Registered Nishinada. 938 n, 1585 g.
1920   Sold to Maeda Ruchi, Toba. Registered Toba. 954 n, 1598 g.
1921   Sold to Kusakabe Kisen Kabushiki Kaisha, Kobe. Registered Minamittonda. 938 n, 1567 g.
1924   Sold to Kusakabe Kyutaro, Gifu.
1925   18 August, wrecked off Kamchatka, Far Eastern Area, Russia, voyage Hakodete (Japan) to Kamchatka (Russia).

LAGUNA

113 EBANI (I)
O.N. 105383   1897–1898

Steel screw steamer, two decks
260.0′×36.4′×20.4′   1093 n   1738 g
Built by William Gray & Co Ltd, West Hartlepool, Yard No 515, for African Association Ltd (Thomas Rogerson, Manager), London. Registered Liverpool. T 3 cyl 22″, 35″, 59″–39″ by Central Marine Engine Works, West Hartlepool. 245 nhp, 10 K.
1896   14 March, launched. April, completed.
1897   Acquired by African Steamship Co. Registered London.
1898   October, sold to Indo-China Steam Navigation Co Ltd (William Keswick, Manager), London. Renamed **LOONG SANG**. Registered London.
1923   September, in collision off Hong Kong and sank.
Ebani is the ancient native name of the Bonny district, Nigeria.

114 LANDANA (II)
O.N. 106841   1897–1898

Steel screw steamer, one deck and spar deck
310.0′×44.1′×15.1′   1827 n   2834 g
Built by Sir Raylton Dixon & Co Ltd, Middlesbrough, Yard No 440, for Elder, Dempster & Co. Registered Liverpool. T 3 cyl 23″, 36″, 59″–42″ by North Eastern Marine Engineering Co Ltd, Newcastle. 244 nhp, 9 K.
1896   21 December, launched.
1897   February, completed.
1898   Aground near Blankenese on leaving Hamburg. Transferred to African Steamship Co. 8 September, sank after collision with ss KNARWATER (1705 g/built 1883) off Ushant, voyage Tyne via Hamburg to West Africa, general cargo (Captain J. Clare).

YORUBA

115 YORUBA (III)
O.N. 104597   1897–1911

Steel screw steamer, one deck and spar deck
322.0′×42.3′×16.8′   1937 n   2992 g
Built by Barclay, Curle & Co Ltd, Glasgow, Yard No 392, as **STRAITS OF SUNDA** for N. McLean & Co, Glasgow. Registered Glasgow. T 3 cyl 23½″, 39″, 64″–42″ by the builders. 277 nhp, 10 K.
1895   January, completed.
1896   Sold to Robert B. Stocker, London. Registered Glasgow.
1897   November, acquired by Alfred Lewis Jones Esq (Elder, Dempster & Co, Managers), Liverpool. Renamed **YORUBA**. Registered Liverpool.
1899   Transferred to Elder Line Ltd. 1913 n, 3000 g.

1911 17 August, aground at Turtle Island, Sherbro River, Sierra Leone, voyage Libreville to Continental ports with a cargo of general West African produce. Became a constructive total loss.

ASHANTI

116 ASHANTI
O.N. 106847   1897–1919

'Ashanti' class
Steel screw steamer, one deck and spar deck
330.0′×45.2′×18.2′   2186 n   3389 g
Built by C. S. Swan & Hunter Ltd, Newcastle, Yard No 218, for G. B. Hunter Esq and W. J. Davey Esq (Elder, Dempster & Co, Managers). Registered Liverpool. T 3 cyl 24″, 40″, 64–42″ by North Eastern Marine Engineering Co Ltd, Newcastle. 293 nhp, 11 K.
Passenger accommodation: 6 first class, 50 steerage.
Intended for the Avonmouth–Canada service.
1897   19 February, launched. April, completed.
1899   Transferred to Elder Line Ltd.
1900   Chartered to Canada Shipping Co Ltd (Beaver Line).
1906   4 October, whilst lying at Forcados, main stop valve of starboard boiler failed. Four men lost their lives.
1914   3 August, sailed from Hamburg for Las Palmas, thus escaped internment as war broke out next day. 30 August, reported sighting s.m.s. KARLSRUHE off Cape Verde but succeeded in eluding her and arrived Dakar 31 August (Captain D. Evans).
1919   19 August, on fire at Dakar—beached and abandoned.
1922   June, refloated and broken up at Marseilles.
Ships of the 'Ashanti' class: ASHANTI (116), LOKOJA (117).
Ashanti is the inland region of Ghana.

LOKOJA

117 LOKOJA (I)
O.N. 109413   1898–1899

'Ashanti' class
Steel screw steamer, one deck and spar deck
330.0′×45.3′×18.2′   2219 n   3458 g
Built by C. S. Swan & Hunter Ltd, Newcastle, Yard No 225, for Elder, Dempster & Co, Liverpool. Registered Liverpool. T 3 cyl 24″, 40″, 64″–42″ by North Eastern Marine Engineering Co Ltd, Newcastle. 292 nhp, 11 K.
Passenger accommodation: 6 first class, 50 steerage.
Designed for Avonmouth–Canada service.
1898   28 April, sea trials, average speed 12 knots.
1899   October, sold to Cie des Vapeur de Charge Francais, Marseilles. Renamed **VESPER**. Registered Marseilles, 2086 n, 3552 g. Employed on the wine trade between Algeria and France.
1903   27 October, left Oron for Rouen and Dunkirk with a cargo of wine in casks. Encountered dense fog in Bay of Biscay. 2 November, proceeding dead slow, at 0300 sighted Ushant light right ahead and ran aground on the rocky coast. Crew abandoned ship in the lifeboats and all survived. Wreck broke up a few days later.
Lokoja (formerly Lairdstown, renamed by Baikie about 1860) is the market town on the west bank of the River Niger at the River Benue confluence, 337 miles upstream from Forcados, Nigeria.

VEGA, formerly GAMBIA

118 GAMBIA (IV)
O.N. 109414   1898–1899

Steel screw steamer, one deck and spar deck
310.0′×44.1′×15.7′   1853 n   2877 g
Built by Sir Raylton Dixon & Co Ltd, Middlesbrough, Yard No 448, for Elder, Dempster & Co. Registered London. T 3 cyl 23″, 36″, 59″–42″ by T. Richardson & Sons Ltd, Hartlepool. 253 nhp, 9 K.
Limited passenger accommodation.
Intended for the Hamburg–West Coast of Africa service.
1898   27 April, trials.
1899   Sold to H. Bergassa & Co, Marseilles. Renamed **VEGA**. Registered Marseilles 1687 n, 3027 g.
1900   Sold to Cie des Vapeur de Charge Francais, Marseilles.
1914   Sold to Cie de Navigation Mixte, Marseilles. 1889 n, 2957 g.
1916   12 April, torpedoed and sunk by German submarine U34, 60 miles to the east of Barcelona, voyage Santos to Marseilles, cargo not recorded.

YOLA

119 YOLA
O.N. 109432   1898–1917

Steel screw steamer, one deck and spar deck
356.0′×45.2′×18.7′   2246 n   5700 d   3504 g
Built by Sunderland Shipbuilding Co Ltd, Sunderland, Yard
No 193, for Elder, Dempster & Co. Registered Liverpool.
T 3 cyl 24″, 40″, 64″–42″ by North Eastern Marine Engineering
Co Ltd, Newcastle. 296 nhp, 11½ K.
Passenger accommodation: 12 first class.
1898   30 March, launched. 2 June, trials.
1899   Transferred to Elder Line Ltd.
1904   High pressure cylinder bored out to 24⅝″ diameter.
1910   April, 2249 n, 3533 g.
1917   26 January, sailed from New York, cargo grain with a
         crew of 33 (Captain H. Owen). 28 January, reported
         missing. Disappeared without trace. Not considered a
         war loss.
Yola is the chief town of the Adamawa Province, Nigeria,
situated on the south bank of the Benue River, 467 miles
upstream from Lokoja.

120 ANDONI
O.N. 109451   1898–1917

Steel screw steamer, one deck
329.2′×45.5′×16.2′   2034 n   5400 d   3188 g
Built by Wm Hamilton & Co Ltd, Port Glasgow, Yard No 135,
for Elder Line Ltd. Registered Liverpool. T 3 cyl 24″, 40″, 65″–
42″ by D. Rowan & Sons, Glasgow. 301 nhp, 9½ K.
1898   24 June, launched. August, completed.
1910   Operated the first direct sailing from Lagos to Cape
         Town and Durban, carrying a cargo of palm oil, kernels,
         skins and livestock.
1917   8 January, torpedoed and sunk in position 35°.19′N
         15°.07′E by U35 (Kapitänleutnant Lothar von Arnauld
         de la Perière), voyage Karachi to the United Kingdom.
         ANDONI was sighted at 0645 on a westerly course.
         U35 dived at 0658 for an underwater attack, firing a
         stern tube at a range of 380 metres. The torpedo struck
         her amidships and she immediately began to settle. At
         0735 her crew abandoned ship, taking to the two
         lifeboats. U35 surfaced at 0745, approached the boats
         and took the Master prisoner (Captain Dennitts). Von
         Arnauld then gave the survivors a course and distance for
         Malta and allowed them to proceed. Shortly afterwards
         ANDONI broke in two and sank. According to her
         Master, who had not saved the ship's papers, **ANDONI**
         had been bound for London from India with a cargo of
         grain. He also stated that she was armed with a three-
         inch quick-firing gun.

U35, then under the command of Kapitänleutnant Heino von
Heimburg, returned from the Mediterranean to Kiel on 9
October 1918. The boat surrendered at Harwich on 27 Nov-
ember and was later sold for scrap to Hughes, Bolckow and Co
Ltd. Von Arnauld left U35 in March 1918 to assume command
of one of the U-cruisers, U139, until the end of the war.
Andoni is a tribal name in the Oil Rivers. The River Andoni
enters the Bight of Biafra to the east of Bonny and west of
Opobo.

ANDONI

OLENDA

121 OLENDA
O.N. 108762   1898–1913

'Oron' class
Steel screw steamer, two decks
345.0′×42.2′×23.0′   2015 n   3171 g
Built by Barclay, Curle & Co Ltd, Glasgow, Yard No 411,
for British & African Steam Navigation Co Ltd. Registered
Glasgow. T 3 cyl 23″, 38″, 63″–45″ by the builders. 300 nhp,
12 K.
Passenger accommodation: 70 first class, 20 second.
1898   7 May, launched. October, completed.
1901   Registered Liverpool. First ship to be dry docked in No
         4 Herculaneum, Liverpool.
1913   Touched wreck of SANSU off Cesstown, Liberia. Decem-
         ber, sold to Messageries Maritime, Marseilles. Renamed
         MOSSOUL. Registered Marseilles. 1953 n, 3135 g.
1917   21 November, torpedoed and sunk in a submerged attack
         by U63 (Kapitänleutnant Otto Schultze), 14 miles north,
         80 miles east of Cap Bon, Mediterranean.
U63 survived the war and, then under the command of Kapitänleutnant Kurt Hartwig, she surrendered at Harwich on 16
January 1919. She was sold for breaking to Hughes, Bolckow
& Co Ltd, who removed her from Harwich on 3 May 1919.

Schultze left U63 in December 1917 to join the staff of Flag Officer U-Boats in the Mediterranean. He survived the war, remained in the navy, and during the Second World War was Commanding Admiral in France from 1941 to 1942, in which year he was promoted to Generaladmiral, shortly before his transfer to the retired list.

Ships of the 'Oron' class: OLENDA (121), ORON (122), SOKOTO (123), BORNU (124).

ORON

122 ORON (I)
O.N. 108769   1898–1914, 1919

'Oron' class
Steel screw steamer, two decks
345.0′×42.2′×23.0′   2015 n   3171 g
Built by Barclay, Curle & Co Ltd, Glasgow, Yard No 412, for British & African Steam Navigation Co Ltd. Registered Glasgow. T 3 cyl 23″, 38″, 63″–45″ by the builders. 300 nhp, 12 K.
Passenger accommodation: 68 first class, 20 second.
1898   23 June, launched. November, completed.
1900   Registered Liverpool.
1914   Detained at Hamburg.
1919   Released and returned to owners. July, sold to Cia Naviera Bidason, Bilbao (Candina y Echevarria, Managers). Renamed **PAZ DE EPALZA**. Registered Bilbao.
1920   Management transferred to R. Echevarria.
1921   December, wrecked on Hornigas Island, voyage Swansea to Leghorn.
Oron is a minor port on the Cross River, Nigeria (15 miles from Calabar).

123 SOKOTO (I)
O.N. 111177   1899–1915

'Oron' class
Steel screw steamer, two decks
345.0′×42.2′×23.0′   1976 n   3080 g
Built by Vickers Sons & Maxim Ltd, Barrow, Yard No 270, for British & African Steam Navigation Co Ltd. Registered Glasgow. T 3 cyl 23″, 38″, 63″–45″ by the builders. 300 nhp, 12 K.
Passenger accommodation: 71 first class, 36 second.
1899   25 February, launched by Mrs Dempster. April, completed.
1900   Registered Liverpool.
1915   26 October, sold to the Admiralty. Converted into a submarine depot ship. 1969 n, 3092 g.
1919   August, sold to Cia Naviera Sevillana SA, Seville. Renamed **TABLEDA**. Registered Seville.
1925   January, sold for demolition in Spain.
Sokoto is a province and its chief township in the north-west of Nigeria.

SOKOTO

BORNU

124 BORNU
O.N. 111196   1899–1916

'Oron' class
Steel screw steamer, two decks
345.0′ × 42.2′ × 23.0′   2074 n   3232 g
Built by Vickers, Sons & Maxim Ltd, Barrow, Yard No 271, for British & African Steam Navigation Co Ltd. Registered Glasgow. T 3 cyl 23″, 38″, 63″–45″ by the builders. 300 nhp, 12 K.
Passenger accommodation: 70 first class, 20 second.
1899   9 May, launched by Mrs Wilson. June, completed.
1900   Registered Liverpool.
1913   August, 2102 n, 3259 g.
1915   May, requisitioned by HM Government.
1916   28 October, foundered 25 miles west of Ushant, voyage Rotterdam to West African coast as an Army Transport.
Bornu is a province in the north-east of Nigeria.

125 JEBBA (I)
O.N. 109969   1898–1907

'Jebba' class
Steel screw steamer, two decks
352.0′ × 44.2′ × 23.4′   2997 n   3953 g
Built by Sir Raylton Dixon & Co Ltd, Middlesbrough, Yard No 421, for Cie Belge Maritime du Congo, as **ALBERTVILLE**. Registered Antwerp. T 3 cyl 27″, 43″, 72″–48″ by T. Richardson & Son Ltd, Hartlepool. 419 nhp, 12 K.
Passenger accommodation: 108 first class, 52 second.
1896   30 June, trials.
1898   Acquired by African Steamship Co, Liverpool. Renamed **JEBBA**. Registered London. 2460 n, 3812 g.
1907   18 March, wrecked near Bolt Tail, South Devon, voyage West Africa to Liverpool via Las Palmas and Plymouth with passengers and a cargo of palm oil, rubber and ivory (Captain J. J. C. Mills). **JEBBA** went ashore in dense fog in the early hours. In the darkness, two local men—Isaac Jarvis and John Argeat, climbed down the 200-feet cliffs and rigged a bosun's chair to effect the rescue of all the 155 passengers and crew. Both men were later awarded the Albert Medal by King Edward VII. Mails and much of the rubber and ivory cargo were salvaged. The vessel became a total loss. The wreck was sold 'as is/where is' to Exploitation and Recovery Venture for £100.
1971   A skin diver found one of the **JEBBA** dining room plates, patterned on which was the original name of **ALBERTVILLE**.
Ships of the 'Jebba' class: JEBBA (125), ARO (126), SEKONDI (127), NIGERIA (128), AKABO (129).
Jebba is a town on the Niger River, 536 miles above Forcados.

*A distant view of **JEBBA** ashore*

JEBBA (S.S.).

The Merchant Shipping Act, 1894.

IN the matter of a formal investigation held at the Magistrates' Room, Liverpool, on the 7th, 8th, and 9th days of May, 1907, before W. J. STEWART, Esq., assisted by Commander L. M. WIBMER, R.N.R., and Captain JENKIN THOMAS, into the circumstances attending the stranding and loss of the British s.s. "JEBBA," of London, which ran ashore near Bolt Tail, Devon, on 18th March, 1907.

Report of Court.

The Court, having carefully inquired into the circumstances attending the above-mentioned shipping casualty, finds, for the reasons stated in the annex hereto, that the stranding and loss of the said vessel were due to the default of the master, Mr. James John Cornish Mills, whose certificate, numbered 015332, the Court suspends for a period of three months from the date hereof.

Dated this 9th day of May, 1907.

W. J. STEWART,

Judge.

We concur in the above report,

L. M. WIBMER, } Assessors.
JENKIN THOMAS, }

Annex to the Report.

This inquiry was held in the Magistrates' Room, Dale Street, Liverpool, on the 7th, 8th, and 9th days of May, 1907, when Mr. Paxton, solicitor, appeared for the Board of Trade, Mr. W. Bateson for the owners, and Mr. A. Miller for the master, chief, and second officers.

The s.s. "Jebba," official number 109969, was a British screw steamship, schooner rigged, built of steel, by Sir Raylton Dixon & Co., at Middlesbrough, in 1896, and was registered at the port of London.

Her dimensions were :—Length, 352 feet ; breadth, 44 feet ; and depth, 23 feet. She was of 3812·55 gross, and 2438·86 net registered tonnage, and was fitted with triple expansion surface condensing engines of 253 nominal horse power, three cylinders 24 in., 43 in., and 72 in., with 48 in. length of stroke, all constructed by Messrs. J. Richardson & Sons, Hartlepool, giving a speed of 10 knots. She was owned by the African Steamship Company ; Mr. E. B. Coarten, of 21, Great St. Helens, London, being the person to whom the management of the vessel was entrusted by advice received 7th September, 1898. She was fitted with steam steering gear, carried 3 lifeboats, 2 surf boats, and a gig capable of accommodating 263 persons, and, in addition to this, 212 life belts and 6 life buoys, all of which had been inspected by the surveyor appointed by the Board of Trade on 24th December last, and a short passenger certificate granted. Mr. Stevenson in his evidence was perfectly satisfied with the condition of the life-saving appliances. In regard to navigating instruments and compasses she was well equipped and observations to ascertain the deviation of the standard compass had been taken from time to time and were recorded in a book. She was fitted with Sir William Thomson's patent sounding machine, the ordinary deep sea and hand lead, and a patent log. In the matter of charts and sailing directions for the British Channel she was also well found.

The s.s. "Jebba" left Las Palmas on 11th March, 1907, at 7.30 p.m., bound for Plymouth, under the command of Mr. J. J. C. Mills. She was loaded with a general cargo, and had a crew of 49 hands all told and 79 passengers. All went well till 17th March, when a position at noon was obtained by observations, and at 3 p.m. Ushant lighthouse was abeam distant 6½ miles as ascertained by a four-point bearing. At this time the course was altered to N.E. by standard compass, with 1° westerly deviation, and the patent log was reset. The master stated that he expected to make good this course, which would take him 9 miles east of the Eddystone lighthouse, and he expected to pick up the light about 12.30 a.m. During the night a strong S.W. wind, with misty weather, appears to have been experienced, and at 11.45 p.m. a cast of the patent log was taken, which gave 37 fathoms, with a fine sandy bottom. This being less than the master expected, he concluded that the vessel had travelled more than the 97½ miles registered on the patent log. After midnight the weather seems to have got thicker, and at 12.40 a.m. two steamers were passed steering down Channel, one of which was seen about a mile off. The second was not visible, and only the steam whistle was heard. At 12.45 a.m. the whistle began to be used at irregular intervals, and the telegraph put at "Stand by," but the vessel continued at full speed till 12.55, when the engines were eased to half speed. At this time the patent log was taken and showed 106 miles, and a cast of the patent lead obtained, which showed 11 fathoms. The master at once gave an order to put the helm hard-a-port, and telegraphed the engines to slow. Shortly after breakers were reported ahead, and the engines reversed to full speed astern, but before this had any effect the vessel took the ground, with her head about S.E., and remained fast. Signals of distress were at once made, and eventually communication with the shore was established by means of the rocket apparatus and lines made fast to the rocks. All the passengers and crew reached the land in safety, but the vessel became a total loss.

There is some discrepancy in the evidence as to what occurred after the sounding of 11 fathoms had been obtained. On the one hand both the master and chief officer agreed that the helm was put hard-a-port, and remained so till the engines were put full-speed astern. On the other hand, the quartermaster, who was at the wheel, stated in his evidence that he received an order from the master to port, and shortly after was directed to steady the ship at E. by N., and that after this had been done he received instructions from the chief officer to bring the ship's head to east, which was done, and her head remained in that direction till she grounded. After careful consideration, the Court is of opinion that the statement of the master and chief officer is most to be relied upon, and that the helm was put hard-a-port, as stated in their evidence. This opinion is strengthened by the fact that from the evidence produced it appears that when the ship grounded her head was in a south-easterly direction.

At the conclusion of the evidence, Mr. Paxton submitted the following questions for the opinion of the Court :—

(1) Were proper measures taken to ascertain and verify the position of the vessel at or about 3 p.m. of the 17th March last? Was a safe and proper course then set and thereafter steered, and was due and proper allowance made for tide and currents ?

(2) Were proper measures taken to ascertain and verify the position of the vessel at or about 11.45 p.m. of the 17th March last, and from time to time thereafter ?

(3) Having regard to the state of the weather after 11.45 p.m. of the 17th March last, was the vessel navigated at too great a rate of speed, and was the lead used with sufficient frequency ?

(4) Was a good and proper look-out kept?

(5) Was the Eddystone Light seen and the fog signal heard by those on board the ship before the stranding? If not, to what cause or causes can this be ascribed?

(6) What was the cause of the stranding and loss of the vessel?

(7) Was the vessel navigated with proper and seamanlike care?

(8) Was the stranding and loss of the s.s. " Jebba " caused by the wrongful act or default of the master and chief officer, or of either of them?

(9) What was the value of the vessel? What were the insurances effected, and how were they apportioned?

Mr. Miller having addressed the Court on behalf of the master, the Court gave judgment as above, and returned the following answers to the questions submitted by the Board of Trade :—

(1) Safe and proper measures were taken to ascertain and verify the position of the vessel at 3 p.m. on the 17th March last, by a four-point bearing of Ushant lighthouse. A course was then set to pass 9° East of the Eddystone lighthouse, and the Court is of opinion that, under the circumstances of wind, weather, and the probable time of approaching close to the land, this course in the absence of a chain of soundings was not a safe and proper one. A course should have been steered directly for the Eddystone light. No allowance was made for tide or current.

(2) Proper measures were taken to ascertain and verify the position of the ship at 11.45 p.m. on the 17th March by a cast of the lead, but after that time none were taken till too late to prevent the accident. Had soundings been taken more frequently the master would have been warned of his approach to the land in time to have avoided the casualty.

(3) The vessel was navigated at too great a rate of speed after 11.45 p.m. of the 17th March last, and the lead was not used with sufficient frequency.

(4) A good and proper look-out was kept.

(5) The Eddystone light was not seen, nor was the fog signal heard by those on board the ship before the stranding, the causes being the state of the atmosphere, and the well-known uncertainty of sound signals.

(6) The cause of the stranding and loss of the s.s. " Jebba " was due to the vessel having over-run her distance, and the failure of the master to ascertain this by a proper use of his lead.

(7) The vessel was not navigated with proper and seamanlike care.

(8) The stranding and loss of the s.s. " Jebba " was caused by the wrongful act or default of the master only.

(9) The value of the vessel at the time of the accident was £32,500. She was valued for the purposes of insurance at £36,000. She was insured in outside policies for £30,600, the balance remaining at the owner's risk.

W. J. STEWART,
Judge.

We concur in the above report.

L. M. WIBMER, } Assessors.
J. THOMAS,

Liverpool, 10th May, 1907.

(Issued in London by the Board of Trade on the 31st day of May, 1907.)

JEBBA seen from the clifftop

ALBERTVILLE, *subsequently* **JEBBA**, *in happier days* (Photo McRoberts collection)

ARO

126 ARO
O.N. 118446   1898, 1904–1914

'Jebba' class
Steel screw steamer, two decks
351.9′×44.1′×23.3′   2417 n   3805 g
Laid down by Sir Raylton Dixon & Co Ltd, Middlesbrough,
Yard No 449, for Elder, Dempster & Co, as **EBOE**. Transferred
after launching to Cie Belge Maritime du Congo. Renamed
ALBERTVILLE. Registered Antwerp. T 3 cyl 27″, 43″, 72″–
48″ by T. Richardson & Sons Ltd, Hartlepool. 432 nhp, 13 K.
Passenger accommodation: 100 first class, 60 second.
1898 9 May, launched as **EBOE**. August, completed as
      ALBERTVILLE.
1904 Transferred to African Steamship Co. Renamed **ARO**.
      Registered London. 2388 n, 3794 g.
1914 Sold to HM Government.
1919 Sold to W. R. Davis, Liverpool.
1921 Sold to Cie des Vapeur Francaise, Paris. Renamed
      STELLA. Registered Havre. 2299 n, 3734 g.
1924 Sold to SA 'Res Affreteurs Reunes', Paris.
1925 Owner's company in liquidation. Broken up in Italy.
Aro is a town 58 miles by rail from Lagos, Nigeria. A quarry
nearby supplied the stone for the Lagos harbour moles.

SEKONDI

127 SEKONDI (I)
O.N. 106837
                                                1901–1910
'Jebba' class
Steel screw steamer, two decks
352.0′×44.2′×23.4′   2421 n   3761 g

Built by Sir Raylton Dixon & Co Ltd, Yard No 430, for Cie
Belge Maritime du Congo as **LEOPOLDVILLE**. Registered
Antwerp. T 3 cyl 27″, 43″, 72″–48″ by T. Richardson & Son
Ltd, Hartlepool. 419 nhp, 12 K.
Passenger accommodation: 108 first class, 52 second.
1896 6 November, launched.
1897 January, completed.
1898 3011 n, 3962 g.
1901 April, acquired by African Steamship Co. Renamed
      SEKONDI. Registered London. 2424 n, 3765 g.
1910 Sold to Bombay & Persia Steam Navigation Co Ltd,
      Bombay. Renamed **KHOSROU**. Registered Bombay
      under British flag.
1922 Sold to Murao Zosensho Goshi Kaisha, Tottori Ken,
      Renamed **AKASHI MARU**. Registered Kobe. 2384 n,
      3831 g.
1928 Sold to Murao Dock Goshi Kaisha, Osaka. Registered
      Tarumi.
1933 Sold for demolition in Japan.
Sekondi is a surf port in Ghana.

128 NIGERIA
O.N. 114747   1901–1920

'Jebba' class
Steel screw steamer, two decks
351.9′×44.1′×23.5′   2391 n   3755 g
Built by Sir Raylton Dixon & Co Ltd, Middlesbrough, Yard
No 479, for African Steamship Co. Registered London. T 3 cyl
27″, 43″, 72″–48″ by Richardson Westgarth & Co Ltd, Hartlepool. 436 nhp, 13 K.
Passenger accommodation: 108 first class, 52 second.
1901 August, completed.
1916 Sold to HM Government (The Shipping Controller),
      (Elder, Dempster & Co Ltd, Managers).
1917 While serving as an accommodation ship at Murmansk,
      caught fire, scuttled and later refloated. Damage exten-
      sive but engine room intact.
1919 Returned to United Kingdom for refit.
1920 Sold to Claude Langdon, London.
1921 Sold to Cie Marseillaise de Navigation a Vapeur (Cie
      Fraissinet), Marseilles. Renamed **NIGER**. Registered
      Marseilles. 2212 n, 3666 g.
1931 Sold for 260,000 Francs for demolition in Italy.
Name derived from Nigeria.

NIGERIA, *from an old postcard*

In April 1918 Ken Redmore arrived in Murmansk to assume
the position of Second Officer.

MY VOYAGE TO MURMANSK

After a few delays, we embarked at Newcastle on the ss PORTO (a captured German passenger vessel) operated by the Cunard Line. Forces Personnel also embarked for duty at Murmansk.

The 'PORTO' made an uneventful voyage, calling at Lerwick en route, arriving at Murmansk during April 1918, berthing alongside a wooden jetty.

The Kola Inlet is ice free throughout the Winter months, but it was very cold with plenty of snow around on our arrival. However we had been supplied with thick woollen underwear and duffle coats and trousers. On boarding NIGERIA we were astounded by the damage caused to the vessel by the fire—from the waist to the stern was just buckled deck houses and decks, with all wood fittings and decks non-existent. The bridge had disappeared, and the after deck completely open, with only the deck beams showing, and to reach the stern section, one had to claw along the stringer plate.

The galley and a large house abaft the engine room casing were in good shape and the engine room practically undamaged and engines intact. There was no accommodation on board for the deck, engine and catering staffs and none ashore.

The steel main-mast, about 3 ft. above the deck, had sunk into itself, and the hull plating from the water line to the sheer strake was also badly buckled, the length of the after deck.

After inspecting the vessel and being informed via the naval officer in charge that there was no intention of the vessel returning to the U.K., we held a meeting and decided that we had been sent out under false pretences and demanded to be returned home on the s.s. PORTO. However after some discussion with the Naval Authorities, the Senior Officer, Admiral Kemp, informed us that a crew was necessary to take charge of the ship, and if we still insisted on being returned to the U.K., he would conscript us all into the Navy.

We decided to stay, and take charge.

No stores had been supplied, except for mattresses and bedding, so everything in the way of food had to be obtained from the Navy.

For accommodation we were offered a choice of one of 4 classes of passenger railway coaches. We chose the 4th Class, as it was absolutely un-upholstered, as there may well have been vermin in the higher classes of coach, and we had our own bedding. The coach was large enough to accommodate all our midship company and had a wood-burning stove at each end. We berthed on board the PORTO until our coach had been placed on the rails by the NIGERIA and had been thoroughly disinfected, cleaned and prepared for our use. Due to the Russian Revolution, there was some unrest ashore, and for the first few weeks during the dark hours, it seemed that bullets were flying perilously close to our position. However that eventually died away. The town was built up with wood dwellings and the streets just quagmires with slush and mud from the melting snow.

Well we settled down, the Engineers got busy with overhauling the engines and we had electricity for lighting. There were piles of 3" deals stacked on the wharves, so we requested the Naval Authority to provide timber, so we could construct accommodation on board. We were told to help ourselves to the timber on the wharf. On doing so we fell foul of the Russian owners of the timber; but that was finally cleared up between the Navy and the owners, and we got ahead with the accommodation. The Engineers' accommodation was constructed first where the passenger accommodation had been in the midship shelter deck. The deck was badly buckled in parts but was safe. A small room was fixed up for Captain Sullivan on the port side of the engine room casing on the promenade deck. The Catering Department was also suitably accommodated, and for the three Deck Officers we built a fairly large room on the starboard side of the casing on the promenade deck. The large room standing on the after part of the deck was utilised for meals and evening recreation.

We were all granted permission to obtain our personal necessities from the canteen on H.M.S. GLORY and a launch was supplied for our use between the vessels. The engines were overhauled and prepared for trial run. A navigation bridge had been built on a very damaged room just forward of the funnel, with a steering wheel and a 3" pipe to the engine room, with a wide open funnel at the top. This was the only means of communication with the engine room.

On the trial trip along the Kola Inlet, the speed registered was 10 knots per hour. On returning to the wharf, I was perched on the wrecked houses aft, the NIGERIA was closing in to the wharf stern first. I signalled to go ahead, but the order was apparently mis-understood in the engine room, and the engines went astern and our counter crashed into the wooden wharf, damaging same, but the rudder was O.K. I suffered a few bruises by being shaken from my perch.

During our occupation of the coach, very early one morning, we were all shaken out of our beds, by what we thought had been a heavy

explosion. However no one was injured, and on investigation we discovered that some bright spark had released a couple of coaches at the shore end of the rails and sent them crashing into our coach. As we were near the end of the wharf, it was well for us that the buffers held, otherwise that would have been the end of our little company.

For the first 3 months, we seemed to exist mostly on rock salmon and corned beef, with some meat doled out by the Navy for our main meal. Otherwise the catering was decent, as we had an efficient Chief Steward and Cook. Our own stores arrived just after the 3 months had elapsed and our meals were more varied than hitherto. Also we were able to disperse with the coach and live on board, to everybody's relief. Another vessel arrived just after our stores, carrying 50,000 cases of V.O.B. Whisky, also cases of wines etc. When landed, we were all allowed a ration of whisky and wine. However I wasn't interested in whisky at that period. During the evening we made our own entertainment in the dining room, there being nothing ashore to interest us.

Well the Summer came, with glorious warm weather and a 24 hour sunshine. The flowers bloomed, and the ground firm and dry. However mosquitoes blossomed forth, rather large ones too, and it was found necessary to wear nets over our heads during the hot days. We fished from the launch quite a great deal in the upper reaches of the Inlet, catching flat fish, and dog fish, the latter being ugly and uneatable. On deck we continued to obtain suitable timber, and roughly re-decked the whole of the after deck, which made it much easier for us to move around.

During the Summer, a terrible epidemic of 'flu occurred, causing quite a loss of life amongst crews of vessels in port and on the naval vessels. We were all very lucky, not sustaining even one case of 'flu. It must have been the hard conditions in which we were living. The Americans came to Murmansk, and requiring a store room, were given permission to build a store room at the fore end of No.3 Hold. The stores that were brought on board to be stowed away made our months water. A man-hole door, somehow, from the after bulkhead of the engine room gave access to the store room, and it was too much for us to ignore, so the Americans lost a few of their good things. Autumn came, dreary weather commenced, with mud and slush ashore, snow falling and ice forming, so the NIGERIA seemed a pleasant spot to be in. As the weather became worse our thoughts went more and more to our homes. We felt that we had had enough, so we commenced to send requests to be relieved.

Armistice Day arrived, November 11th, and a grand spree and rejoicing were had by all in the port. After another request to be relieved, we received the news that our relief would arrive during early December. That lightened our hearts, and our reliefs were received with joy and acclamation on being sighted. That was another occasion for a grand celebration, the evening before embarking for home. The following morning we all trooped over to our returning vessel. When all on board the roll call was made, and one of our members was discovered to be missing. Some of us went to search and found our missing member, sound asleep, in the deep snow. The previous evening had been a little too much for him. Our homeward vessel (another captured German passenger vessel) was operated by the Union Castle Line, and we had a grand run home, arriving at Hull about 3 days prior to Christmas 1918. That is the end of an episode that we were all very pleased to have completed.

I may add that a third crew had to be sent to the NIGERIA to return her to the U.K.

Despite all the damage the vessel sustained, she was stripped down, and repaired. She was then sold to a French company, re-named **NIGER**, and again traded on the West Coast of Africa as a cargo vessel.

From the Elder of Elders Magazine 1976

129 AKABO
O.N. 115268   1902–1926

'Jebba' class
Steel screw steamer, two decks
352.2′ × 44.2′ × 23.6′   2418 n   3806 g
Built by Sir Raylton Dixon & Co. Ltd, Middlesbrough, Yard No 482, for British & African Steam Navigation Co Ltd. Registered Liverpool. T 3 cyl 27″, 43″, 72″–48″ by Richardson Westgarth & Co Ltd, Hartlepool. 436 nhp, 13 K.

Elder Dempster and Co. Limited

PLAN OF SALOONS
AND
PASSENGER ACCOMMODATION
OF THE

S.S. "AKABO"

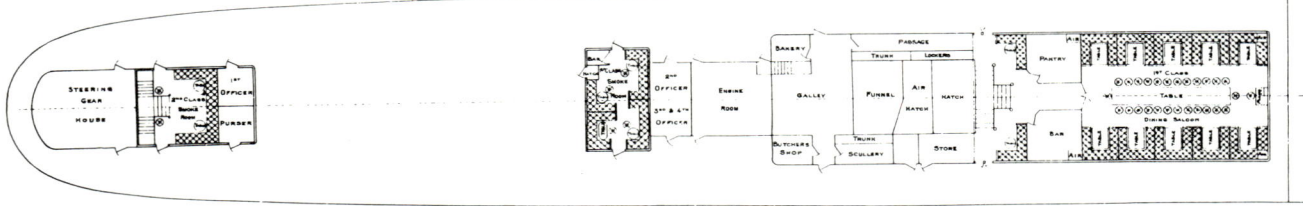

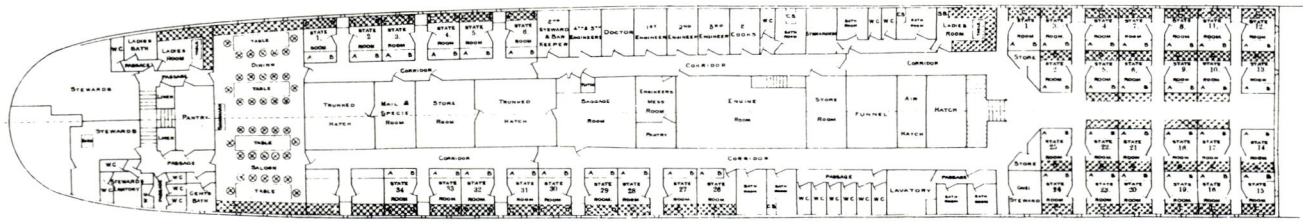

Passenger accommodation: 108 first class, 52 second.

1902	April, completed.
1916	High pressure cylinder bored out to $27\frac{7}{16}''$ diameter.
1917	9 June, attacked by submarine off south-west Ireland. Escaped undamaged, three torpedoes missed, after a prolonged chase. Captain D. Evans was awarded the Distinguished Service Cross for this action.
1925	5 July, entering Lagos harbour ran down and capsized Nigeria Marine tug HERCULES (366 g/built 1906). One European and a number of Africans lost.
1926	December, sold to United Baltic Corporation Ltd. Renamed **BALTONIA**. Registered London. 2390 n, 3839 g.
1927	Fitted for oil fuel. Passenger accommodation: 86 cabin class, 500 third.
1932	Intermediate pressure cylinder bored out to $43\frac{1}{4}''$ diameter.
1936	March, sold for £7700 for demolition at Ghent.

Akabo is a word of greeting in the Yoruba language (Nigeria).

AKABO

DEGAMA

130   DEGAMA
O.N. 110557   1899–1914

'Degama' class
Steel screw steamer, one deck and spar deck
337.5′×45.2′×18.8′   2245 n   3507 g
Built by Furness Withy & Co Ltd, West Hartlepool, Yard No 240, for Elder, Dempster & Co. Registered Liverpool. T 3 cyl $23\frac{1}{2}''$, 38″, 64″–42″ by T. Richardson & Sons Ltd, West Hartlepool. 271 nhp, 9 K.
Passenger accommodation: 10 first class, 6 second.

1899	March, completed.
1911	May, first deep sea vessel to enter Lagos harbour. Transferred to Elder Dempster Shipping Ltd.
1914	6 November, wrecked at Caroline Castle, Las Palmas, voyage Rotterdam to Port Harcourt with general cargo (Captain Cooper).
1915	February, declared a constructive total loss.

Ships of the 'Degama' class: DEGAMA (130), SANGARA (131).
Degama is the old Oil Rivers port of New Calabar, 28 miles through the creeks to the west of Port Harcourt.

131 SANGARA (I)
O.N. 106998   1899

'Degama' class
Steel screw steamer, one deck and spar deck
337.5'×45.2'×18.8'   2265 n   3538 g
Launched by Furness Withy & Co Ltd, West Hartlepool, Yard
No 242, for Elder, Dempster & Co. Registered West Hartlepool.
T 3 cyl 23½", 38", 64"–42" by Sir C. Furness, Westgarth & Co
Ltd, Middlesbrough. 281 nhp, 9 K.

1899   8 April, launched. Sold to West Hartlepool Steam
       Navigation Co Ltd, West Hartlepool and renamed
       DALTONHALL. June, completed.
1901   Sold to Furness Withy & Co Ltd, West Hartlepool.
1915   Sold to Oxton Steamship Co Ltd (Wm Roberts,
       Manager), Liverpool. 2280 n, 3534 g.

SANGARA

1916   Sold to Commonwealth Government Lines of Steamers,
       London. Renamed **AUSTRALSTREAM**. Registered
       Sydney, NSW (British flag).
1919   Sold to Soc Maritime Belge, Ghent. Renamed
       GENERAL DEGOUTTE. Registered Ghent.
1922   Sold to N. D. Rallias, Andros. Renamed **DIMITRIOS
       N. RALLIAS**. Registered Andros.
1935   Broken up.

SOBO

132 SOBO (I)
O.N. 110056   1899–1915

'Sobo' class
Steel screw steamer, one deck and spar deck
345.0'×44.0'×14.3'   2313 n   3652 g
Built by Barclay, Curle & Co Ltd, Glasgow, Yard No 416, for

African Steamship Co. Registered London. T 3 cyl 25", 41",
67"–48" by the builders. 370 nhp, 12½ K.
Passenger accommodation: 70 first class, 40 second.

1898   29 September, launched.
1899   January, completed.
1906   20 January, in collision with tug SANDON in River
       Mersey. Tug capsized and sank, all eight crew members
       lost.
1908   Transferred to Elder Line, Ltd.
1915   Sold to Admiralty, converted into a spare torpedo depot
       ship for the Grand Fleet. Registered London.
1920   Sold to SA les Affreteurs Reunis (Jean Stern, Manager),
       Paris. Renamed **JUPITER**. Registered Rouen.
1924   Registered Havre.
1925   Sold for demolition.

Ships of the 'Sobo' class: SOBO (132), FANTEE (133).

Note—Tug SANDON was salvaged and was again in collision,
capsized and sunk on 6 September 1914. Subsequently salvaged
and renamed HUSKISSON. Broken up 1961.

Sobo is the name of a Niger delta tribe of the Warri-Sapele
area.

SOBO—another view

FANTEE

133 FANTEE (I)
O.N. 110090   1899–1913

'Sobo' class
Steel screw steamer, one deck and spar deck
345.0'×44.0'×14.2'   2301 n   3649 g
Built by Barclay, Curle & Co Ltd, Glasgow, Yard No 417, for
African Steamship Co. Registered London. T 3 cyl 25", 41",
67"–48" by the builders. 370 nhp, 12½ K.
Passenger accommodation: 120 first class, 50 second.

1899   April, completed.

1901 Severely damaged striking submerged rock at Cape Palmas, Liberia. Looted by Kroo labour and local inhabitants until arrival of HMS DWARF.
1904 3 May, ashore at Cameroon. Refloated with the assistance of *EGGA*.
1913 Sold to Ellerman Papayanni Line (F. Smith, Manager), Liverpool. Renamed **ITALIAN**. Registered London. 2302 n, 3647 g.
1921 Transferred to Ellerman Wilson Line, Hull. Renamed **ROLLO**. Registered London. 2225 n, 3647 g.
1932 September, sold for demolition at Copenhagen.
The Fanti are a tribe who inhabit the Accra region of Ghana.

MONTENEGRO

134   MONTENEGRO
O.N. 108386   1899–1922
Steel screw steamer, two decks
375.0′ × 50.0′ × 26.0′   2856 n   4408 g
Built by D. & W. Henderson & Co Ltd, Glasgow, Yard No

404, for Harris & Dixon, London. Registered London. T 3 cyl 25″, 41″, 67″–48″ by the builders. 368 nhp, 10 K.
1898 July, completed.
1899 Acquired by Elder Line Ltd. Registered Liverpool.
1900 Chartered to H.M. Government.
1901–1904 Operated on London–Quebec and Montreal service.
1914 December, reboiled. 2877 n, 4451 g.
1917 Employed as collier, army transport and food supply vessel.
1922 April, sold to Schulte & Bruns, Emden. Registered Emden. 2884 n, 4466 g.
1924 Sold to 'Atlas' Reederei Aktiengesellschaft, Emden. Renamed **EUROPA**. Registered Emden. 2784 n, 4584 g.
1927 January, wrecked near Rervick, voyage Antwerp to Narvik.

135   WHYDAH (II)
O.N. 112632   1899–1902
Steel screw steamer, one deck and spar deck
235.2′ × 33.2′ × 15.2′   896 n   1381 g
Built by Flensburger Schiffahrts-Gesellschaft, Yard No 72, as **JOHANN** for Witt & Busch, Hamburg. Registered Hamburg. C 2 cyl 28½″, 52″–30″ by the builders. 120 hp.
1884 Completed.
1899 Acquired by African Steamship Co. Renamed **WHYDAH**. Registered London.
1902 Sold to Actiesilsk Argo (Donveg & Davidsen, Managers), Christiania. Renamed **ARGO**. Registered Christiania. 878 n, 1394 g.
1905 Sold to Go Kindo, Kobe. Renamed **KINSEI MARU**. Registered Kobe. Now reported as: 241.9′ × 32.2′ × 15.2′, 1024 n 1427 g.
1906 Registed Osaka. November, wrecked on Quelpart Island, Korea (33°.20′N 126°.30′E).
Whydah is a port on the coast of Dahomey.

BOUTRY *towing* **PRAH** *afloat at Grand Bassam*

PRAH

136 PRAH (I)
O.N. 110548   1898–1924

Steel screw steamer, two decks
325.0′×45.2′×19.5′   1593 n   2520 g
Built by W. Dobson & Co, Newcastle, Yard No 101, for Elder, Dempster & Co. Registered Liverpool. T 3 cyl 23″, 37″, 61″–42″ by Wallsend Slipway Co Ltd, Newcastle. 245 nhp, 9½ K.
1898   28 December, launched.
1899   March, completed.
1901   Transferred to British & African Steam Navigation Co Ltd.
1915   Employed as Army Transport. 2418 n, 3326 g.
1916   Taken over by Liner Requisition Scheme. 2466 n, 3339 g.
1920   Aground at Grand Bassam, refloated with assistance from *BOUTRY*.
1924   July, sold to C. Cosmas, Syra, for £7,250. Renamed **TALANTON**. Registered Syra. 2073 n, 3457 g.
1930   Sold to A. N. Valmas & S. L. Athanassoulias (A. N. Valmas, Manager). Renamed **KALLIRROY.V**. Registered Syra.
1932   Sold to Minas M. Didiacakis, Syra. Renamed **VELLA M. DIACAKIS**. Registered Syra.
1934   Broken up at Trieste.
Prah is a Ghanaian river; it enters Gulf of Guinea at Chama.

137 STANLEYVILLE
O.N. Not allocated   1900

Steel twin screw steamer
370.0′×46.2′×22.8′   2588 n   4051 g
Built by Sir Raylton Dixon & Co Ltd, Middlesbrough, Yard No 466, for African Steamship Co as **ELFREDA** and transferred to Cie Belge Maritime du Congo on completion and renamed **STANLEYVILLE**. Registered Antwerp. 2×T 3 cyl 21½″, 34″, 59″–42″ by Wallsend Slipway Co Ltd, Newcastle. 584 nhp, 13 K.
1899   25 July, launched. December, completed.
1900   30 March, transferred to the African Steamship Co but almost immediately, transferred back to Cie Belge Maritime du Congo.
1902   23 May, wrecked at Hoeven Rocks, Axim, Gold Coast.
Stanleyville, now Kisangani, is a town on the Zaire River.

STANLEYVILLE half submerged at Axim

138 ASABA (II)
O.N. 110641   1900

Steel twin screw steamer
320.0′×44.8′×15.3′   1901 n   2931 g
Laid down by Sir Raylton Dixon & Co Ltd, Middlesbrough, for British Maritime Trust Ltd, London, as **ADRIANA**. Acquired by Elder, Dempster & Co whilst on the stocks and renamed **ASABA**. Resold to Union Steamship Co of New Zealand prior to launching and renamed **WHANGAPE**. 2×T 3 cyl 23″, 36″, 59″–42″ by T. Richardson & Sons Ltd, Hartlepool. 255 nhp.

STANLEYVILLE at Antwerp (Photo Cie Maritime Belge)

1900 November, completed.
1902 Registered Dunedin.
1929 Sold to Chun Young Zan, Shanghai. Renamed **NANKING**. Registered Shanghai.
1934–5 Broken up.

ASABA as *WHANGAPE* (Photo Captain E. Whitehead)

139 NYANGA
O.N. 113423   1900–1914

Steel screw steamer, one deck and spar deck
325.7′×45.2′×15.9′   1967 n   3066 g
Built by W. Dobson & Co, Newcastle, Yard No 111, for Elder, Dempster & Co. Registered Liverpool. T 3 cyl 23″, 37″, 61″–42″ by North Eastern Marine Engineering Co Ltd, Newcastle. 252 nhp, 9½ K.

1900 27 September, launched. 3 November, trials.
1903 Transferred to Elder Line Ltd.
1914 16 August, captured and scuttled by the armed merchant cruiser KAISER WILHELM DER GROSSE in position 24°.00′N 16°.30′W, voyage West Africa to Liverpool, general cargo. Crew of **NYANGA** taken prisoner and later transferred to a German collier, and eventually landed at Las Palmas. On 26 August HMS HIGH-FLYER surprised KAISER WILHELM DER GROSSE off Rio del Oro and demanded her surrender. This was refused, and the raider was sunk in the ensuing battle.

Nyanga is a river and port in Gaboon.

NYANGA

140 SANGARA (II)
O.N. 113362   1900–1914, 1919

'Sangara' class
Steel screw steamer, two decks
325.0′×45.0′×19.6′   1563 n   2497 g
Built by Tyne Iron Shipbuilding Co Ltd, Newcastle, Yard No 128, for Elder, Dempster & Co. Registered Liverpool. T 3 cyl 23″, 37″, 61″–42″ by North Eastern Marine Engineering Co Ltd, Newcastle. 254 nhp, 9½ K.

1900 26 May, trials. Transferred to British & African Steam Navigation Co Ltd.
1914–19 Detained in Hamburg throughout World War I.
1919 Sold to Skjelbreds Rederi Aktieselskab Dampskibssel-skab, Christiansand, for £118,500. Registered Christiansand.
1922 Sold to Matsuoka Kisen Kabushiki Kaisha, Osaka. Renamed **NISSHIN MARU**. Registered Shikitsu (Osaka). 2498 n, 3292 g.
1925 Registered Nishinomiya.
1926 Sold to K. Tsutsui (Yamashita Kisen Kabushiki Kaisha, Managers, Kobe. Registered Tokyo. 1788 n, 2573 g.
1928 Registered Kobe.
1929 Sold to Tsutsui Seimatsu (Managers as above), Hyogo Ken.
1933 Registered Tarami.
1934 Sold for demolition.

Ships of the 'Sangara' class: SANGARA (140), WARRI (141), SANSU (142), ADANSI (143), ANCOBRA (144), BOULAMA (145), LOKOJA (146), EGWANA (147).

SANGARA

141 WARRI (I)
O.N. 113482   1901–1927

'Sangara' class
Steel screw steamer, one deck and shelter deck
325.0′×45.1′×19.5′   1558 n   2493 g
Built by Tyne Iron Shipbuilding Co Ltd, Newcastle, Yard No 134, for Elder, Dempster & Co. Registered Liverpool. T 3 cyl 23″, 37″, 61″–42″ by Wallsend Slipway Co Ltd, Newcastle. 252 nhp, 9½ K.

1901 15 June, launched.
1903 Transferred to British & African Steam Navigation Co Ltd.
1915 14 July, attacked by German submarine three miles south-west from Shipwash. Torpedo missed. **WARRI** unarmed at the time. Captain A. E. Webster was awarded the Distinguished Service Order

WARRI

1917 Tonnage opening closed. 2698 n, 3571 g.
1918 14 April, while at Bonny, donkey boiler pipe burst, killing one man.
1927 Sold for £5,500 to G. E. Panas & S. A. Michaelides, Cephalonia. Renamed **RITA**. Registered Argostoli. 1560 n, 2495 g.
1931 Transferred to the ownership of G. E. Panas.
1937 Sold for demolition in Italy.

Warri is a port on river of same name in the Niger delta, 26 miles upstream from Forcados.

142   SANSU (I)
O.N. 113499   1901–1908
'Sangara' class
Steel screw steamer, one deck and shelter deck
325.0′×45.1′×19.6′ 1556 n 2495 g
Built by Tyne Iron Shipbuilding Co Ltd, Newcastle, Yard No 135, for Elder, Dempster & Co. Registered Liverpool. T 3 cyl 23″, 37″, 61″–42″ by Wallsend Slipway Co Ltd, Newcastle. 252 nhp, 9½ K.
1901 29 August, launched. 28 September, trials.
1903 Transferred to British & African Steam Navigation Co Ltd.
1908 9 January, capsized and sank after stranding at Cesstown, Liberia, while on voyage to the United Kingdom with a cargo of palm kernels and cocoa. No casualties, all crew taken on board *BURUTU* but no salvage recoverable. Wrecks of **SANSU** and ASCON WOERMANN lie close to each other.

143   ADANSI
O.N. 113485   1901–1917
'Sangara' class
Steel screw steamer, one deck and shelter deck
325.5′×45.2′×19.6′ 1643 n 2644 g
Built by A. McMillan & Son, Ltd, Dumbarton, Yard No 377, for Elder, Dempster & Co. Registered Liverpool. T 3 cyl 23″, 37″, 61″–42″ by Muir Houston Ltd, Glasgow. 257 nhp, 9½ K.
1901 July, completed.
1903 Transferred to British & African Steam Navigation Co Ltd.
1917 6 May, sunk in 50°.40′N 11°.05′W by U21 (Kapitänleutnant Otto Hersing), voyage North America to Liverpool, cargo food. Hersing sighted the **ADANSI** at 0200 on 6 May and dived at 0220 for an underwater attack. He fired a single torpedo at 0241, which, although it broke surface three times on account of the sea then running, struck the **ADANSI** in the forward hold. The crew immediately abandoned ship. Although the master had left the ship's papers on board, Hersing was able to ascertain that the **ADANSI** had been bound for Liverpool from America with a cargo of foodstuffs, mainly cocoa. She sank at 0350.

U21 became a training boat on 22 March 1918 and survived the war. It was inspected by the Admiralty at Kiel on 14 December 1918 and on 20 February 1919 left Heligoland for Harwich in tow of the German tug LABOE and in company with the German cruiser GRAUDENZ and eight other U-boats. Early on 22 February, however, U21 foundered some 30 miles south of Dogger Bank South. Hersing became an inspector at the U-boat School in April 1918, where he remained until the war ended.

Adansi is a mining town in Ghana.

SOKOTO formerly ANCOBRA

144 ANCOBRA (I)/SOKOTO (II)
O.N. 112841   1901–1923

'Sangara' class
Steel screw steamer, two decks and shelter deck
325.6′×45.2′×19.6′   1642 n   2646 g
Built by A. McMillan & Son Ltd, Dumbarton, Yard No 376, for Elder, Dempster & Co. Registered London. T 3 cyl 23″, 37″, 61″–42″ by Muir & Houston Ltd, Glasgow. 257 nhp, 9½ K.
1900   26 December, launched.
1901   April, completed.
1908   Transferred to African Steamship Co.
1917   Tonnage opening closed. 2811 n, 3698 g.
1921   August, renamed **SOKOTO**.
1923   28 December, sank at Blohm and Voss shipyard, Hamburg, due to bursting of after peak during heavy frost.
1924   Refloated. Sold for demolition in Belgium.
Ancobra is a Ghanaian river; the open anchorage of Axim is situated at the mouth.

BOULAMA

145 BOULAMA
O.N. 115213   1901–1923

'Sangara' class
Steel screw steamer, two decks and shelter deck
324.8′×45.0′×19.6′   1625 n   2613 g
Built by Londonderry Shipbuilding & Engineering Co Ltd, Londonderry, Yard No 49, for Elder, Dempster & Co. Registered Liverpool. T 3 cyl 23″, 37″, 61″–42″ by Clyde Shipbuilding & Engineering Co Ltd, Port Glasgow. 257 nhp, 9½ K.
1901   29 August, launched. October, completed.

1903   Transferred to British & African Steam Navigation Co Ltd.
1909   23 August, stranded on Forcados Bar fracturing stern-post. Refloated with the assistance of *OSHOGBO, MAYUMBA, LOKOJA, ILORIN*.
1917   Tonnage opening closed. 2777 n, 3678 g.
1923   January, sold to Germany. Name retained but Lloyd's do not record owners nor registry port.
1925   Sold for demolition in Germany.
Boulama is a small port in Portuguese Guinea.

146 LOKOJA (II)
O.N. 115236   1902

'Sangara' class
Steel screw steamer, two decks and shelter deck
325.6′×45.6′×19.6′   1614 n   2640 g
Built by Clyde Shipbuilding & Engineering Co Ltd, Port Glasgow, Yard No 247, for Elder, Dempster & Co. Registered Liverpool. T 3 cyl 23″, 37″, 61″–42″ by the builders. 252 nhp, 9½ K.
Passenger accommodation: 12 first class.
1901   28 September, launched.
1902   27 January, wrecked on maiden voyage at Half Assini, Gold Coast, when outward bound from Liverpool.

LOKOJA

147 EGWANGA
O.N. 115284   1902–1927

'Sangara' class
Steel screw steamer, two decks and shelter deck
325.9′×45.0′×19.6′   1614 n   2600 g
Built by Clyde Shipbuilding & Engineering Co Ltd, Port Glasgow, Yard No 248, for Elder, Dempster & Co. Registered Liverpool. T 3 cyl 23″, 37″, 61″–42″ by the builders. 252 nhp, 9½ K.
1902   27 April, launched.
1903   Transferred to British & African Steam Navigation Co Ltd.
1917   Tonnage opening closed. 2804 n, 3658 g.
1925   Ashore at Cape Three Points, Gold Coast. Refloated.
1927   Sold to Rederi Aktiebolag Iris (C. Abrahamsen, Manager). Renamed **ORION**. Registered Stockholm. 2670 n, 3696 g.
1932   6 November, wrecked at Hernossand, Gulf of Bothnia.
Egwanga is the old native name for the Opobo district, near the mouth of the Imo River, Eastern Nigeria.

EGWANA

148 NEMBE (I)
O.N. 114427   1905–1919

Steel screw steamer, two decks and shelter deck
325.0′×45.1′×22.8′   1808 n   2842 g
Built by Tyne Iron Shipbuilding Co Ltd, Newcastle, Yard No
139, for G. H. Elder & Co, Newcastle, as **CROXDALE**.
Registered Newcastle. T 3 cyl 24″, 40″, 64″–42″ by North Eastern
Marine Engineering Co Ltd, Newcastle. 282 nhp, 9½ K.
1902   June, completed.
1904   Sold to Tyne Iron Shipbuilding Co Ltd, Newcastle.
1905   Acquired by Elder, Dempster & Co, Liverpool.
       Renamed **NEMBE**. Registered Liverpool.
1908   Transferred to British & African Steam Navigation Co
       Ltd.
1917   Tonnage opening closed. 2847 n, 3855 g.
1918   23 January, chased by submarine off Scilly Isles, saved
       by weather conditions.
1919   11 August, gutted by fire during loading at Accra for
       USA. Declared a constructive total loss.

Nembe was one of the old Niger Delta trading stations. It is
situated 20 miles up river from Brass.

NEMBE on fire at Accra

149 DELTA
O.N. 111263   1900–1915

Steel screw steamer, one deck
195.5′×28.1′×11.8′   352 n   585 g
Built by C. S. Swan & Hunter Ltd, Newcastle, Yard No 255,
for British & African Steam Navigation Co Ltd. Registered
Liverpool. C 2 cyl 21″, 42″–27″ by J. P. Reynoldson & Sons,
South Shields. 75 hp, 10 K.

Designed for operation on West African coastal services.
1900   Completed. Subsequently transferred to Elder, Demps-
       ter & Co.
1901   Transferred to Imperial Direct West India Mail Service
       Co Ltd. Stationed at Jamaica.
1902   26 April, ashore at Greater Breaker, later refloated.
1903   22 January, ashore on a reef in the harbour of Savannah
       la Mer in exposed position. Refloated.
1909   5 February, returned to West African coastal services.
1915   27 May, hull scuttled (after dismantling) off Forcados,
       Nigeria.

150 ABEOKUTA
O.N. 113464   1901–1915

Steel screw steamer, one deck and lower deck in fore hold
280.2′×40.1′×18.2′   1156 n   1817 g
Built by Robert Duncan & Co, Port Glasgow, Yard No 294, for
Elder, Dempster & Co. Registered Liverpool. T 3 cyl 20″, 33″,
54″–36″ by Rankin & Blackmore, Greenock. 199 nhp, 9 K.
1901   April, completed.
1902   Transferred to Elder Dempster Shipping Ltd.
1915   14 February, foundered, during hurricane in bay of
       Biscay, 70 miles south-west of Ushant (48°.30′N
       07°.30′W), voyage Liverpool to West Africa, general
       cargo. Crew of 18 saved.

Abeokuta, capital of the Egba tribe, is a Provincial Headquarters township 63 miles north of Lagos, Nigeria.

151 KANO
O.N. 113462   1901–1907

Steel twin screw steamer, one deck and teak awning deck
220.0′×36.2′×13.2′   920 n   1452 g
Built by Caledon Shipbuilding & Engineering Co Ltd, Dundee,
Yard No 157, for Elder, Dempster & Co. Registered Liverpool.
2×C 2 cyl 18″, 36″–24″ by the builders. 114 nhp, 9 K.
1901   April, completed.
1902   Transferred to British & African Steam Navigation Co
       Ltd.
1907   28 July, wrecked on Lagos Bar. Went to the assistance
       of *LLANDULAS* aground on Lagos Bar and in so doing
       collided with her, both became total wrecks. Both vessels
       carried cargo ex *MENDI* and *TARQUAH*.

Kano is an ancient walled town of Northern Nigeria, 700 miles
by rail from Lagos, altitude 1617′ above sea level.

152 BIDA (I)
O.N. 113483   1901–1903

'Bida' class
Steel twin screw steamer, one deck and teak awning deck
219.8′×36.1′×13.2′   946 n   1477 g
Built by John Jones & Sons, Birkenhead, Yard No 178, for
Elder, Dempster & Co. Registered Liverpool. 2×C 2 cyl 17″,
36″–24″ by the builders. 121 nhp, 9 K.
Passenger accommodation: 8 first class.
1901   August, completed and transferred to Elder Dempster
       Shipping Ltd.
1903   29 September, voyage Lagos to Hamburg, abandoned
       on fire, 45 miles south by east of Maas lightship, North
       Sea (Captain F. Colbeck, crew 27). Subsequently
       foundered.

Ships of the 'Bida' class: BIDA (152), HAUSSA (153), EGGA
(154).
Bida is a Divisional Headquarters town in the Niger Province
of Nigeria, about 80 miles east of Jebba.

153 HAUSSA
O.N. 113494   1901–1903

'Bida' class
Steel twin screw steamer, one deck and teak awning deck
219.8'×36.1'×13.2' 948 n 1477 g
Built by John Jones & Sons, Birkenhead, Yard No 179, for
Elder Dempster Shipping Ltd. Registered Liverpool. 2×C 2 cyl
17", 36"–24" by the builders. 121 nhp, 9 K.
Passenger accommodation: 8 first class.
1901   September, completed.
1903   15 June, struck submerged rock off Garraway, Liberia,
       voyage Lagos to Hamburg, cargo palm kernels. Fore
       hold flooded. 5 October, declared a constructive total
       loss.
Haussa is the early spelling of Hausa—the major tribe of
Northern Nigeria.

EGGA

154 EGGA
O.N. 114663   1901–1908

'Bida' class
Steel twin screw steamer, one deck and teak awning deck
219.8'×36.2'×13.1' 897 n 1445 g
Built by Londonderry Shipbuilding & Engineering Co Ltd,
Londonderry, Yard No 48, for African Steamship Co. Regis-
tered London. 2×C 2 cyl 18", 36"–24" by Mackie & Baxter,
Glasgow. 119 nhp, 9 K.
Passenger accommodation: 8 first class.
1901   22 May, trials.
1908   17 June, ran aground on Lagos Bar whilst operating
       on Nigerian Branch service. Part cargo (ex *FALABA*)
       jettisoned. Attempts to refloat failed and vessel declared
       constructive total loss.
Egga is a town on the River Niger, 417 miles upstream from
Forcados. Material for building the railway was offloaded here.

155 LLANDULAS
O.N. 113455   1901–1907

Iron screw well deck steamer, engines aft, one deck
200.0'×32.0'×14.2' 447 n 847 g
Built by Selby Shipbuilding & Engineering Co Ltd, Selby, Yard
No 47, for Elder, Dempster & Co. Registered Liverpool. T 3 cyl
17", 28½", 46"–30" by McColl and Pollock, Sunderland. 129 nhp,
10 K.

1901   February, completed.
1902   Transferred to Elder Dempster Shipping Ltd.
1907   26 July, aground on Lagos Bar (see *KANO*). Captain
       Richards in command. Anchors and chains lost. Decla-
       red constructive total loss.
Llandulas is a village in North Wales where Sir Alfred Jones
had a country house.

BURUTU

156 BURUTU (I)
O.N. 115280   1902–1918

'Burutu' class
Steel screw steamer, one deck and spar deck
360.0'×44.2'×14.4' 2441 n 3863 g
Built by Alexander Stephen & Sons Ltd, Glasgow, Yard No
394, for Elder, Dempster & Co. Registered Liverpool. T 3 cyl
27", 43", 72"–48" by the builders. 525 nhp, 14 K.
Passenger accommodation: designed for 100 first class and 50
second; later altered to 60 first class, 20 second and a limited
number of steerage.
1902   May, completed.
1903   Transferred to British & African Steam Navigation Co
       Ltd.
1908   9 January, rescued crew of capsized *SANSU* (179), off
       Cesstown, Liberia. 2468 n, 3902 g.
1914   Operated as special service vessel by British Government
       and then as an army transport.
1917   27 November, (Captain W. Walker) attacked by sub-
       marine, escaped undamaged.
1918   10 April, four days out from Lagos bound for Liverpool,
       attacked by submarine, torpedo missed. Gun fight last-
       ing one and a quarter hours ensued, **BURUTU** (Captain
       H. A. Yardley) was holed two feet above water line on
       starboard side but escaped and arrived Freetown 12
       April. Captain Yardley was awarded the Distinguished
       Service Order. Two men were killed during the engage-

BURUTU from an old postcard

ment. 19 September, (Captain W. Potter) departed Freetown in convoy for Liverpool with a full cargo of African produce, 103 passengers and 95 crew, escorted by HM AMC ALMANZORA. The night of 3 October was dark and squally, with rough sea. At 2250 when about 25 miles south-west of Bardsey, **BURUTU** collided with CITY OF CALCUTTA (7636 g/built 1903) and sank within ten minutes. Only No 1 port boat got safely away, 25 passengers and 25 crew members survived, and 148 lives being lost.

Ships of the 'Burutu' class: BURUTU (156), TARQUAH (157).

Burutu, a port on the River Forcados five miles above the port of Forcados, was the headquarters of the Niger Company.

157 TARQUAH
O.N. 115293   1902–1917

'Burutu' class
Steel screw steamer, one deck and spar deck
360.4′×44.3′×14.3′   2441 n   3859 g
Built by Alexander Stephen & Sons Ltd, Glasgow, Yard No 395, for Elder, Dempster & Co. Registered London. T 3 cyl 27″, 43″, 72–48″ by the builders. 525 nhp, 14 K.
Passenger accommodation: designed for 100 first class and 50 second class, later modified to 60 first class, 20 second class and limited steerage.
1902   23 April, launched. June, completed.
1903   February, transferred to African Steamship Co.
1915   In collision with *APPAM* in Cameroon River.
1917   7 July, torpedoed without warning and sunk by submarine U57 (Kapitanleutnant Ritter Carl-Siegfried von Georg), about ten miles south-west from Bull Rock (51°.29′N 10°.25′W), voyage Sierra Leone to Liverpool with passengers and West African produce. No loss of life.

von Georg later commanded U101 and survived the war. On 24 November 1918 U57, under command of Öberleutnant zur See der Reserve Walter Stein, surrendered at Harwich. Later allocated to France and left Harwich 8 December under tow of French tug.

A COMMENDABLE COMPLIMENT

An incident, which is of considerable interest to all who appreciate a good understanding between Great Britain and Germany, took place at Forcados on October 17. When the Elder Dempster liner *Tarquah* reached the mouth of the Niger the German man-of-war *Sperber* was lying there. Captain Wyndham, of the *Tarquah*, utilised the opportunity to invite the officers of the *Sperber* to dinner, which was accepted cordially, and a very enjoyable evening was spent aboard the British steamer. The band of the *Tarquah* played German airs.—*The African World*, November 24th, 1906.

The *Tarquah* was sunk by German submarine on July 7th, 1917. "A Commendable Compliment"!!!

From the *Elder Dempster House Magazine* 1922

Note—**TARQUAH** is depicted on the 31 cents postage stamp of Sierra Leone issued during 1980.

Tarquah (Tarkwa) is a mining town in Ghana to the north of Sekondi.

MELVILLE (Photo WSPL)

158 MELVILLE
O.N. 115255   1902–1926

Steel screw steamer, two decks
385.0′×48.8′×26.9′   2872 n   4439 g
Built by R. Duncan & Co Ltd, Port Glasgow, Yard No 297, for Elder, Dempster & Co. Registered Liverpool. T 3 cyl 27″, 43″, 72″–48″ by Rankin & Blackmore, Greenock. 359 nhp, 10½ K.
1902   9 January, launched.
1902   18 April, commenced maiden voyage, London to Table Bay.
1904   April, transferred to Elder Line Ltd.
1905   Placed on the Canada–Cape service.
Passenger accommodation: 14 first class (later removed).
Refrigerated chamber fitted and provision made for the carriage of cattle. 2899 n, 4484 g.

TARQUAH

CHARITAS, *formerly* ***MELVILLE***

1917   Requisitioned by HM Government and operated as an army supply ship, later as a collier for both British and Russian Governments. Made two round voyages to Australia during the war period.
1922   Aground at Sekondi on the Gold Coast—refloated.
1926   29 July, sold to SA per L'Industria ed il Commercio Marrittimo, Genoa. Renamed **CHARITAS**. Registered Genoa. 2725 n, 4408 g.
1927   Sold to SA di Navigazione la Tirrenia, Genoa.
1931   Sold for demolition in Italy.

ZARIA as built

159   PORTO NOVO
O.N. 118026   1903–1921

Steel screw steamer, one deck, engines aft
202.5'×30.1'×9.9   328 n   603 g
Built by David J. Dunlop & Co, Port Glasgow, Yard No 254, for Elder Dempster Shipping Ltd. Registered Liverpool. C 2 cyl 22", 44"–27" by the builders. 99 rhp, 9 K.
Designed for operation on the Lagos to Forcados service.
1903   Completed.
1910   Transferred to Elder Line Ltd.
1921   April, dismantled and scuttled off Lagos.
Porto Novo is a town on Badagry Creek near the Dahomey border, approximately 55 miles to the west of Lagos.

160   CANADA CAPE
O.N. 118073   1904–1912

Steel screw steamer, one deck and spar deck
360.0'×48.0'×20.2'   2795 n   4286 g
Built by Northumberland Shipbuilding Co Ltd, Newcastle, Yard No 110, for Elder Dempster Shipping Ltd. Registered Liverpool. T 3 cyl 25", 41", 69"–48" by Richardsons Westgarth & Co Ltd, Sunderland. 372 nhp, 10 K.
1904   February, completed.
1911   Transferred to Elder Line Ltd.
1912   June, fire damage at Cape Town. Sold to H. & C. Grayson Ltd, Liverpool. 2802 n, 4283 g.
1915   Sold to Union Steam Ship Co of New Zealand Ltd, London. Renamed **WAIHEMO**. Registered London.
1918   17 March, torpedoed without warning by submarine and sunk in the Gulf of Athens, voyage Durban to Piraeus, cargo maize. No loss of life.
Name derived from the service for which the vessel was built and operated: Montreal/St John N.B. to Cape Town and beyond.

161   ZARIA
O.N. 118078   1903–1928

'Muraji' class
Steel screw steamer, one deck
350.6'×48.5'×19.7'   2023 n   3243 g
Built by Clyde Engineering & Iron Shipbuilding Co Ltd, Port Glasgow, Yard No 257, for British & African Steam Navigation Co Ltd, Liverpool. Registered Liverpool. T 3 cyl 27", 43", 72"–48" by Clyde Engineering & Iron Shipbuilding Co Ltd, Port Glasgow. 570 nhp, 13 K.
Passenger accommodation: 36 first class, 18 second.
1903   Launched 21 December.
1904   Completed.
1910   Hull lengthened by 30 feet at Port Glasgow to 380.6'.
1914   Employed as a naval supply vessel throughout the war.
1928   Sold for £10,000 for demolition in Norway.
Ships of the 'Muraji' class: ZARIA (161), MURAJI (162).
Zaria is a Provincial Headquarters and railway junction, 613 miles north of Lagos, Nigeria.

CANADA CAPE

ZARIA after lengthening

Elder Dempster and Co. Limited

PLAN OF SALOONS
AND
PASSENGER ACCOMMODATION
OF THE
R.M.S. "ZARIA"

FIRST CLASS
"A" DECK
Cabins No. 1/12, 18, 20 ... ... B 1 rate per passenger
Cabins No. 14/17 ... ... B 2 rate per passenger
"B" DECK
Cabins No. 1 and 2 ... ... A B rate per passenger

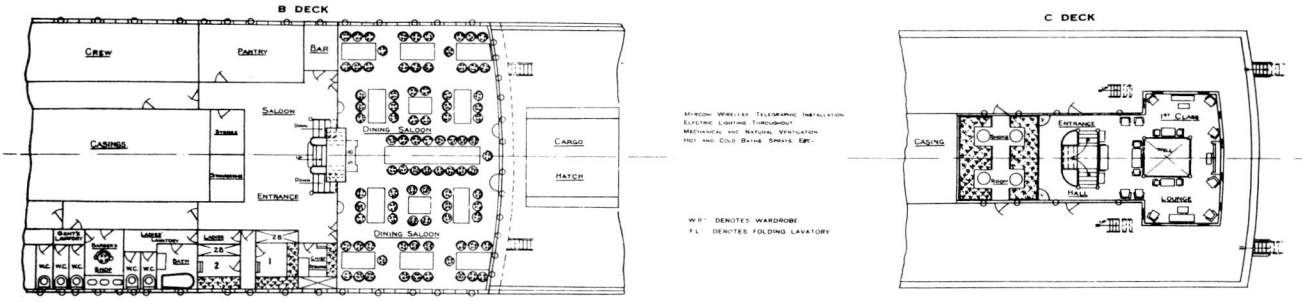

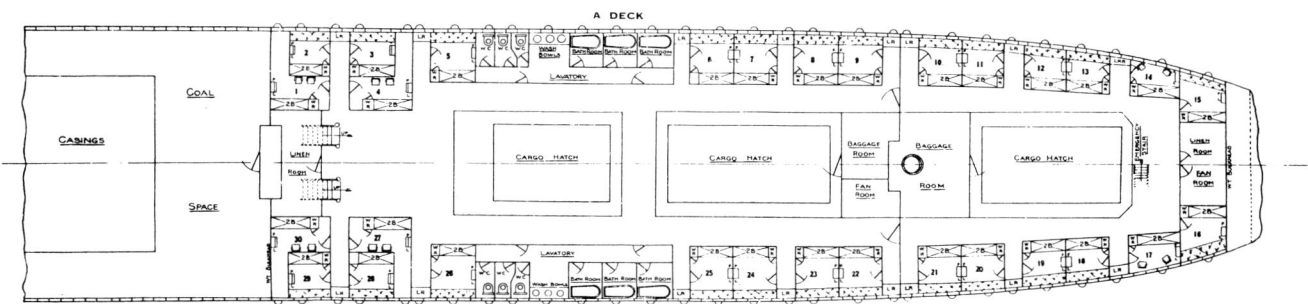

162 MURAJI

O.N. 118095   1904–1914

'Muraji' class
Steel screw steamer, two decks
350.1'×48.5'×19.7'   2016 n   3243 g
Built by Clyde Shipbuilding & Engineering Co Ltd, Port Glasgow, Yard No 258, for Elder Line Ltd. Registered Liverpool. T 3 cyl 27", 43", 72"–48" by Clyde Engineering & Iron Shipbuilding Co Ltd, Port Glasgow. 570 nhp, 13 K.
Passenger accommodation: 36 first class, 18 second.
1904   12 April, launched.
1911   Hull lengthened by 30 feet at Port Glasgow to 380.3'. 2197 n, 3547 g.

1914   23 July, bunkers on fire at Cape Palmas. 10 August, sank at Grand Bassam, voyage Liverpool to West African ports.
Muraji (Mureji) is a town on the Niger River at its confluence with the Kaduna, 459 miles from Forcados, Nigeria.

163 ZUNGERU (I)

O.N. 118107   1904–1906, 1909–1910

Steel twin screw steamer
375.4'×47.0'×23.3'   2578 n   4075 g
Built by Sir Raylton Dixon & Co Ltd, Middlesbrough, Yard No 503, for Elder Dempster Shipping Ltd. Registered Liverpool. 2×T 3 cyl 21½", 36", 59"–42" by Wallsend Slipway Co Ltd, Newcastle. 589 nhp, 13 K.
Passenger accommodation: 90 first class, 50 second.
1904   17 March, launched.
1906   March, transferred to Cie Belge Maritime du Congo. Renamed **BRUXELLESVILLE**. Registered Antwerp.
1909   Transferred to African Steamship Co Ltd. Renamed **ZUNGERU**. Registered London. 2563 n, 4059 g.
1910   December, sold to Cia Transalantica, Cadiz & Barcelona. Renamed **LEGAZPI**. Registered Barcelona. 2565 n, 4349 g.

MURAJI

ZUNGERU

1937   19 May, attacked and disabled by insurgent aircraft during the Spanish Civil War. 24 May, again bombed at Castellon. Later beached and declared a constructive total loss.

Zungeru is a town on the Kaduna River, a railway junction 426 miles north of Lagos.

164   LANDANA (III)
O.N. 125749   1908–1910

Steel twin screw steamer
375.3′×47.0′×23.2′   2690 n   4152 g
Built by Sir Raylton Dixon & Co Ltd, Middlesbrough, Yard No 503, for Cie Belge Maritime du Congo as **LEOPOLDVILLE**.

Registered Antwerp. 2 × T 3 cyl 21½″, 36″, 59″–42″ by Wallsend Slipway Co Ltd, Newcastle. 589 nhp, 13 K.
1904   April, completed.
1908   Transferred to African Steamship Co. Renamed **LANDANA**. Registered London. 2586 n, 4070 g.
1910   November, sold to Cia Transalantica Barcelona. Renamed **C de EIZAGUSRAE**. Registered Barcelona.
1915   2551 n, 4376 g.
1917   25 May, on voyage Barcelona–Manila via Cape Town, when steaming at reduced speed in bad weather, an explosion occurred at 0300 when the vessel was a few miles of Robben Island (Cape Town). The vessel broke her back and with bow and stern pointing into the air plunged beneath the waves within five minutes. Only one boat was able to get away, with 23 persons, and these were rescued nine hours later and taken to Cape Town. The Chief Engineer was rescued on 27 May after

LANDANA

34 hours on a raft. These were the only survivors out of 50 passengers and 100 crew. The mine had been laid by the German raider WOLF some weeks previously.

Note—A model of **LEOPOLDVILLE** is on display in the Antwerp Office of the Cie Maritime Belge.

165 SAPELE (I)
O.N. 120819   1904–1917

'Sapele' class
Steel screw steamer, two decks and shelter deck
350.4′×48.3′×20.5′   1982 n   3152 g
Built by Palmers Co Ltd, Newcastle, Yard No 779, for British & African Steam Navigation Co Ltd. Registered Liverpool. T 3 cyl 25″, 42″, 70″–45″ by the builders. 478 nhp, 12 K.
Passenger accommodation: 10.

1904   December, completed.
1917   9 June, chased by submarine, escaped undamaged. 26 October, (Captain J. Macdonald) voyage Liverpool to Sierra Leone, general cargo, torpedoed without warning and sunk 100 miles north-west from Tory Island, by U104 (Kapitänleutnant Kurt Bernie). Three lives lost. U104 was sunk on 25 April 1918 in 51°.59′N 06°.26′W by HMS JESSAMINE who sighted U-boat on the surface and attacked with depth-charges as it was diving. One survivor was picked up.

Ships of the 'Sapele' class: SAPELE (165), BENUE (166), CHAMA (167), ADDAH (168).
Sapele is a port near the confluence of the Jamieson and Ethiope Rivers, 68 miles from the entrance to Escravos River.

BENUE

1917   December, transferred to African Steamship Co.
1930   Sold to Cie Genovese di Navigazione a Vapore, SA, Genoa. Renamed **CAPO PINO**. Registered Genoa. 1902 n, 3209 g.
1937   February, sank after collision in the Dardanelles.
The River Benue is the major tributary of the Niger. It rises in the Cameroons and flows west to the confluence at Lokoja.

ELDER DEMPSTER AND CO., LIMITED,
COLONIAL HOUSE, 20. WATER STREET,
LIVERPOOL.

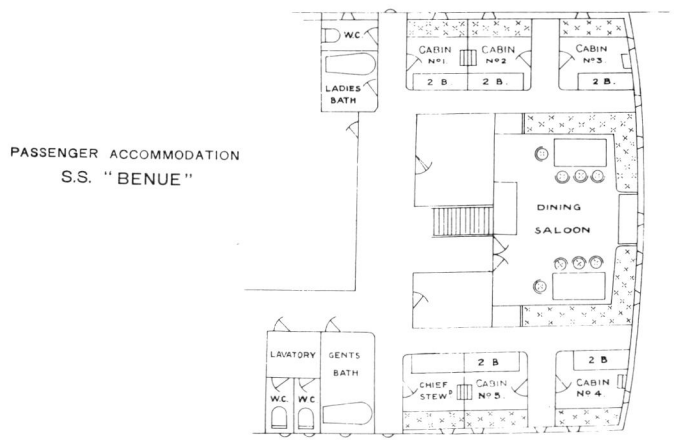

PASSENGER ACCOMMODATION
S.S. "BENUE"

SAPELE

166 BENUE (I)
O.N. 120838   1905–1930

'Sapele' class
Steel screw steamer
350.0′×48.4′×20.8′   1951 n   3212 g
Built by Swan Hunter & Wigham Richardson Ltd, Newcastle, Yard No 773, for Elder Dempster Shipping Ltd. Registered Liverpool. T 3 cyl 25″, 41″, 68″–48″ by Wallsend Slipway Co Ltd, Newcastle. 320 nhp, 11 K.
Passenger accommodation: 10.

1905   12 January, launched.
1914   Chartered to Russian Government, then to Ministry of Shipping.
1915   Took part in the evacuation from the Dardanelles.

167 CHAMA
O.N. 120508   1905–1930

'Sapele' class
Steel screw steamer
350.0′×48.3′×20.7′   1977 n   3152 g
Built by Palmers Co Ltd, Newcastle, Yard No 781, for African Steamship Co. Registered Liverpool. T 3 cyl 25″, 42″, 70″–45″ by the builders. 478 nhp, 12 K.
Passenger accommodation: 10.

1905   April, completed.
1916   Hull damaged due to being ice-bound at Archangel.
1930   Sold to Raffaele Rizzuto, Naples. Renamed **ASSUNZIONE**. Registered Rome. 1948 n, 3195 g.
1933   Sold to Cia Genovese di Vapore SA, Genoa. Renamed **CAPO ARMA**. Registered Genoa. Fitted for burning oil fuel.

BENUE *in 1925*

1938   1939 n, 3172 g.
1942   29 May, torpedoed and sunk 70 miles NNW of Benghazi
        in a dawn attack on an Axis convoy by HMS TUR-
        BULENT (Commander J. W. 'Tubby' Linton). The
        Italian destroyer PESSAGNO was torpedoed and sunk
        in the same attack.
HMS TURBULENT was lost on her last war patrol before
returning to the UK for a refit, when on 12 March 1943 she
was sunk with all hands off Corsica by Italian anti-submarine
vessels. Linton was awarded the Victoria Cross for his very
successful patrols in TURBULENT during 1942.
Chama is one of the Ghanian surf ports, to the east of Sekondi.

CHAMA

168   ADDAH
O.N. 120828   1905–1917

'Sapele' class
Steel screw steamer
350.0′×48.3′×20.7′   1977 n   3149 g
Built by Palmers Co Ltd, Newcastle, Yard No 780, for British
& African Steam Navigation Co Ltd. Registered Liverpool.
T 3 cyl 25″, 42″, 70″–45″ by the builders. 478 nhp, 12 K.
Passenger accommodation: 10.
1905   May, completed.
1915   2826 n, 4396 g.
1917   15 June, (Captain F. C. Clarke) sunk 35 miles south-
        west of Point de Penmarch by UC69 (Kapitänleutnant
        Erwin Wassner) in a submerged torpedo attack followed
        by gunfire, voyage Montreal to Cherbourg, general
        cargo, eight crew lost their lives. After the torpedo struck
        Captain Clarke ordered his crew to abandon ship, but
        he and the gunner E. W. Swan opened fire with the stern
        gun and hit UC69 although not seriously damaging her.
        There followed a brief exchange of fire until **ADDAH**'s
        gun was put out of action, and both men jumped over-
        board and were picked up by one lifeboat. UC69 then
        rammed and sank the lifeboat and fired on the survivors,
        killing eight crewmen.
On 6 December 1917 UC69, then under the command of
Oberleutnant zur See Hugo Thielmann, was accidentally rammed by U96, some 8½ miles north of Cap Barfleur. UC69's
stern was badly damaged and she sank rapidly. On touching
bottom the torpedo in the stern tube exploded and 11 of the
crew were lost with the boat. Wassner went on to command

114

ADDAH

two other U-boats (UB59 and UB117) and survived the war. A submarine depot ship of World War II was named after him. The name Addah is derived from a port in Ghana.

169 KARINA

O.N. 120573   1905–1917

'Karina' class
Steel screw steamer
370.0′×46.2′×23.3′   2638 n   4222 g
Built by Alexander Stephen & Sons Ltd, Glasgow, Yard No 406, for African Steamship Co. Registered London. T 3 cyl 29″, 46″, 77″–51″ by the builders. 422 nhp, 13 K.

Passenger accommodation: 100 first class, 70 second.
1905 4 May, launched.
1917 30 July, attacked by submarine off west of Ireland, torpedo missed. 1 August, sunk 25 miles south of Hook Point, Waterford, by UC75 (Oberleutnant zur See Johannes Lohs) in a submerged torpedo attack, voyage Sierra Leone to Liverpool, with passengers, cargo palm oil and kernels. Eleven lives lost.

On 31 May 1918 UC75, then under the command of Oberleutnant zur See Walter Schmitz, was attacking convoy TU29 off Flamborough Head, when sighted and rammed by the destroyer FAIRY. UC75 sank in 53°.57′N 00°.09′E. There were 14 survivors. Lohs' fate is described under *BENITO*.

Ships of the 'Karina' class: KARINA (169), MENDI (170).
Karina is a town in the north of Sierra Leone.

KARINA

MENDI

170 MENDI
O.N. 120875   1905–1917

'Karina' class
Steel screw steamer
370.2′×46.2′×23.3′   2639 n   4230 g
Built by Alexander Stephen & Sons Ltd, Glasgow, Yard No
407, for British & African Steam Navigation Co Ltd. Registered
Liverpool. T 3 cyl 29″, 46″, 77″–51″ by the builders. 424 nhp,
13 K.
Passenger accommodation: 100 first class, 70 second.
1905   19 June, launched.
1916   Requisitioned for service as an army transport ship.
1917   16 January, (Capt. H. A. Yardley) sailed from Cape
Town for Havre via Plymouth carrying a South African
Native Labour Corps battalion for service in France. 20
February, sailed from Plymouth at 1610. Dense fog
developed during the night, and at 0457 on 21 February,
when about 12 miles off the Isle of Wight, **MENDI** was
rammed between Nos 1 and 2 hatches by *DARRO* (ex-
Elder Dempster), causing an immediate and heavy list
to starboard which prevented launching of the port
lifeboats. Many of the Africans were crushed in their
berths by the impact of the collision or drowned by the
sudden inrush of water. **MENDI** sank 20 minutes after
the collision occurred, amid scenes of great heroism as
members of her crew gave up places in the few and
overcrowded lifeboats to Africans struggling in the icy
water, but owing to the fog many more could not be
located. At the subsequent Court of Inquiry special
mention was made in particular of the gallant conduct
of Q/M H. J. Wilson, 4th Engineer J. W. Pascoe, and
Ordinary Seaman V. Capter. In all, 656 of the 894
personnel on board lost their lives in what was Elder
Dempster's worst disaster of the War, and South Africa's
worst maritime disaster. The fog itself lifted at about
0630, too late to be of any help to the victims.
Mendi is a tribe and dialect of Sierra Leone

Engine-room telegraph salvaged from **MENDI**, *now in
Bembridge Museum*

A plate recovered from **MENDI**

R.M.S. "MENDI," AT CALABAR, TAKING NATIVE TROOPS ON BOARD FOR DAR-ES-SALAAM.

PATANI

171 PATANI
O.N. 120872   1905–1930

'Agberi' class
Steel screw steamer, two decks and shelter deck
370.3'×49.3'×21.8'   2178 n   3465 g
Built by Workman Clark & Co Ltd, Belfast, Yard No 219, for
Elder Line Ltd. Registered Liverpool. T 3 cyl 26", 44", 74"–48"
by the builders. 379 nhp, 13 K.
Passenger accommodation: 10.
1905   6 June, launched. 4 August, trials.
1916–17   Operated for the French Government, Canada–
          France.
1918   Transferred to African Steamship Co. 3087 n, 4810 g.
1924   2173 n, 3487 g.
1930   March, sold to Cia Genovese di Navigazione a Vapore,
       SA, Genoa. Renamed **CAPO FARO**. Registered Genoa.
       2137 n, 3476 g.
1939   Fitted to burn oil fuel.
1941   30 November, bombed and sunk by British aircraft in
       the Ionian Sea in position 37°.28'N 19°.20'E.
Vessels of the 'Agberi' class: PATANI (171), AGBERI (172),
ABURI (173), FULANI (174), PRAHSU (175), SIERRA
LEONE (176).
Patani is a town 70 miles above Forcados on the Forcados
River.

172 AGBERI
O.N. 120880   1905–1917

'Agberi' class
Steel screw steamer, two decks and shelter deck
370.3'×49.3'×21.8'   2324 n   3730 g
Built by Workman Clark & Co Ltd, Belfast, Yard No 220, for

Elder, Dempster & Co. Registered Liverpool. T 3 cyl 26", 44",
74"–48" by the builders. 379 nhp, 13 K.
Passenger accommodation: 10.
1905   6 July, launched.
1909   2177 n, 3463 g.
1912   Transferred to Elder Line Ltd.
1915–16   Completed four round voyages to Arctic—Russian
          troops to Brest for the Imperial Russian Government.
1917   Transferred to African Steamship Co. 3098 n, 4812 g. 25
       December, sunk 18 miles N30W from Bardsey Island
       by U87 (Kapitänleutnant Freiherr Rudolf von Speth-
       Schülzburg) in a submerged torpedo attack, voyage
       Dakar to Liverpool, with passengers and general cargo.
The fate of U87 is described in connection with the *TAMELE*.
Agberi is one of the old trading towns in the Niger Delta.

AGBERI

AGBERI with Russian troops aboard at Brest

173 ABURI
O.N. 123765   1907–1917

'Agberi' class
Steel screw steamer, two decks
370.6′×49.3′×21.8′   2324 n   3730 g
Built by Harland & Wolff Ltd, Belfast, Yard No 383, for African Steamship Co. Registered London. T 3 cyl 26″, 44″, 74″–48″ by the builders. 528 nhp, 13 K.
Passenger accommodation: 10.

1906   18 October, launched.
1907   2 January, trials.
1917   17 April, sunk 125 miles north-west of Tory Island by U61 (Kapitänleutnant Victor Dieckmann) in a submerged torpedo attack, voyage Liverpool to West Africa, general cargo. Twenty-five lives lost, 25 survivors landed at Larne, Ireland.

U61 was sunk with all hands on 26 March, 1918 in 51°.48′N 05°.52′W by HMS P51 in a depth-charge attack.
Aburi is a town in Ghana 26 miles to the north of Accra.

174 FULANI (I)
O.N. 124068   1907–1914

'Agberi' class
Steel screw steamer, two decks
370.6′×49.3′×21.8′   2326 n   3731 g
Built by Harland & Wolff Ltd, Belfast, Yard No 386, for Elder, Dempster & Co. Registered London. T 3 cyl 26″, 44″, 74″–48″ by the builders. 528 nhp, 13 K.
Passenger accommodation: 10.

1907   31 January, launched. Transferred after completion to African Steamship Co.
1914   3 June, stranded on Carpenter Rock, near Freetown, Sierra Leone, voyage West Africa to Liverpool, cargo palm oil.
       The mid-ship section and funnel (which was kept painted E-D buff) was a permanent landmark until the beginning of World War II. The engines were still visible in 1982.

The Fulani is a tribe of Northern Nigeria.

ABURI

FULANI

119

FULANI firmly aground, taken in 1930

175 PRAHSU (I)
O.N. 124075   1907–1931

'Agberi' class
Steel screw steamer, two decks
370.6′×49.3′×21.8′   2311 n   3756 g
Built by Harland & Wolff Ltd, Belfast, Yard No 387, for Elder, Dempster & Co. Registered Liverpool. T 3 cyl 26″, 44″, 74″–48″ by the builders. 528 nhp, 13 K.
Passenger accommodation: 10.
1907   June, completed.
1911   Transferred to African Steamship Co.
1917   3181 n, 5072 g.
1924   2305 n, 3791 g.
1931   December, sold for £3300 to Anglo Maritime Shipping Ltd for breaking-up at Rosyth.
Prahsu is a town on the River Prah in Ghana.

PRAHSU

176 SIERRA LEONE
O.N. 123767   1907–1910

'Agberi' class
Steel screw steamer, two decks
370.6′×49.3′×21.8′   2327 n   3730 g
Built by Harland & Wolff Ltd, Belfast, Yard No 384, for African Steamship Co. Registered London. T 3 cyl 26″, 44″, 74″–48″ by the builders. 528 nhp, 13 K.
Passenger accommodation: 10.
1906   15 November, launched.
1907   16 January, sailed on maiden voyage.
1910   1 July, wrecked at the entrance to Axim, outward bound from Liverpool with general cargo.
Sierra Leone is a country in West Africa.

PRAHSU, from a colour drawing

SIERRA LEONE, *from a postcard*

177   COALING/ETHIOPE (III)
O.N. 120930   1906–1915

Steel screw steamer, one deck and spar deck
340.0′×47.1′×27.4′   2475 n   3794 g
Built by Furness Withy & Co Ltd, West Hartlepool, Yard No
286, for Elder Dempster Shipping Ltd. Registered Liverpool.
T 3 cyl 24″, 39″, 66″–45″ by Richardsons, Westgarth & Co Ltd,
Hartlepool. 317 nhp, 11½ K.
1906   March, completed.
1911   2 August, transferred to Elder Line Ltd. Renamed
       ETHIOPE. Registered Liverpool.
1915   28 May, sunk in position 49°39.′N 04°16.′W by U41
       (Kapitänleutnant Klaus Hansen). **ETHIOPE** (Captain
       J. McDonald) voyage Hull and London to Calabar,

general cargo, was sighted bearing 4° on U41's port bow
at 0955. As the U-boat pursued, **ETHIOPE**'s crew were
seen to abandon ship. At 1008 Hansen fired one of
his stern tubes at a range of 300 metres. The torpedo
porpoised but ran straight and struck the steamer
beneath the funnel, and she went down within nine
minutes. Although her name had been painted over,
Hansen was able to identify his victim as **ETHIOPE**.
U41 was sunk on 24 September 1917 by the Q-ship
BARALONG in 49.°10′N 07°.33′W. There were only two survivors from a crew of 37, Hansen being one of the casualties.

178   CLARENCE/DAKAR
O.N. 123658   1906–1915

'Dakar' class
Steel twin screw steamer, two decks and well deck
370.1′×46.1′×22.8′   2602 n   4081 g
Built by Sir Raylton Dixon & Co Ltd, Middlesbrough, Yard
No 457, as **CLARENCE** for African Steamship Co. Transferred
to Cie Maritime Belge du Congo before completion and renamed **ANVERSVILLE**. Registered Antwerp. 2×T 3 cyl 21½″,
34″, 59″–42″ by Wallsend Slipway Co Ltd, Newcastle. 584 nhp,
14 K.
Passenger accommodation: 100 first class, 70 second.
1898   Launched 12 December.
1899   Completed May.
1906   Transferred to African Steamship Co. Renamed
       DAKAR. Registered London. 2518 n, 3987 g.
1913   15 February, in collision with LYNG (Norwegian) 15
       miles south by west of Eddystone light.
1915   31 March, at Forcados with tween deck bunker fire.
       31 May, abandoned, burnt out.

COALING *in 1912* (Photo M. C. Crossley Evans)

DAKAR

1918   Owned by HM Government (The Shipping Controller).
1920   Salved by Nigeria Marine. Registered Lagos. Returned to United Kingdom (Captain T. E. Williams).
1922   Sold to NV Hollandsche Zuid Africkaansche Stoomvaat Maatschappij, Amsterdam. Renamed **BLOEMFON-TEIN**. Registered Rotterdam. 2958 n, 4654 g.
1926   Sold to Ho Hong Steamship Co Ltd (Lim Kian Beng, Manager), London. Renamed **HONG PENG**. Registered Singapore (British flag). 2525 n, 4055 g.
1942   Hulked at Singapore.
1947   March, broken up at Singapore.

Ships of the 'Dakar' class: DAKAR (178), MANDINGO (179). Dakar is an important port situated at the tip of Cape Verde peninsula, the westernmost point of Africa.

MANDINGO, *from a postcard*

179 MANDINGO (III)

O.N. 123693   1906–1914

'Dakar' class
Steel twin screw steamer, two decks and well deck
370.1′×46.2′×22.8′   2814 n   4091 g
Built by Sir Raylton Dixon & Co Ltd, Middlesbrough, Yard No 458, as **PHILIPPEVILLE**, for Cie Belge Maritime du Congo. Registered Antwerp. 2×T 3 cyl 21½″, 34″, 59″–42″ by Wallsend Slipway Co Ltd, Newcastle. 584 nhp, 14 K. Passenger accommodation 100 first class, 70 second.
1899   August, completed. 2 September, trials.
1906   Transferred to African Steamship Co. Renamed **MANDINGO**. Registered London. 2504 n, 3986 g.
1914   Sold to Royal Mail Steam Packet Co. Renamed **CHAUDIERE**. 2504 n, 4019 g.
1927   Sold to T. W. Ward Ltd.
1928   September, broken up at Ardrossan.

180 FALABA (I)

O.N. 124000   1906–1915

'Falaba' class
Steel screw steamer, two decks and shelter deck
380.5′×47.4′×22.9′   3011 n   4806 g
Built by Alexander Stephen & Sons Ltd, Glasgow, Yard No 414, for Elder, Dempster & Co. T 3 cyl 29″, 46″, 77″–51″ by the builders. 424 nhp, 14 K.
Passenger accommodation: 120 first class, 70 second.
1906   22 August, trials, speed 15½ K.
1907   Transferred to Elder Line Ltd.
1915   28 March, (Captain F. J. Davis) sunk by U28 (Kapitänleutnant Baron Georg-Günther von Forstner), 38 miles west from the Smalls, voyage Liverpool to West Africa, 145 passengers, 95 crew. At about 1300, von Forstner sighted a large steamer right ahead, whereupon he dived for a submerged attack, which, however, had to be abandoned owing to the rather high seas. U28 thus surfaced and set off in pursuit. When the U-boat had closed to within two to three miles, the steamer clearly noticed she was being chased by a U-boat, since she attempted to escape. U28, however, continued to gain on the steamer until von Forstner was able to force her to stop under threat of bombardment. U28 then went alongside, but at a safe distance, and von Forstner communicating through a loud-hailer instructed the passengers and crew to leave the ship, for which he was allowing ten minutes. Considerable confusion reigned on board, and out of consideration for the passengers, who were running helplessly about the deck looking for a lifeboat, von Forstner extended his deadline to 20 minutes, after which he ordered a torpedo tube to be ready, but waited a further three minutes before giving the order to fire, since he could see that people were still on board. At 1353 he fired one stern tube, since a lookout had reported the smoke of an approaching vessel. The torpedo struck the FALABA aft. At the last moment a boat full of survivors, which von Forstner had not previously noticed, was being lowered. The ship on being hit capsized to starboard and sank by the stern within ten minutes. Her master had remained on the bridge and continued to sound the steam whistle to attract the attention of a nearby trawler, which then undertook rescue operations. Von Forstner found to his regret that he was unable to assist, for the steamer had W/T and he was mindful of the fast approaching vessel whose smoke had been sighted by the lookout. He identified his victim as the FALABA from Liverpool and estimated she was carrying 300 to 400 passengers. He praised the Master's conduct, 104 lives, including that of the Master, were lost when the FALABA was sunk.

U28, then under the command of Kapitänleutnant Georg Schmidt, was sunk in 72°.34′N 27°56′E on 2 September 1917. The circumstances were somewhat bizarre. U28 had attacked and torpedoed the ss OLIVE BRANCH. The steamer, however, refused to go down, so U28 opened fire at a range of 250 yards to finish her off with gunfire. The second shot entered the OLIVE BRANCH's No 4 hold, which contained ammunition. The OLIVE BRANCH blew up, the explosion wrecking U28. Although a number of the U-boat's crew survived the explosion, some ending up in the water, others on the wreck of the U-boat, none were rescued. Von Forstner had left U28 in June 1916 to take up an appointment in July as an instructor at the U-boat school. In December 1917 he transferred to surface ships and when the war ended, then a Korvettenkapitän, he was serving as First Lieutenant in the light cruiser KÖNIGSBERG. Ships of the 'Falaba' class: FALABA (180), ELMINA (206). Falaba is a town in the north of Sierra Leone, 60 miles from the source of the River Niger.

FALABA

181　BENDU
O.N. 123995　　　　　　　　　　1906–1929

'Bendu' class
Steel screw steamer, one deck and spar deck
375.2′×47.3′×18.9′　2821 n　4319 g
Built by Swan Hunter & Wigham Richardson Ltd, Newcastle,
Yard No 773, for Elder, Dempster & Co. Registered Liverpool.
T 3 cyl 25½″, 42″, 70″–48″ by North Eastern Marine Engineering
Co Ltd, Newcastle. 396 nhp, 12 K.
1906　September, completed.
1912　Transferred to Elder Line Ltd.
1928　4 May, voyage West Africa to Boulogne, lost propeller
　　　and towed into Las Palmas by *BOMA*.
1929　January, sold to D. Tripcovich & Co, SA di Navigecione
　　　(Rimorchi & Salataggi, Managers), Trieste for £18,000.
　　　Renamed **ARCADIA**. Registered Trieste (Italian flag).
1934　December, wrecked off Dakar.
Ships of the 'Bendu' class: BENDU (181), BENIN (182).
Bendu is situated at the mouth of River Taia, near Sherbro
Island, Sierra Leone.

182　BENIN (III)
O.N. 124067　　　　　　　　　　1907–1929

'Bendu' class
Steel screw steamer, one deck and spar deck
375.2′×43.7′×18.8′　2788 n　4313 g
Built by Swan Hunter & Wigham Richardson Ltd, Newcastle,
Yard No 785, for Elder, Dempster & Co. Registered Liverpool.
T 3 cyl 25½″, 42″, 70″–48″ by North Eastern Marine Engineering
Co Ltd, Newcastle. 396 nhp, 12 K.
1907　September, completed.
1911　18 March, departed from New York, inaugurating Elder
　　　Dempster's service USA–West Africa. This was under
　　　the direction of Mr C. W. Cook, later Traffic Manager
　　　of Elder Dempster Lines (who died in 1956, aged 82).
1912　May, transferred to Imperial Direct Line Ltd. 2815 n,
　　　4348 g.
1929　December, sold to I. C. Pateras & Co, Chios, Greece
　　　(Rethmuis & Kulundis Ltd, Managers). Renamed
　　　HARALAMPOS P. Registered Syra.
1932　Sold for demolition in Spain.

BENDU

BENIN

183   BADAGRI

O.N. 124056   1907–1918

'Badagri' class
Steel screw steamer, two decks and shelter deck
325.0′×46.0′×22.8′   1825 n   2952 g
Built by Tyne Iron & Shipbuilding Co Ltd, Newcastle, Yard
No 163, for Elder, Dempster & Co. Registered Liverpool. T
3 cyl 24″, 40″, 66″–45″ by J. Dickenson & Sons Ltd, Sunderland.
311 nhp, 10 K.

1907   28 February, launched by Mrs Brunton.
1909   Transferred to Elder Line Ltd.
1918   13 July, sunk 425 miles west-north-west of Cape St
       Vincent by U91 (Kapitänleutnant Alfred von Glasen-
       app) in a submerged torpedo attack. The **BADAGRI**
       was bound from Liverpool to Sierra Leone with 5000
       tons of piece goods, 370 tons of munitions and £25,000
       in gold, silver and other coins. Her Chief Officer was
       taken prisoner by the U-boat.

U91 survived the war and surrendered at Harwich on 27
November 1918 in accordance with the peace treaty. She was
later removed to a French port.
Ships of the 'Badagri' class: BADAGRI (183), ABONEMA
(184), PALMA (185).
Badagri is the name of an old slave port 50 miles on a creek of
the same name to the west of Lagos lagoon.

ABONEMA

184   ABONEMA/SAPELE (II)

O.N. 124076   1907–1929

'Badagri' class
Steel screw steamer, two decks and shelter deck
324.7′×45.9′×22.7   1865 n   2982 g
Built by Irvine's Shipbuilding & Drydock Co Ltd, West Hartlepool, Yard No 157, for Sir Alfred Lewis Jones, KCMG (Elder,
Dempster & Co, Managers). Registered Liverpool. T 3 cyl 24″,
40″, 66″–45″ by Richardson Westgarth & Co Ltd, South Shields.
311 nhp, 10 K.

1907   25 May, launched. July, completed.

1909   Transferred to British & African Steam Navigation Co
       Ltd.
1917   2600 n, 3969 g.
1920   25 October, renamed **SAPELE**. Registered Liverpool.
1929   August, sold to Weigel Bohnen & Cia Ltda, SA, Com-
       mercial Buenos Aires. Renamed **SAN JORGE**.
       Registered Buenos Aires. Converted to oil fuel.
1933   Sold to Delgardo & Cia, Buenos Aires.
1935   Sold to Cia Argentina de Navegacion Mihanovich Ltda,
       Buenos Aires. Renamed **SANTA CATHARINA**.
       2224 n, 3903 g.
1941   sold to Bowaters Newfoundland Pulp & Paper Mills
       Ltd. Renamed **KITTY'S BROOK**. Registered St
       John's, Newfoundland (British flag). 2973 n, 4031 g.
1942   9 May, 0310 hours torpedoed and sunk by U588
       (Kapitanleutnant Victor Vogel) in position 42°.56′N
       63°.59′W, voyage Newfoundland to Argentina. Nine
       lives lost.
1942   31 July, U588 sunk by HMCS ST EEMA.

Abonema is a minor port in the Niger Delta, 28 miles to the
west of Port Harcourt through the creeks.

SAPELE, *formerly* **ABONEMA**

PALMA

185 PALMA
O.N. 124080   1907–1930

'Badagri' class
Steel screw steamer, two decks and shelter deck
325.0′×45.9′×22.7′   1864 n   2981 g
Built by Irvine's Shipbuilding & Dry Docks Co Ltd, West
Hartlepool, Yard No 160, for Elder, Dempster & Co. Registered
Liverpool. T 3 cyl 24″, 39″, 66″–45″ by Richardson, Westgarth
& Co Ltd, West Hartlepool. 310 nhp, 10 K.
1907   August, completed.
1909   February, transferred to British & African Steam Navi-
        gation Co Ltd.
1928   2 May, (Captain F. Clegg) stranded at Outer Tom Shot
        Buoy, Calabar River, fouled anchor caused hull damage.
        Refloated with assistance from Branch vessels.
1930   January, sold to T. Fonaris, Syra, (Rithymnis & Kulu-
        kundis Ltd, London, Managers). Renamed **FONARIS**.
        Registered Syra.
1931   July, sold for demolition at Savona.
Palma was a beach village east of Lagos.

186 SALAGA (I)
O.N. 124035   1907–1930

'Salaga' class
Steel screw steamer, two decks and shelter deck
380.5′×50.3′×22.4′   2394 n   3879 g
Built by Workman Clark & Co Ltd, Belfast, Yard No 238, for

SALAGA

Elder, Dempster & Co. Registered Liverpool. T 3 cyl 26″, 44″,
74″–48″ by the builders. 379 nhp, 13 K.
Passenger accommodation: 30 first class.
1907   17 February, trials.
1910   6 May, collided with cutter SALLY half mile north of
        Cape Sierra Leone lighthouse.
1911   Transferred to Imperial Direct Line Ltd. 3285n, 5134g
1930   21 June, sold for demolition in Italy.
Ships of the 'Salaga' class: SALAGA (186), GANDO (187).
Salaga is in Ashanti, Ghana, 60 miles south of Tamele.

187 GANDO
O.N. 124047   1907–1917

'Salaga' class
Steel screw steamer, two decks and shelter deck
380.5′×50.3′×22.4′   2393 n   3809 g
Built by Workman Clark & Co Ltd, Belfast, Yard No 239, for
Elder, Dempster & Co. Registered Liverpool. T 3 cyl 26″, 44″,
74″–48″ by the builders. 379 nhp, 13 K.
Passenger accommodation: 30 first class.
1907   12 March, trials.
1911   February, transferred to African Steamship Co.
1914   August, requisitioned for military duties. 2451 n, 3895 g.
1916   Returned to owners' commercial service.
1917   24 January, on passage from New York, wrecked on
        Bruni Rock, Sinoe, Kroo Coast, Liberia.
Gando is a Northern Nigerian town situated about 55 miles
south-west of Sokoto.

GANDO

188 NIGER (III)
O.N. 124106   1908–1916

'Niger' class
Steel twin screw steamer, one deck
225.0′×36.1′×13.2′   606 n   980 g
Built by D. J. Dunlop & Co, Port Glasgow, Yard No 264, for
African Steamship Co. Registered Liverpool. 2×T 3 cyl 13″,
21″, 34″–24″ by the builders. 114 nhp, 9½ K.
Passenger accommodation: four cabins off saloon under poop.
Designed for West African coastal service.
1907   5 December, launched.
1908   January, completed.
1916   2 August, wrecked at Grove Point, 11 miles east of Accra
        while operating on the Lagos–Gold Coast service.
Ships of the 'Niger' class: NIGER (188), BARO (189),
LOKOJA (190), UROMI (191), BIDA (192).

BARO, *subsequently renamed* **ILORIN**

189 BARO (I)/ILORIN (II)
O.N. 127905   1908–1933

'Niger' class
Steel twin screw steamer, one deck
225.0′×36.2′×13.1′   551 n   957 g
Built by W. Harkess & Son Ltd, Middlesbrough for Elder, Dempster & Co, Yard No 174. Registered Liverpool. 2×T 3 cyl 13″, 21″, 34″–24″ by MacColl & Pollock Ltd, Sunderland. 132 nhp, 10 K.
Passenger accommodation: four cabins off saloon under poop.
1908   23 March, trials. June, transferred to British & African Steam Navigation Co Ltd.
1919   29 December, renamed **ILORIN**.
1932   Laid up in Badagri Creek.
1933   3 May, dismantled and scuttled off Lagos.
Baro is a town on the river Niger, 65 miles above Lokoja.

190 LOKOJA (III)
O.N. 127903   1908–1934

'Niger' class
Steel twin screw steamer, one deck
225.0′×36.1′×13.2′   576 n   981 g
Built by D. J. Dunlop & Co, Port Glasgow, Yard No 265, for Elder, Dempster & Co. Registered Liverpool. 2×T 3 cyl 13″, 21″, 34″–24″ by the builders. 114 nhp, 9½ K.
1908   May, completed. June, transferred to British & African Steam Navigation Co Ltd.
1909   23 August, assisted in refloating *BOULAMA* at Forcados.
1911   5 May, stranded on Lighthouse Beach, refloated without damage (Captain J. A. J. Williams).
1932   April, laid up at White House Wharf, Apapa.
1933   Transferred to Elder Dempster Lines Ltd.
1934   5 September, dismantled and scuttled off Lagos.

191 UROMI
O.N. 127978   1909–1936

'Niger' class
Steel twin screw steamer, one deck
225.0′×36.2′×13.1   556 n   962 g
Built by W. Harkess & Son Ltd, Middlesbrough, Yard No 177, for Elder, Dempster & Co. Registered Liverpool. 2×T 3 cyl 13″, 21″, 34″–24″ by MacColl & Pollock Ltd, Sunderland. 133 nhp, 10 K.
Passenger accommodation: 8.

1909   Completed May. Trial speed 11¼ K.
1922   July, transferred to Cie Belge Maritime Belge du Congo (Agence Maritime Internationale, SA, Managers). Renamed **KINSHASA**. Registered Antwerp 618 n, 941 g.
1925   November, transferred to African Steamship Co. Renamed **UROMI**. Registered Liverpool. 556 n, 969 g.
1933   Transferred to Elder Dempster Lines Ltd.
1936   22 April, dismantled and scuttled outside Lagos.
During her later years **UROMI** was engaged in transporting coal from Port Harcourt to Takoradi.
Kinshasa was the original and is the present name of Leopoldville, Zaire. Uromi is a town 55 miles north-east of Benin City, Nigeria.

UROMI

192 BIDA (II)/IBADAN (II)
O.N. 127915   1908–1932

'Niger' class
Steel twin screw steamer, one deck
225.0′×36.2′×13.1′   554 n   963 g
Built by W. Harkess & Son Ltd, Middlesbrough, Yard No 176, for African Steamship Co. Registered Liverpool. 2×T 3 cyl 13″, 21″, 34″–24″ by MacColl & Pollock Ltd, Sunderland. 133 nhp, 10 K.
Passenger accommodation: 8.
1908   13 June, launched by Mrs Weatherhead. 16 July, trials. 25 August, aground at Aboh Crossing.
1920   April, renamed **IBADAN**.
1932   Laid up in Badagry Creek, Lagos. 2 November, scuttled off Lagos after stripping.

193 JAMAICA
O.N. 127063   1908–1912

Steel screw steamer, two decks
220.0′×34.0′×14.9′   602 n   1138 g
Built by W. Harkess & Son Ltd, Middlesbrough, Yard No 175, for Elder Line Ltd. Registered Bristol. T 3 cyl 18″, 29″, 48″–33″ by MacColl & Pollock Ltd, Sunderland. 171 nhp, 12 K.
Passenger accommodation: 44 first class amidships, 20 second class poop.
1908   11 August, launched. October, completed.
1912   Sold to Royal Mail Steam Packet Co.
1914   Sold to Pacific Steam Navigation Co. Registered Liverpool.
1929   Sold to Soc Industrial del Aysen. Renamed **COYHAIQUE**. Registered Valparaiso. 647 n, 1099 g.
1942   January, wrecked off Puerto Aysen.
Jamaica is a West Indies island.

JAMAICA

T 3 cyl 26″, 42″, 70″–48″ by Richardsons Westgarth & Co Ltd, Middlesbrough. 339 nhp, 10½ K.
Passenger accommodation: 12.
1910 16 March, trials.
1911 April, transferred to Imperial Direct West India Mail Line Ltd.
1923 May, sold to St Mary Steamship Co Ltd (Williams Bros, Managers), Cardiff. Renamed **DEANSWAY**. Registered Cardiff.
1931 Managers Pardo Williams & Co, Cardiff.
1932 June, sold for £1800 for demolition at Dunston-on-Tyne.
River Kaduna is a tributary of the Niger. A township of the name stands on the river and is a railway junction 561 miles from Lagos at 1,961 feet altitude.

194 KONAKRY
O.N. 127929   1908–1918

Steel screw steamer, one deck and shelter deck,
self trimming top side tanks
360.3′×52.3′×25.9′ 2331 n 4406 g
Built by Sir Raylton Dixon & Co Ltd, Middlesbrough, Yard No 538, for British & African Steam Navigation Co Ltd. Registered Liverpool. T 3 cyl 26″, 42″, 70″–48″ by North Eastern Marine Engineering Co Ltd, Sunderland. 339 nhp, 10½ K.
Passenger accommodation: 12.
1908 30 July, launched by Mrs Roxburgh. 23 September, trials.
1916 Operated by H.M. Government as fleet oiler. 4255 n, 5743 g.
1918 1st December, in collision with ORDUNA (15,499 g, built 1914), 16 miles off Galley Head, County Cork. Beached at Garrettstown, later declared a constructive total loss.
Konakry is a port in Guinea.

KADUNA

196 KWARRA (II)
O.N. 128047   1910–1924

Steel screw steamer, one deck and shelter deck, cantilever framed, self trimming tanks
360.0′×52.0′×26.1′ 2304 n 4441 g
Built by Sir Raylton Dixon & Co Ltd, Middlesbrough, Yard No 548, for Elder Dempster & Co. Registered Liverpool. T 3 cyl 26″, 42″, 70″–48″ by North Eastern Marine Engineering Co Ltd. 428 nhp, 10½ K.
Passenger accommodation: 12.
1910 30 May, launched.
1911 2 January, returned to Tyneside for examination after grounding in the Pentland Firth when proceeding to USA. May, transferred to Imperial Direct Line Ltd.
1916 Operated as East African military transport. Later taken over by Government under Liner Requisition Scheme.
1917 January, 3220 n, 5816 g. 19 May, chased by German submarine in Atlantic, saved by gun fire.

KONAKRY

195 KADUNA (I)
O.N. 128029   1910–1923

Steel screw steamer, two decks and shelter deck,
self trimming top side tanks
360.1′×52.0′×26.2′ 2308 n 4455 g
Built by Sir Raylton Dixon & Co Ltd, Middlesbrough, Yard No 547, for Elder Dempster & Co. Registered Liverpool.

KWARRA

1924 January, sold to St Mary Steamship Co Ltd. Renamed **BROOKWAY**. Registered Cardiff. 2225 n, 4426 g.

1926 Sold to Charter Shipping Co Ltd., Cardiff. Renamed **CHARTERHOUSE**. Registered Cardiff.

1932 April, sold for demolition.

1933 Broken up at Port Glasgow.

197 SHONGA (I)
O.N. 127994   1909–1928

'Shonga' class
Steel screw steamer, two decks and shelter deck
340.1'×46.0'×23.0'   1911 n   3044 g
Built by Irvines Shipbuilding & Dry Docks Co Ltd, West Hartlepool, Yard No 170, for Elder, Dempster & Co. Registered Liverpool. T 3 cyl 25", 40", 67"–45" by Richardson, Westgarth & Co Ltd. 335 nhp, 11 K. Fitted with ten 5-ton derricks and two 15-ton derricks

1909 Launched 19 July by Mrs Antrobus (wife of Senior Crown Agent). Trials 4 September.

1910 October, transferred to Elder Line Ltd.

1915 December, transferred to African Steamship Co.

1918 20 December, when in position 36°.04'N 63°34'W low pressure eccentric rod fractured. One man killed.

1920 December, grounded off east coast of Ireland.

1928 17 February, wrecked two miles north of Ymuiden, voyage West Africa to Amsterdam and Hamburg.

Ships of the 'Shonga' class: SHONGA (197), WINNEBA (198), BASSAM (199).

Shonga is a town in Nigeria.

198 WINNEBA (I)
O.N. 128002   1909–1913

'Shonga' class
Steel screw steamer
340.1'×46.0'×23.0'   1908 n   3040 g
Built by Irvines Shipbuilding & Dry Docks Co Ltd, Yard No 171, for Elder, Dempster & Co. Registered Liverpool. T 3 cyl 25", 40", 67"–45" by Richardson, Westgarth & Co Ltd, Hartlepool. 335 nhp, 11 K. Fitted with ten 5-ton derricks and two 15-ton derricks.

1909 2 September, launched by Mrs Furness. 18 October, trials.

SHONGA (Photo Ship society of South Africa, Leendertz Collection)

1910 May, transferred to British & African Steam Navigation Co Ltd.

1913 26 July, wrecked on Basha Point Rock, Ivory Coast, voyage West Africa to Hamburg.

Winneba is a surf port in Ghana, West of Accra.

199 BASSAM/SULIMA (I)
O.N. 128006   1909–1927

'Shonga' class
Steel screw steamer, two decks and shelter deck
340.3'×46.0×23.0'   1909 n   3040 g
Built by Irvines' Shipbuilding & Dry Docks Co Ltd, West Hartlepool, Yard No 313, for Elder, Dempster & Co. Registered Liverpool. T 3 cyl 25", 40", 67"–45" by Richardson Westgarth & Co Ltd, Hartlepool. 335 nhp, 11 K.
Passenger accommodation: limited.

1909 14 October, launched. 13 November, trials.

SHONGA in the Elbe, 1927

1910 May, transferred to British & African Steam Navigation Co Ltd.
1921 8 January, renamed **SULIMA** to release name for 'B' boat.
1927 October, sold for £10,000 to A. & P. Scitto, Fils & Co, Oran. Renamed **GEORGES ET HENRI**. Registered Oran.
1934 Registered Marseilles.
1937 Sold to Compagnia Genovese de Navigazione a Vapore, SA, Genoa. Renamed **CAPO MELE**. Registered Genoa. 1848 n, 3058 g.
1949 Sold to Sukru Yakup Uzner, Istanbul. Renamed **KAPTAN YAKUP**. Registered Istanbul. 1888 n, 3060 g.

BASSAM

1953 Sold to Fuad Akbasoglu, Istanbul. Renamed **CAYIRKOY**. Registered Istanbul.
1960 May, broken up in Turkey at Penner by owners.
Bassam is a port on the Ivory Coast of West Africa.
Sulima is a town in Sierra Leone.

200 HARTLEY
O.N. 118616   1909–1917
Steel screw steamer, one deck and well deck, engines aft
229.0'×33.5'×14.7'   725 n   1150 g
Built by Wood Skinner & Co Ltd, Newcastle, Yard No 114, for Burnett Steamship Co, Newcastle. Registered Newcastle.
T 3 cyl 18½", 30", 49"–33" by North Eastern Marine Engineering Co Ltd, Newcastle. 151 nhp.
1903 August, completed.
1906 12 April, collided with GEORGETTE (Worms Line) in Grimsby Roads.
1909 Chartered for service at Forcados. Returned to UK in December.
1910 May, purchased by British & African Steam Navigation Co Ltd. Returned to Lagos Branch Service.
1917 9 July, attacked by seaplane in North Sea, torpedo missed.
1918 26 January, sunk two miles north-east from Skinningrove by UB34 (Oberleutnant zur See Helmuth Ruckteschell) in a submerged torpedo attack, voyage Boulogne to Tyne in ballast. No lives lost.
UB34 survived the war and, then under the command of Leutnant zur See der Reserve Hans Illing, surrendered at Harwich on 27 November, 1918 in accordance with the peace treaty. In 1919 she was sold to G. Cohen, Sons & Co for scrap. Von Ruckteschell assumed command of U54 after leaving UB34 and survived the war to command the surface raiders WIDDER and MICHEL in 1939–1942.
Hartley is a mining village between Whitly Bay and Blyth. A traditional name of the Burnett Steamship Co.

SIR GEORGE

201 SIR GEORGE
O.N. 129012   1909–1935
Steel twin screw steamer, two decks and shelter deck
240.0'×38.1'×14.1'   733 n   1254 g
Built by D. J. Dunlop & Co, Port Glasgow, Yard No 267, for Niger Co Ltd. Registered London. 2×T 3 cyl 13", 21", 34"–24" by the builders. 113 nhp.
1909 Completed.
1911 Purchased by African Steamship Co for Branch Service.
1933 April, transferred to Elder Dempster Lines Ltd. Registered Liverpool.
1935 21 June, dismantled and scuttled off Lagos.
Named after Sir George Goldie (1845–1925), who as Captain Goldie-Taubman, formed the United African Company in 1879 by the amalgamation of four British firms. The United African Co became National African Co in 1882 and then the Royal Niger Co in 1886.

202 TAMELE (I)
O.N. 128032   1910–1917
'Tamele' class
Steel screw steamer, two decks and shelter deck
360.1'×50.2'×22.7'   2420 n   3924 g
Built by Irvine's Shipbuilding & Dry Docks Co Ltd, Hartlepool, Yard No 487, for Elder, Dempster & Co. Registered Liverpool. T 3 cyl 25", 40", 68"–48" by Richardson, Westgarth & Co Ltd, Hartlepool. 370 nhp, 11½ K.
1910 26 January, launched (without ceremony owing to the death of Sir Alfred Jones). October, transferred to British & African Steam Navigation Co Ltd.
1917 2422 n, 3932 g. 16 July, (Captain T. H. Beard) sunk. 65 miles west by south from the Fastnet by U87 (Kapitänleutnant Rudolf Schneider) in a submerged torpedo attack, voyage West Africa to Liverpool, with passengers and West African produce, with the loss of one life. When off the south-west coast of Ireland at 0545 a submarine was sighted which discharged a torpedo, but by a skilful manoeuvre of **TAMELE**, it missed and passed harmlessly 30 feet astern. The submarine then appeared right astern at 0605 and opened fire at a distance of about 1000 yards. **TAMELE**, which was hit seven times, none being dangerous, replied with 20 rounds, all of which fell short. Immediately the submarine had been sighted, wireless messages were sent out for assistance, and at this point in the combat a destroyer appeared on the scene. The submarine hurriedly submerged, and the liner continued on her way. The whole day passed uneventfully, but at 2040 without

the slightest warning **TAMELE** suddenly shook from stem to stern; she had been hit by a torpedo right amidships, wrecking the engine-room. In order to stop the engines 4th Engineer A. J. Brian, climbed down the telegraph stanchions, as the ladders had been blown away, while the engine-room had been flooded through the gaping hole rent in the ship's side. The discipline of the men was excellent, and out of a crew of 59 only one man lost his life. For their services on this occasion Captain Beard received the Distinguished Service Cross and the Distinguished Conduct Medal was awarded to Mr A. J. Brian.

U87, then under the command of Kapitänleutnant Freiherr Rudolf von Speth-Schülzburg, was sunk with all hands by HMS P56 in 52°.56′N 05°.07′W on 25 December 1917. P56 forced the U-boat, which was at periscope depth, to the surface by attacking with depth-charges and then gunned and rammed her. On 13 October 1917 Schneider had been washed overboard from U87 in heavy seas in the central North Atlantic. Although picked up he failed to respond to efforts at resuscitation.

Ships of the 'Tamele' class: TAMELE (202), AKASSA (203), ONITSHA (204).

Tamele is a town in the northern territories of the former Gold Coast.

AKASSA

TAMELE

203 AKASSA (II)
O.N. 131275   1910–1917

'Tamele' class
Steel screw steamer, two decks and shelter deck
360.2′×50.1×22.7′   2420 n   3919 g
Built by Irvine's Shipbuilding & Dry Docks Co Ltd, West Hartlepool, Yard No 489, for Elder Line Ltd. Registered Liverpool. T 3 cyl 25″, 40″, 60″–48″ by Richardson, Westgarth & Co Ltd, Hartlepool. 370 nhp, 11 K.
Passenger accommodation: 30.

1910 9 May, launched. 7 July, trials, speed 13 K.
1917 13 August (Captain T. H. Beard), sunk eight miles south-east from Galley Head by UC33 (Oberleutnant zur See Alfred Arnold) in a submerged torpedo attack, voyage Liverpool to West Africa, with passengers and general cargo. Nine lives lost.

UC33 was sunk on 26 September 1917 by HMS P61 in 51°.55′N 06°.14′W, shortly after it had torpedoed the ss SAN ZEFERINO, which was being escorted by P61. There were only two survivors from the U-boat, one of whom was the captain.

ONITSHA

204 ONITSHA (I)
O.N. 128048   1910–1932

'Tamele' class
Steel screw steamer, two decks and shelter deck
360.2′×50.1′×22.7′   2422 n   3921 g
Built by Irvine's Shipbuilding & Dry Docks Co Ltd, West
Hartlepool, Yard No 488, for Elder, Dempster & Co. Registered
Liverpool. T 3 cyl 25″, 40″, 68″–48″ by Richardson, Westgarth
& Co Ltd, Hartlepool, 370 nhp, 11 K.
Passenger accommodation: 30.

1910   15 March, launched (without ceremony owing to the
death of Sir Alfred Jones). May, transferred to British
& African Steam Navigation Co Ltd on completion. 2
June, trials, speed 12 K.
1917   8 July, attacked by submarine off west of Ireland, torpedo
missed.
1932   27 January, sold for £2600 for demolition at Haverton-
on-Tees.

See also *OBUASI (I)* for details of 8 July 1917 action.
Onitsha is an important township on the east bank of the River
Niger 201 miles upstream from Forcados.

*ONITSHA laid up on 25 May 1920. **BURUTU** and
JEBBA also visible*

205 BENGUELA (II)
O.N. 131366   1910–1930

Steel screw steamer, two decks
425.5′×53.0′×29.2′   3534 n   5520 g
Built by Swan Hunter & Wigham Richardson Ltd, Newcastle,
Yard No 789, for Imperial Direct Line Ltd. Registered Liver-
pool. T 3 cyl 28″, 46″, 77″–54″ by Wallsend Slipway Co Ltd,
Newcastle. 566 nhp, 14 K.

1910   Completed July.
1914–1917   Transported South African troops to France and
later employed as food carrier and collier.
1917   17 April, attacked by submarine off west coast of Ireland,
torpedo missed. 16 July, attacked by submarine off
north-west Ireland. A torpedo missed and gun battle
ensued from 1130 until 1900. This is the longest action
on record between a merchantman and a German submarine. The U boat, damaged by gunfire, was unable
to submerge and later taken in tow of an RN destroyer.
Captain W. Purdon was awarded the Distinguished
Service Cross.
1930   15 April, laid up in the River Dart.
1933   27 May, sold for £4200 to Italian interests. September,
sold for demolition.

206 FULANI (II)/ELMINA (III)
O.N. 129183   1910–1928

'Falaba' class
Steel screw steamer, two decks and shelter deck
380.4′×47.7′×22.9′   2997 n   4792 g
Built by Alexander Stephen & Sons Ltd, Glasgow, Yard No
413, as **FULANI** for African Steamship Co. Transferred to Cie
Maritime Belge du Congo and renamed **ALBERTVILLE** prior
to completion. Registered Antwerp. T 3 cyl 29″, 46″, 77″–51″ by
the builders. 424 nhp, 14 K.
Passenger accommodation: 138 first class, 72 second.

BENGUELA

Elder Dempster and Co. Limited

PLAN OF PASSENGER ACCOMMODATION
OF THE
S.S. "ONITSHA"

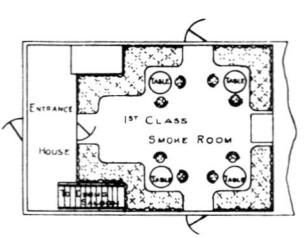

UPPER BERTH, A
LOWER BERTH, B
SOFA BERTH, C
ELECTRIC LIGHT.
HOT & COLD BATHS, ETC|

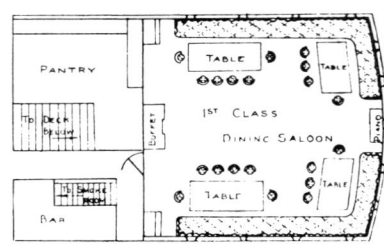

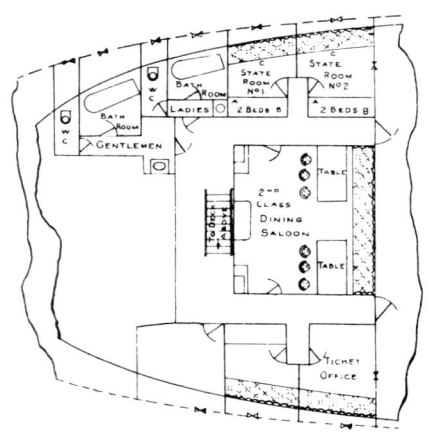

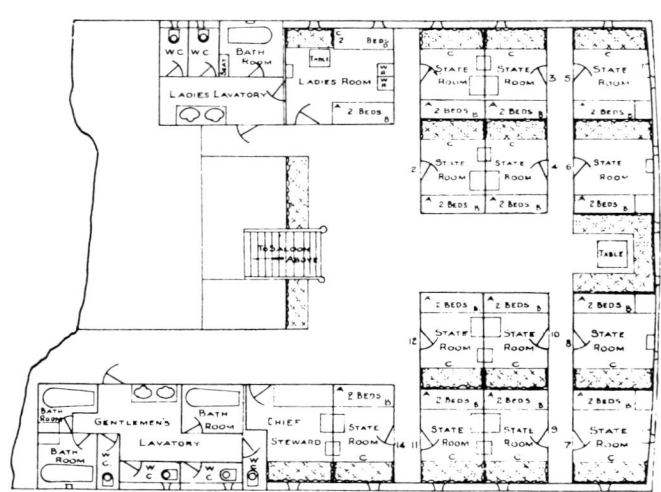

S.S. "ELMINA"

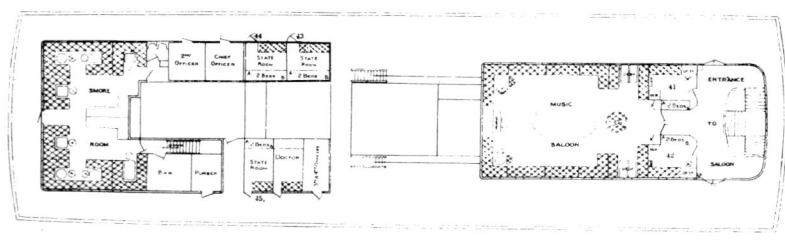

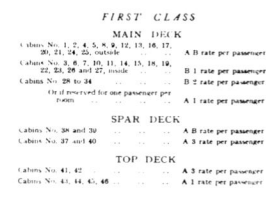

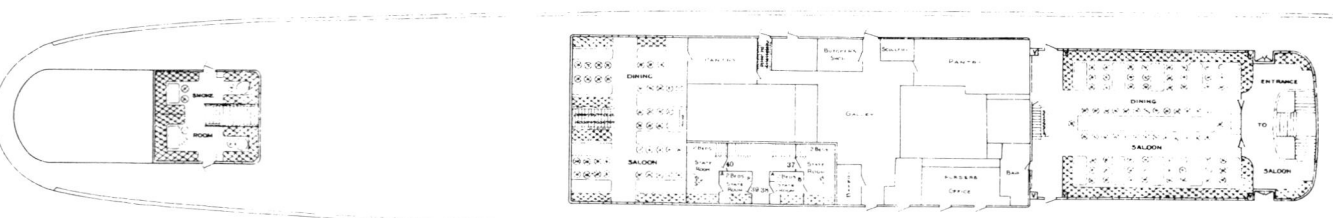

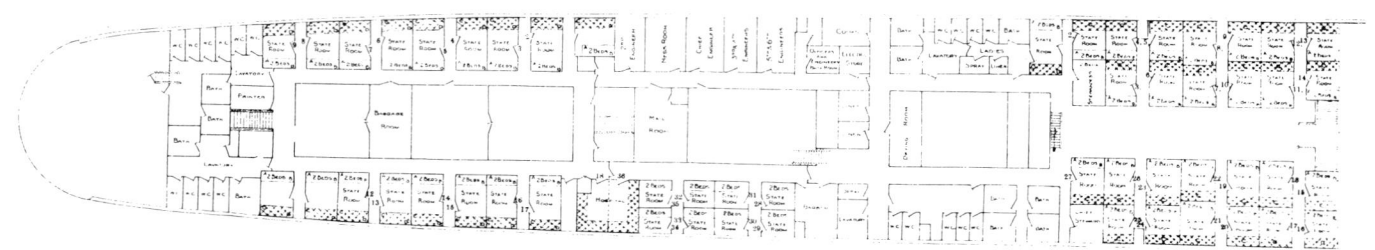

132

ELMINA

1906 Completed. Trial speed 15½ K.
1910 Acquired by African Steamship Co. Renamed **ELMINA**. Registered London.
1928 Sold for £20,000 to Mrs M. Vardy, London. Renamed **IPHIGENIA**. Registered London.
1932 P. G. Callimanopulos, Piraeus, appointed manager.
1933 Sold to Fenton SS Co, London. Renamed **CAIRO CITY**. Registered London.
1940 Used as blockship at Port Tewfick.
1946 Laid up in the Blackwater River.
1949 Sold for demolition. 24 September, whilst under tow fouled the Cross Sands Lightship. 27 September, arrived Blyth for demolition by Hughes, Bolckow Ltd.

Ships of the 'Falaba' class: FALABA (180), ELMINA (206).

Another view of **ELMINA**

207 VIERA Y CLAVIJO (II)
O.N. Not allocated   1912–1930

'Viera y Clavijo' class
Steel screw steamer, one deck and shelter deck
210.2′×30.0′×9.9′   501 n   862 g
Built by Caledon Shipbuilding & Engineering Co Ltd, Dundee, Yard No 224, for Cia de Vapores Correos Interinsulares Canarios. Registered Las Palmas. T 3 cyl 16½″, 27″, 44″–28″ by the builders. 139 nhp, 11 K.
Passenger accommodation: 176.

1912 Completed February.
1930 Sold to Cia Trasmediterranea, Las Palmas.
1945 505 n, 880 g.
1956 March, fitted to burn oil fuel.
1978 Sold to B. van der Marel BV, Nieukerk. Renamed **JOMAR** and deleted from Lloyd's Register as non-sea-going. Subsequently reverted to original name.
1984 Reported moved to Zierikzee, Rotterdam, for preservation.

Ships of the 'Viera y Clavijo' class: VIERA Y CLAVIJO (207), LEON Y CASTILLO (208), LA PALMA (209).

208 LEON Y CASTILLO (II)
O.N. Not allocated   1912–1930

'Viera y Clavijo' class
Steel screw steamer, one deck and shelter deck
210.0′×30.0′×10.2′   486 n   871 g
Built by W. Harkess & Son Ltd, Middlesbrough, Yard No 191, for Cia de Vapores Correos Interinsulares Canarios. Registered Las Palmas. T 3 cyl 16½″, 27″, 44″–28″ by MacColl & Pollock Ltd, Sunderland. 140 nhp, 11 K.
Passenger accommodation: 190.

1912 March, completed; 9 March, sailed on maiden voyage to Puerto de la Luz, arriving 17 March.
Resume, Engineer's Log: total revolutions 1,030,460; revolutions per minute 98.7; total distance 1867; speed 10.7 knots; slip 10%; total coal used 111 tons; coal used per day, including auxiliaries 15 tons; navigation time 7 days, 6 hours, 26 minutes.
1930 Sold to Cia Trasmediterranea, Las Palmas. Registered Santa Cruz.
1952 August, fitted to burn oil fuel.
1981 Sold to Martin Juan Arkey, shipbreaker. October, broken up at Las Palmas.

209 LA PALMA
O.N. Not allocated   1912–1930

'Viera y Clavijo' class
Steel screw steamer, one deck and shelter deck
210.0′×30.0′×10.2′   468 n   871 g
Built by W. Harkess & Son Ltd, Middlesbrough, Yard No 192, for Cia de Vapores Correos Interinsulares Canarios, Las

Two studies of Canary Isles inter island ships, with **LEON Y CASTILLO** *above, and* **PALMA**, *below, alongside the Las Palmas Marina in the 1980s*

Palmas. Registered Santa Cruz. T 3 cyl 16½", 27", 44"–28" by MacColl & Pollock Ltd, Sunderland. 140 nhp, 11 K.
Passenger accommodation: 190.
1912 April, completed. 10 April, sailed Middlesbrough on maiden voyage. 16 April, sailed Bremen. 24 April, arrived Las Palmas.
1930 Sold to Cia Trasmediterranea, Barcelona.
1935 April, 513 n, 894 g.
1951 February, fitted to burn oil fuel, 523 n, 894 g.
1972 514 n, 894 g.
1976 24 September, reported laid up at Las Palmas. 12 November, sold to Mrs H. Flick.
1979 Reported still laid up at Las Palmas and deteriorating.
1982 2 February, reported still laid up. 22 December, reported moored at a marina in Las Palmas for possible use as a floating yacht club.
La Palma is a port in Grand Canary.

210 LANZAROTE
O.N. Not allocated   1912–1932
'Lanzarote' class
Steel screw steamer, one deck and shelter deck
160.0'×25.9'×10.4'   189 n   475 g
Built by Smith's Dock Co Ltd, Middlesbrough, Yard No 500, for Cia de Vapores Correos Interinsulares Canarios, Las Palmas. Registered Las Palmas. T 3 cyl 13", 22", 36"–26" by the builders. 100 nhp, 10 K.
1912 Completed March.
1932 Sold to Cia Trasmediterranea, Barcelona.
1967 Reported demolition by Aguilar y Peres commenced December at Valencia.
Ships of the 'Lanzarote' class: LANZAROTE (210), GOMERA HIERRA (211), FUERTEVENTURA (212).
Lanzarote is an island of the Grand Canary.

211 GOMERA HIERRA
O.N. Not allocated   1912–1932
'Lanzarote' class
Steel screw steamer, one deck and shelter deck
160.3'×26.0'×10.3'   237 n   447 g
Built by Caledon Shipbuilding & Engineering Co Ltd, Dundee, Yard No 225, for Cia de Vapores Correos Interinsulares Canarios, Las Palmas. Registered Las Palmas. T 3 cyl 13", 21½", 35"–27" by the builders. 100 nhp, 10 K.
1912 March, completed. 8 March, sailed Dundee on maiden voyage. 16 March, arrived Las Palmas.
1932 Sold to Cia Trasmediterranea, Barcelona. Renamed **GOMERA**. Registered Las Palmas.
1965 September, demolition commenced by J. Castillo, Barcelona.

212 FUERTEVENTURA
O.N. Not allocated   1912–1932
'Lanzarote' class
Steel screw steamer, one deck and shelter deck
160.0'×25.9'×10.4'   187 n   478 g
Built by Smith's Dock Co. Ltd, Middlesbrough, Yard No 501, for Cia de Vapores Correos Interinsulares Canarios, Las Palmas. Registered Santa Cruz. T 3 cyl 13", 22", 36"–26" by the builders. 100 nhp, 10 K.
1912 April, completed and departed South Shields for Las Palmas via Dover, arriving Las Palmas 24 April.

1932 Sold to Cia Trasmediterranea, Barcelona.
1934 Registered Las Palmas.
1952 September, 272 n, 574 g.
1967 Passenger accommodation: 38.
1968 Sold for demolition at Valencia. July, work by Aguilar y Peris commenced.

ABOSSO

213 ABOSSO (I)
O.N. 135176   1912–1917
'Abosso' class
Steel twin screw steamer, two decks and awning deck
425.6'×57.3'×31.4'   4762 n   7782 g
Built by Harland & Wolff Ltd, Belfast, Yard No 430, for African Steamship Co. Registered London. 2×Q 4 cyl 20½", 29½", 42", 61"–48" by the builders. 516 nhp, 14 K.
Passenger accommodation: 400 first and second class, including the first single passenger cabins in the Elder Dempster fleet.
1912 12 August, launched. 19 December, completed.
1913 8 January, maiden voyage Liverpool to West Africa.
1917 Departed Bathurst 14 April for Liverpool (Captain J. T. Toft), with 127 passengers and 134 crew, cargo mails and 3500 tons West African produce. At 2105 24 April, in position 57.10'N 14.58'W was torpedoed by U43 (Korvettenkapitan Helmuth Jurst), the torpedo striking the after part of the engine room and No 3 hold, U43 having shadowed **ABOSSO** for most of the day. Immediately the torpedo struck an SOS was sent, and **ABOSSO**, after listing briefly to port, recovered and took a pronounced list to starboard. Within a very short time everyone aboard was at his allotted station. Unfortunately, although the engines had been ordered to be stopped **ABOSSO** was still moving at some speed, but Nos 1, 3 and 7 boats, carrying 41 passengers and 23 crew, were launched in advance of any order being given by Captain Toft. Inevitably they were swamped on reaching the water with the loss of all aboard bar six. A RN destroyer arrived about an hour later and Captain Toft decided to risk launching the remaining boats although **ABOSSO**, listing heavily, was still moving in a circle. Their occupants, together with six survivors found clinging to No 1 lifeboat, were rescued by the destroyer, the final death toll being 65. U43, meanwhile crash-dived and made good her escape.
U43, then commanded by Kapitanleutnant J. Kirchner, surrendered at Harwich on 20 November 1918 and was sold to G. Cohen, Sons & Co for scrap and towed from Chatham on 20

May 1919. Jurst was transferred to the staff of Captain (U Boats) in May 1917 and ended the war as Navigating Officer of SMS DERFFLINGER.

Ships of the 'Abosso' class: ABOSSO (213), APPAM (214), APAPA (215).

Abosso is a town in Ghana, north of Tarkwa.

214 APPAM/MANDINGO (IV)
O.N. 135442   1912–1936

'Abosso' class
Steel twin screw steamer, two decks and awning deck
425.6'×57.3'×31.4' 4761 n 7781 g
Built by Harland & Wolff Ltd, Belfast, Yard No 431, for British & African Steam Navigation Ltd. Registered Liverpool. 2×Q 4 cyl 20½", 29½", 42", 61"–48" by the builders. 516 nhp, 14 K.
Passenger accommodation: 400 first and second class (later 250).

1912   10 October, launched.

1913   March, completed. Trials 16 knots. 12 March, commenced maiden voyage.

1916   11 January, sailed from Dakar for Liverpool with a large number of passengers including 40 Germans taken prisoner in the Cameroons. 15 January, in perfect weather, smoke was sighted on the horizon at about 1230 and a vessel gradually came into sight, apparently a tramp steamer in need of painting. By about 1500 she was 1200 yards off the port beam of **APPAM** when she hauled round and signalled 'Stop instantly'. It was assumed on the liner that she was in need of assistance and Captain Harrison instructed the Radio Officer to signal her. The signal was jammed, and the 'tramp' dropped her gun screens, unfurled her battle ensign and fired a shell across **APPAM**'s bows. It was the raider MOEWE (Kapitan Graf zu Dohna-Achlodien). The Germans sent a boarding party across, and seized the ships papers (Captain Harrison had thrown the code books overboard as soon as he realised what was going on). The Germans meanwhile took all **APPAM**'s officers back to the MOEWE except for the Purser, who was instructed by the senior German officer to reassure the passengers that they were in no danger. From MOEWE came the crews of six ships previously sunk by the raider. At about 1800 both vessels got under way, the erstwhile German prisoners aboard **APPAM** serving as guards. At midnight, after steaming westwards there was another delay while bedding and two passengers, Sir E. W. Merewether, Governor of Sierra Leone, and Mr F. S. James, CMG, were transferred to the raider. They were returned next morning, assured by the Commander of MOEWE that although he could not guarantee not to sink **APPAM** he did guarantee passengers and crew a safe landing. That evening (16 January) MOEWE sunk CLAN McTAVISH in a running battle, the survivors being taken aboard the British liner.

17 January, the ship, including mails and personal baggage, was thoroughly searched and a parole sheet was demanded with the names and full identity of all non-combatants on board. On the advice of Sir E. W. Merewether, after much deliberation, parole was given, some 143 mainly captured crews, but including 31 of **APPAM**'s passengers who were in HM Forces, were

transferred to MOEWE, and the raider then steamed away, leaving much relief but also high respect for the humanity of the German officers. **APPAM**, now under command of Leutnant Berg, duly equipped with scuttling charges, made for America at low speed, with all on board on limited rations, and avoiding other ships, arriving at Newport News on 1 February.

APPAM was interned by the United States authorities, and a lengthy legal battle ensued to regain her. In this the Elder Dempster New York agent Daniel Bacon played a crucial part, and his successful efforts were rewarded by the presentation of a silver model of the ship. The capture of **APPAM** was regarded by the Germans as a signal achievement, and Leutnant Berg's family subsequently added the name Appam to their own.

1917   Returned to owners. 20 August, renamed **MANDINGO** and renumbered O.N. 140664 in view of the strenuous German opposition.

1919   4 June, reverted to original name and Official Number: **APPAM**.

1933   May, transferred to Elder Dempster Lines Ltd.

1936   14 February, sold for £14,500 for demolition to Thos Ward & Co Ltd, and sailed from Liverpool 24 February for Milford Haven.

After the war MOEWE surrendered to HM Government and in July 1921 was owned by Elders & Fyffes and, as GREENBRIAR, was employed carrying West Indies bananas to Britain. Appam is an old surf port in Ghana, west of Winneba.

COMMUNION SET

The photograph shows the Communion Chalice, Paten and Wine Vessel presented to the passenger ship, R.M.S. *Appam* by M. E. L. Accra in 1921. The inscription on the base of the silver chalice reads "To the Glory of God and for use in His Service on board the R.M.S. *Appam*—M. E. L. Accra 1921".

The set was found recently when clearing the passenger filing room in the basement of India Buildings and was contained in a small black box inscribed, M.V. *Aba*. It is assumed that the set was transferred to *Aba* in 1936 when *Appam* was broken up after twenty-three years' service.

The set was presented on loan to the Mersey Missions to Seamen last September. The identity of "M. E. L. Accra" is not known and any readers having information as to the unknown donor are requested to contact the Editor of *Sea*.

APPAM

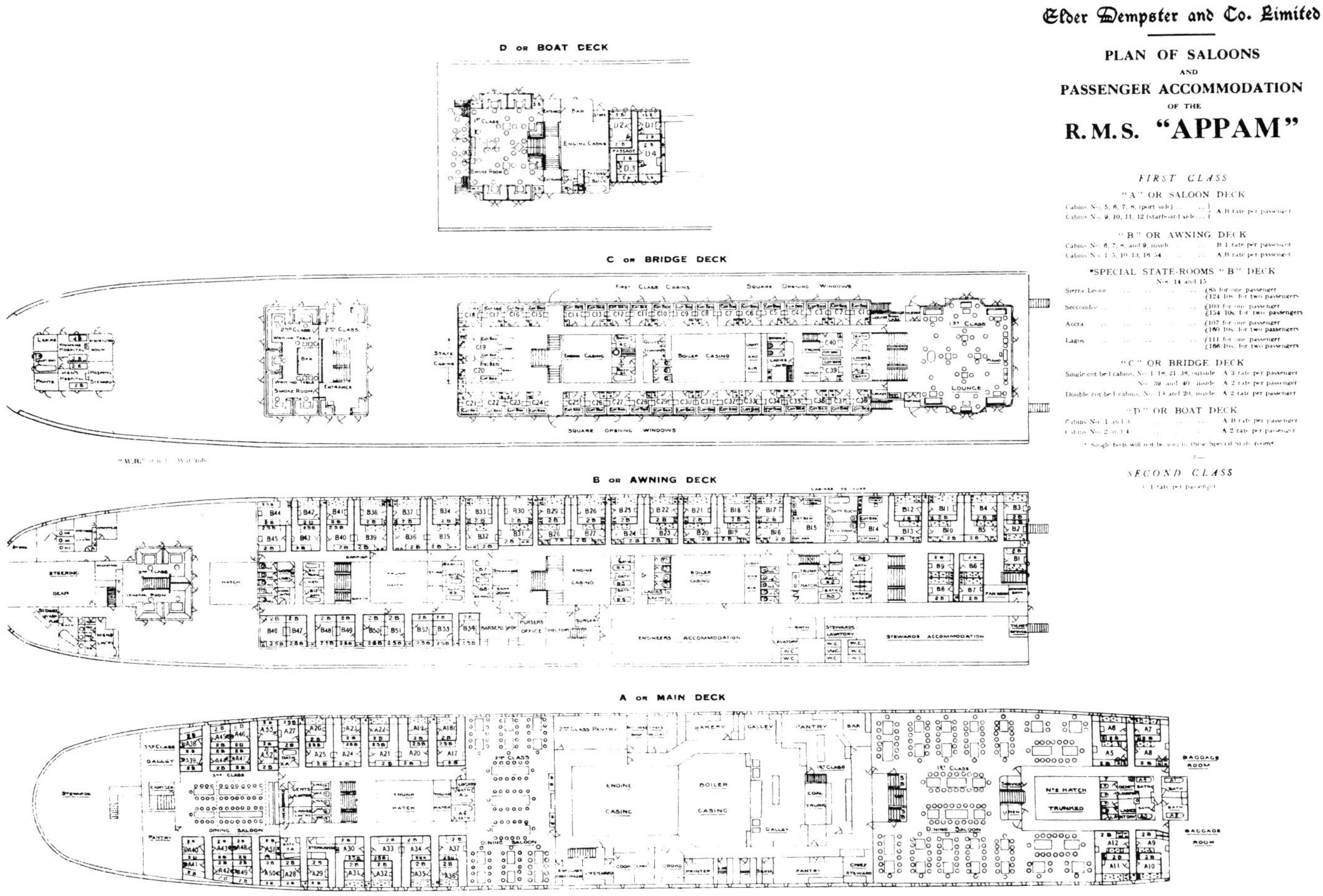
Elder Dempster and Co. Limited
PLAN OF SALOONS
AND
PASSENGER ACCOMMODATION
OF THE
R.M.S. "APPAM"
FIRST CLASS
"A" OR SALOON DECK
"B" OR AWNING DECK
Cabins No. 6, 7, 8, and 9, inside
B 1 rate per passenger
Cabins No. 1-5, 10-13, 16-34
A B rate per passenger
*SPECIAL STATE-ROOMS "B" DECK
Nos. 14 and 15
Sierra Leone
£85 for one passenger
£124 10s. for two passengers
Seccondee
£103 for one passenger
£154 10s. for two passengers
Accra
£107 for one passenger
£160 10s. for two passengers
Lagos
£111 for one passenger
£166 10s. for two passengers
"C" OR BRIDGE DECK
Single cot-bed cabins, No. 1-18, 21-38, outside
A 3 rate per passenger
No. 39 and 40, inside
A 2 rate per passenger
Double cot-bed cabins, No. 19 and 20, inside
A 2 rate per passenger
"D" OR BOAT DECK
SECOND CLASS
D OR BOAT DECK
C OR BRIDGE DECK
B OR AWNING DECK
A OR MAIN DECK

APPAM

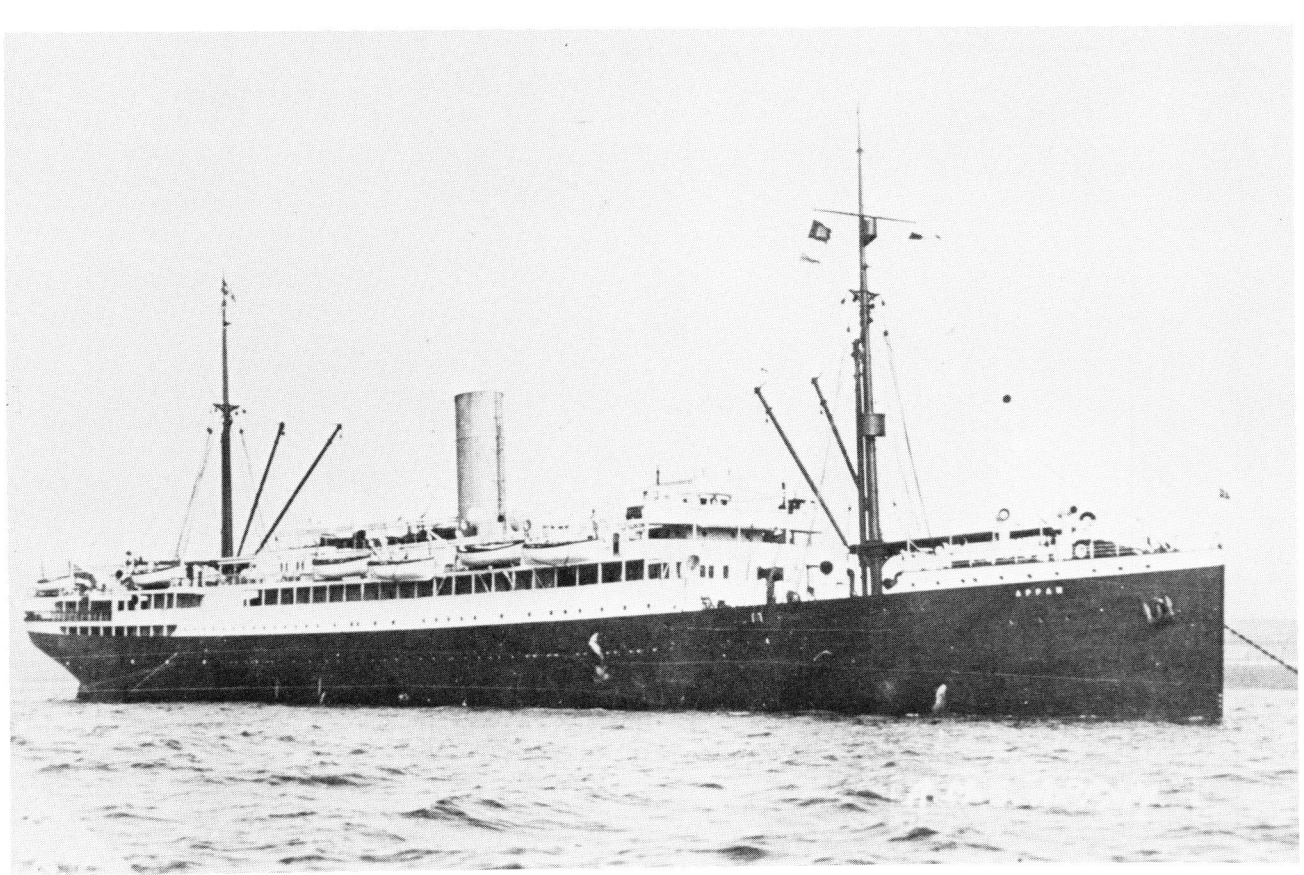

Another view of ***APPAM***

Weather forecasting services in the thirties had not reached the standards they have today by quite a long way. There was no means of knowing, when Elder Dempster's *Appam* left Liverpool on a scheduled sailing in March 1935, that we were heading into the worst gale I have ever seen in all my 36 years of service with the Company.

Sailing day was quiet and gloomy with nothing to distinguish it from any other Wednesday in March. I was Chief Officer, under Captain P. Sola, and in my third year of completely uneventful voyages in *Appam*. Captain Haigh, now a retired Marine Superintendent, was Second Officer and the Third was the late Captain Cleator.

On the second day out, as we were approaching

STORM AT SEA

by Capt. R. K. Palmer

the Bay of Biscay, the glass began to fall rapidly and by late that afternoon we knew we were in for a good blow, at least. But it was more than that. Very soon the high winds and seas made it necessary to stream the log-line astern. From its usual place, streamed from the midship's boom, it blew right over the boat deck.

Conditions grew rapidly worse and that evening, during dinner, Captain Sola ordered me to turn out all hands to secure lifeboats. We were already too late to save the emergency boat, which

was normally kept slung out. This was the first to go. By this time the wind had reached hurricane force and the seas were sweeping right over the ship. We had altered course to go to the assistance of an Italian ship in distress, but it was soon evident that we could not be of much help in such seas.

Our lifeboats were already in danger as the heavy seas sweeping over them tore away the bolts holding the chocks to the deck. Some of the boats were swinging free in the davits as the waves battered them. I asked Captain Sola if he would heave to and give us a better chance to secure the boats, but he replied that we were already late and could not afford further loss of time.

By this time all hands, including officers, were trying desperately to secure the wildly swinging boats. A massive sea caught one boat and brought it crashing on top of us, pinning some men against the deckhouse. One AB, a last minute replacement or 'Pier-head jump' as they were called, was washed overboard and lost. One moment he was there and the next he had gone. There was just nothing we could do.

All except myself managed to scramble to the shelter of a deckhouse, but I was struck by someone's sea boot and unable to follow them. I heard afterwards that they all thought I had gone over the side, but I hung on to a stanchion and inched my way to a bridge ladder. I made my report to

APPAM ENCOUNTERS HEAVY WEATHER

Top:
Appam *built in 1913*

Above right:
Lifeboat being jettisoned

suffered extensively. Over 100 deck chairs which had been lashed under shelter on the after-end of the promenade deck were smashed up and lost, while below, the crockery and furniture were wrecked.

One brave passenger, who was determined to stay in the smoke room, ended up with a broken arm and a pile of furniture on top of him. Among the passengers were a number of missionaries who could be heard singing hymns in their cabins.

The condition of the ship when daylight came was appalling. There were smashed boats and awning spars, bent stanchions, boat-falls trailing astern, as well as wire reels and ventilators missing from the forecastle head. The boat which had been washed high up on the top of the stokehold ventilator had to be hauled down with a rope and a coaling winch. But it was beyond repair and had to be put over the side.

After the worst night I have ever spent at sea in peace time, the next morning was almost windless, though with a mountainous swell, and it came on to blow hard again in the next day or so.

Incredibly, the crew did not sustain any real

the Master and again asked him to heave to, but he said it was now too late as the ship would answer neither helm nor engines. We just lay there, wallowing and rolling, the main deck rail under and the seas sweeping right over the ship. Some even went down the funnel, which was quite a tall one, some 80 or 90 feet above the waterline.

Two of the lifeboats had by now disappeared completely and several others were smashed beyond repair. We were amazed to see one boat lodged on top of one of the stokehold ventilators, washed there by a freak wave. Where boats and guard-rails had been swept away there was no protection against being washed overboard until we had a chance to rig life-lines. The Fourth Officer was just going over the side when the Second and Third grabbed him by the arms and hauled him back to safety.

The loss of the lifeboats was, of course, the most serious part of the damage, but awning spars, stanchions, ventilators and wire reels had also

injuries, apart from cuts and bruises, except, of course, for the poor AB washed overboard. He was a fine seaman, one of the old sailing ship types. We heard afterwards that there had been 39 calls for assistance that night, one ship having gone down with all hands.

We were two days late on the outward voyage because of that storm but managed to make up a day homeward, picking up spare lifeboats at Takoradi and crockery from the outward bound mail liner. That was all.

Appam *of 7,781 gross tons, was built in 1913. Her sister ships* Apapa *and* Abosso *were both sunk during World War I. Captured by the German cruiser* Moewe *in January 1916 off Madeira and taken to America (then neutral) by a German prize crew, she was immediately seized by the US authorities and, after a long series of trials in the courts, returned to her owners. In February 1939 she was broken up at Milford Haven.*

—The editor, SEA.

*This postcard emphasises the importance attached by the Germans to the capture of **APPAM** and Leutnant Berg*

APAPA

215 APAPA (I)
O.N. 136797

'Abosso' class
Steel twin screw steamer, two decks, awning deck
and shelter deck
425.7′×57.3′×31.3′ 4812 n 7832 g
Built by Harland & Wolff Ltd, Govan, Glasgow, Yard No
443GB, for African Steamship Co. Registered London. 2×Q
4 cyl 20½″, 29½″, 42″, 61″–48″ by builders. 516 nhp, 14 K.
Passenger accommodation: 400 first and second class.

1914 Completed.
1917 28 November, voyage West Africa to Liverpool with 119
passengers, 132 crew and general cargo, sunk three miles
north by east from Point Lynas by U96 (Kapitänleutnant
Heinrich Jess). **APAPA** had sailed in convoy from Sierra
Leone. The convoy separated into two sections escorted
by three destroyers each, one bound for Channel ports
and the other consisting of, **APAPA**, CITY OF GLAS-
GOW, and CIRCASSIA bound for Liverpool. The
escort was withdrawn in the evening of 27 November
and **APAPA** lost contact with the other two ships about

2000 hrs. Proceeding at 13½ knots, she rounded the Skerries, and made a course to pass two miles to seaward of Point Lynas. The night was brightly moonlit, with a rough sea, and Captain James Toft was on the bridge with the second and fourth officers. Early in the morning **APAPA** shuddered violently as a torpedo struck and exploded on the starboard side, aft, and as she began to settle, fortunately on an even keel, the engines were stopped and orders were given to lower the boats. A second torpedo struck when almost all the complement were safely in the boats. The ensuing explosion caused some of the boats to be swamped, while **APAPA** heeled over to starboard, paused briefly, and then went down. Unfortunately, in doing so, her funnel caught a lifeboat and sank it with all 30 on board, while others became entangled in the radio aerials or rigging. Scarcely ten minutes had elapsed since the first torpedo struck. The surviving six boats cruised around picking up survivors and were eventually rescued, but 40 passengers and 39 crew lost their lives.

U96 survived the war and, then under the command of Kapi-tänleutnant Karl Jasper, surrendered at Harwich on 20 November 1918 under the terms of the peace treaty. In 1919 she was sold to the Forth Shipbreaking Co for scrap. Jess commanded U90 after U96 and survived the war.

The wreck of **APAPA** was located in 1931 in position 53°.26'N 04°.18'W at a depth of 112 feet. Subsequently Risdon, Beazley & Co Ltd carried out diving expeditions to recover part of the cargo and one propellor. In the late 1970s the wreck was acquired by E. Hutton, Esq.

1984 Wreck acquired by George Rose Esq.

Apapa is on the mainland opposite Lagos Island, part of the Lagos port complex.

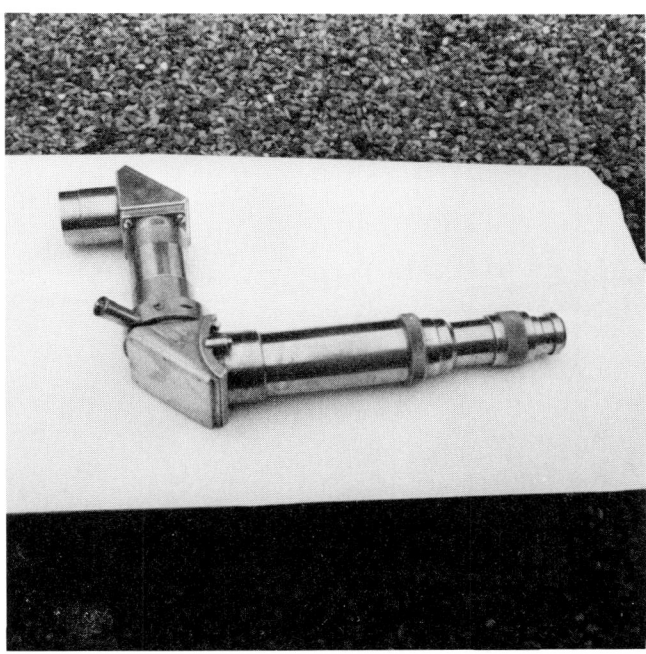

A gunsight from **APAPA** *recovered in 1984* (Photo R. Smith)

Recovery

An article on Nautical Archaeology by Dr. Davies which appeared in Liverpool University's staff and students publication 'Precinct', recalls an up-to-date recovery from the wreck of Elder Dempster's 'Apapa'

RMS 'Apapa' was torpedoed in November 1917 when she was within two miles off Point Lynas, Anglesey. Thirty-nine Elder Dempster men and many passengers were killed.

Last August a team of divers from the Chorley Sub-Aqua Club led by Mr. Boyd Harris recovered from the wreck an electric light bulb which was intact and marked "ED & Co. Ltd." so helping to identify the wreck. The bulb, with other items, was recovered from a depth of 120 feet.

216   EGORI (I)

O.N. 135588   1914–1939

'E' class
Steel screw steamer, two decks
405.6'×54.3'×23.5'   3023 n   4995 g
Built by Harland & Wolff Ltd, Glasgow, Yard No 445, for British & African Steam Navigation Co Ltd. Registered Liverpool. T 3 cyl 26", 44", 74"–51" by the builders. 574 nhp, 12 K. Passenger accommodation: 12.

1914   22 April, launched. June, completed.
1915   April, transferred to Elder Line Ltd. On Government service, Canada–Mediterranean. Tonnage openings closed. 4876 n, 6649 g.
1917   December, transferred to African Steamship Co.
1925   3023 n, 4998 g.
1933   April, transferred to Elder Dempster Lines Ltd.
1939   23 March, sold for £14,000 to G. E. Marden (Wheelock & Co, Managers). Renamed **EGORLOCK**. Registered Shanghai (British flag).
1942   Taken over by Ministry of War Transport. Registered London.
1947   Sold to Williamson & Co, Hong Kong. Registered Hong Kong (British flag).

1949   Sold to Inchona Steamship Co Ltd (Williamson & Co, Managers). Renamed **INCHONA**. 3023 n, 4998 g.
1950   Laid-up pending repairs.
1951   April, sold for demolition to Lai Chai Kok, Hong Kong.
Ships of the 'E' class: EGORI (216), EBANI (217), EBOE (218), ELELE (219), ELOBY (220), EGBA (221).
Egori is a town on the river Niger, 285 miles above Forcados.

EGORI

217 EBANI (II)
O.N. 131462   1912–1938

'E' class
Steel screw steamer, two decks and shelter deck

405.1' × 54.0' × 23.5'   2963 n   4862 g
Built by Palmers Shipbuilding & Iron Co Ltd, Jarrow, Yard No 820, for British & African Steam Navigation Co Ltd. Registered Liverpool. T 3 cyl 26″, 44″, 74″–51″ by the builders. 566 nhp, 12 K.

Passenger accommodation: 12.
1912   12 June, launched. 21 October, trials.
1915–1918   Requisitioned as hospital ship.
1933   April, transferred to Elder Dempster Lines Ltd.
1938   30 November, sold to Fratalli Ruzzato, Naples, for £12,000. Renamed **MARISTELLA**. Registered Naples.
1940   Registered Genoa. 2940 n, 4872 g.
1942   Taken over by Argentine Government (Flota Mercante del Estado). Renamed **RIO ATUEL**. Registered Buenos Aires. 1754 n, 3342 g.
1946   Ownership regained by Fratalli Ruzzato. Renamed **MARISTELLA**. Registered Genoa. 2949 n, 4872 g.
1948   3 August, damaged by mine off Borkum.
1950   June, sold for demolition at Bruges, Belgium.

FIVE YEARS AS A HOSPITAL SHIP

There are but few ships in the Mercantile Marine that can boast of a record such as that possessed by the R.M.S. *Ebani*. To serve the Empire as a hospital ship for within forty-eight hours of five years, during which period she steamed close upon 200,000 miles and carried 50,000 sick and wounded and yet only have a death-roll of 74 is a record of which any ship may well be proud.

Nevertheless, such is her record, and she served for an unbroken stretch of over three years on the South-East Coast of Africa during the campaigns in those regions.

PASSENGER ACCOMMODATION
S.S. "EBANI" & S.S. "EBOE"

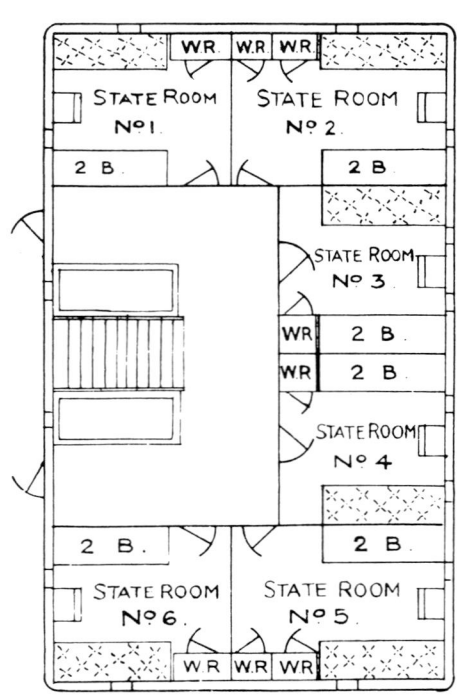

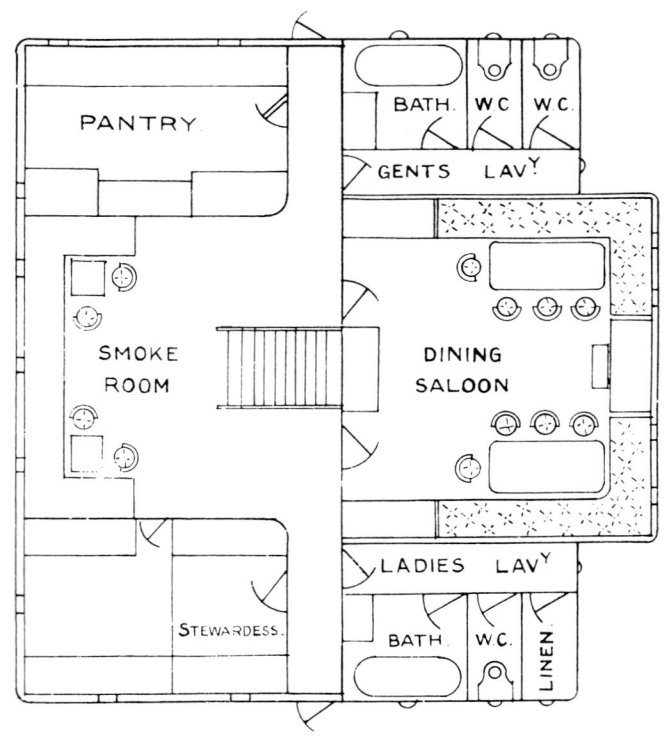

Other parts of her service were spent in the Mediterranean; on the South-West Coast of Africa; and her final commission was that of carrying 500 German women and children from Walfish Bay and Luderitzbricht to Rotterdam at the close of hostilities.

Ebani left Liverpool eight days before the outbreak of war, on her usual service to West Africa. The news that war had broken out was received when she was leaving the Canary Islands on her way to the West African ports.

The outward voyage was made without event, and while lying in Forcados, Nigeria, loading for home, her Commander, Captain A. Faill, received instructions to unload what cargo and mails he had on board and proceed without delay to Capetown. The Union Government were anxious to fit out a hospital ship, and on the recommendation of Captain Lambert, R.N., Naval Transport Officer at Capetown, they decided to charter the *Ebani*. Alterations were commenced on her arrival on October 24th, 1914, and on December 2nd she was officially opened by Lady Buxton.

Ebani left for Walfish Bay, and for seven months continuously carried the sick and wounded of the German South-West campaign from Walfish Bay and Luderitzbricht to Capetown, making in all seventeen voyages.

After completing this service to the Union Government, she was handed over to the Imperial Government and ordered to Gibraltar.

On the voyage from South Africa to Gibraltar the *Ebani*, when nearing her destination in company with the steamer *Buresk*, was stopped by an enemy submarine which commenced shelling the *Buresk*, eventually sinking her, the crew taking to the boats. The submarine then signalled the *Ebani* to send a boat alongside with an officer. Captail Faill obeyed, sending a boat in charge of the Chief Officer with the principal Medical Officer. Whilst the Germans were examining the ship's papers, a French destroyer appeared. Those on board the submarine espied the oncoming war vessel and ordered the boat to clear off whilst she hurriedly submerged.

Captail Faill rescued the crew of the *Buresk*. On arrival at Gibraltar *Ebani* was ordered to carry out hospital work in the Mediterranean, and was engaged for three months running between Mudros and Alexandria. At the end of this period, which was October 24th, 1915, she was ordered to Liverpool via Southampton, carrying 350 sick and wounded from Mudros.

At Liverpool a complete refit was carried out, and on November 23rd, she set out for Malta carrying 62 V.A.D. nurses.

At Malta she again took on board 350 sick and wounded for Southampton, and after safely landing these men left for Alexandria, where she embarked the 19th Stationary Medical Unit.

Proceeding via Suez, the *Ebani* arrived on March 4th, 1916, at Mombasa, and was engaged continuously in carrying the sick and wounded of the German South-East campaign from the East African ports to Durban and Capetown.

EBANI

During this service, which occupied three years and one month, she carried 37,000 sick and wounded. In March, 1919, as if destined to see the haunts of her peaceful trading days while still in her war-paint, she was ordered from Dar-es-Salaam to the West Coast of Africa, carrying 250 wounded to Lagos, 17 to Seccondee, and 240 to Sierra Leone.

In April, 1919, she discharged the Medical Unit at Capetown, and proceeded home to England.

On May 7th, 1919, she arrived in London, but her good work was not completed. Her name had become a household word in South Africa, and the Union Government were anxious that the *Ebani* should place the hall-mark on her war record by carrying home to Capetown some of the gallant wounded South Africans who had fought in France. Accordingly, on July 1st, she sailed from Havre with a number of wounded South Africans, and after landing them at Capetown, the *Ebani* bid farewell to Capetown, and proceeded to Walfish Bay and Luderitzbricht, embarking there 500 German women and children for Rotterdam.

On October 22nd, 1919, she was returned to her owners. During her five years of noble record the ship was under the same Commander, Captain A. Faill, who with Chief Officer Downs, Chief Engineer Lumsden and Purser Lecky, these four being the only members of the crew when she left Liverpool in July, 1914 who remained throughout her war service.

The carrying of the German women and children was surely a fitting termination to a long period of humanitarian work.

From *The Elder Dempster Fleet in the War*

EBANI *as a Hospital ship*

EBOE, from a 'Captain's Painting'

218   EBOE (IV)
O.N. 135174   1912–1938

'E' class

Steel screw steamer, two decks and shelter deck
405.1′×54.1′×23.5′   2965 n   4866 g
Built by Palmers Shipbuilding & Iron Co Ltd, Jarrow, Yard
No 821, for African Steamship Co. Registered London. T 3 cyl
26″, 44″, 74″–51″ by the builders. 566 nhp, 12 K.
1912   25 September, launched.
1916   Employed as Army Transport.
1918   7 April, (Captain T. H. Beard) (unarmed), attacked by
submarine gunfire off the coast of Sierra Leone, saved
by speed.
1933   April, transferred to Elder Dempster Lines Ltd. Registered Liverpool.

EBOE

1938   Sold to Fratelli Rizzuto, Naples, for £12,000. Renamed
FORTUNSTELLA. Registered Genoa.
1941   Sold to Argentine Government. Renamed **RIO
TERCERO**. Registered Buenos Aires. 2934 n, 4864 g.
1942   22 June, torpedoed by U202 (Kapitänleutnant Hans
Heinz Linder) position 39°.15′N 72°.32′W, voyage New
York to Buenos Aires, cargo mail and coal.

219   ELELE
O.N. 135462   1913–1917

'E' class

Steel screw steamer, two decks and shelter deck
405.0′×54.1′×23.4′   2963 n   4831 g
Built by Irvines Shipbuilding & Dry Dock Co Ltd, West Hartlepool, Yard No 521, for British & African Steam Navigation
Co Ltd. Registered Liverpool. T 3 cyl 26″, 44″, 74″–51″ by
Richardson, Westgarth & Co Ltd, Hartlepool. 577 nhp, 12 K.
Passenger accommodation: 12.
1912   23 December, launched.
1913   May, completed.
1914   Carried troops from Mauritius to England, afterwards
between Britain and France.
1917   18 June, sunk by U24 (Kapitänleutnant Walter Remy)
in 52°.16′N 17°.20′W. Remy sighted **ELELE** at 1240
bearing one point on the starboard bow, steering eastward and zigzagging. U24 dived for a submerged attack
at 1247 and fired a single bow tube at 1357 at an
estimated range of 2000 metres with a 70° track angle.
The torpedo struck abaft the bridge after running for 2
minutes 19 seconds, indicating a true range of 2650
metres. **ELELE**, which Remy subsequently learnt was
bound for Liverpool from Boston with wheat and

munitions, capsized and quickly sank amid a series of explosions. There was no loss of life.

U24 survived the war, having been employed since the autumn of 1917 as a training boat. Then under the command of Kapitänleutnant Ernst Bücker, she surrendered at Harwich on 22 November 1918. Remy also survived the war, having left U24 in July 1917 to command U90, with which he remained until the end of hostilities.

Elele is a town in Eastern Nigeria to the north of Port Harcourt.

220 ELOBY
O.N. 135437   1913–1917

'E' class
Steel screw steamer, two decks and shelter deck
405.0'×54.1'×23.4'   2958 n   4820 g
Built by Irvines Shipbuilding & Dry Dock Co Ltd, West Hartlepool, Yard No 520, for British & African Steam Navigation Co Ltd. Registered Liverpool. T 3 cyl 26", 44", 74"–51" by Richardson, Westgarth & Co Ltd, Hartlepool. 577 nhp, 12 K.
Passenger accommodation: 12.
1912 12 September, launched.
1913 22 February, trials. 30 August, grounded on Bonny Bar, floated off undamaged.
1915 Operated as Government transport between Britain and France.
1916 26 June, attacked by submarine in Mediterranean, torpedo missed.
1917 19 July, sunk in position 35°.11'N 15°58'E by U38 (Kapitänleutnant Max Valentiner), voyage details not recorded. At 1355 on 19 July Valentiner sighted a convoy consisting of two steamers escorted by two fleet sweeping vessels of the 'Foxglove' class on his port beam. The ships were zigzagging about a mean easterly course. At 1356 U38 dived for an underwater attack and at 1440, U38 having then closed to 1500 metres, Valentiner fired a single bow tube at the leading steamer, estimated to be of some 6000 grt. As the torpedo struck the ship there was an exceptionally powerful explosion, which shook the U-boat violently, breaking some of the gauge glasses. Valentiner thus deduced his target had been carrying ammunition. Several splinters were heard to land on the U-boat's deck and large pieces of wreckage fell into the water nearby. Some five minutes later, U38 was the target of a depth-charge attack, three being dropped, but managed to slip away unscathed at a depth of 40 metres. After half an hour, U38 came up to periscope depth and Valentiner observed the other steamer and the two escorts steaming away eastwards at high speed. Fifty-six of the **ELOBY**'s crew, including the Master, (Captain Wright) lost their lives in this attack.
Eloby is an island in the Corisco Bay off the coast of Gabon.

EGBA

221 EGBA
O.N. 136655   1914–1943

'E' class
Steel screw steamer, two decks and shelter deck
405.9'×54.3'×23.5'   3024 n   4989 g
Built by Harland & Wolff Ltd, Glasgow, Yard No 444, for African Steamship Co. Registered London. T 3 cyl 26", 44", 74"–51" by the builders. 574 nhp, 12 K. Decks strengthened for heavy cargoes.
Passenger accommodation: 12.
1913 17 December, launched.
1914 4 April, trials.
1915 Engaged on trooping duties.
1933 April, transferred to Elder Dempster Lines Ltd. Registered Liverpool.
1940 Tonnage opening closed. 4815 n, 6681 g.
1941 10 May, **EGBA** in position 10°.57'N 29°.13'W, came across and rescued survivors in boat No 3 from Lamport and Holt ss LASSELL which had been torpedoed on the evening of 30 April about 300 miles south-west of Cape Verde Islands.
1942 12 May, at 10.10 voyage UK to Halifax (Captain H. Welton) attacked by submarine, torpedo passed 150 feet ahead of vessel.
1943 9 August, sold for £4989 to Ministry of War Transport. Renamed **EMPIRE SEVERN** (Elder Dempster Lines Ltd, Managers).
1946 12 October, scuttled in Atlantic, loaded with high explosives.

Egba is the name of one of the Yoruba sub-tribes inhabiting the Abeokuta area of Western Nigeria, and of a town 36 miles north of Lokoja.

ELOBY

EGBA off Economia, White Sea, April 1918

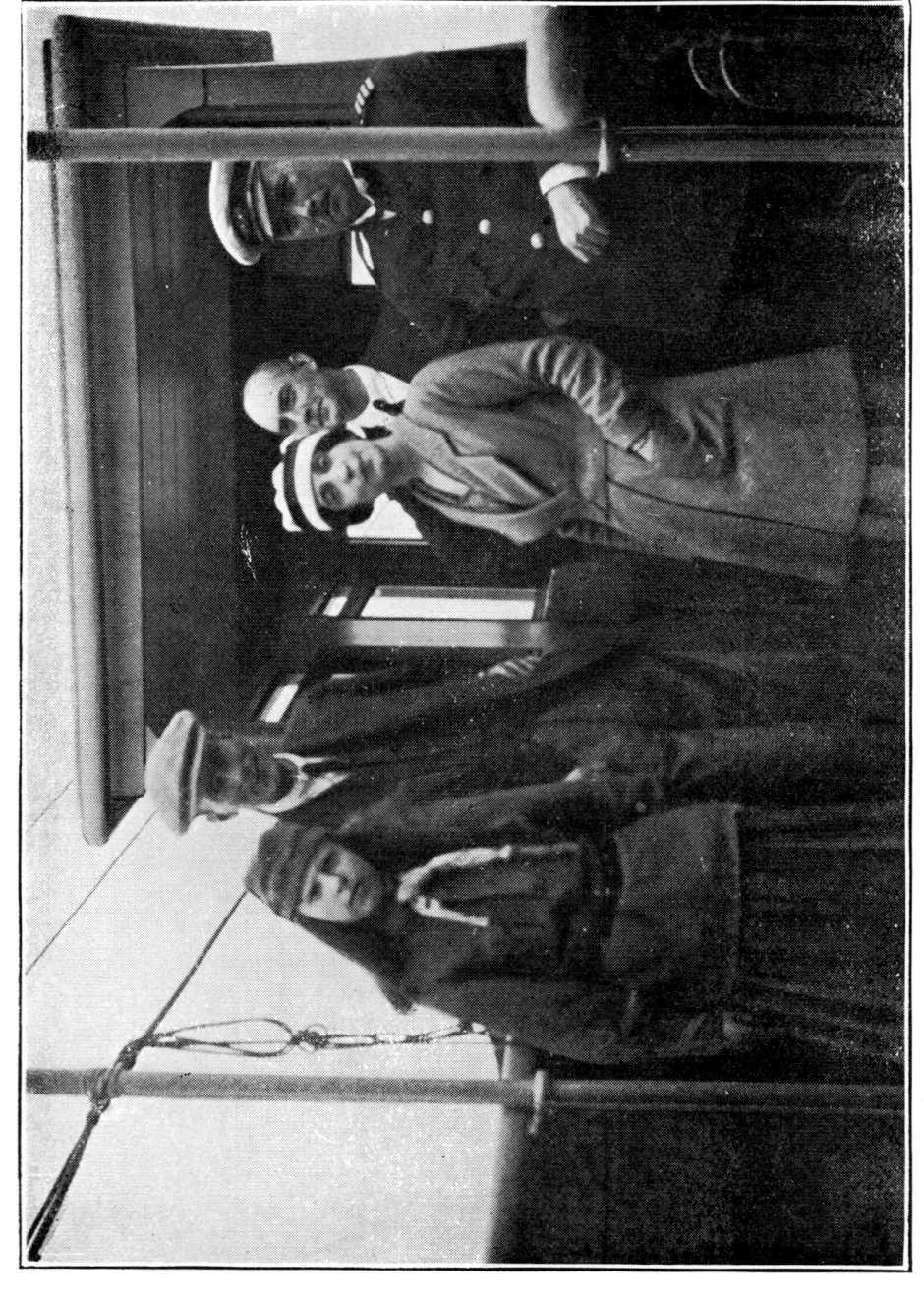

On Board R.M.S. "Egba," at Archangel.
(Right to Left) Captain Millson, Mr. Reed, Baroness D'Accurti,
Major McGrath, Tamara (Daughter of Baroness D'Accurti).

APRIL, 1918.   R.M.S. " EGBA " ASSISTING H.M.S. " ALEXANDRA "
(ICE-BREAKER), THROUGH EXTRA THICK ICE IN THE WHITE SEA.

ABINSI

C DECK

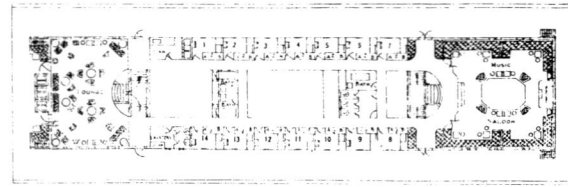

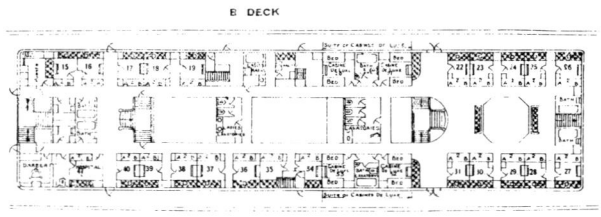
B DECK

A DECK

222 ABINSI

O.N. 137388   1914–1933

Steel twin screw steamer, two decks and shelter deck
400.5′×53.5′×31.5′   3914 n   6365 g
Built by Harland & Wolff Ltd, Belfast, Yard No 402, for Cie Belge Maritime du Congo, as **LEOPOLDVILLE**. Registered Antwerp. 2×Q 4 cyl 21″, 30″, 43″, 61″–48″ by the builders. 816 nhp, 13½ K.
Passenger accommodation: 120 first class, 18 second.

1910   April, completed.
1910   24 May, ran aground on Shebar Shoal, Sierra Leone, voyage Matadi to Antwerp.
1914   July, acquired by Elder Line Ltd. Renamed **ABINSI**. Registered Liverpool.
1917   Transferred to African Steamship Co. 15 July, attacked by submarine off south-west of Ireland, torpedo missed.
1919   January, ran ashore on Pluckington bank, River Mersey.
1920   January, in collision with ss PATRICIAN (T. & J. Harrison) whilst undocking at Liverpool.
1927   5 October, ran ashore on Pluckington bank, River Mersey.
1933   26 March, sold for £6100 to Smith, Houston & Co, Glasgow, for demolition. 2 August, towed from Liverpool to Glasgow by tugs FLYING FOAM and FLYING KITE. 5 August, sold for £6000 to Douglas and Ramsey and subsequently broken up.

Abinsi is a township on the River Benue, to the east of Makurdi.

ABINSI

223 OBUASI (I)

O.N. 128041   1914–1917

Steel screw steamer, two decks and shelter deck
360.0′×50.1′×22.8′   2576 n   4143 g
Built by Tyne Iron Shipbuilding Co Ltd, Newcastle, Yard No 173, as **CHRISTOPHER** for Booth Steam Ship Co Ltd. Registered Liverpool. T 3 cyl 25″, 40″, 68″–48″ by North Eastern Marine Engineering Co Ltd, Newcastle. 367 nhp, 11 K.
1910   April, completed.

OBUASI

1914   Acquired by British & African Steam Navigation Co Ltd. Renamed **OBUASI**. Registered Liverpool. 4 August, departed from Liverpool for West Africa. Requisitioned as army transport and later carried troops from Accra, Gold Coast, to Keta and Lome in Togoland (German Colony) and then returned to Southampton with German prisoners captured at Lome.

1917   8 July, sunk in approximately 52°.N, 17°.30′W by U49 (Kapitänleutnant Richard Hartmann), voyage Dakar to Liverpool, cargo general. At 1215 Hartmann saw the funnel smoke of two steamers and at 1218 he dived for an underwater attack. At 1414 he fired at the first* of the two steamers, but the torpedo missed, owing to miscalculation of the target's speed. He then turned his attention to the other steamer, which was **OBUASI**, firing one torpedo at 1416, which struck in the forward part. The crew proceeded to abandon ship, except for the gunners, who were firing at U49's periscope. As **OBUASI** showed no sign of going down, Hartmann fired one stern tube at 1430 to finish her off, but the torpedo, which was fitted with a 'propeller' pistol, failed to detonate. Hartmann thus reloaded with a bronze torpedo†, which he fired at 1530. This time the torpedo found its mark and **OBUASI**'s gun crew finally abandoned ship. Ten minutes later, U49 surfaced just ahead of the steamer, with the object of finishing her off with gunfire, but the forward deck gun was defective and thus Hartmann resorted to explosive charges‡. **OBUASI** went down at 1635 and Captain P. Sola and her gun crew were made prisoner.

U49 was sunk with all hands on 11 September 1917 in 46°.17′N 14°.42′W when rammed by ss BRITISH TRANSPORT. Obuasi is a town in Ghana, south of Kumasi.

* The first ship was Elder Dempster's **ONITSHA**. She succeeded in eluding the enemy and arrived safely at Liverpool.
† The bronze torpedo, so named because it was wholly made of bronze, dated back to 1895–8 and was the oldest type in use by the Germans during the First World War. It was shorter than the more modern steel torpedoes and was reserved for short-range use against merchant ships. The pistol fitted was of a relatively simple design and incorporated no safety fan. The 'propeller' pistol referred to earlier was, judging by its designation, fitted with such a device, which would appear to have malfunctioned and hence prevented the torpedo from detonating.
‡ These were cylindrical bombs under a foot long that were hung to the ship's side outside the hull in the neighbourhood of the engine-room. They were also used as scuttling charges for the U-boat itself, when they were attached to torpedo warheads or placed in the torpedo tubes.

224   GABOON (II)

O.N. 137434   1915–1933

'G' class
Steel screw steamer, two decks
337.0′×48.5′×22.6′   2005 n   3297 g
Built by Tyne Iron Shipbuilding Co Ltd, Newcastle, Yard No 193, for British & African Steam Navigation Co Ltd. Registered Liverpool. T 3 cyl 25″, 41″, 68″–45″ by North Eastern Marine Engineering Co Ltd, Newcastle. 429 nhp, 11 K.
Passenger accommodation: 8.

1915   March, completed.

1917   9 June, beat off submarine gun attack in Atlantic with own gunfire.

1933   January, sold for £8500 to Cia Uruguaya de Navegacion Ltda. Renamed **PARANA**. Registered Montevideo. Fitted to burn oil fuel.

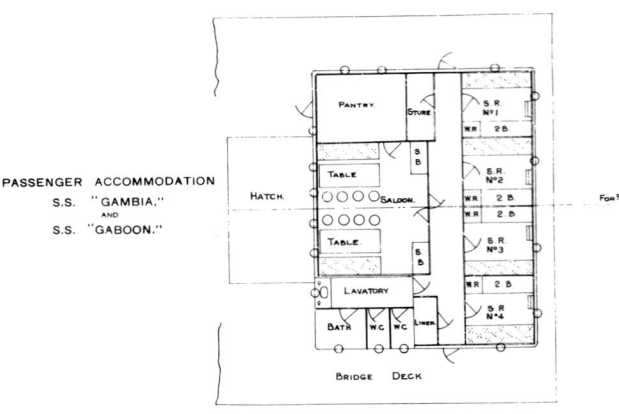

ELDER DEMPSTER AND CO., LIMITED,
COLONIAL HOUSE, 20, WATER STREET,
LIVERPOOL.

PASSENGER ACCOMMODATION
S.S. "GAMBIA,"
AND
S.S. "GABOON."

GAMBIA

1936 Registered Buenos Aires.
1942 Sold to Cia Argentina de Navegacion Mihanovich Ltda.
1960 Sold to Flota Argentina Navegacion de Ultramer.
1964 Sold to Empresa Lineas Maritimas Argentinas.
1966 Sold to Ayasa SA. Renamed **SIDERCA**.
1968 December, demolition completed by Ayasa Campana.
Ships of the 'G' class: GABOON (224), GAMBIA (225).

GABOON

225 GAMBIA (V)
O.N. 137484   1915–1933

'G' class
Steel screw steamer, two decks
337.0′×48.5′×22.6′   1997 n   3296 g
Built by Tyne Iron Shipbuilding Co Ltd, Newcastle, Yard No
194, for British & African Steam Navigation Co Ltd. Registered
Liverpool. T 3 cyl 25″, 41″, 68″–45″ by North Eastern Marine
Engineering Co Ltd, Newcastle. 429 nhp, 11 K.
Passenger accommodation: 8.
1915 October, completed.
1917 22 February, chased by submarine in English Channel
     but escaped by superior speed.
1933 June, sold to 'Adria' Societe Anonima di Navigation
     Marittima (Riva E. Filberto, Manager), Fiume, for
     £8500. Renamed **LEOPARDI**. Registered Fiume.
1937 Sold to 'Tirrenia' Societa per Azioni di Navigazione,
     Naples. Registered Genoa. 1971 n, 3289 g.
1940 14th August, mined and sunk, six miles east of Tolmettoc
     32°.39′N 21°.03′E.

226 MANXMAN
O.N. 93825   1915–1916

Steel screw steamer, two decks
White Star's first cattle carrier
430.7′×45.2′×30.0′   3055 n   4639 g
Built by Harland & Wolff Ltd, Belfast, for Oceanic Steam
Navigation Co Ltd, Liverpool, Yard No 210, as **CUFIC**. Registered Liverpool. T 3 cyl 27″, 44½″, 74″–60″ by the builders.
520 nhp, 13 K.
1888 10 October, launched. 8 December, maiden voyage,
     Liverpool–New York.
1896–98 Chartered to Cia Transatlantica Espanola. Renamed
     NUESTRA SENORA DE GUADALOUPE. Reverted
     to **CUFIC** on return to owners.
1900 December, lost propeller in North Atlantic, towed into
     Queenstown by ss KANSAS CITY. £6800 salvage paid.
1901 Sold to Dominion Line, Liverpool, renamed
     MANXMAN. Registered Liverpool.
1915 Acquired by Elder, Dempster & Co. 3122 n, 4827 g.
1916 Acquired by P. Lawrence Smith, Toronto. Registered
     Montreal. Sold to United States & Canada Trans-
     portation Co Ltd, New York.
1918 Registered Toronto (British flag).
1919 18 December, foundered in North Atlantic with loss of 45
     lives in position 41°.53′N 59°.51′W on voyage Portland,
     Maine, to Gibraltar, cargo wheat.

MANXMAN

MONTEZUMA

227 MONTEZUMA (III)
O.N. 137812   1915–1916

Steel twin screw motorship, two decks and shelter deck
435.9′×55.3′×35.2   4593 n   7237 g
Built by Harland & Wolff Ltd, Irvine, Yard No 467, for Elder, Dempster & Co Ltd. Registered Liverpool. 2×4 SCSA Burminster and Wain 6 cyl 26⅜″–39⅜″ by builders. 655 nhp, 10½ K.
1915   Completed May.
1916   Sold to Glen Line (McGregor, Gow & Holland & Co Ltd), London. Renamed **GLENARTNEY**. Registered Glasgow. 4599 n, 10160 d, 7263 g.
1918   5 February, torpedoed and sunk in convoy by UC54 (Kapitänleutnant Heinrich XXXVII, Prinz Reuss), 30 miles north-east of Cape Bon, with the loss of two lives, voyage Singapore and Alexandria to UK.

UC54 was one of a number of U-boats that were not ready to proceed to sea when the order came in October 1918 to evacuate the Mediterranean and return to Home Waters. Hence, on 28 October UC54, then under the command of Oberleutnant zur See Otto Loycke, was blown up at Trieste. After leaving UC54 Prinz Heinrich XXXVII commanded UB130 until the end of the war.

228 BENITO (II)
O.N. 124225   1917

Steel screw steamer, two decks
390.0′×52.2′×26.4′   3021 n   4712 g
Built by Scotts' Shipbuilding & Engineering Co Ltd, Greenock, Yard No 415, as **FALLS OF NITH**, for Falls Line Steamship Co Ltd, (Wright Graham & Co Managers), Glasgow. Regis-

tered Glasgow. T 3 cyl 26½″, 44″, 72″–48″ by the builders. 471 nhp, 10 K.
1907   September, completed.
1917   Acquired by Imperial Direct Line Ltd (Elder, Dempster & Co Ltd). Renamed **BENITO**. Registered Liverpool. 26 December, sunk 9 miles south of Dodman Point by U57 (Kapitänleutnant Otto Steinbrinck). **BENITO** was damaged by U57 in an underwater torpedo attack and was taken in tow of trawlers before being finished off with another torpedo, voyage from Newcastle with Admiralty cargo, coal and coke. No loss of life.

U57, then under the command of Oberleutnant zur See Johannes Lochs, was sunk with all hands on 14 August 1918 off Zeebrugge on a British mine.

BENITO

INDORE

IKBAL

229 INDORE
O.N. 109447   1918–1925

Steel screw steamer, two decks and spar deck
480.0′×52.3′×27.0′   4775 n   7300 g
Built by Workman Clark & Co Ltd, Belfast, Yard No 145, for
Indore Steam Ship Co Ltd (J. H. Welsford & Co Ltd,
Managers). Registered Liverpool. T 3 cyl 29½″, 50″, 82″–60″ by
the builders. 665 nhp, 13 K.

1898   10 March, launched.
1913   Sold to Gulf Transport Co (Liverpool) Ltd (J. H. Welsford & Co, Managers), Liverpool.
1915   September, on charter to Canadian Pacific Railway Co.
1918   25 July, torpedoed by submarine off Northern Ireland. Two lives lost. Beached, later refloated and repaired. Acquired by Elder, Dempster & Co Ltd.
1925   December, sold for £13,250 for demolition in Italy.

230 IKBAL
O.N. 102146   1917

Steel twin screw steamer, two decks
445.2′×49.1′×30.2′   3490 n   5434 g
Built by Harland & Wolff Ltd, Belfast, for Ikbal Steam Ship
Co (E. Bates & Co, Managers), Liverpool, Yard No 279.
Registered Liverpool. 2×T 3 cyl 18½″, 31″, 52″–48″ by the
builders. 469 nhp, 11½ K.

1894   22 February, launched.
1902   29 November, ashore Taylor's Bank, River Mersey, refloated undamaged by PATHFINDER.
1913   Sold to Gulf Transport (Liverpool) Ltd (J. H. Welsford & Co, Managers).
1915   Army supply ship on charter to Canadian Pacific Railway Co.
1917   March, acquired by Elder, Dempster & Co Ltd. April 29, torpedoed and sunk in a surface attack by U93 (Kapitänleutnant Baron Spiegel v. u. zu Peckelsheim) 250 miles west of Ushant, having sailed from St Johns, New Brunswick. Captain Clegg and two gunners made prisoner.

U93, then under the command of Kapitänleutnant Helmut
Garlach, was lost with all hands in January 1918. She is
recorded as having been sunk on 7 January after having been
rammed˙by the ss BRAENEIL. However, this assessment is
almost certainly incorrect, since the U-boat rammed and sunk
in this incident was much more likely to have been U95, which
was also lost with all hands in January 1918. U93, therefore,
was very probably sunk on 31 January off the Channel Islands
by an aircraft of the French Maritime Seaplane Squadron.
Spiegel became a prisoner of war on 30 April 1917, the day

after he sank the **IKBAL**, when U93 intercepted, and was
engaged by a Q-ship, the PRIZE, which was the former German
schooner ELSE. U93 escaped with some damage, but her
Commanding Officer and two of her crew were blown overboard
by the blast from a shell and picked up by the PRIZE. U93
was brought back to Wilhelmshaven by her First Lieutenant,
Oberleutnant zur See Ziegner.

231 ROQUELLE (III)
O.N. 140582   1918–1927

Steel screw steamer, one deck
348.6′×49.9′×23.6′   2761 n   4364 g
Built by Campbeltown Shipbuilding Co Ltd, Campbeltown,
Yard No 107, for Imperial Direct West India Line Co Ltd
(Elder, Dempster & Co Ltd, Managers). Registered Liverpool.
T 3 cyl 25″, 40″, 65″–45″ by J. G. Kincaid & Co Ltd, Greenock.
327 nhp, 10 K.

1918   May, completed. Sailed from the Clyde in ballast for Cardiff to load for maiden voyage (Captain D. Evans), attacked by submarine when passing St John's Point of Greenore at 0215 on 3 June. Two torpedoes aimed, both missed.
1927   October, sold to Britain Steam Ship Co Ltd, (Watts, Watts & Co Ltd, Managers), London. Renamed **DATCHET**. Registered London. 2239 n, 3610 g.
1933   Sold to Goulandris Bros, Athens. Renamed **MARIONGA J. GOULANDRIS**. Registered Andros. 2259 n, 3610 g.
1934   14 November, stranded at Necochea, Argentine, position 38°.32′S 58°.44′W. Later declared a constructive total loss.

ROQUELLE

Another view of **ROQUELLE**

232 BASSA (II)
O.N. 142341   1919–1940

'B' class
Steel screw steamer, War 'B' type, two decks
400.1′×52.3′×28.4′   3202 n   5267 g   8075 d
Built by Armstrong Whitworth & Co Ltd, Newcastle, Yard
No 932, as **WAR POINTER** for the Shipping Controller.
Registered London. T 3 cyl 27″, 44″, 73″–48″ by G. Clark Ltd,
Sunderland. 517 nhp, 11 K.

1918   March, completed.
1919   Acquired by African Steamship Co. Renamed **BASSA**.
        Registered London.
1933   Transferred to Elder Dempster Lines Ltd. Registered
        Liverpool.
1936   12 to 23 September, aground in Sherbro River.
1940   29 September, (Captain G. E. Anderson) sunk by U32
        (Kapitänleutnant Hans Jenisch) in position 54°.N21°.W
        approx, voyage Liverpool to New York in ballast. At
        0053 Jenisch fired a single torpedo that struck **BASSA**
        just abaft the engine room after running for 57 seconds,
        which corresponds to a range of 850 metres. **BASSA**
        immediately began to settle by the stern, which was soon
        awash, her bows coming up out of the water. Boats were
        lowered. U32 closed to within a few yards and read her
        name with the aid of a searchlight. She went down at
        0105 with all hands.

U32 was sunk on 30 October 1940 in the North Atlantic by
HMS HARVESTER and HIGHLANDER. Thirty-three of her
crew of 42 survived, including Jenisch, and they were taken
prisoner.
Ships of the 'B' class: BASSA (232), BATHURST (233),
BONNY (234), BOUTRY (235), BIAFRA (236), BODNANT
(237), BAKANA (238), BEREBY (239), BATA (240),
BADAGRY (241), BARRACOO (242), BURUTU (243),
BOMA (244).

BASSA

BATHURST

233 BATHURST (II)
O.N. 140610   1919–1933

'B' class
Steel screw steamer, War 'A' type, one deck
400.1′×52.3′×28.5′   3181 n   5233 g   8075 d
Launched by Caird & Co Ltd, Greenock, Yard No 354, as
WAR ALYSSUM for the Shipping Controller. Completed for
British & African Steam Navigation Co Ltd as **BATHURST**.
Registered Liverpool. T 3 cyl 27″, 44″, 73″–48″ by the builders.
517 nhp, 11 K.

1919   20 February, launched. March, completed. Whilst on
        passage from the United Kingdom to West Africa
        (Captain A. E. Webster, Chief Officer W. Munt),
        BATHURST took in tow the American ss *ATLANTIC*
        CITY, which had sustained an engine failure, and safely
        towed her to Funchal.
1920   December, transferred to Elder Line Ltd.
1931   2 June, laid up at Barrow.
1933   31 July, sold for £6200 to B. E. Benierakis, Patras.
        Renamed **KOSTIS**. Registered Chalcis.
1939   Sold to Panagos D. Pateras, Chios. Renamed
        DIAMANTIS. Registered Patras.
1948   24 July, fire in cargo and explosion, voyage Sydney NSW
        to Three Rivers. Abandoned in Caspe Bay. 25 July, fire
        extinguished and aground. Refloated two days later and
        repaired. Sold to Ponticos and Lemos, Piraeus. Renamed
        THORROS. Registered Patras.
1951   29 November, aground near Honningsvaag, voyage
        Archangel to Cardiff, cargo timber. 12 December,
        refloated but subsequently developed severe list during
        heavy weather and sank.

234 BONNY (III)
O.N. 140615   1919–1928

'B' class
Steel screw steamer, War 'B' type, two decks
400.0′×52.3′×28.4′   3165 n   5173 g   8075 d
Launched by Irvines Shipbuilding & Dry Dock Co Ltd, West
Hartlepool, Yard No 593, as **WAR STOAT** for the Shipping
Controller. Completed for British & African Steam Navigation
Co Ltd as **BONNY**. Registered Liverpool. T 3 cyl 27″, 44″, 73″–
48″ by Richardson, Westgarth & Co Ltd, 369 nhp, 11 K.

1918   December, launched.
1919   14 April, completed. Subsequently transferred to Elder,
        Dempster & Co Ltd.
1920   Transferred to Elder Line Ltd.
1921   Transferred to British & African Steam Navigation Co
        Ltd.
1928   10 April, (Captain M. Woolwright) on passage from
        London to Douala struck outer rock at Cape Palmas,
        Liberia. Beached one mile to the east. 3 May 1928,
        declared a constructive total loss, abandoned.

BONNY

BOUTRY

235 BOUTRY
O.N. 143295   1919–1933
'B' class
Steel screw steamer, War 'B' type, two decks
400.0′ × 52.3′ × 28.5′   3192 n   5182 g   8075 d
Launched by Irvines Shipbuilding & Drydock Co Ltd, West
Hartlepool, Yard No 597, as **WAR GULL** for the Shipping
Controller. Completed for Elder, Dempster & Co Ltd as
BOUTRY. Registered London. T 3 cyl 27″, 44″, 73″–48″ by
Richardson, Westgarth & Co Ltd, West Hartlepool. 517 nhp,
11 K.

1919	16 April, launched. 18 June, trials, 12 K.
1920	Transferred to African Steamship Co.
1931	Laid up in Blackwater River.
1933	15 November, sold for £7500 to Margaronis Bros and others, Piraeus. Renamed **MOUNT RHODOPE**. Registered Piraeus.
1942	Sold to Oceanos Maritime Steamship Co, Piraeus.
1945/47	Operated by Ministry of War Transport.
1957	Sold to Potamianos Brothers, Piraeus. Renamed **CAPTAIN GIORGIS**.
1960	Sold to Sidiremboriki Ltd, Piraeus. 20 June, demolition commenced.

BOUTRY *at Bordeaux*

236 BIAFRA (IV)

O.N. 143285   1919–1951

'B' class
Steel screw steamer, War 'B' type, two decks
400.4′×52.3′×28.5′   3299 n   5405 g   8075 d
Launched by Caird & Co Ltd, Greenock, Yard No 570, as
WAR DAHLIA for the Shipping Controller. Completed as
BIAFRA for Elder, Dempster & Co Ltd. Registered London.
T 3 cyl 27″, 44″, 73″–48″ by Harland & Wolff Ltd, Greenock.
517 nhp, 11 K.

1919 29 April, launched. 20 June, completed.
1920 Transferred to African Steamship Co.
1933 April, transferred to Elder Dempster Lines Ltd. Registered Liverpool.
1935 HP cylinder relined 25½″ diameter.
1940 January, collided in Liverpool Bay with Lackenby (Ropners Ltd) during snowstorm.

BIAFRA

1941 12 July, while steaming in convoy as Commodore Ship from Halifax to the United Kingdom collided with BRITISH DILIGENCE (Tanker, 8408 g / built 1937) and COMANCHEE (tanker, 5601 g / built 1912) in dense fog about 2200 near the Cabot Straits, with severe damage. Towed to Louisburg and beached.
1942 January, completed repairs.
1943 4 January, together with *DAVID LIVINGSTONE* unsuccessfully attempted to re-float PIERRE LOTI, aground at Libreville, French Equatorial Africa. PIERRE LOTI eventually broke up.
1951 23 August, sold for £95,000 to Meridian Shipping Co, Panama. Renamed **GEORGE**. Registered Panama. 3320 n, 5283 g.
        During first voyage for new owners considerable boiler troubles were experienced off Ushant, followed soon after, when loading at Lules, by a crew walk-off led by Second Mate, alleging ship to be insanitary.
1956 Sold to Unity Compania Navegacion Sociedad Anonima (Faros Shipping Co Ltd, Managers), London. Renamed **UNITY**.
1957 Sold to Linea Adriatico, Gulfo Persa Ltd, Trieste. Renamed **MAHFUZ**.
1958 Sold to Cia Mar di Isola Spetsia, San Jose, Costa Rica. Renamed **SPETSAI STAR**.
1959 6 April, sold to Okushaji Co, Osaka, for demolition.

REPORT BY CAPTAIN BERNARD HEATON HOLT

Certificate—Ordinary Master.
In command 5 years—at sea 30 years.
Joined "Biafra" as Master 24 October 1940.
  "Biafra" loaded at Quonset Rhode Island various articles for building an American base in Northern Ireland consisting of machinery, timber of various sorts, pile drivers, stores etc and Gasoline Gelignite.

We left Quonset on 4 July 1941 alone and arrived 6 July at Halifax to take bunkers and water and to join a convoy for crossing the Atlantic.

On 10 July a conference was held in the Naval Control at Halifax by the Masters of all the vessels in the convoy, some 45 or 46, and the Conference Commander, a Naval Officer in charge of the convoy system, the Admiral who was going as Commodore of the convoy (Mackay) and his staff P.O. signals, the Commander of the local escort and Commander of sea escort and Commander in charge of the air escort.

The Conference Commander reminded the Captains of the necessity of station keeping and of promptly carrying out orders. Then the Admiral spoke of station keeping, and strict attention to signals. He stated that if he blew K on the whistle in fog it meant all ships to stop engines, he also requested the 3rd line of the convoy to repeat signals. He emphasized the leaders of the columns would sound the column numbers when the Commodore did so,—this is also in fog to ensure good station keeping. The Masters were then invited to ask questions. There was no further discussions about fog, the Masters' questions relating to speeds and other minor matters. I did not ask any questions. I was told that mine was to be the Commodore ship. The plan of the convoy was given to each Master in duplicate, one for the bridge and one for the wireless room. This showed 9 columns of 5 vessels in each column. The distances given were, columns 3 cables apart in daylight, 5 at night if signal given, and 2 cables in line ahead. Such signals are given by flag by the Commodore and this is relayed down each line and the last in each line gives the answering pennant.

We left Halifax at 10.25.a.m. on 11 July in single line, "Biafra" leading, and formed the convoy outside the harbour. Here the sealed orders were opened. Those orders give the series of positions to be made during the voyage and the true course from one position to another. From this one could plot the track for the voyage. The convoy speed was 5¾ knots—the "Biafra" was No 5—1 having 4 ships on her starboard beam and four on her port beam.

After forming convoy we steered for a short time a South easterly course and then made a course of 60° true which would take us to the position in which we were to make a 73° alteration of courses to port. The general Admiralty instructions which every Master has directs that at night time in fog alterations of course are to be carried out by altering 20° at a time and that the allowance of time between alterations is from 15 to 20 minutes to allow each vessel to get into station before the next turn and when each turn is completed all vessels are to resume the convoy speed and that prior to making each turn the Commodore will blow a four blast signal followed at an interval by the executive signal. In daylight all signals are given by flag; at night in the absence of fog lights but only in emergency, otherwise night time alterations are given by flag in daylight, and when the time for alteration arrives only the executive signal is given.

Shortly after noon on 12 July fog developed and by 1 o'clock it was dense and continued so and visibility was practically nil—at times we could see the ships on our beam and at other times we could not, so we streamed fog buoys.

About 6 o'clock or a little after I said to the Commodore in the presence of the Chief Officer that I thought it would be dangerous to make the turn of 73° due about 10 o'clock if the fog continued. He replied that all the Masters knew how to carry out the turns and he would carry out the manoeuvre. A little later we were discussing the turns and he agreed that as confusion might arise about the final turn of 13° he would not order this but order only the 3 turns of 20° each and leave the other until daylight.

About every 15 minutes we sounded column numbers on the siren—first the Commodore, followed by the other leaders and judging from these signals the leaders were keeping good station.

The Commodore and I remained on the bridge all the time. Again about 9 o'clock in the presence of the 3rd Officer I reminded the Commodore about giving the K signal in fog, and said as we were in hand with time why not give the signal now and wait until daylight before altering course as the convoy was capable of fast speed and we could easily make up any time lost. His reply was "We will make the turn". I then said to him that as the convoy was covering a large area would it not be a good plan to start the turns at 9.30 (instead of 10 o'clock), at which time I estimated we would reach the actual turning point) so that the last vessels of the convoy would be nearer to the correct position on completion of the turn of 60°. To this he agreed.

There had been no alteration of convoy clocks since leaving Halifax. At 9.26 the Commodore blew 4 long blasts on the siren, repeated by all leading ships. At this time we could not see any other vessel. As soon as the last leader had sounded the 4 blasts the Commodore ordered a 2 short blast signal which was given and repeated by all leaders. I sent the 3rd Officer to the monkey bridge to check the new course by the standard compass and he steadied the ship on that course and came back to the bridge. I told the Commodore "We are right on now"—meaning 40. In making the turn the vessels on our starboard hand increased their speeds according to their distance from us from about ½ knot for the nearest to about 2 knots for the farthest and those on the port hand decreased to about the same extent. In making a turn the Commodore always reduces speed by a knot.

At 9.37 we heard the crash of a collision somewhere astern of us. I told the Commodore "that sounded like a collision" but he made no remark.

At 9.45 the second 4 long blasts was given which was repeated by the leaders and then the executive signal of 2 short. I sent the 3rd Officer again on the monkey bridge to steady her on the new course and he called out she was right on. At this time and whilst coming round we heard a number of 1 and 2 blast signals from vessels astern. I suggested to the Commodore that he might now give the column signal and he agreed and did so; we heard some of the leaders give their column signal numbers and at the same time a whole series of blasts of different kinds from various directions in the convoy.

At 9.59 the bridge look-out and I simultaneously observed a vessel approaching our port side distant about 150 feet bearing almost at a right angle. I first saw his masthead and side lights and then the hull. I ordered full ahead and hard-a-starboard and the helmsman repeated the order and I saw him put the wheel over. The vessel came on and struck us amidships, penetrated the hull in the boiler room. I do not think our helm or engines had any time to make appreciable alteration as it was a matter of seconds only before he struck us. Engine room and stokehold began immediately to flood—put out the fires and all lights (electric) failed. I ordered the 2 red "not under command" oil lamps to be lighted and hoisted and this was at once done—the lamps are kept handy on the bridge. I ordered rockets to be fired and the klaxon horns, one on the bridge, one on the poop, to be sounded continuously and this was done. The other vessel dropped astern.

At 10.07 another vessel was sighted at about 150 feet approaching our port side but at a lesser angle and she struck us with her stem and starboard bow in almost the same place as the first vessel. We had bunker coal on our bridge deck which acted as a buffer otherwise I believe this second vessel with her raking stem would probably have cut deeply into us and sunk us.

About 10 minutes later as nearly as I can judge the fog had thinned slightly and we sighted yet another vessel heading towards our port side distant some 200/300 yards, but he saw us in time and ported and cleared us.

B. H. HOLT, Master.

237 BODNANT

O.N. 140631   1919–1940

'B' class
Steel screw steamer, War 'B' type, two decks
401.0′×52.3′×28.5′   3177 n   5258 g   8075 d
Launched by John Brown & Co Ltd, Clydebank, Yard No 417, as **WAR CRANE** for the Shipping Controller. Completed for Elder, Dempster & Co Ltd as **BODNANT**. Registered Liverpool. T 3 cyl 27″, 44″, 73″–48″ by the builders. 517 nhp, 11 K.

1919   May, launched. 3 July, trials. November, transferred to African Steamship Co. 3230 n, 5342 g.
1933   Transferred to Elder Dempster Lines Ltd.
1940   30 December, collided with *CITY OF BEDFORD*, position approximately 62°.N 23°.W, voyage Hull to Freetown, cargo government stores. Both vessels sunk.

Bodnant sailed from Hull on December 28, 1940 bound for Freetown and Lagos, via Methil and Oban, having a crew of 52 (including two gunners) 10 passengers, and 1,150 tons of Government stores.

She was in a convoy of about 30 vessels in nine columns of three or four each, distances between columns being five cables and that between ships in column two cables. The *Bodnant* was leading ship in the starboard column.

On the night of December 29, 1940 the convoy was proceeding into the North Atlantic at a speed of nine knots course of South 76 deg. West true. The following day, at 0900 B.S.T. in about 62 deg. North, 21 deg. West, 280 miles South of Iceland, the weather conditions were very dark, the wind being a moderate gale from the South East and there was a rough and heavy swell. No lights were exhibited, but the loom of the vessel in the first column on the port beam of the *Bodnant* could just be observed.

The Chief Officer, (D. Haigh) was in charge of the bridge, with a helmsman at the wheel, one seaman on lookout, and two passengers, one on each wing, also on lookout on the lower bridge. At 0920 hours he observed right ahead and at a distance of about four to five cables the shape of a vessel whose navigation lights were switched on immediately after the Chief Officer sighted her.

The lights were two side lights and foremast head light. They were bright and from their position the oncoming vessel appeared to be on an exactly opposite course.

BODNANT

156

PASSENGER ACCOMMODATION

S.S. "BOMA"   S.S. "BODNANT"

S.S. "BIAFRA"   S.S. "BATA"

S.S. "BATHURST"

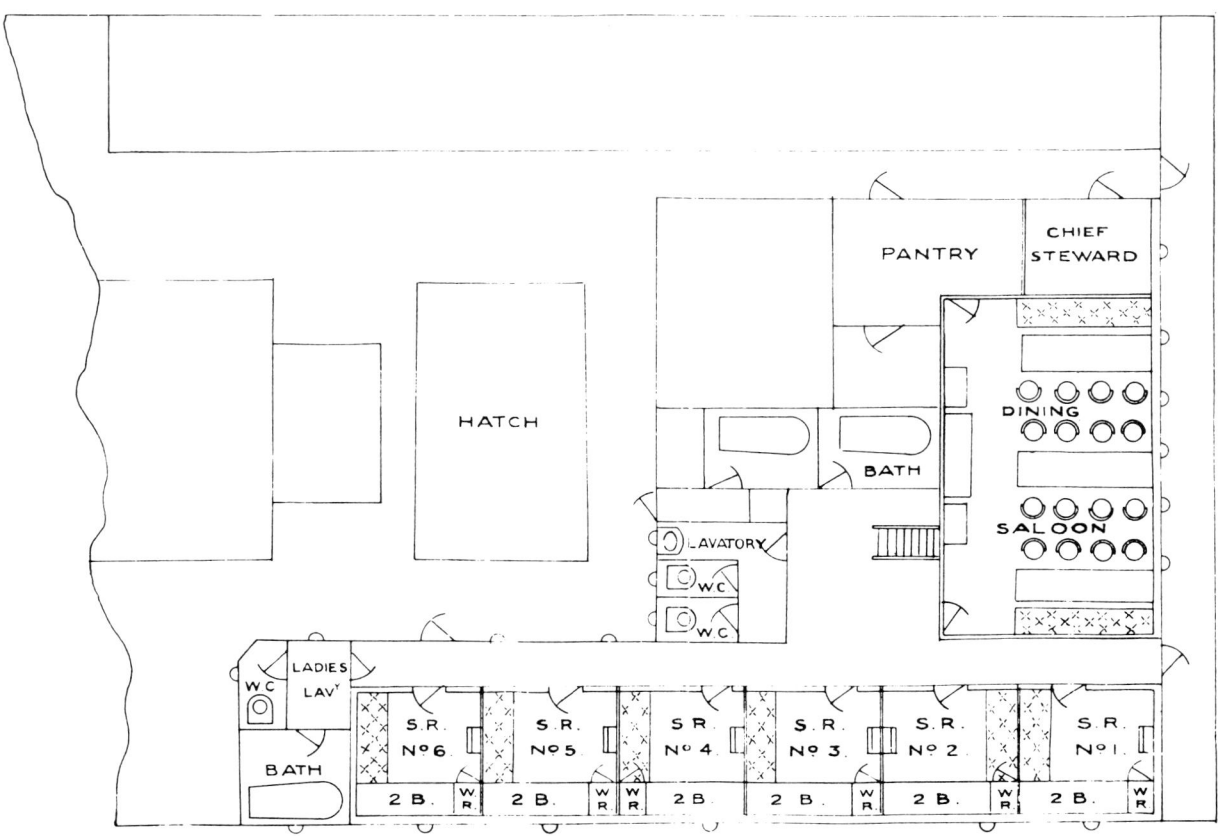

SCH. 3 FORM 37

3/23-5

It would appear that this vessel (the *City of Bedford*, Ellerman Lines) switched on her lights, having seen the *Bodnant* almost at the same moment that the *Bodnant* saw her.

The Chief Officer, who was at the starboard side of the wheelhouse, immediately ordered the helm hard-a-starboard, sounded a short blast on the whistle and stepped into the wheelhouse and switched on the navigation lights using the dimmer switch. He then left the wheelhouse and found Captain Harding who had at that time been taking breakfast in his cabin, standing at the top of the starboard ladder, asking "What's up?".

No sound signal was heard from the *City of Bedford* but she was altering course to port rapidly, shutting out her red light. The *Bodnant* gave another short blast on her whistle without response from the *City of Bedford*.

The interval between the two blasts was apparently 30 seconds and when the second blast was given, the distance between the two vessels was about two cables. At the same time, Captain Harding rang the telegraph full ahead, a double ring, and repeated the order hard-a-starboard.

The *City of Bedford* continued to go to port and the vessels collided; the points of impact being the *City of Bedford*'s starboard side between the fo'c'sle and the foremast and the *Bodnant*'s stem. The blow was a heavy one and the *Bodnant* seemed to ride over the *City of Bedford* as if she were on the crest of the wave and the *City of Bedford* in the trough. The *Bodnant* was a near light ship having only 1,150 tons of cargo, whereas the *City of Bedford* was low in the water and appeared to be heavily laden. The two vessels fell together, the bows of each being close together as far as the foremasts. They then drifted apart and cleared one another.

About the time of the collision a number of navigation lights appeared and abeam, those lights being in some cases from vessels forming the *Bodnant*'s convoy and in others in the convoy of which the *City of Bedford* was part. The two convoys were proceeding on almost directly opposite courses and presumably they were making the same speed of nine knots. The two vessels would, therefore, be meeting at a combined speed of 18 knots—1,800 ft. a minute, that is four cables = 2,400 ft.—80 seconds.

Both vessels suffered considerable damage, with the result that some hours afterwards they both foundered.

From *The Price of Peace*

Bodnant is a town in North Wales.

238   BAKANA (II)

O.N. 140638   1919–1929

'B' class

Steel screw steamer, War 'A' type, one deck

400.4′×52.3′×28.5′   3253 n   5384 g   8175 d

Built by Ropner & Sons Ltd, Stockton, Yard No 529, as **WAR PRIMULA** for the Shipping Controller. Completed for Elder, Dempster & Co Ltd as **BAKANA**. Registered Liverpool. T 3 cyl 27″, 44″, 73″–48″ by Richardsons, Westgarth & Co Ltd, Middlesbrough. 369 nhp, 11 K.

1919 July, launched. September, completed. Subsequently

transferred to British & African Steam Navigation Co Ltd.

1920 Transferred to Elder Line Ltd.
1929 November, sold to Fratelli Lagorara, Genoa. Renamed **HONOR**. Registered Genoa.
1943 8 September, seized by the Germans at Genoa.
1944 12 September, scuttled at San Remo.
1946 Raised.
1947 Broken up at San Remo.

HONOR, formerly BAKANA

239 BEREBY
O.N. 143416   1919–1941
'B' class
Steel screw steamer, War 'B' type, two decks
400.2′×52.3′×28.5′   3179 n   5248 g   8075 d
Laid down by Irvines Shipbuilding & Drydock Co Ltd, West Hartlepool, Yard No 600, as **WAR RAVEN** for the Shipping Controller. Launched as **BEREBY** for Elder, Dempster & Co

Ltd. Registered London. T 3 cyl 27″, 44″, 73″–48″ by Richardsons, Westgarth & Co Ltd, West Hartlepool. 517 nhp, 11 K.
1919 27 June, launched. 9 October, trials, 12 K.
1923 Aground at Mazagan Harbour.
1924 Transferred to African Steamship Co.
1931 January, laid up in Blackwater river.
1933 April, transferred to Elder Dempster Lines Ltd.
1941 24 September, ran ashore on Ringfad Point (north of Dundrum Bay), County Down, Ireland, voyage Liverpool to Takoradi and Port Harcourt (Captain H. Harding). Declared a constructive total loss.
Name taken from port of Bereby in Ghana.

240 BATA
O.N. 143446   1919–1933
'B' class
Steel screw steamer, War 'B' type, two decks
400.8′×52.3′×28.5′   3212 n   5260 g   8075 d
Launched by John Brown & Co Ltd, Clydebank, Yard No 491, for the Shipping Controller. Completed as **BATA** for Elder, Dempster & Co Ltd. Registered London. T 3 cyl 27″, 44″, 73″–48″ by Harland & Wolff Ltd, Glasgow. 517 nhp, 11 K.
1919 10 September, launched. 14 October, trials.
1920 Transferred to African Steamship Co. 3278 n, 5328 g.
1926 June: "By arrangement with the Sierra Leone Government, two African boys from Freetown, M. L. Margai and F. A. A. Johnson, joined the *Bata* as cadets, and will serve the usual term of apprenticeship in our ships. They are now making their second voyage and it is hoped that they will ultimately become qualified pilots for the run between Freetown and Sherbro. So far as is known, this is the first time in the history of the Mercantile Marine that African boys have become cadets on a British ship."
(From *Elder Dempster House Magazine*).

BEREBY

BATA

BADAGRY

1930   September, laid up at Dartmouth.

1933   15 November, sold to Tower Steamship Co, London, for £7500. Renamed **TOWER ABBEY**. Registered London.

1935   September, sold to Wm Crosby & Co Pty Ltd, Melbourne. Renamed **WILLANDRA**.

1938   Sold to Taihei Kisen KK (Yamashita Kisen KK, Managers), Kobe. Renamed **UTIDE MARU**. Registered Kobe.

1944   29 February, sunk by US Submarine SARGO in position 08°.57′N 132°.52′E.

Bata is the name of a township in Rio Muni.

241   BADAGRY (II)

O.N. 143602   1919–1933

'B' class

Steel screw steamer, War 'B' type, two decks

400.2′×52.4′×28.5′   3149 n   5161 g   8075 d

Built by Irvines Shipbuilding & Drydocks Co Ltd, West Hartlepool, Yard No 601, as **WAR CROW** for the Shipping Controller. Completed as **BADAGRY** for British & African Steam Navigation Co Ltd. Registered Liverpool. T 3 cyl 27″, 44″, 73″–48″ by Richardsons, Westgarth & Co Ltd. 517 nhp, 11 K.

1919   24 September, launched. 11 December, completed.

1930   Laid up at Dartmouth. Transferred to Imperial Direct Line Ltd in December.

1933   November, sold to Tramp Shipping Development Co Ltd.

1934   Sold for £7500 to Tower Steam Ship Co Ltd, London. Renamed **TOWER BRIDGE**. Registered London.

1935   September, sold for £18,500 to Ben Line Steamers Ltd. Renamed **BENALDER**. Registered Leith.

1942   8 November, attacked by U-boat off Gold Coast, (position 04°.19′N 02°.44′W, voyage Freetown to Takoradi and Lagos. Reached Takoradi in damaged condition two days later. Subsequently towed to Cape Town.

1944   August, repairs completed at Cape Town and returned to service.

1947   Sold to New Dholera Steamships Ltd, Bombay. Renamed **JAYBRAHMA**. Registered Bombay (British flag).

1955   Sold to Sigma Shipping Co Ltd, Hong Kong. Renamed **SIGMA TRADER**. Registered Hong Kong (British flag).

1958   5 March, arrived Hong Kong to be broken up by Hong Kong Chip Hua Manufactory Co (1947) Ltd.

BADAGRY, *from an oil painting*

159

BARRACOO

Dempster & Co Ltd as **BARRACOO**. Registered London. T 3 cyl 27″, 44″, 73″–48″ by North Eastern Marine Engineering Co Ltd, Sunderland. 517 nhp, 11 K.

1919 10 September, launched. 12 December, trials.
1920 Transferred to African Steamship Co.
1931 15 September, laid up at Bideford.
1933 31 August, sold for £6225 to Nicolas Eustathion & Co, Piraeus. Renamed **MICHALAKIS**. Registered Syra.
1939 Sold to Yamashita Kisen KK, Kobe. Renamed **KUSUYAMA MARU**. Registered Kobe. 3779 n, 5307 g.
1943 8 February, torpedoed and sunk by US Submarine TUNNY west of Formosa in position 22°.40′N 119°.12′E.

242 BARRACOO
O.N. 143914   1919–1933
'B' class
Steel screw steamer, War 'B' type, two decks
400.3′×52.3′×28.5′   3155 n   5234 g   8075 d
Launched by R. Thompson & Sons Ltd, Sunderland, Yard No 310, for the Shipping Controller. Completed for Elder,

243 BURUTU (II)
O.N. 142732   1920–1934
'B' class
Steel screw steamer, War 'B' type, two decks
400.1′×52.4′×28.4′   3220 n   5275 g   8075 d
Built by Sunderland Shipbuilding Co Ltd, Sunderland, Yard No 319, as **WAR SWAN** for the Shipping Controller (Bigland & Co, Managers). T 3 cyl 27″, 44″, 73″–48″ by Blair & Co Ltd, Stockton. 517 nhp, 11 K.

1918 Completed.
1920 January, acquired by British & African Steam Navigation Co Ltd. Renamed **BURUTU**. Registered Liverpool.

BURUTU

1926 15 January, on fire at Hull. In February involved in two collisions in two days, first with German GENERAL BILGRANDO (800 emigrants for Brasil) near Blankenese in fog. The German had stranded and the collision occurred as she freed herself. The second was off Nordeney with Neptune Co's POLLOX which had to be towed in, machinery space flooded. 25 December, in collision with French barque EUGENE SCHNIEDER off Portland; the sailing ship sank in three minutes with 24 lives. Four survivors scrambled aboard **BURUTU** which was undamaged.

1927 10 October, aground in Sherbro River. Refloated December.

1930 Laid up in River Dart.

1934 7 February, sold to D. Inglessi Fils SA Nav. de Samos. Renamed **DEMETRIOS INGLESSES**. Registered Samos.

1949 November, laid up Piraeus. Later recommissioned (Frinton Shipping Ltd, Managers).

1959 4 July, sold to Asahi Bussan Co Ltd and arrived Osaka on that date for demolition.

244 BOMA (II)

O.N. 143615   1920–1940

'B' class
Steel screw steamer, War 'B' type, two decks
400.6′ × 52.3′ × 28.5′   3313 n   5408 g   8075 d
Launched by Harland & Wolff Ltd, Glasgow, Yard No 561, for the Shipping Controller. Completed for British & African Steam Navigation Co Ltd as **BOMA**. Registered Liverpool. T 3 cyl 27″, 44″, 73″–48″ by the builders. 517 nhp, 11 K.
Passenger accommodation: 6 first class.

1919 23 October, launched.
1920 26 February, trials.
1928 4 May, towed *BENDU* after loss of propeller to Las Palmas.
1933 Transferred to Elder Dempster Lines Ltd.
1940 5 August, **BOMA** was struck by a torpedo at 2048 while proceeding from Milford Haven to Freetown with 1000 tons of coal in convoy OB193 (Captain E. C. Anders). **BOMA** was sunk by U56 (Kaptainleutnant Otto Harms). U56 fell in with OB193 on the evening of 5 August. At 2138 (U-boat time was one hour ahead of the convoy's time) Harms fired two torpedoes at a range of 1500 metres at a tanker of 8–9000 grt. A single explosion was heard after a running time of 7 minutes 25 seconds. As German torpedoes were designed to explode at the end of their run, Harms naturally assumed this to have been the case here. In fact, the explosion was due to one of the torpedoes striking **BOMA**. The Germans' time and position correspond almost exactly with the British time and position and the German description of the convoy (course, speed, details of escort) fits OB193 perfectly. Three lives were lost.

U56 was destroyed in an air raid on Kiel on 28 April 1945. Harms had left her on 16 October 1940 and subsequently commanded U464, one of the U-tankers. He was taken prisoner on 20 August 1942 when U464 was sunk. After the war he went to live in Kiel.

245 BOMPATA

O.N. 145845   1921–1934

Steel screw steamer, two decks
410.4′ × 54.3′ × 27.9′   3352 n   5570 g   8200 d
Built by Harland & Wolff Ltd, Belfast, Yard No 560, for Elder, Dempster & Co Ltd. Registered Liverpool.

BOMA (Photo J. Clarkson)

BOMPATA

MATADI

2 steam turbines DR gearing by the builders. 590 nhp, 11 K.
Passenger accommodation: 6 first class.
1920 28 October, launched.
1921 April, completed, and laid up at builders yard.
1923 27 January, maiden voyage. Transferred to British &
African Steam Navigation Co Ltd.
1927 December, bunker fire, voyage Calabar to New York.
1930 7 November, laid up in River Dart.
1933 Transferred to Elder Dempster Lines Ltd.
1934 July, sold for £8500 to Downs Steamship Co Ltd (Basil
M. Mavroleon, Manager), London. Renamed **TOWER
DALE**. Registered London.
1935 sold to A/S Finland-Amerika Linjen O/Y, Helsinki.
Renamed **NAVIGATOR**. Registered Helsingfors. Re-
engined by North Eastern Marine Engineering Co Ltd,
Newcastle. T 3 cyl 22½", 37", 63"–45". 2000 ihp 3212 n,
5656 g.
1937 Grounding damage on passage Rosario to Helsinki.
1946 June, converted to burn oil fuel.
1952 Sold to Finska Angfartygs.
1956 Sold to General Sea Transport & Navigation Co Inc.
Renamed **KEFALOS**. Registered Monrovia.
1959 Sold to James A. Dow (Newcastle) Ltd. Renamed
FALKOS. Sold for demolition. 12 December, work commenced at Osaka.

246 MATADI (II)
O.N. 140633   1919–1921
'M' class
Steel screw steamer, War 'C' type, one deck
331.3′×46.8′×23.2′   1879 n   3097 g   5050 d
Launched by R. Thompson & Sons Ltd, Sunderland, yard No
309, as **WAR RAVINE** for the Shipping Controller. Completed
for Elder, Dempster & Co Ltd as **MATADI**. Registered Liverpool. T 3 cyl 25", 41", 68"–45" by North Eastern Marine Engineering Co Ltd, Sunderland. 358 nhp, 11½ K.
1919 18 March, launched.
1921 November, sold to Cie Africaine de Navigation,
Antwerp. Registered Antwerp.
1929 Transferred to Cie Maritime Belge (Lloyd Royal) SA.
1937 Sold to J. M. Lyras & Co (Rethymnis and Kulukundis,
Managers), Piraeus. Renamed **LYRAS N**. December,
sold to Cie Africaine de Navigation, 'Francafrica' (SA
de Gerance Armement, Managers), Rouen. Renamed
BRESTOIS. Registered Rouen.
1942 Seized by Italians. Renamed **VERCELLI**.

1943 29 January, attacked by aircraft—bomb damaged.
Taken in tow next day (30 miles off Cape Bon, Tunisia)
for Bizerta but sank one and a half miles off Cape Farina.
Ships of the 'M' class: MATADI (246), MATEBA (247).

247 MATEBA
O.N. 140647   1919–1921
'M' class
Steel screw steamer, War 'C' type, one deck
331.2′×48.0′×22.1′   1757 n   2955 g   5050 d
Launched by W. Dobson & Co Ltd, Walker-on-Tyne, Yard No
212, as **WAR CRATER** for the Shipping Controller. Completed
for Elder, Dempster & Co Ltd as **MATEBA**. Registered Liverpool. T 3 cyl 25", 41", 68"–45" by North Eastern Marine Engineering Co Ltd, Wallsend, Newcastle. 358 nhp, 11½ K.
1919 28 May, launched.
1921 November, sold to Cie Africaine de Navigation,
Antwerp. Registered Antwerp.
1930 Transferred to Cie Maritime Belge (Lloyd Royal) SA.
1937 Sold to Cie Delmas Vieljeux, La Rochelle. Renamed
MAURICE DELMAS. Registered La Rochelle. 1873 n,
3161 g.
1938 Fitted to burn oil fuel.
1942 December, seized by Italians. Renamed **MODICA**.
1943 15 February, sunk during air raid on Naples.
1947 Salvaged, repaired and put back into service. Owner:
Pietro Longobardo, Naples. 1749 n, 2896 g, 4700 d.
Registered Naples.
1960 Sold to Salvaton Carlino Industrie, Naples, for demolition. Work commenced January.
The name is derived from the Mateba Pass, River Zaire.

MATEBA

NEW BRUNSWICK

248 NEW BRUNSWICK

O.N. 140632   1920–1942

'N' class
Steel screw steamer, War 'N' type, one deck and shelter deck
412.6′×55.8′×34.4′   4028 n   6529 g   10,500 d
Launched by Harland & Wolff Ltd, Belfast, Yard No 555, as
WAR LIBERTY for the Shipping Controller. Completed for
Elder, Dempster & Co Ltd as **NEW BRUNSWICK**. Registered
Liverpool. T 3 cyl 27″, 44″, 73″–48″ by the builders. 517 nhp,
10 K.

Passenger accommodation: 2 first class.
1919   15 May, launched. 26 June, trials.
1920   December, transferred to Elder Line Ltd.
1933   April, transferred to Elder Dempster Lines Ltd.
1942   21 May, (Captain C. H. Whalley) torpedoed and sunk
       by German submarine U159 (Kapitanleutnant Helmut
       Witte) off Rio del Oro, in position 36°.53′N 22°.55′W,
       voyage Glasgow to Lagos, cargo military stores and
       general, with the loss of three lives. Witte sighted the
       convoy just after midnight on 21 July, at a distance of
       some eight miles. He proceeded to haul ahead on the
       dark side, with the object of attacking when the moon
       went down. At 0324 U159 penetrated the screen astern
       of the leading escort on the convoy's port side and fired
       all six tubes in succession at five-overlapping steamers.
       Witte claimed hits for all four bow tubes and one hit for
       the two stern torpedoes. Three steamers in a sinking
       condition were seen to sheer out of station. A fourth was
       observed to be down by the head. In all, Witte claimed
       three steamers definitely sunk. For an hour after the
       attack the area was illuminated by starshell, despite
       which U159 was able to retire unseen on the surface.

       Witte returned to the attack at 0510. However, on this
       occasion, while trying to penetrate the screen, U159 was
       picked up by the leading port wing escort, who turned
       her searchlight on the U-boat and opened fire. U159
       crash dived and was attacked by two escorts with depth-
       charges, which although accurately aimed caused only
       very minor damage.

FILE ADM 237/141

YEAR 1942   CONVOY No OS 28   DATE DEP 12th Nov. 1942

CONVOY COMMODORE: A. J. DAVIES, C.B., R.N.R. SS "INCHANGA" for Freetown

VICE-COMMODORE: MASTER OF SS "BARON VERNON" for Takoradi
REAR-COMMODORE: MASTER OF SS "EMPIRE SIMBA" for Freetown

EMPIRE RAVEN 8½K 96ft	DRAMATIST 9½K 96ft	EMPIRE SIMBA 10½K 87ft	DOVERHILL 9K 99ft	INCHANGA 12K 109ft	ALDERMIN 10K (Du) 110ft	BARON VERNON 8½K 82ft	BLOOMERSDIJK 12K (Du) 118ft	CITY OF EXETER 12½K 120ft			
CHRISTINE MARIE 8½K 115ft	BRUXELLES (Bel) 8½K 89ft	KIRUNA 9K 90ft	CADUCEUS	TORONTO (Nor) 11½K 84ft	NYANZA 10K 87ft	ST. ROSARIO 10K 78ft	SANTOS (Nor) 11½K 70ft	CITY OF JOHANNESBURG 11½K 100ft			
PRINS WILLEM VAN ORANJE 9K (Du) 70ft	DARONIA 10K 105ft	MONTENOL 14K 90ft	NEW BRUNSWICK 10K	BEACONSFIELD 10½K 86ft		QUEEN VICTORIA 10K 87ft	GLENAPP 12K 113ft	CAPE HAWKE			
EL CIERVO 9½K 95ft	ATHEL KNIGHT 9½K 100ft	.	.	OCEAN VESPER 10½K 74ft	FORT ST. JAMES 10K 73ft	SABOR 9½K 89ft	CITY OF CORINTH 11K 105ft	.			
			ROSEWOOD oiler for escorts 10½K 100ft	OBSERVER 10½K 92ft	BENALDER 10½K 90ft	ERRINGTON COURT 8½K 93ft		ASTREL (Nor)			

ESCORT HMS WESTON (s/o): GORLESTON: TOTLAND: WELLINGTON

Local escort HMS MOLDE (ex RNN "Kos xx")

Note: Two signalmen on board "BARON VERNON"

▶ SHIPS BOUND FOR FREETOWN
▷ SHIPS BOUND FOR CAPE & ONWARDS
| SHIPS BOUND FOR TAKORADI

NEW BRUNSWICK *was lost in Convoy OS28 (Plan L. Norbury-Williams)*

NEW GEORGIA

In fact, only **NEW BRUNSWICK** and one other ship were hit in U159's attack, namely RFA MONTENOL, which was damaged and had to be sunk by HMS WOODRUFFE with gunfire. Three torpedoes were seen by the ships to miss the **NEW BRUNSWICK** and two to miss the MONTENOL, which, when added to the two hits, makes one torpedo too many. A possible explanation is that one of those seen to miss the **NEW BRUNSWICK** subsequently hit the RFA, which was torpedoed about two minutes beforehand.

Kapitanleutnant Helmut Witte, of U159, sank **NEW BRUNSWICK** *(Photo Bundesarchiv)*

The escort vessel that saw U159 when the U-boat later returned to the convoy was the GORLESTON, which, with the sloop WESTON, carried out the depth-charge attack described in U159's war diary.

U159, then under the command of Oberleutnant zur See Hermann Beckmann, was sunk with all hands on 15 July 1943 in 15°.58′N 73°.44′W by US aircraft VP/32. Witte survived the war.

Ships of the 'N' class: NEW BRUNSWICK (248), NEW GEORGIA (249), NEW MEXICO (250), NEW TEXAS (251), NEW TORONTO (252), NEW BRIGHTON (253), NEW BROOKLYN (254), NEW COLUMBIA (255).

The 'N' class was of a special build, having straight frames, bevelled bilge, and triangular stern.

Name derived from a town in New Jersey, USA.

249   NEW GEORGIA
O.N. 140645   1919–1933

'N' class

Steel screw steamer, War 'N' type, one deck and shelter deck
412.6′×55.8′×34.4′   4044 n   6566 g   10,400 d

Launched by Harland & Wolff Ltd, Belfast, Yard No 556, as **WAR TRIUMPH** for the Shipping Controller. Completed for Elder, Dempster & Co Ltd as **NEW GEORGIA**. Registered Liverpool. T 3 cyl 27″, 44″, 73″–48″ by the builders. 517 nhp, 11 K.

1919   12 June, launched. 14 August, trials.
1921   Transferred to British & African Steam Navigation Co Ltd.
1930   6 February, laid up at Dartmouth.
1933   30 March, sold for £6750 to Nausicaa Shipping Co, Athens. Renamed **PENELOPE**. Registered Piraeus.
1939   Sold to Polar Cia de Navegacion Ltda, Panama City. Renamed **PENELOPI**. Registered Panama. Depth 28.6′. 2899 n, 4787 g.

1956 February, sold to Pacific Bulk Carriers Inc, Hong Kong. Renamed **PACIFIC CARRIER**. 4073 n, 6495 g. July, transferred to Atlantic Bulk Carriers Inc, Hong Kong. Renamed **ATLANTIC CARRIER**.
1959 February, sold for demolition at Mukaishima.
Name derived from one of the United States of America.

NEW MEXICO

250 NEW MEXICO
O.N. 140651   1919–1933
'N' class
Steel screw steamer, War 'N' type, one deck and shelter deck
412.6′×55.8′×34.4′   4044 n   6566 g   10,400 d
Launched by Harland & Wolff Ltd, Belfast, Yard No 557, as **PHILADELPHIAN**. Completed for Elder, Dempster & Co Ltd as **NEW MEXICO**. Registered Liverpool. T 3 cyl 27″, 44″, 73″–48″ by the builders. 517 nhp, 11 K.
1919 26 June, launched. 28 August, trials.
1920 December, transferred to Elder Line Ltd.
1931 8 June, laid up at Dartmouth.
1933 April, transferred to Elder Dempster Lines Ltd. August, sold to S. G. Razis, London. Renamed **ANDREAS**. Registered Argostoli.
1936 Sold to Ionion Steam Ship Co Ltd, Piraeus, Registered Argostoli.
1942 4 November, shelled and sunk by Italian submarine DA VINCI (Commander Gazzana) off the coast of Pernambuco, approximately 02°.00′S 30°.30W on voyage St Johns (New Brunswick) and Trinidad to Cape Town and Alexandria, cargo ammunition and general.
Name derived from one of the United States of America.

251 NEW TEXAS
O.N. 140653   1919–1955
'N' class
Steel screw steamer, War 'N' type, one deck and shelter deck, second deck in forward holds and after main hold
412.6′×55.8′×34.4′   4044 n   6568 g   10,400 d
Launched by Harland & Wolff Ltd, Belfast, Yard No 559, unnamed, for the Shipping Controller. Completed for Elder, Dempster & Co Ltd as **NEW TEXAS**. Registered Liverpool. T 3 cyl 27″, 44″, 73″–48″ by the builders. 517 nhp, 11 K.
Passenger accommodation: one double berth stateroom.
1919 14 August, launched. 18 September, trials.

NEW TEXAS

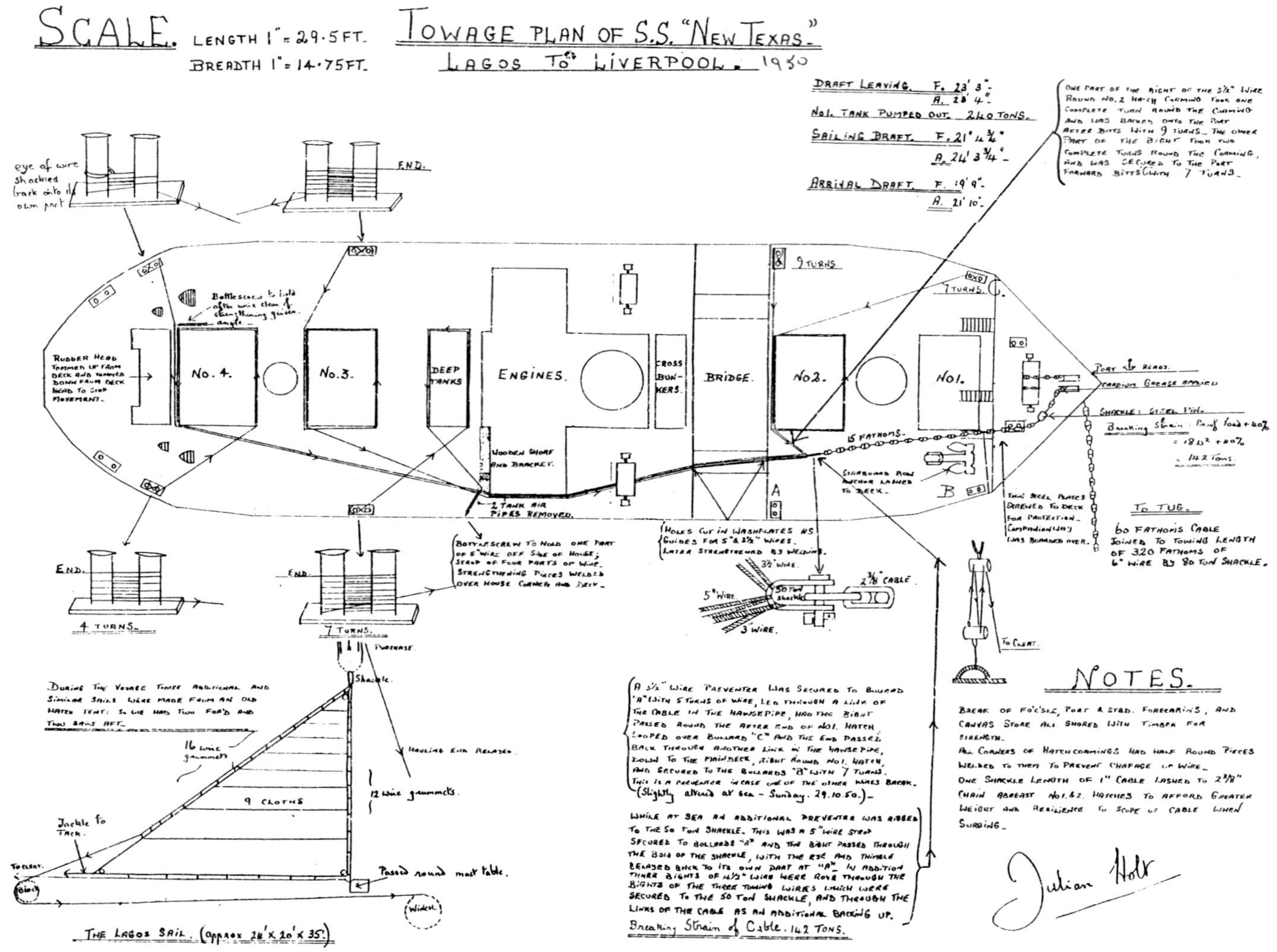

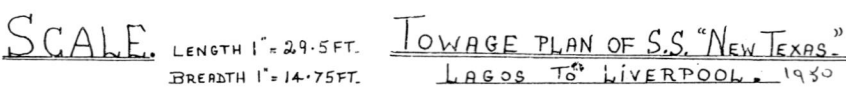

Towage Plan of S.S. "New Texas"
Lagos to Liverpool. 1950

1921 February, transferred to British & African Steam Navigation Co Ltd.

1933 April, transferred to Elder Dempster Lines Ltd.

1950 8 August (Captain C. H. Whalley), grounded while discharging at Accra, refloated and proceeded to Lagos. Sternpost and rudder carried away entering harbour. Departed Lagos 6 October, under tow of tug BUSTLER and arrived at Liverpool 6 November.
Voyage data
Total distance steamed—4097 miles
Total distance port to port—4212 miles
Total steaming time—26d, 19h, 02m
Total time port to port—28d, 8h, 08m
Voyage average speed homewards—6.37 knots
Delays

Date	Stop	Slow ahead	Tug repairs
9/10/50	1438 hrs	1455 hrs	,,
14/10/50	0600 hrs	1039 hrs	,,
14/10/50	1914 hrs	1958 hrs	,,
23/10/50	0435 hrs	0629 hrs	Various engine ,,
23/10/50	0820 hrs	0828 hrs	movements to ,,
26/10/50	2258 hrs	2303 hrs	keep clear of tug ,,
1/11/50	0433 hrs	0508 hrs	,,
1/11/50	2315 hrs	0925 hrs	,,

Total time **NEW TEXAS** not steaming due to tug repairs, 18h, 32min

1955 January, sold for £59,000 to British Iron & Steel Corporation for demolition. 14 January, arrived Barrow.
Name derived from one of the United States of America.

252 NEW TORONTO
O.N. 140658   1919–1942
'N' class
Steel screw steamer, War 'N' type, one deck and shelter deck
412.6′×55.8′×34.4′   4044 n   6568 g   10,400 d
Launched by Harland & Wolff Ltd, Belfast, Yard No 558, unnamed, for the Shipping Controller. Completed for Elder, Dempster & Co Ltd as **NEW TORONTO**. Registered Liverpool. T 3 cyl 27″, 44″, 73″–48″ by the builders. 517 nhp, 11 K.

1919 28 August, launched. October, trials.

1920 December, transferred to British & African Steam Navigation Co Ltd.

1924 Grounded on Coffin Patches.

1933 April, transferred to Elder Dempster Lines Ltd.

1942 5 November, (Captain C. J. Kewley) escorted by ML263 **NEW TORONTO** was bound for Accra from Lagos with African produce when torpedoed by U126 (Kapitanleutnant Ernst Bauer). Bauer sighted the **NEW TORONTO**'s mastheads at 1800 (Central European Time). She was zigzagging between 240° and 280°. At 2059 in a surface night attack Bauer fired a spread salvo of two torpedoes at a range of 300 metres, one of which struck the target beneath the forward mast. Just before he fired, Bauer caught sight of a small motor launch astern of the steamer, which after the explosion rapidly closed the ship in her wake and when abreast stopped to carry out a listening pursuit. U126 initially withdrew to observe the results of the attack. The motor launch's attempts at hunting were obviously ineffectual, and as there appeared to be no great effect on the target from

NEW TORONTO

the torpedo hit, Bauer ran in for a second surface attack. On this occasion the torpedo struck abreast the after end of the bridge. The motor launch then began to chase the U-boat around the stricken vessel, while aimlessly dropping depth-charges. Eventually the **NEW TORONTO** sank. Three crew and one cattle drover lost their lives.

U126, then under the command of Oberleutnant zur See Kietz, was sunk with all hands on 3 July 1943 to the north-west of Cape Ortegal by Wellington 'R' of 172 Squadron Coastal Command. Bauer survived the war.

Name derived from Canadian city of Toronto.

253 NEW BRIGHTON
O.N. 144348   1920–1933

'N' class

Steel screw steamer, War 'N' type, one deck and shelter deck, second deck in forward holds and after main hold

412.6′×55.8′×34.4′   4044 n   6538 g   10,400 d

Launched by Harland & Wolff Ltd, Belfast, Yard No 577, unnamed. Completed for African Steamship Co as **NEW BRIGHTON**. Registered London.

2 steam turbines DR gearing by the builders. 678 nhp, 11 K.

1919   6 November, launched.
1920   31 January, trials.
1932   1 May, laid up at New York.
1933   Transferred to Elder Dempster Lines Ltd. Registered Liverpool. 16 June, sold to T. K. King, Shanghai. Renamed **CHIN YUEN**. Registered Shanghai. 4004 n, 6524 g.
1938   Sold to Kinryu Kisen KK, Totteri-Ken, Japan. Renamed **KINRYU MARU**. Registered Sakai.
1951   Sold to Toyo Kaiun KK. Registered Kobe.
1952   June, broken up in Japan.

254 NEW BROOKLYN
O.N. 143625   1920–1954

'N' class

Steel screw steamer, War 'N' type, one deck and shelter deck, second deck in forward holds and after main hold

412.6′×55.8′×34.4′   4023 n   6546 g   10,400 d

Launched by Harland & Wolff Ltd, Belfast, Yard No 566, as **WAR ROMANCE** for the Shipping Controller. Completed for Elder, Dempster & Co Ltd as **NEW BROOKLYN**. Registered Liverpool. T 3 cyl 27″, 44″, 73″–48″ by the builders. 517 nhp, 10 K.

NEW BRIGHTON

NEW BROOKLYN

1919 11 December, launched.
1920 31 March, trials. Subsequently transferred to British & African Steam Navigation Co Ltd.
1932 16 June, laid up at Bideford.
1933 April, transferred to Elder Dempster Lines Ltd.
1954 17 November, sold to Mageolia Navegacion SA (Southern Shipping & Finance Co Ltd, London, Managers). Renamed **MARIANNA**. Registered Panama.
1956 Sold to John S. Latsis, Athens. Registered Piraeus.
1959 Sold to shipbreakers. 6 August, arrived Spezia for demolition by Terrestre Maritima Spa.
Name derived from town in New York state.

NEW COLUMBIA (Photo J. Clarkson)

255 NEW COLUMBIA
O.N. 144601   1920–1943
'N' class
Steel screw steamer, War 'N' type, one deck and shelter deck, second deck in forward holds and after main hold
412.6′×55.8′×34.4′   4044 n   6574 g   10,400 d
Launched by Harland & Wolff Ltd, Belfast, Yard No 567, as **WAR PAGEANT** for the Shipping Controller. Completed for African Steamship Co as **NEW COLUMBIA**. Registered London. T 3 cyl 27″, 44″, 73″–48″ by the builders. 517 nhp, 10 K. Fitted for either coal or oil burning.
1920 25 March, launched. 30 June, trials.
1928 Pioneered the bulk palm oil trade from West Africa to USA. Two fuel oil tanks filled with palm oil as an experiment.
1933 Transferred to Elder Dempster Lines Ltd. Registered Liverpool.
1943 31 October, torpedoed and sunk by U68 in position

04°.25′N 05°.03′E, voyage Libreville to Lagos, cargo copper and general, no lives lost. At 1832 (Central European Time) on 31 October U68 (Oberleutnant Albert Lauzemis) had just surfaced when Lauzemis sighted the **NEW COLUMBIA** (Captain F. B. Kent) some 10,000 metres away steaming in his direction. In view of that and the fact that it was still light U68 dived, altered onto the target's course and resurfaced some time later, at 1914, to haul ahead for an attack. At 2124, having achieved an attacking position, Lauzemis fired one FAT torpedo set to run straight (a FAT torpedo, christened 'curly' by the Royal Navy during the war, was designed to describe a to-and-fro course, as required, to increase the chances of a hit when attacking convoys). After running for just under 40 seconds the torpedo struck abreast the forward mast, the steamer began to settle by the bows, but failed to sink. Lauzemis thus fired a second straight-running FAT, which hit in the engine-room and at 2200 the **NEW COLUMBIA** went down by the head. Her crew told Lauzemis that she was the *TROILUS* bound for Lagos with cotton.

U68 was sunk on 10 April 1944 to the west-north-west of Madeira by aircraft from the US carrier GUADALCANAL. There was only one survivor, an Ordinary Seaman.

JEBBA

256 JEBBA (II)
O.N. 142300   1919–1933
'J' class
Steel screw steamer, Japanese War Standard type, two decks and awning deck
385.3′×51.2′×25.5′   4278 n   5875 g   9160 d
Built by Kawasaki Dockyard Co, Kobe, Yard No 398, as **WAR LION** for HM Government (Furness Withy & Co Ltd, Managers). Registered London. T 3 cyl 26″, 43½″, 72″–48″ by the builders. 440 nhp, 10 K.
1917 September, completed.
1919 October, acquired by African Steamship Co. Renamed **JEBBA**. Registered London.
1928 October, lost propeller and towed into Lagos by *BENDU*.
1930 12 May, laid up at Dartmouth.
1933 22 March, sold for £4000 to Tramp Shipping Development Co Ltd, London (Xilas Bros & A. Constantinidis, Piraeus). Renamed **THALIA**. Registered Syra. 2768 n, 4574 g.
1940 19 October, torpedoed and sunk by U99 (Korvettenkapitan Otto Kretschmer) in position 57°.N 11°.30′W approximately, voyage Montreal to Garston, cargo steel.
1941 17 March, U99 sunk by HMS WALKER.
Ships of the 'J' class: JEBBA (256), JEKRI (257).

JEKRI in the River Dart

257 JEKRI

O.N. 142316   1920–1933

'J' class
Steel screw steamer, Japanese War Standard type,
two decks and awning deck
385.3′×51.2′×25.5′   4278 n   5875 g   9160 d
Built by Kawasaki Dockyard Co Ltd, Kobe, Yard No 401, as
WAR PILOT for HM Government (Furness Withy & Co Ltd,
Managers). Registered London. T 3 cyl 26″, 43½″, 72″–48″ by
the builders. 440 nhp, 10 K.
1917   October, launched. November, completed.
1920   7 January, acquired by Elder, Dempster & Co Ltd.
        Renamed **JEKRI**. Registered London.
1921   Transferred to British & African Steam Navigation Co
        Ltd. Registered Liverpool.

1930   7 April, laid up at Dartmouth
1933   22 March, sold for £4500 to Tramp Shipping Devel-
        opment Co Ltd, London. Registered Liverpool. Sep-
        tember, sold for £4150 for demolition at Genoa.
Jekri is the name of a tribe in the Forcados area of the Niger
Delta.

258 ABA

O.N. 141887   1920–1947

Steel twin screw motorship, two decks and shelter deck
450.5′×55.8′×36.6′   4623 n   7347 g   8000 d
Laid down by Barclay, Curle & Co Ltd, Glasgow, Yard No 519,
to the order of the Imperial Russian Government. Construction
suspended when the revolution took place. Purchased by Glen
Line Ltd and completed as **GLENAPP**. Registered Glasgow.
2× B & W oil engines 4 SCSA 8 cyl 29½″–43$\frac{5}{16}$″ by Harland &
Wolff Ltd, Glasgow. 1140 nhp, 14 K.
1918   September, completed.
1920   Acquired by British & African Steam Navigation Co
        Ltd. Rebuilt as a passenger liner, accommodation 225
        first class, 140 second and third class, masts reduced to
        two and one traditional type funnel fitted. Renamed
        ABA. Registered Liverpool. 4596 n, 7937 g, 4858 d.
1921   8 August, trials. November, commenced first voyage,
        Liverpool to West Africa.
1922   27 August, 1600 hours **ABA** (Captain Johnston Hughes
        [see Appendix 2]) took in tow the disabled Portuguese
        destroyer, GUADIANA, arriving at Las Palmas 2030
        on 30 August.
1929   4 December, left Liverpool (Captain T. E. Williams) for
        Lagos with 128 passengers and the Christmas mails. The

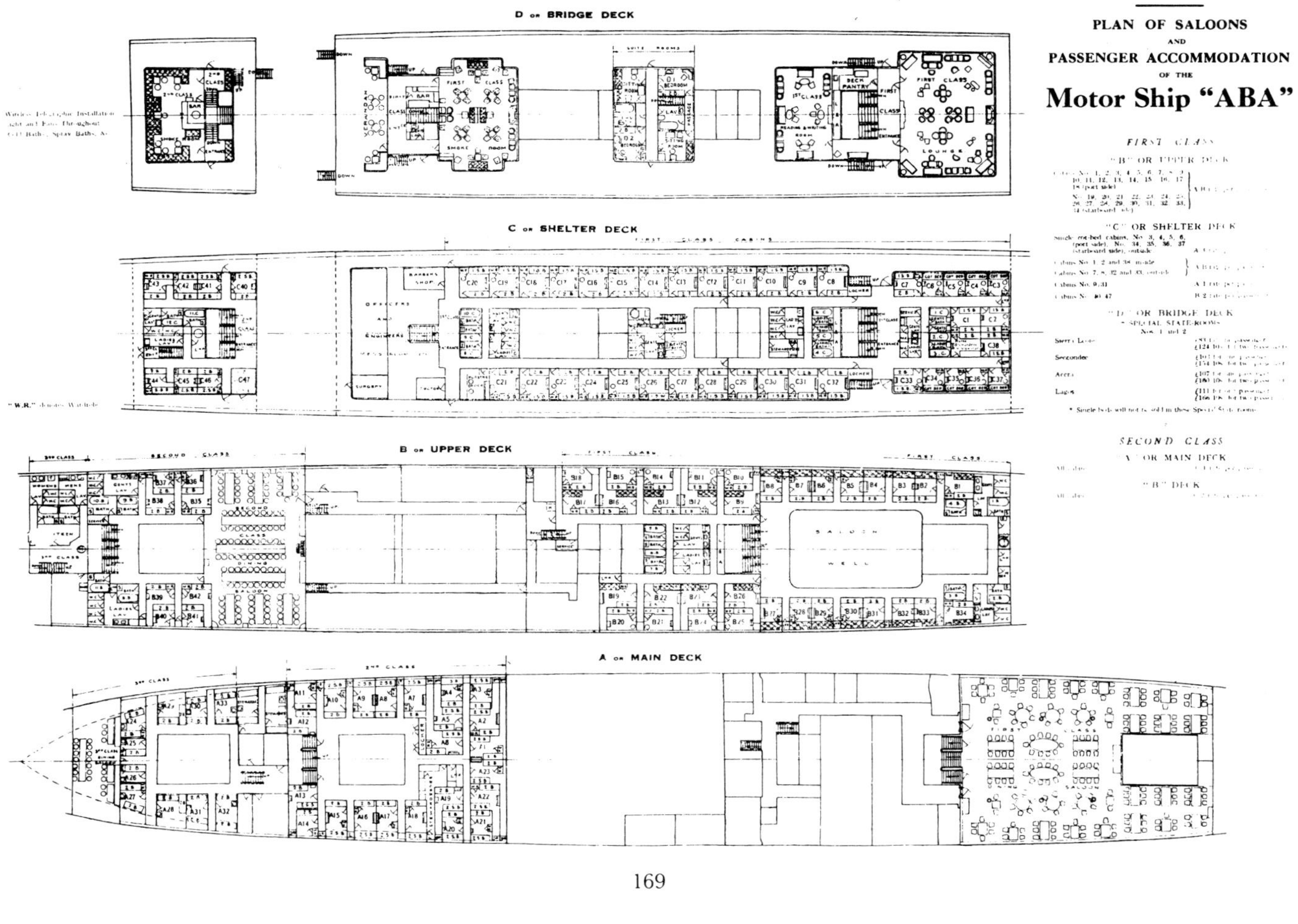

ABA lying off Sekondi, c. 1929–1930

following day **ABA** ran into severe weather conditions which badly damaged the steering engine and buckled the after portion of the steering house, causing plates to start from the deck. Hand steering gear was put into use, but successive pounding also damaged this, rendering **ABA** almost helpless. A call for assistance was sent out which was answered by the *APAPA* and *EGBA*. Later the salvage tug ZWARTE ZEE put a line aboard **ABA** and towed her towards Queenstown, where she was assisted into the harbour by the local tug MORSECOCK.

1931   4 June, grounded off Customs Wharf, Lagos lagoon. Refloated with assistance of *BARRACOO* after efforts of Nigerian-Marine tugs failed. Subsequently laid up.

1931–32   Laid up at Dartmouth.

1933   April, transferred to Elder Dempster Lines Ltd.

1939   Requisitioned by the Admiralty, converted as a hospital ship.

1941   17 May, damaged by bombs in aircraft attack 50 miles south of Crete.

1944   15 March, damaged by bombs during aircraft attack on Naples. One crew, one RAMC orderly and one patient killed.

1945   Made two round trips Liverpool–Ireland transporting Royal Air Force Personnel.

1947   7 January, returned to owners. 29 April, sold to Bawtry Steamship Co Ltd for £55,000. Renamed **MATRONA**. Registered Liverpool. 31 October, capsized in Bidston Dock, Birkenhead, due to the removal of pig iron ballast.

1948   8 June, vessel righted, declared beyond economic repair and sold for demolition. 4 October, arrived at Barrow-in-Furness for demolition by T. W. Ward Ltd.

Two views of **ABA** *in the River Mersey*

DEPARTURE AND ARRIVAL DATES OF HM HOSPITAL SHIP **ABA** SINCE THE COMMENCEMENT OF HOSTILITIES IN SEPTEMBER 1939

Sailed Liverpool 9.9.1939. Arrived Scapa Flow 11.9.1939. Anchored at Scapa as a Hospital Carrier until 28.10.1939 when she left for Invergordon with wounded.

Arrived Invergordon 28.10.1939 and left again on 1.11.1939 for Scapa. Was at anchor at Scapa until 6.12.1939 when she left for Dundee.

Arrived Dundee 7.12.1939 and after discharging wounded, refuelling and storing, left Dundee on 14.12.1939, back again for Scapa, arriving there 15.12.1939.

Remained anchored as a Hospital Carrier until 5.2.1940 when she left for Greenock, arriving there 7.2.1940. Remained at the Tail of the Bank until 28.2.1940 when she sailed for Liverpool.

During all the above period she was running for the Admiralty, and whilst at Liverpool was transferred to a Military Hospital Ship.

Arrived Liverpool on 1.3.1940 and undocked for River Mersey 9.5.1940. Remained at anchor until 25th May.

Time and date arrived	Time and date departed	Port or anchorage
	0656 25. 5.1940	Mersey River
1415 27. 5.1940	0800 28. 5.1940	Kirkwall
2000 31. 5.1940	1000 1. 6.1940	Hardstad
1700 4. 6.1940	1350 7. 6.1940	Scapa Flow Anchorage
1835 7. 6.1940	1050 8. 6.1940	Scapa Flow Anchorage— orders to return
0130 10. 6.1940	0450 10. 6.1940	Bar Light River Mersey
0712 10. 6.1940	1340 5. 7.1940	River Mersey
0730 10. 7.1940	1115 10. 7.1940	Gibraltar
1125 13. 7.1940	1900 8. 8.1940	Gibraltar (orders to return
	28. 8.1940	to Table Bay, Capetown)
0805 30. 8.1940	1512 4. 9.1940	Capetown
0800 22. 9.1940	1800 22. 9.1940	Aden
0800 28. 9.1940	0450 3.10.1940	Suez
1415 8.10.1940	1515 8.10.1940	Malta
1400 12.10.1940	1100 13.10.1940	Haifa
1700 14.10.1940	1510 15.10.1940	Alexandria
0830 16.10.1940	0950 16.10.1940	Port Said
2140 16.10.1940	1430 17.10.1940	Suez
0900 23.10.1940	1020 24.10.1940	Aden
1700 30.10.1940	1300 4.11.1940	Bombay
1800 18.11.1940	1844 10.12.1940	Durban
0743 28.12.1940	0605 19. 1.1941	Suez
1145 19. 1.1941	0635 23. 1.1941	Ismailia
1215 23. 1.1941	1830 24. 1.1941	Port Said
0800 26. 1.1941	1800 29. 1.1941	Sollum (to anchor in Bay)
1400 30. 1.1941	1400 4. 2.1941	Alexandria
0805 7. 2.1941	1000 7. 2.1941	Bardia
1740 7. 2.1941	1530 9. 2.1941	Tobruk
1600 10. 2.1941	1630 11. 2.1941	Alexandria
0800 12. 2.1941	1718 19. 2.1941	Port Said
0900 21. 2.1941	1400 23. 2.1941	Tobruk
1640 24. 2.1941	1900 27. 2.1941	Alexandria
1830 28. 2.1941	1230 16. 4.1941	Haifa
1845 17. 4.1941	1845 17. 4.1941	Alexandria
1230 20. 4.1941	1830 20. 4.1941	Piraeus
0800 21. 4.1941	1218 21. 4.1941	Suda Bay
0815 23. 4.1941	1547 25. 4.1941	Alexandria
1820 26. 4.1941	1715 2. 5.1941	Haifa
0715 5. 5.1941	0715 5. 5.1941	Suda Bay
1005 5. 5.1941	1840 5. 5.1941	Canea
1430 7. 5.1941	1500 8. 5.1941	Alexandria
1730 9. 5.1941	1730 13. 5.1941	Haifa
0914 16. 5.1941	1845 16. 5.1941	Canea
0830 19. 5.1941	1740 16. 6.1941	Haifa
1200 17. 6.1941	1000 22. 7.1941	Port Said
0642 24. 7.1941	0020 28. 7.1941	Zenima
0940 29. 7.1941	0818 30. 7.1941	Suez
1510 2. 8.1941	0702 3. 8.1941	Port Sudan

Time and date arrived	Time and date departed	Port or anchorage
1005 6. 8.1941	1441 8. 8.1941	Aden at Anchor
	0735 9. 8.1941	Aden
0950 23. 8.1941	1042 23.10.1941	Durban
0800 8.11.1941	1800 11.11.1941	Aden
0800 18.11.1941	1000 19.11.1941	Suez
1205 25.11.1941	1740 25.11.1941	Aden
0800 11.12.1941	0700 2. 2.1942	Durban—remained at Durban
0935 14. 2.1942	0736 24. 2.1942	Aden
0727 1. 3.1942	1333 2. 3.1942	Suez
0817 8. 3.1942	1442 8. 3.1942	Aden
1910 14. 3.1942	0700 15. 3.1942	Mombasa
0740 22. 3.1942	1800 24. 3.1942	Durban
1615 25. 3.1942	0706 14. 4.1942	East London
1800 15. 4.1942	1645 23. 4.1942	Durban
0715 7. 5.1942	1615 7. 5.1942	Aden
1800 12. 5.1942	0600 13. 5.1942	Suez
1700 13. 5.1942	1500 16. 5.1942	Port Said
1200 18. 5.1942	1935 30. 5.1942	Alexandria
0805 1. 6.1942	1500 2. 6.1942	Tobruk
0800 3. 6.1942	1905 7. 6.1942	Alexandria
0800 9. 6.1942	1530 9. 6.1942	Tobruk
1730 10. 6.1942	1930 13. 6.1942	Alexandria
0800 15. 6.1942	1130 16. 6.1942	Tobruk
1830 18. 6.1942	1630 30. 6.1942	Alexandria
0845 2. 7.1942	0600 4. 7.1942	Haifa
1537 5. 7.1942	1800 6. 7.1942	Alexandria
0800 8. 7.1942	1844 8. 7.1942	Haifa
1450 9. 7.1942	1100 10. 7.1942	Port Said
0900 11. 7.1942	0830 25. 7.1942	Haifa
1700 25. 7.1942	1810 19. 8.1942	Beirut
1540 22. 8.1942	1500 25. 8.1942	Alexandria
0840 27. 8.1942	1712 27. 8.1942	Beirut
1300 29. 8.1942	1942 29. 8.1942	Alexandria
0807 31. 8.1942	1430 31. 8.1942	Haifa
1545 1. 9.1942	1730 2. 9.1942	Port Said
1455 3. 9.1942	1010 4. 9.1942	Haifa
1610 4. 9.1942	1720 5. 9.1942	Port Said
1235 6. 9.1942	1805 6. 9.1942	Haifa
1045 8. 9.1942	1915 8. 9.1942	Alexandria
0745 10. 9.1942	1415 10. 9.1942	Haifa
1214 11. 9.1942	1700 13. 9.1942	Port Said
1700 14. 9.1942	1900 15. 9.1942	Beirut
1000 17. 9.1942	1800 17. 9.1942	Alexandria
0900 19. 9.1942	1100 23. 9.1942	Haifa
0933 24. 9.1942	1845 24. 9.1942	Port Said
1430 25. 9.1942	1800 25. 9.1942	Haifa
0947 27. 9.1942	1828 27. 9.1942	Alexandria
0813 29. 9.1942	0910 30. 9.1942	Haifa
1000 1.10.1942	1812 1.10.1942	Port Said
1730 2.10.1942	1230 3.10.1942	Beirut
1330 5.10.1942	1645 6.10.1942	Port Said
1630 7.10.1942	1700 8.10.1942	Beirut
1010 11.10.1942	1730 11.10.1942	Alexandria
1050 13.10.1942	1945 15.10.1942	Beirut
1051 16.10.1942	1710 16.10.1942	Port Said
1212 17.10.1942	1800 22.10.1942	Haifa
1043 24.10.1942	1719 24.10.1942	Alexandria
0749 26.10.1942	1720 26.10.1942	Beirut
1032 28.10.1942	1800 28.10.1942	Alexandria
0803 29.10.1942	1700 29.10.1942	Beirut
0934 1.11.1942	1710 1.11.1942	Alexandria
0829 3.11.1942	1600 6.11.1942	Haifa
1300 8.11.1942	1700 8.11.1942	Alexandria
0835 10.11.1942	1600 11.11.1942	Haifa
0950 13.11.1942	1630 13.11.1942	Alexandria
0810 15.11.1942	1600 16.11.1942	Beirut
0849 18.11.1942	1630 18.11.1942	Alexandria
0736 20.11.1942	0727 21.11.1942	Beirut
0900 23.11.1942	1630 23.11.1942	Alexandria
0900 25.11.1942	0405 14.12.1942	Haifa
0930 17.12.1942	1645 17.12.1942	Tobruk
1025 19.12.1942	1223 24.12.1942	Alexandria
1000 25.12.1942	0725 27.12.1942	Port Said
1000 2. 1.1943	1800 2. 1.1943	Aden
1535 15. 1.1943	0737 18. 1.1943	Durban

Time and date arrived		Time and date departed		Port or anchorage
1900	19. 1.1943	0739	20. 5.1943	Port Elizabeth
1300	22. 5.1943	1300	30. 5.1943	Durban
0706	10. 6.1943	1524	10. 6.1943	Aden
1650	15. 6.1943	1753	17. 6.1943	Suez (in Canal)
1217	18. 6.1943	0741	20. 6.1943	Alexandria
1339	23. 6.1943	1845	23. 6.1943	Tripoli
0735	27. 6.1943	1532	5. 7.1943	Alexandria
0854	9. 7.1943	1240	9. 7.1943	Tripoli
1035	10. 7.1943		10. 7.1943	Valencia
1840	10. 7.1943	0722	11. 7.1943	Sicily (Cape Ognina)
2000	13. 7.1943			Ras El Hallab
1010	14. 7.1943	0610	26. 7.1943	Tripoli
1115	27. 7.1943	1534	28. 7.1943	Syracuse
1826	29. 7.1943		29. 7.1943	Ras El Hallab
1217	30. 7.1943	1626	6. 8.1943	Tripoli
0942	8. 8.1943	1830	8. 7.1943	Syracuse
1155	10. 7.1943	1642	12. 7.1943	Tripoli
0845	14. 7.1943	1600	14. 7.1943	Syracuse
1747	15. 7.1943	1301	16. 7.1943	Tripoli
1800	20. 8.1943	1800	23. 8.1943	Alexandria
0900	27. 8.1943		28. 8.1943	Catania
0844	30. 8.1943	1827	5. 9.1943	Phillippeville
0930	6. 9.1943	1847	7. 9.1943	Bizerta
0822	7. 9.1943	0737	9. 9.1943	Bizerta
Between 10th/12th September 1943 lying in the Gulf of Salerno				
0843	14. 9.1943	2145	16. 9.1943	Bizerta
Between 18th/19th September 1943 lying in the Gulf of Salerno				
1710	21. 9.1943	2010	21. 9.1943	Bizerta
		0810	11.11.1943	Alexandria

Time and date arrived		Time and date departed		Port or anchorage
0910	18.11.1943	0950	19.11.1943	Algiers
0920	24.11.1943	1605	27. 2.1944	Liverpool
0735	4. 3.1944	1827	4. 3.1944	Gibraltar
0740	7. 3.1944	1121	7. 3.1944	Bizerta
1700	9. 2.1944	1625	11. 3.1944	Taranto (disembarking patients)
0900	13. 3.1944	1647	15. 3.1944	Naples
1808	15. 3.1944	0340	1. 4.1944	Castellanmario di Stalna
0705	1. 4.1944	1455	1. 4.1944	Naples
0835	5. 4.1944	1957	5. 4.1944	Gibraltar
2215	10. 4.1944		14. 5.1944	Avonmouth
	26. 5.1944	1600	29. 5.1944	New York
0845	1. 6.1944	1825	2. 6.1944	Halifax
1640	12. 6.1944	1713	25. 6.1944	Mersey River
1350	26. 6.1944	1300	9. 9.1944	Milford Haven
2130	9. 9.1944	1117	10. 9.1944	Barry Roads
1445	10. 9.1944	1810	12. 9.1944	Avonmouth
2020	12. 9.1944	1200	13. 9.1944	Barry Roads
1840	24. 9.1944	0900	3.10.1944	Halifax
0746	14.10.1944	1900	14.10.1944	Clyde
1513	15.10.1944	0915	27.10.1944	Liverpool
0700	2.11.1944	1630	3.11.1944	Punta Delgada (Azores)
1000	13.11.1944	1300	22.11.1944	Halifax
1918	5.12.1944	1430	6.12.1944	Gibraltar
0730	10.12.1944	1630	11.12.1944	Naples
1925	14.12.1944	1300	15.12.1944	Oran
1000	16.12.1944		16.12.1944	Gibraltar
1700	21.12.1944			Mersey River

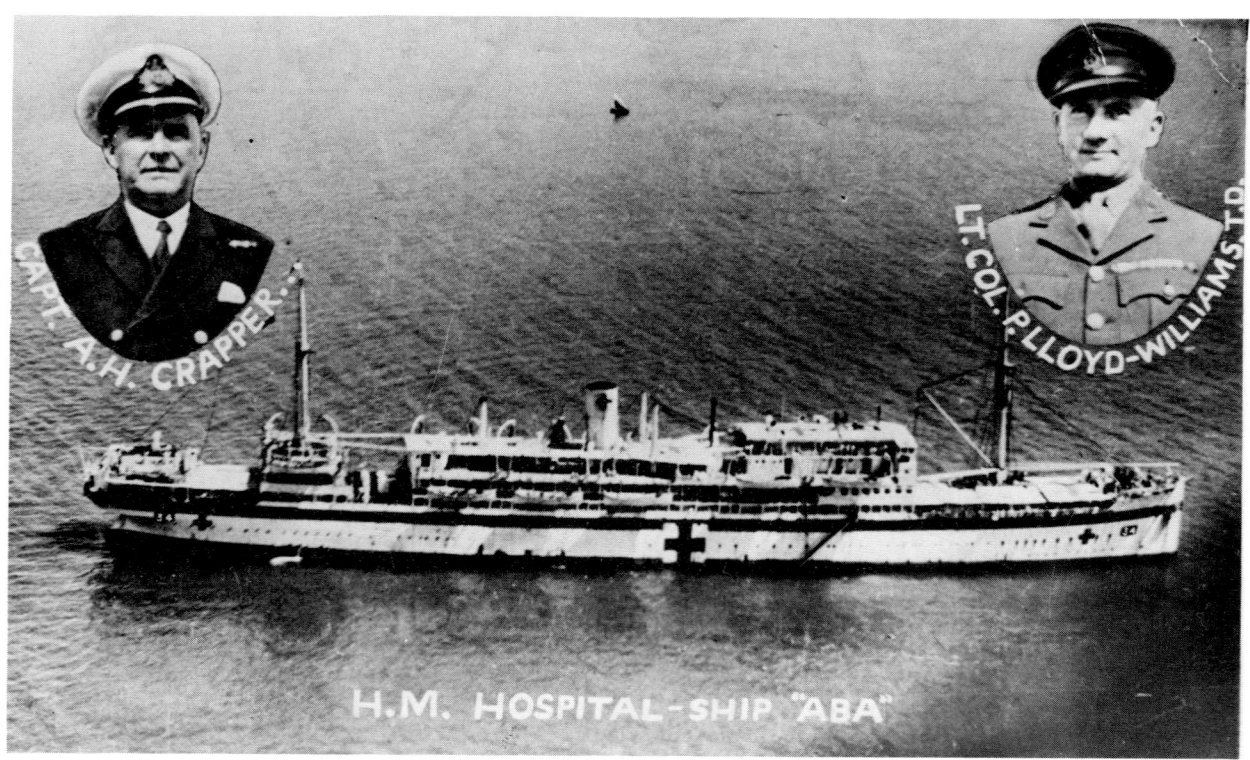

HM Hospital Ship **ABA** *with her Captain and Senior Medical Officer*

Port	Arrived	Departed	Information
Liverpool	23.12.1944	29.1.1945	Awaiting orders
	1945	*1945*	
Southampton	1st February	3rd February	Transferring sick
Cherbourg	5th February	7th February	Transferring sick
Southampton	7th February	8th February	Transferring sick
Cherbourg	12th February	12th February	Transferring sick
Southampton	13th February	15th February	Transferring sick
Cherbourg	17th February	18th February	Transferring sick
Southampton	20th February	21st February	Transferring sick
Cherbourg	28th February	3rd March	Transferring sick
Southampton	3rd March	7th March	Transferring sick
Southampton	12th March	24th March	Awaiting orders and engine repairs
Cherbourg	25th March	25th March	Transferring sick
Southampton	26th March	28th March	Transferring sick
Southampton	9th April	28th April	Awaiting medical patients
Glasgow	1st May	10th July	Repairs and survey
Trondheim	16th July	17th July	Repatriation Russian patients
Trenco	19th July	19th July	
Murmansk	21st July	29th July	Disembarking patients
Trenco	24th July	29th July	
Trondheim	29th July	30th July	Awaiting orders
Faslane	3rd August	20th August	Awaiting orders
Freetown	1st September	2nd September	
Ango Ango (Congo)	9th September	10th September	Patients
Matadi	10th September	13th September	Patients
Boma	13th September	14th September	Patients
Freetown	21st September	22nd September	
Las Palmas	27th September	28th September	
Antwerp	6th October	7th October	
Southampton	9th October	22nd October	Repairs—awaiting orders
Algiers	29th October	29th October	Embarking patients
Taranto	2nd November	3rd November	Embarking patients
Port Said	7th November	10th November	Embarking patients
Beirut	11th November	11th November	Embarking patients
Piraeus	14th November	18th November	Disembarking and embarking patients
Beirut	18th November	18th November	Called for onward routeing
Port Sibenik	19th November	19th November	Disembarking patients
Naples	23rd November	24th November	Disembarking patients
Marseilles	26th November	27th November	Disembarking patients
Port Said	3rd December	10th December	Embarking patients
Algiers	16th December	17th December	Embarking patients
Freetown	28th December	28th December	
	1946	*1946*	
Takoradi	1st January	1st January	Disembarking patients
Lagos	2nd January	18th January	Disembarking patients/cleaning/repairs
Congo River Mouth	21st January	22nd January	Awaiting daylight
Boma	22nd January	23rd January	Embarking patients
Ango Ango (Congo)	23rd January	29th January	Embarking patients
Freetown	1st February	1st February	Embarking patients
Las Palmas	7th February	7th February	Embarking patients
Downs	13th February	14th February	Awaiting orders
Antwerp	15th February	16th February	Disembarking patients
River Clyde	20th February	21st February	Entered dock
Southampton		23rd April	Embarking P.O.W. patients
Antwerp	25th April	27th April	Disembarking/embarking patients
Southampton	28th April	7th May	Disembarking/embarking patients
Hamburg	10th May	12th May	Disembarking/embarking patients
Southampton	14th May	19th May	Disembarking patients
Hamburg	21st May	22nd May	Embarking patients
Southampton	24th May	26th May	Disembarking/embarking patients
Hamburg	1st June	4th June	Disembarking/embarking patients
Southampton	6th June	18th June	Disembarking/embarking patients
Hamburg	20th June	23rd June	Disembarking/embarking patients
Southampton	25th June	4th July	Disembarking/embarking patients
Hamburg	6th July	9th July	Disembarking/embarking patients
Southampton	11th July	19th July	Disembarking/embarking patients
Hamburg	21st July	23rd July	Disembarking/embarking patients
Southampton	25th July	9th August	Disembarked 25/7, awaiting orders, engine repairs. Embarked 9/8
Hamburg	11th August	13th August	Disembarked 11th. Embarked 12/13th
Southampton	16th August	26th August	Disembarked 16th. Awaiting orders. Embarked 25/8
Port Said	6th September	12th September	Disembarked 7th Embarked 10/11th
Valletta Malta	16th September	16th September	Embarked patients
Naples	17th September	18th September	Disembarked 17th Embarked 18th
Gibraltar	22nd September	22nd September	
Southampton	27th September	16th December	Awaiting orders
Liverpool	18th December	18th December	Embarking troops only
Belfast	19th December	20th December	Disembarking troops only

Port	Arrived	Departed	Information
Liverpool	21st December	21st December	Embarking troops only
Belfast	22nd December	30th December	Disembarking/embarking troops
Liverpool	31st December *1947*	31st December *1947*	Disembarking troops only
Belfast	1st January	1st January	Embarking troops only
Liverpool	2nd January	2nd January	Disembarking troops only
Belfast	3rd January	4th January	Embarking troops only
Liverpool	6th January		Hove to—bad weather
River Mersey	7th January		
Birkenhead	7th January		Tide Time = 1108 hours

REDELIVERED FROM HM SERVICE 1700 HOURS 7TH JANUARY 1947
ABA WAS SOLD 1ST MAY 1947

OPERATIONAL OCCASIONS OF H.M.H.S. "ABA"

The War Years, 1940 to 1943

Taken over by the Government on the outbreak of war, "ABA" first rendered her services as a Naval Hospital Carrier, and was stationed at the Naval Base of Scapa Flow. Whilst on this station she was able to give succour to the survivors of the ROYAL OAK and IRON DUKE, when these vessels were sunk by enemy action, landing the injured at Kirkwall.

Early in 1940, ABA was ordered to proceed to Liverpool, to fit out as a fully equipped Military Hospital Ship, resulting in her being rated as the finest vessel in the Hospital Ship Service.

Leaving for Norway during April 1940, she played her part in rendering merciful aid to the sick and wounded of that ill starred campaign, and worked there until the evacuation was completed, then with a full load of patients, plus the Harstadt Medical Staffs, Doctors and Nurses, she returned to Liverpool.

May 1940 was spent in improving the Hospital Fittings of the vessel, in the light of the experience gained in Norway, most of this work being carried out whilst the ship lay at anchor in the River Mersey.

On July 5th, "ABA" was ordered to the Middle East, her first stop being Gibraltar, where she had to await a Safe Conduct Permit from the Italian Government to proceed through the Mediterranean. This must at first have been granted, and then later rescinded, for we received our orders to sail for Alexandria, and were actually off Oran when we were recalled by Wireless and instructed to return to Gibraltar, from where we were routed to Egypt via the Cape and Red Sea Route.

On our arrival in Egypt, "ABA" conveyed wounded from Solum, Mersa Matruh, or Tobruk as the line of battle ebbed and flowed, taking patients to Alexandria or Haifa as required. The run from Alexandria to Tobruk was well named "The Bomb Alley of the Middle East".

Then Greece fell to the Nazis, and "ABA" sailed to Piraeus to pick up the wounded. She was the last ship to leave that devastated port, and when she did so, she brought away everyone and everything possible, even though Dive Bombers hurtled around wreaking great destruction wherever their bombs fell, apparently our own aircraft were in no position to cope with them.

Next came the Battle of Crete, and "ABA" voyaged to Suda Bay, but fortunately she left Crete just before the storm broke. On the way to Alexandria from Crete she was heavily bombed twice in one day. About noon on the 17 May, an Italian bomber rained down a stick of 8 bombs, all scoring near misses, and about 6-30 P.M., she was very heavily attacked by twelve Junkers 85(s) who would have undoubtedly sunk her but for the protection then afforded by the Cruisers "Coventry" and "Dido" and the seven Destroyers that were accompanying them. The German Radio stated that these attacks were made because we had the King of Greece aboard and also his entire Suite. This was untrue.

When Rommel pushed the Eighth Army to Alexandria, and that port was vacated, "ABA" was the last to steam out of the deserted harbour. When the Tide of Victory turned in our favour and General Montgomery (whose brother was Church of England Padre aboard our ship) drove the enemy back "ABA" was again ready and for these services, she and her staff was cited in a Special Order of the Day by General Montgomery.

Under strict adherence to the Laws of the Geneva Convention, little can be done for the protection of a Hospital Ship, for the one and sufficient reason that they should not require any form of protection at all. Whilst I was Master of "ABA" I felt that in view of any further damage to her by bombing it would be in the Company's interests if I could view the ship from the air at various altitudes and so satisfy myself that her Red Cross Markings were as efficient as possible, and visible at every angle of approach. At Aden, through the courtesy of the R.A.F. I was able to arrange to go up in a Bomber and see how the ship appeared from the air for myself. We flew over at various altitudes, and I asked the Pilot to make a Mock Dive Bombing Attack on the ship, but at all altitudes and under all conditions she could be very clearly identified as a Hospital Ship.

Two suggestions I would like to make for the safety of Hospital Ships, and "ABA" in particular; and they are these.

In the first place, when a hospital ship is in a Blacked-out Port, and especially so on moonlight nights, she should be permitted to put to sea, and to switch on her lights when well clear of the port. Anyone will readily realise that a white ship, on a moonlit sea, or harbour is too good a mark to miss, and we have had this experience only far too often in various ports. The ship can return at daylight to complete the loading of the wounded in safety.

Secondly, and most important point of all, is that the Engines should be maintained in as near perfect order as possible, ready for any emergency. This can only be the case if time to do repairs and the necessary overhauls is granted the Engineers.

During my three years aboard "ABA" it was my experience that we were far too often, needlessly and casually put on such Short Notice of Readiness as four and six hours, and only on very rare occasions being granted a definite time of say several clear days in which the Engineers could work on the repairs.

These short Notices of readiness were virtually useless to the Engine Room Staff, and repairs that were urgently needed had to be postponed indefinitely. These conditions caused the Engines to deteriorate seriously and finally repairs that took many weeks, and must have proven very expensive to the Company had to be undertaken, whereas if time had been allowed us to effect these repairs before they became so urgent, a few days would have sufficed, and the general running and efficiency of the machinery improved.

In conclusion, I would like to mention the very satisfactory relationship and co-operation that existed at all times between the Ships personnel and the Military Staff.

G. W. Neely, Chief Officer

January, 1943

To:—O.C. TROOPS H.M. Hospital Ship "ABA"

SPECIAL ORDER OF THE DAY BY P. S. TOMLINSON, C.B., D.S.O., K.H.P.

Major-General Commanding Royal Army Medical Corps & Army Dental Corps, Middle East Forces

On the occasion of H.M. Hospital Ship "ABA" leaving the Mediterranean Station I should like to convey to all ranks my appreciation of the very hard work carried out by them over long hours during the past twenty-seven voyages.

The work carried out by the "ABA" during the past seven months is a record unequalled by any Hospital Ship and although most of it was away from the scene of the main fighting, it has none the less, formed part of a cog, the operation of which set the machinery in action which culminated in the Eighth Army's great victory.

Also a little appreciation from the Principal Sea Transport Officer, (Middle East)

28th November, 1942

I should like to take this opportunity of congratulating you and your Chief Engineer on having kept the ship running so long.

Signed. Hugh T. England
COMMODORE

Captain A. H. Crapper,
Master, H.M.H.S. "ABA"

REPORT OF CAPTAIN E. BROWN OF H.M. HOSPITAL SHIP "ABA"

The ship has been away from the United Kingdom for approximately 3 years 4 months and Captain Brown proceeded to South Africa in order to join her on the 17th July, 1943.

He left U.K. per a Troop Ship. On arrival at Durban he was informed by our Agents, Messrs. Mitchell Cotts that 7 Junior Engineers had been at that port for 10 weeks awaiting transport. Captain Brown immediately got in touch with the S.T.O. (lady). After seeing her three times, she eventually arranged for the party to join the "STRATHMORE" 4 days later for Suez. On arrival at Suez the Master got in touch with the S.T.O. and found that he had not reported the party's arrival to the C. in C. Captain Brown pressed the matter and got him to pass the message through. He then arranged for them to proceed to Algiers per the same ship.

On arrival at Algiers they were informed by the S.T.O. that the "ABA" was working from Phillipville. As there was no train for 3 days, and it took 3 days to make the journey, Captain Brown was able to arrange with the S.T.O. for a lorry convoy going to Constantine to take them along, and he later received permission from Movement Control at Constantine to take one of the lorries to Phillipville, where they eventually arrived 48 hours after leaving Algiers. The journey was uncomfortable to say the least as it was necessary for them to sleep on their baggage in the lorry. The food was provided by the Army Authorities and the drivers assisted in every way possible in the cooking.

On arrival at Phillipville they were informed that the "ABA" was then working from Bizerta, but as there was no accommodation there it was necessary to proceed to Tunis, again by lorry, but this time an open lorry. The journey took 36 hours and they spent each night at an Officers Transit Camp where meals were supplied. They were 6 days at Tunis and again the "ABA's" orders were changed and she went to Phillipville, but as Tunis was on her return route, on Captain Brown's suggestion, it was arranged she would call in for the party.

Captain Brown states that Captain Crapper gave him every assistance when taking over the ship, but there was only 2 hours available in which to do this.

Later on going round the ship the first thing that struck Captain Brown was the condition of the Lifeboats and gear. They had been swung out and powsed to the deck for practically 3 years she has been a Hospital Ship. This had tended to push in the strakes. The davits were also in an unsatisfactory condition being very difficult to move.

E.D. personnel on board appeared to be quite happy, but there seemed to be a certain amount of discontent amongst the Army Staff. For some time there had been trouble about the Bar Sales and Captain Brown found that they had kept their own stocks when possible. He was going to write to the Company for permission to alter the system and run the ship as a Naval Mess.

Note: Mr. Sharrock, who was present at the interview, stated that that whole of the Bar question will be thoroughly gone into.

Liquor and cigarettes were difficult to obtain in North Africa. The Master had not had any complaints about the food but a large quantity of C.T.C. cigarettes had been purchased by the previous Chief Steward in South Africa. Captain Crapper had condemned a quantity of Clipper cigarettes and after examination Captain Brown condemned these C to C cigarettes which were found to be green and smelling.

Whilst in the Mediterranean the ship was on service between Tunis to Catania and Catania to Taranto and return to Phillipville, and then back to Taranto and return to Phillipville. Another voyage was made to Taranto and then to Tripoli and from there to Alexandria, Algiers and home. The ship made all these passages alone without escort. She was fully lit up, position and speed being broadcast every 4 hours. Her movements were entirely in the hands of the S.T.O.

The master reports that you usually find that hospital ships when attacked are mixed up with other craft. It is not permissible for the position of mines to be reported by wireless, but these can be reported by visual signal when an H.M. Ship is in sight, also when the ship reaches port. Every endeavour is made to keep clear of ships at anchor and in convoy.

HM Hospital Ship **ABA**

Captain Brown reported that when boarding the ship alongside the quay at Taranto on October the 12th, the vessel was unable to moor close alongside owing to shoal water and it was necessary to heave on the starboard anchor to keep the bow off and allow the stern to come alongside. The ship was drawing approximately 22'9" aft and 21'.9" forward.

Liverpool. With regard to the damage sustained through the dummy barge at No. 4 Hatch being moved aft, no one on board the ship gave authority, and in fact it was not known to the Officers that the barge had been moved. When Captain Brown's attention was called, the damage had already been done. This was caused through the corner of the barge ranging on the ship's side.

Personnel. All personnel on board were satisfactory.

The ship was on Sea Transport service and took Italian prisoners of war from Algiers to Taranto and Poles from Taranto to Port Said. At Port Said they picked up Greeks, Yugo-Slavs and Italians and proceeded to Beirut where they embarked Frenchmen.

From Beirut they went to Piraeus to land the Greeks, calling at Bari for routing instructions to the Port of Sibenik, where they dropped the Yugo-Slavs. Sibenik is a small port in the Adriatic on the Coast of Yugoslavia.

From Sibenik they proceeded to Naples where they disembarked Italians and then onwards to Marseilles with the Frenchman. They went back to Port Said in ballast where they effected engine repairs, and took oil and water. Had to wait at Port Said for the "ATLANTIS" that was bringing from Burma West Africans. They left Port Said with the West Africans for Algiers from which port they took Fuel Oil and water, then on to Freetown, Takoradi and Lagos disembarking patients at all ports. After storing ship and engine repairs, they proceeded to the River Congo to the Port of Ango-Ango to take on board 400 Belgian repatriated civilians for Antwerp.

On the voyage to Bari, they experienced some heavy weather and again on the way to Naples they had a very severe gale off the south of Italy. A heavy sea which broke aboard badly damaged the port accommodation ladder, also breaking a couple of windows and flooding some of the wards.

The ship covered a distance of 20,340 miles with an average speed of 10.19 knots.

Aba is an important trade centre in Owerri Province of Nigeria.

ABA *at Lagos buoys, 4 January 1946*

H.M.H.S. "ABA"   Oct. 1943 to Oct 1945.

Joined Aba at Tunis Oct 8" 1943.
She was then on a voyage from Phillipville in North
Africa to Catania + Taranto to pick up wounded &
transport them to Phillipville.
She had been on this run for two or three voyages, having
previously taken part in the Salerno landing & other
landings in Sicily + Italy, but as Capt Chapman was
then in command, I recommend you to apply to him.

After two trips to Catania & Taranto we were ordered to
Tripoli + loaded wounded for Alexandria. Discharging
the wounded, we then picked up a full load (485) for U.K.
Arriving Liverpool on 11" Nov 1943.
This was the first, the "Aba" had been to a U.K port for
about three years.

An extensive overhaul at Cammell Lairds.

Left fitting out dock 13" Feb 1944, loaded 400 Italians
at L'pool Landing Stage, but defects to engines delayed
final departure until 27" Feb. an Gibraltar for water &
oil 4" Mar + left 6pm same day. an Bizerta for orders
7" Mar & left after half hour's wait. an Taranto 9" Mar
Discharged Italians on the 10" and loaded about 180
British patients & proceeded to Naples to fill up.
an Naples 13" Mar and anchored outside breakwater.
at 10.30 AM received orders to shift anchorage to North
side of Naples Bay. This anchorage was just
inshore from men-of-war anchored in the bay.
on the 14" received orders to clear harbour at 7 AM
on the 15.

at 1.25 AM of the 15th the alert sounded. It was a bright moonlight night, the men-of-war had put up a very effective smoke screen but it was some time before the screen covered the "Aba" and at 1.35 we received a direct hit from a dive bomber. He made two attacks on the ship & there were three very near misses which did damage to the after part of the ship. The white paint of the "Aba" must have stood out clearly in the bright moonlight & the red crosses on the decks and upper structure should also have been seen, but we did not carry our Geneva lights when in harbour.

Some troop ships had arrived on the 14th & no doubt the raid took place on their account.

The bomb struck the ship on the Stbd side outside the 3rd officers cabin on 'A' deck. It travelled from Stbd to Port passing through A. B & C decks and exploded on 'D' deck. Considerable damage was done, the shell plating blown out, D deck depressed & C deck blown up. There were three fatal casualties, the RAMC orderly on duty in DI ward received the full explosion, his body being badly mutilated, one patient in D.1 port was decapitated, and the ship's quarter-master on duty at the gangway on C deck was also badly mutilated when C deck was blown up. The main staircase caught fire, but this was quickly put out by the crew under Mr Bird the chief officer and the bosun Mr Bawden.

One sister on the staircase was very badly burned but not fatally. There were about 20 of the patients suffering from shock in various forms. The senior surgeon had both ankles broken and the junior medical officer one ankle.

All patients were quickly evacuated from the forward
wards with the assistance of the ship's crew including
~~stewards~~ stewards, who all played their part in
helping the RAMC to get the patients comfortable in
the after wards which were not damaged.
The patients were truly patient showing great courage
and fortitude under the trying conditions and
some were suffering from very bad wounds received
in action.
On the evening of the 15th Mar the Aba was ordered to
Castel le Mare at the south of Naples Bay for
repairs.   The patients remained on board
during the repairs, there were several alarms but no
further raids took place.
Mount Vesuvius started an eruption on the
night of the 18th Mar and continued during our stay
at Castel le Mare.   Whilst being a magnificent
sight, the ash became a serious menace to the
stability of the ship, and had to be cleared from
the upper deck every few hours. It also did
considerable damage to boat falls and the upper deck
generally.
Left Castel le Mare at 5.30 AM 1st April and proceeded
to Naples + filled up the undamaged wards a total
number of patients of about 400. Left same day.
One patient died + was buried at sea on the 4th April.
Called Gib for fresh water April 5th + proceeded to U.K.
Arrived Avonmouth 11th April + discharged patients.
Further repairs were carried out at Avonmouth.
Lt Col P Lloyd Williams recd the OBE. The RAMC. Quarter master Sergeant + the
Sergeant major recd the MBE + two sisters mentioned in despatches after Naples.
14 May loaded full with American wounded (480)
Left same day for New York following hospital ship
route as given by Routing officer on 30th Parallel.
Arr New York 26th May.
American wounded received with bands playing, flags
flying

[...] [...] [...] At Halifax N.S. 1st June.
Loaded Canadian Army Medical Corps. (409)
Left Halifax 2nd June. At Liverpool 12 June.

17 June Ship taken over by Sea Transport and all
crew signed for volunteering in any ship during emergency.
Left Liverpool 25 June & arrived Milford Haven 26th
The ship was on 24 hours notice to proceed to
Cherbourg when required. We learned later that
wounded were being evacuated by plane & L.S.T.s
Left Milford Haven 10th Sept & at Avonmouth same day.
Loaded Canadian wounded Sept 12th. Left 13th.
Followed usual route on 30° Parallel & then due North to
Halifax.   At Halifax 24th Sept Band & Flag [...] [...]
Dry docked 27th Sept. Undocked 2nd Oct. Embarked
Canadian Army Medical Corp about 300. Left Halifax
3rd Oct. Usual route. Directed by Admiralty 9 Oct 30
miles further South.   Hospital ships gave position
course & speed every day in Atlantic & every 4 hours
in [...]

At Gourock 14th Oct & left same day, arrived Liverpool
landing stage 15th Oct & discharged C.R.A.M.C.
Docked 16th Oct.   Sent to landing Stage 26th Oct &
embarked Canadian wounded about 400.
Left 27 Oct for Halifax N.S. via Ponte Delgardo in
the Azores.   At Ponte Delgardo 1st Nov for fresh
water. Left 3rd Nov. At Halifax 13th Nov. Usual
band & flag.   Engine Overhaul. Left Halifax
22nd Nov. Very bad weather on this voyage, 500
patients on board. At Gibralter for fresh water
5 Dec Left 6th Dec. & At Naples 10th Dec
Embarked British patients 11th Dec & left same day.
Called Oran 14th Dec for fresh water & left 15th Dec
At L'Pool 21st Dec Disembarked 22nd Dec.
Docked Brunswick Dk 23rd Dec.

Remained at Liverpool for eng. repairs
and ____ instructions.
Left Liverpool ___ Southampton 28ᵗʰ Jan 1945.
An Cowes Roads 31ˢᵗ Jan + Southampton 2ⁿᵈ Feb.
Took up service carrying wounded of all
nationalities incls. German ~ from Cherbourg to Southampton. Remained on
this service until 28ᵗʰ April 1945, when we left
for Glasgow. + an 1ˢᵗ May.
VE day in King Geo V dock Glasgow. Service on
board attended by a large party of local N.F.S.
Proceeded to Faslane in farewell 10ᵗʰ May. Took on a few
sick Norwegians + Russians. Left Faslane 12ᵗʰ July.
An Trondhjeim 16ᵗʰ July. discharged sick and
loaded 300 Russian sick + wounded. These men
had been prisoners of war + were in a very low state.
Left Trondhjeim 17ᵗʰ July. Tromso 19ᵗʰ July + picked
up escort to proceed to Murmansk. An 21ˢᵗ July.
Five patients died on the voyage from Tromso. +
many of those landed were very near to death
as result of starvation.

79 + 30
General
Hospitals

Left Murmansk 22ⁿᵈ July. An Tromso 24ᵗʰ July.
Ship thoroughly fumigated, all wards + beds + bedding
treated as the Russians had been in terrible state.
Started embarking British Hospital Personnel ✱
Left Tromso 27ᵗʰ July + an Trondhjeim 29ᵗʰ July.
Embarked more British Personnel + left 30ᵗʰ July.
An Gourock Aug 2ⁿᵈ Faslane 3ⁿᵈ + discharged
Personnel.
Left Faslane 20ᵗʰ Aug for Belgian Congo.
Freetown Sept 1ˢᵗ Fresh water + fuel oil.
An Boma Sept 9ᵗʰ + Ango Ango same day.
Left Ango Ango Sept 10ᵗʰ + made fast to Matadi
wharf same day

Embarked 400 Belgians, male & female &
children. All more or less sick.
Left Matadi 13 Sept. one patient died 26 Sept.
Freetown Sept 21, left Sept 22.
Las Palmas Sept 27 left Sept 28.
At Antwerp 6 Oct & disembarked.
Senior officers of ship & R A M C entertained to
lunch by Belgian Minister for Colonies.
Left Antwerp Oct 7 at Southampton Oct 9.
Left the ship on Oct 11 & Capt Cave took the
ship until the end of the voyage.

For total number of casualties carried &
further details on particular voyages of
numbers & class of wounded carried. Lt Col
P Lloyd-Williams may be able to help.

    Lt. Col. P. Lloyd-Williams O B E.
      "Canezla"
        Bangor
       Caernarvonshire

MATRONA, *formerly*
ABA, *capsized*

MATRONA,
ready for righting

MATRONA *after righting*

182

ABA, *in her heyday*

FANTEE

EKARI

259 FANTEE (II)
O.N. 144410   1920–1933

Steel screw steamer, War 'F1' type, one deck and shelter deck
399.5′×53.0′×32.8′   3527 n   5663 g   9000 d
Launched by Northumberland Shipbuilding Co, Howden-on-Tyne, Yard No 277, unnamed, for the Shipping Controller. Completed for Elder, Dempster & Co Ltd as **FANTEE**. Registered London. T 3 cyl 27″, 44″, 73″–48″ by Palmers Shipbuilding & Iron Co Ltd, Hebburn-on-Tyne. 517 nhp, 11 K.
1919   21 November, launched.
1920   4 March, completed. April, collided with and sank tug WHITE ROSE (125 g/built 1885).
1932   January, laid up in Blackwater River.
1933   22 March, sold for £9,000 to Kassos Steam Navigation Co Ltd, Greece. Renamed **AKTI**. Registered Syra. 2593 n, 4261 g.
1938   4 December, in collision with LA PLATA (8056 g/built 1922) off Ushant, voyage Rio de Janeiro to Antwerp, cargo ore. Sank in position 47°.40′N 06°.20′W.

260 EKARI
O.N. 144502   1920–1926

Steel screw steamer, two decks and shelter deck
405.2′×54.2′×23.9′   4090 n   6741 g
Built by John Brown & Co Ltd, Clydebank, Yard No 519c, for Elder, Dempster & Co Ltd. Registered London. 3 steam turbines, DR gearing, by the builders. 630 nhp, 11½ K.
Passenger accommodation: 45 double berth cabins.
1920   April, completed.
1921   Transferred to African Steamship Co.
1926   November, sold to Cie Belge Maritime du Congo SA (Agence Maritime Internationale SA), Belgium. Renamed **STANLEYVILLE**. Registered Antwerp. 4499 n, 6612 g.
1932   December, sold for £10,000 for demolition in the United Kingdom.
1933   July, re-sold for demolition in Japan.

Another view of **FANTEE**, *at Hamburg in 1930*

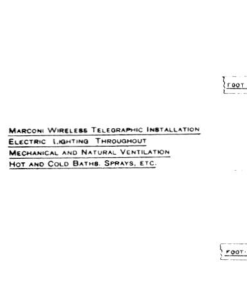

'B' OR SHELTER DECK.

MARCONI WIRELESS TELEGRAPHIC INSTALLATION
ELECTRIC LIGHTING THROUGHOUT
MECHANICAL AND NATURAL VENTILATION
HOT AND COLD BATHS, SPRAYS, ETC.

'W R' DENOTES 'WARDROBE'
'F L' DENOTES 'FOLDING LAVATORY'

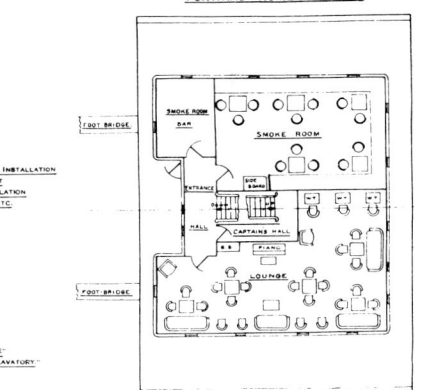

FORWARD PROMENADE DECK.

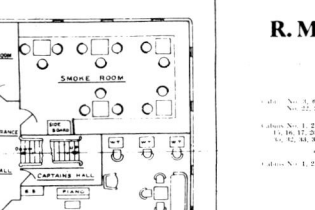

Elder Dempster and Co. Limited

PLAN OF SALOONS
AND
PASSENGER ACCOMMODATION
OF THE
R.M.S. "EKARI"

FIRST CLASS

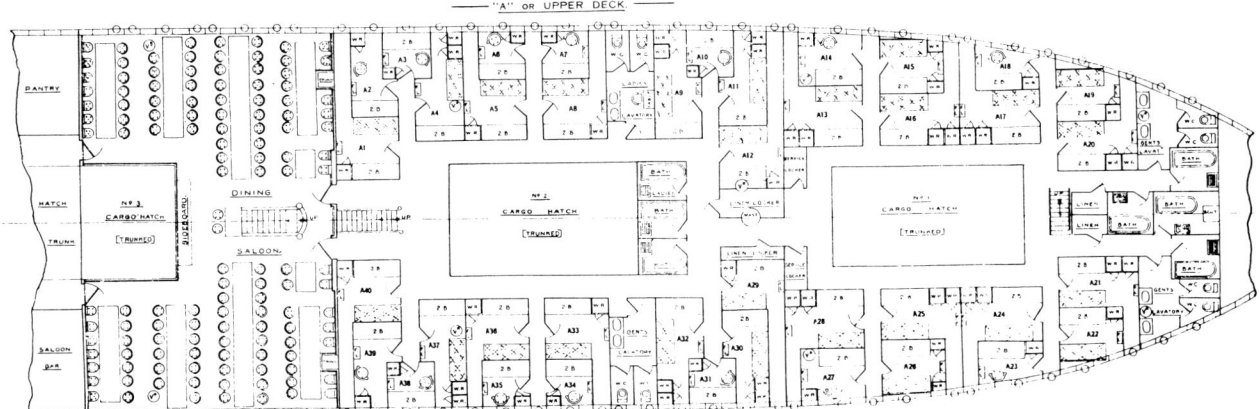

"A" OR UPPER DECK.

EKARI

CALGARY

261 CALGARY
O.N. 143707   1921–1958

'C' class
Steel screw steamer, two decks
440.1′×59.2′×31.1′   4486 n   7206 g   10,600 d
Built by John Brown & Co Ltd, Clydebank, Yard No 596c,
for British & African Steam Navigation Co Ltd. Registered
Liverpool. 3 Curtiss steam turbines, DR gearing, by the
builders. 667 nhp, 12 K.
Passenger accommodation: 8 first class in double berth cabins.
1921   February, completed.
1933   May, transferred to Elder Dempster Lines Ltd.
1947   Converted to burn oil fuel.
1957   Sold for £57,050 to British Iron & Steel Corporation.
        Allocated to T. W. Ward Ltd for demolition.
1958   19 April, delivered at Grays, Essex.
Ships of the 'C' class: CALGARY (261), COCHRANE (262),
CALUMET (263), CARIBOO (264).
Calgary is a town in Alberta, Canada.

Extract from a report submitted by Captain W. R. Brown following a
voyage in convoy from Freetown to the United Kingdom in October
1942:

In the course of the convoy navigation my attention was particularly
attracted by the movements of a Swedish vessel. I noticed that after
getting the Night Intentions Signal, which was given from the Commodore vessel by flag signal in the course of the afternoon, she always fell
well behind the convoy, generally at distances of between 5 to 7 miles.
She always returned to the convoy in daylight in time to get the Night
Intentions signal for the next day. I formed the impression that she was
perfectly capable of maintaining the convoy speed if she wished to do
so, but that she deliberately fell out of the convoy at the most dangerous
time. When the convoy got off the coast of Ireland this vessel disappeared and I do not know where she went to.

I regard the movements of the Swedish vessel which I have mentioned as suspicious and I should like to see Swedish vessels excluded from our convoys.

ELDER DEMPSTER LINES, LIMITED

S.S. "CALGARY"
S.S. "CALUMET"
S.S. "COCHRANE"

PLAN OF
PASSENGER ACCOMMODATION

A postwar view of **CALGARY** (Photo Skyfotos)

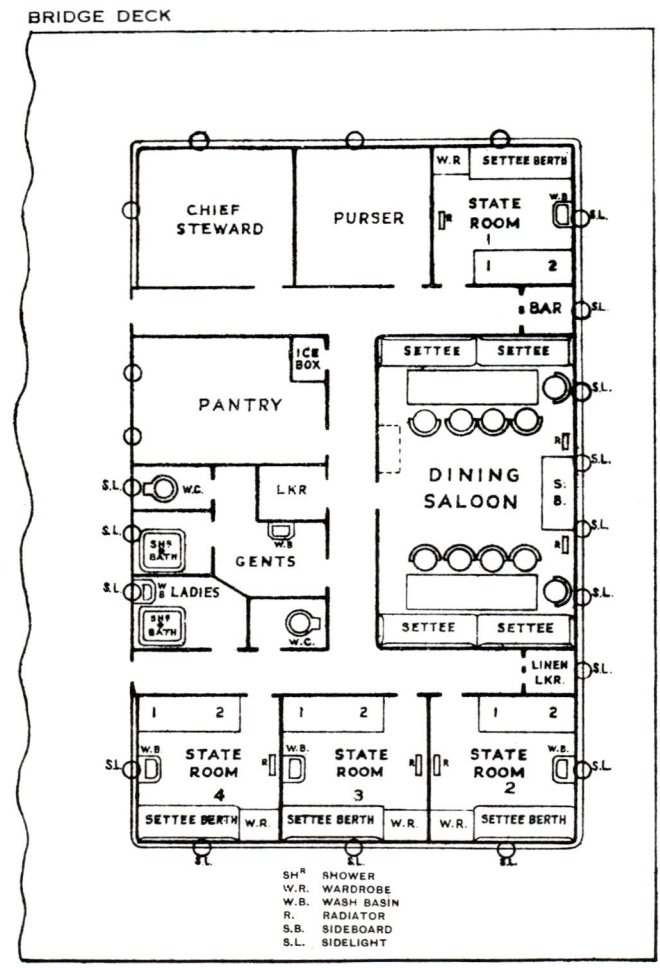

CALGARY *in the breakers' yard at Grays, Essex* (Photo G. A. Game, of Killick Martin's staff) (*From* Sea *magazine*)

Cabin plan of the three surviving 'C' class ships

COCHRANE

262 COCHRANE
O.N. 146705   1923–1957

'C' class
Steel screw steamer, two decks
440.0′×59.2′×31.1′   4485 n   7203 g   10,600 d
Built by John Brown & Co Ltd, Clydebank, Yard No 597c, for African Steamship Co. Registered London. 3 Curtiss steam turbines, DR gearing, by the builders. 667 nhp, 12 K.
Passenger accommodation: 8 first class in double berth cabins.

1923   March, completed.
1926   March, first vessel to berth alongside Apapa wharf.
1933   April, transferred to Elder Dempster Lines Ltd. Registered Liverpool. 4431 n, 7276 g.
1947   Converted to burn oil fuel.
1957   5 April, sold for £58,200 to Frank Rijsdijk Industries, Hendrik Ido Ambacht, Holland, for demolition.

Cochrane is a town in Ontario, Canada.

CALUMET, *engaged on the Canada–Cape route*

263 CALUMET

O.N. 147204   1923–1955

'C' class
Steel screw steamer, two decks
440.2′×59.2′×31.1′   4462 n   7268 g   10,627 d
Built by John Brown & Co Ltd, Clydebank, Glasgow, Yard No
598C, for Imperial Direct Line Ltd. Registered Liverpool. 3
Curtiss steam turbines, DR gearing, by the builders. 667 nhp,
12 K.
Passenger accommodation: 8 first class in double berth cabins.
1923   March, completed.
1933   April, transferred to Elder Dempster Lines Ltd.
1936   February, arrived Freetown with starboard side lower
       cross bunker on fire. Extinguished after off-loading 150
       tons of coal.
1955   30 August, sold for £130,000 to Cia Maritime Asiatic
       Panamense, SA. Renamed **PACIFIC CONCORD**.
       Registered Panama. 4427 n, 7347 g.
1956   Sold to Pacific Bulk Carriers Inc, Hong Kong. Renamed
       OCEANIC ENTERPRISE. Registered Panama.
1960   Sold to Nichimen Sitagyo KK for demolition 4 February,
       arrived Mihara.
Calumet is a town on Lake Superior in Michigan, USA.

264 CARIBOO

O.N. 147267   1924–1928

'C' class
Steel screw steamer, two decks
440.4′×59.2′×31.1′   4463 n   7275 g   10,600 d
Built by John Brown & Co Ltd, Clydebank, Yard No 599c, for
Elder, Dempster & Co Ltd. Registered Liverpool. 3 Curtiss
steam turbines, DR gearing, by the builders. 667 nhp, 12 K.
Passenger accommodation: 8 first class in double berth cabins.
1924   August, completed.

1928 22 November, arrived at East London, on charter to the
Union-Castle Mail Steamship Co Ltd, voyage Beira to
New York, cargo chrome ore and general, and remained
off the port until early morning 23 November when she
entered the roadstead to work cargo. There was a high
wind and confused sea and loading was only carried out
with difficulty. At 1550 it was decided that further work
was impossible on account of the increasingly heavy
swell and wind, and **CARIBOO** shortly afterwards put
to sea, following the RMS WINDSOR CASTLE. By
now there was torrential rain and by 2000 a moderate
gale and high seas, with bad visibility. The intention of
the Master (Captain A. Mitchell) was to make for the
100 fathom line and then turn towards the coast. At 2255
this was done, and soundings at midnight indicated 70
fathoms.
24 November, soundings were regularly taken as
CARIBOO steamed at 3–3½ knots, but when soundings
at 0200 indicated 19 fathoms the ship was turned. Shortly
after 0215 five bumps were felt, indicating that she
had struck an underwater obstruction. It soon became
apparent that there was substantial damage, and within
an hour of striking speed fell off and **CARIBOO** was
making water rapidly in the after hold, stokehold and
bunker. Accordingly Captain Mitchell anchored in
about 28 fathoms to prevent the ship from being driven
ashore, the coast being some 5–6 miles distant. The
order to abandon ship was given at 0630 by which time
the after deck was awash. Shortly afterwards WINDSOR
CASTLE, which had received **CARIBOO**'s distress
signals, arrived and took the survivors aboard, Captain
Mitchell remaining on his ship. The harbour tug BUF-
FALO now arrived and attempts were made to take
CARIBOO in tow but by 1245 it became obvious that
the ship was doomed and she sank stern first shortly
afterwards, Captain Mitchell being taken aboard BUF-
FALO. At the subsequent Court of Enquiry it was found
that **CARIBOO** had struck an object between Keiskama

187

Point and the mouth of the Golana River in 7 fathoms and was badly holed. No blame was attached to Captain Mitchell or his officers and crew, but recommendations were made for the fitting of radio direction-finders at East London. Captain Mitchell, in his turn, paid tribute to his own crew and also to that of WINDSOR CASTLE (Captain Sir Benjamin Chave) whose prompt action in coming to the rescue at no little risk to his own ship was in the highest standards of seamanship.

1981   December, the *Cape Times* reported that the wreck of **CARIBOO** had been located in 20 fathoms, two nautical miles off the Bigha River mouth. The wreck was completely demolished but some copper and a fragment of a plate bearing the Elder Dempster crest was recovered during a 12 month operation.

Cariboo is a town and port on the Northumberland Strait, Nova Scotia.

CARIBOO

ADDA

265   ADDA
O.N. 146664   1922–1941

Steel twin screw motorship, two decks and awning deck
435.3′×57.3′×31.3′   4663 n   7816 g   6405 d
Laid down as **ANCOBRA** by Harland & Wolff Ltd, Greenock, Yard No 608, for African Steamship Co, but launched as **ADDA**. Registered Liverpool. 2×B & W oil engines 4 SCSA 8 cyl 29⅛″–45¼″ by the builders. 1317 nhp, 14 K.
Passenger accommodation: 225 first class, 74 second, 32 third.

1922   November, completed. 29 November maiden voyage.
1923   April, collided with *BATA* in river Mersey.
1933   28 April, transferred to Elder Dempster Lines Ltd. Registered Liverpool.
1941   8 June, (Captain J. T. Marshall) torpedoed and sunk by U107 (Korvettenkapitan Gunther Hessler), voyage Liverpool to West Africa, general cargo and 490 pass-

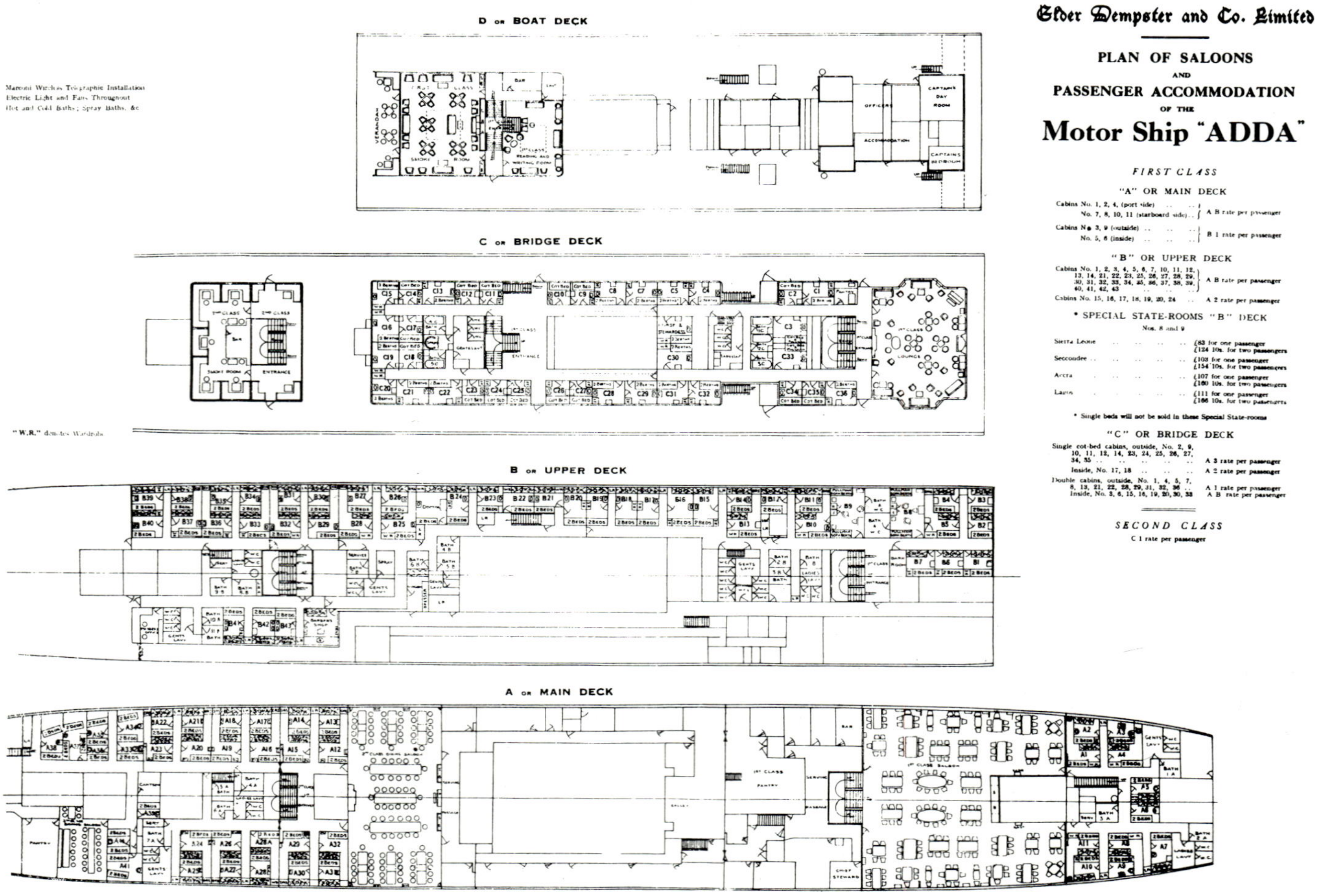

188

Above, Kapitanleutnant Gunther Hessler sitting on the wind deflector of U107 (complete with four aces badge), and top right, receiving a warm welcome at Lorient on 2 July 1941 after U107's record breaking cruise during which she sank ADDA, ALFRED JONES, DIXCOVE, and 11 other ships, aggregating 86,699 gross tons (Photo Bundesarchiv)

engers and crew, in position 8°.30′N 14°.39′W. Hessler, patrolling off Freetown, sighted **ADDA** at 2230 in bright moonlight, as she was zigzagging towards Freetown. U107 hauled ahead and dived at 0114 for an underwater attack, which, however, was frustrated by **ADDA**'s execution of a particularly large zig to starboard, as a result of which Hessler lost contact, which was not easy to re-establish, as U107's multiple hydrophones were not working satisfactorily. On the assumption, therefore, that the ship must sooner or later alter course for Freetown, Hessler headed south and soon fell in with her again. By now they were quite close to Freetown and there was the danger to U107 of patrol vessels. **ADDA** was still zigzagging, so Hessler had instinctively to choose the right moment to attack. U107 dived at 0313 and Hessler fired one bow tube at 0442 (British Double Summer Time), the torpedo striking **ADDA** some 25 metres from the stern. She stopped and began to settle. Boats were lowered. At 0515 she sank by the stern and U107 withdrew. Ten crew and two passengers lost their lives.

U107 (Kapitanleutnant Karl-Heinz Fritz) sunk 8 August 1944 by RAF Liberator of Squadron 201 at 46°.46′N 03°.49′W. Hessler is the son-in-law of Grand Admiral Karl Dönitz. Adda is an old surf port in Ghana.

ADDA

266 EDIBA/MATTAWIN
O.N. 147465   1923–1942

Steel twin screw motorship, two decks and shelter deck
406.0′×54.2′×32.9′ 4220 n 6919 g 9190 d
Built by Harland & Wolff Ltd, Glasgow, Yard No 582G, for
Elder, Dempster & Co Ltd. Registered London. 2× B & W oil
engines 4 SCSA 6 cyl 26$\frac{3}{8}$″–39$\frac{3}{8}$″ by the builders. 810 nhp, 11 K.
Passenger accommodation: 12 first class in two berth cabins.

1923 April, completed.
1924 Transferred to African Steamship Co.
1929 September, renamed **MATTAWIN**. Registered London
following transfer to the Canada–Cape service.
1933 April, transferred to Elder Dempster Lines Ltd. Registered Liverpool.
1942 2 June (Captain C. H. Sweeny), torpedoed and sunk by
U553 (Korvettenkapitan Karl Thurmann) in position
40°.14′N 66°.01′W while sailing independently from
New York to Cape Town with military stores. Thurmann
had sighted the **MATTAWIN** at 0345 and proceeded
to haul ahead for an attack. At 0548 he fired a spread
salvo of two torpedoes at a range of 1800 metres. One of
the torpedoes, which was a surface-runner, missed,
owing to a gyro failure having caused it to run too far
left. The other appeared to strike the ship, giving off a
metallic sound, but failed to explode. Thurmann thus
manoeuvred for another attack, which was commenced
at 0718, when he again fired two torpedoes at about the
same range as before. One of the torpedoes hit forward,
the ship turned to starboard and stopped. She began to
settle by the bow. A distress call was transmitted on the
600-metre band and seven boats were seen to be lowered.
At 0730 Thurmann fired a final torpedo to finish her off.
MATTAWIN was hit aft and sank by the stern. No
lives were lost.
U553 was lost with all hands through unknown cause in the
North Atlantic during January 1943.
Ediba and Mattawin are place names, the former a town on
the Cross River, Nigeria, 115 miles from Calabar, and the latter
a town in Quebec province of Canada.

M.S.S. "EDIBA"

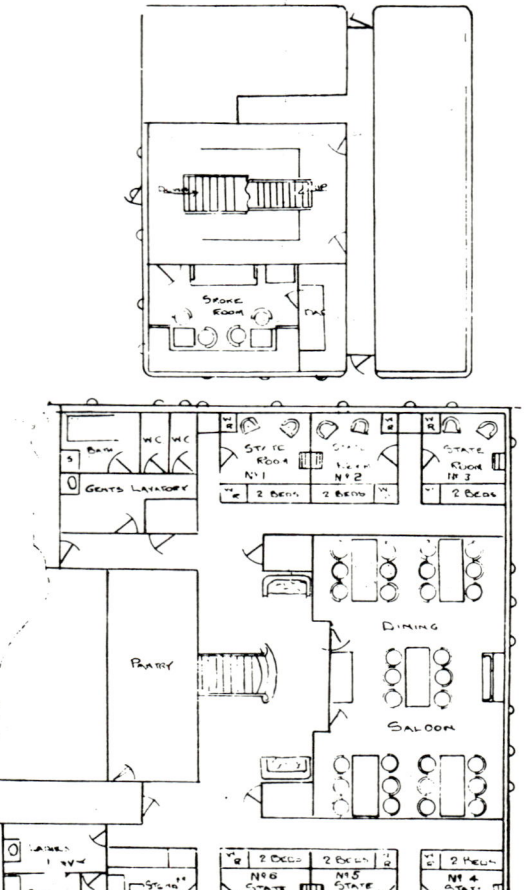

MATTAWIN (Photo F. W. Hawks)

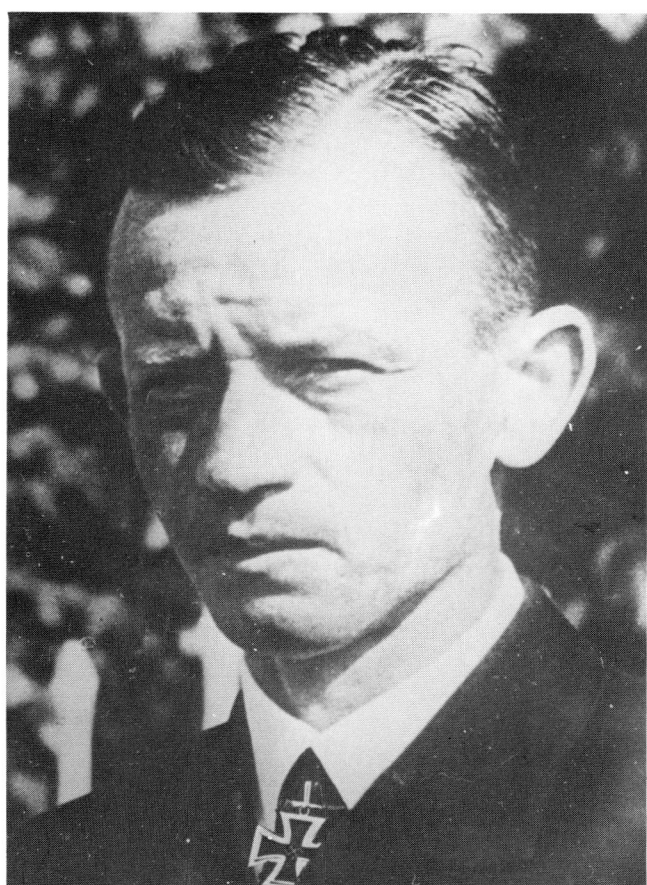

Korvettenkapitan Karl Thurmann sank **MATTAWIN**

MATTAWIN *seen from a different angle* (Photo A. Duncan)

This pencil sketch by E. Hamilton was used to depict **ACCRA** *and* **APAPA** *on this pre-war postcard*

Apapa wharf, shortly before the outbreak of war, with **ACCRA** *or* **APAPA** *embarking passengers for the voyage to Great Britain*

267 ACCRA (II)

O.N. 149595   1926–1940

'Accra' class

Steel twin screw motorship, two decks and weather deck
450.8′×62.3′×31.3′ 5471 n 6512 d 9337 g
Built by Harland & Wolff Ltd, Belfast, Yard No 616, for British
& African Steam Navigation Co Ltd. Registered Liverpool. 2×
B & W oil engines 4 SCDA 6 cyl 26¾″–55⅛″ by the builders.
1651 nhp, 14 K.

Passenger accommodation: 243 first class, 76 second.

1926   18 March, launched. 28 August, commenced trials (Cap-tain J. B. Wright), carrying 200 guests to the Scottish Islands.

1928   First ship to berth at the new port of Takoradi.

1933   May, transferred to Elder Dempster Lines Ltd.

1940   26 July (Captain J. J. Smith), torpedoed and sunk by U34 (Korvettenkapitan Wilhelm Rollman) in position 55°.40′N 16°.28′W, voyage Liverpool to West Africa with 333 passengers, 163 crew, and general cargo. Eleven passengers and eight crew lost their lives. In his war diary Rollman described the sinking.

At 1300 have achieved favourable position ahead of the convoy. Commence run-in. Dived at 1330. The convoy alters course about every 4–10 minutes. Formation is six columns, each of five steamers in line abreast. Escort consists of two gun-boats and two patrol-boats. All vessels are armed. Average size about 7–8000 grt, among them a very large passenger liner, several tankers and large freighters. Mostly in ballast, few laden. Steamers have bow protection gear. Last course steered by convoy is 290°.

191

ACCRA

Commence attack on the passenger liner, which is leading ship in the port wing column. She is modern, with three-colour camouflage, armed (number of guns not discernible) one funnel, two masts. Deduce she must be armed merchant cruiser, for as a passenger liner she would take up station in the middle of the convoy. 1447. After the leading ship of the third column has passed I am able to aim between the third and second columns. Spread salvo of three G7e torpedoes. Inclination 90°, range 1170 metres, speed of target 9 knots. Centre torpedo strikes right amidships. The left one hits a freighter astern of her, and which initially was concealed from view, at a point some 50 metres ahead of the stern, at a range of 2300 metres. The explosion on the AMC was followed by a second violent explosion, presumably a boiler explosion. Heavy list to starboard and extensive damage amidships (all lifeboats rendered useless) was the immediate result, she also began to settle gradually by the stern.

U34 sank on 5 August 1943 in the Baltic following a collision with the tender LECH. By that time Rollmann had assumed command of U848, in which boat he was killed when she was sunk with all hands on 5 November 1943 in the South Atlantic by US aircraft.

Ships of the 'Accra' class: ACCRA (267), APAPA (268).

*Kapitanleutnant Wilhelm Rollmann, of U34, wrote finis to **ACCRA**'s career (Photo Bundesarchiv)*

ACCRA

ELDER DEMPSTER LINES

List of Passengers

M.V.
"ACCRA"
(9,336 Tons)

OFFICERS.

Commander ...	...	...	...	...	...	...	J. C. SHOOTER
Chief Officer...	...	...	...	...	...	...	... R. JONES
Chief Engineer	...	...	...	...	...	...	R. B. YOUNG
Purser	...	...	...	...	...	...	J. STUART
Surgeon	...	...	...	...	...	... DR. J. McD. ECKSTEIN
Chief Steward	...	...	...	...	... A. F. BARNARD, O.B.E.

PORTS OF CALL

Madeira...	...	...	... (arr.)	Aug.	12
Las Palmas	...	...	...	,,	,, 13
Bathurst	...	...	...	,,	,, 16
Freetown	...	...	...	,,	,, 18
Takoradi	...	...	...	,,	,, 21
Accra	...	...	...	,,	,, 22
Lagos	...	...	...	,,	,, 23
Port Harcourt	...	...	,,	,, 26

Sailing from
LIVERPOOL
ON
WEDNESDAY, 8TH AUGUST
1934

*Cover and title page of an **ACCRA** passenger list*

Elder Dempster Lines

Passenger List

M.V. "ACCRA"
AUGUST 8, 1934

268 APAPA (II)
O.N. 149611   1927–1940

'Accra' class
Steel twin screw motorship, two decks and weather deck
450.7'×62.3'×31.3'   5472 n   9333 g   6512 d
Built by Harland & Wolff Ltd, Belfast, Yard No 695, for British
& African Steam Navigation Co Ltd. Registered Liverpool. 2×
B & W oil engines 4 SCDA 6 cyl 26¾"–55⅛" by the builders.
1651 nhp, 14 K.
Passenger accommodation: 243 first class, 76 second.

1926   26 August, launched.
1927   January, completed. Maiden voyage (Captain J. Hughes).
1933   May, transferred to Elder Dempster Lines Ltd.
1939   Ladies hairdressing salon opened on board.
1940   June, with *DAVID LIVINGSTONE* rescued Polish and Czech Air Force Officers in the Gironde River, near Bordeaux. At the Warplane Wreck Investigation Group

APAPA

APAPA or *ACCRA* approaching the landing stage, Liverpool
(Photo Light Impressions)

APAPA in service

Museum, Fort Perch Rock, New Brighton, there are photographs and newspaper cuttings covering this action. The airmen were brought to Liverpool via Gibraltar and later encamped at Chalmondley and Malpas near Chester. 15 November (Captain E. V. Davies), bombed and sunk in convoy by Focke-Wulf FW200 (Gruppe I, KG40) in position 54°.34'N 16°47'W, voyage Freetown to Liverpool with 261 passengers and crew and general cargo. Twenty-four lives were lost. Captain Davies, aware that **APAPA** was in an area frequented by enemy aircraft, had alerted passengers and ordered the crew to action stations at 0800, but ordered a stand down an hour later after talking to the convoy Commodore. At about 1000 engine noises were heard and an aircraft was seen at about 150 feet above the ship, well below the cloud level of 1500 feet. The aircraft crossed the ship diagonally from aft port to forward starboard, dropping two bombs. One landed to starboard, amidships, at a distance of 20 feet, causing some water and blast damage, but the other proved lethal, penetrating No. 3 hatch and exploding with sufficient force to blow out a substantial part of the port hull plating and wrecking the engines. More seriously, the cargo of palm kernels in No. 3 hold was ignited and, owing to the loss of power, all efforts to control the fire proved unavailing, and, despite much heroism by the crew, it proved necessary to abandon **APAPA**, which ultimately broke in two and sank, still blazing. Survivors were taken aboard *MARY KINGSLEY, NEW COLUMBIA,* BOULDERPOOL, HMS BROKE and a corvette.

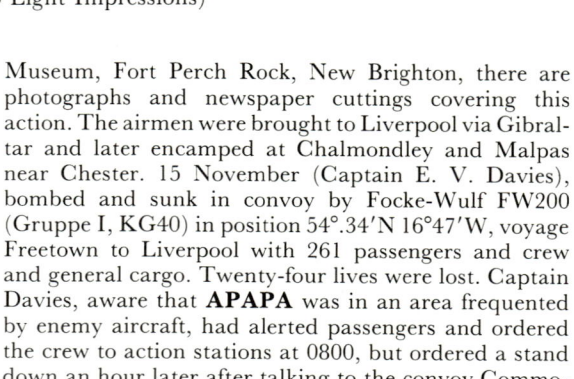

APAPA blazing after the attack

HEROISM IN ATLANTIC: SEAMEN BRAVE PERILS OF U-BOAT-INFESTED WATERS TO RESCUE CREW OF TORPEDOED MERCHANTMAN

The above pictures, just released for publication, show a dramatic incident that occurred in 1941 during the Battle of the Atlantic. The ship Apapa was bombed by a German aircraft and caught fire. The captain of an accompanying ship, the Highland Star, promptly brought his vessel stern on to the Apapa, and with amazing skill kept her there until most of the Apapa's crew had leapt on to the after deck of the rescue ship. Four U-boats were known to be prowling close by. The lower picture shows the Apapa breaking in half and sliding be...... waves.

The last of **APAPA**. *Standing by,* MARY KINGSLEY *with her distinctive silhouette*

269   DUNKWA (I)
O.N. 149636   1927–1941

'D' class
Steel screw motorship, two decks and shelter deck
355.3' × 49.2' × 22.4'   1996 n   3789 g   5870 d
Built by A. McMillan & Son Ltd, Dumbarton, Yard No 735,
for British & African Steam Navigation Co Ltd. Registered
Liverpool. B & W oil engine 4 SCSA 6 cyl $29\frac{1}{8}''$–$59\frac{1}{16}''$ by Harland
& Wolff Ltd, Glasgow. 489 nhp, 10 K.
Passenger accommodation: 12 first class.
1927   August, completed.
1933   May, transferred to Elder Dempster Lines Ltd.

1940   Tonnage opening closed. 2841 n, 4752 g.
1941   6 May (Captain J. W. Andrew), torpedoed and sunk by
U103 (Freggatten-Kapitan Victor Schültze) in position
08°.43'N 17°.13'W, voyage Glasgow to Freetown, general cargo. At 1534 Schütze sighted **DUNKWA** zigzagging about a mean course for Freetown. U103 hauled
ahead and at 1635 dived for an underwater attack. U103
had only one tube clear for firing, since it had not been
possible to reload during daylight after the sinking of
the ms SURAT earlier that day. So, at 1717 (British
Double Summer Time) Schütze fired one of his stern
tubes, the **DUNKWA** was struck aft and she went down
by the stern within eight minutes. Schütze noticed that

Kapitanleutnant Victor Schültze became the first U-Boat Commander to be awarded the highly prized Knights Cross. Above, his Officer of the Watch invests him with a 'home-made' version. Below on 9 March 1941 Grand Admiral Karl Dönitz invested him with the genuine Cross (Photos Bundesarchiv)

the crew were crammed into only one lifeboat, so he had U103's crew right one that had capsized and provided the survivors with extra water before making off. Seven crew members lost their lives.

Ships of the 'D' class: DUNKWA (269), DIXCOVE (270), DARU (271), DAGOMBA (272), DEIDO (273).

Dunkwa is a town and railway junction to the south of Obuasi in Ghana.

DUNKWA

270   DIXCOVE (I)

O.N. 149641   1927–1941

'D' class

Steel screw motorship, two decks and shelter deck

355.4′×49.2′×22.4′   1995 n   3790 g   5870 d

Built by A. McMillan & Son Ltd, Dumbarton, Yard No 736, for British & African Steam Navigation Co Ltd. Registered Liverpool. B & W oil engine 4 SCSA 6 cyl 29⅛″–59 1/16″ by Harland & Wolff Ltd, Glasgow. 489 nhp, 10 K.

Passenger accommodation: 12 first class.

1927   October, completed.

1933   May, transferred to Elder Dempster Lines Ltd.

1941   19 May, damaged by mine in position 51°.36′N 01°.11′E (off Foulness Island, Essex). 24 September (Captain R. Jones), torpedoed and sunk by U107 (Korvettenkapitan Gunther Hessler) in position 31°.12′N 23°.41′W, voyage Freetown to Liverpool, with general cargo. One life was lost. **DIXCOVE** was torpedoed in Hessler's second attack on the convoy. In the first, earlier on the same day, U107 had missed two ships with a salvo of four torpedoes. Having reloaded, U107 approached on the dark eastern horizon, and running in on the convoy's starboard side fired, at 0633 (British Double Summer Time), all four bow tubes at three ships—two torpedoes at a 'tanker' and one each at two steamers—in a surface night attack. After firing Hessler turned away and on hearing no explosions immediately, he was convinced, in view also of the earlier unexplained misses, that he was suffering torpedo failures. However, four minutes had elapsed when two torpedoes were observed to strike the tanker amidships, very close together, a third hit one of the steamers beneath the bridge and a fourth hit the other steamer amidships. Lights appeared on the decks of the steamers and boats were seen being lowered. (The ship described as a 'tanker' by Hessler was most probably the **DIXCOVE**, the ships referred to in the war diary as No 2 and No 3 were probably the LAFIAN and the JOHN HOLT respectively, both of which were torpedoed simultaneously with the **DIXCOVE**.) Following the attack Hessler was forced to avoid an escort

DIXCOVE

and was thus unable to observe the torpedoed vessels fully. When he was able to take another look he had lost sight of the 'tanker' and thus assumed she had gone down. He could see the other two ships were still afloat and in the process of being abandoned. Unable to close the convoy again owing to the firing of starshell by the escorts, which lasted until 0800, Hessler decided against risking any further attacks, since his potential target was only a small steamer and there were seven escorts screening her.

Dixcove is an old surf port in Ghana to the east of Cape Three Points.

DARU

271   DARU (I)

O.N. 149652   1927–1941

'D' class

Steel screw motorship, two decks and shelter deck

355.4′×49.2′×22.4′   2106 n   3839 g   5870 d

Built by A. McMillan & Son Ltd, Dumbarton, Yard No 737, for British & African Steam Navigation Co Ltd. Registered Liverpool. B & W oil engine 4 SCSA 6 cyl 29⅛″–59 1/16″ by Harland & Wolff Ltd, Glasgow. 489 bhp, 10 K.

Passenger accommodation: 12 first class.

1927   December, completed.

1933   May, transferred to Elder Dempster Lines Ltd.

1940   2127 n, 3894 g.

1941   19 May, in collision with ss BEECHVILLE in Loch Ewe. 15 September (Captain W. Rowlands), bombed and sunk in position 51°.56′N 05°.58′W, while bound for Liverpool from Duala and Sherbro with West African produce. She was sunk when convoy HG72 was attacked by aircraft of Gruppe 406, Luftflotte 3. She was hit forward in a dive-bomb attack by one of two 250 kg or 500 kg HE bombs (reports differ on the size of bomb) and set on fire, the other bomb having holed **DARU** forward when exploding just off the starboard side, resulting in a heavy list and the loss of the ship. No lives were lost.

It was originally intended to call this ship *DUALA* or *DODO*. Daru is a district in Sierra Leone.

272 DAGOMBA

O.N. 149669   1928–1942

'D' class
Steel screw motorship, two decks and shelter deck
355.3' × 49.2' × 22.4'   2100 n   3845 g   5870 d
Built by A. McMillan & Son Ltd, Dumbarton, Yard No 738, for British & African Steam Navigation Co Ltd. Registered Liverpool. B & W oil engine 4 SCSA 6 cyl 29⅜"–59¹⁄₁₆" by Harland & Wolff Ltd, Glasgow. 489 nhp, 10 K.
Passenger accommodation: 12 first class.

1928   March, completed.
1933   May, transferred to Elder Dempster Lines Ltd.
1935   Grounded at St Ann Shoals, subsequently grounded off Akassa.
1942   3 November, (Captain J. T. Marshall) torpedoed and sunk by Italian submarine AMMIRAGLIO CAGNI (Capitano Di Fregata Carlo Liannazza) in position 02°.30′N 19°.00′W, voyage Freetown to Liverpool via the West Indies and Canada, cargo palm oil, timber and

tin ore, with the loss of seven lives. **DAGOMBA**, bound for Trinidad from Takoradi, sailed in convoy TS23, but the convoy dispersed some three days before **DAGOMBA** was torpedoed.

AMMIRAGLIO CAGNI survived the war until the Italian armistice, when, under the command of Capitano di Corvetta Giuseppe Roselli Lorenzini, she entered Durban on 20 September 1943 to surrender. She returned to Italy via Mombasa, Aden and Haifa, arriving in Taranto on 2 January 1944. After refitting she was transferred to Palermo, where she was used for the training of Allied and Italian anti-submarine forces until the end of the war.

CAPTAIN'S REPORT—LOSS OF m.v. "DAGOMBA"

By John Tate Marshall

I have been at sea since 1906.
I took my Master's Certificate in 1914.
I have been in command for 18 years.
I joined the m.v. "Dagomba" on the 19th August 1942 at Liverpool.
She was lost on the 3rd November 1942 in Lat.2.29° N, Long. 19° W, about 450 miles west of Freetown as a result of being struck by 3 torpedoes all on the starboard side, the first one in the way of No.3 hatch into the deep tanks, the second one between Nos. 1 and 2 and the third immediately under the bridge, in the course of a voyage from the West Coast of Africa to Liverpool via the West Indies and Canadian ports at 18.00 G.M.T. and foundered within 3 minutes.

There are four missing as a result of the casualty, 1 Ordinary Seaman, 1 Electrician, 1 Steward's Boy, and 1 Assistant Cook. In addition 3 died on rescue ships—they were the Ship's Clerk, from exhaustion, the 2nd Mate who died from injuries received at the time of abandoning ship and a Native Steward's Boy.

The vessel was laden with a full cargo of approximately 5000 tons, consisting of African produce including palm oil in bulk, kernels, tin and timber.

DAGOMBA *laid up in the River Dart* (Photo F. W. Hawks)

She had a crew of 49 all told and one male passenger, a total of 50 lives.

Included in the crew were 6 gunners, 4 Naval and 2 Army.

The Deck Officers and crew were Master, 3 Mates, Carpenter, Bosun, 8 ABs, 1 Ordinary Seaman, 2 Deck Boys, 3 Radio Operators and a ship's Clerk; the Engineers were, Chief, 2nd 3rd 4th and 5th, 1 Electrician, Chief Steward and 2nd Steward, European cook, 2 assistant Cooks (Natives) 3 Stewards Boys, 9 Greasers.

The Dagomba had 3 continuous decks, lower tween deck, upper tween deck and main deck and above the main deck the boat deck; above that the navigating bridge and above that the monkey island.

The Officers' accommodation was on the starboard side of the main deck; the Engineers' on the port side of the main deck, the Wireless Operators—two on the after end of the Boat deck and one, the senior, on the navigating bridge adjacent to the wireless room; the accommodation for the seamen was forward and the gunners aft in the poop. My cabin was on the lower bridge which is on the boat deck. The chart room was on the navigating bridge abaft the wheelhouse which was protected by concrete.

During the voyage we had regular gun drills several times each week when the crew practised loading and management of the guns. The 2nd Officer was appointed Gunnery Officer and he conducted the practices under my supervision and gave the training to members of the deck crew.

In addition we carried 4 P.A.C. rockets—these are rockets which when they are fired carry out with them a wire. When these rockets reach a certain height they explode and release two parachutes, one at either end of the wire and the wire is suspended between them. These rockets were fitted 2 on either side of the monkey island with boxes of wire beside them. These rockets are operated by means of lanyards which are passed through the deck to a position in the wheelhouse immediately about the helmsman's head, and alternate lanyards, two on each side of the wheelhouse protection. In order to fire them all that one has to do is to cock one lanyard and pull the other. It is the duty of the officer in charge on the bridge at the time to fire them when enemy aeroplanes are approaching. If I am on the bridge I give the order.

We also carried about a dozen snowflake rockets for use at night time, in the event of an alert. These rockets go up to a considerable height, some 1200 feet, and then explode and throw out a high illuminant which lights up a considerable area. We were also supplied with 4 kites, which are ordinarily flown from the main mast head. The kite is held by a wire let out and hauled in from the winch. Kites were not flown during the voyage owing to unfavourable weather.

We commenced the outward voyage from Liverpool on the 19th August 1942 and before leaving Liverpool a thorough examination of the vessel's equipment, lifeboats and other apparatus was made by the Company's Superintendent and the officers of the vessel including myself and the crew exercised at Boat drill. Every member of the crew was supplied with a protective suit. This is an oiled silk waterproof suiting, and consists of a one piece suit, which is opened and closed by zip fasteners. The orders in regard to the use of this suit are that every man is to carry it with him when he is ordered to boat situations and to have it ready for use. We had regular weekly lifeboat drills, the first on leaving Liverpool and continued them throughout the voyage out and home.

On the homeward voyage a further thorough inspection of the boats and equipment was made, and the boats put into the water at Forcados River, and they were found to be in good condition and fully watertight. At these drills everybody mustered at their stations with their lifejackets and lifebelts on and with their protective suiting, and were allotted their various duties. The 3rd Officer entered the boats and inspected the gear. I supervised these boat drills. On the same occasions we also had fire drills, at which all the crew attended and carried out their allotted duties, and all fire fighting appliances were brought into use and tested, and the watertight door was opened and shut under the supervision of the Chief Engineer.

We left Takoradi on the 29th October 1942 in convoy, the convoy consisting of 7 vessels in all, with an escort of an armed trawler and a motor boat, and for the first 36 hours an air escort.

She had 4 holds, two forward and two aft, and 6 deep tanks all situated in No.3 lower hold. These were used for carrying bulk oil.

She had 6 watertight bulkheads, 5 fully watertight and No.4 (abaft the engine room) with a watertight door leading into the shaft tunnel. This door was opened and shut by a ratchet situated on the top floor of the engine room and was under the control of the Chief Engineer. This door was always kept locked, except that it was partly opened at each watch for the purposes of inspection with an Engineer standing by.

The bulkheads were as follows: No.1 (Collision bulkhead) between

the fore peak and No.1 hold, No.2 between Nos.1 and 2 holds, No. 3 between No.2 hold and the engine room, No. 4 between the engine room and No.3 hold, No. 5 between No.3 and 4 holds, No.6 between No.4 hold and the after peak. These bulkheads extended from the tank tops to the upper 'tween deck, with the exception of No.1 where a new steel bulkhead had been erected from the upper 'tween deck to the main deck.

She had 4 lifeboats carried in davits on the boat deck, number 1 and 3 on the starboard side of the boat deck, Nos. 2 and 4 on the port side. No.3 was a motor boat.

Each boat had mast and sail, blankets, first-aid set, corned beef, milk, biscuits, fresh water and a dozen red lights. There was one portable wireless set which was in charge of the 2nd Wireless Operator and was taken into No.4 boat, it was a receiving and sending set. The boats were lowered by hand and always kept swung out at sea. The capacity was—of Nos. 1 and 2, 21 persons each, No.3 29 persons and No.4 32 persons. A total capacity of 103 persons.

We had 6 rafts, each capable of accommodating in my opinion about 25 people. These rafts were carried, two in the forward, 2 in the after rigging, one on the foredeck and one on the after deck. These rafts float on drums and have beckets. Each raft also had a self igniting buoyancy light and a lifebuoy. We had rope ladders and life lines—these fitted in such a way that by cutting a rope they dropped and fell down the side of the ship. There were a rope ladder and 4 knotted life lines for each boat; also scramble nets one on port side and one on starboard side.

Everyone on board had a new improved pattern life jacket, fitted with a small electric bulk and battery. My orders were that these lifejackets were to be carried at all times. In addition to the lifejackets each man had a cork lifebelt; we had a total of about 120 lifebelts.

The vessel was fitted with degaussing gear.

We carried the following armament—on the gun platform aft a 4″ breech-loading gun and also a twelve pounder, on the boat deck 2 twin Marlins—one on each side—and on the bridge two twin Hotchkiss, one in each wing.

The convoy proceeded towards Freetown and I left it about 150 miles south of Cape Palmas at midnight of the 31st October. I proceeded on my course towards Trinidad alone.

The weather continued fine and clear, moderate wind, and the voyage proceeded without incident until the 3rd November at 18.00 hours G.M.T.

There was on the bridge at the time the Chief Officer in charge; the senior Cadet who always takes the watch with the Chief Officer and who was at the particular time engaged in an inspection of the lifeboats. I also was on the bridge at the time; an A.B. at the wheel. There was an A.B. on lookout in the crow's nest; 2 gunners were continuously on the lookout aft standing by the guns. We were making about 9 knots. It was daylight and clear.

I was standing in the starboard wing of the bridge when the first torpedo struck us, followed almost immediately by the second and third.

The explosion blew the hatches off Nos. 1, 2 and 3 and it was obvious to me that the deep tanks had been penetrated because quantities of bulk oil were filling the after deck. She took a list to starboard immediately and commenced to founder rapidly by the stern.

Nos. 1 and 3 boats were demolished by the force of the explosion.

All personnel came to their boat stations and I gave the order to abandon ship.

The two port boats (numbers 2 and 4) were lowered away with some difficulty owing to the heavy list, but were in fact lowered without mishap.

All the members of the crew and the passenger, except the 4 who were missing, got into these two boats. The Chief Engineer and myself were taken down with the ship. We each came to the surface and were picked up by the Chief Officer in No.2 boat.

The vessel foundered within 3 minutes of the explosions.

We were unable to send a wireless message from the ship because the wireless room was wrecked.

After we got into the boats and the vessel had disappeared the submarine surfaced, ordered us alongside and asked if anyone was injured and the name of the ship was given by the 3rd officer; it was an Italian submarine, manned by Italians, but from their appearance 4 of the crew struck me as being Germans. The Captain of the submarine who spoke English said he was sorry to have to sink the ship but it was war and asked if we required any stores, water &c. He gave us two kegs of water, two tins of corned beef, 2 tins of biscuits, cigarettes and matches, and 2 bottles of cognac. He then gave us a bearing of Freetown as 450 miles to the east; then he submerged.

In the meantime the 3rd Officer had got up his sail and got a start of my boat; we hoisted the sail and got under way shaping a course for Freetown.

By daybreak the next morning the 3rd Officer's boat (number 4) was not in sight. We carried on with a good sailing breeze for about 5½ days, after which the wind fell light and the only means of locomotion was the oars; we had sailed approximately 300 miles. Owing to the intense heat it was impossible to row during the day and we rested during the daylight and rowed at night time.

On the early morning of the 14th November the lights of a steamer were sighted ahead distant about 6 miles. We burned red flares and the vessel threw a searchlight onto us and turned away. About 4 or 5 hours afterwards this vessel returned and picked us up. She was the "Bartholomew Dias" a Portuguese Naval Sloop. She took us on board. This was 150 miles W S W of Freetown.

There were 21 in my boat. The Clerk, Bennett, was suffering from exposure and sunburn, and he was immediately attended to by the sick bay on the sloop. My left hand had become poisoned at the wrist and the ship's surgeon attended to my hand immediately, and the rest of the crew were also attended to, given spirits to wash in and dry clothing and coffee. We were treated very well and could not have been treated better. Sleeping accommodation was allotted to everyone and a full list of the survivors' names of this boat was immediately radioed by the sloop to N C O Freetown and also to Lisbon. Bennett, the Clerk, died in his sleep the same evening, the cause of death being syncope; he was buried the next day, which was Sunday the 15th November.

We proceeded then until the 21st November when we arrived at Luanda, Portuguese West Africa. We were taken ashore there, accommodation was found immediately and we remained there until noon on Monday, 23rd November. Then we were put aboard the Portuguese Mail Boat bound for Freetown. I received hospital treatment while I was at Luanda.

The Portuguese Mail Boat sailed the same day, 23rd, and we reached Freetown a week later on the 30th November 1942, and we were all landed at Freetown and were accommodated there. Myself and 8 ratings came home from Freetown on H.M.T. "Franconia", the remaining members of the crew were left at Freetown awaiting transport.

We were landed at Liverpool on Thursday, 17th December 1942.

No.4 boat I have heard was picked up on the 10th November by a Vichy French Patrol vessel and taken to a Vichy French port (Dakar, I believe) and the men put into a concentration camp.

Two of the members of No.4 I heard died on the rescue vessel; they were the 2nd Mate and a native Steward's boy. I believe that the 2nd Mate died as a result of injuries sustained by him in carrying out his duties at the time of the explosion and I do not know what was the cause of the Steward's boy's death.

I desire to add that there was no panic whatever on my vessel at the time of the casualty everybody acted in a perfectly orderly and seamanlike manner, including the passenger, and I desire also to state that we were treated with the greatest kindness and consideration on the Portuguese sloop and also on the Portuguese mail boat which took us to Freetown.

(sgd) J. T. MARSHALL

REPORT FROM MR. W. C. BIRD, CHIEF OFFICER OF THE "DAGOMBA"

The ship sank at 17.55 G.M.T. 3rd November, 1942. Mr. Bird was on watch at the time and the Master was on the Bridge with him. The first explosion hit the ship on the starboard side of No. 3 Hatch, the Palm oil Tanks. The tanks were pierced and oil immediately commenced to flow from them. The engines stopped immediately. There were two other explosions all on the starboard side. The ship took a list of 25° to Starboard and all the boats on that side were smashed. They had great difficulty in lowering the Port boats owing to the heavy list.

No. 2 Boat was the Mate's boat and by the time he had rung "Off Engines" and sounded "Abandon ship" and got to his boat, the 3rd Mate was already at No. 4 boat with his boat's crew attempting to lower.

Mr. Bird, assisted by Bosun Ellis, who was attending at the after fall, commenced to lower No. 2 boat. Shortly afterwards Court, A.B. came along and Mr. Bird handed the Fall to him whist he attended and assisted in the lowering of the boat into the water. When the Chief Officer saw that the boat had almost reached the water he then went along to the raft in the Port Fore Rigging knowing it would be required for the ship was by this time sinking rapidly. After releasing the raft he went back to the boat deck and saw the Chief Engineer Mr. Frost being carried along by a hugh sea whilst the Captain was crawling from his Cabin along the boat deck. The Chief Officer seeing the position was by this time hopeless jumped into the water but missed the water and landed into the boat. By this time the ship had upended and was visible only from Bridge to Bow.

The Master, Chief Engineer, Bosun Ellis and Court, A.B. failed to jump in time and went down with the ship. The Chief Officer then fended off the lifeboat from the ship as she sank stern first alongside of them and remained on the spot to rescue survivors.

The sea for a considerable area was thick with Palm Oil and Logs from No. 2 Lower Hold were shooting out all over the place. Mr. Bird saw the Captain's topee floating on the water and surmised that he was somewhere near it. He paddled towards it and found the Captain in a state of complete exhaustion in a doubled up position. He dragged him into the boat and then proceeded to pick up Bosun Ellis and Waters A.B. He kept searching the wreckage for further survivors and next reached Carpenter Lewis and being a big man had great difficulty in getting him aboard. The next he picked up was Chief Engineer Frost. They rescued him with the aid of a boat hook. He was almost finished and said afterwards he couldn't have held on much longer. He was also a very heavy man and they had great difficulty in getting him aboard. They next picked up the Chief Radio Officer Johnson, another heavy weight whose back was badly cut and lacerated from debris floating near. P. Bennett (Pursers Clerk) was also picked up. He was quite naked and suffering terribly from immersion and swallowing palm oil. He died shortly after being rescued by the Portuguese ship.

They next attempted to pick up Court but he was too far away and as he was nearer the 3rd Mate's Boat he hailed Mr. Wicksteed, 3rd Officer, to pick him up.

By this time he had in the boat 7 sick and injured men all which tended to prevent getting the Lifeboat properly trimmed and the sail set. Although Bosun Ellis was violently sick, he managed to handle an Oar and was of great assistance. During the subsequent 5 days in the Lifeboat, Captain Marshall was delirious and on two occasions in his delirium went to strike certain members of the Lifeboat crew for no apparent reason. Mr. Bird had great difficulty with him and eventually had to use very strong measures in point of fact he had to tie him down and it was the chafing of the rope on his wrists that caused the poisoning.

Purser Bennett was also delirious and remained so during the whole of the 11 days. His delirium made the task of sustaining the crew more difficult. After 5 days the Captain improved, but was not able to take any active part in the navigation of the boat and was dreadfully weak when eventually rescued and had to go to bed immediately on getting aboard the Portuguese Sloop.

Carpenter Lewis helped considerably when Captain Marshall was at his worst. He was raving at times and endeavoured on two occasions to jump overside. He did succeed once and would have drowned only for the prompt action of Mr. Frost, Chief Engineer, who siezed him by the foot when drifting away. This incident occurred in the middle of the night and it was after this that the Chief Officer tied him down in the bottom of the boat.

During this period when the Chief Officer's time was occupied in looking after the Captain and other sick men, A.B. Swinburne steered the boat under the Chief Officer's orders.

Mr. Bird would like to make special mention of Carpenter Lewis, A.B. Swinburne and Cadet Corneille who was at all times most helpful being cheerful and most useful. Army Gunner Marsden showed great fortitude as an Oarsman.

Mr. Bird had a touch of Sun Stroke himself on the 9th day and Captain Marshall and Cadet Corneille tended him with the greatest care.

(sgd) W. C. BIRD

REPORT OF NO. 4 LIFEBOAT EX M.V. "DAGOMBA"

November 3rd, 1942

At 16.50 hours on November 3rd 1942, in position 02°.30′N, 17°50′W (approx.) the "DAGOMBA" was struck on the starboard side by two torpedoes. One hit forward of the forward engineroom bulkhead and the other exploded in the palm oil tanks astern of the after engineroom bulkhead. Immediately the vessel took a heavy list to starboard and commenced sinking rapidly. The accommodation in the starboard alleyway was immediately flooded out, and the Second Officer, Mr. R.M. Mail and myself, were washed out of our rooms and into the alleyway. Together we ran up on to the boat deck, and found that the only boats left intact were Nos. 2 and 4 on the port side. No. 1 boat was completely wrecked, and the motorboat, No. 3, was badly damaged. All the rafts were also damaged, and two were blown right into the water by the explosions.

The 2nd Officer and myself then took charge of No. 4 boat and with the assistance of A.Bs. Owen and Flett commenced getting the boat away.

The gripes were slipped without any trouble, but then we found that owing to the heavy starboard list, the boat was leaning heavily against its boom, and the after falls were jammed. At this stage Mr. Williams, the Second Radio Officer, ran up with the portable W/T transmitter and receiver, and together we tried to push the boom off, but found it too heavy. Mr. Mail then left the forward fall, which he had been tending, to one of the A.B.s and bracing himself against the scupper edge, held the boom off whilst A.B. Owen lowered away forward and I lowered away the after fall.

When the boat was level with the bulwarks all the crew who were mustered got inside, and then seeing that the "DAGOMBA" was going, we dropped the boat the last four or five feet into the water, just letting the falls run, and then jumped after her. The boat swung well clear and the painter was immediately cut by Hyde (R.N.Gunner) and I swam to her, clambered aboard and took the tiller.

The total time between the explosions and the boat getting clear of the ship was about two minutes, and a few seconds later the "DAGOMBA" finally disappeared, the suction being amazingly slight.

At once we got the oars out, and commenced picking up the people in the water. We picked up Mr. Grainger, Second Engineering, Mr. Christie, Chief Steward; A.B. Court, and Mr. Mail, Second Officer, and then salvaged a tank of water from one of the damaged rafts.

Mr. Mail had obviously hurt himself badly whilst holding the boat boom clear, and had been hit whilst in the water by one of the logs which had been shooting through the gap in No. 2 hold, where one of the torpedoes had exploded, to the surface of the water. He was very badly injured, as was Peter Okorie, Steward's Boy, so I decided to go alongside the submarine which had surfaced and request medical attention.

During all this time the Chief Officer's boat No. 2, was also cruising around, picking up survivors, including among others Captain J. T. Marshall, O.B.E., the Master, and the First Radio Officer, Mr. Johnston.

The submarine was an Italian of some 1300 tons, with eight torpedo tubes, two 3.9″ guns, net cutter forward and was of the modern welded type. All her paintwork was new and unstained, and she had a realistic wolfhead on the starboard side of the conning tower. The Italians threw us a line, and after some trouble, owing to the swell, we managed to get alongside.

The first Lieutenant, who spoke English well, said that he could give us no medical attention, as they had no doctor, but he handed over two bottles of cognac, two water barricoes, some biscuits and some cigarettes and matches. I thought that we had lost a boat compass when dropping the boat into the water, and so I asked him if he had a spare one. After some delay he produced one and gave it to me. The Italians filmed all this—doubtless for propaganda purposes.

We spent about three quarters of an hour alongside the submarine, and then, as it was growing dusk, we drew away from him and went alongside the other boat, which was lying close by.

We then checked over the numbers and found that three of the natives were missing—members of the galley staff who had been working in the starboard alleyway, outside the galley, at the time of the explosion.

The Chief Officer instructed me to keep in company with him and we decided to steer E.N.E. till morning. We handed over a bottle of cognac and offered them one of the barricoes of water, but were told to keep it till morning.

The Chief Officer's boat, which was the smaller of the two had twenty-two in it, and there were twenty-six in mine.

Names and Ratings of Men in No. 4 Boat

D. G. Wickstead, 3rd Officer.
H. W. Grainger, 2nd Engineer.
J. H. James, 4th Engineer.
F. White, Extra 4th Engineer.
J. Williams, 2nd Radio Officer.
T. Christie, Chf. Steward.
F. Brodigan, 2nd Steward.
C. Murphy, A.B.
E. Owen, O.S.
D. Flett, A.B.
C. Court, A.B.
E. Pettit, O.S.
C. Phillips, Deckhand (R.N.)
C. Hyde, Deckhand (R.N.)
E. Powell, Deckhand (R.N.)
G. Waddington, Deckhand (R.A.)
L. McGrath, Deckhand (R.A.)
C. Smith, Passenger.
Etim, Cleaner (Nigerian).
Bassey, Cleaner (Nigerian).
Kolo, Steward's Boy (Nigerian).

Madegwa, Steward's Boy (Nigerian).
Taire, Steward's Boy (Nigerian).
Roberts, Steward's Boy (Kroo)
Okorie, Steward's Boy (Nigerian).

R.M. Mail, Second Officer, died in the boat on November 4th and was buried at sea on that day.

By the time we had cleared the submarine and been alongside No. 2 boat, it was rapidly getting dark, so we stepped the mast, hoisted the sails, and commenced to steer the course agreed—viz. E.N.E. We last observed the other boat about three hundred yards astern, also sailing.

The tiller snapped as soon as the boat started moving, so I had to improvise a tiller from a piece of bottom board until morning.

All hands were very wet and cold during the night, so I issued a small tot of cognac all round. Many of the crew were very sick from the Palm Oil which they had swallowed whilst in the water, and altogether it was a very miserable night. The 2nd Officer was groaning badly and passing up portions of his intestine, but all we could do was to keep him as warm as possible and moisten his lips with cognac.

November 4th

Shortly after midnight Mr. Mail died, but I decided to leave him for a few hours, and bury him just before dawn.

05.00 hours I burned one red flare and the lookout reported an answering flare from the southward. We then lowered Mr. Mail's body over the side, and I think most of us said a few quiet prayers as a silent tribute to a very gallant man. Just before dawn we burned another red flare as a guide for the other boat, but received no answer.

When dawn broke there was no sign of her, and I must accept the responsibility for missing her during the night, but would point out that the difficulty in steering, organising watches, attending to the injured men etc., did not leave much time or opportunity for keeping a good lookout. It was very unfortunate, because we had a great amount of extra water and the other boat had only its bare complement, but, under the circumstances, it was unavoidable.

As soon as it was light the engineers commenced making a tiller which was screwed on to the rudder head, and was a very sturdy job, then we organized watches on the tiller and lookout, and I handed over to Mr. Grainger the Second Engineer, and with the help of Messrs. Christie and Brodigan, issued the first meal to the crew. It consisted of one prune, two Horlock's tablets, one biscuit, pemmican and one dipper of water.

I decided to make for the West African Coast between Cape Palmas and Freetown, as the breeze was blowing steadily from the S.S.E. and the Guinea Current would help. I laid off our approximate position on the boat chart and set course 055° (T) Error 20°W (Note: by observation our compass was nearly magnetic) Leeway 25° = EAST—(Compass) wind S.S.E. The lookouts worked hourly watches and the helmsmen two hours each. The W/T mast was hoisted at 10.00 hours and the Second Radio Officer transmitted a message giving our position, course and speed. The text of the message was as follows:

"S.O.S. S.O.S. S.O.S. de GNQX torpedoed in 02° 30′ N. 17° 50′ W, two lifeboats steering N.E. speed 2½ knots (approx) Please send immediate aid".

Messrs. Christie and Brodigan took stock of our food and all water tanks were opened up and the water was tasted—everything was found in good order. They were then screwed up tightly and the tank spanner was kept aft.

Okorie, the Nigerian steward was badly lacerated from the explosions and was very lightheaded, but all the rest of the boat's crew were unhurt, and when the sun dried their clothing and warmed them a little, all were in good spirits.

I decided to ration the food on a six weeks' basis as I anticipated making a landfall within a month. Three meals were issued throughout, and three dippers of water—the prunes, raisins and peanuts being particularly acceptable.

The sun was very hot towards mid-day so headgear was improvised from the spare canvas in the boat and the spray hood was rigged forward. This hood proved too great a temptation, however, as during the night a lot of the crew crowded under it, thus pulling the boat down by the head and making her difficult to sail. Accordingly I decided to rig it amidships, and this the engineers contrived to do on the following day, and it made a very useful awning.

Several W/T messages were transmitted throughout the day, and Freetown could be heard on the receiver.

At night we held a singsong, which was ably led by L. McGrath, an R.A. Gunner, whose good spirits and cheerfulness were irrepressible during the whole voyage.

By this time all hands had recovered from shock and morale was really good. The boat was sailing easily and well, and the helmsmen were all becoming quite expert at their job.

November 5th

Course was maintained EAST (c) all night and the boat sailed very well and was taking very little helm to keep her on her course.

At daylight I threw overboard small pieces of wood and found the leeway was still about 25°, and then commenced to make a log line from the twine we had in the boat. Later we took casts of the log every watch and found the boat was making good from 2½/3 knots. This was very heartening to all the crew, and the log reading was always eagerly awaited. We were fortunate in having a watch on board to time the observations.

Morale was growing better and better as all hands settled down to their various jobs and watches were always relieved on the minute.

We had used a lifebelt light minus the red glass to illuminate the compass at night, and found it very satisfactory, so all these lights were collected and stored aft for this purpose. All the "Etagone" tablets from the lifebelts were also collected, and I decided to keep these as an emergency ration for when everything else was finished.

Up to this time no one had managed to sleep at all, as the boat was so full and everyone was very cramped, so we attempted to organise the complement, so that two or three could get a sleep, but it was very difficult to find room.

We held another singsong this night, it seemed to hearten everyone, and also kept us a bit warm. We all suffered from cold during the nights, as the majority of us were very poorly clothed.

November 6th

Course was maintained throughout the night as usual, and the boat logged a steady 3 knots. At dawn breakfast was served as usual, and then another W/T message was transmitted.

Watches, etc. were maintained as usual throughout the day, and in the evening, by general consent, I held a short service and prayers were said for Mr. Mail, our safety and the safety of those in the other boat, also for those who had been killed by the explosions when the ship sank. All hands sang a few hymns, and seemed considerably heartened.

Later the breeze freshened a great deal and the boat began to make real progress. Preventer stays were rigged on the mast, and I decided to hang on to all sail. As many of the hands as possible crowded on to the windward side of the boat to keep her trimmed, and for four consecutive hours we had some first-class sailing, logging a steady 5 knots. Fortunately, nothing carried away.

November 7th

Course was maintained, as usual, throughout the night, the wind dropping to the normal force shortly after 0.100 hours.

Okorie was caught drinking salt water during the early hours of the morning, by Mr. Christie. He was severely warned. However, at daybreak he was obviously worse, and, where before he had been merely light-headed, he was now obviously crazy.

Two W/T messages were transmitted on this day. The boat continued logging 2½/3 knots throughout the day, and continued sailing easily and well.

It commenced raining in the afternoon and early evening, so, knowing too well the discomfort of sitting in damp clothes throughout the chilly night, we adopted the practice of taking off our clothes and keeping them as dry as possible whilst the rain continued. We caught as much water as possible, although we were well stocked already.

November 8th

Course was still maintained EAST (e) throughout the day and log readings were still 2½/3 knots. There were several heavy rain showers throughout the morning and afternoon, and the breeze was no longer blowing steadily.

At 17.30 hours we were struck by a severe squall and had to let fly the sheet, lower away, and quickly we hove the sea anchor over. For the next five hours a severe storm raged and we lay to the sea anchor all night, finding the best place for this was over the stern leading slightly on the starboard quarter. On three occasions the boat almost capsized, her lee gunwale being completely submerged, and we had to do a great deal of fast pumping with the semi-rotary to keep the boat clear of water.

All hands, with the exception of the man on the anchor watch, huddled under the sail, but it was a most miserable night and rather disheartening as we were drifting fast to the N.N.W.

November 9th

By 02.00 the wind had died down quite a lot and by 05.00 there was only a gentle breeze. We then got the sea-anchor in, and found that it was torn into shreds. We hoisted the sails again, but the breeze was very light and we did not make much more than 1 knot. The sun was very hot towards noon, and the breeze dropped until a flat calm prevailed. We were now being constantly followed by three sharks.

At 16.00 hours we commenced rowing, doing half-hourly spells on the oars, but at 20.00 hours we had to give up as all were too exhausted to carry on. Sails were again hoisted, but the breeze was too light to make any appreciable progress.

A W/T message was transmitted in the evening, but it was now necessary to conserve the batteries in the transmitter, in case we sighted anything.

November 10th

There was still very little breeze on this day, so at 05.00 we commenced rowing and continued until the sun became too hot. By this time many of the crew were suffering from severe sunburn, and it was only by constantly bathing the head and neck with seawater that sunstroke was avoided.

In the early evening we again commenced rowing, but only managed to keep going for four hours, then we hoisted the sail and endeavoured to utilise what evening breeze there was.

November 11th

The same course was maintained throughout the night, and in the early morning we again commenced rowing. We decided to keep rowing very easily all day to try to get clear of the calm belt, so we manned four oars continuously.

At 13.00 hours smoke was sighted on the horizon by Mr. James. All the oars were immediately manned, and I headed up for the bearing of the smoke which only appeared at intervals. A W/T message was immediately transmitted, and I ignited one smoke float. At 13.30 I fired another smoke float, and could now make out a convoy in the distance. Mr. Williams, Second Radio Officer, was continuously flashing with the mirror.

We observed the escorting warship detach from the convoy and proceed slowly towards us. We naturally assumed that the convoy was British, and so were in no wise perturbed when we saw the French flag flying on the sloop—assuming that she was Free French. The rest of the convoy were by now out of sight.

We pulled alongside the warship which was the Vichy "AVISO ANNAMITE" and I climbed her Jacob's ladder and went up to the Captain to thank him. I held out my hand and commenced to thank him, but he rapped out in French, "Impossible", and told his First Lieutenant to explain the circumstances. I then had my first news of the North African affair and was told that this was a French man of war under the orders of the Vichy Government and that we were thus Prisoners of War. I protested that we were Merchant Seamen, and therefore, civilians, but merely received a shrug of the shoulders—a method of evading the issue with which I was to become well acquainted in the near future.

We were searched and then put in the Capstan flat under a heavy guard. We were given a small quantity of drinking water, but were not allowed to wash. Okorie was put in the sick bay and the badly sunburned cases were treated with some of our own calamine lotion. Our boat was put aboard one of the ships in the convoy the s.s. "VILLE D'ORAN".

The Capstan flat, our prison for the next five days, was a room under the forecastle measuring about 15' × 13' with a large and extremely dirty capstan motor in the middle. The whole twenty-four of us were kept in this place day and night, there was little ventilation, several rats, and we ate and slept on the very dirty deck. In actual fact there was not sufficient floor space for everyone to lie down.

At 17.00 hours they brought us some food, rice and bits of meat cooked in peanut oil, but quite palatable. We had, however, to eat with our very dirty hands, and we were not allowed to wash. The Doctor came in and dosed us with laxative, then the Captain came, and made a long speech, which I translated to the best of my ability, in which he said that he was going to treat us as Prisoners of War but *with humanity*. We were then locked in.

The deadlights were closed, and there was no other ventilation and the stench arising from the twenty-four unwashed men in that hot, confined space was dreadful. Soon the laxative began to do its work, and one of the crew knocked on the door and requested permission to go to the W.C. He was very roughly answered and shortly afterwards the guards brought 3" × 4" battens and jammed the door with them. Had anything happened we would have been caught like rats in a trap.

November 12th

At 07.00 the door was opened and those who had managed to hold out tried to get out to the W.C. However, they would only allow us to go one at a time accompanied by two guards with revolvers—some of the men were in something very nearly approaching agony by this time.

We were given two tins of sardines, bread and coffee for breakfast—the ratings gave us cigarettes and matches while the officers were not looking. The lower deck ratings and Petty Officers were very sympathetic throughout, and kept us supplied with cigarettes, matches, and the latest news, but they were scared of being caught.

At 10.00 hours we were allowed on the forecastle head and "washed" in a tub of salt water. We were then allowed half-an-hour's exercise before being sent below.

I was interrogated by the First Lieutenant, but gave him no information except a list of names and the name of the Owners.

We had a meal at 11.00 hours and another at 16.30, and were once more locked and battened in at 19.00 hours. I protested vigorously to the Officer of the Watch about the lack of air, so, after removing all light fuses, he allowed the lifting of the deadlights about half an inch and the guards brought us a tub to use as a latrine—this occupied some of our valuable space, but was a slight improvement on the previous night.

November 13th

This day was similar to the preceding one, but later I was called in by the Captain and Surgeon to go and see Okorie in the sick-bay. He was obviously dying and did not speak and the Surgeon said that as he had no drugs he could do nothing.

At 19.00 hours we were locked and battened in as usual.

November 14th

Peter Okorie died in the early hours of this day and at 09.00 we were drawn up on the quarter deck to hold the burial service. Four of our Nigerians acted as bearers and I conducted a short service. The ship's Officers and men were also drawn up on the quarter deck and the ship's bugler played the French equivalent to the "Last Post". The colours were then lowered, and Okorie was dropped over the stern into the sea.

We were again allowed a short exercise period on the forecastle head and at 19.00 were again locked and battened in.

November 15th

At 07.5 we were given breakfast, two tins of sardines and bread once again. We were now nearing Dakar, as the N.E. trades were freshening, and the ship's crew were rigging boat booms etc. This day proceeded in much the same manner as the preceding ones, but we were allowed to wash with fresh water later in the day.

November 16th

We arrrived at Dakar at 08.30 hours, and later in the morning observed that a very large armed guard was being drawn up on the quay opposite the "ANNAMITE". We counted them, and found that there were one hundred and twenty men with rifles and bayonets, and another guard of "Police Arsenal" with light sandbags.

At 14.30 hours a lorry arrived, we boarded her, and were taken under heavy guard to Sebikotane Internment Camp. On arriving at the Camp all money and valuables were taken from us, and full particulars taken. Each one was given a number, and we were then marched off to our quarters.

I protested against our imprisonment as being contrary to International Law, but was given no answer.

The camp was a disused school, surrounded with a barbed wire entanglement. On arrival there each man was issued with a pair of trestles, planks to lay across the top, "donkey's breakfast" a sheet and a blanket. I was told to appoint a cook, and Brodigan, Second Steward volunteered for the job.

The only cooking "facilities" were a large iron pot, some wood, and a couple of small dishes. The evening dinner consisted of a small piece of goat's meat, a pumpkin and two gallons of water—for twenty four men.

At 20.00 hours we marched four hundred yards across rough ground, most of us barefooted, and had our first meal. We had to wait until the French natives had finished and then ate from the same tin plates with the same utensils, which were not washed, but merely dipped in cold water and put back on the filthy tables.

Ten guards with rifles and bayonets and a sergeant stayed with us all the time, and then marched us back. At 22.00 lights were extinguished and we were able to sleep in the comparative comfort for the first time since we were torpedoed. Outside the Camp was floodlit and guards paraded round all night.

November 17th

At 07.00 we turned out and cleaned the place for inspection. At 08.00 we lined up in threes for inspection with myself at the front, and the O.C. Camp and I then proceeded round the Camp. I pointed out the dreadful condition of the latrines to him—they were crawling with maggots and infested with toads, blowflies etc., and asked him for disinfectant so that we could get them cleaned up. He replied that it was impossible to obtain any.

Later in the day I had a fatigue party working on the latrines and eventually we managed to get them clear, but the stench while doing it was appalling.

The sanitary conditions at the camp were very bad; all drains were simply open trenches in which water and sewage merely stagnated, and there was only one washbasin for all hands. However, we all took advantage of an issue of soap to wash what remained of our clothes, and it was a very scantily dressed party that marched across to the schoolroom for "lunch".

The meal was, if anything, rather worse than that of the preceding day. The O.C. Camp came in whilst we were attempting to stomach it, and I got up and made a lengthy and vigorous protest about the food and cooking and eating conditions. The reply I received was: "Ici il n'y a rien; bientot vous allez manger comme des sauvages"—but the evening meal was slightly better, and he gave me ten eggs later in the day which we had boiled for the morrow's breakfast.

As the French authorities had taken good care not to put a single English speaking man among the Camp Officers and N.C.Os, all the burden of translating, filling in the prison forms etc., fell on my shoulders and wearisome work it was. I received an average of twenty individual requests and protests from the men for the first two days, until the O.C. Camp eventually refused to see me any more, or listen to any more protests.

I demanded proper feeding, permission to see the American Vice-Consul, permission to write to the Red Cross at Dakar about the vile conditions, permission to cable the Company our names and whereabouts, protested against our summary imprisonment without cause, against the insanitary conditions, about our lack of shoes and clothing etc., etc., but all to no avail.

We received only two meals per day all the time we were there. The procedure never varied. At 10.00 hours the Senegalese soldiers dragged along a miserable goat or sheep, cut its throat and hacked off a lump of bleeding meat and gristle which our cook boiled for three hours or so with ersatz macaroni or pumpkin, or filthy, maggot-ridden lentils. The liquid was served as "soup" and the meat was our lunch. We also received from 150–200 grammes of bread per day, which was usually kept till morning to eat for breakfast and had a similar meal at 20.00 hours.

I should like to take this opportunity of complimenting Mr. Brodigan, Second Steward, for the good work he did during our stay in the internment camp. He acted as cook throughout and always did his best to make the very bad food as palatable as possible.

November 19th

All hands turned out at 07.00 and at 07.30 all fatigue parties went on duty, cleaning up the accommodation. Inspection was again held at 08.00 hours.

In the afternoon two new arrivals were brought to the Camp—they had been in the Dakar hospital with dysentery and malaria. They had been allowed to listen to the news, and they told us that the general opinion in Dakar was that we would be released within two or three weeks. They also told how three of their ship's company, who had been at this camp a short while before, had died from sheer neglect from malaria and dysentery.

Our kit arrived on the lorry with them, and we were later issued with a native solider's rig, viz:

    1 Sun Helmet.
    2 prs. Cotton shorts.
    2 cotton shirts.
    2 prs socks.
    1 pr army boots
    1 French army greatcoat.
    1 Haversack.

We had not been allowed any cigarettes for many days, even though Messrs. Christie, James and Smith offered to pay for them with the money which was taken from them when we arrived. The bolder spirits, therefore, bartered their army kit with the guards for packets of cigarettes which they distributed, very generously, around the camp.

November 19th–November 24th

During the next four days there was no change in the usual routine, but on the 24th our temporary O.C. Camp was replaced by the permanent officer who had returned from Bamako, where he had escorted the crews of the "ORONSAY" and the "SITHORIA" together with some R.A.F. personnel.

He had the reputation for being a hard man, which he undoubtedly was, but he had the saving grace of being exceedingly garrulous and he used often to send for me to discuss the latest news and follow the campaign in North Africa using his excellent ordnance maps. I was thus able to keep the Camp abreast of all new developments and this caused a great improvement in general morale, as the men were by now suffering from chronic boredom. At this time I also instituted French and signalling lessons which were quite well attended.

I also managed to get news and occasional "Paris–Dakar" from the little native "Medicin-Auxiliaire", who was attached to the Camp as Doctor, and to whom I was giving daily English lessons.

The new O.C. Camp told me that provided the Camp was run on strictly military lines, he would not interfere as he was satisfied with the good state of internal discipline.

I immediately organised the camp on the lines he indicated appointing Orderly Officers of the day—Messrs. Grainger, James and Christie in rotation, arranging regular fatigue parties, also in daily rotation, and appointing Bombardier McGrath as Quartermaster Sergeant under Mr. Christie. The Camp ran very smoothly on these lines, the orderly Officers being most attentive to their duties, thus leaving me more time to "wangle" little extras of food from the Sergeant Caterer, and also to learn the latest news.

On this day we received the news that Senegal had joined the African bloc under Admiral Darlan, and this cheered everyone immensely although, at the same time, all began to get rather restless as it seemed unfair that we should be interned under such conditions when we were actual *de facto* allies.

November 25th–November 27th

There was nothing of importance occurring during these three days, although the food became steadily worse under the new O.C. One night everyone was so hungry that we cut cards for one square inch of bread left over from that day's ration. The midday meal on the 27th was the worst to date—the meat was rotten and stinking, so I took my plate and marched into the C.O's room, where he was having quite a good meal, and shoved it under his nose. When he started to stammer out that he could not see anything wrong with it I got really annoyed and told him that if nothing was done I would request all my men to eat the rotten meat, and he would then have twenty hospital cases. This rather weak bluff worked, and he hastily issued ten tins of sardines.

Our natives were now drawing separate rations, as they were constantly ill on our fare. They were getting rice and meal in lieu of bread and the half-litre of wine we received daily.

Two of the men went down with dysentery on this day and one man had malaria. The medical attention was very poor but I managed to get the Native doctor down to see them, and he gave one injection. He dropped his hypodermic needle on the earth floor, but made no attempt to sterilize it—just wiping it on his sleeve before using it.

November 28th–December 2nd

Conditions continued to grow worse many of the men had acute diarrhoea and the dysentery and malarial cases did not improve. One man collapsed on sick-parade on the 29th but received no attention. We heard that Boisson had gone to North Africa to negotiate, and we had hopes of being released on his return.

December 3rd

At last the American Vice-Consul arrived—Mr. Du Mont. We made our protests to him and he took my log-book away with him to forward to the Foreign Office. He was most guarded in his statements, but did say that he thought we should be out shortly, and told us not to try to escape until the situation clarified.

He also promised to get us ration cards for cigarettes, matches, razors, toothbrushes etc., and issued Officers with £2 of francs and men with £1 worth.

I was allowed to walk back to his car with him, without guards and I asked him for his personal opinion of the whole affair. He replied that he considered it a "phoney set-up" but that as his Government seemed satisfied, he had to concur.

None of his promises ever came to anything—we did not receive cigarettes, razors or anything else.

We did, however, have a good evening meal on the evening the Vice-Consul came, but that was the only *real* result of his coming.

December 3rd–December 9th

There was no news and no change in the situation for the next week and everyone became rather restless—the life was so monotonous as there was nothing to do.

At 05.00 hours on the 9th, however, the O.C. Camp wakened me and told me to get dressed and come and listen to the Swiss Radio as he expected good news for us. We hurried off to the house of a big local landowner—M. Roche—where I heard the announcement that Governor-General Boisson had agreed to release Allied Merchant ships and seamen interned in French West Africa.

I hastily ran back to the camp and told the good news. All the men were naturally very jubilant, but at the same time highly indignant that the armed guard was still kept on, and they were not allowed out of the camp.

Later in the day the rules were relaxed a little and in the evening we were taken to see a cinema show. In the early evening two more men, Clemance and Rigney were carried from Dakar Hospital. Rigney was a mass of suppurating sores and Clemance was simply a living skeleton.

December 10th

On this day the brass band of the 7th Regiment de Tirailleurs Senegalaise came to the Camp to play. They gave a fairly good rendering of "Tipperary" amidst cheers from the local civilian population, who were clustered outside the barbed wire. Most of the restrictions were relaxed, and the men were allowed into the field outside the camp.

December 11th

In the early morning I was sent in a lorry to Rufisque to Area Intelligence H.Q. and after an interview with Capitaine Druiard—the Intelligence Officer, was told that on the following morning we would be sent by train to Kaolack and thence taken across the Gambia frontier.

I also received all the ration cards for cigarettes, razors etc., which had been withheld from us and went around the town spending the francs which the American Vice-Consul had paid us.

When I returned to the Camp all the men had already been told the news and were in the local club where all the townspeople were holding an impromptu party. The civilians seemed as pleased as we were, most of the women had embroidered union-jacks on their dresses, and some had tears of joy in their eyes. They seemed very glad indeed to have this direct confirmation that the African bloc really did *mean* something, and all that day nearly every house in the little town was wide open to all. We were told to make free use of their wireless sets to listen to the English programmes and I personally was so deluged with invitations that I was only able to stay about half-an-hour at each house.

December 12th

At 09.00 hours we entrained at Sebikotane—a first class sleeper had been reserved for us and we were provided with a guide.

At two stations on the route the Chef du Gare sent his compliments to me and requested a few moments conversation with me. They were very anxious for news of the de Gaullist movement but the general opinion amongst the civil population, junior Army Officers and N.C.Os was that Giraud was the only man for the position of High Commissioner. No one seemed to have any faith in Admiral Darlan.

At the last stop before Kaolack a large crowd gathered around our carriage to see "les prisonniers Anglais", and brought out jugs of wine and beer for us. We arrived at Kaolack at 23.00 hours were given a quick meal and then boarded a lorry en route for the Gambia. The lorry was of the usual Senegalese type i.e. driven by a charcoal gas producer unit and as soon as it got outside the town it broke down. After much stoking it consented to run a little further and then broke down again. The driver told the Police Supt. who was accompanying us that we would have to wait till morning for repairs. In the morning the lorry ran an average of four hundred yards between breakdowns, and the driver did not once get out of bottom gear. We were now driving along bush tracks and in every sandy patch the lorry stuck, all hands had to then get down and push.

At about 11.00 hours on the 13th we arrived at a village some ten miles from the Gambia border, the track was very sandy and we were doing far more pushing than walking, and therefore decided to walk the rest of the way and told the Police Supt. that we had had enough of pushing his lorry. He seemed quite relieved, called two guards and told them to take us to the frontier post. We had to assist Clemance the sick man but despite that fact arrived at the frontier at 14.00 hours. There was nothing but a solitary Customs post and a native Customs Officer. He offered to send a man to the nearest British army post but I decided to accompany the guide myself to ensure contacting the Army before nightfall. The rest of the party were given water and lay down in the shade of a tree to get some rest. After walking through the thick bush for an hour I arrived at a native village, but none of the inhabitants could speak English or French neither could the guide. Just outside the village were some tyre marks of Army vehicles, so I decided to follow these, and after a few minutes found a lorry and rest-house, where a Mr. Gordon of the Gambia Agricultural Department was having his lunch. He gave me his lunch then we went back to the border for the sick man sending a runner to the nearest Army post. We collected the sick man and took him down to Nijara, where he was put to bed in the District Commissioner's Rest House. A short while after the Army brought the rest of the party down to Nijara wharf, where we were all met by Mr. Pemberton the Company's Marine Superintendent and taken by launch to Bathurst.

NOTES
1. The total distance sailed between torpedoing and being picked up by the "AMMANITE" was about 420 miles.
2. The sea anchor, which was almost new, proved quite inadequate to stand up to a really severe storm.
3. Preventer stays are necessary for prolonged sailing with a good wind the only fore-stay on a boat provided with standing lug and jib sails is the jib itself, and this is not really adequate.

4. A half-minute sandglass would be very useful in a boat to time the casts of any improvised log.

5. The most nourishing and eatable food in the boat was definitely the prunes, raisins and peanuts.

6. The boat tool kit was most useful throughout.

7. The morale and discipline both whilst in the boat and in captivity were really excellent there was never any difficulty in obtaining volunteers for extra fatigues, A.Bs Court, Murphy and Flett, O.S. Owen and Gunners Phillips, McGrath and Waddington being particularly keen and willing.

The Africans only gave trouble on one occasion, although they were in very low spirits whilst in captivity, and when threatened with disciplinary action, they soon obeyed orders.

> D. G. Wickstead,
> 3rd Officer,
> m.v. "DAGOMBA"

Dagomba is a Ghanaian tribal name.

DAGOMBA in service

273 DEIDO (I)

O.N. 160370   1928–1959

'D' class

Steel screw motorship, two decks and shelter deck
356.6′×49.2′×22.4′   2122 n   3878 g   5851 d
Built by Ardrossan Dockyard Ltd, Ardrossan, Yard No 337, for African Steamship Co. Registered London. B & W oil engine 4 SCSA 6 cyl 29⅛″–59 1/16″ by J. G. Kincaid & Co Ltd, Greenock. 489 nhp, 10 K.
Passenger accommodation: 8 first class.

1928   March, completed. Funnel subsequently heightened.
1933   April, transferred to Elder Dempster Lines Ltd. Registered Liverpool.
1940   2143 n, 3894 g.
1958   2 September, sold (after voyage 95) for £27,200 to Eckhardt & Co GmbH, Hamburg, for demolition.

THE INCREDIBLE LAUNCHING OF 'DEIDO'
by Peter McEvoy

What was probably one of the most incredible launchings in the annals of shipbuilding took place at Ardrossan on the Firth of Clyde. In short, this arose from complications attached to the launching of the African Steam Ship Company's motorship *Deido* in the early winter of 1928.

A squad of experienced shipbuilders had been appointed to the launch on that winter's day. As usual, they looked forward to the jovial company in the "local" afterwards for it was then customary to drink the ship's health and perhaps a drop more.

Beforehand there would be much exacting work to do. The actual launching party consisted of those directly concerned with both the ownership and building of the vessel. These were gathered on the gaily decorated platform specially erected below the *Deido's* bow. Naturally,

DEIDO as built with short funnel

they expected a beautiful launch followed by an equally beautiful lunch. Like the workmen, their expectations suffered an alarming setback.

The routine preparatory work progressed. All the complex network of staging was removed, and the *Deido* was at last in full view. Proudly she stood, shining new and massive with that unique pre-baptismal aura, inviting the photographers for a prize picture. The tide was at its height, the sea calm, there was no wind and everything was perfect.

A series of orders rang out and the carpenters worked furiously with their large hammers, removing all the wedges and keel blocks so that the *Deido* could be free. Down the ways and into the sea she was then expected to go but the lady though differently. She seemed stuck to the launchway and cries of "She's stuck!". "It's the frost," were heard amid the excited clamour.

Started to move
Those in close proximity, however, could see that the vessel had in fact started to move although ever so slowly. The launching squad were unconcerned, knowing as they did that all ships start off slowly. All 355 ft. of the 3,878-ton *Deido* had given everyone a fright; a little hitch to provide the pressmen with something to write about.

A voice cried "She's away", and a great cheer rang out from the platform as a bottle of rich champagne crashed upon her bow, showering the assembly below. The shipbuilders were thirsty and longed for a speedy launch but the *Deido* made them wait.

There was plenty of room in the sea and even the island of Ailsa Craig looming in the background wouldn't have stopped her. No check chains were required in Ardrossan's South Yard but check chains or not, the *Deido* continued. Crawling on her way like a crippled old monster, she went leisurely and nonchalantly towards the sea.

The tide was gradually receding and inevitably there would soon be no water left. Something would have to be done, but what? This ship would have to be coaxed, cajoled, pushed or even rammed into the water.

Time was rapidly running out and *Deido* lumbered on. Unbelievably, her speed was estimated at only one eighth of an inch every few minutes. Surely she would not come to a bad end at such an early age?

While they waited, some chatted about the fate of the *Daphne* which turned turtle after being launched on the Clyde by Stephens of Linthouse near the end of the last century. One of these men had been there although this particular situation was something quite different.

If only something could be done which would speed the ship on her way. The launchway declivity at that time was five-eighths of an inch to one foot and it was quite astonishing that a ship could rest on such a slope with no means of support.

Push the ship
At last came a suggestion and all were asked to push the ship. The *Deido*, however, proved herself stubborn as the proverbial mule and still only inched downhill. Her telescopic mast was dropped in a bid to cause vibration. Workmen danced on her decks and a strong wire was fastened between her and a travelling crane. The men cursed quietly but the *Deido* still never gathered speed.

For those who had come to watch, the fun was now over as the spectacle of the African Steam Ship Company's order defying the ingenuity of these men who boasted of Clyde built ships continued. The *Deido*, one of a class of five motorships, behaved badly while her sisters—built by McMillan of Dumbarton—went down to the sea normally.

Now there would have to be some exceptionally quick thinking. It was no longer a matter of getting the ship into the water but of keeping her out of it. Merely watching this present performance as the tide

This early view of **DEIDO** *shows her surf boats to advantage*

withdrew was simply courting disaster, for, the ship would then land on a hard concrete berth which had otherwise been covered by a good high tide.

The ensuing order summoned all available labour to toil throughout the night in a desperate effort to postpone her outward progress. The idea was to shore her up again and hold her fast. The previously discarded keel and bilge blocks were hastily gathered up for re-insertion under the ship but these tumbled like ninepins because the vessel was still moving. The men worked like Trojans and finally captured and secured the *Deido* to be dealt with another day. Meanwhile, the townspeople slept on and dreamed of the launch they never saw.

In the clear light of the following day the next assault was planned. Experts from larger shipyards in the upper reaches of the Clyde were invited to visit and examine the launchways to check whether they were fault-free. Maybe the ship had been lying in a hollow or perhaps the declivity was wrong? On the other hand could it be the tallow had frozen? No one really knew.

Launch No. 2
However these men did. They had many years of experience in launching ships of literally all shapes and sizes. They decided the tallow had indeed frozen and instructions were given to light flares up and down both sides of the slipway the next morning. Oil was liberally applied to the existing grease which was usually reliable and all was made ready for launch number two.

Tomorrow came or rather another day. The various shoring materials were again removed and the men were jokingly told not to throw them too far away. No one appreciated the humour for they were sure that this time the *Deido* would go. The suggested preparations were made and the usual orders given but still she remained motionless and defiant.

There was no panic—just silence. In spite of all the hard work the tallow remained frozen. Even the oil saturation had made no difference. It seemed then that the *Deido* would just not go down to the sea. The ice-cold atmosphere which prevailed over the Ayrshire coast was blamed and the term "an act of God" was generally used to sum up the event.

With growing publicity the real pressure was now on. Those responsible for the launching could have no peace. There was nothing for it but to start all over again.

Every item of equipment was overhauled and tested in readiness for the renewed attempt. A new type of grease was to be used and experiments were conducted with this on a series of miniature slipways which had to be specially constructed.

The miniature launch was a great success. A large bucket was filled with scrap iron and attached to a crane by means of a long wire. This was lifted and then lowered onto the slipway whereupon the taut wire was slackened thereby allowing the bucket, aided by declivity, to speed to the end of the launchway like a torpedo before being lifted clear again by the crane. By this time the talking point had got round to whether or not the ship would be broken up where she stood.

The news soon spread that the *Deido* was still high and dry. She had adamantly refused to stir even an inch this time and seemed glued to her launchways. The following day was comparable to a football cup final. The ship was making history and it became a case of the "do or die" *Deido*. On this latest occasion the augmented crowd would at least be of greater assistance if pushing was again required.

Third attempt
This was to be the third attempt and the hugh crowd stood quietly in expectation. They didn't have long to wait. The by now familiar commands rang out and sure enough the *Deido* set off but very, very slowly. Two powerful hydraulic rams had been securely bolted to the standing ways at the bow of the ship. These were switched into life and their sudden impact upon the once hesitant ship caused her to almost leap down the slipway and into the sea.

The *Deido* had become waterborne at long last. People sighed, smiled and cheered tumultuously at the end of this unprecedented marathon. She had made the ideal departure. A perfect picture at the end of a truly perfect day.

The "do or die" *Deido* did not die but survived for another 30 years. She was in fact the only motorship of her class to survive the war. Elder Dempster Lines Ltd. employed her on their West African services during those long years so instead of being broken up at her birthplace in 1928, she was scrapped a long time later in 1958. Her story in service could best be told by those who sailed in her but the launching drama enacted at Ardrossan lives on in memory.

Reprinted from *Sea Breezes*

Deido is a district of Douala on the Wuri River, Cameroon.

ELDER DEMPSTER LINES, LIMITED

M.V. "DEIDO"

PLAN OF
PASSENGER ACCOMMODATION

A postwar cabin plan of **DEIDO**, *seen (below left) with raised funnel*

MILVERTON was hastily acquired from the then associated Glen Line Ltd to replace CARIBOO

274 MILVERTON
O.N. 144193   1929–1934

Steel twin screw motorship, two decks and shelter deck
406.0′×54.2′×32.9′ 4123 n 6754 g 9030 d
Built by Harland & Wolff Ltd, Glasgow, Yard No 513G,
for Glen Line Ltd as **GLENTARA**. Registered Glasgow.
2× B & W oil engines 4 SCSA 6 cyl 26⅜″–39⅜″ by the builders.
810 nhp, 10½ K.
Passenger accommodation: 12.

1920	April, completed.
1929	7 January, acquired by British & African Steam Navigation Co Ltd for the Canadian–West Africa service. Later renamed **MILVERTON**. Registered Liverpool.
1930	Laid up on the Tyne River.
1931	Transferred to Elder, Dempster & Co Ltd.
1933	April, transferred to Elder Dempster Lines Ltd.
1934	24 May, sold for £12,750 to W. R. Carpenter & Co Ltd, Sydney, New South Wales. Renamed **SALAMAUA**. Registered Liverpool.

1938   Registered Suva, Fiji (British flag).
1941   6 October, bombed by German aircraft and damaged when at anchor in Straits of Jubal, Suez.
1948   Sold to Pacific Shipowners Ltd, Suva, Fiji Islands. Renamed **LAUTOKA**.
1953   September, sold for demolition in Japan.

275   HENRY STANLEY
O.N. 161382   1929–1942

'Explorer' class
Steel screw motorship, two decks and shelter deck
370.5′×51.6′×20.1′   2188 n   4028 g   5650 d
Built by Ardrossan Dockyard Ltd, Ardrossan, Yard No 342, for African Steamship Co. Registered London. B & W oil engine 4SCSA 8 cyl 29⅛″–59 1/16″ by J. G. Kincaid & Co Ltd, Greenock. 652 nhp, 12½ K.
Passenger accommodation: 12.
1929   April, completed.
1935   Transferred to Elder Dempster Lines Ltd. Registered Liverpool.
1940   3044 n, 5026 g.
1942   7 December, torpedoed and sunk by U103 (Kapitanleutnant Gustav-Adolf Janssen) in position 40°.35′N 39°.40′W, voyage Liverpool to Freetown, cargo general and dynamite. Janssen first sighted **HENRY STANLEY** at 1945 (Central European Time) on 6 December, but then lost sight of her at 2030 in a rain squall. She was resighted after dark, and Janssen attacked on the surface, firing one bow tube. For no apparent reason the torpedo missed, so Janssen fired a second bow tube. That torpedo, too, missed, as the ship having obviously seen the torpedo's wake in the phosphorescent sea went hard a-port. **HENRY STANLEY**'s Master (Captain R. Jones) later confirmed that the torpedo passed 5 to 10 metres astern of his vessel. At 2224 a signal from Rasch (U106) reported the sighting of a steamer, which Janssen thought might be the same one as he had attacked (this was not in fact the case; Rasch had seen another ship). At 2359 Janssen fired a third bow torpedo at a range of 1000 metres. On this occasion **HENRY STANLEY** was hit forward, whereupon she stopped engines, put on a red masthead light and lowered the boats. At 0037 on 7 December her Master was picked up from one of the boats and taken on board U103 (it was a common practice of the Germans to take the Master prisoner whenever possible). Janssen learnt the name of his victim, her port of departure and her destination, and also some details of her cargo, said to have been cement and vehicles. The Master stated that only the forward compartment was flooded and that the ship could thus remain afloat without too much difficulty. In order to sink her therefore, Janssen fired a fourth torpedo at 0140 from one of the stern tubes. **HENRY STANLEY** was hit beneath the bridge, a huge explosion followed as the ship blew up. The Master then revealed that **HENRY STANLEY** was also carrying dynamite. He also stated that she had sailed independently from Liverpool, which was not believed by Janssen. 52 crew and 10 passengers (in four boats), were never heard of again, and were presumed lost in the gale which followed the sinking. Captain Jones was released in April 1945.

HENRY STANLEY (Photo F. W. Hawks)

U103 was bombed and sunk in Kiel on 15 April 1945. She had been paid off in the previous year. Janssen survived the war. Name commemorates the great African explorer, Henry Morton Stanley.

Ships of the 'Explorer' class: HENRY STANLEY (275), MARY KINGSLEY (276), DAVID LIVINGSTONE (277), MARY SLESSOR (278), WILLIAM WILBERFORCE (279), EDWARD BLYDEN (280), MACGREGOR LAIRD (281), ALFRED JONES (282).

Miss Mary Kingsley

276 MARY KINGSLEY
O.N. 162510   1930–1954

'Explorer' class
Steel screw motorship, two decks and shelter deck
370.5'×51.6'×20.1'   2175 n   4017 g   5650 d
Built by Ardrossan Dockyard Ltd, Ardrossan, Yard No 346, for African Steamship Co. Registered London. B & W oil engine 4SCSA 8 cyl $29\frac{1}{8}''-59\frac{1}{16}''$ by J. G. Kincaid & Co Ltd, Greenock. 640 nhp, $12\frac{1}{2}$ K.
Specially fitted with 100 ton derricks for heavy lift cargoes, particularly locomotives.
Passenger accommodation: 12.
1930   27 September launched.
1933   Laid up at Dartmouth.
1935   1 January, transferred to Elder Dempster Lines Ltd. September, in severe equinoctial gales, when on passage Liverpool to West Africa, one of a number of locomotives stowed on deck broke adrift. Ship was turned about and proceeded to Falmouth, arriving 19 September for repair and relashing.
1940   3037 n, 5021 g.
1947   2166 n, 4083 g.
1952   December, major engine breakdown. Returned to Liverpool.

1954   Sold for £25,000 to the British Iron & Steel Corporation. 18 September arrived at T. W. Ward Ltd, Preston, for demolition.
Named to commemorate Mary Henrietta Kingsley (1862–1900) whose travels in West Africa made her famous.

MARY KINGSLEY, *with her distinctive derricks*

DAVID LIVINGSTONE *at anchor (above) and getting under way (below) (Photo J. Clarkson)*

209

277 DAVID LIVINGSTONE

O.N. 161146   1930–1953

'Explorer' class
Steel screw motorship, two decks and shelter deck
370.6'×51.6'×20.1'   2175 n   4022 g   5860 d
Built by A. McMillan & Son Ltd, Dumbarton, Yard No 853,
for British & African Steam Navigation Co Ltd. Registered
Liverpool. B & W oil engine 4SCSA 8 cyl 29⅛"–59⅟₁₆" by Harland
& Wolff Ltd, Glasgow. 652 nhp, 12½ K.
Passenger accommodation: 12.

1930 April, completed.
1935 1 January, transferred to Elder Dempster Lines Ltd.
1940 3032 n, 5031 g. June, together with *APAPA* rescued Pol-
      ish and Czech Air Force Officers in the Gironde River
      near Bordeaux. At the Air Force Museum, Fort Perch
      Rock, New Brighton, there are a number of photographs
      and newspaper cuttings covering this action. The airmen
      were brought to Liverpool via Gibraltar and later
      encamped near Chester.
1943 4 January, **DAVID LIVINGSTONE** together with
      BIAFRA attempted to re-float PIERRE LOTTI,
      aground off Libreville. PIERRE LOTTI eventually
      broke up.
1947 2168 n, 4091 g.
1953 3 September, sold for £20,000 to British Iron & Steel
      Corporation. 11 September, arrived at T. W. Ward Ltd,
      Grays, Essex, for demolition.

Named to commemorate the celebrated explorer.

Convoy position:

Port	Starboard
MARY SLESSOR	SALVESTRIA
CITY OF EDINBURGH	PUCK
CAMBRIA	STORK

One destroyer each side. Convoy position changed later
which put CITY OF EDINBURGH four cables abreast
of **MARY SLESSOR**'s port side. Purser Pritchard (look-
out) reported to the Chief Officer that the City liner was
coming toward **MARY SLESSOR**. As Chief Officer
dashed to the portside wing the CITY OF EDIN-
BURGH came into contact forward of Number One
Hold.

1940 3041 n, 5027 g.
1942 28 January, enquiry held: Justice Buckenile, Captain
      W. R. Crumplin, Captain R. L. F. Hubbard. **MARY
      SLESSOR** one-third to blame, CITY OF EDIN-
      BURGH two-thirds.
1943 7 February, (Captain C. H. Sweeny) mined at 2358
      off Gibraltar in position 35°.55'N 6°.02'W on voyage
      Gibraltar to United Kingdom, cargo sardines, 32 lives
      were lost. The mines had been laid on 1 and 2 February
      by U118 (Korvettankapitan Werner Czygan). **MARY
      SLESSOR** detonated two mines almost simultaneously,
      and within 90 seconds was heeled to starboard in excess
      of 45°. Captain Sweeny was able to have one boat
      launched before abandoning his ship which sank within
      15 minutes.

U118 was sunk with all hands on 12 June 1943 to the south-
west of the Azores by aircraft from the US carrier BOGUE.
Name commemorates the pioneer missionary, Mary Slessor,
(1848–1915) who spent nearly forty years at Calabar, Nigeria.

*A memorial to David Livingstone at Ujiji, Tanganyika,
where Stanley met Livingstone* (Photo Mrs J. O. C. Duffy)

MARY SLESSOR

278 MARY SLESSOR

O.N. 161149   1930–1943

'Explorer' class
Steel screw motorship, two decks and shelter deck
370.6'×51.1'×20.1'   2163 n   4016 g   5650 d
Built by A. McMillan & Son Ltd, Dumbarton, Yard No 864,
for British & African Steam Navigation Co Ltd. Registered
Liverpool. B & W oil engine 4SCSA 8 cyl 29⅛"–59⅟₁₆" by Harland
& Wolff Ltd, Glasgow. 652 nhp, 12½ K.
Passenger accommodation: 12.

1930 May, completed.
1934 12 July, laid up at Dartmouth.
1935 1 January, transferred to Elder Dempster Lines Ltd.
1939 29 October, under the command of Captain R. W. Tate,
      Chief Officer Kenyon, Purser E. G. Pritchard—came
      into collision with CITY OF EDINBURGH.

*June 1930 saw **MARY SLESSOR** at Opobo, waiting to load
palm oil*

MARY SLESSOR

MARY SLESSOR *at Opobo, June 1930*

Miss Mary Slessor, above, and, left, her grave at Calabar
(Photos Mrs J. O. C. Duffy)

WILLIAM WILBERFORCE (Photo F. W. Hawks)

279   WILLIAM WILBERFORCE
O.N. 161406   1930–1943

'Explorer' class
Steel screw motorship, two decks and shelter deck
370.2'×51.7'×20.1'   2165 n   4013 g   5650 d
Built by D. & W. Henderson & Co Ltd, Glasgow, Yard No
855M, for African Steamship Co. Registered London. B & W
oil engine 4SCSA 8 cyl 29⅛"–59¹⁄₁₆" by Harland & Wolff Ltd,
Glasgow. 652 nhp, 12½ K.
Passenger accommodation: 12.

1930   May, completed.
1934   4 January, 2355 hours in collision with ss BRONZITE.
1935   1 January, transferred to Elder Dempster Lines Ltd.
       Registered Liverpool.
1940   3032 n, 5004 g. 4 July, bombed and damaged by aircraft
       in Portland Harbour.
1943   9 January, (Captain J. W. Andrew) torpedoed and sunk
       by U571 (Kapitanleutnant Fritz Schneewind) in position
       29°.20'N 26°.53'W while on voyage Lagos to Liverpool,
       general cargo. Schneewind saw **WILLIAM WIL-
       BERFORCE**'s mastheads at 1725 (Central European
       Time). She was steering a mean course of 325° at 11
       knots, while zigzagging by 30° to 40°. U511 hauled ahead
       until 2045, at which time the ship executed a large zig
       for nightfall, before returning to her original course 15
       minutes later. U511 then ran in on the surface from
       down moon, firing at 2142 a salvo of two bow torpedoes,
       which ran for 55 seconds before striking the target, one
       amidships, the other forward. The ship took a list to port
       and within five minutes had capsized, sinking by the
       head at 2154. U511 closed the lifeboats, of which there
       were four, and found out the name of the vessel and her
       port of departure and destination. Three crew members
       lost their lives.

U511 was handed over to Japan in July 1943 and was com-
missioned in the Japanese navy as RO500. She surrendered at
Maizuru in August 1945 and was later broken up.
Schneewind assumed command of U183 and was killed on 23
April 1945 when his boat was sunk with all hands in the Java
Sea by the US Submarine BESUGO.
Ship so named to honour the great opponent of the slave trade.

280   EDWARD BLYDEN
O.N. 161156   1930–1941

'Explorer' class
Steel screw motorship, two decks and shelter deck
370.6'×51.6'×20.1'   2155 n   4022 g   5860 d
Built by Harland & Wolff Ltd, Glasgow, Yard No 867G,
for British & African Steam Navigation Co Ltd. Registered
Liverpool. B & W oil engine 4SCSA 8 cyl 29⅛"–59¹⁄₁₆" by the
builders. 652 nhp, 12½ K.
Passenger accommodation: 12.

1930   June, completed.
1935   1 January, transferred to Elder Dempster Lines Ltd.
1940   3024 n, 5003 g.
1941   22 September, (Captain W. Exley) torpedoed and sunk
       by U103 (Kapitanleutnant Werner Winter) in position
       27°.36'N 24°.29'W on voyage Freetown to Liverpool,
       general cargo. **EDWARD BLYDEN** was proceeding in
       convoy SL87 when torpedoed. Winter had fallen in with
       the convoy on that morning and by noon had taken up
       a position ahead to await nightfall before attacking. At
       2315 he ran in on the convoy's port bow and at 2346
       fired a salvo of four torpedoes at four steamers. Three
       hits were recorded at various intervals; the fourth tor-
       pedo was assumed to have missed. Winter then brought

EDWARD BLYDEN

Kapitanleutnant Werner Winter (Photo Bundesarchiv)

the ship was coming back to her original course, she was struck by the second torpedo, this time on the starboard side under the bridge. The ship commenced to settle rapidly by the stern and sank within a few minutes. Despite that, the 51 members of the crew and the 12 passengers got safely away from the ship. The other two of the first four torpedoes missed. The two stern torpedoes both hit the NICETO DE LARRINAGA, which was astern of **EDWARD BLYDEN**.

Edward Blyden was named to commemorate a West Indian negro, who at one time was Native Agent for Lagos. A great Arabic scholar, he was Director of Mahommedan Education on the Gold Coast. He addressed the Liverpool Chamber of Commerce in September 1901 on 'West Africa Before Europe'.

Founder of the African Steamship Co, Macgregor Laird

U103 round for a stern shot and at 2347 fired both stern tubes at two more steamers, claiming hits for both torpedoes, the latter on a lone ship at the rear of the convoy. As a result of the attack Winter claimed to have seen and heard a total of five torpedo explosions and to have observed a freighter of about 7000 grt capsize and sink, two other freighters totalling some 11,000 grt sink by the stern, a torpedo explosion on another ship of about 5000 grt, and a large blue-green explosion on the rear ship. At 2354 a destroyer was sighted approaching the position of the attack, so Winter placed her astern of U103 and made off to the south at high speed.

In reality, two of U103's first salvo of four torpedoes struck the **EDWARD BLYDEN**. The first hit the port side aft, whereupon the ship sheered to port towards the next column. Hard a-starboard was ordered, and just as

281 MACGREGOR LAIRD (II)
O.N. 161450   1930–1953

'Explorer' class

Steel screw motorship, two decks and shelter deck

370.1′×51.7′×20.1′   2167 n   4015 g   5650 d

Built by D. & W. Henderson & Co Ltd, Glasgow, Yard No 859, for African Steamship Co. Registered London. B & W oil engine 4SCSA 8 cyl 29⅛″–59 1/16″ by Harland & Wolff Ltd, Glasgow. 652 nhp, 12½ K.

Passenger accommodation: 12.

1930   July, completed.

1935   1 January, transferred to Elder Dempster Lines Ltd. Registered Liverpool. September, sustained severe weather damage, deck cargo shifted. Returned to Falmouth to carry out repairs.

ELDER DEMPSTER LINES, LIMITED
DAVID LIVINGSTONE
M.V. "MACGREGOR LAIRD"
MARY KINGSLEY
PLAN OF
PASSENGER ACCOMMODATION

DR. DRAWERS
W.R. WARDROBE
W.B. WASH BASIN
R. RADIATOR
S.B. SIDEBOARD

BOAT DECK

SHELTER DECK

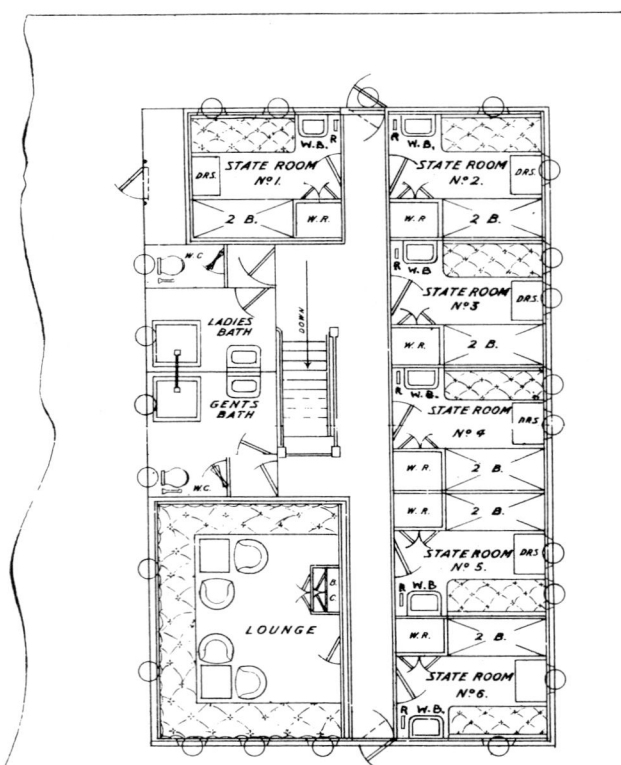

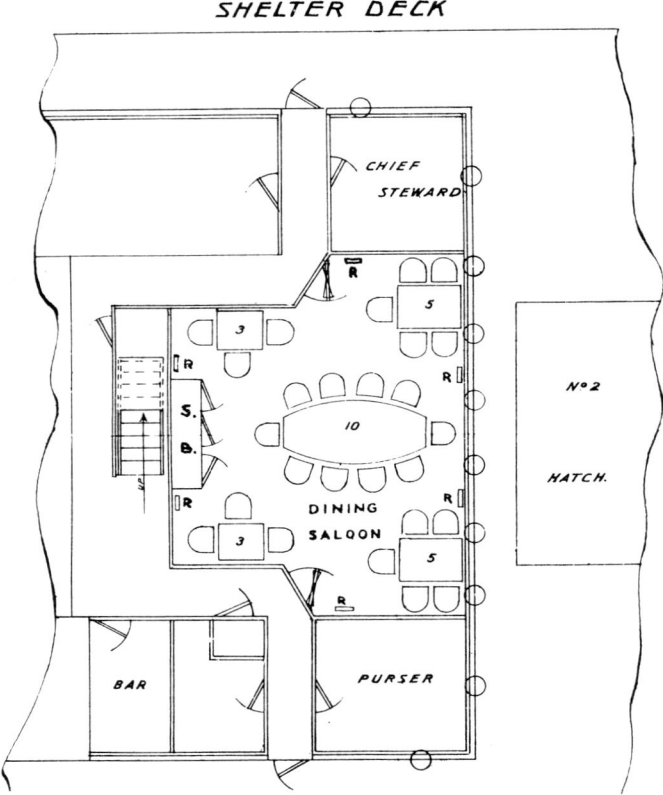

MACGREGOR LAIRD, *peacetime* (Photo F. W. Hawks)

1941   3026 n, 4992 g.
1953   24 February, sold for £95,000 to Anglo-Saxon Petroleum Co Ltd, London. Renamed **SHELL QUEST**. Registered London. 2215 n, 4105 g.
1954   Transferred to Shell Co, Quator Ltd, London. Fitted

out at Grayson, Rollo & Clover Docks for service in the Persian Gulf as an undersea exploration vessel. Accommodation for 120 men was installed in the tween decks.
1956   Sold to Stanhal Navigation Ltda, Panama (N. & J. Vlassopulos Ltd, London, Managers). Renamed **SALAMAT**. Registered Panama.
1961   October, sold to Yugoslav shipbreakers for demolition.

The same ship, the same angle, but here **MACGREGOR LAIRD** *is down to her marks and armed*

Above, **ALFRED JONES**, *and, below right Sir Alfred Lewis Jones, KCMG*

282 ALFRED JONES
O.N. 162322   1930–1941

'Explorer' class
Steel screw motorship, two decks and shelter deck
370.6′×51.6′×20.1′ 2155 n 4022 g 5650 d
Built by Harland & Wolff Ltd, Glasgow, Yard No 868G,
for British & African Steam Navigation Co Ltd. Registered
Liverpool. B & W oil engine 4SCSA 8 cyl 29$\frac{7}{8}$″–59$\frac{1}{16}$″ by Harland
& Wolff Ltd, Glasgow. 652 nhp, 12$\frac{1}{2}$ K.
Passenger accommodation: 12.

1930 September, completed.
1932 Laid up at Dartmouth.
1935 1 January, transferred to Elder Dempster Lines Ltd.
1940 3028 n, 5018 g. 27 October (Convoy B234), bombed by
aircraft and badly damaged when in position 56°.00′N
12°.08′W. Eleven lives were lost but ship reached the
Clyde under escort.
1941 1 June, (Captain H. Harding) torpedoed and sunk by
U107 (Korvettenkapitan Gunther Hessler) in position
8°N 15°W approximately, voyage Liverpool to Takoradi,
cargo aircraft and military stores. Hessler sighted
ALFRED JONES at 1140 off Freetown as she emerged
rapidly from the haze. U107 hauled ahead of **ALFRED
JONES**, who was zigzagging irregularly, which caused
difficulties for Hessler, as he was unable to determine
her speed. Hessler therefore decided to use a salvo of
two torpedoes, which he fired at 1409 (British Double
Summer Time) at a range of 800 metres. Although
spread, both appeared to hit at the same point, some 20
metres from the stern, enveloping the after part of the
ship in a cloud of smoke. **ALFRED JONES** took on a
list to starboard and the crew began to abandon ship on
the port side. Hessler took a closer look and was convinced he had torpedoed a Q ship or an armed merchant
cruiser. He waited half an hour, but as after that time
she was still afloat and now on an even keel, he assumed
she was being kept afloat on barrels or the like and
decided to use another torpedo, which was fired at 1438.

It struck some 30 metres from the bow, blowing the
ship's side open. Many of **ALFRED JONES**'s crew
swarmed on deck but they had no opportunity to lower
any boats before the ship capsized and sank by the head.
Two crew members lost their lives.

U107 was sunk in the Bay of Biscay on 18 August 1944 by
Sunderland W of 201 Squadron. There were no survivors.
Hessler, who at that time was no longer her CO, survived the
war.

Named to commemorate Sir Alfred L. Jones, Shipping Entrepreneur par Excellence.

Two scenes in the Toxteth Dock, Liverpool, early 1930s. Note the steam lorry, above. Below, casks of palm oil

ALFRED JONES *bows, November 1940, after alterations by the Luftwaffe*

217

ACHIMOTA leaving Belfast for trials (Photo Harland & Wolff Ltd)

ACHIMOTA on trials (Photo Harland & Wolff Ltd)

WANGANELLA, formerly ACHIMOTA (Photo Wellington Harbour Board Maritime Museum)

1961 September, taken over by McIlwraith McEachern, Melbourne.
1962 April, sold to Hang Fung Shipping Co, Hong Kong. November, sold to Utah Construction Co Inc.
1963 Sold to New Zealand Government (Ministry of Works) for use as a hostel at Manapouri hydro-electric project, Doubtful Sound, New Zealand.
1970 Sold by Australian Pacific Shipping Co (Hong Kong) Ltd, Panama, to Taiwan shipbreakers. 17 April, left Deep Cove, New Zealand for Hong Kong. 5 June, arrived Kaohsiung, Taiwan, for demolition, by Shyeh Sheng Fuat Steel & Iron Works. 10 June, demolition commenced, completed 5 July.
Name derived from the University town in Ghana.

Andrew Bell built these models of ACHIMOTA and CALABAR

283   ACHIMOTA
O.N. 153940   1931–1932
Steel twin screw motorship, two decks and weather deck
461.2′×63.9′×31.3′   5625 n   9576 g   6238 d
Launched by Harland & Wolff Ltd, Belfast, Yard No 849, for British & African Steam Navigation Co Ltd. Registered Liverpool. 2×B & W oil engines 4SCSA 8 cyl 29⅛″–59 1/16″ by the builders. 1385 nhp, 15 K.
The first set of engines were lost on passage between Glasgow and Belfast; this caused considerable delay in delivery.
Passenger accommodation: 236 first class, 68 second
1929   17 December, launched.
1931   September, completed. Trials (Captain A. H. Crapper) ran under Elder Dempster supervision but due to financial difficulties ownership was not taken up, and the ship was laid up at Belfast.
1932   September, sold to Huddart Parker Ltd, Melbourne for £345,376. Renamed **WANGANELLA**. Registered Melbourne. November, sailed for Australia and 12 December arrived Melbourne to enter the Australia–New Zealand service.
1940   19 June, received survivors of NIAGARA (13,415 g), mined and abandoned in position 35°.53′S 174°.54′E.
1941   May, requisitioned for conversion to hospital ship.
1944   April 14, at Bombay when ss FORT STIKINE (7142 g/ built 1942) blew up. Served as emergency hospital.
1946   Returned to owners. 5741 n, 9876 g.
1947   19 January, (Captain R. Darroch) aground on Barrett's Reef at entrance to Wellington Harbour on first post war voyage (to Vancouver). Towed off 18 days later. Repaired and laid up.
1948   November, resumed service.

284   ILORIN (III)
O.N. 143527   1934–1942
Steel screw steamer, one deck and well deck
189.4′×30.3′×12.6′   413 n   815 g
Built by London and Montrose Shipbuilding & Repair Co Ltd, Montrose, Yard No 86, as **MARION MERRETT**, for Trowbridge Steam Navigation Co Ltd (D. R. Llewellyn Merrett & Price Ltd, Cardiff, Managers). Registered Cardiff. T 3 cyl 14½″, 24″, 40″–27″ by Wm Beardmore & Co Ltd, Glasgow. 99 hp, 9 K.
1920   December, completed.
1926   Sold to McIntyre, Inglis & Co Ltd, Glasgow. Renamed **KIRKWYND**. Registered Glasgow. 12 July, aground at Rhoscolya, attended by lifeboat RAMOS CANRERA. Later re-floated.
1927   Sold to J. P. Hutchison Ltd, Glasgow. Renamed **SMERDIS**.
1933   Sold to Moss Hutchison Line Ltd, Liverpool.
1934   7 July, purchased for £7750 by Elder Dempster Lines Ltd. Renamed **ILORIN**. Registered Liverpool. Employed on West African coastal trade (Takoradi–Port Harcourt).
1942   1 September, (Captain C. H. Bott) torpedoed and sunk by U125 (Kapitanleutnant Ulrich Folkers) in position 05°N 01°W approximately, voyage Lagos to Takoradi, with the loss of Captain Bott and 29 crew. That evening U125 had just surfaced after having dived because of an aircraft when Folkers sighted **ILORIN** on his starboard beam. The **ILORIN** was steering a straight course and steaming at 6–7 knots. While working to achieve a position ahead Folkers noticed the steamer put on her navigation lights as darkness fell, but otherwise she proceeded darkened. At 2156 U125 went to action sta-

Kapitanleutnant Ulrich Folkers sank **ILORIN**
(Photo Bundesarchiv)

tions and at 2206 Folkers fired one bow tube at a range of 800 metres, aimed at **ILORIN**'s bridge. The torpedo struck just abaft the bridge, the ship heeled over to port and sank within three minutes in 45 metres of water. No lifeboats were seen, or any sign of survivors. Folkers considered the steamer's behaviour to have been somewhat carefree, since she had not been zigzagging and had put on her navigation lights, presumably for recognition purposes as she approached Takoradi. Apparently no U-boat had been in the area for some time, hence the minimal anti-submarine measures.

U125 was sunk with all hands in a hedgehog attack by HM Destroyer VIDETTE in 52°.31′N, 44°.50′W on 6 May 1943.

ILORIN

CALABAR

285   CALABAR (III)
O.N. 164255   1935–1953
Steel screw motorship, one deck
249.4′×41.2′×16.3′   1097 n   1932 g
Built by Harland & Wolff Ltd, Belfast, Yard No 954, for Elder Dempster Lines Ltd. Registered Lagos (British flag). B & W oil engine 2SCSA 5 cyl $19\frac{5}{8}''$–$35\frac{3}{8}''$ by the builders. 404 nhp, 13 K.
Passenger accommodation: 40 first class, 12 third.
Passenger vessel for West African coastal service
1935   19 March, completed. Maiden voyage Captain J. J. Smith.
1939   October, registered Liverpool. Employed on the Takoradi–Lagos–Cape Town route after the outbreak of war.
1948   Returned to United Kingdom (Captain C. E. Edge) for refit and survey by builders. 1058 n, 1964 g.
1953   5 May, returned to Liverpool and placed on sale list. 27 July, sold for £42,000 to Epirotiki Steamship Navigation Co (George Potamianos SA, Managers), Piraeus. Renamed **SEMIRAMIS**. Registered Piraeus.
1954   Opened first service between Greece and Italy, on charter to National Tourist Organisation of Greece. Later made cruises to Greek Islands and also operated on owner's services to Piraeus, Crete, Rhodes, Cos Patmos, Delos, Myconas, the round voyage being of five days duration.
1969   March, 1600 n, 2269 g. 937 d, Passenger accommodation: 337.
1978   June, called at Freetown, Sierra Leone.
1980   Sold to Shobokshi Maritime Co, Saudi Arabia. Sold to National Shipbreakers Pte Ltd, Singapore shipbreakers and 8 April, arrived Singapore for demolition, 19 October work commenced.

286   ABOSSO (II)
O.N. 164265   1935–1942
Steel twin screw motorship, three decks and shade deck
460.8′×65.2′×31.5′   6743 n   11,330 g
Built by Cammell Laird & Co Ltd, Birkenhead, Yard No 1006, for Elder Dempster Lines Ltd. Registered Liverpool. 2 B & W oil engines 2SCSA 8 cyl $24\frac{7}{16}''$–$45\frac{1}{4}''$ by J. G. Kincaid & Co Ltd, Greenock. 1660 nhp, 15 K.
Passenger accommodation: 251 first class, 74 second, 32 third.
1935   19 June, launched by Mrs Elizabeth L. Holt. 8 September, completed.
1935   16 October, commenced maiden voyage (Captain J. C. Shooter).
1939   27 June, in collision with ss YEWFOREST (794 g/built 1910) in dense fog 22 miles off Ushant.

Dressed overall, **CALABAR** *departs from Lagos, bound for Liverpool and a refit, after 13 years on the West African coast*

221

An E. Hamilton sketch of **ABOSSO**, as seen on a postcard

ABOSSO in the Mersey

1941   24 May, attacked by Focke-Wulf Kondor, sustaining slight damage.

CAPTAIN TATE'S REPORT ON ATTACK OF 24 MAY 1941

I have to report that an attack was made on this vessel by a Focke-Wulf aircraft on the morning of the 24th May last.

At about 8.28 a.m., the plane was sighted approaching at high speed from about four points abaft the port beam, and she subsequently passed directly over the centre of the vessel.

At approximately 400 yards, I ordered all machine guns that would bear, to open fire. Her bombing attack was preceded by heavy machine gun and cannon fire, and 'ABOSSO' was hit many times by both bullets and cannon-shells, some armour-piercing bullets penetrating the superstructure.

Our machine-gunners behaved with remarkable steadiness, and, during the plane's attack, kept up an intensive fire.

Two bombs were released, but missed by a narrow margin. They exploded close on the port side, and the ship was violently shaken.

Her attack was in a diagonal direction that would have taken her in line with three ships; 'ABOSSO' being the first, but she was so roughly handled by 'ABOSSO's' guns, that I do not think she was in any shape to carry out her full intentions.

After the bombs had exploded, both engines stopped, and the vessel fell rapidly astern of the convoy. Shortly afterwards the starboard engine was restarted at half speed ahead, and at 9.30 a.m. this engine had worked up to full speed. At 11.34 a.m. the port engine was put to slow ahead, gradually increasing its revolutions until at 11.58 a.m. both engines were again working at full speed.

When it was possible to do so I consulted with Mr. Mylrea the Chief Engineer, and we decided that it was possible to continue the voyage, and so I rejoined the convoy.

I am glad to be able to say that during this action the discipline of the passengers and crew was excellent, and there were no casualties, but I would like to stress the courage of the machine-gunners, most of whom are Naval and Air Force ratings, and also the fine work done by Mr. Mylrea and his Engine-room staff. There is no doubt in my mind that had the gunners not stuck so well to their job the bombs would not have missed, and would have entered the vessel amidships. The engineers too, worked extremely hard under what might easily have been dangerous conditions, and that we were able to continue the voyage due largely to their efforts.

1942   29 October, torpedoed and sunk by U575 (Kapitan-leutnant Gunther Heydemenn) in position 48°.30'N 28°.50'W on voyage Cape Town to Liverpool with 182 crew, 189 passengers and 200 tons wool. One hundred and seventy two passengers and 168 crew, including Captain R. W. Tate and all his officers, died. Heydemann had first sighted **ABOSSO** as she emerged from a rain squall. She was steaming at about 12 knots and zigzagging. U575 hauled ahead for an attack, but by the time twilight was beginning the U-boat was still astern of the **ABOSSO**. Heydemann thus increased speed to close and by 2212 he had manoeuvred into an attacking position. One minute later he fired a spread salvo of four torpedoes at a range of 1200 metres. **ABOSSO** was hit amidships, stopped, and took an increasing list. Hey-demann identified his victim as of the **ABOSSO**-type of motorship. At 2228 he fired another torpedo to give her the coup de grâce, which struck abreast the forward edge of the bridge. She sank by the head at 2305. Heydemann then closed the position of sinking and with the aid of his searchlight saw a mass of rafts and boats, some with lights, all fully loaded with soldiers in uniform. Owing to the prevailing weather making communication with the survivors difficult, he was unable to ascertain the identity of the ship. He then withdrew to rendezvous with U463, a U-tanker, for refuelling, as by then his diesel oil had fallen to less than three tons.

U575, then under the command of Oberleutnant zur See Wolf-gan Boehmer, was destroyed on 13 March 1944 in 46°.18'N 27°.34'W by the RCN frigate RUPERT, the US destroyers HAVERFIELD and HOBSON, Wellington B/172, Fortresses R/206 and J/220 and aircraft from USS BOGUE. Heydemann survived the war.

REPORT ON SINKING

Albert Victor May. Formerly Quartermaster on m.v. "Abosso"

The "Abosso" was homeward bound from the Cape carrying a number of passengers in addition to her crew. She was in light trim carrying about 200 tons of, I think, Wool, which had been loaded at Capetown.

She was navigating alone and without escort. At 6 p.m. (ship's time) on 29th October, 1942, I took over the wheel. Immediately before taking over the wheel I got the 4 p.m. position from the Chart on the Chartroom table. It was 49°00' N. and 28°00' W.

When I took the wheel the ship had just ceased zig-zagging and our course was about N. 80° E. true.

It was dark. There was not much wind but there was a heavy sea. The wind was from about N.W. The Chief Officer Mr. Kenyon was in charge of the bridge. We were keeping double watches, the other Officer on watch being Mr. Allitt, the Senior third Mate.

The troop Officer, Mr. Wright was also on the bridge.

At 6.5 approximately I got the order to alter course 90° to port. This was so far as I know in accordance with our usual practice every night of evasive steering. I expected we would get back on to our course and start zigzagging at about 9 p.m. when the moon rose. When the vessel was steadied up I was ordered to steer a steady course till further orders.

Just after I got this order which was about 6.15 p.m. the ship was struck by a torpedo on the port side just abaft the bridge.

Immediately after the explosion the lights went out and the main engines stopped. The vessel took a heavy list to port.

Everybody on the bridge including myself proceeded to put on their lifebelts and make for their boat stations. My boat station was No. 5 on the starboard side. As I left the bridge I saw the Captain leaving his cabin and going towards the Wireless room. It was told by Q.M. J. Arundell who was in No. 5 boat with me that he had heard the Captain telling the Wireless Operator to get an S.O.S. away.

I met Mr. Wright the Troop Officer and a lady passenger Mrs. Franklyn, whom I told to get into the boat and she did so.

I then proceeded to the after fall to assist in lowering the boat but I was told by Mr. Wright to get into the boat and take charge which I did. The boat was then ready for lowering. Difficulty was experienced in lowering the boat owing to the heavy list of the ship. When the boat was lowered to the Promenade Deck the remainder of the passengers whose station was No. 5 boat got in. I assumed that they belonged to No. 5 boat. I do not know for certain. The behaviour of everybody concerned was quite orderly.

Owing I suppose to the extra weight of these passengers and the rolling of the ship, the boat took charge and dropped straight into the water.

She landed on an even keel.

I took charge of the boat. I was the Senior Member of the crew in the boat.

There were 31 all told in the boat of whom 14 were members of the crew.

One of those in the boat was Lieut. Commander Commou, Royal Netherlands Navy. It is not correct to say that he cut the boats painter.

He was singing out to cut the painter but to the best of my belief he never left the after end of the boat at this time.

The painter was in fact let go by one of the crew in the bows releasing the toggle by which it was secured to the fore end of the boat.

We were carried well away from the ship by a sea. We got the oars out and whilst doing so we were engaged in picking up survivors from the water.

These came out of No. 3 boat which had upended whilst still hanging by the forward falls, the after ones having been let go.

We picked up 4 survivors who are included in the total 31 previously given by me.

When we got the oars out we pulled about 300 yards away from the ship where we busied ourselves in getting the pump going and baling out with buckets and anything we could get hold of. The boat had sprung a leak owing to coming down so hard on the water.

We tried on the following day to stop the leaks by using some composition which was supplied as part of the boats equipment but it was too cold to get the stuff in a plastic condition.

Whilst we were lying off the ship I noticed the motor launch No. 9 boat coming round looking for survivors. She came close to us a couple of times.

I saw lights indicating the presence of about 3 other boats, my impression being that 5 boats at least got away.

I had also noticed that all the falls on the starboardside of the ship except No. 3 were empty.

Whilst lying off the ship I saw that they had got the emergency generator going and the flood lights which illuminate the boat stations were on. By that time the "Abosso" was on an even keel again. Very shortly after she had righted herself and I would say about 20 minutes after the first torpedo she was struck by another torpedo and about 5 minutes after that she went down bow first.

Shortly after the "Abosso" sank the submarine surfaced and she turned her search light on the position where the ship went down and on the boats in the vicinity.

She remained surfaced for about 5 minutes flashing her lights on and off. She may have continued on the surface longer than this but I saw no more of her lights.

During the night all we could do was to keep the boat head to sea

and continue baling which we did till daylight. The light of one of the other boats was in sight up to about 1.30 a.m. but by daylight there were none of them in sight.

At daybreak on the 30th October we put the sail up and continued sailing till about 4 p.m. when the weather got too bad. We then lowered the sail and streamed the sea anchor, which worked satisfactorily in assisting us to keep head to wind. The weather was very bad and I used the oil bag.

This was the worst night I have spent at sea. It was very cold and wet.

The men at the oars got worn out trying to keep the boat head to sea. I make no complaint against them in the circumstances. They were mostly stewards and not accustomed to handling oars.

The lady passenger, Mrs. Franklyn was very helpful in every possible way.

I had decided to put the sail up as soon as possible to relieve the work at the oars and when dawn came I did so.

The wind by that time had shifted to the westward and had moderated but there was still a heavy sea.

We steered approximately N.E. sailing before the wind all the time.

About an hour before we were picked up we sighted the masts of a convoy right ahead. We exhibited red flares to attract attention.

After that we spotted a corvette coming towards us on the port side a good way off.

She did not appear to have sighted us. Shortly afterwards we saw H.M.S. "Bideford", ahead coming in our direction.

We then dropped the sail and got our oars out in order to go alongside.

We were picked up at 11 o'clock by the "Bideford's" time.

We were told on the "Bideford" that they spotted our red sails but that they had not seen our flares.

We received every kindness from the "Bideford".

As regards the boats equipment the pump was not of sufficient capacity to meet the weather conditions which we experienced. I would also suggest that an electric torch would be a handy addition to the equipment.

In other respects I was well satisfied with the boats equipment including the food.

I was told on the "Bideford" that a destroyer had been detached from the U.K./Canada convoy to look for survivors.

The 'Bideford's' convoy was from the U.K. to North Africa. I presume she communicated with the U.K./Canada convoy.

I was also told on the "Bideford" that they had received a message from the Admiralty instructing them to look out for survivors.

I should mention that before the ship sank we had passed a couple of small rafts. I do not know personally what happened to the Regulation rafts but Kelly O.S. who was in my boat told me that he had seen the bosun and the lamp trimmer releasing them.

Some of the occupants in my boat were suffering from injuries. In particular Capt. Reaks (R.A.M.C.) had hurt his back. J. Tyrer Asst. Steward had a foot injury. Also D. Thomas (foot injury) and a Dutch sailor who had burnt his hand coming down the lifeline into the boat.

MV ABOSSO

LENGTH 479 Feet   BREADTH 65 Feet   DEPTH 37 Feet   GROSS TONNAGE 11,329

A further view of the pre Second World War flagship

11 32/1/28

OCEAN ARCHIVES.

Film l.   No 28   COMMANDER - IN - CHIEF,
WESTERN APPROACHES,
LIVERPOOL, 3.

28th December 1942

Dear Mr Holt,

Thank you for your letter of the 22nd December.

I fully appreciate the concern you must feel, which we fully share, over the sad loss of so many passengers and crew from the ABOSSO, and am glad that I am able to reassure you that, although the casualty took place so far from land, immediate steps were taken to endeavour to find the remaining survivors.

You will appreciate that the importance of the convoy to which H.M.S. TIDEFORD was attached prohibited any search being made by escorts of this convoy, but the search was, in fact, continued with all the forces at our disposal for some days, unfortunately with no success.

I hope to have the pleasure of meeting you soon.

Yours Sincerely,

Max Horton.

A D M I R A L

L. Holt Esq.
    54 Ullet Road,
        Liverpool 17.

224

287 SOBO (II)

O.N. 164319 1937–1963

'Sobo' class
Steel screw motorship
379.0′×52.7′×21.3′ 2321 n 4124 g 5987 d
Built by Scotts' Shipbuilding & Engineering Co Ltd, Greenock, Yard No 566, for Elder Dempster Lines Ltd. Registered Liverpool. Oil engine, opposed pistons, 2 SCSA 4 cyl $22\frac{1}{16}''$–$85\frac{1}{16}''$ by Wm Doxford & Sons, Sunderland. 3100 bhp, $12\frac{1}{2}$ K.
Passenger accommodation: 12.
1937 3 April, maiden voyage (Captain J. R. Jones).
1940 3154 n, 5353 g.
1943 27 March, unsuccessfully attacked by four torpedo bombers when bound for Bone, North Africa, in a convoy consisting of 20–25 vessels (Commodore ship INVENTOR) escorted by two destroyers, three corvettes and light cruiser CARLISLE. **SOBO** was singled out and attacked at 1000. HMS CARLISLE signalled **SOBO**, advising that a German surface raider was also in the vicinity.

My last two voyages in the *Sobo* occurred during the attack on North Africa.

On the first of these, in the longest convoy I had ever seen, we sailed from Gourock with the 158th American Brigade. What a contingent they were—all from the Middle West and I don't think any one of them had ever seen a ship until the crossing. They were good chaps really, but like most soldiers they hated ships.

The *Sobo* was the leading assault ship of her section and just before we were to pass through the Straits of Gibraltar, I was studying my

ELDER DEMPSTER LINES, LIMITED
M.V. "SOBO"
PLAN OF
PASSENGER ACCOMMODATION

PROMENADE DECK

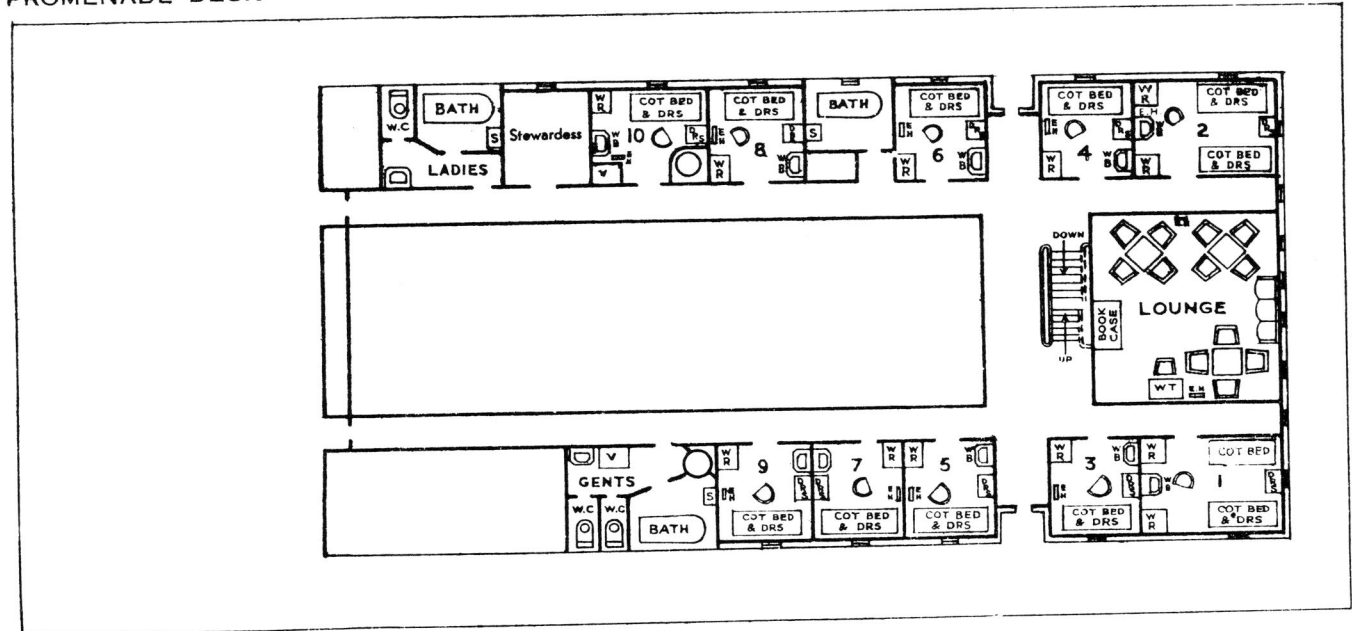

SHELTER DECK

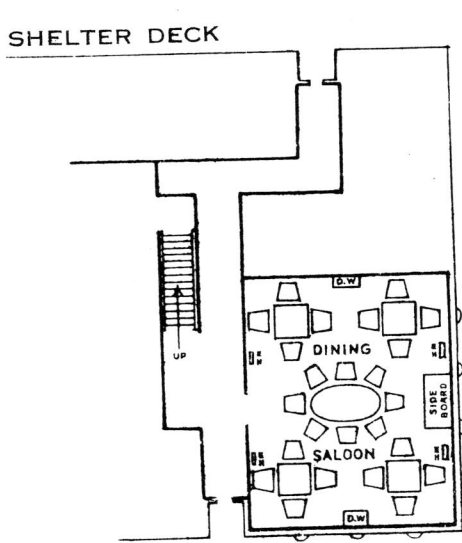

INDEX

W.B. Wash Basin
W.R. Wardrobe
Drs. Drawers
W.T. Writing Table
E.H. Electric Heater
D.W. Dumb Waiter

SOBO

orders for the attack on Algiers. Suddenly my cabin door burst open and the American C.O. appeared, looking wildly excited.

"Say, Cap." he shouted, "one of my boys has just told me he has seen a big shark passing by. What the hell are you going to do about it?"

Not thinking, I said: "One?—there are lots of them around here, why worry?" This seemed really to unnerve him.

"Well," he replied, "I can tell you brother, if we're hit none of your boys will see the life-boats—you fellows can have the landing barges."

Apparently he thought it would take a day to get the lashing off the barges. I had to show him how quickly they could be freed by touching a stern hawse slip. At that he felt obviously relieved and turning round said: "Well, I take my hat off to you dog-gone Limeys." The thought had obviously not occurred to him that if a torpedo hit us there would have been no question of taking to the boats: the cargo on board needed but a spark for the *Sobo* to disintegrate—600 tons of high octane, barrels of heavy oil, bombs and ammunition of all kinds.

On the morning of the day fixed for the attack our job was to zig-zag across the stern of the convoy. At daybreak a plane came along and dropped a torpedo on our stern side. With the helm hard a-port the *Sobo* turned so quickly that the torpedo shot alongside about ten feet off. We could see its track in the water and were thankful for the *Sobo's* manœuvrability.

We landed our troops the following morning 15 miles from Algiers and not a single shot was fired from the shore. All the ships were hard at work landing troops, guns, tanks, oil, ammunition and so on. The following day we went to Algiers, which had been captured by our forces.

Our first night in the anchorage was a bad one with the German and Italian Air Force over in hundreds, bombing and blasting in high and low level attacks. But the *Sobo* kept clear of everything, and though some of the bombs fell very close we did not lose even a light bulb. Apart from all her other work, the *Sobo* came gaily through two further voyages with me, and several more with Captain J. S. Cowan.

Captain J. J. Smith, OBE, *Sea* magazine

1947   2413 n, 4173 g.
1963   16 August, arrived Bruges for demolition by Van Heyghen Freres.

Ships of the 'Sobo' class: SOBO (287), SWEDRU (288), SEA-FORTH (289), SANSU (290), SANGARA (291).

SWEDRU

288   SWEDRU (I)
O.N. 164321   1937–1941
'Sobo' class
Steel screw motorship
379.0′×52.7′×21.3′   2321 n   4124 g   5987 d
Built by Scotts' Shipbuilding & Engineering Co Ltd, Yard No 567, for Elder Dempster Lines Ltd. Registered Liverpool. Oil engine, opposed pistons, 2 SCSA 4 cyl $22\frac{1}{16}''$–$85\frac{1}{16}''$ by Wm Doxford & Sons Ltd, Sunderland. 3100 bhp, $12\frac{1}{2}$ K.
Passenger accommodation: 12.

1937   May, completed.
1940   3172 n, 5379 g.
1941   16 April, bombed by a Focke-Wulf Kondor in position 55°.21′N 12°.50′W, voyage Freetown to Liverpool with 47 crew, two gunners, 12 passengers and general cargo including timber. The Kondor, from Gruppe I of KC40, was severely damaged by anti-aircraft fire from the convoy and forced to ditch. Seven passengers and 17 crew, including Captain Little, lost their lives. The attack set **SWEDRU** ablaze and the burning hull was torpedoed and sunk by a British warship.
Swedru is a town to the north of Winneba, Ghana.

226

Launch of *SEAFORTH* (Photo D. C. Thomson & Co Ltd)

Elder Dempster representatives aboard **SEAFORTH**, *Captain J. R. Jones on left* (Photo B.S. Marine Design Services Ltd)

289 SEAFORTH

O.N. 166259   1939–1941

'Sobo' class
Steel screw motorship
378.0′×52.7′×21.3′   3211 n   5459 g
Built by Caledon Shipbuilding & Engineering Co Ltd, Dundee, Yard No 369, for Elder Dempster Lines Ltd. Registered Liverpool. Oil engine, opposed pistons, 2 SCSA 4 cyl $22\frac{1}{16}''-85\frac{1}{16}''$ by Wm Doxford & Sons Ltd, Sunderland. 3100 bhp, $12\frac{1}{2}$ K.
Passenger accommodation: 12.

1938   22 November, launched by Miss Rosemary Hughes Jones.
1939   23 and 24 February, trials. 3650 bhp, 14·827 K. Maiden voyage (Captain J. R. Jones).
1941   18 February, torpedoed and sunk by U103 (Fregatten-Kapitan Victor Schütze) in position 58°.48′N 18°.17′W, voyage Liverpool to West Africa, with the loss of Captain W. Minns, all 48 crew and ten passengers. Schütze sighted the **SEAFORTH**'s mastheads at 1355 (Central

European Time) on 18 February 1941. She was steering east and periodically zigzagging by some 40° to 50°. U103 hauled ahead of her in squally weather that made it difficult to maintain contact. By 1930 U103 had achieved a favourable attacking position, but was prevented from carrying out an underwater attack by the high sea. Schütze therefore waited for darkness, when he could attack on the surface. During a heavy rain squall he fired two torpedoes, at 2130 and 2131. The first missed, probably due to an aiming error, as the U-boat was yawing violently. The second struck amidships, there was a heavy explosion, **SEAFORTH** stopped and boats were lowered. U103 closed **SEAFORTH** on the ship's lee side. There was no sign of a list and she seemed not to be sinking, so Schütze fired one of his stern tubes. Despite aiming problems due to yawing the torpedo struck **SEAFORTH** in the after hold. Several explosions followed and she sank rapidly by the stern.

SEAFORTH *on trials* (Photo B.S. Marine Design Services Ltd)

Passengers aboard were: Mr Thomas Hughes (Elder Dempster Lines Ltd), Miss Read (Scottish Mission, Calabar), Mr & Mrs McKendrick (Scottish Mission, Calabar), Mr & Mrs Greig (Scottish Mission, Calabar), Mr J. Trudjeon (care of Holman Bros Ltd, Takoradi), Captain E. G. Pyke (Gold Coast Regiment, Accra), Mr & Mrs G. W. Roberts (UAC, Takoradi).

U103 was sunk by aircraft bombs in an attack on Kiel on 15 April 1945. She had been paid off in 1944. Schütze survived the war.

Seaforth chosen at the request of Hon. L. H. Cripps—one of his family had a home in Seaforth, near Liverpool.

SEAFORTH. *A deck scene*
(Photo B.S. Marine Design Services Ltd)

290 SANSU (II)
O.N. 166261   1939–1961

'Sobo' class
Steel screw motorship
378.0′×52.7′×21.3′   3196 n   5446 g   5927 d
Built by Scotts' Shipbuilding & Engineering Co Ltd, Greenock, Yard No 573, for Elder Dempster Lines Ltd. Registered Liverpool. MAN oil engine 2 SCDA 6 cyl 23$\frac{5}{8}$″–35$\frac{7}{16}$ by the builders. 3100 bhp, 12$\frac{1}{2}$ K.
Passenger accommodation: 12.
1939   April, completed.
1943   March, involved in convoy OS44 but avoided attack.
1955   2345 n 4174 g.
1961   13 January, sold for demolition to British Iron & Steel Corporation for £38,000 and broken up by T. W. Ward Ltd at Preston.

Attack by U107 on Convoy OS44 (times are Z–I)—Following several listening watches in the early hours of 13 March weak HE was picked up at 0400 bearing 030 degrees. U107 surfaced and altered towards. At 0508 Gelhaus sighted the silhouette of a destroyer to starboard and then those of several steamers to port and concluded he was between the escort ahead of the convoy and the merchantmen. He thus altered onto the convoys' course of 180 degrees and dropped astern into its midst. His intention was first to empty his bow tubes at the column on his port side and then to turn to starboard and bring his stern tubes to bear on the same side of the convoy. At 0530 he altered to run in for a surface attack and fired his first four bow tubes in quick succession at a range of 1200 metres, one torpedo each

SANSU

at a different steamer, whose outlines in the mist were difficult to make out. While turning for the stern shots he heard four muffled explosions. One steamer was seen to fire a rocket and No 84's SSS was picked up on the 600-metre band. Gelhaus fired his stern tubes at 0537 and 0538 at a large four-masted steamer. A huge explosion occurred after 1$\frac{1}{2}$ minutes, immediately followed by an even larger explosion, which produced a bursting cloud that glowed red, from which Gelhaus considered he may have hit an ammunition ship. At that stage Gelhaus found himself between the red glowing cloud and an escort vessel, and being lit up by the glow he crash-dived, initially travelling away at high speed before slowing and adopting silent routine.

Counter-attacks followed, one pattern was close, another somewhat farther away, which indicated to Gelhaus that the escorts did not have a firm contact. At 0917 a pattern of four depth-charges exploded, followed at 0930 by a single charge. Then, continuously from 0940 to 1050, unexplained explosions, like gunfire. Gelhaus came up to periscope depth for an all-round look but saw nothing and so dived again for trim before surfacing once more at 1300 and setting off in pursuit, in the hope of being able to carry out another attack that night before any air patrols arrived. At 1425, U107 passed through several masses of floating wreckage, which included empty lifeboats and rafts. Having been forced to dive repeatedly for aircraft, Gelhaus did not sight the convoy's smoke until 1141 the next day but was unable to catch it owing to continued harassment by air patrols.

SANSU *from a picture postcard*

Four ships of OS44 were hit in quick succession and must all have been victims of U107's first attack. They were CLAN ALPINE (No 84), whose SSS was picked up by Gelhaus between the first and second attacks, the OPORTO (No 74), which crumpled and rapidly sank, the SEMBILANGAN (No

YEAR 1943   **OS 44**

Convoy No. ~~(crossed out)~~

SS SANSU for Freetown

Convoy Commodore
F.A. MARTEN, CB, CMG, RNR

VICE-COMMODORE
Captain of
SS SILVER BEECH
for Freetown & TAKORADI

DATE DEP. 6th March 1943   **DATE ARRIVE**

11 G. GNGPELN-GESBY / BARON / Zuidmeek Ramsey / 9½K 83' 90'	21 R/T G. QUSS / NEW CALEDONIA / 9½K 95'	31 R/T	41 ESTABELLA 9K 89'	51 Commodore SANSU 11½K 92'	61 ISIPINGO 12K 93'	71 MAKRANA 12K 55'	81 SILVER BEECH 12K 70'	91 EMPIRE GLADE 12K 80'	101	111 TORBORG	121
12 BEGUM 10K 100' 13K	22 HENRI JASPAR 11K 108'	32 ALPHARD (Du.) 11K 108'	42 MATADIAN 11K 97'	52 DEIDO (circled) 9½K 95'	62 COPACABANA (Bel.) 14K 113'	72 CITY OF WORCESTER 10½K 131'	82 AFRICAN PRINCE 9½K 93'	92 SEMBILANGAN TORP 10K	102 ST. JUST LOUREST 10K	112 AMBERTON	122
13 CAP CARINI / DANAE II 9½K 58' 10K	23 CELTIC STAR 9½K 75'	33 URANIEN BORG 9K 72'	43	53 DORDRECHT (Du.) 9½K 66'	63 TJILAMBI "sunk collision" 10K 105'	73 ASPHALION 11½K 118'	83 MENELAUS 13K 98'	93 SEMBILAN 10½K 114'	103 CITY OF SYDNEY 13½K	113 HOLLENDGE 11K 31'	123
14 LINDEEN / BACTRIA 8½K 80' 10K 70'	24 EMPIRE SUNBEAM / GUDRUN MAERSK 13K 67'	34 PETROL	44 PETROL	54 PETROL / RONAN 9K	64 MARCELLA TORP 9½K 84'	74	84 CLAN ALPINE TORP 10½K 95'	94 CITY OF WINDSOR 11K 110'	104 BAHARISTAN 9½K 95'	114 FORT WEDDERBURNE ND 10K 9d	124
15 8½K 80'	25 BARON NAPIER 9½K 72'	35 CITY OF LANCASTER 9K 36'	45 ALGERIAN 8½K 72'	55 GENERTON 8½K 82'	65	75	85 OPORTO TORP (circled) 9½K 82'	95	105	115	125

ESCORT

◢ — Ships for Freetown
∇ — Ships for WALVIS BAY, Capetown ...
⊘ — Bathurst
⌦ — S. America

—— Ships inside

P.T.O.

(Plan by L. Norbury-Williams)

92) and the MARCELLA (No 64), both of whom blew up. The CLAN ALPINE, which was only damaged in the first attack, was subsequently very probably hit by one of the stern torpedoes, since she experienced a second explosion a few minutes after the first. Even then, the CLAN ALPINE, poop and after-deck awash, remained afloat and had to be sunk by HMS SCARBOROUGH with two depth charges. U107's other stern torpedo presumably missed.

*Kapitanleutnant Jost Metzler, of U69
(Photo Bundesarchiv)*

291   SANGARA (III)

O.N. 166270   1939–1943: 1944–1960

'Sobo' class
Steel screw motorship
378.0′×52.7′×21.3′   3196 n   5445 g
Built by Scotts' Shipbuilding & Engineering Co Ltd, Greenock, Yard No 574, for Elder Dempster Lines Ltd. Registered Liverpool. MAN oil engine 2 SCDA 6 cyl 23⅝″–35⁷⁄₁₆″ by the builders. 3100 bhp, 12½ K.
Passenger accommodation: 12.

1939   June, completed. Maiden voyage (Captain A. A. Smith).
1941   30 May, torpedoed in Accra Roads by U69 (Kapitanleutnant Jorst Metzler) with the loss of Captain S. Themens. **SANGARA** sank by the stern in 33 feet of water. 12 August, Italian submarine ENRICO TAZZOLI (Capitan-Fregatta Carlo Fecia di Cossato) fired a torpedo at the wreck. It missed.

U69 was sunk by HMS VISCOUNT off St Johns, Newfoundland, on 17 February 1943 with the loss of all hands. Metzler, who was no longer in command, survived the war.

1943   1 April, sold, as is/where is, to two locally based engineers for the sum of £500 (excluding some fittings). After re-floating **SANGARA** was towed to Lagos Roads; it

SANGARA

M.V. "SANGARA"

PLAN OF
PASSENGER ACCOMMODATION

PROMENADE DECK

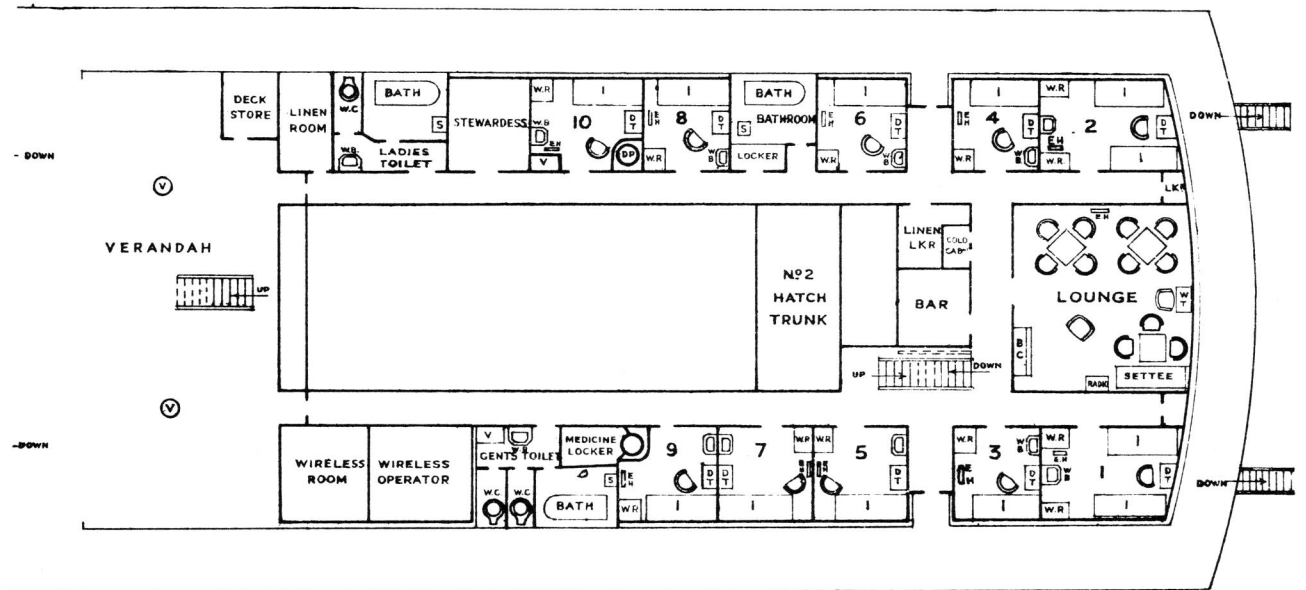

S.	Seat
W.B.	Wash Basin
W.R.	Wardrobe
E.H.	Electric Heater
D.T.	Dressing Table
W.T.	Writing Table
B.C.	Bookcase
S.B.	Sideboard
D.W.	Dumb Waiter

SHELTER DECK

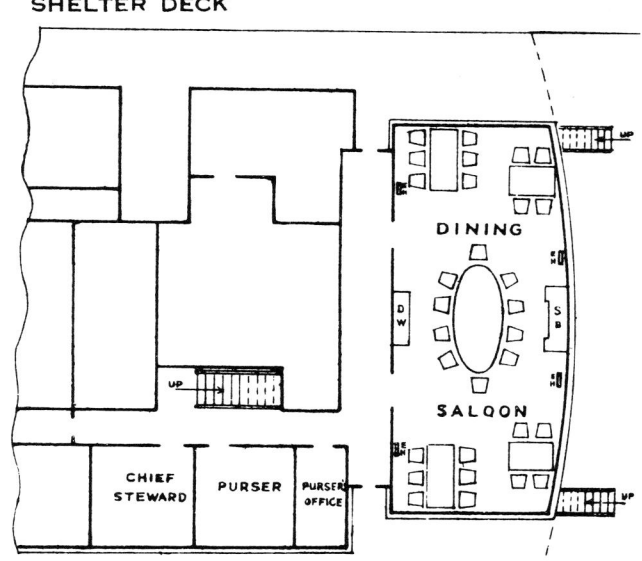

SANGARA laid up at Lagos

was decided that owing to port congestion and her condition it would be unwise to allow her to enter port. She was then towed to the Cameroon River until it was decided what to do with her, she being the property of the salvors. Whilst at Douala (Cameroon) her cargo was sold, after which Elder Dempster repurchased **SANGARA** and she was then towed to Lagos, where a berth had been prepared just above Wilmot Point (Elder Dempster shipyard). At the end of the war she was stripped of all engines and woodwork fittings, i.e. hatches and decking, which was renewed. **SANGARA** was then chipped from stem to stern, and the damage to the ship aft (where the torpedo had struck) repaired.

1946 Departed Lagos under the tow of the tug SEAMAN, destination Middle Docks, South Shields. Speed averaged $2\frac{1}{2}$ knots and took 62 days to complete the passage (Captain John J. Smith). All repair work carried out in

Lagos was under the supervision of Mr T. Beckerleg, Superintendent Engineer. The original engines were retained.

1947 10 April, departed Liverpool on 'second maiden voyage' under the command of Captain Stanley John Bristow. 2329 n, 4189 g, 5927 d.

1960 14 September, sold for £38,000 to British Iron & Steel Corporation. 17 September, arrived at Preston for demolition by T. W. Ward Ltd.

FANTEE

At 0820 **FANTEE** struck the Seven Stones Reef and was abandoned eight minutes later. Back broken before arrival of salvage tug. Declared a constructive total loss. Court of Enquiry found casualty caused by wrongful act of the Master (Captain J. W. Andrew). His Certificate was suspended for six months. The crew of 56 and two passengers, Mr and Mrs F. G. Pemberton, were rescued by Scilly Isles launches BITTERN and GOLDEN SPRAY.

Ships of the 'FANTEE' class: FANTEE (293), FULANI (294).

ARETE

292 ARETE
O.N. 145407   1937–1947

Steel screw steamer
197.7′×30.6′×12.2′   509 n   898 g
Built by Mistley Shipbuilding & Repairing Co, Mistley, Yard No 5, for F. W. Horlock's Ocean Transport Co Ltd, Mistley. Registered Harwich. T 3 cyl 16″, 27″, 44″–30″ by G. Clark, Sunderland. 106 nhp, 9 K.

1925 Completed.
1937 5 June, purchased by Elder Dempster Lines Ltd for £16,000. Registered Liverpool. Employed carrying coal from Port Harcourt, Nigeria to Takoradi.
1947 September, broken up at Lagos.

FULANI

293 FANTEE (III)
O.N. 161104   1943–1949

'Fantee' class
Steel twin screw motorship
464.6′×60.3′×25.8′   3870 n   6369 g
Built by Cammell Laird & Co Ltd, Birkenhead. Yard No 947, as **PENRITH CASTLE** for Lancashire Shipping Co Ltd (J. Chambers & Co, Managers). Registered Liverpool. 2 × Werkspoor oil engines 4 SCSA 6 cyl 28¾″–59$\frac{1}{16}$″ by North Eastern Marine Engineering Co Ltd, Newcastle. 4600 bhp, 13½ K. Passenger accommodation: 4.

1929 9 May, launched by Mrs T. Regram. July, completed.
1943 9 February, rescued 28 survivors from American liberty ship RODGER B. TANEY, sunk by U169 (Kapitanleutenant Georg Lassen), voyage Saldanha Bay to Bahia. Eighteen crew and 13 gunners lost. 24 September, acquired by Elder Dempster Lines Ltd.
1946 Renamed **FANTEE**.
1949 6 October, encountered dense fog when rounding Land's End, voyage from Matadi via Amsterdam to Liverpool.

294 FULANI (III)
O.N. 161100   1943–1958

'Fantee' class
Steel twin screw motorship
464.6′×60.3′×25.8′   3807 n   6369 g   9710 d
Built by Cammell Laird & Co Ltd, Birkenhead, Yard No 946, as **THURLAND CASTLE** for Lancashire Shipping Co Ltd (J. Chambers & Co, Managers). Registered Liverpool. 2 × Werkspoor oil engines 4 SCSA 6 cyl 28¾″–59$\frac{1}{16}$″ by North Eastern Marine Engineering Co Ltd, Newcastle. 4600 bhp, 13¼ K. Passenger accommodation: 4.

1929 26 March, launched by Mrs M. Wilson. Trials 14.253 K.
1943 24 September, acquired by Elder Dempster Lines Ltd.
1946 Renamed **FULANI** (at New York). 3833 n, 6359 g.
1949 13 January, in collision with DELAWARE SUN in Delaware Bay (8964 g built 1922, owners Sun Oil Co, registered Philadelphia).
1950 21 June, on fire in Brunswick Dock, Liverpool. Passenger accommodation increased to 8 (4×2 berth).

M.V. "FULANI"

PLAN OF
PASSENGER ACCOMMODATION

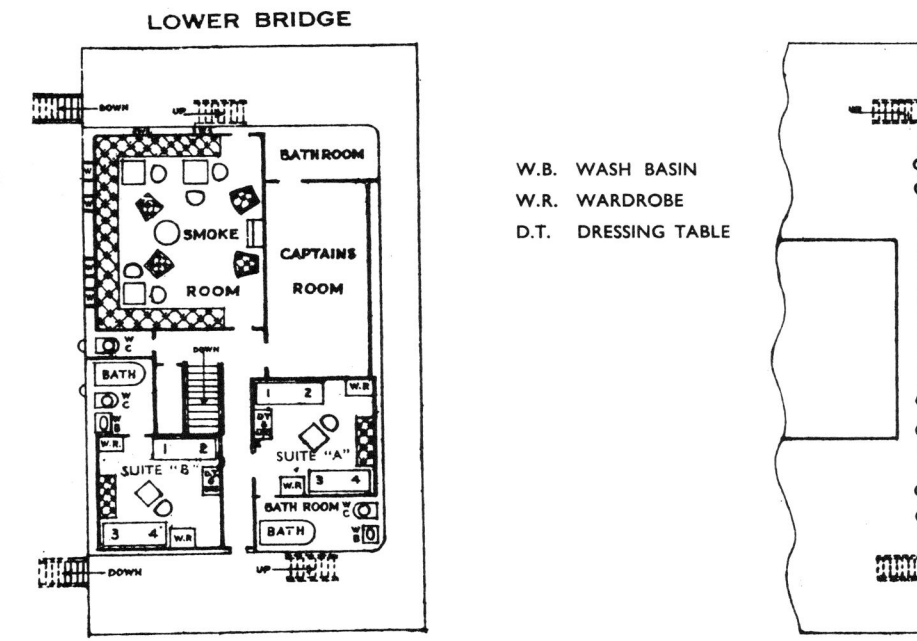

W.B. WASH BASIN
W.R. WARDROBE
D.T. DRESSING TABLE

FULANI accommodation plans before (above) and after (below) the fire in 1950

ELDER DEMPSTER LINES, LIMITED

M.V. "FULANI"
PASSENGER PLAN

D.T. - DRESSING TABLE
W.B. - WASH BASIN
WR.F. - PULL-OUT WRITING FLAP
E.H. - ELECTRIC HEATER
B.C. - BOOK CASE
C.T. - COFFEE TABLE
H.S. - HINGED SEAT

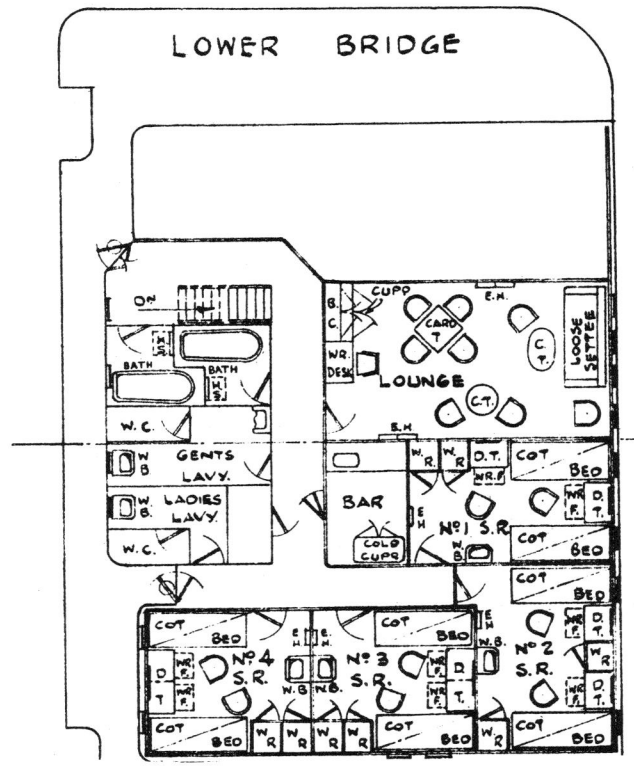

1958 14 October, sold to H. J. Hansen, Odense, Denmark. 7 November, arrived Odense for demolition.

CHAIRMAN'S REPORT ON THE "FULANI" FIRE

WEDNESDAY, JUNE 21ST, 1950

PERSONS ON BOARD AT TIME OF FIRE:
Mr. Corfe—Night Officer
Night Engineer
Junior Engineer (back from leave)
Electrician
1 Native Engineroom hand
Stewards

The vessel arrived in Liverpool from West Africa on June 5th 1950 and docked in Canada dock where she discharged her cargo. On completion of dis-charge on June 15, the holds were inspected by Mr. Farrell and Mr. Wilson, the relieving Officer. Everything was found to be in order with the cargo completely discharged, dunnage stacked ready for use and hatches cleaned ready for loading. The vessel moved to the loading berth, S. W. Brunswick Dock on June 15th, Cargo gear was rigged during the afternoon of June 15th and work commenced on the morning of June 16. The Foreman was Mr. Harper, and the gang foreman in No. 2 hatch was Mr. Sennett, and in No. 3 hatch, Mr. Egan throughout the loading period.

HOURS OF CARGO WORK:

Thursday,	15.6.50.	Rigging gear
Friday,	16.6.50.	8 a.m.–7 p.m.
Saturday,	17.6.50.	8 a.m.–noon
Monday,	19.6.50.	8 a.m.–7 p.m.
Tuesday,	20.6.50.	8 a.m.–7 p.m.
Wednesday,	21.6.50.	8 a.m.–7 p.m.

At 9.05 p.m. approximately on Wednesday, June 21st, the fire was first observed.

REPAIRS:
Minor voyage repairs were being done throughout the vessel. Burning work was being done on the bridge structure when the ship started to load and repairs were finished down below in the forward hatches on Friday, June 16th, and in No. 5 hatch welding finished at 5 p.m. on June 16th. The usual fire watchman was always in attendance during these operations; this man is additional to the Fire Security Patrolman. The only cargo loaded in No. 2 on June 16th was asbestos sheets in the fore end of the orlop deck against the bulkhead.

PERSONNEL:
Mr. Williams was the day officer and his hours of duty were 9 a.m. to 5 p.m. Mr. Wilson, the relieving officer, was also on board daily from 9 a.m. to 5 p.m. Mr. Corfe was the night officer; he came on duty at 5 p.m. and remained till 9 a.m. next morning. The relieving officer signs a book on taking over to say that he is satisfied with the work, and the day officer rings up the Dock Office to say he has been relieved.

In the engine room one engineer, who does alternate nights, is on duty all night from 5 p.m. to 8 a.m. The following morning, while during the day all the engineers who are not on leave are aboard. The engine room hands live on board so they are available day or night. A man is stationed on the gangway from 6 p.m. to 6 a.m., and the Dock watching service provides a man who is concerned with the Fire Security of the vessel at night from 5 p.m. to 8 a.m. next morning. The duties of the night watchman are to keep undesirable people off the ship, and to inspect the vessel's moorings. The fire patrol arrives before the vessel finishes work, is provided with accommodation aboard and takes an hourly patrol round the vessel. While the vessel is working, they are on deck continually passing from hatch to hatch, as they are also responsible for preventing pilferage on deck.

CARGO WATCHING:
A watchman is provided down each hatch to stop either smoking or pilferage. During the vessel's loading, nothing out of the ordinary was reported, and there was no smoking. At 7 p.m. the watchman is the last man out of the hatch when the top deck hatches are replaced, the tarpaulins drawn over the hatch and a few wedges knocked into place. This was done on the night of the fire. The hatches are then inspected by the responsible officer.

In No.3, the forward deep tanks were full of cargo and the deep tanks lids were lowered and the four corner bolts were in place; this would not make a watertight joint. The manhole lids were, however, securely in place.

SHIP'S FIRE APPLIANCES:
Mr. Calder informed the inquiry that repairs were being done to the vessel's deck water service, and so two hoses were connected ready for use to the shore water supply. There was a point of disagreement here when the ship's officers said they were not informed of these repairs. The fire pump was always ready for instant use in the engine room, and there were sufficient people on board to operate it. As it was a motor, it was impossible to say how long it would take to bring it into action but it would only be a few minutes.

The Master last had a fire inspection at sea on May 31st 1950. As he signed the Log, it can be taken that he was satisfied with the condition of the vessel's fire-fighting equipment.

CARGO ON BOARD:

	No. 1		No. 2	No. 3 Deep Tanks
For'd.	Bags salt	For'd.	B/s Cotton	c/s window
	Stoneware pipes		c/s	frames
			machinery	Rolls wire mesh
Mid-ships	B/s Stockfish	Mid-ships	B/s Cottons	c/s earthenware
	c/s cycles		c/s machinery	Scrap tyres
	c/s earthenware		Railway	Dms. caustic
			chassis	General
			frames	
			cigarettes etc.	
Aft.	Dms. caustic	Aft.	c/s machinery	
	soda		dms. dyes	
	Bags salt		c/s refrigerators	
	c/s machinery		c/s cigarettes	
	General		c/s biscuits	
			dms. sodium	
			hydrosulphite	

Vessel lay port side to wharf.

	Hatches	Tonnage Loaded				
	No. 1	2	3	4	5	6
Shelter deck				19		
Orlop Deck		63		30		
Lower Hold	572	407	280	231	460	332
Total of cargo	572	470	280	280	460	332

7 p.m. June 21st   Total Deadweight 2,394 tons.

STATE OF TANKS: 21st June, 1950.

Fore Peak	Full	
No. 1 tank	3″	
No. 2 Tank P. & S.	Full	
No. 3 Tank Oil P. & S.	3′8″	3′10″
No. 4 Tank Oil P. & S.	2′0″	2′0″
No. 5 Tank Oil P. & S.	Dry	0′2″
No. 6 Tank Oil P. & S.	0′2″	0′2″
No. 7 Tank Oil	3″	
After Peak	Full	
Feed Tank	3′2″	
Domestics	Full	

VESSEL'S DRAFT: 15′5″ forward   18′8″ aft.
Vessel had an approximate list of 1½°–2° to port.

DISCOVERY OF FIRE:
Mr. Corfe said he was on deck at intervals up to 9 p.m. and noticed nothing, and it was also stated that the Dock Master had noticed the vessel at 9 p.m. and had seen nothing wrong. The night watchman discovered the fire. At 9 p.m. he was aft and about to commence his rounds, when he saw smoke coming from No. 2 ventilators.

He tried to descend No. 2 but the fumes and smoke drove him back. He told the Electrician to 'phone for the fire brigade which arrived at 9.17 p.m. Meanwhile the rest of the personnel were employed in fetching the hoses on board, and the Dockmaster who had noticed the smoke—telephoned for Commodore Lane, who arrived about 9.35 p.m.

On arrival, the fire brigade put four hoses down the ventilators and also took off the top hatches in order to pour water down below. Breathing apparatus was used but the heat drove the firemen from the hatch. Mr. Clitherow, Liverpool's Chief Fire Superintendent, was in control, and he worked in close conjunction with Commodore Lane, when he arrived, and the Dock Master. In reply to a supplementary question, it was ascertained that the fire was observed in No. 3 deep tanks at about 10.15 p.m. and that in order to save the oil fuel double bottom tanks catching fire and endangering the whole ship, Commodore Lane flooded the two forward tanks. Captain Sinclair stated that, in his view, this was a material factor in saving the after part of the ship from fire. Immediate orders were given to the engine room staff to close all water-tight doors. The vessel assumed a gradual list to port until at approximately 1 a.m. the Dock and Fire Authorities ordered the vessel to be abandoned. Sprinklers were left in Nos. 1 and 2 lower holds and the firemen then concentrated on saving the shed from alighting. The Salvor also concentrated on putting water aboard from the dock. As the morning progressed, the vessel, of her own accord, gradually righted herself for, with the water level in the dock run down, the vessel took to the mud. There had been a small local fire in the engine room that was quickly brought under control. At 6 a.m. fire fighting was resumed aboard, but the bridge structure had meanwhile caught fire, and efforts were made to extinguish this. It was then decided to flood the ship in order to quench the fire, and the Mersey Dock Board formally took over control of the vessel from the owners. The bilge lines could not be used for this purpose, and the fire brigade undertook the flooding with the use of their hoses. Inadvertently the valve on No. 6 bilge line had been left open when the water-tight doors were closed the previous evening, and, when No. 6 was flooded, the tunnel filled as well. The fire was finally quenched on Thursday afternoon. The vessel was then resting on the bottom some ten feet from the dockside with about a 1° list to starboard. Extra moorings had been put out during the course of the fire, and at 11 a.m. on Thursday forenoon, there were 9 parts of rope leading forward, 6 parts leading aft from the forecastle, with 11 parts of rope aft together with the fore and aft wire backsprings that had doubled up.

HAZARDOUS CARGO IN NO. 2:

There was nothing of an absolute inflammable nature in the cargo stowed in this compartment. The railway chassis were encased in creosoted timber, but this is not liable to spontaneous combustion. There were galvanised wares done up in tarred lagging and, in the after part of the No. 2 hold against the bulkhead in either wing 100 drums of sodium hydrosulphite for Hatadi. These drums were loaded on June 19th and were exposed in the stowage up to covering-up time on June 21st. This chemical was packed in thin steel drums enclosed in cardboard containers. It is liable to combustion when in contact with water, when it quickly emits a fierce heat. Before the material could be fixed, however, it would be necessary for the steel drums to be perforated, and water introduced into the stowage. The Ministry of Transport allows it to be carried in Passenger ships, and on or under deck in a cool, well ventilated space away from acids or combustible materials. In a supplementary circular, the Ministry says it must be separated from any explosives by the engine and boiler rooms space, or by one complete hold in a horizontal plane. It is a more dangerous compound than sodium hydrosulphide. When carried by rail, it is marked with a yellow label that is a warning of its inflammable nature.

SALVAGE OPERATIONS:

These commenced on the afternoon of Tuesday, June 27th. By 4.15 p.m. the major salvage pumps were stopped, and pumping was continued with small auxiliary pumps. The dock level had been specially run down in order that the vessel's floating could be a controlled movement, and water was run from the North end system as required through the paddles. Water was not taken from Toxteth Dock on account of a deeply laden Italian ship. No. 1 hold was partially pumped out, No. 2 had about 9 feet of water in it, No. 3 deep tanks were still flooded, No. 4 and 5 holds were nearly out, the tunnel was still full, No. 6 was dry and the after Peak tank was full of water. At 6.30 p.m. pumping was commenced on the after peak tank in order to lighten her aft. By 7.10 p.m. the vessel was afloat fore and aft with the dock reading at Toxteth sill at 24′6″; the draft fore and aft being approximately 20′6″ and 26′3″ respectively, and the tide levels in the dock and river being now level. It would now be possible to fill the dock to its natural level without imperilling the floating operations.

WEDNESDAY AFTERNOON, JUNE 28TH:

This afternoon, with the vessel moored alongside the quay, an inspection was made of the vessel's forward hatches. In No. 2 lower hold it was possible to see that the cargo on the starboard side was far more severely burnt than that on the port side. This would partly be due to the water building up on the port side as the vessel listed, but it would also show that the seat of the fire would probably be found on the starboard side, especially the after end where there was more general devastation than in the forward wing. There were no signs of the sodium hydrosulphite containers. The deep tanks in No. 3 were still full of water but the water marks in No. 2 and No. 3 orlop deck and 'tween deck showed that a

large amount of water had found its way into these decks rather than the lower holds. The angle on the bulkhead—unmeasured—was approximately 25°–30°. This water would have been a material factor contributing to her list.

RECOMMENDATIONS:

1. Mr. Greenwood asked that the Outward Freight Department should supply them with more details concerning the nature and quantity of hazardous cargo booked for each vessel besides the gross quantity which is all they receive at present. It was said that the necessary steps would be taken at once to cover this important point.

2. Mr. Davies suggested that Chemical Fire Extinguishers might be made use of to a greater extent in fighting fires by the shore brigade.

3. It was stated that the arrangements that were made were adequate and that everyone worked in close co-operation with one another.

POINTS THAT OCCUR TO ME:

1. It should be considered whether it is desirable that a vessel's tunnel should be accidentally flooded at a time of emergency due to other vital matters exercising the mind of the responsible officer so that the valve on No. 6 hatch of the scupper pipe to the tunnel was now closed. Would it be possible to construct a proper hold well, or hat-box suction in No. 6 hatch that would be controlled on its own bilge line and would therefore, avert the flooding? Is the valve kept open or shut at sea?

2. The sodium hydrosulphite must remain a fairly strong suspect of the cause of the fire. As this type of chemical is frequently shipped to Matadi, it is liable to receive bottom stowage, and the drums might, therefore, be crushed. This would assist any sweat or moisture to interact on the contents causing another fire. Consideration might be given to stowing this type of cargo in some forecastle deck cabin where any conflagration would be localised. If the shipments are too large to be stowed, should these drums receive 'tween deck stowage where, in the event of fire, they would be easily accessible? In this event good dunnaging would be an essential.

3. When repairs are being effected to the ship that materially imperil her safety whilst in port, the fact should be noted daily in the mate's log so that they will be continually brought to the attention of the responsible officer on board.

295 FREETOWN (I)

O.N. 149667   1943–1958

Steel twin screw motorship
428.0′×56.1′×28.9′   3622 n   5853 g   8944 d
Built by Cammell Laird & Co Ltd, Birkenhead, Yard No 928, as **GREYSTOKE CASTLE**, for Lancashire Shipping Co Ltd (J. Chambers & Co, Managers). Registered Liverpool.
$2 \times$ Werkspoor oil engines 4 SCSA 6 cyl $28\frac{3}{4}''$–$59\frac{1}{16}''$ by North Eastern Marine Engineering Co Ltd, Newcastle. 4000 bhp, $13\frac{1}{2}$ K.

Passenger accommodation: 12.

1927   8 December, launched by Mrs A. Chambers.

1928   Completed.

1938   26 November, aground on Verde Island, Philippines. Damage considerable, temporary repairs at Olangapo, Subic Bay, completed at Hong Kong.

1940   17 February, in collision with and sank CHELDALE (4218 g/built 1925), 24 miles off Durban. Sixteen lives lost. Admiralty Court held **GREYSTOKE CASTLE** was three-quarters to blame.

1943   24 September, acquired by Elder Dempster Lines Ltd. Passenger accommodation removed.

1946   Renamed **FREETOWN**.

1948   31 January (Captain E. Moore) grounded at Northfleet Hope Flats in the Thames and re-floated without damage. 1 February, 0515 hours when proceeding up the Thames came into collision with two ships in Erith Reach, CORCREST and YEWCREST. The former was badly damaged and two lives lost.

1956   Laid up for engine repairs in Harrington Dock, Liverpool, 17 October to 7 December. New bed plate fitted.

1958   19 August, sold for £42,500 to Eissen und Metall, K. G. Lehr, Hamburg, for demolition, arriving 22 August.

Freetown is the capital and main seaport of Sierra Leone.

An Incident of the Royal Visit

Her Majesty thanks the Krooboys of M.V. Freetown

THE M.V. *Freetown* was one of the five Elder Dempster vessels tied up alongside Apapa Wharf on the day Her Majesty the Queen officially opened the Apapa Wharf Extension.

On the day before the official opening Captain W. L. Kay, Master of M.V. *Freetown*, was approached by the Headman of the Krooboys aboard. 'The Headman informed me,' writes Captain Kay, 'that he had heard that the "boys" would not be allowed to shout "Welcome" when the Queen passed the ship. I told him that they could "Shout their heads off."'

'Shortly afterwards Mr J. O. Jones, the Chief Officer, mentioned that the "boys" would like a notice on the ship expressing their loyalty and suggested a canvas strip along the fore deck rail. I agreed to this and the job was handed over to the Cadets who, despite the advice of all and sundry, made an excellent job of it.

The sign read "Welcome Your Majesty from Loyal Sierra Leone Subjects". The next morning it was whipped to the rail and the Krooboys lined up behind it.

'H.R.H. The Duke of Edinburgh noticed it and pointed it out to the Queen. The "boys" were highly delighted when the Queen turned around in her car and gave them a special wave and smile.

'Just before the Queen's arrival, I was handed the Loyal Address and requested to send it to the Queen. I was able to get it to Government House through the good offices of Mr and Mrs Whittaker of John Holts who were my guests that day.'

The author of the Loyal Address, Thomas S. M. Weah, was naturally delighted when Captain Kay was able to show him a letter from Major Edward Ford, Assistant Private Secretary to the Queen, conveying Her Majesty's thanks to the Sierra Leone members of his crew.

The Krooboys' message on the rail of the *Freetown*. Photographed by H. A. Ross, Second Officer

FREETOWN

1967 7 March, sold to Guan Guan Shipping (Pte) Ltd, Singapore, for £115,000. Renamed **GOLDEN LION**. Registered Singapore. 4303 n, 7414 g. 135 passengers.

1971 Sold to Chinese mainland shipbreakers. 9 May, left Singapore Roads en route Shanghai, arriving 18 May for demolition by China National Machinery Import and Export Co.

Tarkwa (Tarquah) is a town in Ghana.

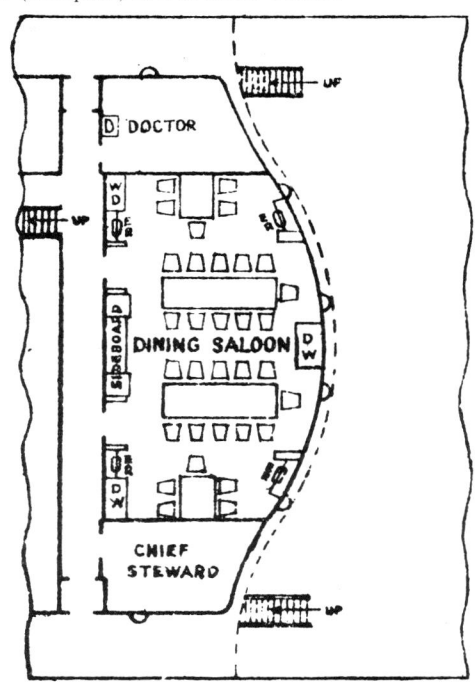

296 TARKWA

O.N. 168877   1944–1967

Steel screw motorship

458.9′×59.3′×26.1′   4272 n   7416 g   7620 d

Built by Caledon Shipbuilding & Engineering Co Ltd, Dundee, Yard No 399, for Elder Dempster Lines Ltd. Registered Liverpool. B & W oil engine 4 SCSA 8 cyl $29\frac{1}{8}''$–$59\frac{1}{16}''$ by J. G. Kincaid & Co Ltd, Greenock. 4400 bhp, $13\frac{1}{2}$ K.

Passenger accommodation: 40 in four-berth cabins.

1944 April, completed. Maiden voyage (Captain W. Baxter-Jones).

1957 Former DEMS accommodation converted to 8 four-berth third class cabins.

M.V. "TARKWA"

PLAN OF
PASSENGER ACCOMMODATION

PROMENADE DECK

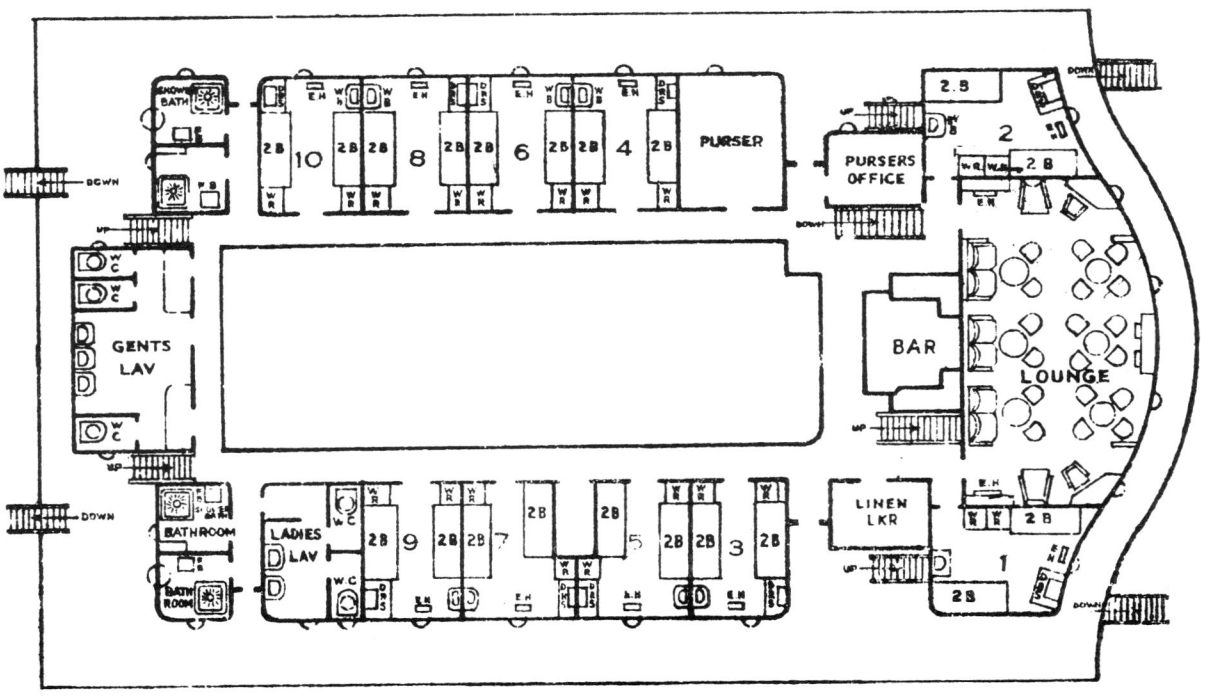

TARKWA (left) and TAMELE (right, above) were the first ships built to restore the Elder Dempster passenger services after the War. Note the difference in layout between TAMELE (below) and TARKWA (previous page)

M.V. "TAMELE"

PLAN OF
PASSENGER ACCOMMODATION

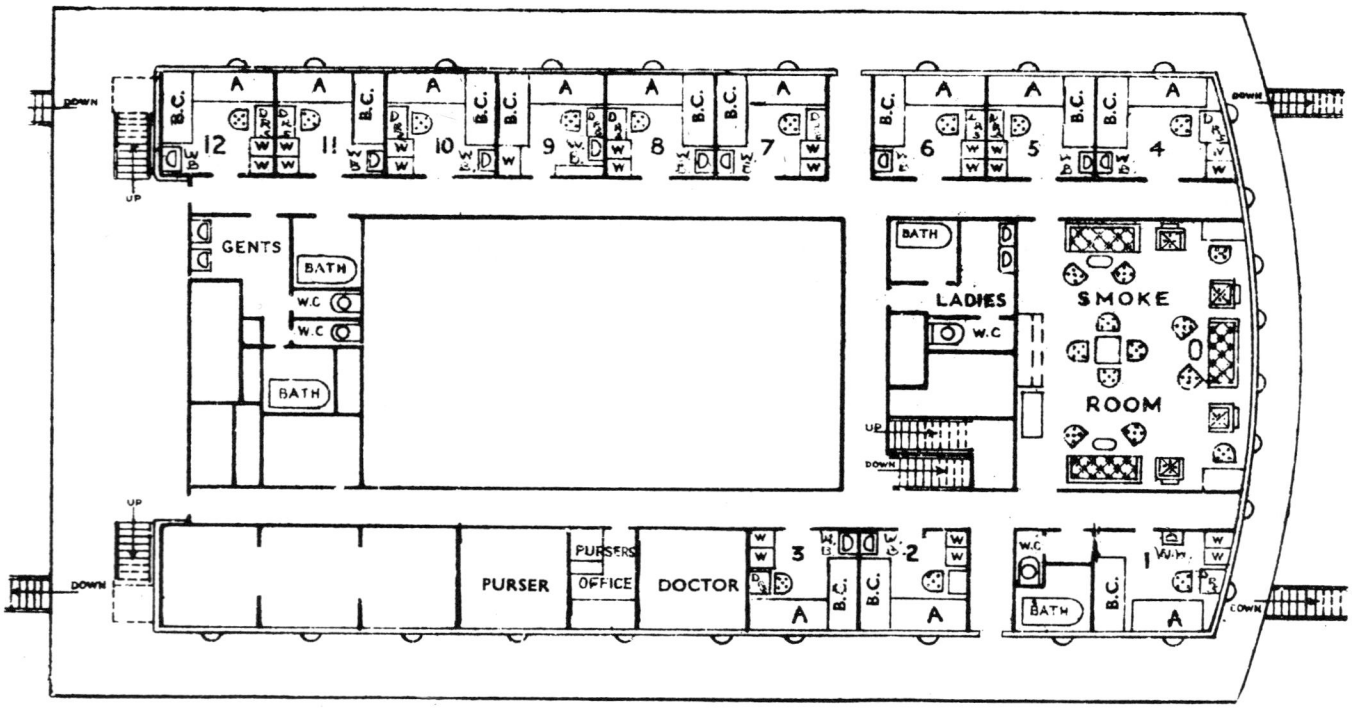

297 TAMELE (II)
O.N. 168889   1945–1967

Steel twin screw motorship
452.5′×58.7′×26.1′ 4140 n 7172 g 8170 d
Built by Cammell Laird & Co Ltd, Birkenhead, Yard No 1151, for Elder Dempster Lines Ltd. Registered Liverpool. 2× Oil engines, opposed pistons, 2 SCSA 3 cyl 23⅝″–91⁵⁄₁₆ by Wm Doxford & Sons Ltd, Sunderland. 5950 bhp, 14½ K.
Passenger accommodation: 36 in three-berth cabins.
1944 3 August, launched by Mrs Marion Smye.

1945 January, completed. Maiden voyage (Captain G. D. Simpson, OBE). 6 May, voyage 2, Glasgow to Far East and military service as troopship.
1946 Ballast and troop fittings removed, loaded gunny bags for West Africa and later employed on Liverpool to Port Harcourt service.
1967 22 March, sold to Guan Guan Shipping Ltd, Singapore. Renamed **GOLDEN CITY**. Registered Singapore. 4127 n, 7173 g, 8110 d.
1973 6 April, arrived Hong Kong after sale to Leung Yau Shipbreaking Co Ltd. May, demolition commenced.

CABANO

CAMBRAY

298 CABANO
O.N. 174802   1946–1960

'Cabano' class
Steel screw steamer, War 'Park' type
441.5′×57.2′×26.9′   4244 n   7157 g   10,109 d
Built by Burrard Drydock Co Ltd, North Vancouver, British Columbia, Yard No 184, as **STRATHCONA PARK** for Canadian Government (Parks Steam Ship Co Ltd, Managers). Registered Montreal (British flag). T 3 cyl 24½″, 37″, 70″–48″ by John Inglis Co Ltd, Toronto, Ontario. 2500 ihp, 11 K.
1943   September, completed.
1946   Acquired by Elder Dempster Lines (Canada) Ltd. Renamed **CABANO**.
1950   10 June, transferred to Elder Dempster Lines Ltd, Liverpool. Registered Liverpool. 4319 n, 7157 g.
1951   Accommodation re-designed.
1959   4307 n, 6708 g.
1960   15 February, sold to Sure Shipping Co Ltd, Hong Kong. Renamed **HAPPY VOYAGER**. Registered Hong Kong (British flag).
1965   Sold to Ideal Shipping Co Ltd (World Wide (Shipping) Ltd, Managers), Hong Kong. Renamed **HITAKA**. Registered Hong Kong.
1966   14 September, reported leakages and hull fractures during voyage from Chalna to Cheba—on arrival was found not to be worthy of repair. 17 October, arrived Hirao for demolition by Matsukara Kaiji KK.

Ships of the 'Cabano' class: CABANO (298), CAMBRAY (299), CARGILL (300), CHANDLER (301), COTTRELL (302).
These vessels were purchased for C$2,825,000 in an 'en bloc' agreement from HM Canadian Government.

299 CAMBRAY
O.N. 175593   1946–1960

'Cabano' class
Steel screw steamer, War 'Park' type
441.6′×57.2′×26.9′   4299 n   7165 g   10,310 d
Launched as **FORT GREEN LAKE** by North Vancouver Ship Repairs Ltd (Pacific Dry Dock Co Ltd, Vancouver), British Columbia, Yard No 145, for Canadian Government (Parks Steamship Co Ltd, Managers), completed as **BRIDGELAND PARK**. Registered Montreal (British flag). T 3 cyl 24½″, 37″, 70″–48″ by Dominion Engineering Works Ltd, Montreal. 2500 ihp, 11 K.
1944   14 September, delivered.
1946   Acquired by Elder Dempster Lines (Canada) Ltd. Renamed **CAMBRAY**. Registered Montreal (British flag).
1950   July, transferred to Elder Dempster Lines Ltd, Liverpool. Registered Liverpool.

1951   Accommodation redesigned.
1956   October, 4338 n, 7209 g.
1960   23 August, sold to Cia de Navegacion 'Somerset', SA, Lugano, Switzerland. Renamed **SIMETO**. Registered Panama. 4204 n, 6947 g, 10,700 d.
1971   16 May, arrived Bilbao for demolition by Hierros Ardes.
CAMBRAY became the last Elder Dempster vessel to operate on the Canada–Cape service.

CARGILL

300 CARGILL
O.N. 174798   1946–1960

'Cabano' class
Steel screw steamer, War 'Park' type
441.6′×57.2′×26.9′   4240 n   7152 g   10,190 d
Built by Burrand Drydock Co Ltd, South Yard (Vancouver Dry Dock Co), Vancouver, British Columbia, Yard No 183, for Canadian Government (Parks Steam Ship Co Ltd, Managers) as **WASCANA PARK**. Registered Montreal (British flag). T 3 cyl 24½″, 37″, 70″–48″ by John Inglis Co Ltd, Toronto. 2500 ihp, 11 K.
1943   28 August, completed.
1945   April, new starboard boiler fitted.
1946   Acquired by Elder Dempster Lines (Canada) Ltd. Renamed **CARGILL**. Registered Montreal (British flag).
1950   June, transferred to Elder Dempster Lines Ltd, Liverpool. Registered Liverpool. 4313 n, 7152 g.
1951   Accommodation redesigned.
1959   4334 n, 7216 g.
1960   19 October, sold to Interocean Shipping Co Ltd, Hong Kong. Renamed **MARINE NAVIGATOR**. Registered Hong Kong (British flag).

1962 Sold to Prestige Shipping Co Ltd, Hong Kong. Renamed **MARINE ACE**.
1966 6 December, arrived Hirao for demolition by Matsukara Kaiji KK.

Cargill owned the largest grain elevator company in Canada. As part of World War II war effort Cargill Company built an inland shipyard on the Minesota River where ships were launched sideways and then towed down river for fitting out.

301 CHANDLER
O.N. 175384   1944–1960

'Cabano' class
Steel screw steamer, War 'Park' type
441.6′×57.2′×26.9′   4221 n   7161 g   10,246 d
Built by North Vancouver Ship Repairs Ltd, North Vancouver, British Columbia, Yard No 140, for Canadian Government (Parks Steam Ship Co Ltd, Managers) as **CRYSTAL PARK**. Registered Montreal (British flag). T 3 cyl 24½″, 37″, 70″–48″ by John Inglis Co Ltd, Toronto. 2500 ihp, 11 K.
1944 2 May, delivered.
1946 Acquired by Elder Dempster Lines (Canada) Ltd. Renamed **CHANDLER**. Registered Montreal (British flag).
1950 6 June, transferred to Elder Dempster Lines Ltd, Liverpool. Registered Liverpool.
1951 Accommodation redesigned.
1956 Chartered by HM Government for service during the Suez operations.
1959 4339 n, 7212 g.
1960 22 April, sold to Cia de Nav 'Indomitus' SA, Panama. Renamed **NATALE**. Registered Panama. 4223 n, 6940 g.
1969 9 August, sold for demolition at Spezia, by Spa Cant. Navali Santa Maria.

Chandler is a port between the Pabos river and Newport, Gaspé Peninsula, Nova Scotia.

CHANDLER

302 COTTRELL
O.N. 175609   1944–1961

'Cabano' class
Steel screw steamer, War 'Park' type
441.6′×57.2′×26.9′   4218 n   7163 g   10,310 d
Built by North Vancouver Ship Repairs Ltd, North Vancouver. British Columbia, Yard No 147, for Canadian Government (Parks Steam Ship Co Ltd, Managers), as **FORT HARRISON**. Delivered as **GOLDSTREAM PARK**. Registered Montreal (British flag). T 3 cyl 24½″, 37″, 70″–48″ by Canadian Allis-Chalmers Ltd, Montreal. 2500 ihp, 11 K.
1944 7 November, delivered.

1946 Acquired by Elder Dempster Lines (Canada) Ltd. Renamed **COTTRELL**. Registered Montreal (British flag).
1950 August, transferred to Elder Dempster Lines Ltd, Liverpool. Registered Liverpool.
1951 Accommodation redesigned.
1959 4335 n, 7217 g.
1961 14 February, sold for £85,000 to Cia de Navegacion 'Somerset', SA, London. Renamed **SANTAGATA**. Registered Panama. 4198 n, 6930 g, 10,869 d.
1971 27 January, arrived Blyth for demolition by Hughes Bolckow Ltd.

COTTRELL

303 KNOWLTON
O.N. 150709   1946–1951

Steel screw Canadian Great Lakes steamer
251.2′×43.0′×16.6′   1219 n   2068 g
Built by Fraser Brace Ltd, Three Rivers, Province of Quebec, for Geo. Hall Coal & Shipping Corporation, Montreal, as **N. H. BOTSFORD**. Registered Montreal (British flag). T 3 cyl 19″, 32″, 56″ by Worthington Pump & Machinery Corporation, Buffalo, NY. 188 nhp, 8 K.
1922 August, completed.
1926 Sold to Canada Steamships Ltd, Montreal. Renamed **KNOWLTON**.
1946 24 October, acquired by Elder Dempster Lines Ltd for £5000 for the West African coastal services. Registered London.
1951 February, towed to United Kingdom—July, sold for demolition at Milford Haven by T. W. Ward Ltd.

Knowlton is a small town in Cowansville, Quebec.

N. H. BOTSFORD, *subsequently* **KNOWLTON**, *in drydock at Montreal (left)* (Photo R. C. Griffin)

SOKOTO II, *formerly **ANCOBRA*** (ship No. 144), *from an original painting by an unknown artist*

APPAM (ship No. 214), from a painting by Odin Rosenvinge

An impression of **ACCRA** *(ship No. 267) by Odin Rosenvinge*

FIRST-CLASS SMOKING LOUNGE. T.M.S. "ACCRA."

A LOFTY central dome, with large cut glass bowl electric light filling the centre, surmounts the Smoking Lounge in the "ACCRA," which is designed in the style of William and Mary. The walls are coloured in warm old gold with panels of gold and ivory. The furniture is in black and gold and vermilion lacquer with silk damask cushions to match.

ACCRA & APAPA

Extract from a brochure of the 1920s

FIRST-CLASS SMOKING LOUNGE. T.M.S. "APAPA."

THE Smoking Lounge in the "APAPA" is decorated in shades of cream and ivory. The overmantel contains a fine copy of an old painting of the French school as a centrepiece.

ACCRA & APAPA

Extract from a brochure of the 1920s

EBOE V (ship No. 325) *and* ***EKET*** (ship No. 523) *at Calabar, from a painting by John Stobart*

FREETOWN II (ship No. 371), from a painting by John Stobart

IDOMENEUS *(ship No. 388) in the Bonny River* (Photo M. Wild)

MENESTHEUS *(ship No. 419)* (Photo Fotoflite)

KNOWLTON

Launch of GLENORVIE (above) and (below) towards the end of her career as OXFORD (Photos R. C. Griffin)

304 OXFORD
O.N. 145515   1946–1950

Steel screw Canadian Great Lakes steamer
252.0'×42.5'×17.5   1125 n   1893 g
Built by Swan Hunter & Wigham Richardson Ltd, Sunderland, Yard No 1209, as **GLENORVIE** for Glen Line Ltd (J. Playfair, Manager), Midland, Ontario. Registered Montreal (British flag). T 3 cyl 16", 27" 44"–33" by McColl Pollock Ltd, Sunderland. 111 nhp, 8 K.
1923   May, completed.
1926   Sold to Canada Steamships Ltd, Montreal. Renamed **OXFORD**.
1946   24 October, acquired by Elder Dempster Lines Ltd for £5000 for the West African coastal services. Registered London.
1950   19 November, scuttled 20 miles south-south-east of Lagos.
Oxford is named after the county of Oxford, Ontario.

305 SAPELE (III)
O.N. 165022   1946–1962

'Sapele' class
Steel screw steamer, War 'B' Coaster type
224.5'×36.7'×14.0'   370 n   974 g   1219 d
Built by Blyth Dry Dock & Shipbuilding Co Ltd, Blyth, Yard No 312, as **EMPIRE PAVILION** for Ministry of War Transport. Registered Blyth. T 3 cyl 13½", 22¾", 38"–27" by Geo. C. Clark (1938) Ltd, Sunderland. 900 ihp, 12 K.
Passenger accommodation: one double-berth cabin.
1945   November, completed.
1946   Acquired by Elder Dempster Lines Ltd for £80,000. Renamed **SAPELE**.
1962   7 June, sold for £33,000 to Ocean Industries Ltd, Karachi. Renamed **MAHIA**. Registered Karachi. Converted into a shrimp factory. 590 n, 1359 g.
1970   Sold to Pan-Islamic Steamship Co Ltd, Karachi. Renamed **SAFINA-E-AHMAR**. Registered Karachi. Converted into dry cargo ship. 332 n, 906 g, 1037 d.
1973   Sold to Pakistani shipbreakers. 22 March, arrived Karachi for demolition by Heudnare Manufacturing Corp Ltd.
Ships of the 'Sapele' class: SAPELE (305), FORCADOS (306), WARRI (307).

FORCADOS

306 FORCADOS (III)
O.N. 169148   1946–1962

'Sapele' class
Steel screw steamer, War 'B' Coaster type
224.5'×36.7'×14.0'   371 n   974 g   1219 d
Built by Smiths Dock Co Ltd, Middlesbrough Yard No 1135, as **EMPIRE PATTERN** for Ministry of War Transport (Euxine Shipping Co Ltd, Managers). Registered Middlesbrough. T 3 cyl 13½", 22¾", 38"–27" by the builders. 900 ihp, 12 K.
Passenger accommodation: one double-berth cabin.
1945   July, completed.

FORCADOS at Oil Wharf, Lagos

1946   December, acquired by Elder Dempster Lines Ltd for £83,300. Renamed **FORCADOS**.
1962   7 September, sold to S. Leriotis & I. Anghelatos of Greece. Renamed **BARBALIAS**. Registered Piraeus.
1965   Sold to G. Tzortzis & C. Sykias, Piraeus. Renamed **AGIA VARVARA**. 632 n, 1253 g.
1966   8 August, foundered off Cyprus during heavy weather, voyage Ashdod to Biscay. No loss of life.

FORCADOS loading oil at Lagos

FORCADOS at Lagos

307   WARRI (II)
O.N. 169149   **1946–1956**

'Sapele' class
Steel screw steamer, War 'B' Coaster type
224.5′×36.7′×14.0′   380 n   974 g   1219 d
Built by Smiths Dock Co Ltd, Middlesbrough, Yard No 1154, as **EMPIRE PAMPAS** for Ministry of War Transport. Registered Middlesbrough. T 3 cyl 13½″, 22¾″, 38″–27″ by the builders. 900 ihp, 12 K.
Passenger accommodation: one double-berth cabin.
1945   November, completed.
1946   Acquired by Elder Dempster Lines Ltd. Renamed **WARRI**.
1956   12 June, stranded near Iwerekun, 20 miles east of Lagos, and became a constructive total loss (Captain A. A. Thomas), voyage Sapele to Lagos, cargo kernels.

WARRI

The *Warri* on the steep sandy coast twenty miles East of Lagos. A photograph taken at 2.30 on the afternoon of June 13 at low tide about thirty-four hours after the *Warri* was stranded

The Loss of the S.S. Warri

AT 0520 hours on the morning of June 12, the *Warri* stranded on the steep sandy coast twenty miles east of Lagos. In the opinion of the Master, Captain A. A. Thomas, his little ship was a 'total loss' within minutes of stranding, and events subsequently confirmed this view. The *Warri* was bound from Sapele to Lagos with a full cargo of Palm Kernels. She left Sapele at 0922 hours on June 11, crossed Escravos Bar that evening, rounded the Fairway Buoy at 1930, and set a course for Lagos. At 2040 hours a departure bearing was taken of Escravos Light dipping below the horizon. This was the last anyone on the *Warri* saw of the shore until an appreciable time *after* she had stranded and become a total loss.

The moon, of which an azimuth bearing was taken after passing Escravos Fairway Buoy during a break in the clouds when the course was set for Lagos, was in its first quarter, and set at 21.15 hours. Thereafter the night was pitch dark, the sky overcast, and there were frequent rain squalls, and almost continuous light rain between. The sea was calm, however, and there was little swell. The Second Officer, who was on watch when the ship stranded, said afterwards that the darkness was so intense, especially from ahead and to starboard, that he was unable to distinguish the horizon even with night glasses. Captain Thomas was called suddenly by the Second Officer a few moments before his ship struck the beach. The Second Officer had 'sighted breakers close to starboard'. Captain Thomas rushed to the bridge but the vessel grounded and lurched heavily before he reached it.

'On coming on deck I found conditions of "extreme darkness" with light rain still falling and visibility almost nil. As it proved we were some sixty yards from the beach but it was impossible to see any signs of land or bush and it was only with the aid of "Aldis Lamp" that I realized that we were so very close inshore. I have no clear recollection of the time the rain ceased, but when daylight came in, the visibility was about normal except in an East and West direction where it was impaired due to high surf spume along the line of beach.'

From the instant of stranding the *Warri* was continuously pounded by heavy surf and swept by heavy breaking seas. She had a list of 10 degrees to port, seaward. Captain Thomas' report goes on:

She was bound from Sapele to Lagos with a full cargo of palm kernels. A photograph, taken about one hour before low tide on June 14, showing the pounding by the surf . . .

. . . and the 'heavy breaking seas.'

The heavy breakers had distorted the hull

The buckling of the hull is shown in these two photographs, taken at low tide on the day after she was stranded

'Second Officer Harrison had Ported helm prior to calling me but engines were still on Full Ahead, and there was no further movement in Ship's head which remained at approximately 250 degrees T. I stopped engines and hove the lead to ascertain depth of water; engines were then put to Full Astern at 0526 hours but with no response. At 0538 hours engines were stopped and the crew ordered to emergency stations. The vessel by this time was heeling over to Port approximately 10 degrees and was subjected to heavy pounding by surf along Port side. Orders were then given to prepare No. 1 Lifeboat for lowering and at 0605 hours Mr Fairbairn, Chief Engineer, informed me that the Shell plating in Port Boiler-room Store had opened up and that water was gaining rapidly in Stokehold and Engine-room despite the efforts of two Pumps.

'After examination of shell plating with the Chief Engineer I gave him orders to draw fires and ease the Boilers down and to abandon the Engine-room as I feared an explosion. At this juncture there was 5 feet of water in Stokehold, No. 2 Hold sounding 2 feet 9 inches and No. 1 Hold still dry. List was increasing perceptibly and at 0630 hours I ordered No. 1 Lifeboat away in charge of Second Officer Harrison with 20 Africans; this boat capsized in the heavy surf but all hands were able to swim ashore. As the list was increasing rapidly no attempt was made to launch No. 3 Lifeboat, but contact with the beach was established by "Schermuly Rocket Line" and the remainder of the African crew were landed by means of an improvised "Breeches Buoy" and all accounted for.

'At 0830 hours Chief Engineer and Chief Officer reported that water was gaining rapidly in Holds and Engine-room, bulwarks along Port side were flattened and vessel taking a severe pounding.'

Captain Thomas' report outlines in terse simple language yet another tragic drama of the sea. Fortunately, very fortunately, no lives were lost and there was no serious injury, but a fine little ship was lost, and the loss of a ship is very akin, as seamen know well, to the loss of something human, intimate and vital. By now the Masters, Officers of our Fleet and all those whose responsibilities are concerned with the safety and well-being of our ships, their crews, passengers and cargoes, have been made aware of the causes of this sad disaster. I use the plural in 'causes' because long experience has shown that it is rare in marine casualties for a single cause to be sole reason for the loss of or serious damage to a ship. We have taken pride in our principles and practices of sound and safe navigation. We have striven to learn, and to train future generations of navigators, our Midshipmen and young Officers to learn, that the sea is a jealous mistress, never to be taken lightly or for granted, always demanding the utmost care, constant alertness and scrupulous skill, if she is to be served well, rightly and in safety. 'The Price of Admiralty is Eternal Vigilance.'

From the Company's point of view, and the men who sail our ships, in the difficult and challenging seas off the coasts of Africa, the United Kingdom, the Continent and North America, and the great expanses of the Atlantic Ocean, there is one good that can arise from the loss of the *Warri*—a renewed determination to learn well the lessons of the loss, and to ensure that henceforward, so far as human skill, courage and strong endeavour, linked with the fund of knowledge and experience gained for us by our predecessors, never again will we suffer a marine casualty like the *Warri*.

From a different point of view, the loss of our little ship brought not a lesson but an inspired illustration of warm humanity, kindliness and generous help to those in distress and danger. The *Warri* was lost on the coast of Nigeria, twenty miles east of Lagos, virtually on the doorstep of the village of Iwerekun. She was cast on the beach in the dark hours before dawn. As soon as the awakened villagers were aware of the disaster, they hastened, the whole community, to render assistance. Although Iwerekun is only twenty odd miles from Lagos, it is almost inaccessible by any ordinary means from the capital city or other urban centre. The only accepted means of communication is by a trek of five or six miles inland through dense bush, crossing swamps and creeks, waist deep to the walking traveller —and there is no other way—to a village on Omu creek from which a canoe can be taken to wind its way through inland channels and lagoons to Lagos. This journey, seldom attempted by the villagers except in cases of urgent need, is the only way goods and supplies can reach them, head porterage for all the land journey, and the trip invariably takes two or three days. The only possible alternative, and this was the way taken by the villagers to help two of the African crew of the *Warri*, and later that night the Second Officer and Third Engineer, to bring the news of the disaster to Lagos, was to walk along the soft sandy beach; over twenty miles of difficult slow footslogging, with the surf breaking a few yards away to seaward and dense bush, swamp, mangroves and palms a few yards to landward. The news reached our office in Lagos via Wilmot Point, late in the afternoon of June 12. Immediately arrangements were made for the N.P.A. tug, the Senior Pilot and two of our Masters to proceed the following day, to see if there was any prospect of salvaging the *Warri*. Mr Neville, Branch Vessels' Superintendent, after hours of inquiring and questioning, ascertained that it might be just possible for a Land Rover to make the journey to Iwerekun along the shore from Victoria Beach. Through the generous help of B.E.W.A.C, Agents for Land Rovers in Nigeria, a vehicle was promised for the following day with Mr

The Land Rover making tricky progress towards the *Warri*

'Even the four wheel drive Land Rover could make no progress in the soft sand above high water mark.'

Some of the snags encountered on the way

Higgins, Chief Mechanic to B.E.W.A.C. in charge and an African co-driver, to take Mr Neville, and emergency supplies, to the *Warri* and her crew.

This journey to Iwerekun, and the two further trips on successive days, proved highly adventurous and not a little hazardous. When the Land Rover reached Victoria Beach it was found that the journey would have to be made on wet sand, as even the four wheel drive Land Rover could make no progress in the soft sand above high water mark. This and other factors compelled the trips to be timed in relation to the tide, roughly between half ebb and half flood. At many places along the beach tree trunks and thick branches extended to below the water's edge; in some instances it was possible with axes and saws to hack a way through these snags, but in many other places it was necessary to wait until the surf momentarily receded and then to make a dash for

'Going to sea in a Land Rover!' The wheel tracks tell their own story

it round the seaward side of these obstructions and turn swiftly back on to the higher sand before—it was hoped—the surf broke again! It was in fact 'going to sea in a Land Rover'! Mr Neville, the writer, and others who made these trips came back with the firm conviction that nothing was impossible to a Land Rover in work of this kind. On innumerable occasions the vehicle was virtually under water, caught in the breaking of heavy surf spray, but it always got through, though the plugs had to be dried out frequently.

As a result of these three visits to the *Warri*, during which Lloyd's Surveyor, Captain Simpson of the *Accra*, the Salvage Association's Surveyor, the Government Marine Officer, Lloyd's Agent, the writer, as well as Mr Neville, visited the *Warri* on one or more occasions, coupled with the reports received earlier from the Senior N.P.A. Pilot, Captain Gwilym Jones and two of our Masters who went to the wreck of the *Warri* in the Marine tug, it was finally confirmed that any salvage attempt of the *Warri* was impracticable. Almost within a few hours of her stranding the sand started to build up, both inside and outside of the little ship, and four days after she was ashore she was embedded in sand to a depth of about 14 feet on the seaward side. In addition, the heavy pounding of the breakers had made her common with the sea throughout her entire

length, the hull itself was badly distorted and fractured, and the superstructure broken away along the whole length of the port side. The question then arose of the possibility of salvaging the more valuable and readily portable equipment, and transporting this, the Captain and five other European Officers, and their gear (including a parrot!) back to Lagos. This was finally accomplished through the courtesy and help of the Nigerian Military Authorities who made available two Army jeeps and three four wheel drive Army trucks, and full service personnel for the operation.

The difficulties of the beach transit were already known and much had been done on the previous three trips in the Land Rover to improve the journey by the removal of snags and trees. Despite this, and the very fine efforts of the military personnel, only the two jeeps and one three ton truck eventually succeeded in reaching the *Warri* on the first occasion, the outward journey to Iwerekun taking three hours. As the result of the experience gained then, the remaining several journeys necessary to complete the evacuation of personnel and salvaged equipment was undertaken by one of the Army jeeps. The proven hazards of getting a big three ton truck through did not warrant their further use.

The villagers at Iwerekun proved kindly, effective and hospitable hosts to the ship's company. Mr Bankole, the schoolmaster, was the only African who spoke English fluently and he and the village heads combined to do everything humanly within their power to alleviate the inevitable hardships which the crew were encountering. The village school house was put at the disposal of the crew and every service it was practicable for the villagers to render, both to the crew itself and in assisting in the salvaging of equipment from the *Warri*, was given promptly and willingly. The villagers built a hut right alongside the *Warri* and maintained watches with the ship's personnel for many days. The gratitude of the Captain and crew has already been expressed to the villagers, and the ship's bell and clock were presented by Captain Thomas in remembrance.

The sandspit made by the *Warri* is clearly shown. By the time this photograph was taken, the *Warri* was embedded into the sand to a depth of about fourteen feet on the seaward side

'As soon as the awakened villagers were aware of the disaster they hastened . . . to help.'

Elder Dempster Lines are making a presentation to the village through the local authority concerned, with the expressed wish that as the school room, and Mr Bankole the schoolmaster, did so much in succouring the ship's company, the money should be expended in the interests of the school.

This brief account would be incomplete if it did not record the fine behaviour of the ship's company when the stranding occurred. Captain Thomas and Mr Fairbairn, Chief Engineer, both report that the African crew under their European Officers carried out every order and stood by their posts as required, often at serious personal hazard, until the *Warri* was abandoned on the Captain's orders. Thereafter too, all hands willingly carried out every order given. This, of course, is in accord with the finest traditions of the sea, and seamen, and it is what we expect at all times. Nevertheless, it is good to put on record that there were no failures this time, that everything human endeavour could accomplish was done, and no doubt as a result, the loss of the *Warri* brought with it no tragedy in the way of human loss or injury.

We should like to record our gratitude to those others outside the Company who helped us in many ways, and who sent us their genuine messages of sympathy in the loss of our ship. Not least amongst these were the Government Officers of the Ministry of Transport, the Officers of the N.P.A., Lloyd's Surveyor in Lagos, the firm of B.E.W.A.C., and the Army Authorities and personnel, both European and African.

M.B.G.

Mr Bankole, the schoolmaster of Iwerekun, is seen in the centre. On the right is the guide who walked with the first party along the beach from Iwerekun to Lagos on June 12

From Sea *magazine*

ZINI

308 ZINI

O.N. 169674   1944–1947, 1947–1959

'Z' class
Steel screw steamer, War 'Liberty' type
441.7′×57.0′×27.8′   4380 n   7291 g   10,642 d
Built by Bethlehem Fairfield Shipyard Inc, Baltimore, Maryland, Yard No 2218, as **TENCH TILGHMAN** for the United States Maritime Commission. On completion, bare boat chartered to Ministry of War Transport (Elder Dempster Lines Ltd, Managers). Renamed **SAMOS**. Registered London. T 3 cyl 24½″, 37″, 70″–48″ by General Machinery Corporation, Hamilton. 2500 ihp, 10 K.

1943   September, completed.
1947   22 April, acquired by Elder Dempster Lines Ltd for £135,261. Renamed **ZINI**. Registered Liverpool. 4447 n, 7256 g.
1959   15 September, sold to Dorset Shipping Co, Liberia, for £74,000. Renamed **SAN SALVADOR**. Registered Monrovia. 4409 n, 7221 g.
1968   October 26, arrived at Spezia for demolition by Cantieri di Portovenere SpA.

Ships of the 'Z' class: ZINI (308), ZUNGERU (309), ZUNGON (310).

ZUNGERU

309 ZUNGERU (II)

O.N. 169654   1944–1947, 1947–1958

'Z' class
Steel screw steamer, War 'Liberty' type
441.7′×57.0′×27.8′   4380 n   7219 g   10,642 d
Built by Bethlehem Fairfield Shipyard Inc, Baltimore,

Maryland, Yard No 2248, as **ADOLPH LEWISOHN** for United States Maritime Commission. On completion bare boat chartered to Ministry of War Transport (Elder Dempster Lines Ltd, Managers). Renamed **SAMOTA**. Registered London. T 3 cyl 24½″, 37″, 70″–48″ by General Machinery Corporation, Hamilton. 2500 ihp, 10 K.

1943 October, completed.
1947 Acquired by Elder Dempster Lines Ltd. Renamed **ZUNGERU**. Registered Liverpool. 4236 n, 7255 g.
1958 24 November, sold for £115,000 to Casa Blanca Shipping Corporation of Liberia. Renamed **POROS**. Registered Monrovia. 4444 n, 7257 g.
1966 Sold to Marestela Cia, Nav SA, Greece. Renamed **MERY**. Registered Piraeus.
1968 Sold to Toula Shipping Co Ltd, Limassol. Registered Famagusta. 4322 n, 7214 g.
1971 14 September, arrived Aviles for demolition by Jose Heres.

SHERBRO

ZUNGON

310 ZUNGON
O.N. 169764   1947–1958

'Z' Class
Steel screw steamer, War 'Liberty' type
441.8′×57.0′×27.8′   4444 n   7267 g   10,642 d
Built by Bethlehem Fairfield Shipyard Inc, Baltimore, Maryland, Yard No 2288, as **HUGH L. KERWIN** for United States Maritime Commission. On completion, bare boat chartered to Ministry of War Transport (Booth Steamship Co Ltd, Managers). Renamed **SAMYALE**. Registered London. T 3 cyl 24½″, 37″, 70″–48″ by General Machinery Corporation, Hamilton, Ohio. 2500 ihp, 10 K.

1943 December, completed.
1947 Acquired by Elder Dempster Lines Ltd. Renamed **ZUNGON**. Registered Liverpool.
1958 2 October, sold to Sociedad Pacifica Marina SA, Liberia. Renamed **AEGINA**. Registered Monrovia.
1961 Sold to Augusta Shipping Corporation, Liberia. 4462 n, 10,881 d, 7257 g.
1966 Sold to Marancho Cia Nav SA, Greece. Renamed **IRINI**. Registered Piraeus.
1967 10 June, in collision, ten miles north of Cape Spartel, with tanker RUSSELL N. GREEN (31,975 g/built 1965), on voyage Gdynia towards Mediterranean ports, cargo sulphate. Arrived Cadiz seriously damaged. 6 December, arrived Valencia in tow for demolition by Revalorizacion de Materials SA.

311 SHERBRO (II)/MATRU
O.N. 181103   1947–1967

'Sherbro' Class
Steel screw motorship
408.0′×57.2′×22.4′   2636 n   4810 g   6181 d
Built by Furness Shipbuilding Co Ltd, Haverton Hill-on-Tees, Yard No 405, for Elder Dempster Lines Ltd. Registered Liverpool. Doxford oil engine, opposed pistons, 2 SCSA 4 cyl 22$\frac{1}{16}$″–85$\frac{1}{16}$″ by Richardson Westgarth & Co Ltd, Hartlepool. 3100 bhp, 12½ K.
Passenger accommodation: 12.

1947 16 May, launched by Mrs W. L. Robinson. Completed November. Maiden voyage Captain J. N. McNae.
1965 April, transferred to Guinea Gulf Line Ltd. Renamed **MATRU**.
1966 Passenger accommodation withdrawn.
1967 Sold for £100,000 to Agia Eftichia Shipping Co. Renamed **AGIA EFTCHIA**. Registered Famagusta. 2420 n, 4805 g.
1971 Sold to Inchop Shipping Corporation, Somalia. Renamed **MOKA**. Registered Mogadishu. 28 November, arrived Karachi for demolition by United Ship-breaking Industries.

Ships of the 'Sherbro' class: SHERBRO (311), SHONGA (312), SALAGA (313), SEKONDI (314), SULIMA (315), SWEDRU (316). All built at a cost of £450,000 each.

SHONGA

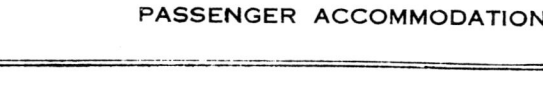

M.V·s.
"SALAGA"
"SEKONDI"
"SHERBRO"
"SHONGA"
"SULIMA"
"SWEDRU"

PLAN OF
PASSENGER ACCOMMODATION

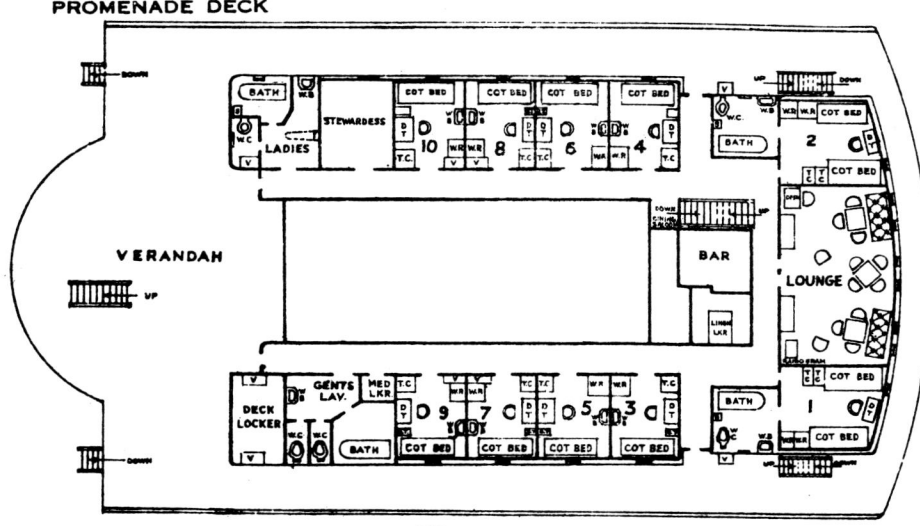

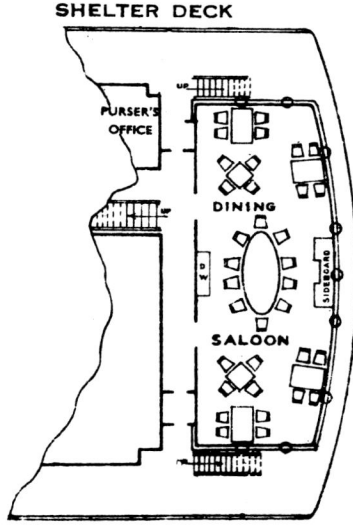

D.W.	Dumb Waiter
T.C.	Tallboy Compactum
D.T.	Dressing Table
W.R.	Wardrobe
B.T.	Bedside Table
W.B.	Wash Basin
S.	Seat

Compare the accommodation layout of the post-war 'S' ships with that of their pre-war counterparts (see page 225)

---

312 SHONGA (II)/MALLAM
O.N. 181110   1947–1967
'Sherbro' class
Steel screw motorship
408.0′×57.2′×22.4′   2656 n   4810 g   6330 d
Built by Scotts' Shipbuilding and Engineering Co Ltd, Greenock, Yard No 642, for Elder Dempster Lines Ltd. Registered Liverpool. Doxford oil engine, opposed pistons, 2 SCSA 4 cyl 22$\frac{1}{16}$″–85$\frac{1}{16}$″ by the builders. 3100 bhp, 12$\frac{1}{2}$ K.
Passenger accommodation: 12.
1947   19 August, launched by Mrs C. T. J. Cripps. November, completed. Maiden voyage, Captain G. D. Simpson, OBE.
1965   April, transferred to Guinea Gulf Line Ltd. Renamed **MALLAM**.
1966   Passenger accommodation withdrawn.
1967   25 November, sold for £100,000 to Pacific International Lines (Pte) Ltd, Singapore. Renamed **KOTA MAJU**. Registered Singapore. 2419 n, 4804 g.
1977   Sold to Pakistani shipbreakers. 14 October, arrived Karachi.
Note—SHONGA was the only one of the post-war 'S' class to have her name painted on the white half-rounds. The other five ships' names were painted on the black hull.

313 SALAGA (II)/MAMFE
O.N. 182393   1947–1968
'Sherbro' class
Steel screw motorship
408.0′×57.2′×22.3′   2634 n   4810 g   6350 d
Built by Hawthorn Leslie & Co Ltd, Newcastle, Yard No 688, for Elder Dempster Lines Ltd. Registered Liverpool. Doxford oil engine, opposed pistons, 2 SCSA 4 cyl 22$\frac{1}{16}$″–85$\frac{1}{16}$″ by the builders. 3100 bhp, 12$\frac{1}{2}$ K.
Passenger accommodation: 12.
1947   18 June, launched by Mrs J. G. Beazley. December, completed. Maiden voyage, Captain A. A. Smith.
1965   March, transferred to Guinea Gulf Line Ltd. Renamed **MAMFE**.
1966   Passenger accommodation withdrawn.
1968   9 February, sold for £115,000 to Singapore Shipping Development Co (Pte) Ltd, Singapore. Renamed **LUCKY TRADER**. Registered Singapore. 2419 n, 4804 g.
1973   12 March, arrived Hsinkiang for demolition by China National Machinery Import/Export Corp. (See also page 455).
Mamfe is a district of Cameroun.

SALAGA

SALAGA *discharging cargo at Accra, 1953*

251

ELDER DEMPSTER LINES 'S' CLASS

SEKONDI

1967   22 September, sold to Peseta Shipping Corp SA, Panama. Renamed **JAVA SEA**. Registered Panama.

1968   July, sold to Fortunewind Maritime Ltd, Hong Kong. Renamed **FORTUNE CARRIER**. Registered Mogadishu. 2413 n, 6201 g. 1 October, foundered in position 22°.02′N 116°.33′E (approximately 120 miles east of Hong Kong) in hurricane 'Elaine', voyage Hong Kong to Hsinkiang. Two crew lost.

Mampong is a town 25 miles north of Kumasi, Ghana.

314 SEKONDI (II)/MAMPONG
O.N. 182402   1948–1967

'Sherbro' class
Steel screw motorship
408.0′×57.2′×22.4′   2634 n   4811 g   6201 d
Built by Furness Ship Building Co Ltd, Haverton Hill on Tees, Yard No 406, for Elder Dempster Lines Ltd. Registered Liverpool. Doxford oil engine, opposed pistons, 2 SCSA 4 cyl $22\frac{1}{16}″$–$85\frac{1}{16}″$ by Richardson, Westgarth & Co Ltd, West Hartlepool. 3100 bhp, $12\frac{1}{2}$ K.
Passenger accommodation: 12.

1947   17 June, launched by Mrs Marion Smye.

1948   February, completed February. Maiden voyage (Captain W. H. Newton).

1965   Transferred to Guinea Gulf Line Ltd. Renamed **MAMPONG**.

1966   Passenger accommodation withdrawn.

315 SULIMA (II)/MANO (I)
O.N. 182432   1948–1967

'Sherbro' class
Steel screw motorship
408.6′×57.2′×22.3′   2636 n   4810 g   6235 d
Built by Scotts' Shipbuilding and Engineering Co Ltd, Greenock, Yard No 643, for Elder Dempster Lines Ltd. Registered Liverpool. Doxford oil engine, opposed pistons, 2 SCSA 4 cyl $22\frac{1}{16}″$–$85\frac{1}{16}″$ by the builders. 3100 bhp, $12\frac{1}{2}$ K.
Passenger accommodation: 12.

1948   27 January, launched by Mrs A. M. Bennett. May, completed. Maiden voyage (Captain J. S. Cowan).

1959   Passenger accommodation used to house African cadets.

1965   February, transferred to Guinea Gulf Line Ltd. Renamed **MANO**.

1966   Passenger accommodation withdrawn.

1967   26 June, sold for £115,000 to Efnaval Cia SA, Greece. Renamed **ANNA F**. Registered Piraeus. 2419 n, 4804 g, 6314 d.

1972   March, arrived Antwerp with severe engine trouble.

1973   September, towed to Gdansk for repair which proved too costly. Later in the year sold for demolition at Bilbao. When under tow broke adrift, stranded to the south of Klaipeda on 4 December in position 54°.58′N 20°.17′E.

SULIMA

SWEDRU

Three of the post-war 'S' ships, **SWEDRU, SHONGA** and *(on right)* **SALAGA**, *with* **FREETOWN** *and* **TAMELE** *in the background*

316 SWEDRU (II)/MARADI
O.N. 182443   1948–1967

'Sherbro' class
Steel screw motorship
408.0′×57.2′×22.4′   2637 n   4809 g   6325 d
Built by Scotts' Shipbuilding and Engineering Co Ltd, Greenock, Yard No 644, for Elder Dempster Lines Ltd. Doxford oil engine, opposed pistons, 2 SCSA 4 cyl 22$\frac{1}{16}$″–85$\frac{1}{16}$″ by the builders. 3100 bhp, 12$\frac{1}{2}$ K.
Passenger accommodation: 12.

1948   22 April, launched by Mrs J. H. Joyce. August, completed. Maiden voyage (Captain W. Rowlands).

1949   In collision with *COCHRANE* when entering Lagos harbour, causing damage to propeller. After examination certified fit to proceed to United Kingdom under own power. Outward bound on same voyage a case of new Nigerian shilling coins worth £400 was reported missing from strong room.

1965   July, transferred to Guinea Gulf Line Ltd. Renamed **MARADI**.

1967   19 June, sold to Kavalaris Shipping Co Ltd, Greece. Renamed **KABALARIS**. Registered Piraeus.

1969   Transferred to Kavalaris Shipping Co Ltd, Nicosia. Registered Famagusta. 2402 n, 4804 g, 6313 d.

1972   7 June, sold to Revalorizaci de Materiales, Bilbao. Demolition commenced August.

317 ACCRA (III)
O.N. 181100   1947–1967

'Accra' class
Steel twin screw motorship
471.0′×66.2′×25.6′   6448 n   11,599 g   7112 d
Built by Vickers Armstrong Ltd, Barrow, Yard No 948, for Elder Dempster Lines Ltd. Registered Liverpool. 2× Doxford oil engines, opposed pistons, 2 SCSA 4 cyl 26$\frac{3}{8}$″–91$\frac{5}{16}$″ by the builders. 9400 bhp, 15 K.
Passenger accommodation: 245 first class, 24 second, 150 deck.

1947   24 February, launched by Mrs Creech-Jones. September, completed, cost £900,000. Trial speed 16.89 K at 119 rpm. 24 September, maiden voyage (Captain C. C. Cave). On completion and for some eighteen months **ACCRA** was painted black overside with red boot-topping. Later changed to grey overside with green boot-topping.

1949   6 November. Arrived Liverpool from Lagos on one engine 6 days late following broken crankshaft. Repaired by builders.

1960   Accommodation fitted with air-conditioning, at Antwerp.

1967   After completing 171 round voyages sold to shipbreakers. 8 November, departed Liverpool (Captain L. L. James), 13 November, arrived Cartagena for demolition by J. Navarro Frances.

Ships of the 'Accra' class: ACCRA (317), APAPA (318).

ACCRA *sailing on her maiden voyage, 24 September 1947, and (next page) the embarkation notice*

Elder Dempster Lines, Limited

<u>Maiden voyage</u>

EMBARKATION NOTICE.

M.V. "ACCRA."

Liverpool, Wednesday, 24th September, 1947.

We are pleased to inform you that a First Class passage has been reserved for you to Freetown/Takoradi/Lagos by this opportunity.

Kindly note you are required to report, with baggage, for examination by the Controls, to the Princes Landing Stage, Liverpool, at 12.30 p.m. on Wednesday, 24th September.

Passengers from the South of England are advised that should there be a sufficient number travelling by rail from London the Company will endeavour to arrange a special train from Euston Station to Riverside Station, Liverpool, on the morning of embarkation, otherwise arrangements will be made for such passengers to travel by the 8.30 a.m. train from Euston Station on the 24th September, due Lime Street Station, Liverpool, at 12.45 p.m. Motor coaches will be available at Lime Street Station to convey passengers to the place of embarkation and lorries will be provided to transport baggage.

If, therefore, you intend to travel from Euston on the morning of sailing, please complete and return the form attached to this notice, and you will be advised due course of the train arrangements made.

Unfortunately, existing conditions preclude baggage from being sent forward in advance for shipment, but for the benefit of those travelling from other areas and from London, other than on sailing morning, we will be pleased to arrange for Baggage Agents to meet them at the Liverpool main line stations to relieve them of heavy baggage, provided the time, date and station of arrival and number of packages for transportation to the Landing Stage are advised in reasonable time.

The Free Baggage allowance per adult passenger is 40 cu. ft. and children's allowances are in proportion. Excess baggage is charged for at the following rates:—

Freetown ...	...	130/- per ton of 40 cubic feet.
Takoradi ...	...	135/- per ton of 40 cubic feet.
Lagos ...	...	140/- per ton of 40 cubic feet.

A freight charge of £2 2s. 0d. is made for a bicycle.

We enclose, herewith:—

1.—Declaration Form.

2.—"Special Instructions to Passengers," which should be carefully studied and complied with.

3.—Supply of baggage labels.

Please complete attached Acknowledgment and "Declaration" Form, posting them to this office BY RETURN POST whereupon Passage Ticket will be issued. Should there be insufficient time to post your Passage Ticket to you, it will be issued on embarkation at Liverpool.

When embarking, you are required to present:—

PASSPORT.

NATIONAL REGISTRATION IDENTITY CARD.

FOOD RATION BOOK **WITH PAGE 5 DULY FILLED IN.**

It is to be emphasised that Travellers' Cheques are only to be used on board to supplement the currency allowance of £5 Sterling plus £10 in the currency of the country to which you are proceeding, as otherwise their unrestricted use may embarrass the ship's resources. It is preferable that they should be of small denominations.

It is regretted that official restrictions do not permit passengers to board the ship prior to examination by the Controls and, after embarkation, their return ashore is not allowed. Also, relatives or friends are not permitted to accompany passengers to the point of embarkation.

It is essential that we be kept informed of any change of address, but in the event of any postponement of sailing the Company cannot accept responsibility for any Hotel or incidental expenses incurred.

ELDER DEMPSTER LINES, LIMITED.

(DRESS OPTIONAL)

Name...

ACKNOWLEDGMENT.

I acknowledge receipt of your letter and embarkation instructions concerning my passage in the M.V. "ACCRA," embarking Liverpool, 24th September, 1947.

I *will / *will not travel *First / *Third Class by rail from Euston Station, London.

*Delete words not applicable.

Signature ....

Mrs Creech-Jones naming **ACCRA**

ACCRA, _now with grey hull (above) and (below) First Class Smoke Room_

ACCRA _First Class Dining Room (above) and Library (below)_

ACCRA First Class Lounge *(top left)*, Swimming Pool *(top right)*, Games Deck *(below left)* and Card Room *(below right)*

The Sierra Leone Dance Troupe aboard *ACCRA* at Freetown

TYPE OF ACCOMMODATION	DECK	CABINS NUMBERED	GRADE PER PASSENGER
SUITE with Private Sitting Room and Bathroom	C	17 and 19 (Combined)	"A6"
SUITE without Sitting Room	C	17	"A4"
SITTING ROOM used separately as Two Berth Cabin	C	19	"A1"
SINGLE BERTH CABINS with Showers	C C D	3, 9, 11, 13, 15, 41, 51, 53, 55, 57, 59, 61, 63, 65, 67 4, 10, 12, 54, 56, 58, 60 51, 53, 55, 57, 67 (D 67 "A" rate for 2 passengers)	"A2"
TWO BERTH CABINS with Private Bathroom	D D	11, 13, 15, 17, 19, 21 23 *, 25 *, 27 *, 29 * 12, 14, 16, 18, 20, 22 24 *, 26 *, 28 *, 30 *	"A1"
TWO BERTH CABINS with Showers	C C D D	1, 5, 7, 21, 23, 25, 27, 29, 31, 33, 35, 37, 39, 43, 45, 47, 49 2, 6, 8, 14, 16, 18, 20, 22, 24, 26, 28, 30, 32, 34, 36, 38, 40, 42, 44, 46, 48, 50, 52 1, 3, 5, 7, 9, 31, 33, 35, 37, 39, 41, 43, 45, 47, 49, 59 *, 61 *, 63 *, 65 * 2, 4, 6, 8, 10, 32, 34, 36, 38, 40, 42, 44, 46, 48, 50, 52, 54, 56, 58 *, 60 *, 62 *, 64 *, 66 *, 68 *, 70 *, 72 *, 74 *	"A"
TWO BERTH CABIN (without Shower)	C	62	"B"
THIRD CLASS FOUR BERTH CABINS	E	1, 2, 3, 4, 5, 6	Third Class Rate

*Rooms marked with an asterisk have additional pullman berth for emergency use

PROMENADE DECK B.

BRIDGE DECK C.

UPPER DECK D.

MAIN DECK E.

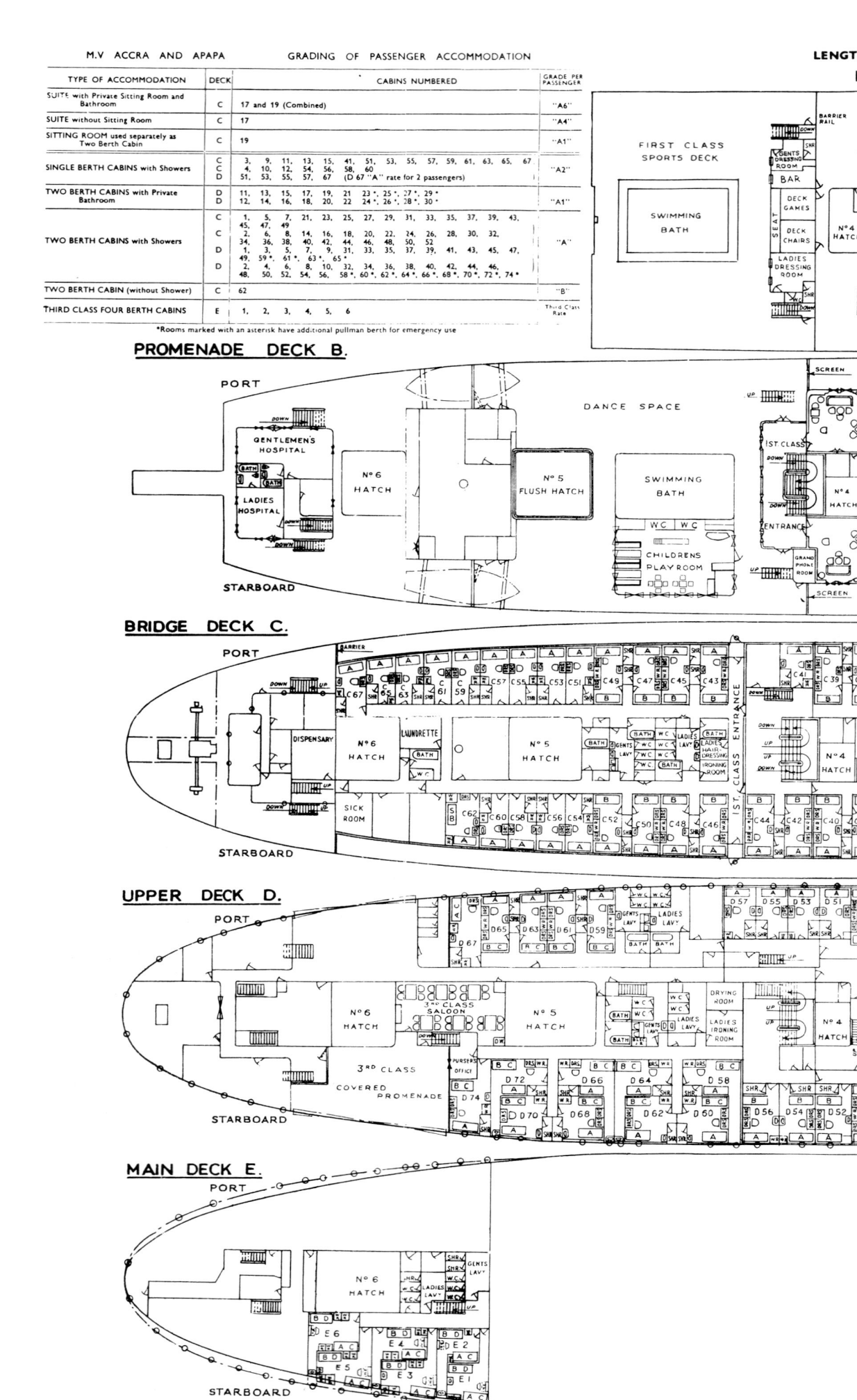

PASSENGER ACCOMMODATION

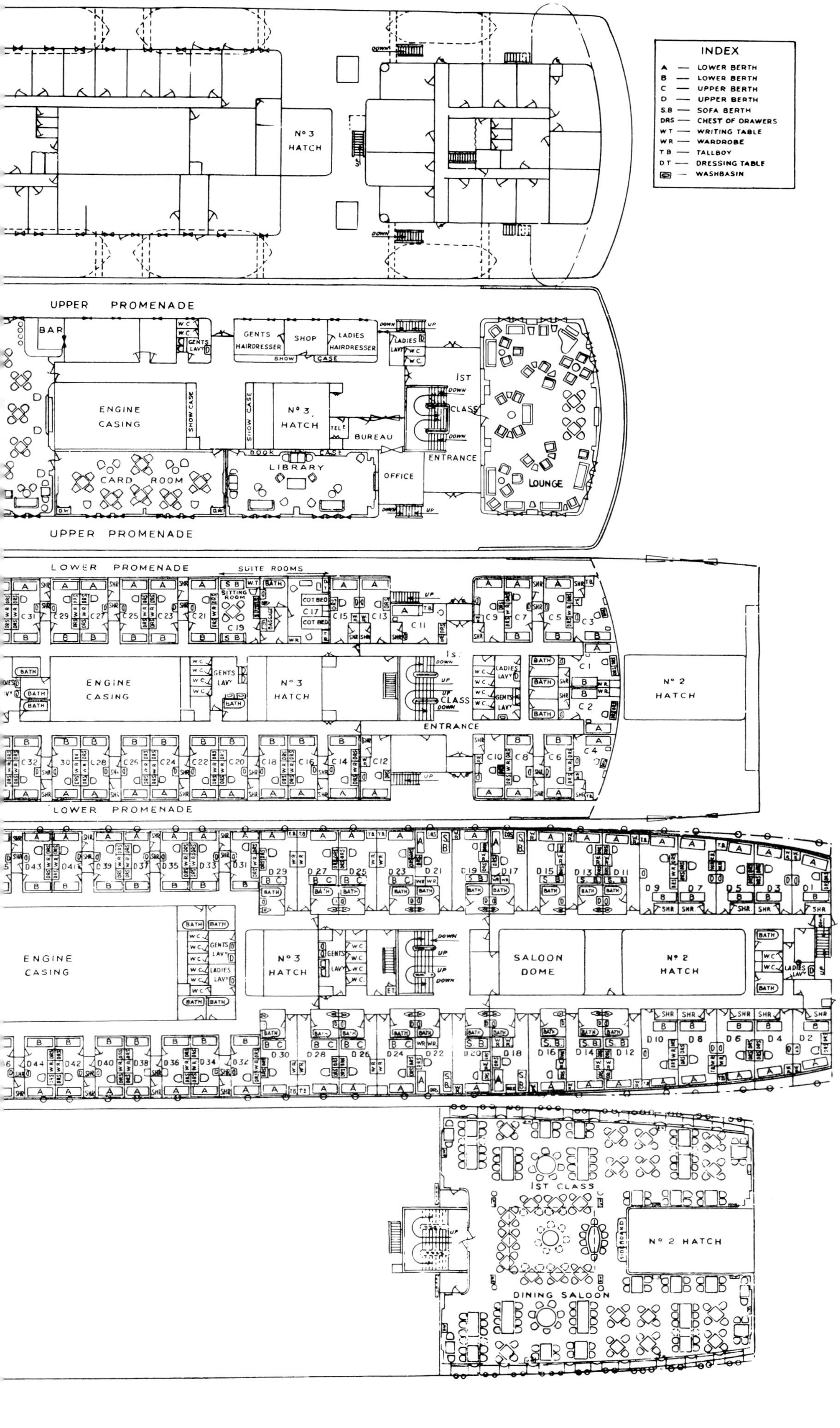

INDEX		
A	—	LOWER BERTH
B	—	LOWER BERTH
C	—	UPPER BERTH
D	—	UPPER BERTH
S.B	—	SOFA BERTH
DRS	—	CHEST OF DRAWERS
W T	—	WRITING TABLE
WR	—	WARDROBE
T B	—	TALLBOY
D T	—	DRESSING TABLE
▭	—	WASHBASIN

No 3 HATCH

UPPER PROMENADE

BAR · W C · W C · GENTS LAV · GENTS HAIRDRESSER · SHOP · SHOW CASE · LADIES HAIRDRESSER · LADIES LAV · W C · W C · DOWN · UP

ENGINE CASING · SHOW CASE · SHOW CASE · No 3 HATCH · BUREAU · TEL · 1ST DOWN DOWN CLASS ENTRANCE

CARD ROOM · BOOK CASE · LIBRARY · OFFICE · LOUNGE

UPPER PROMENADE

LOWER PROMENADE · SUITE ROOMS

SITTING ROOM · COT BED · COT BED · SB · WT · BATH

C31 C29 C27 C25 C23 C21 C19 · C17 C15 C13 C11 · C9 C7 C5 C3 · C1

ENGINE CASING · W C · GENTS LAV · W C · BATH · No 3 HATCH · 1ST UP UP CLASS DOWN ENTRANCE · LADIES LAV · W C · W C · GENTS LAV · BATH · BATH · C2 · No 2 HATCH

C32 30 C28 C26 C24 C22 C20 C18 C16 C14 C12 · C10 C8 C6 · C4

LOWER PROMENADE

D43 D41 39 D37 D35 D33 D31 · D29 D27 D25 D23 D21 D19 D17 D15 D13 D11 · 09 07 05 03 01

ENGINE CASING · BATH BATH · W C · GENTS LAV · W C · LADIES LAV · W C · BATH BATH · No 3 HATCH · GENTS W C · LAV W C · DOWN UP UP DOWN · SALOON DOME · No 2 HATCH · BATH · W C · LADIES LAV · BATH

6 D44 D42 D40 D38 D36 D34 D32 · D30 D28 D26 D24 D22 D20 D18 D16 D14 D12 · D10 D8 D6 D4 D2

1ST CLASS · No 2 HATCH · DINING SALOON

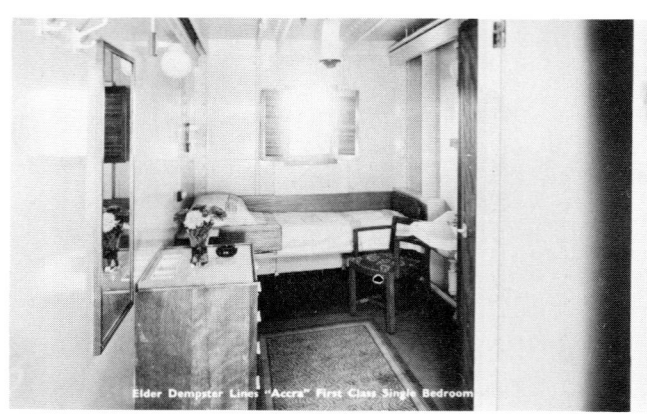

ACCRA cabins. First Class single (top left), Suite sitting room (top right), Suite bedroom (below left) and Two berth cabin (below right)

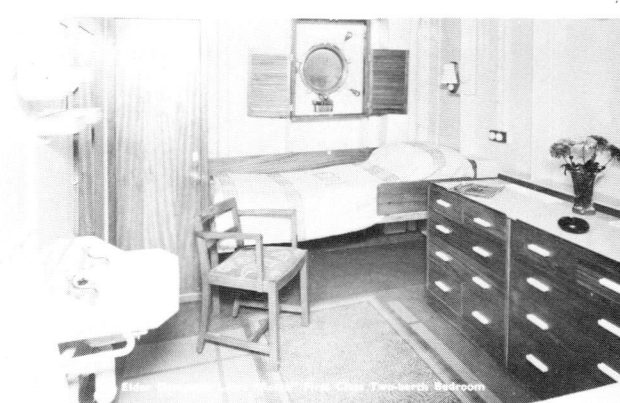

ACCRA and AUREOL at Liverpool during the 1966 Seamans' strike

APAPA at Bathurst, 1964

318 APAPA (III)
O.N. 182411   1948–1968

'Accra' class
Steel twin screw motorship
471.0′×66.2′×25.5′   6453 n   11,607 g   7112 d
Built by Vickers Armstrong, Barrow, Yard No 949, for Elder Dempster Lines Ltd. Registered Liverpool. 2× Doxford oil engines, opposed pistons, 2 SCSA 4 cyl $26\frac{3}{8}''$–$91\frac{5}{16}''$ by the builders. 9400 bhp, 15 K.
Passenger accommodation: 245 first class, 24 second, 150 deck.

1947 18 August, launched by Mrs A. C. Tod.
1948 March, completed. Maiden voyage (Captain J. J. Smith) commenced 12 March. On completion and for some 18 months **APAPA** was painted black overside with red boot-topping. Later changed to grey overside with green boot-topping.
1949 Between Freetown and Takoradi, on voyage Liverpool to Lagos, three members of the Catering Department broke into the strongroom by knocking out the pins from the hinges. They opened a case containing £10,000 West African Currency Board notes, re-stuffing the case with kitchen paper. The case was landed at Takoradi and signed for as intact by the authorities. It was only when the case was opened at the bank at Sekondi was the theft discovered. Culprits apprehended and eventually brought to trial at Liverpool.
1955 Leslie Gordon Vining, first Archbishop of West Africa, died on board **APAPA** whilst travelling home to the United Kingdom on sick leave.
1956 6412 n.
1960 Accommodation fitted with air-conditioning at Antwerp.
1968 After the completion of her 177th voyage (Captain D. Campbell) offered for sale and 12 November, sold to Shung Cheong Steam Navigation Co Ltd, Hong Kong. Renamed **TAIPOOSHAN**. 6455 n, 11,651 g.
1975 23 February, sold for demolition by Yun Shen Steel & Iron Works, Kaohsiung.

Note—**APAPA** and ACCRA were designed some 25 feet longer but built to a reduced length due to steel shortage.

King Neptune (alias Purser J. E. Cowden) and the Barber (alias Chief Officer M. R. Foster) aboard **APAPA** *(above), and (below) contemplating their clientele*

APAPA *at Liverpool*

APA *officers for her final voyage. From left: D. Haworth (Third Officer), D. Thomson (Third Officer), J. Binnie (Second Officer), I. Lowden (Second Officer), M. R. Foster (Chief Officer) and Captain D. Campbell*

S.S. "PRAH"
PASSENGER PLAN

W.R. - WARDROBE
DRS. - CHEST OF DRAWERS
D.T. - DRESSING TABLE
E.F. - ELECTRIC FIRE

UPPER DECK

PRAH

1950 20 March, acquired by Elder Dempster Lines Ltd. Renamed **PRAH**. Registered Liverpool. Passenger accommodation: 8. First voyage (Captain W. (Teapot) Brown).

1959 19 February, sold for £100,000 to Atlantska Plovidva, Dubrovnik, Yugoslavia. Renamed **NAPRIJED**. Registered Dubrovnik.

1967 Sold to Splosna Plovba, Piran. Registered Koper (Yugoslav flag). 4524 n.

1969 13 May, sold to Brodospas Shipbreakers for demolition at Split.

319 PRAH (II)
O.N. 182971   1950–1959

Steel screw steamer
447.9′×56.2′×26.9′ 5278 n 7339 g 9711 d
Built by William Grey & Co Ltd, West Hartlepool, Yard No 1166, as a naval auxiliary and launched as HMS **HOLM SOUND**. T 3 cyl 24½″, 39″, 70″–48″ by Duncan Stewart & Co Ltd, Glasgow (built 1942), 2825 ihp, 11 K.

1944 Completed.

1949 Recommissioned and converted into cargo ship. Renamed **EMPIRE LABUAN**. Purchased by Aviation & Shipping Co Ltd (N. W. Purvis, Manager), London. Renamed **AVISBAY**. Registered London.

320 BARO (II)
O.N. 183766   1950–1961

Steel screw steamer
250.0′×38.2′×14.9′ 684 n 1517 g 1530 d
Built by Blyth Dry Docks & Shipbuilding Co Ltd, Blyth, Yard No 348, for Elder Dempster Lines Ltd. Registered Liverpool. T 3 cyl 16½″, 27″, 46″–30″ by North Eastern Marine Engineering Co (1938) Ltd, Sunderland. 1000 ihp, 11 K.

1949 6 December, launched by Mrs F. Clegg.

1950 May, completed. Maiden voyage (Captain W. B. R. Bryan).

1961 2 June, sold to Marvalor Cia Armadora SA, Greece. Renamed **SOPHIE MARIS**. Registered Andros.

1965 Sold to Ambassador Steamships (Pte) Ltd (F. Collis & Co Ltd, Managers), India. Renamed **ANTON**. Registered Cochin.

1970 Sold to Collis Line Pte Ltd, Cochin.

1972 June, sold to Indian Metal Industries Ltd, Bombay, for demolition.

BARO at Port Harcourt

BENUE at Port Harcourt

BENIN

321 BENIN (IV)

O.N. 183786   1950–1960

Steel screw steamer
312.0′×44.2′×17.7′ 1282 n 2483 g 3130 d
Built by J. Lamont & Co Ltd, Port Glasgow, Yard No 374, for
Elder Dempster Lines Ltd. Registered Liverrool. T 3 cyl 17½″,
28″, 48″–33″ by Rankin & Blackmore Ltd, Greenock. 1100 ihp,
11 K.
1950   5 April, launched by Miss J. Joyce. Completed August.
        Maiden voyage (Captain W. E. Humphreys).
1960   30 November, sold to Tynedale Shipping Co Ltd (Joseph
        Constantine Steamship Line Ltd, Managers),
        Middlesbrough, for £80,000. Renamed **YORKWOOD**.
        Registered Middlesbrough.
1964   Sold to Mediterranean & Baltic Shipping Corp, Piraeus.
        Renamed **NOUFARO**. Registered Piraeus.
1968   Sold to Agia Irene Steamship Corp, Piraeus. Renamed
        AGIA IRENE. 1233 n, 2484 g.
1969   23 July, foundered in Corunna Roads (position 43°.10′N
        9°.32′W) after developing leaks in heavy weather, when
        on voyage Huelva to Ghent. No lives lost.

322 BENUE (II)

O.N. 169563   1951–1952

'Benue' class
Steel screw steamer, US 'Jeep' type
259.0′×42.1′×18.0′ 1026 n 1814 g 2843 d
Built by Pacific Bridge Co, Alameda, California, Yard No 7,
for United States Maritime Commission as **BENJAMIN TAY**.
Registered London. T 3 cyl 19″, 32″, 56″–36″ by the builders.

1300 ihp, 11 K. On completion chartered by Ministry of War
Transport and placed under management of Joseph Constantine Steamship Line Ltd.
1943   Completed.
1951   5 February, acquired by Elder Dempster Lines Ltd.
        Renamed **BENUE**. Registered London.
1952   2 October, sold to Anglo D/S, A/S (Valdemar Skogland
        A/S, Managers), Norway, for £46,000. Renamed
        ANGLO. Registered Haugesund.
1953   Steam engines replaced by 2 Sulzer oil engines 2 SCSA
        8 cyl 360 mm–600 mm, 1200 bhp, 11 K. 1008 n, 1845 g.
1965   Sold to D/S A/S Ryvingen (Alf Lindo, Manager),
        Norway. Renamed **LINDVANG**.
1969   Sold to Mrs Pigi Alexatos (G. H. Valsamakis & A.
        Alexatos, Managers), Greece. Renamed **DANAOS**.
        Registered Piraeus.
1974   Sold to Greek Eastern Shipping Co, Greece. Renamed
        VETA.
1977   Sold to Fanouri Cia Naviera SA. Renamed **AGHIOS
        FANOURIOS III**.
1978   Reported sold to Greek shipbreakers—6 October,
        arrived Piraeus and laid up.
1985   31 August, still reported laid up at Piraeus.
Ships of the 'Benue' (US 'Jeep') class: BENUE (322), BIDA
(323).

BIDA

323 BIDA (III)

O.N. 169573   1951–1952

'Benue' class
Steel screw steamer. US 'Jeep' type
259.0′×42.1′×18.0′ 1023 n 1791 g 2843 d

Built by Walter Butler Shipbuilders Inc, Superior, Wisconsin (western tip of Lake Superior), Yard No 1, for United States Maritime Commission as **JOHN W. AREY**. Registered London. T 3 cyl 19″, 32″, 56″–36″ by Prescot Co, Menominee, Michigan. 1300 ihp, 11 K. On completion, bare boat chartered to Ministry of War Transport, under management of Stone & Rolf Ltd.

1943 Completed.
1951 24 April, acquired by Elder Dempster Lines Ltd. Renamed **BIDA**. Registered London.
1952 30 October, sold to Anglo D/S, A/S (Valdemar Skogland A/S, Managers), Norway, for £45,000. Renamed **BASRA**. Registered Haugesund.
1953 High pressure cylinder rebored to 19¼″ diameter.
1964 Sold to Union Maritime Steamship Co, Piraeus, Greece. Renamed **PLEIAS**. Registered Piraeus. 1046 n, 2843 g.
1968 Renamed **ATLANTIC CONTRACTOR**. Sold to Reyes & Lim Co, Inc, Philippines. Renamed **TIMBER COAST**. Registered Manila.
1971 12 January, foundered in heavy weather when on voyage Canabayon to Limay in position 12°.39′N 125°.07′E.

324 AUREOL
O.N. 183819   1951–1974

Steel twin screw motorship, three decks
537.1′×70.2′×25.1′   7718 n   14,083 g   6937 d
Built by A. Stephen & Sons Ltd, Glasgow, Yard No 629, for Elder Dempster Lines Ltd. Registered Liverpool. 2× Doxford oil engines, opposed pistons, 2 SCSA 4 cyl 26⅜″–91 5/16″ by the builders. 9400 bhp, 16 K.
Passenger accommodation: 269 first class, 76 cabin.

1949 17 November, keel laid.
1951 28 March, launched by Mrs E. Tansley. Completed October. 8 November, maiden voyage (Captain J. J. Smith).
1954 1 May, officially opened Queen Elizabeth II Quay, Freetown.
1960 Air conditioning extended throughout.
1964 24 August, first mail vessel to berth alongside the new passenger terminal at Takoradi; opened by Mr Ofora Atta, Ghana Minister of Communications.
1969 Passenger accommodation: 451. 6827 n.

Mrs E. Tansley launching **AUREOL**

AUREOL

*The camera captures **AUREOL's** yacht-like lines to perfection as she approaches the quayside at Las Palmas*

1972 16 March, **AUREOL** became the last regular liner to sail from the port of Liverpool. The service was then transferred to Southampton.

1974 21 October, arrived Southampton, laid up, and offered for sale after completing 203 round voyages. 15 November, sold to Marianna Shipping & Trading Corporation, Athens. Renamed **MARIANNA VI**. Registered Panama. In service as accommodation ship at Jeddah— 402 berths.

1979 22 February, arrived Piraeus in tow from Jeddah.

1980 24 February, arrived Rabegh for service as accommodation ship.

1985 Bilinder Marine Corp SA, Athens, appointed Manager. 31 August, in service.

Named after Mount Aureol, Sierra Leone.

ALEXANDER STEPHEN & SONS, LTD
"AUREOL"—SHIP NO. 629
SEA TRIAL PROGRAMME

1951
Summertime

Wed. 10th Oct.	Leave Shieldhall for Tail of Bank (M.W.10.8).	9.00 a.m.
	Anchor Trial.	11.30 a.m.
	Adjust Compasses.	12.30 p.m.
	Commence D/F Calibration. Approx.	1.30 p.m.
	Tug leaves Gourock Pier for ship to Embark and Land Personnel as required.	2.30 p.m.
	Commence Builders' Trials for Engine Adjustment. Approx.	3.00 p.m.
	Test Wireless, Radar and Echo Sounding Equipment, as convenient.	
	Anchor at Tail of Bank. Approx.	7.00 p.m.
	Tug in attendance at Princes Pier, Greenock, while vessel at Anchorage.	
	Commence endurance trial approx. 12 hours.	8.00 p.m.
Thur. 11th Oct.	Commence 4 Double Runs on Arran Mile at the following R.P.M.s 81.5 R.P.M. 97.5 R.PM. 111 R.P.M. and 118.5 R.P.M. Approx.	8.00 a.m.
	Stopping and Astern Trials with and without the Brake on Main Engines. (Observations to be taken on Mile Post.) Steering Gear Trial. On completion of trials, proceed to Anchorage.	
	Anchor at Tail of Bank. Approx.	3.00 p.m.
	Tug in Attendance at Princes Pier Greenock to land Builders Personnel etc., as required.	4.30 p.m.
	Embark Owners Guests.	6.00 p.m.
	Commence 8 hours Consumption Trial at 111 R.P.M. followed by 4 hours Consumption Trial at 118 R.P.M.	
	Approx.	7.00 p.m.

Fri. 12th Oct.	Return to Anchorage at Tail of Bank.	
	Approx.	9.30 a.m.
	Hand Over.	
	Builders' Staff leaves vessel as required.	
	Vessel leaves Anchorage for Liverpool.	P.M.
Sat. 13th Oct.	Vessel Berths at Liverpool.	A.M.

'AUREOL' AIDS PADDLE TUG IN BISCAY

Homeward-bound from West Africa, *Aureol* met up with the 55-year-old paddle tug *Eppleton Hall* in distress in the Bay of Biscay. *Eppleton Hall*, believed to be the world's last steam paddle tug, was on her way from the Tyne to San Francisco Maritime Museum. Manned by a volunteer crew and delayed by bad weather in the Bay of Biscay, she had run out of fuel and needed 500 gallons of fuel oil in drums. Although *Aureol* was unable to supply the amount in drums, she stood by for an hour and a half until a Spanish trawler took the tug in tow.

Senior electrician Frank James took the photograph

One of the more unusual episodes in the life of a modern liner. From Sea *magazine*

PRESENTATION CEREMONY ON BOARD M.V. AUREOL

Sir Alan Tod was asked by the photographers present at the ceremony to hold up the cheque for £75,000. Right: The scene on M.V. Aureol during Alhaji Abdulmaliki's speech. The seal was fixed to the deed of the trust fund by Mr Michael Smye, left, company secretary, and was signed by Mr J. H. Joyce, second left, chairman of Elder Dempster Lines Ltd. Mr S. A. Cotton, right, is one of the trustees, and a director of Elder Dempster Agencies Ltd.

Elder Dempster marked the Independence of Nigeria by establishing the Elder Dempster Nigeria Independence Trust. This page in Sea magazine records the ceremony when Elder Dempster's chairman Sir Alan Tod handed over the cheque

CABIN CLASS SMOKE ROOM

CABIN CLASS STATEROOM

AUREOL's accommodation is shown on the following pages

1st CLASS DINING SALOON

1st CLASS LOUNGE

CHILDREN'S PLAYROOM

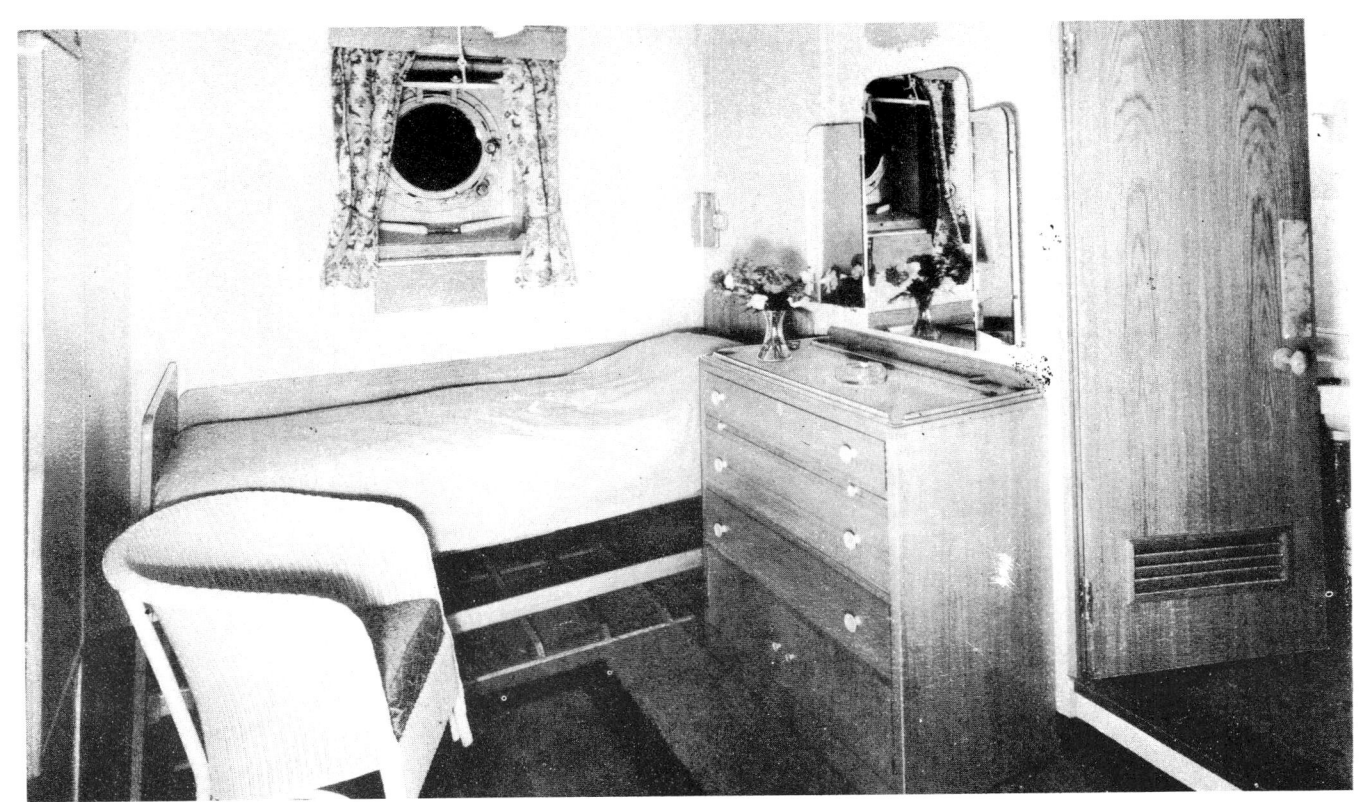

1st CLASS SINGLE BERTH CABIN & TOILET

ELDER DEMPSTER LINES, LIMITED

T.S.M.V. "AUREOL"

LENGTH 538 FT: BREADTH 70 FT: DEPTH 36 FT: 6 INS:

PLAN OF PASSENGER ACCOMMODATION

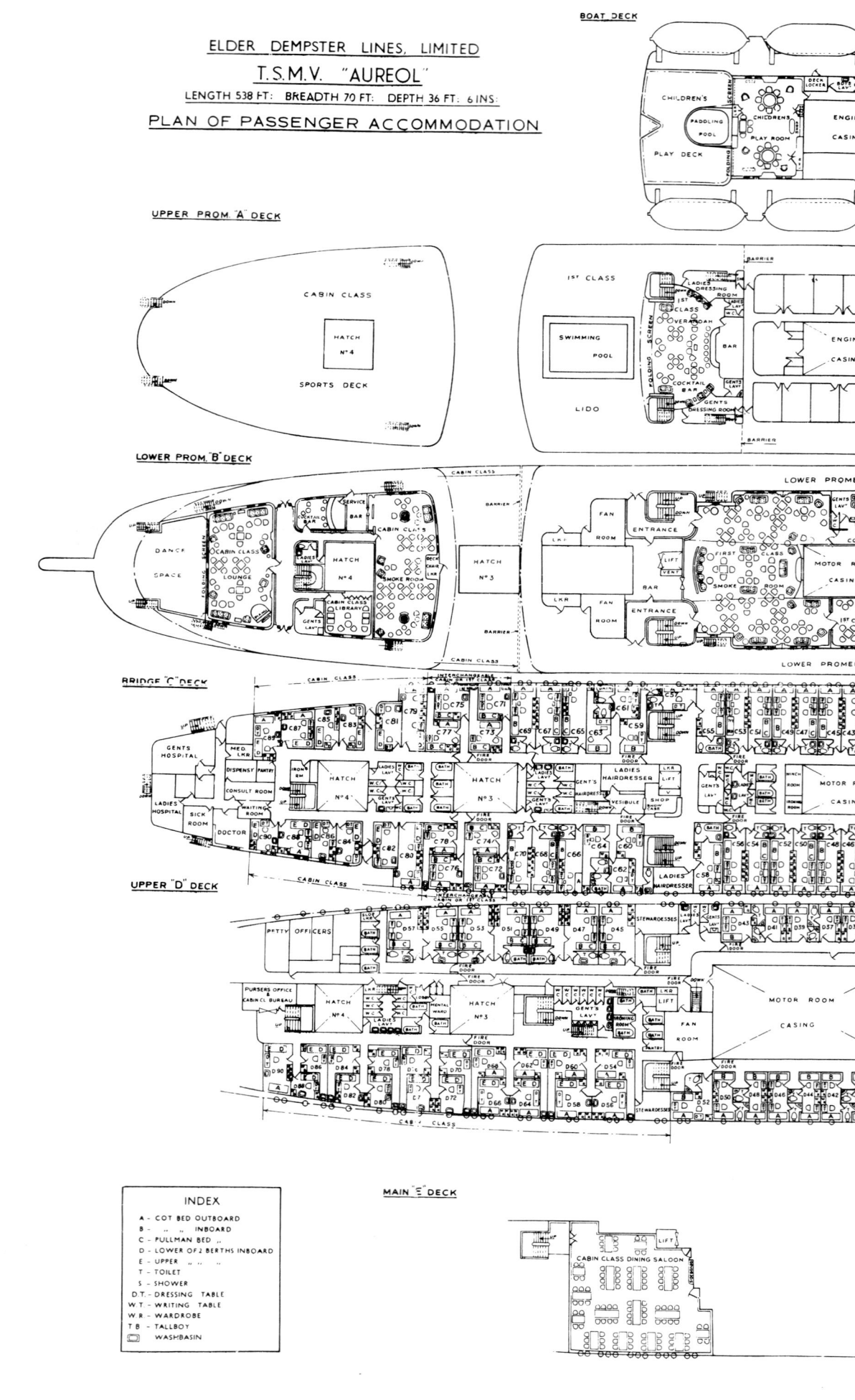

BOAT DECK

UPPER PROM. "A" DECK

LOWER PROM. "B" DECK

BRIDGE "C" DECK

UPPER "D" DECK

MAIN "E" DECK

INDEX

A - COT BED OUTBOARD
B - „ „ INBOARD
C - PULLMAN BED „
D - LOWER OF 2 BERTHS INBOARD
E - UPPER „ „ „
T - TOILET
S - SHOWER
D.T. - DRESSING TABLE
W.T. - WRITING TABLE
W.R. - WARDROBE
T B - TALLBOY
▭ WASHBASIN

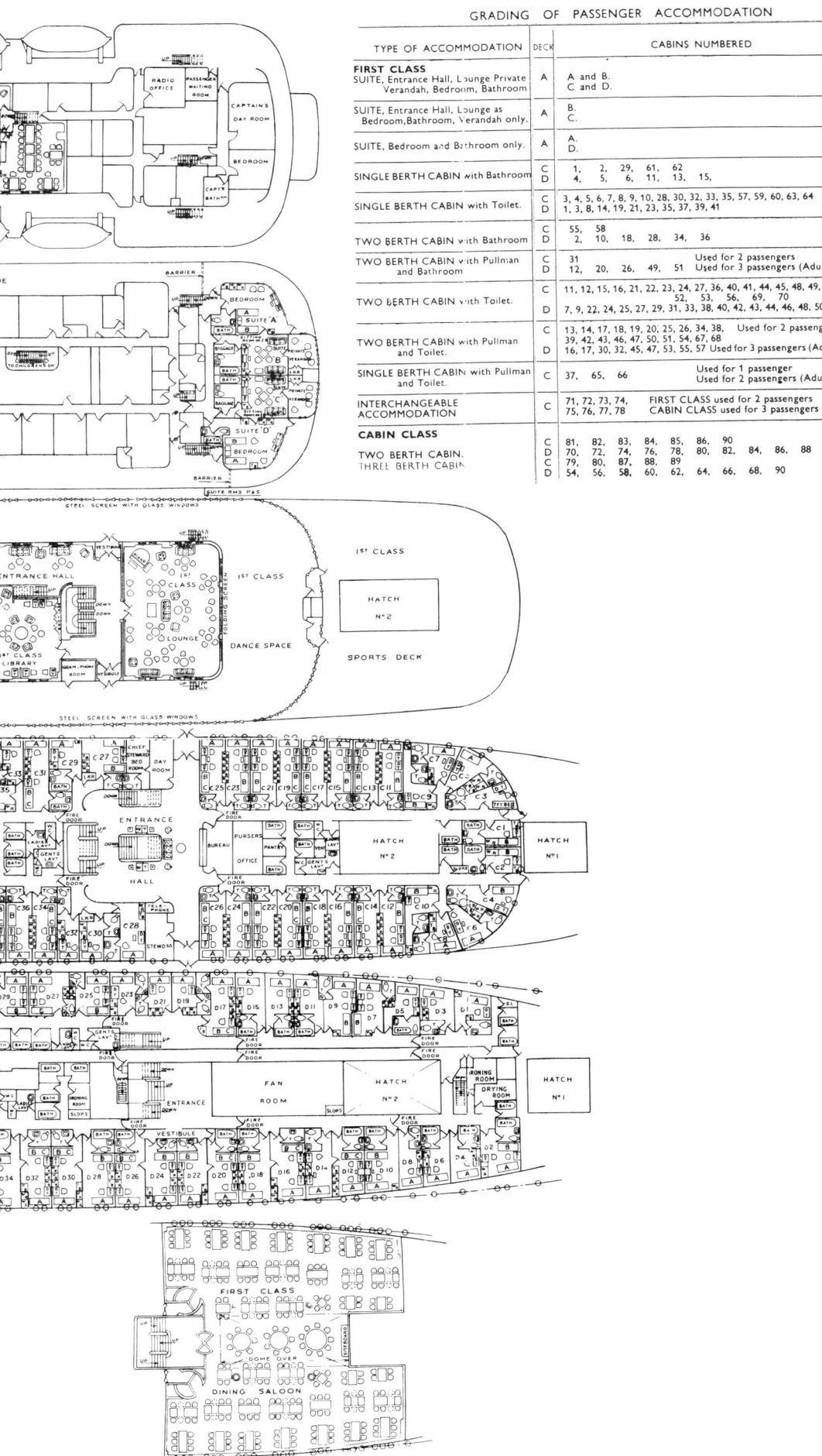

GRADING OF PASSENGER ACCOMMODATION

TYPE OF ACCOMMODATION	DECK	CABINS NUMBERED		Grade Per Passenger
FIRST CLASS				
SUITE, Entrance Hall, Lounge Private Verandah, Bedroom, Bathroom	A	A and B. C and D.		"A7"
SUITE, Entrance Hall, Lounge as Bedroom, Bathroom, Verandah only.	A	B. C.		"A5"
SUITE, Bedroom and Bathroom only.	A	A. D.		"A4"
SINGLE BERTH CABIN with Bathroom	C	1, 2, 29, 61, 62		"A3"
	D	4, 5, 6, 11, 13, 15,		
SINGLE BERTH CABIN with Toilet.	C	3, 4, 5, 6, 7, 8, 9, 10, 28, 30, 32, 33, 35, 57, 59, 60, 63, 64		"A2"
	D	1, 3, 8, 14, 19, 21, 23, 35, 37, 39, 41		
TWO BERTH CABIN with Bathroom	C	55, 58		"A1"
	D	2, 10, 18, 28, 34, 36		
TWO BERTH CABIN with Pullman and Bathroom	C	31	Used for 2 passengers	"A1"
	D	12, 20, 26, 49, 51	Used for 3 passengers (Adult)	"A"
TWO BERTH CABIN with Toilet.	C	11, 12, 15, 16, 21, 22, 23, 24, 27, 36, 40, 41, 44, 45, 48, 49, 52, 53, 56, 69, 70		"A"
	D	7, 9, 22, 24, 25, 27, 29, 31, 33, 38, 40, 42, 43, 44, 46, 48, 50, 52		
TWO BERTH CABIN with Pullman and Toilet.	C	13, 14, 17, 18, 19, 20, 25, 26, 34, 38, 39, 42, 43, 46, 47, 50, 51, 54, 67, 68	Used for 2 passengers	"A"
	D	16, 17, 30, 32, 45, 47, 53, 55, 57	Used for 3 passengers (Adult)	"B"
SINGLE BERTH CABIN with Pullman and Toilet.	C	37, 65, 66	Used for 1 passenger	"A2"
			Used for 2 passengers (Adult)	"A"
INTERCHANGEABLE ACCOMMODATION	C	71, 72, 73, 74,	FIRST CLASS used for 2 passengers	"B"
		75, 76, 77, 78	CABIN CLASS used for 3 passengers	CABIN
CABIN CLASS				
TWO BERTH CABIN.	C	81, 82, 83, 84, 85, 86, 90		CABIN
	D	70, 72, 74, 76, 78, 80, 82, 84, 86, 88		
THREE BERTH CABIN.	C	79, 80, 87, 88, 89		
	D	54, 56, 58, 60, 62, 64, 66, 68, 90		

AUREOL

*In the Middle East, **MARIANNA VI** still has the grace she enjoyed as **AUREOL** (Photo M. Mitchell)*

325   EBOE (V)
O.N. 185423   1952–1977

'Eboe' class
Steel screw motorship
508.3′×64.3′×27.8′   5242 n   9397 g   10,060 d
Built by Scotts' Shipbuilding & Engineering Co Ltd, Greenock, Yard No 655, for Elder Dempster Lines Ltd. Registered Liverpool. Doxford oil engine, opposed pistons, 2 SCSA 6 cyl $28\frac{9}{16}''$–$88\frac{9}{16}''$ by the builders. 8000 bhp, 16 K.

*Lady Milverton about to christen **EBOE***

EBOE

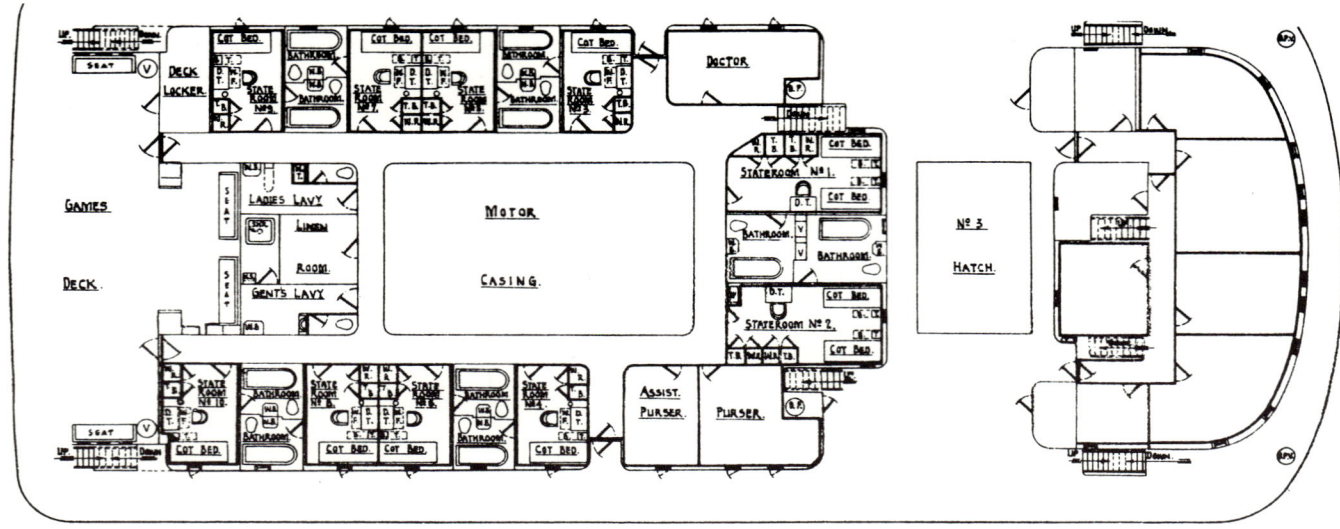

PROMENADE DECK.

ELDER DEMPSTER LINES, LIMITED

M.V.s "EBANI" AND "EBOE"

PLAN OF PASSENGER ACCOMMODATION

KEY TO ABBREVIATIONS

WR.	-	WARDROBE
T.B.	-	TALLBOY
D.T.	-	DRESSING TABLE
W.F.	-	WRITING FLAP
B.T.	-	BEDSIDE TABLE
W.B.	-	WASHBASIN
H.S.	-	HINGED SEAT
W.T.	-	WASH TUB
WR.T.	-	WRITING TABLE
C.T.	-	COFFEE TABLE
B.C.	-	BOOKCASE

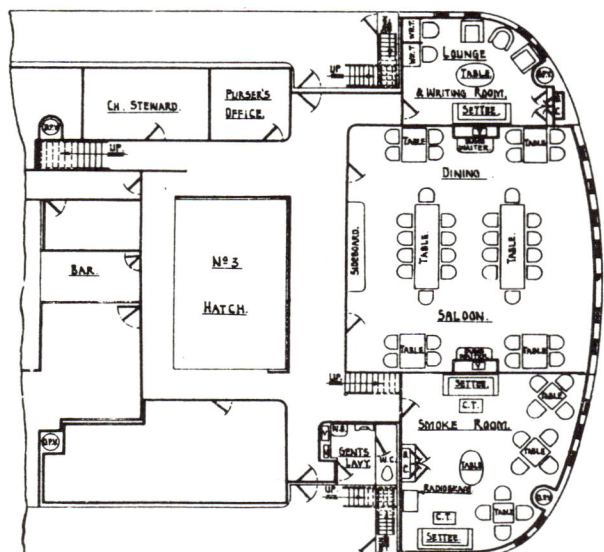

Passenger accommodation: 12.

Strengthened to Government standards for possible use as an Armed Merchant Cruiser.

1951 19 September, launched by Lady Milverton.

1952 March, completed. Maiden voyage (Captain R. A. Roberts).

1977 19 September, sold to Triton Navigation Corporation, Monrovia (Maldive Shipping Ltd, Managers). Renamed **GEORGIOS**. 5198 n, 9380 g, 10,347 d. Before delivery the ship's bell was removed and presented to Lady Milverton.

The above sale is not recorded in *Lloyds' Register*.

1978 Sold to Maldives Shipping Ltd, Panama. Renamed **GEORGIA**. Registered Panama. Sold to Pakistani shipbreakers (Zenith Management Corp, Bombay Managers), 19 February, arrived Gadani Beach. Demolition commenced almost immediately.

Ships of the 'Eboe' class: EBOE (325), EBANI (326).

326 EBANI (III)

O.N. 185437   1952–1977

'Eboe' class
Steel screw motorship
508.3′×64.3′×27.8′   5241 n   9396 g   10,010 d

EBANI

Built by Scotts' Shipbuilding & Engineering Co Ltd, Greenock, Yard No 656, for Elder Dempster Lines Ltd. Registered Liverpool. Doxford oil engine, opposed pistons, 2 SCSA 6 cyl $28\frac{9}{16}''$–$88\frac{9}{16}''$ by the builders. 8000 bhp, 16 K.
Passenger accommodation: 12.
Strengthened to Government standards for possible use as an Armed Merchant Cruiser.

The 'Ebani' . . .

heads for the Bay

Prizewinning photographs by F. N. Dalzell, Extra Second Officer, M.V. *Ebani*; taken homeward bound after leaving Las Palmas during February 1956.

From Sea *magazine*

1952　13 March, launched by Miss J. Tod. June, completed.
　　　Maiden voyage (Captain W. R. Rowlands).
1956　5200 n.
1973　Transferred for one round Far East voyage to China
　　　Mutual Steam Navigation Co Ltd (Blue Funnel Line
　　　Ltd, Managers). 5201 n, 9376 g, 10,576 d.
1977　Sold for demolition to Shipbreaking Industries Ltd and
　　　arrived Faslane 15 August.

327　ONITSHA (II)
O.N. 185435　　　　　　　　　　　　　　1952–1972

'Onitsha' class
Steel screw motorship
449.4′×62.3′×22.5　3171 n　6972 d　5802 g
Built by Harland & Wolff Ltd, Belfast, Yard No 1448, for Elder
Dempster Lines Ltd. Registered Liverpool. B & W oil engine
2 SCSA 5 cyl $24\frac{7}{16}''$–$55\frac{1}{2}''$ by the builders. 3750 bhp, 13 K.
Designed for the carriage of heavy locomotives.
Passenger accommodation: 12.
1952　29 January, launched by Miss Susan Tod. June,
　　　completed. Maiden voyage (Captain J. S. Cowan).
1971　Tmk 2619 n, 5386 g, 6972 d. Tmk 3798 n, 7269 g, 9463 d.
1972　26 May, sold to Cisne Cia Nav SA, Piraeus, Greece.
　　　Renamed **AMVOURGON**. Registered Piraeus. Closed
　　　shelter deck. Tmk 3798 n, 7267 g, 9134 d.
1975　8 January, voyage Quebec to Baltimore, fire in the engine
　　　room and crew abandoned ship seven miles off Fox river,
　　　near Cape Gaspé. **AMVOURGON** taken in tow. 11
　　　January, arrived Halifax. 7 May, left Halifax in tow. 29
　　　May, arrived Santander for demolition. 9 June, work
　　　commenced.
Ships of the 'Onitsha' class: ONITSHA (327), OBUASI (328),
OWERRI (344).

ONITSHA (above) and (below) with ITU aboard

ONITSHA unloading locomotives at Apapa wharf

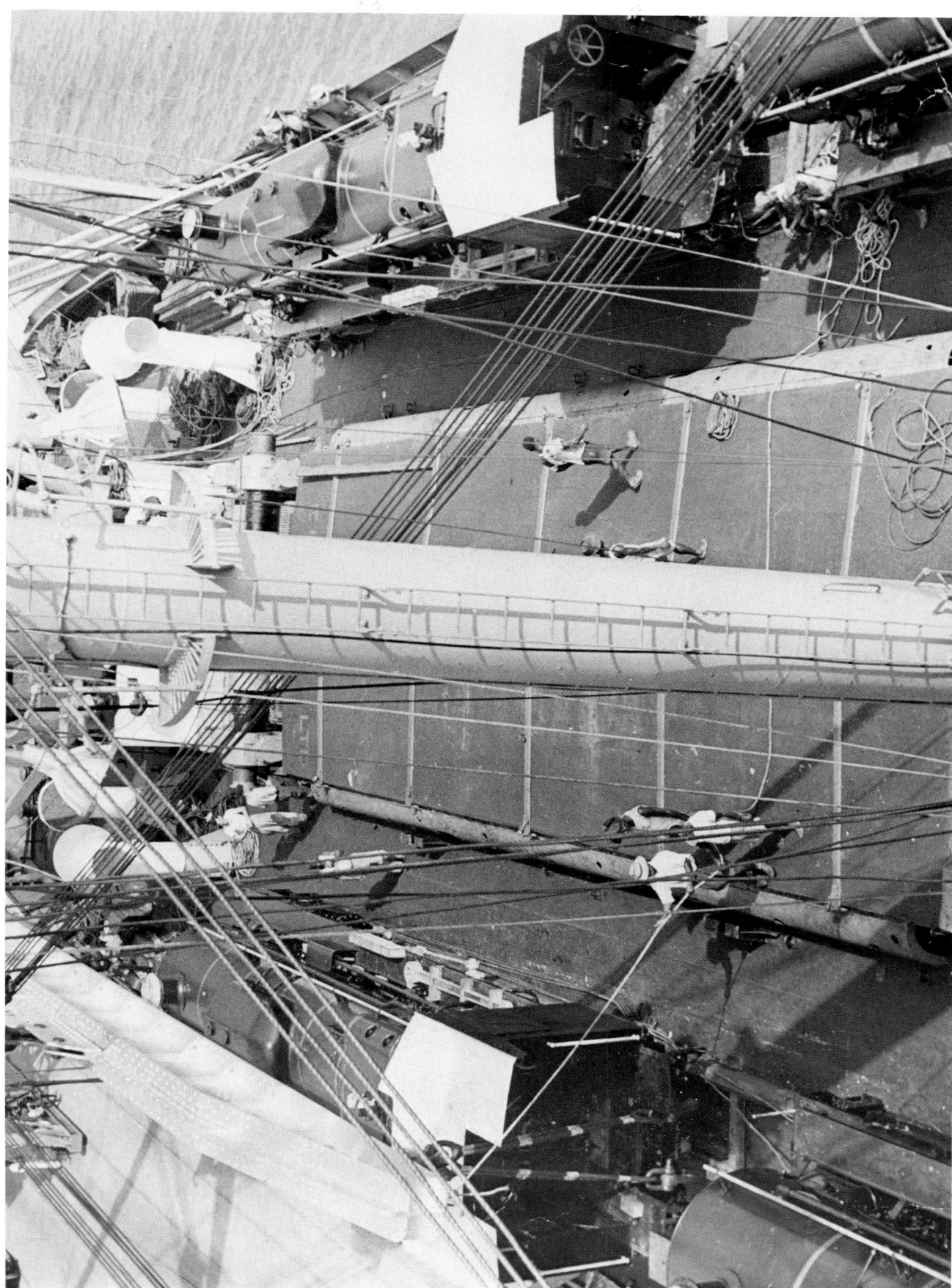

ONITSHA showing locomotives stowed on deck

ONITSHA outward bound, 1965

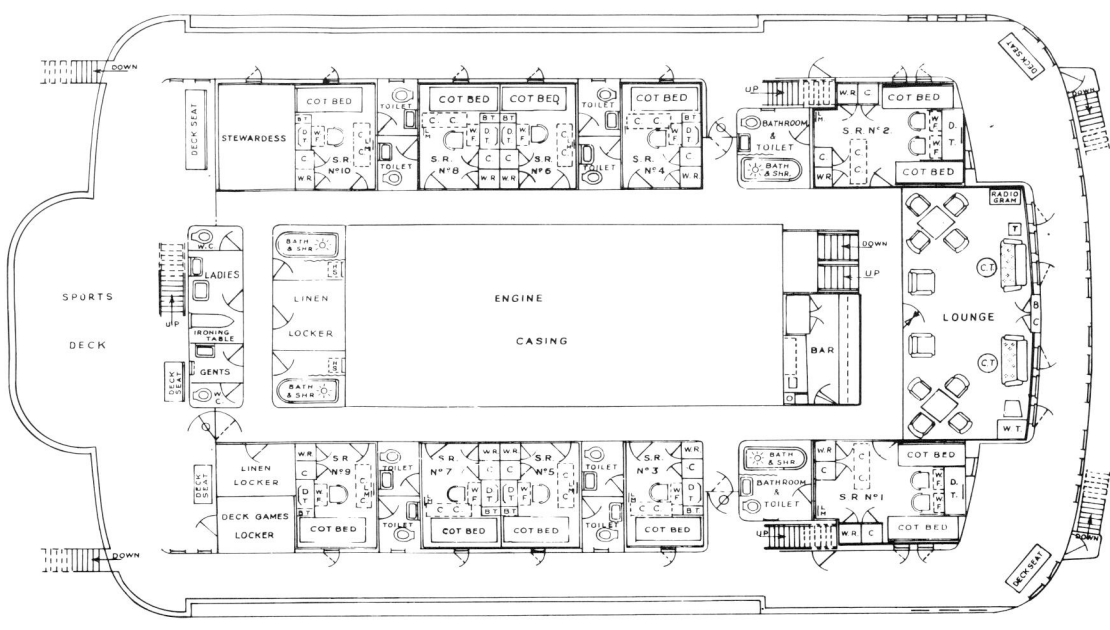

BRIDGE DECK

ELDER DEMPSTER LINES, LIMITED

M.V. "OBUASI"

PLAN OF PASSENGER ACCOMMODATION

KEY TO ABBREVIATIONS

W.R.	-	WARDROBE
C.	-	COMPACTUM
D.T.	-	DRESSING TABLE
B.T.	-	BEDSIDE TABLE
L.M.	-	LONG MIRROR
W.F.	-	WRITING FLAP
S.R.	-	STATE ROOM
H.S.	-	HINGED SEAT
C.C.	-	POSITION FOR CHILDS COT
C.T.	-	COFFEE TABLE

Issued March, 1953.

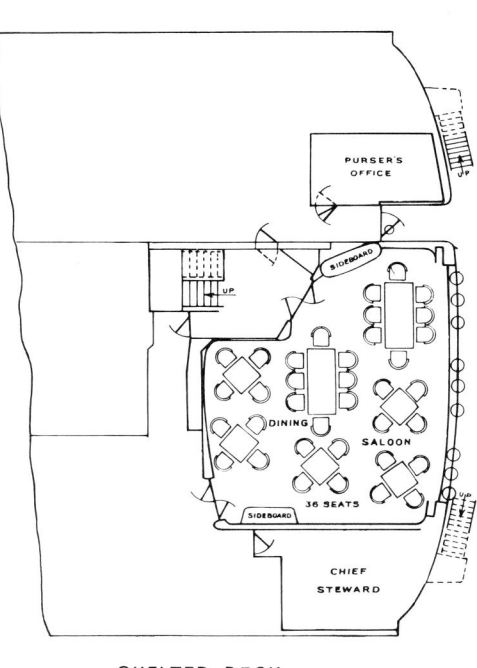

SHELTER DECK

OBUASI

328 OBUASI (II)
O.N. 185449   1952–1972

'Onitsha' class
Steel screw motorship
449.8′×60.3′×23.3′   3147 n   5883 g   7089 d
Built by Harland & Wolff Ltd, Belfast, Yard No 1449, for Elder Dempster Lines Ltd. Registered Liverpool. B & W oil engine 2 SCSA 5 cyl 24$\frac{7}{16}$″–55$\frac{1}{8}$″ by the builders. 3750 bhp, 13 K.
Passenger accommodation: 12.

1952   24 June, launched by Mrs M. B. Glasier. November, completed. Maiden voyage (Captain R. A. Roberts).
        OBUASI served as a Cadet Training Ship for a number of years.
1966   Passenger accommodation withdrawn. 3117 n, 5895 g.
1972   Sold to Anglo-Pacific SA (Anglo Eastern Shipping Co Ltd, Managers), Victoria, Hong Kong. Renamed **AMOY**. Registered Mogadishu. 2959 n, 5895 g. 9 August, stranded and subsequently abandoned near Cape Negrais at the mouth of the Irrawaddy River, in position 16°.10′N 94°.15′E, voyage Calcutta to Rangoon, and declared a constructive total loss.

329 PROME
O.N. 164119   1952–1962

'Prome' class
Steel screw steamer

462.0′×59.2′×27.3′   4334 n   7043 g   9400 d
Built by Wm Denny & Bros Ltd, Dumbarton, Yard No 1295, for British & Burmese Steam Navigation Co Ltd (P. Henderson & Co, Managers). Registered Glasgow. Three Parsons steam turbines, SR gearing, by the builders. 4700 shp, 14 K.
Passenger accommodation: 75 first class.

1937   May, completed.
1940   Requisitioned and converted for service as a mine depot ship.
1952   30 January, acquired by Elder Dempster Lines Ltd with the purchase of the British & Burmese Steam Navigation Co Ltd.
1955   October. In collision with CYCLOPS in Liverpool Bay inward from Burma. Minor damage sustained.
1962   30 September, arrived Bruges for demolition by Van Heyghen Freres.

Note—**PROME** did not trade on the West African service.
Ships of the 'Prome' class: PROME (329), SALWEEN (330).

330 SALWEEN
O.N. 165926   1952–1962

'Prome' class
Steel screw steamer
462.0′×59.2′×27.3′   4355 n   7063 g   9400 d
Built by Wm Denny & Bros Ltd, Dumbarton, Yard No 1307, for British & Burmese Steam Navigation Co Ltd (P. Henderson & Co, Managers). Registered Glasgow. Three Parsons steam turbines, SR gearing, by the builders. 4700 shp, 14 K.

*The Henderson liners **PROME** (above) and **SALWEEN** (below) came under the Elder Dempster umbrella in 1952, but continued to serve on their owners Burmese service*

HENDERSON LINE

s.s. "PROME"—Plan of Passenger Accommodation

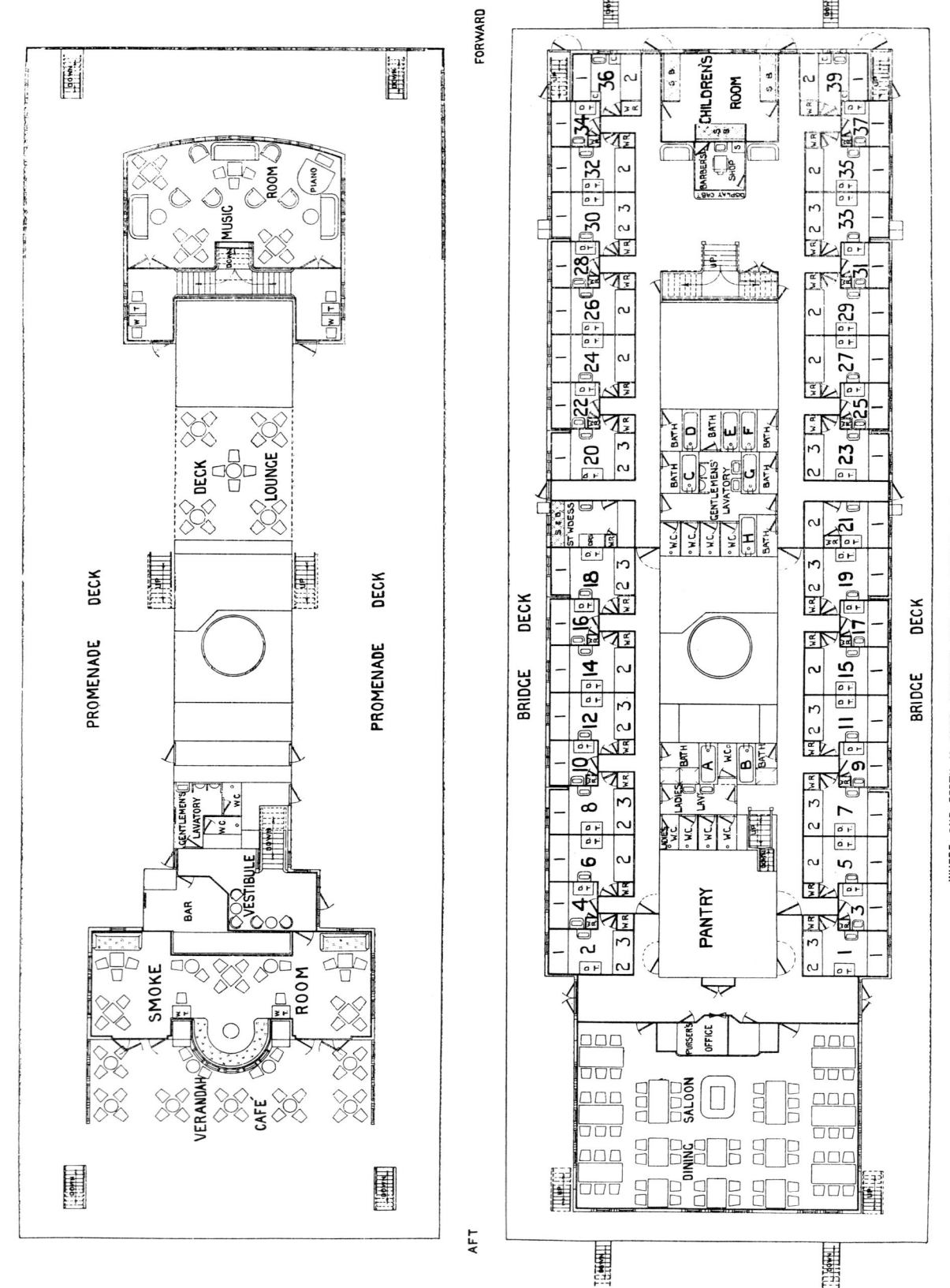

FORWARD

PROMENADE DECK

DECK

PROMENADE DECK

LOUNGE

MUSIC ROOM

PIANO

GENTLEMEN'S LAVATORY

W.C.

W.C.

VESTIBULE

BAR

SMOKE ROOM

VERANDAH CAFE

AFT

BRIDGE DECK

BRIDGE DECK

CHILDREN'S ROOM

BARBERS SHOP

DISPLAY CABT

PANTRY

DINING SALOON

PURSER'S OFFICE

LADIES LAV.

GENTLEMEN'S LAVATORY

BATH   A   B   BATH

BATH   C   D   BATH
E
BATH   F   BATH
G
H   BATH

WHERE ONE BERTH IS OVER ANOTHER THE ODD NUMBER IS THE UPPER BERTH

W.R.—WARDROBE   C.—LOCKER CABINET

D.T.—DRESSING TABLE

284

Passenger accommodation: 75 first class.
1938 February, completed.
1940 Requisitioned for service as a troopship.
1952 30 January, acquired by Elder Dempster Lines Ltd, with the purchase of the British & Burmese Steam Navigation Co Ltd.
1962 Sold to shipbreakers for £78,000 and arrived Hong Kong 30 May for demolition by Shiu Wing Hong.
Note—**SALWEEN** did not trade on the West African service.

331 KALEWA
O.N.169491   1952–1963

'Kalewa' class
Steel screw motorship
446.3′ × 56.2′ × 24.9′   2855 n   4876 g   8950 d
Built by Lithgows Ltd, Port Glasgow, Yard No 1019, for British & Burmese Steam Navigation Co Ltd (P. Henderson & Co, Managers). Registered Glasgow. Doxford oil engine, opposed pistons, 2 SCSA 3 cyl $23\frac{5}{8}''$–$91\frac{5}{16}''$ by D. Rowan & Co Ltd, Glasgow, 2400 bhp, 11 K.
1946 26 December, launched by Miss Brown.

KALEWA

1947 March, completed. 3 April, commenced maiden voyage, United Kingdom to Burma, thereafter on charter to Elder Dempster Lines Ltd on the West African trade.
1952 30 January, acquired by Elder Dempster Lines Ltd with the purchase of the British & Burmese Steam Navigation Co Ltd.

KALEWA after launching

1963 Sold to Cia de Nav Anderson SA, London, for £82,500. Renamed **SINCERITY**. Registered Panama. 2794 n, 4882 g.

1971 February, Tmk 2838 n, 4775 g. 4255 n, 6775 g.

1977 Sold for demolition and arrived 18 May at Dalmuir for demolition by W. H. Arnott Young & Co Ltd.

Ships of the 'Kalewa' class: KALEWA (331), KATHA (332), KANBE (333), KALADAN (334).

KATHA (Photo W. Ralston Ltd)

332 KATHA
O.N. 182077   1952–1962

'Kalewa' class
Steel screw motorship
446.5′ × 56.2′ × 24.9′   2851 n   4878 g   8950 d
Built by Lithgows Ltd, Port Glasgow, Yard No 1024, for British & Burmese Steam Navigation Co Ltd (P. Henderson & Co, Managers). Registered Glasgow. Doxford oil engine, opposed pistons, 2 SCSA 3 cyl $23\frac{5}{8}''$–$91\frac{5}{16}''$ by D. Rowan & Co Ltd, Glasgow. 2400 bhp, 11 K.

1947 4 September, launched. November, completed. 12 December, commenced maiden voyage, round trip to Indian ports, then chartered by Elder Dempster Lines Ltd for West African trade.

1952 30 January, acquired by Elder Dempster Lines Ltd with the purchase of the British & Burmese Steam Navigation Co Ltd.

1962 25 January, engines disabled whilst on voyage West Africa to United Kingdom. Taken in tow by *DEIDO*. Sold to Cia de Nav 'Ira' SA, Liberia, for £77,500. Renamed **INTEGRITY**. Registered Monrovia. 2791 n, 4883 g.

1970 December, shelter deck closed. 4425 n, 7058 g, 9094 d.

1977 Sold to Osborne Maritime Inc, Panama. Renamed **UNITED CARRIER**. Registered Panama.

1978 Sold to Sohail Breakers Ltd. 30 June, departed Karachi for Gadani beach. August, demolition commenced.

KANBE (Photo W. Ralston Ltd)

333 KANBE
O.N. 182086   1952–1962

'Kalewa' class
Steel screw motorship
446.6′ × 56.2′ × 24.9′   2851 n   4878 g   8950 d
Built by Lithgows Ltd, Port Glasgow, Yard No 1025, for British & Burmese Steam Navigation Co Ltd (P. Henderson & Co, Managers). Registered Glasgow. Doxford oil engine, opposed pistons, 2 SCSA 3 cyl $23\frac{5}{8}''$–$91\frac{5}{16}''$ by D. Rowan & Co Ltd, Glasgow. 2400 bhp, 11 K.

1947 26 December, launched.

1948 April, completed. 14 May, commenced maiden voyage, on charter for one round trip, United Kingdom–Persian Gulf–Australia, then chartered by Elder Dempster Lines Ltd for West African trade.

1952 30 January, acquired by Elder Dempster Lines Ltd with the purchase of the British & Burmese Steam Navigation Co Ltd.

1962 Sold to Cia de Nav 'Ira' SA, Liberia, for £90,000. Renamed **LOYALTY**. Registered Monrovia. 2983 n, 4870 g.

1971 January, Tmk 2993 n, 4812 g. 4048 n, 6481 g.

1974 Sold to Chinese mainland shipbreakers and sailed Tokyo 17 January, arriving Shanghai 6 February for demolition by China National Machinery Import/Export Corp.

334 KALADAN
O.N. 182158   1952–1963

'Kalewa' class
Steel screw motorship
447.5′ × 56.2′ × 24.9′   2844 n   4916 g   8950 d
Built by Lithgows Ltd, Port Glasgow, Yard No 1056, for British & Burmese Steam Navigation Co Ltd (P. Henderson & Co, Managers). Registered Glasgow. Doxford oil engine, opposed

KALADAN *sliding down the ways after being named by Miss Naismith, a Secretary with Henderson Line for 52 years*

*KATHA safely afloat (above), riding light (below left) and in later life as **ACTIVITY** (below right)*

pistons, 2 SCSA 3 cyl 23⅜″–91 5/16″ by D. Rowan & Co Ltd, Glasgow. 2400 bhp, 11 K.

1950 16 June, launched by Miss Naismith. Completed October. 27 October, commenced maiden voyage (Captain K. S. Marsh), United Kingdom–West Africa, on time charter to Elder Dempster Lines Ltd.

1952 30 January, acquired by Elder Dempster Lines Ltd with the purchase of the British & Burmese Steam Navigation Co Ltd.

1963 Sold for £98,000 to Cia de Nav Candria SA, Panama, Renamed **ACTIVITY**. Registered Panama. 2848 n, 4884 g.

1977 30 June, left Dubai in tow for Karachi. 11 July, arrived Gadani Beach. October, demolition commenced.

335 YOMA (I)

O.N. 182084   1952–1964

'Yoma' class

Steel screw steamer

463.0′×60.8′×26.7′   3385 n   5809 g   9920 d

Built by Wm Denny & Bros Ltd, Dumbarton, Yard No 1410, for British & Burmese Steam Navigation Co Ltd (P. Henderson & Co, Managers). Registered Glasgow. Three Parsons steam turbines, SR gearing, by the builders. 5500 shp, 14 K.

Passenger accommodation: 12.

1947 29 October, launched.

1948 April, completed. Trials on 7139 tons displacement, 5744 shp at 101 rpm, 17.08 K.

287

YOMA

Another view of **MARTABAN**

1952 30 January, acquired by Elder Dempster Lines Ltd with the purchase of the British & Burmese Steam Navigation Co Ltd.

1964 Sold to China Merchants Steam Navigation Co Ltd, Taipei. Renamed **HAI PING**. Registered Kaohsiung. 3000 n, 5846 g.

1970 13 February, departed New York on final voyage bound for Keelung. 13 May, sold prior to this date for demolition at Kaohsiung by Heun China Steel Corp.

Ships of the 'Yoma' class: YOMA (335), MARTABAN (336).

Note—**YOMA** did not trade on the West African service.

336 MARTABAN
O.N. 182141   1952–1963

'Yoma' class
Steel screw steamer
461.6′×60.8′×26.1′   3333 n   5740 g   9895 d
Built by Wm Denny & Bros Ltd, Dumbarton, Yard No 1435, for British & Burmese Steam Navigation Co Ltd (P. Henderson & Co, Managers). Registered Glasgow. Three Parsons steam turbines, SR gearing, by the builders. 5500 shp, 14 K.
Passenger accommodation: 12.

1949 6 September, launched.

1952 30 January, acquired by Elder Dempster Lines Ltd with the purchase of the British & Burmese Steam Navigation Co Ltd.

1963 Sold to China Merchants Steam Navigation Co Ltd, Taipei, for £156,650. Renamed **HAI HO**. Registered Kaohsiung. 3000 n, 5139 g.

1971 Sold to Taiwan shipbreakers. 7 July, arrived Kaohsiung for demolition but later resold for further trading to Ken Hsieng Navigation Co Ltd, Taipei. Renamed **KEN HO**.

1975 Sold to Universal Steel Enterprises Co Ltd, and 5 May, sailed from Singapore Roads for Kaohsiung. 21 July, demolition work commenced.

Martaban is a township on the Bilin River, Burma.

Note—**MARTABAN** did not trade on the West African service.

337 KINDAT
O.N. 182142   1952–1962

'Kindat' class
Steel screw motorship
454.9′×58.2′×25.1′   3204 n   5530 g   9000 d
Built by Lithgows Ltd, Port Glasgow, Yard No 1050, for British & Burmese Steam Navigation Co Ltd (P. Henderson & Co, Managers). Registered Glasgow. Doxford oil engine, opposed pistons, 2 SCSA 4 cyl $23\frac{5}{8}″$–$91\frac{5}{16}″$ by D. Rowan & Co Ltd, Glasgow. 3200 bhp, 12 K.

1949 24 November, launched.

1950 4 June, commenced maiden voyage to Australia via Persian Gulf and return, then chartered by Elder Dempster Lines Ltd for the West African trade.

1952 30 January, acquired by Elder Dempster Lines Ltd with the purchase of the British & Burmese Steam Navigation Co Ltd.

1962 Sold to St Thomas Shipping Co Inc, Panama, for £128,000. Renamed **FIDELITY**. Registered Panama. Tmk 3200 n, 5503 g. 4287 n, 7196 g, 9400 d.

1977 Sold for breaking up. 4 April, arrived Faslane for demolition by Shipbreaking Industries Ltd.

Ships of the 'Kindat' class: KINDAT (337), KOYAN (339).

MARTABAN

KINDAT

KADEIK (Photo W. Ralston Ltd)

KOYAN (Photo W. Ralston Ltd)

338 KADEIK
O.N. 184961   1952–1966

Steel screw motorship
454.9′×58.2′×26.7′   4436 n   7489 g   10,200 d
Built by Lithgows Ltd, Port Glasgow, Yard No 1066, for British & Burmese Steam Navigation Co Ltd (P. Henderson & Co, Managers). Registered Glasgow. B & W oil engine 2 SCSA 6 cyl 29⅛″–59¹⁄₁₆″ by J. G. Kincaid & Co Ltd, Greenock. 3300 bhp, 12 K.

1951	15 November, launched.
1952	January, completed. 30 January, acquired by Elder Dempster Lines Ltd with the acquisition of the British & Burmese Steam Navigation Co Ltd. 17 February, commenced maiden voyage, United Kingdom to West Africa.
1956	4363 n.
1966	13 September, sold to Vronca Cia SA, Liberia, for £230,000. Renamed **KYRA KATINA**. Registered Monrovia. 4390 n, 7415 g.
1975	Sold to Hesperus (Panama) SA, Panama. Renamed **AN MING**. Registered Panama.
1977	Sold to Lycus (Panama) SA, Panama. 28 December, in Lagos Roads. Reported abandoned by crew with water in engine room.
1979	24 July, rolled over and sank in a position about three and a half miles south-west of Lagos lighthouse.

Note—**KADEIK** was the last vessel completed for the British & Burmese Steam Navigation Co Ltd before its acquisition by Elder Dempster Lines Ltd. Unlike other 'K' ships she was completed as a Closed Shelter Deck vessel.

339 KOYAN
O.N. 184978   1952–1966

'Kindat' class
Steel screw motorship
454.9′×58.2′×25.1′   3193 n   5537 g   9300 d
Built by Lithgows Ltd, Port Glasgow, Yard No 1075, to the order of British & Burmese Steam Navigation Co Ltd (P. Henderson & Co, Managers). Completed and delivered to Liner Holdings Ltd. Registered Glasgow. B & W oil engine 4 SCSA 6 cyl 29⅛″–59¹⁄₁₆″ by J. G. Kincaid & Co Ltd, Greenock. 3300 bhp, 12 K.

1952	25 June, launched. September, completed. 10 October, commenced maiden voyage, United Kingdom to West Africa.
1966	Sold to Puntamar SA, Panama. Renamed **AUDACITY**. Registered Panama.

1969	August: Tmk 3196 n, 5491 g. 4379 n, 7271 g.
1979	Sold for demolition. 10 January, arrived Aviles, Spain. 5 February, demolition commenced by Desguacee y Salvamentos.

340 KOHIMA (I)
O.N. 184987   1953–1966

'Kohima' class
Steel screw motorship
454.9′×58.2′×25.1′   3182 n   5597 g   9300 d
Built by Lithgows Ltd, Port Glasgow, Yard No 1073, to the order of British & Burmese Steam Navigation Co Ltd (P. Henderson & Co, Managers). Completed and delivered to Liner Holdings Ltd. Registered Glasgow. B & W oil engine 4 SCSA 6 cyl 29⅛″–59¹⁄₁₆″ by J. G. Kincaid & Co Ltd, Greenock. 3300 bhp, 12 K.

1952	13 December, launched by Mrs J. H. Joyce.
1953	20 May, completed. 16 June, commenced maiden voyage, United Kingdom to West Africa.
1966	1 September, sold to Puntar Maritime SA, Panama, for £360,000. Renamed **FESTIVITY**. Registered Panama. Tmk 3300 n, 5578 g. 4510 n, 7405 g.
1977	18 July, aground off Ulsan in position 35°.35′N 129°.28′E, voyage Hampton Roads, USA to Hamburg. 29 July, refloated, considered beyond repair. 9 November, arrived Bilbao for demolition by Herros Ardes.

Ships of the 'Kohima' class: KOHIMA (340), KENTUNG (341), KANDAW (347).

KOHIMA

Kohima is a Burmese town and the site of a famous battle of World War II. This ship was presented with a commemorative plaque by the Burma Star Association. The plaque is now at 'Aulis', the Ocean Transport and Trading Group's Cadet Training Establishment. The War Memorial at Kohima bears the moving lines:

"Tell them of us, and say
For your to-morrow
We gave our to-day."

PATANI, before heightening of funnel

KENTUNG

341 KENTUNG

O.N. 185017   1954–1966

'Kohima' class
Steel screw motorship
455.1′×58.2′×25.0′   3093 n   5558 g   9325 d
Built by Wm Denny & Bros Ltd, Dumbarton, Yard No 1465, for British & Burmese Steam Navigation Co Ltd (P. Henderson & Co, Managers). Registered Glasgow. B & W oil engine 4 SCSA 6 cyl engine 29$\frac{1}{8}$″–59$\frac{1}{16}$″ by J. G. Kincaid & Co Ltd, Greenock. 3300 bhp, 12 K.

1951   March, ordered.
1954   29 July, launched. October completed. Trials 3215 bhp at 115.75 rpm, displacement 8580 tons, 13.95 K.
1966   9 December, sold to Puntamar SA, Panama. Renamed **TENACITY**. Registered Panama, Tmk 3263 n, 5543 g. 4518 n, 7439 g.
1972   Sold to Cia de Navegacion Jaspes SA, Lugano (International Service Lugano). Registered Panama.
1978   Transferred to Cia de Navegacion Jaspes SA, Panama. Renamed **BERENIX**.
1979   Sold to Five Oceans Shipping Corp, Panama. Renamed **MERCY FIVE**.
1980   Sold to Taiwan shipbreaker. 15 May, sailed from Hong Kong. 5 June, arrived Kaohsiung and broken up by Nan Long Steel & Iron Co.

342 PATANI (II)

O.N. 185495   1954–1972

'Patani' class
Steel screw motorship
449.9′×60.3′×26.0′   3312 n   6183 g   10,417 d
Built by Scotts' Shipbuilding & Engineering Co Ltd, Greenock, Yard No 663, for Elder Dempster Lines Ltd. Registered Liverpool. Doxford oil engine, opposed pistons, 2 SCSA 4 cyl 560 mm×2160 mm by the builders. 2800 bhp, 11 K.

1954   22 April, launched by Mrs A. E. Muirhead. August, completed. 8 September, commenced maiden voyage (Captain R. M. McWilliam).
1964   Funnel heightened.
1972   31 October, sold to Globe Navigation Ltd, Hong Kong. Renamed **PATWARI**. Registered Mogadishu. Tmk 3347 n, 6049 g, 10,310 d, 4479 n, 7877 g.
1977   Sold to Vertigo Shipping Co Ltd, Karachi. Registered Limassol.
1978   Sold to Pakistani shipbreakers. 27 January, arrived Karachi. 9 February, moved to Gadani Beach. May demolition commenced.

Ship of the 'Patani' class: PATANI (342), PERANG (343).

343 PERANG

O.N. 185506   1954–1972

'Patani' class
Steel screw motorship
449.9′×60.4′×26.0′   3439 n   6177 g   10,060 d

KENTUNG

PERANG, after heightening of funnel

Built by Wm Gray & Co Ltd, Hartlepool, Yard No 1267, for Elder Dempster Lines Ltd. Registered Liverpool. Doxford oil engine, opposed pistons, 2 SCSA 4 cyl 560 mm–2160 mm by Scotts' Shipbuilding & Engineering Co Ltd, Greenock. 2800 bhp, 12 K.

1954 30 August, launched by Mrs D. H. Tod. December, Completed.
1955 Maiden voyage (Captain W. R. Brown).
1964 Funnel heightened.
1972 12 June, sold to Agnic Shipping Corp. Renamed **AGNIC**. Registered Piraeus.
1974 10,221 d.
1978 Sold to Pakistani shipbreakers. 3 April, left Mina Gaboos for Karachi. 7 May, arrived Gadani Beach. June, demolition commenced.

344 OWERRI (I)
O.N. 185512   1955–1972

'Onitsha' class
Steel screw motorship, open shelter deck
450.0′×62.3′×23.0′   3371 n   6240 g   7697 d
Built by Harland & Wolff Ltd, Belfast, Yard No 1479, for Elder Dempster Lines Ltd. Registered Liverpool. B & W oil engine 2 SCSA 5 cyl 620 mm–1400 mm by the builders. 3750 bhp, 13 K.
Passenger accommodation: 12.

1954 14 October, launched by Mrs J. C. Cadbury.
1955 January, completed. Maiden voyage (Captain A. M. Scobbie, OBE).
1972 21 July, sold for £110,000 to Maldives Shipping Ltd (Maldivian Nationals Trading Corporation (Ceylon) Ltd, Colombo). Renamed **MALDIVE COURAGE**. Registered Male (Maldivian flag). 2951 n, 5798 g, 7820 d.
1983 Sold to Pakistani shipbreakers. 26 March, left Jeddah for demolition at Gadani Beach, Karachi, and arrived 28 March when demolition by Ali & Co commenced immediately, completed April.

Owerri (corruption of Owera) is a town in Eastern Nigeria, 65 miles to the north of Port Harcourt by road.

Above, Mrs John Cadbury launching **OWERRI**. *Below,* **OWERRI**

The M.V. *Owerri* just after she had been launched on October 14, 1954, at Messrs Harland & Wolff's Belfast Yard by Mrs John Cadbury, wife of Mr John Cadbury, Chairman of the West African Merchants' Freight Association. The *Owerri* will go into service early in 1955.   *From Sea magazine*

345 OTI (I)

O.N. 187135   1956–1972

'Oti' class

Steel screw motorship, open shelter deck

450.0′×62.3′×23.0′   2780 n   5485 g   7840 d

Built by Harland & Wolff Ltd, Belfast, Yard No 1546, for Elder Dempster Lines Ltd. Registered Liverpool. B & W oil engine 2 SCSA 5 cyl 620 mm–1400 mm (exhaust 470 mm) by the builders. 3750 bhp, 13 K.

1955   15 December, launched by Miss Anne Muirhead.

1956   April 25–26, trials. 13 May, commenced maiden voyage from Liverpool (Captain W. E. Humphreys).

1958   15 July, first vessel to enter Tema harbour, Ghana.

1967   October, transferred to Ocean Steamship Co Ltd for 11 days, but intended voyage to Far East did not materialise.

1972   17 May, sold to Mimimeth Shipping Ltd, Greece. Renamed **MIMI METHENITIS**. Registered Famagusta. 2780 n, 5458 g 8009 d.

1976   Sold to Goldbeach Shipping Co Ltd, Cyprus. Renamed **GOLDBEACH**. Registered Limassol.

1977   Sold to Medina Maritime SA, Cyprus. Renamed **NICOLAS K**.

1979   Sold to Valmay Shipping Co Ltd, Cyprus. 26 December, sold for demolition by An Hsiung Iron & Steel Co, Kaohsiung.

Ships of the 'Oti' class: OTI (345), ONDO (346).

Note—**OTI** was the first vessel in the Elder Dempster fleet to be fitted with inert gas fire extinguishers in the cargo holds.

Oti is the name of a large tributary of the Volta River. It flows southerly in the north-east of the territory of Ghana.

Two views of **OTI**

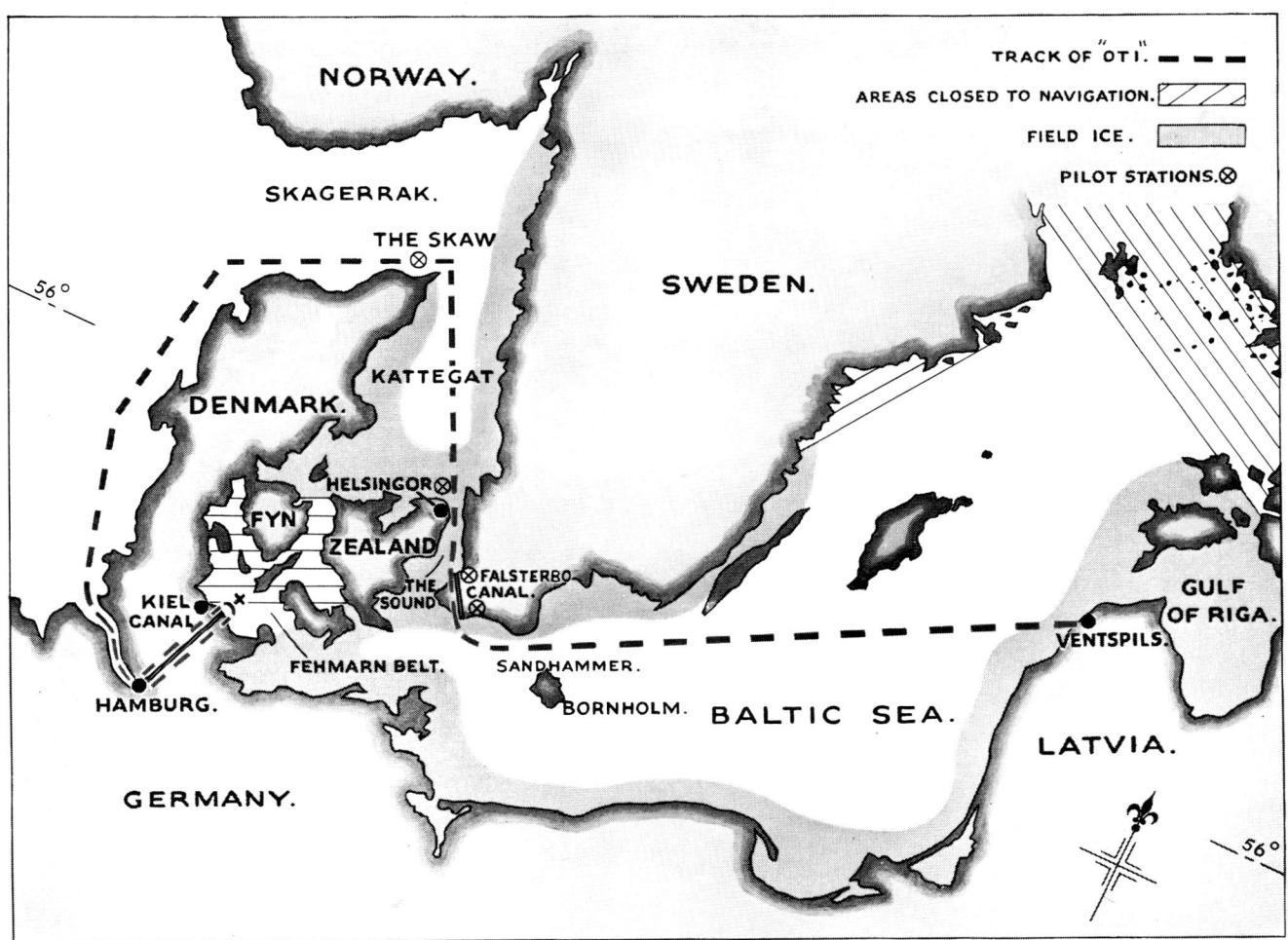

Journey Into Ice

by

Captain F. Weller

(*Who served as Staff Captain for the* Oti's *Baltic voyage*)

IN the severest winter of the century 47,000 tons of cocoa ordered by Russia from Ghana had to be shipped to Baltic ports. The M.V. *Oti* was chosen to carry one cargo from Tema to Ventspils and on February 8, 1963, Captain Ness had to decide which route to take through the ever increasing ice-fields

As a powerful Russian tanker was reported to be going to Kiel next day to convoy the Russian ships in Kiel Bay through the Fehmarn Belt to the comparatively ice-free eastern coasts, Captain Ness made up his mind to use the Canal route. Weather reports were gloomy, but the *Oti* made her way down the Elbe from Hamburg, followed by small coasters making for the sea.

The Brunsbüttel locks had been efficiently cleared of ice but the passage along the Canal was difficult. Ice three

feet thick reduced the *Oti*'s pace to five knots at Full Speed. Progress was a monotonous repetition of stickin g reversing, shaking free and breaking away.

About 5.30 p.m. the *Oti* reached the 71 kilometre passing and got the halt signal. A low-powered ship was ice-bound two miles ahead and the ice soon held us firm. The temperature dropped to 16° F. but coffee or hot soup, thanks to our able Chief Steward, served every two hours or so, kept the cold at bay. The arrival of tugs from Kiel mended matters and the rest of the journey through the Canal was uneventful.

Once inside the locks at Kiel the Master's cabin filled with people. The Agent's representative assured us that the Russian tanker would cut through the ice like a hot knife through butter. The Bay and Baltic pilots were less encouraging: conditions were shocking, they said, and only a breaker from Poland or Russia could clear a passage. The Agent added that conditions had worsened in the previous twenty-four hours, and the tug *Pacific* reported ice a metre thick from the lightship to Buoy 8.

We left the locks in the early hours of February 10 to anchor until day-break in the bay. The 'knife' followed a little later, anchoring slightly ahead of us. Only the officer of the watch and the watchman saw her: the rest of us were tired out and sound asleep. Beyond the four ships stretched the vast expanse of 'butter', blue and white, steely and forbidding. Captain Ness, who was experiencing ice for the first time, awaited the rigours of the day.

At dawn the four ships in the convoy broke easily through the channel cleared by the *Pacific*, West Germany's most powerful tug. At the lightship the Bay pilots disembarked. The tanker led the way into the buoyed channel, the *Oti* followed and the *Pacific* raced on to clear a path to Buoy 8. After one mile the tanker struck the first real pack-ice and stopped dead. The *Oti* raced up and by going hard over to starboard broke a path alongside the helpless knife, which had proved too blunt for such hard butter. Three cables on and the tanker had to be freed again. I glanced over the side and saw rafted ice in a pack three feet thick. No wonder we had made only a mile in three hours. Yet the *Oti* proved the most manoeuvrable of all the ships.

COASTER TO THE RESCUE

About noon the *Pacific* returned and cleared a double track. On the move again we staggered for some three miles and then stuck. The tanker failed to free us. Luckily a very fast and powerful coaster led us all to a wide area where the winter ice had cracked. Here our company broke up. The tanker pressed forward, forced a wide path through the pressure ridge and the belt of hummocky ice and disappeared over the horizon. The two weaker vessels turned round and headed back for Kiel. Captain Ness followed the tanker's track in search of clear water.

One mile forward and we stuck for half an hour. Then we had the best run of the day through smooth winter ice before coming up with our old friend the tanker, stuck once again. For the third time Captain Ness freed the captive. Then, hearing from the *Pacific* that ice ahead was up to three metres thick, he thought it pointless to proceed. With the *Pacific*'s help he turned round. It was 5 p.m.: in ten hours we had covered nine miles. In the wake of the *Pacific* we made our way back to Kiel at a good four knots.

The news of our plight was sent to Head Office that night and we made our way back to Brunsbüttel with the thermometer at 10° F. We were amazed to see workmen building wooden pathways over the Canal at three different points. Through the night ice bulletins followed in disheartening succession:

Flensburg—closed to navigation: Weser—24 hours delay: Little Belt—navigation without breakers not advisable: Drogden Channel—closed; breakers assist all vessels into Copenhagen, an open lead runs down the Swedish coast, navigation by high-powered vessels possible through the Flintrannan Channel: Skaw—open drift ice: Kattegat—new ice drifting, floes, some rafting: southern Entrance to Sound—navigation for high-powered vessels only but not without difficulty, ice-breakers assisting.

At 5 a.m. I handed the decoded messages to Captain Ness and turned in. At anchor in the Elbe the Captain read and re-read the bulletins, wondering whether the northern passage was still possible. One sentence determined his course of action: 'An open lead runs down the Swedish coast.' By 7 a.m. on February 11 the anchor was home and the *Oti* headed down the river.

Throughout the 11th and the morning of the 12th the *Oti* beat north in fairly good weather towards the Skaw. Pilots were working off Skaw station and apart from scattered floes there was little ice between Skaw and the Anholt light. But the outlook in the whole of the Baltic area was depressing with one exception—there was still an open lead off the Swedish coast through the Flintrannan Channel, navigable only by high-powered steamers, and ice-breakers could not guarantee help in the Sound.

Once we were south-east of the Anholt light, new ice, young ice and pancake ice covered wide areas. There were occasional patches of drift ice too. By the time the Kattegat lightship was abeam the *Oti* was vibrating slightly as she broke through ice an inch thick. The temperature was down to 8° F. and rafting worsened the conditions of the ice. Luckily the steam heating modifications to the water lines and the stiffening for the main suction inlets, fitted after the lessons of the *Dunkwa*'s voyage to Leningrad had been studied, were working well.

We approached the pilot station off Helsingor. In these waters, I reflected, Nelson had made history by putting the telescope to his blind eye 160 years ago. But there had been no ice to bar his progress when he attacked the Danish fleet. The pilot came aboard and told the Captain that 40 ships were stuck fast or delayed in the ice at the entrance to the Sound. Ice-breakers could free only six or seven ships a day and the *Oti*'s chances of getting through were remote.

"The Falsterbo Canal is open and the sea off Sandhammer is ice-free," said Captain Ness. "We will go that way."

"I never heard of a ship this size going through the Canal," exclaimed the pilot in surprise.

"Take us to Malmo Roads," insisted the Captain, "and we will contact our Agents."

The Third Mate re-checked the *Oti*'s measurements: 23-ft. draft, 65-ft. beam. The passage through the Canal was possible. We went Full Ahead into the heavy drift and pack ice round Vem. The *Oti* shuddered under the impact of the rafted floes and her speed dropped. A call was put through by radio telephone to the Agent and we were advised to anchor for the night in Malmo Roads. Our Danish pilot called the Swedish pilot station at Malmo, giving the *Oti*'s draft and beam and telling him that the Captain wished to use Falsterbo. The Malmo pilot station replied that the maximum draft was now only 21-ft.

"Master advises that he can lighten to 20.06," answered our Danish pilot.

"Will board you a.m. but can give no assurance that pilot will take you—Goodnight," came the reply.

At 5 a.m. on February 14 the Swedish pilot was on board. We picked up our anchor and set off once more. Ice in the Falsterbo Channel was at least two inches thick but well broken-up. The channel into Falsterbo was also broken up, but fast winter ice over a foot thick clung to both sides. We pressed slowly on, passing several small coasting craft and watching some boys fishing through holes cut in the ice. We entered the western lock gates and passed between edgings of thick ice, cleared the eastern lock and were into the almost open water that stretched towards Trelleborg. The pilot, after telling us that the *Oti* was the biggest ship to have used the Canal, disembarked

As far as the eye can see, a pitiless desert of ice. The Oti *was trapped again and again*

with Captain Ness's thanks. Then came the order: 'Engines Full Ahead!'

What a relief it was to be in the open sea again. We ran happily through young ice and huge areas of pancake and new ice. This tinkled and sparkled when the ship's bow shattered it. Some 40 miles from Ventspils the *Oti* ran into vast blankets of winter ice, but despite vibrations she scarcely lost a knot in speed. Ten miles further on the ice was an inch thick and the thickness increased, with occasional pressure ridges. The wind had been little above force 3 for three days and ice formed with fantastic rapidity.

A buoy ahead warned us to alter course and keep the ship steady for some leading towers. About 2 p.m. on February 16 the Russian pilot came aboard between the breakwater at Ventspils. We had made it! All our hopes had been justified: the *Oti* began to discharge her cargo that night.

The week in Ventspils was full of interest. The ice bulletins were ominous. For three nights in succession the temperature was zero, the waters of the Baltic at freezing point or below. Two days before we left the wind veered slowly from east to south and south-west. Enormous ice areas off East Denmark and further south on the Polish and German coasts began to break and drift northwards. Overnight Malmo Roads were blocked and the Norwegian and Swedish coasts became un-navigable. Trouble loomed everywhere. To crown all, on sailing day, February 20, Russian bulletins reported very close pack and drift ice for 30 miles off the Latvian coast, with navigation for high-powered vessels only.

Doubtful of our fortunes we left Ventspils Full Ahead for two miles—to become stuck in heavy pack ice. Freeing ourselves was a laborious job in a ship lightened of cargo. We went Slow Ahead, now and then giving the engines Full Astern to get a shudder out of the ship. The ballast tanks had to be filled or emptied to alter the ship's water plane, a good two hours' work each time. Sludge ice filled and froze in the injections, which had to be unblocked.

To head north-west up the swept channel was impossible, for the ice was hummocky and we could see jagged vertical ice sheets caused by pressure ridges for miles ahead. Our only hope lay in a lead to the south-west which had to be entered a mile astern of our position. About noon we were free and set out for the open water. For five long hours we heard the reports from the officers: "Lead to Starboard, Sir," or "Pack ice ahead but only a neck; lead opens up beyond, Sir." Twice we failed to break through the necks but about 6 p.m. a westerly lead led to clear waters and we we left the coastal pack ice behind. Only 13 miles in nine hours, but we were free: the *Oti* went Full Ahead again.

Difficulties recurred but we made Falsterbo to find the Canal open despite the ice formations. The pilot came on board without delay and we passed slowly through the Canal. Deserted summer houses on each side stirred memories of forgotten sunny days. Boys waved to us. They were out with guns, helping to free swans or shooting those beyond help. The pilot warned Captain Ness that the southerly wind was making the Sound hourly more dangerous: the Danish side was navigable but hard going. There was no pilot at Halsinborg, though anchorage was safe.

Through the Flintrannan Channel we went, the *Oti* shuddering, her speed sometimes down to three knots. The grinding of the ice along her sides was worse than anything we had yet encountered. After six hours of this gruelling course the pilot disembarked and half an hour later we dropped anchor off the Danish coast. It was about midnight. Weary with their two days' exertions the *Oti*'s crew slept without stirring.

Daylight on February 22 brought new hopes. Ice bulletins showed that Way 36 was the best route west. The East Jutland coasts were comparatively free of ice: those of Norway and Sweden were impassable. The wind was south-west and far away stretched a desert of unbroken ice. A Polish freighter altered course and broke a path down our starboard side as we hove anchor. We appreciated the gesture. Course was set south of the Kattegat lightship, still miraculously in position. A German freighter, the *Gisela Russ*, having a tough time to port, joyfully altered course and fell in behind, to be joined in the next few hours by two other small craft.

Twice we stuck and twice got free immediately. On one occasion when Captain Ness had gone below we came to a halt and the engines were stopped. The Captain returned to the bridge just as a sharp crack was heard and we saw the ice opening up for fully half-a-mile ahead.

By noon the ice-fields were penetrated by great leads which wound through them. The *Oti*'s speed picked up and despite brief encounters with narrow necks or isthmuses progress became easier all the time. By 5 p.m. we had said goodbye to our enemy the ice and were running up the East Jutland coast. Water, water everywhere, and lapping gently along the ship's sides.

Above us in the radio room Sparks was tapping out the happy message: "Our time of arrival at Hamburg is . . ." The *Oti* and her crew were safely back from the ice-fields.

From Sea *magazine*

The M.V. Oti, under the command of Captain W. R. Bayley, was the first ocean-going liner to berth at Tema Harbour last summer

Our M.V. Oti first at Tema

THE M.V. *Oti* is a ship associated with 'first' occasions; not only was she the first ship in the world to be fitted with the 'Pyrene–E.D.–Hol' Fire Fighting System developed by our Company, but she has achieved another 'first' by being the first ocean-going liner to berth in the uncompleted harbour at Tema, under the command of Captain W. R. Bayley, who gave a most impressive performance in the way he put the ship alongside the quay. She berthed at Tema in order to unload heavy lift cranes from the United States which are being used in the construction of the harbour. The cranes cost £110,000 and have a lifting capacity of 110 tons. The cranes were too heavy for road transportation from Takoradi where it was originally planned they should be unloaded. Many prominent people were present to welcome the arrival of the *Oti*, including Mr Justice Van-Lare and his wife, Nene Lanimo Opata II, Hiowe Manche of Shai, Nii Kwabena Bonne III, Osu Alata Manche, and also a member of the Tema Development Corporation, Nii Agbo Kofi Nyado, the Nayo Wulomo of Tema, the Tema Manche, Nii Adjetey Ansah II, Mr Bediako Poku, General Secretary of the Convention People's Party, representing the Prime Minister, Dr Kwame Nkrumah. A libation was poured for the safe arrival of the ship by the Nayo Wulomo, Nii Agbo Kofi. The occasion attracted a large number of journalists and the aerial photograph of the *Oti*, which appears on this page, was printed in many newspapers in this country and throughout the world.

The construction of the twelve and a half million

pound Tema Harbour is being carried out by Parkinson Howard Limited. Sir William Halcrow and Partners are the consulting engineers. The Harbour is due to be completed in 1960. It will have a four-berth quay, dockyard, oil berth, fishing harbour and slipways. It will provide safe anchorage in 42 feet of water. The two cocoa sheds shown on the left of the photograph are the largest clear span buildings outside the United States.

Mr J. C. Lucas, who was present to welcome the Oti *on her arrival at Tema, took this photograph of the heavy lift crane being unloaded*

From Sea *magazine*

EVACUATION FROM SAPELE

by Captain R. Munro, Master of Oti

On August 9, 1967 while we were passing Cowan Estate, on passage from Warri to Sapele, we received a message from the Lobito Palm at Warri, to say that they were evacuating some of the expatriate population of Sapele, mainly women and children, because there had been a coup in the Mid-West State and it was suspected that trouble was heading towards Sapele.

When we arrived at Sapele, women and children had begun to gather with their suitcases on a lawn fronting a house by the river. The Sapele Agent asked me to go ashore immediately to discuss a message he had received from Lagos indicating that, if it was humanly possible, I should embark as many people as were able to leave. We made fast with two slip wires at No. 8 buoys, in case there should be no labour to let go mooring ropes, and left the engines on stand-by I warned the Agent that the embarkation would need to be carried out quickly because the first safe anchorage was nine miles away at Yoruba Island. The second was 15 miles away at Fagan Island. Since there was a possibility of Biafran troops driving down the road from Benin to Nanatown and sealing off the Creek it was advisable to get past Nanatown at night. This depended on how long the embarkation would take and how much daylight remained.

We began embarking in the afternoon by launch and tug from a small pier, and finished in just over an hour. Ten minutes later *Oti* let go her moorings and began her passage downstream with a total of 66 children and 55 adults on board. During the embarkation, all members of the crew had assisted with the children and with the baggage. Officers and Petty Officers cleared their own rooms where possible and arranged to double up with other Officers to make room for the evacuees.

In view of the need to reach a safe anchorage, *Oti* maintained full speed, and at the same time, I noted a Protest against any claims which might arise from the fact that we were proceeding at full speed past log rafts and moored lighters.

We reached the first anchorage while there was still some daylight, and I therefore decided to proceed to the second anchorage at Fagan Island. Floodlights were removed from the main mast and fitted on the fo'c's'le head in case we should be caught in a narrow stretch when it became dark. In actual fact, these proved to be of little use as they did not throw a sufficiently strong beam to light up the banks. It was easier to steam in the dusk without them as the banks showed up quite clearly.

We reached Fagan Island just as it became dark, but as the river widens here, I decided to continue and pass Nanatown. Eventually I anchored off Bluff Point. By this time, conditions were unsuitable for further progress as it began to rain and visibility was reduced. We left at first light the following morning, and from then on the passage was uneventful. *Oti* eventually cleared Escravos Bar and we reached Lagos on the evening of August 10. The following morning we berthed at Apapa. Disembarkation of evacuees began immediately and was completed within the hour.

From Sea *magazine*

346 ONDO
O.N. 187146   1956–1962

'Oti' class
Steel screw motorship, open shelter deck
450.0′×62.3′×23.0′   2758 n   5435 g   8000 d
Built by Harland & Wolff Ltd, Belfast, Yard No 1554, for Elder Dempster Lines Ltd. Registered Liverpool. B & W oil engine 2 SCSA 5 cyl 620 mm–1400 mm (exhaust 470 mm), by the builders. 3750 bhp, 13 K.

1956   7 June, launched by Mrs A. C. Dove. October, completed. 7 November, commenced maiden voyage from Liverpool (Captain R. M. McWilliam).

1961   6 December, whilst on voyage Sapele to Riga (cargo cocoa beans) **ONDO** was making for the Kiel Canal locks at Brunsbuttelkoog. At 1715 as the Cuxhaven pilot boat was approaching in very heavy weather, wind Force 10, it capsized. In an effort to avoid danger to the men in the water, Captain W. L. Farquhar of the **ONDO** stopped the engines and the ship was blown on to the sandbank near Elbe No 2 lightship. The pilot and the boat's crew were lost. **ONDO** was lightened but could not be refloated. The wreck was abandoned in March 1962 and purchased by Helmutts Wolff, Wilhelmshaven, and Uwe Truhen, Cuxhaven, for DM 80,000 in 1968,

ONDO

but all efforts to salvage were unsuccessful. A Dutch company bought the wreck in 1970 for DM 50,000 and also failed to refloat **ONDO**. In 1975 a Herr Fadian of Hamburg purchased the wreck for DM 30,000.

Ondo is both a province and its chief town in the rain forest region of Nigeria.

Two views of **ONDO** *aground*

Another view of the ill-fated **ONDO**

KADUNA

347 KANDAW

O.N. 185021   1955–1967

'Kohima' class
Steel screw motorship
455.0′×58.3′×25.1′   3126 n   5599 g   9300 d
Built by Lithgows Ltd, Port Glasgow, Yard No 1088, for British & Burmese Steam Navigation Co Ltd (P. Henderson & Co, Managers). Registered Glasgow. B & W oil engine 4 SCSA 6 cyl 740 mm–1500 mm by J. G. Kincaid & Co Ltd, Greenock. 3300 bhp, 12½ K.

1954   14 December, launched by Mrs P. J. D. Toosey.
1955   March, completed. 7 April, commenced maiden voyage (Captain J. S. Grassick), Liverpool to West Africa.
1964   1 May, transferred to Elder Dempster Lines Ltd.
1967   14 September, sold for £235,000 to Naviera Ceresio SA, Panama. Renamed **HONESTY**. Registered Panama. Tmk 3199 n, 5479 g. 4442 n, 7379 g, 11,500 d.
1975   Sold to Nogamar SA, Panama.
1977   22 November, laid up at La Spezia.
1978   2 February, sold for demolition by CNS Maria at Spezia.

Ships of the 'Kandaw' class: KANDAW (347), KADUNA (348).

348 KADUNA (II)

O.N. 185039   1956–1973

Steel screw motorship
455.0′×58.3′×25.1′   3126 n   5599 g   9301 d
Built by Lithgows Ltd, Port Glasgow, Yard No 1098, for British & Burmese Steam Navigation Co Ltd (P. Henderson & Co, Managers). Registered Glasgow. B & W oil engine 4 SCSA 6 cyl 740 mm–1500 mm by J. G. Kincaid & Co Ltd, Greenock. 3300 bhp, 12½ K.

1956   16 January, launched. April, completed. 13 April, commenced maiden voyage (Captain J. C. Gibson), United Kingdom to West Africa.
1972   On temporary transfer during the year to China Mutual Steam Navigation Co Ltd.
1973   7 April, sold to Regent Navigation Shipping Corp, Liberia. Renamed **REGENT RELIANCE**. Registered Singapore.
1975   Registry transferred to Panama. Tmk 3095 n, 5412 g. 4283 n, 7236 g, 11,573 d.
1978   February. Sold to Z. M. Industries. 22 April, arrived Gadani Beach for demolition.

KANDAW

Lady Hobhouse about to launch **EGORI** (Photo J. Weir)

349 EGORI (II)
O.N. 187158   1957–1978

Steel screw motorship
509.0′×64.3′×27.8′   4558 n   8586 g   10,300 d
Built by Scotts' Shipbuilding & Engineering Co Ltd, Greenock,
Yard No 673, for Elder Dempster Lines Ltd. Registered Liverpool. Doxford oil engine, opposed pistons, 2 SCSA 6 cyl
670 mm–2320 mm by the builders. 9000 bhp, 16 K.

1956	12 June, launched by Lady Hobhouse.
1957	27 February, completed. 16 March, commenced maiden voyage (Captain A. M. Scobbie, OBE).
1972	Transferred to China Mutual Steam Navigation Co Ltd for one round voyage to Far East, then reverted to Elder Dempster Lines Ltd. Tmk 2734 n, 6241 g, 8315 d. 4493 n, 8331 g, 10,593 d.
1978	6 September, sold to Ali Khalifa Mirchandani Shipping Co Ltd, Kuwait. Renamed **AZZA**. Registered Kuwait.
1979	Sold to A1 Navigation Ltd, Kuwait. Subsequently sold to Li Chong Iron Works Co Ltd for demolition. 9 October, arrived Kaohsiung. 11 October, delivered.

EGORI

CALABAR *as depicted on an Elder Dempster postcard used to illustrate* **CALABAR** *and* **WINNEBA**

350 CALABAR (IV)
O.N. 164664   1957–1963

'Calabar' class
Steel twin screw steamer
451.4′×61.2′×32.1′   5083 n   8162 g   7200 d
Built by Swan Hunter & Wigham Richardson Ltd, Newcastle,
Yard No 1492, for Bullard King & Co Ltd, as **UMTALI**.
Registered London. 2×T 3 cyl 22½″, 38″, 63″–39″ and 2 LP turbines DR gearing by the builders. 7550 hp, 13½ K.
Passenger accommodation: 105, one class.

1936	July, completed.
1940	7 September, damaged in air attack on London. 11 September, again damaged in air attack
1941	26 April, helped rescue survivors from ss MOUNTPARK, which had been bombed and sunk in position 56°.17′N 12°.24′W.
1953	November, fitted for oil burning.
1957	26 April, acquired by Elder Dempster Lines Ltd. Renamed **CALABAR**. Registered Liverpool. 4903 n, 8305 g. Operated on Tilbury–West Africa service. First voyage (Captain P. M. Ralston).
1962	November, sold for £45,000 for demolition.
1963	6 January, arrived at Inverkeithing for demolition by T. W. Ward Ltd.

Ships of the 'Calabar' class: CALABAR (350), WINNEBA (351).
Umtali is a town in Zimbabwe.

351 WINNEBA (II)
O.N. 166451   1957–1963

'Calabar' class
Steel twin screw steamer
451.4′×61.2′×32.1′   5052 n   8180 g   7200 d
Built by Swan Hunter & Wigham Richardson Ltd, Newcastle,
Yard No 1556, for Bullard King & Co Ltd, as **UMGENI**.
Registered London. 2×T 3 cyl 22½″, 38″, 63″–39″ and 2 LP turbines DR gearing by the builders. 7550 hp, 13½ K.
Passenger accommodation: 105, one class.

1938	May, completed.
1940	7 September, severely damaged in air attack on London.
1941	21 May, attacked by Focke-Wulf bomber. This aircraft was shot down with the first round from the ship's 12 pounder.
1954	December, fitted for oil burning.
1957	26 April, acquired by Elder Dempster Lines Ltd. Renamed **WINNEBA**. Registered Liverpool. 4923 n, 8355 g, 7362 d. Operated on Tilbury–West Africa service. First voyage (Captain W. R. Rowlands).
1963	26 January, sold for £50,000 for demolition to Jos de Sweat, Antwerp.

Umgeni is a river in Natal.

ELDER DEMPSTER LINES, LIMITED.

PASSENGER ACCOMMODATION PLAN

s.s. "WINNEBA" & s.s. "CALABAR"

8,300 Tons

GRADING OF PASSENGER ACCOMMODATION

TYPE OF ACCOMMODATION	DECK	CABIN NUMBER	GRADE PER PASSENGER
SINGLE BERTH CABINS	C	1, 2, 3, 4, 5, 6	L 2
TWO BERTH CABINS	C	7, 8, 9, 10, 11, 12, 13, 14, 15, 16, 17, 18, 19, 20, 21	L 2
TWO BERTH CABINS	D	24, 26, 28, 30, 32, 34, 36, 38, 40, 42, 44,	L
THREE BERTH CABINS	D	23, 29, 31, 37, 39, 45, 46, 47	L
THREE BERTH CABINS (with additional Pullman Berth)	D	25, 27, 33, 35, 41, 43	L

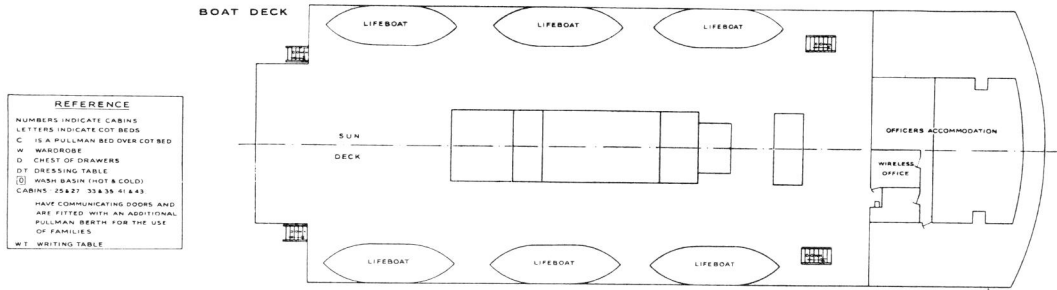

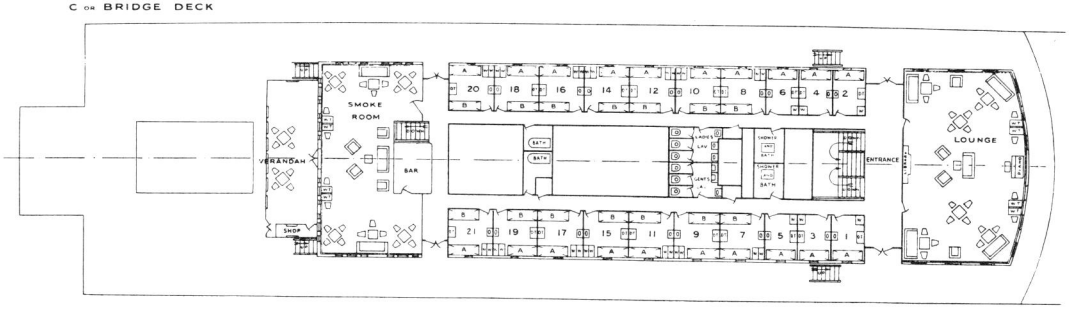

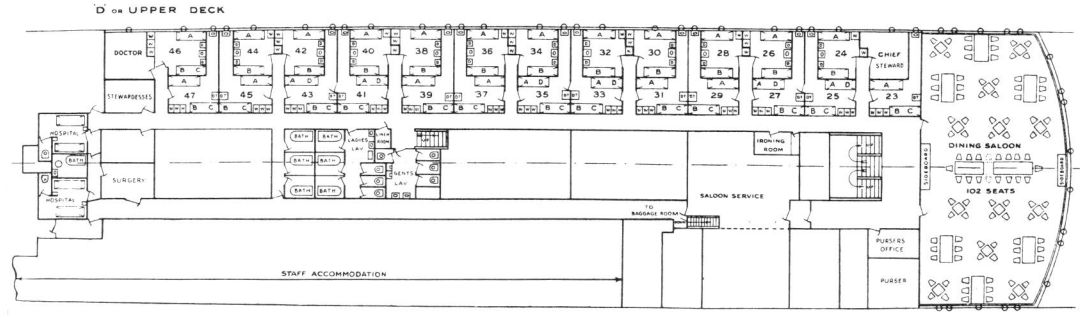

UMGENI, *subsequently* **WINNEBA**, *on a Bullard King & Co Ltd postcard similarly used to portray two ships*

WINNEBA (Photo Kunle Olatunde)

302

HILARY, *with Elder Dempster funnel colour* (Photo K. P. Lewis)

352 HILARY
O.N. 162350   1956–1957

Steel screw steamer
442.0′×56.2′×24.6′   4206 n   7415 g   6179 d
Built by Cammell Laird & Co Ltd, Yard No 975, for Booth
Steamship Co Ltd. Registered Liverpool. T 3 cyl 29″, 48½″,
81½″–57″ and LP steam turbine, DR gearing, by the builders.
6000 ihp, 14½ K.
Passenger accommodation: 80 first class, 250 third.

1931   17 April, launched. August, completed.
1941   January, requisitioned for service as an ocean boarding
       vessel. 3 May, intercepted Italian tanker RECCO about
       350 miles north of the Azores but was unable to prevent
       the crew from scuttling her. 10 May, intercepted Italian
       tanker GINNA M 325 miles north of the Azores and put
       prize crew aboard to sail her to Belfast.
1942   15 April, paid off.
1943   March, converted for service as Infantry Landing ship,
       and bridge armoured and boat deck stiffened. July,
       participated in the invasion of Sicily as HQ ship of Rear-
       Admiral Sir Philip Vian. Subsequently took part in the
       Salerno landings. December, returned to the United
       Kingdom.
1944   Based at Portsmouth. 6 June, served as flagship of Force
       J in the Normandy landings.
1945   January, sailed for the Clyde and subsequently recon-
       ditioned for normal service. Passenger accommodation
       now 93 first, 138 tourist.
1946   September, made a voyage to West Africa on the Elder
       Dempster berth. Subsequently returned to her owners
       South American service.
1956   Chartered by Elder Dempster Lines Ltd for four voyages
       to West Africa while their ACCRA and APAPA were
       undergoing refit. During this time her funnel was painted
       buff. HILARY continued to be manned by her owners
       except that Elder Dempster Pursers R. Worthington and
       T. Flatley joined her. The surgeon, Dr J Llewellyn-

Jones, although a Booth Line employee, had previously
served with Elder Dempster aboard TARKWA and
ACCRA.
1957   Reverted to owners service on termination of charter.
1959   Sold for demolition. 15 September, arrived at T. W.
       Ward Ltd, Inverkeithing. Subsequently slightly dama-
       ged by explosion and fire aboard a tanker lying alongside
       whilst demolition was in progress.

353 BHAMO
O.N. 300188   1957–1979

Steel screw motorship
470.0′×60.0′×26.5′   3098 n   5932 g   9650 d
Built by Lithgows Ltd, Port Glasgow, Yard No 1118, for British
& Burmese Steam Navigation Co Ltd (P. Henderson & Co,
Managers). Registered Glasgow. B & W oil engine 2 SCSA 4 cyl
750 mm–1500 mm (exhaust 500 mm) by J. G. Kincaid & Co
Ltd, Greenock. 5850 bhp, 14 K.

BHAMO on trials (Photo W. Ralston Ltd)

Above, **BHAMO** *entering the water flying both the Elder Dempster and Henderson Line flags. From* Sea *magazine. Below another view of* **BHAMO** *running trials* (Photo W. Ralston Ltd)

1957 24 September launched by Madame Aung Soe. Completed December.
1958 15 January, commenced maiden voyage (Captain J. Walker-Brown), United Kingdom to Burma.
1967 Allocated to Guinea Gulf Line Ltd service.
1968 Transferred to the management of Roxburgh, Henderson & Co.
1975 3098 n, 5932 g, 9801 d.
1979 14 April, sold to Globe Navigation Ltd, Victoria, Hong Kong, for US$390,000. Renamed **BHAMOT**. For final voyage loaded a full cargo of phosphates at Casablanca for the Far East, thence sold to Taiwan shipbreakers. 10 July, arrived Kaohsiung. 20 July, demolition work began by Chi Young Steel Enterprise.

Bhamo is a town in Burma, 60 miles east of Katha.

KABALA

KUMBA (Photo Skyfotos)

354 KUMBA
O.N. 300212   1958–1973

'Kumba' class
Steel screw motorship
454.9′×58.3′×25.1′   2996 n   5439 g   9400 d
Built by Lithgows Ltd, Port Glasgow, Yard No 1114, for British & Burmese Steam Navigation Co, Ltd (P. Henderson & Co, Managers). Registered Glasgow. B & W oil engine 2 SCSA 4 cyl 620 mm–1400 mm (exhaust 470 mm) by J. G. Kincaid & Co Ltd, Greenock. 3300 bhp, 12 K.
1958 1 July, launched by Mrs J. Borland. September completed. 19 October, commenced maiden voyage (Captain W. Fitzgerald), United Kingdom to West Africa.
1964 21 October, transferred to Elder Dempster Lines Ltd.
1973 28 August, sold to Regent Navigation Shipping Corp, Singapore. Renamed **REGENT LIBERTY**. Registered Panama. Tmk 2991 n, 5154 g, 9551 d. 4546 n, 11,786 d, 7377 g.
1980 Sold to Metal Scrap Trade Corp Ltd. 24 January, arrived Vishakhapatnam for demolition by A. P. Andhra Pradesh Industrial Development Corp Ltd. June, work commenced.

Ships of the 'Kumba' class: KUMBA (354), KABALA (355), PRAHSU (356).
Kumba is a town in Cameroun.

355 KABALA
O.N. 301383   1958–1973

'Kumba' class
Steel screw motorship
454.9′×58.3′×25.1′   2995 n   5445 g   9360 d

Built by Lithgows Ltd, Port Glasgow, Yard No 1115, for British & Burmese Steam Navigation Co Ltd (P. Henderson & Co, Managers). Registered Glasgow. B & W oil engine 2 SCSA 4 cyl 620 mm–1400 mm (exhaust 470 mm) by J. G. Kincaid & Co Ltd, Greenock. 3300 bhp, 12 K.
1958 14 October, launched by Mrs M. B. Glasier. December, completed.
1959 11 January, commenced maiden voyage (Captain I. Laing), United Kingdom to West Africa.
1960 Transferred to Elder Dempster Lines Ltd.
1973 26 November, sold for £360,000 to Magnom Maritime Co Ltd (Shiptrade Corporation SA, Managers), Greece. Renamed **PAPAMAURICE**. Registered Famagusta. 2954 n, 5223 g, 9551 d.
1976 Registered Limassol.
1980 Sold for US$809,475 to Mao Chen Iron & Steel Co Ltd. 3 May, arrived Kaohsiung. 10 May, demolition commenced.

356 PRAHSU (II)
KALAW/KOHIMA (II)
O.N. 301293   1959–1973

'Kumba' class
Steel screw motorship
454.9′×58.3′×25.4′   3012 n   5445 g   9400 d
Laid down as **KOKO** for British & Burmese Steam Navigation Co Ltd and launched by Lithgows Ltd, Port Glasgow, Yard No 1116, as **PRAHSU** for Elder Dempster Lines Ltd. Registered Liverpool. B & W oil engine 2 SCSA 4 cyl 620 mm–1400 mm (exhaust 470 mm) by J. G. Kincaid & Co Ltd, Greenock. 3300 bhp, 12 K.
1958 29 December, launched by Mrs A. M. Bennett.

PRAHSU

1959 March, completed. 13 April, commenced maiden voyage (Captain N. Pryce), United Kingdom to West Africa.

1964 6 April, transferred to British & Burmese Steam Navigation Co Ltd. Renamed **KALAW**. Employed on the Burma service.

1966 Transferred to Elder Dempster Lines Ltd. Renamed **KOHIMA** (to perpetuate the name).

1973 20 December, sold for £360,000 to Naves Maritime Co Ltd (Shiptrade Corporation SA), Cyprus. Renamed **PAPAGEORGIS**. Registered Limassol. 2971 n, 5223 g, 9551 d.

1980 3 January, sold to An Hsiung Iron & Steel Co, Taiwan. 17 April, demolition commenced at Kaohsiung.

357 DARU (II)/YOMA (II)

O.N. 187198   1958–1979

'Daru' class
Steel screw motorship
460.0′×62.2′×27.5′   3385 n   6340 g   9970 d
Built by Scotts' Shipbuilding & Engineering Co Ltd, Greenock, Yard No 679, for Elder Dempster Lines Ltd. Registered Liverpool. Doxford oil engine, opposed pistons, 2 SCSA 5 cyl 670 mm–2320 mm by the builders. 5500 bhp, 14 K.

1958 10 April, launched by Mrs M. Harrison. 11 September, completed. 9 October, maiden voyage (Captain W. R. Lightbody, MBE) from Rotterdam to West Africa.

1965 November, renamed **YOMA**. It was intended this vessel be placed on the United Kingdom–Burma service but the voyage was cancelled and **YOMA** reverted to **DARU**.

1966 February, on Guinea Gulf Line service, under management of Roxburgh Henderson & Co Ltd.

1973 Tmk 3425 n, 6175 g, 10,260 d. 4679 n, 8147 g, 10,364 d.

1979 20 April, sold to Soc Maritime, Liberia Ltd for US$575,000. Renamed **LONE EAGLE**. Registered Panama.

1980 Sold to Venture Company Inc, Panama. Renamed **ANJO ONE**. Registered Panama.

1982 Sold for US$105,000 to Pakistani shipbreakers. 14 February, arrived at Karachi for demolition by Waheed Bros. 8 September, work commenced.

Ships of the 'Daru' class; DARU (357), DEGEMA (358), DIXCOVE (359), DUNKWA (360), DEIDO (361), DUMURRA (362).

YOMA, *formerly and subsequently* **DARU**

358 DEGEMA

O.N. 301300   1959–1979

'Daru' class
Steel screw motorship
460.0′×62.3′×26.4′   3112 n   5902 g   9700 d
Built by Wm Gray & Co Ltd, Hartlepool, Yard No 1295, for Elder Dempster Lines Ltd. Registered Liverpool. Doxford oil engine, opposed pistons, 2 SCSA 5 cyl 670 mm–2320 mm by Central Marine Engine Works Ltd, Hartlepool. 5500 bhp, 14 K.

1958 27 November, launched by Mrs P. G. A. Arundel.

1959 7–8 April, trials. Maiden voyage (Captain P. M. Ralston). Whilst homewards on voyage 2 the Chief Officer (W. Crossman) and an Ordinary Seaman (P. D. Long) were swept overboard and lost as they were lashing loose logs during heavy weather in the Bay of Biscay.

DARU

DEGEMA (Photo Skyfotos)

307

ELDER DEMPSTER LINES, LIMITED

M.V. "DEGEMA" Voyage 70

STOWAGE PLAN

SAILED FROM W.C. AFRICA TO LONDON

DATE 16th April, 1977

DRAFT 22' 05" M

STABILITY G.M. = + 2.5

M.V. "DIXCOVE"
M.V. "DEGEMA"
Port ~ Stbd
Deck Aft

ABIDJAN ~ LONDON
19 ROUND IROKO LOGS 122.456 TONNES
B/L 42 'VARIEX' = 9 IROKO → 1 LOG No 5514A = 11 TONNES
" 40 VARIEXB = 10 IROKO WITH No LOG TALLY
Log Tally 'A' 34-51

No 5   No 4

ABIDJAN ~ LONDON
186 BUNDLES SAWN TIMBER 156.820 TONNES

B/L 7. 'A' SGL LOT WHITE' : 22 BDLS FRAMIRE
Lot B/L 36 SMGL LOT C VIOLET : 31 BDLS SAMBA
" 33 SMGL LOT C BLACK : 5 BDLS SAMBA
" 34 SMGL LOT C VIOLET : 17 BDLS SAMBA
" 33 SMGL LOT L BLACK : 8 BDLS SAMBA
B/L 18 SMGL LOT J : 43 BDLS SAMBA
B/L 19 SMGL LOT F YELLOW : 60 BDLS SAMBA

X = STOWED IN AFT END

ABIDJAN ~ LONDON
720 BAGS COFFEE 25.537 TONNES
Plot

ABIDJAN ~ LONDON
4 CASES SUNDRIES 1.108 TONNES
B/L 37 'MOTOR PARTS' 1.43 MACHINERY
" 63 AIRCLEV : 2 CSS EFFECTS
" 38 CODDING'UN : 1 CS EFFECTS

ABIDJAN LONDON
Plot BAGS COFFEE
B/L 4 'SOCIVE' 118

ONE SMILS FORK LIFT STOWED HERE

MONROVIA ~ LONDON
1645 BAGS COFFEE 101.850 TONNES
Plot

MONROVIA ~ LONDON
Plot BAGS COFFEE
B/L 'LPMC'

DOUALA ~ LONDON
5 PALLETS RUBBER
5 BALES RUBBER
4.050 TONNES
B/L 5 'CDC'

ABIDJAN ~ LONDON
6 BDLS MAHOG VENEERS
Plot B/L 30 10.30
1.13

Port
Stbd Bridge
Stars

DOUALA ~ LONDON
58 BUNDLES SAWN TIMBER 62.715 TONNES

ABIDJAN ~ LONDON
59 BUNDLES SAWN TIMBER 54 TONNES

ABIDJAN ~ LONDON
1200 BAGS COFFEE 76.671 TONNES
B/L 4 'SOCIVEX' 115
420 BAGS
B/L 2 'SOCIVE' 116
420 BAGS
B/L 3 'SOCIVE' 117
420 BAGS

DOUALA ~ LONDON
424 BAGS COFFEE 84.647 TONNES
B/L 1 UCCAO : 125 BAGS
" 2 PMO : 375
" 3 PMO : 924

ABIDJAN ~ LONDON
265 BUNDLES SAWN TIMBER 227.60 TONNES

B/L 32 'AB.360' : 17 BDLS TIAMA
B/L : K.S. 'O' : 20 BDLS DIBETOU
Plot B/L 5 : 9748+ RED DANT : 4 BDLS IROKO
" 22 CH 11250 : 36 BDLS IROKO
B/L 43 'AEA' FD 5522' : 78 BDLS IROKO
Plot B/L 5 'ABA/SEBA' : 47 BDLS IROKO
" 11 V.B. SAUD : 9 BDLS IROKO
" 9 D.L.B. 97393 : 11 BDLS IROKO

ABIDJAN ~ LONDON
9 ROUND ACAJOU LOGS 27.254 TONNES
B/L 36 'BTC'
Log Tally H 25-33

DOUALA ~ LONDON
63 ROUND LOGS 195.5 TONNES

Plot B/L 24 'EAGICAM' : 4 BDLS BILOLO
" 22 " : 2 NGOLLON
" 26 E K : 33 BIBONO
" 19 EAGICAM : 7 NGOLLON
" 20 " : 9 NGOLLON
" 25 CTA : 8 NGOLLON

Log Tally 'C' 54-99 (No.81 missing)
H 1-7
H 9-12
H 14-22

MANANI ~ LONDON
31 ROUND HEROMESIA LOGS
126 TONNES Plot B/L 1 : 12 'KD'
" 2 'KD'
" 3 : 18 KD
Log Tally 'C' 25-55

DOUALA ~ LONDON
35 BUNDLES SAPELLI SAWN TIMBER 56.812 TONNES

Plot B/L 13 'SEBC'

ABIDJAN ~ LONDON
35 BUNDLES ROKO SAWN TIMBER
Plot B/L 11 'EFBA 5560D' 36.000 TONNES

ABIDJAN ~ LONDON
265 BUNDLES SAWN TIMBER 28.565 TONNES
Plot B/L 9 'SINGFEL 97393' : 13 BDLS IROKO
B/L 35 SMGL LOT H : 27 BDLS IROKO
Plot B/L 11 'EFBA 5560D' : 1 BDLS IROKO

DOUALA ~ LONDON
59 BUNDLES SAWN TIMBER 54.049 TONNES
Plot B/L 11 'SEBC' : 31 BDLS SILO
" 12 SEBC : 28 BDLS SILO

Aft Coffin

DOUALA ~ LONDON
55 BUNDLES SAWN TIMBER 39.101 TONNES
Plot B/L 10 'TIC 1518' : 15 BDLS MOABI
" 13 SEBC : 40 BDLS SAPELLI

Stbd Coffin

Ref: CP 4

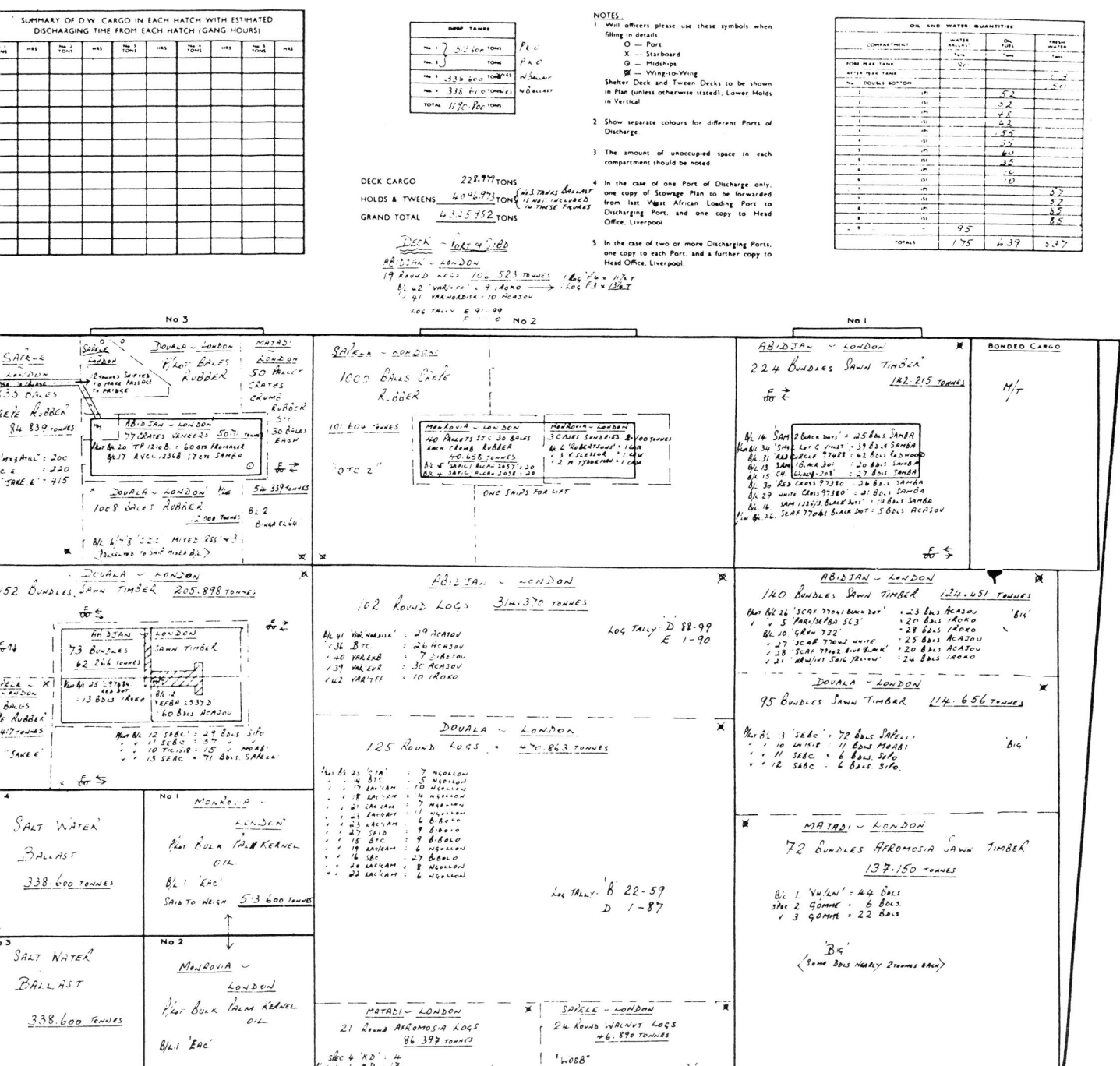

1969 Tmk 3086 n, 5636 g, 9754 d. 4667 n, 8153 g, 10,111 d.
1979 23 February, sold for US$630,000 to Arphaxad SA (Spe-
      cova Cia Naviera SA, Managers), Honduras. Renamed
      VEEJUMBO. Registered Puerto Cortes.
1982 Renamed **DEJEMA**.
1983 January, renamed **DEGEMA**. Sold for demolition and
      broken up by Zulfiqar Metals Ltd at Gadani Beach.
Degema is the name of a Divisional Headquarters town and
port (now closed) on the Sambreiro River in the Niger delta.

359 DIXCOVE (II)
O.N. 301309   1959–1979

'Daru' class
Steel screw motorship
460.0′×62.3′×26.4′   3114 n   5905 g   9430 d.
Built by Wm Gray & Co Ltd, Hartlepool, Yard No 1296, for
Elder Dempster Lines Ltd. Registered Liverpool. Doxford oil
engine, opposed pistons, 2 SCSA 5 cyl 670 mm–2320 mm by
Central Marine Engine Works, Hartlepool. 5500 bhp, 14 K.
1959 25 March, launched by Mrs H. R. Lane. June,
      completed. 17 July, commenced maiden voyage (Cap-
      tain F. St. H. Webber) during which the ship struck
      wharf at Port Harcourt, stem set back 5 feet.
1968 Tmk 3077 n, 5649 g, 9754 d. 4642 n, 8138 g, 10,111 d.
1972 Transferred to China Mutual Steam Navigation Co Ltd
      but reverted to Elder Dempster Lines Ltd.
1979 20 April, sold to Gulf Shipping Lines Ltd (Gulfeast
      Ship Management Ltd), Hong Kong, for US$580,000.
      Renamed **GULF EAGLE**. Registered Liverpool.
1983 Sold to Khalil & Sons Ltd. 14 June, arrived Chittagong.
      June, demolition commenced at Sita-Kunda.

Two views of **DIXCOVE**

GULF EAGLE, *formerly* **DIXCOVE**, *at Djibouti during 1979*

310

From Sea magazine

M.V. DUNKWA

The First Four-cylinder Supercharged Doxford Engine

THE *Dunkwa* is the fourth of the new class of six vessels in the Elder Dempster Lines Fleet. Each bears the name of a West African place beginning with the letter 'D'. Of these the *Daru* was the first and she has been joined in service by the *Degema*, the *Dixcove* and the *Deido*. The *Dumurra* will sail on her maiden voyage in July 1961.

General Particulars of M.V. *Dunkwa*

Length Overall, 460 feet; Breadth Moulded, 63 feet; Loaded Draft, 26 feet 1¼ inches; Total Deadweight, 9,572 tons; Bale Capacity, 577,566 cubic feet; Deep Tank Capacity, 1,267 tons Palm Oil, etc.; 'Tween Deck Tank Capacity, 464 tons Groundnut Oil, etc.; Gross Tonnage, 6,109; Net Tonnage, 3,195; Service Speed, 14 knots.

M.V. *Dunkwa* is fitted with the first supercharged four-cylinder Scott-Doxford engine ever to be built and her entire amidship accommodation is fully air-conditioned.

1. *Above:* M.V. Dunkwa *at her launching in January 1960.*

2. *Right: The Hon. Mrs John Baring sponsored the* M.V. *Dunkwa at the launching ceremony from Scott's Shipbuilding Yard, Greenock, and wished God-speed to all who sail in her.*

3. *Below: On her trials in the Firth of Clyde.*

360 DUNKWA (II)

O.N. 301338   1960–1981

'Daru' class
Steel screw motorship
460.0′×63.3′×26.1′   3195 n   6109 g   9572 d
Built by Scotts' Shipbuilding & Engineering Co Ltd, Greenock, Yard No 685, for Elder Dempster Lines Ltd. Registered Liverpool. Doxford oil engine, opposed pistons, 2 SCSA 4 cyl 670 mm–2320 mm by the builders. (The first supercharged four cylinder Scott-Doxford to be built.) 5700 bhp, 14 K.
First Elder Dempster cargo ship fitted with permanent swimming pool.

1960   10 January, launched by the Hon Mrs J. Baring. July, maiden voyage (Captain R. W. Philip).
1973   Tmk 3208 n, 5909 g, 9716 d. 4653 n, 8254 g, 10,099 d.
1977   July, in collision (Captain B. W. Fowler) with PEARL TRADER (Greek flag) when berthing at Freetown. Minor damage.
1981   Sold to Clare Shipping Corporation, Greece. Renamed **CLARE**. 19 January, engine damage sustained while lying at Rio de Janeiro. Subsequently sold 'as lying' to Resolve Maritime Ltd, Panama. Renamed **RESOLVE**. Registered Panama.
1983   Sold to Pakistani shipbreakers. 28 March, arrived Gadani Beach for demolition by Elahi Shipbreakers Ltd. 28 March, work commenced, completed April.

DUNKWA (Photo W. Ralston Ltd)

361 DEIDO (II)

O.N. 301379   1961–1979

'Daru' class
Steel screw motorship
460.0′×63.3′×26.1′   3195 n   6109 g   9398 d
Built by Scotts' Shipbuilding & Engineering Co Ltd, Greenock, Yard No 686, for Elder Dempster Lines Ltd. Registered Liverpool. Doxford oil engine, opposed pistons, 2 SCSA 4 cyl 670 mm–2320 mm by the builders. 5700 bhp, 14 K.

The Hon. Mrs J. Baring after launching DUNKWA (Photo J. Weir)

DEIDO *Nearing completion. From* Sea *magazine*

1961   1 February, launched by Mrs J. L. Evelyn. 19 April, trials. 21 May, completed. Maiden voyage (Captain D. H. Coughlan, DSO, RNR).

1961   25 January, towed KATHA disabled with engine fault, to Lisbon (see next page).

1967   Tmk 3208 n, 5909 g, 9899 g. 4653 n, 8254 g, 10,287 d.

1979   29 January, sold for US$660,000 to National Glory Cia Nav SA (Canopus Shipping SA, Managers), Athens. Renamed **SAN GEORGIO III**. Registered Panama.

1980   Transferred to Canopus Shipping SA, Greece. Renamed **AGIOS GEORGIOS III**. Transferred to Aetos Maritime Co (Canopus Shipping SA, Managers).

1982   18 January, laid up at Piraeus.

1985   August, reported still laid up at Piraeus.

DEIDO

313

The Deido *Tows the* Katha *to Lisbon*

A Report of the Towing Operation
by Captain D. H. Coughlan, D.S.C., Master of M.V. Deido

AT 10.30 on January 25 we received a message from the Master of the M.V. *Katha* that his engines were disabled and a request for a tow to Lisbon. I agreed to accept this subject to the Company's approval and proceeded to her position. We arrived at the *Katha*'s position (latitude 38° 52½′ North, longitude 11° 42½′ West) about six hours later and began to prepare for the tow. We had been unable to make any advance preparations for the tow because of our full deck cargo of logs and it would have been a well nigh impossible task to take two

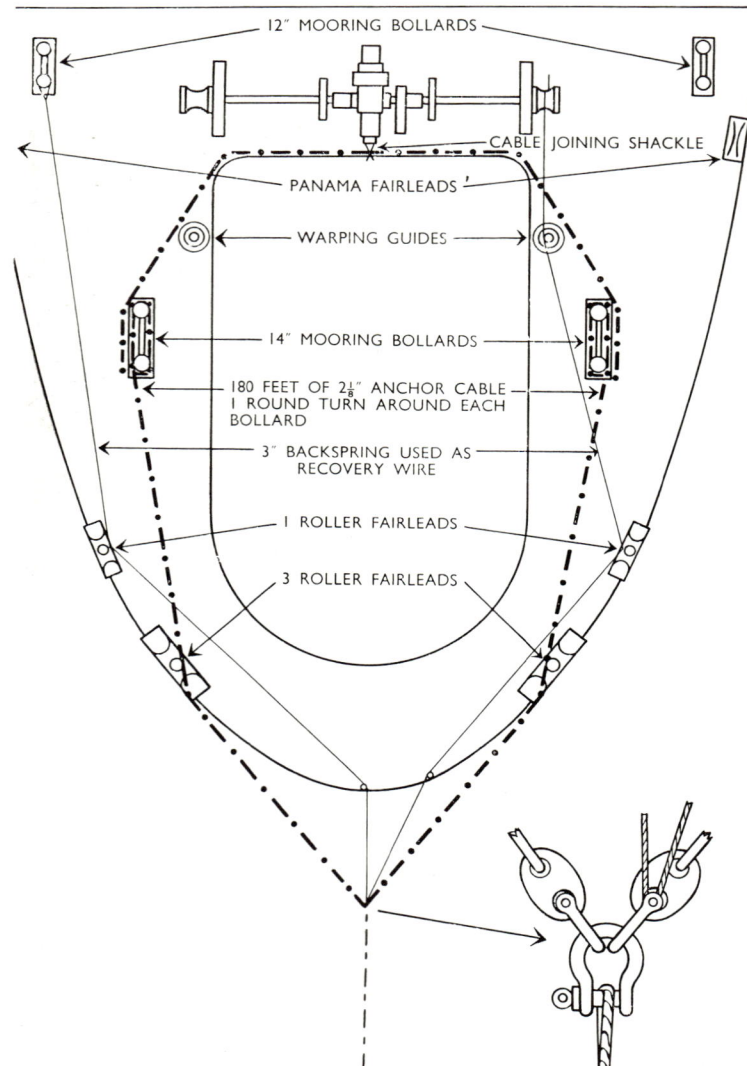

12″ MOORING BOLLARDS

CABLE JOINING SHACKLE

PANAMA FAIRLEADS

WARPING GUIDES

14″ MOORING BOLLARDS

180 FEET OF 2¼″ ANCHOR CABLE
1 ROUND TURN AROUND EACH
BOLLARD

3″ BACKSPRING USED AS
RECOVERY WIRE

1 ROLLER FAIRLEADS

3 ROLLER FAIRLEADS

shackles of cable from forward along the deck to aft. I did, however, suggest to the Master of the *Katha* that he hang off his starboard anchor, make fast his insurance wire to the end of his cable, have his insurance wire on a bight in the water, the soft eye end stoppered on the rail on the port side, his relieving tackles rigged, and that we tow through the hawse. He agreed to these suggestions.

Because of the full deck cargo it was decided to pass the two shackles of cable from forward to aft outside the ship. The second shackle was brought on deck, the cable broken and then put back in the locker. A wire was brought from aft through the panama lead on the forward port side of the poop, through the port fairlead forward, and shackled to the cable. The strain was taken on this wire and the cable veered on the windlass. When the end appeared the compressor was put on, a wire made fast to the other end of the cable, and then veered as the after wire was hove away. Eventually all strain was taken off the forward wire and the cable was up and down from the poop with this wire as a preventer if necessary. On the poop the wire was led through the port panama lead around the forward port bitts across the deck to the starboard forward bitts then aft around the warping guide to the mooring winch. When the end of the cable reached the starboard warping guide the cable was stoppered off on the port forward bitts, the wire shifted to the warping guide on the starboard after fairlead, and the cable again hove in until the end was on deck on the port side. The forward wire was unshackled and hove back in forward, and the cable hove across the deck until the end was on the starboard side. The cable was then passed around the forward part of the deck house and middled on each side. The cable was on the poop by 18.00 hours.

After middling the cable it was led on each side, from the fore part of the deck house, around the outside of the fore part of the midship bitts, one turn round them, and down to the after fairleads. A heavy shackle was on the end of each part with another shackle to join them and take the insurance wire when we received it.

By 19.33 all was ready and the 'run in' to pass the tow was begun. There was a moderately heavy swell running from the W.S.W. with an occasional heavy one, and a light N.E. breeze. The *Katha* was laying heading 150° but swinging between 130° and 170°. The approach was made from her stern along her port side. At 20.09 a rocket was fired across *Katha*'s fore deck and by 20.11 the *Katha* had the ratline. The method was a ratline to the rocket line, followed by a 4 in. rope messenger. The 4 in. messenger was onboard *Katha* by 20.15. By 20.26 it was fast to her insurance wire and we started to bring it aboard. By 20.50 the insurance wire was fast and the bridle paid out over our stern ready for towing. When the bridle was in position it was approximately 8 to 10 feet from the stern at the point of tow. The *Katha* then commenced veering her cable to three shackles forward of her windlass. By 21.23 *Katha* had her cable veered and the relieving tackles fast. The tow had begun.

After the strain had been taken on the tow and *Katha* was moving, speed was increased gradually by 5 r.p.m. until 64 r.p.m. were reached and maintained. Morning sights showed this had given a speed made good of 6½ knots. The tow was laying very easily with no chafing whatever.

At 00.40 the following morning, January 26, the Chief Engineer reported he had a hot side rod, and the engine was stopped. At 02.17 towing was again started at the same speed after repairs had been carried out.

The next morning when I was able to observe the tow properly in daylight I felt that a longer one would be better. At 09.05 the engine was stopped and the *Katha* veered her cable to five shackles forward of her windlass. At 09.23 towing was started again and by 11.28 we had reached 76 r.p.m. in steps of 5 r.p.m. This appeared a good towing speed, the cable laying

Above: M.V. Deido *with her full deck cargo of logs with* M.V. Katha, *a Henderson Line vessel.*

Right: The tow in progress. The inset picture shows the bridle lying eight to ten feet from the stern of the Deido. *In the larger picture a small section of the bridle is just visible at deck level.*

quiet onboard with no chafing and a good catenary in the tow. *Katha* also appeared to be able to steer better. From subsequent visual bearings this gave a speed of 8½ knots made good.

At 14.44 engine was stopped with Cape Roca nearly abeam, and the tow shortened with one shackle just in the water for the approach to shallow water. At 15.01 towing was continued. At 15.53 engine was stopped and, as tugs and pilots had arrived, we started to slip the tow. A recovery wire had been rigged when bridle was first put out. The bridle was brought inboard, the insurance wire unshackled, and the tow slipped at 16.28 in position Fort Santa Marta 027° 2.1 miles. The M.V. *Deido* then proceeded on her voyage.

      *   *   *

(Captain Coughlan quotes as highlights of the tow the chief engineer swinging a 28 lb. hammer on the forecastle which was manned by engineer and purser officers.)

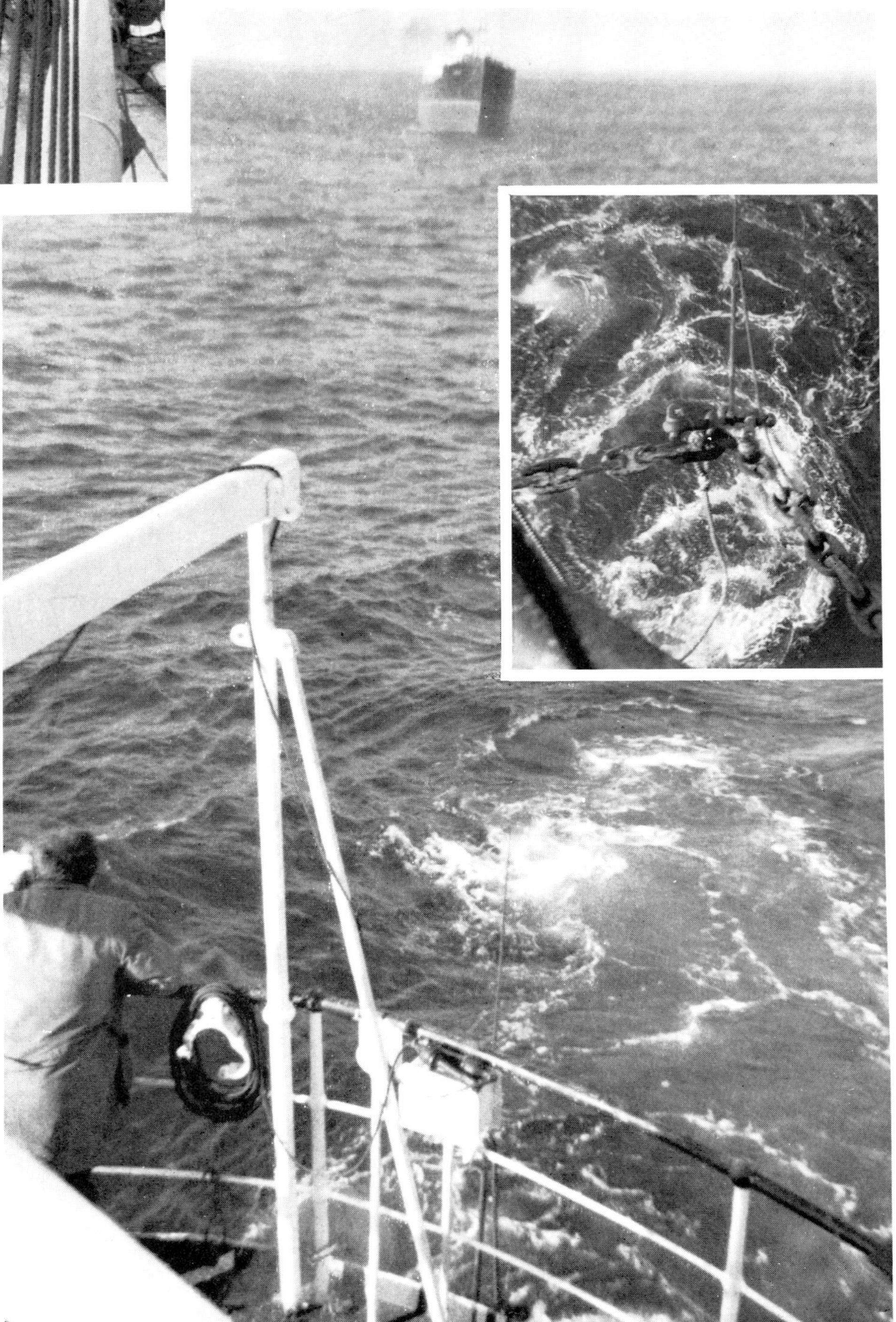

From Sea *magazine*

315

362 DUMURRA
O.N. 303171   1961–1980

'Daru' class
Steel screw motorship
460.0′×63.3′×26.1′   3262 n   6150 g   9550 d
Built by A Stephen & Sons Ltd, Linthouse, Glasgow, Yard
No 677, for Elder Dempster Lines Ltd. Registered Liverpool.
Doxford oil engine, opposed pistons, 2 SCSA 5 cyl 670 mm–
2320 mm by Hawthorn Leslie (Eng) Ltd, Newcastle. 5500 bhp,
14 K.

1961   16 March, launched by Mrs J. D. Robertson. 6 July,
         completed, maiden voyage (Captain W. R. Rowlands).
1970   Tmk 3248 n, 5932 g, 9850 d. 4658 n, 8238 g, 10,078 d.
1980   6 June, sold to Fumurra Ltd, Isle of Man (Dafnoussa
         Compania Naviera SA, Panama, Managers) for US$1.4
         million. Renamed **FUMURRA**. Registered Douglas,
         IOM (United Kingdom flag). Delivered at Abidjan.
1983   Sold for US$376,750 to Jehangir Siddiqi. 2 May, demo-
         lition commenced at Gadani Beach.

Note—This vessel was originally ordered from Cammell Laird
& Co Ltd, Birkenhead, but the order was cancelled and replaced with A. Stephen & Sons Ltd.

*Above, **DUMURRA** seen off Dawes
Island, Port Harcourt in June 1975.
The photograph was taken from
DONGA (Photo M. Wild), and,
right, another view*

BETWEEN TWO GULFS
M V DUMURRA ON CHARTER

Alistair Faulds wrote this article at the end of 1966 when he was Second Officer on the Dumurra. *Since then he has served on the* Onitsha *and flown out to Freetown to join the* Mamfe *on charter to Chargeurs Réunis. He is now studying for his Master's Certificate.*

The beginning of August saw *Dumurra* heading on a great circle track across the expanse of ocean between Northern Ireland and the North

the Eastern seaboard and now became a menace to us and other North Atlantic Track vessels. We therefore headed Southerly, astern of the hurricane and after 41 hours steaming resumed our course. September 8 saw the Azores astern of us and on the 11th we passed Gibraltar making good speed through calm seas along the North African coast. We arrived in Beirut on the 16th and after one day of evading "bumboatmen and barbers" left for Aqaba.

The flat, desolate, unvarying scenery of the Suez Canal passed by and, in contrast, the towering, rocky coast of the Gulf of Aqaba provided fine photographic material for those members of the crew interested in the subject. The port of Aqaba was busy, handling 40,000 imported tons a month and, at the time we were there, had a growing tourist industry concerned mainly with visits to places of religious interest.

West Passage to the Bahamas. Excellent weather speeded our passage and on August 11 we were through the "Hole in the Wall", passing down the straits of Florida and across the Gulf of Mexico to our destination—Houston, Texas.

Our Charterers, Isthmian Lines Inc., received a somewhat inquisitive crew with their ship on August 14. I say inquisitive because none of us had any real idea for which ports we were heading. We soon learned, however, that we were bound for the Mediterranean and the Persian Gulf. We received this news with mixed feelings. On the whole, the Persian Gulf seemed to be held in rather low esteem. However, underlying this, there was excitement at the thought of going "somewhere different". The prospect of lands unvisited has held the imagination of sailors for centuries.

After loading in Houston we stopped off at New Orleans for two days, and then on to the more familiar ports of Norfolk, Baltimore and New York. We completed our loading programme on September 1 and sailed fairly light (2879 tons) for Beirut in The Lebanon some 5200 miles away. Unfortunately, during our stay in America, Hurricane "Faith" had passed up

1 Dumurra *during the voyage*

2 Dumurra *unloading tanks in Banda Shahpour*

3 & 4 *In the Persian Gulf*

5 & 6 *The* Dumurra's *route between two Gulfs*

Three days later we arrived in Assab in Ethiopia, on the coastal region originally called Eritrea. It was federated with Ethiopia in 1952. In contrast with the port which was being built by the Czechs, the town was rather primitive, consisting of two sandy streets.

From Assab we steamed out of the Red Sea and stopped off at Djibouti in French Somaliland. Some two weeks before our arrival, General de Gaulle had visited the city. His visit was followed by independence riots, so we found the city crowded with troops. The Government had deported practically all the experienced dock workers for the part they had taken in the riots, so we found the standard of labour working the ship very poor. As a result it took us some three days to discharge our cargo, bunker and be on our way to the Persian Gulf.

Six hundred miles on we passed the Quoin Islands—"the Coins" as they are known to regular traders—which mark the entrance to the Gulf, on the afternoon of October 1. It was all too apparent that we had entered the Gulf proper, because instead of the usual drop in temperature on the middle watch, it rose to 88° and stayed there. Next day the temperature rose once again and we heard from the radio station at Bahrain that the "high" for the day would be 102° and the "low" 88°. These, of course, were shade

3

October 13.

We berthed near one of the world's first water distillery plants. The plant has a capacity of 7,000,000 gallons of fresh water a day and has been such a success that two more are under construction. A new pipe-line was being laid to divert water from the Shatt-al-Arab for household use. From the amount of money which is being spent on an efficient water supply, it can be imagined just how barren and waterless the whole area is. The valley of the Shatt-al-Arab with its date-groves and thriving export trade during the date season, is the only green spot in the area.

The city of Kuwait proved to be the most modern in every respect that we had so far visited, and many of the crew took a trip in to town with shopping lists ranging from toothpaste to tape recorders.

Kuwait bans every form of alcohol because of its Moslem faith. The rule is strictly enforced and we felt its influence on board since no one was allowed to drink on deck.

October 15 saw us at Kharg Island which now belongs to the Persian Government. The Island was originally owned by one of the many Sheiks of Persia, who, when he was offered 10% of the royalties from the export of crude oil, refused on the grounds that it was too little. Shortly after

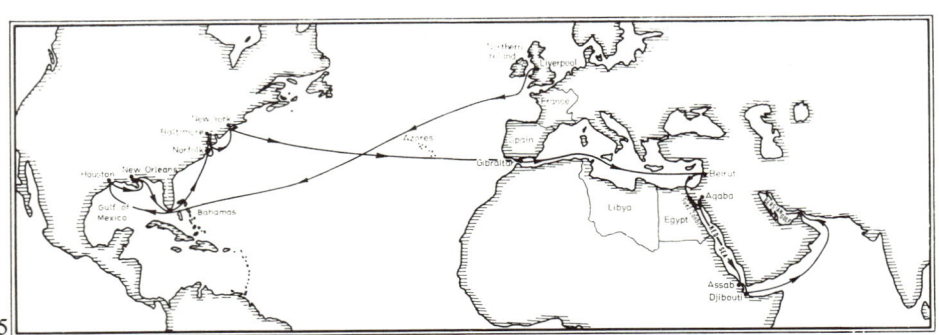

5

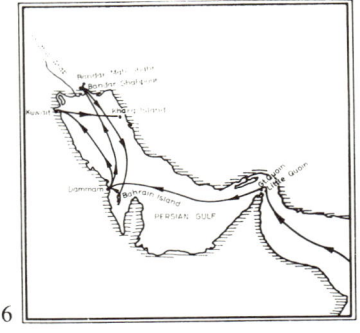

6

4

temperatures, so one hour in the sun was like taking a Turkish bath—or perhaps a Persian bath would be more appropriate in this case. On our way to Bandar Shahpour we were diverted to Dammam in Saudi Arabia with instructions to register our position in the queue of ships awaiting a berth and then to proceed on our way again. Bandar Shahpour, on the Khor Musa, is virtually miles from anywhere, and is completely surrounded by flat desert land. The nearest port is Bandar Mah Shahr which is used solely by tankers. So after our stay here, we returned to the open sea and eventually anchored off Bahrain Island to discharge a small amount of general cargo before returning to Dammam. After three days' discharging at the end of a six-mile-long pier, we went on our way to Kuwait, arriving on

his refusal he was hanged under rather mysterious circumstances, and Kharg Island is now one of the world's largest oil exporting ports. British, French and American aid is still at work there and British Petroleum, who own the controlling shares, are well represented by tugs, tankers and tenders.

On October 16, the ship was finally discharged and we sailed from Kharg Island to Suez and then on to Italy. So we left the Persian Gulf behind, with memories of camels, Arabs, desert, and, of course, heat. Excellent weather followed us all the way out of the Gulf and passing the "Coins" our thoughts turned to what lay ahead in Italy and, naturally, in the familiar West African scene. But this, of course, is another story. . . .

From Sea magazine

318

DONGA in drydock at Brooklyn, 1979

DUMBAIA

363 DONGA

O.N. 301420   1960–1981

'Donga' class
Steel screw motorship
465.0′×63.1′×26.3′   3486 n   6559 g   10,550 d
Built by Lithgows Ltd, Port Glasgow, Yard No 1133, for British & Burmese Steam Navigation Co Ltd (P. Henderson & Co, Managers). Registered Glasgow. B & W oil engine 2 SCSA 4 cyl 750 mm–1500 mm (exhaust 500 mm) by J. G. Kincaid & Co Ltd, Greenock. 5850 bhp, 14 K.

1960   12 April, launched by Mrs R. L. Hodges. 12 July, commenced maiden voyage (Captain N. Taylor), United Kingdom to West Africa. 29 June, on bare boat charter to Elder Dempster Lines Ltd.
1964   6 May, purchased by Elder Dempster Lines Ltd.
1972   Transferred to China Mutual Steam Navigation Co Ltd for one round voyage to Far East. Tmk 3441 n, 6366 g, 10,928 d. 5047 n, 8863 g, 11,715 d. Transferred to Elder Dempster Lines Ltd.
1981   26 March, sold for US$1.3 million to Diamant Merchant Shipping Ltd, (Diamantides Maritime Co Ltd), Piraeus. Renamed **DIAMANT MERCHANT**. Registered Piraeus.
1983   Sold to Seakissed Marine Ltd, Cyprus. Renamed **LYDRA**. Registered Limassol. 27 September, sold for demolition at Karachi. 7 October, arrived Port Along, October, broken up by J. M. Steel Industries.

Ships of the 'Donga' class: DONGA (363), DUMBAIA (364), DALLA (365).

Donga is a north flowing tributary of the River Benue. Also a township on right bank in Benue Province, Nigeria.

DONGA (Photo W. Ralston Ltd)

364 DUMBAIA

O.N. 301426   1960–1981

'Donga' class
Steel screw motorship
465.0′×63.1′×26.2′   3484 n   6558 g   10,550 d
Built by Lithgows Ltd, Port Glasgow, Yard No 1134, for British & Burmese Steam Navigation Co Ltd (P. Henderson & Co, Managers). Registered Glasgow. B & W oil engine 2 SCSA 4 cyl 750 mm–1500 mm (exhaust 500 mm) by J. G. Kincaid & Co Ltd, Greenock. 5850 bhp, 14 K.

1960   8 August, launched by Mrs S. A. Cotton. October, maiden voyage (Captain W. E. Humphreys). 17 October, on bare boat charter to Elder Dempster Lines Ltd.
1964   3 July, purchased by Elder Dempster Lines Ltd.
1968   Tmk 3399 n, 6385 g, 10,755 d. 5112 n, 8876 g, 11,530 d.
1981   10 March, sold to Questnorth Ltd, Isle of Man.
1982   13 August, laid up at Piraeus.
1984   Sold to Chinese shipbreakers. 14 March, reported engine room flooded in position 05°.57′N 90°.51′E, voyage Italy to Far East. 20 April, arrived Shanghai for demolition.

Elder Dempster's last *conventional* general cargo vessel.

365 DALLA

O.N. 301444   1961–1980

'Donga' class
Steel screw motorship
465.0′×63.1′×26.3′   3476 n   6564 g   10,550 d
Built by Lithgows Ltd, Port Glasgow, Yard No 1141, for British & Burmese Steam Navigation Co Ltd (P. Henderson & Co, Managers). Registered Glasgow. B & W oil engine 2 SCSA 4 cyl 750 mm–1500 mm (exhaust 500mm) by J. G. Kincaid & Co Ltd, Greenock. 5850 bhp, 14 K.

1961   1 February, launched. Maiden voyage (Captain J. C. Gibson).
1964   20 March, purchased by Elder Dempster Lines Ltd.
1968   Tmk 3399 n, 6385 g, 10,755 d. 5067 n, 8831 g, 11,530 d.
1972   Transferred to China Mutual Steam Navigation Co Ltd for one round voyage to the Far East. Transferred to Elder Dempster Lines Ltd.
1980   19 March, sold for US$1.5 million to Diamant Engineer Shipping Co Ltd, Greece. Renamed **MARMARAS**. Registered Piraeus.
1981   13 October, left Rostock for Alexandria with 11,903 tons of steel blooms. Deck in No 4 hold collapsed with shift of cargo. Put into Rotterdam.

DALLA

Two views of **PEGU** (Upper photo by W. Ralston Ltd, lower photo by D. Keen)

1982 12 February, laid up at Lefkas. Sold to Seagleam Maritime Ltd, Cyprus.
1983 1 September, substantial fire damage to engine room and accommodation.
1984 Sold to Brodospas for demolition and 19 June, arrived Split.

MARMARAS, *formerly* **DALLA** (Photo D. Keen)

1982 19 February, left Mahon, Minorca 1830 but returned due to propeller shaft bearing trouble. Sold to Salerno Marine Co Ltd. Renamed **NICOL MYLO**.
1983 Sold to Taiwan shipbreakers. 7 November, arrived Kaohsiung for demolition by Nan Hor Steel Ent Co Ltd, completed during that month.

366 PEGU

O.N. 301459   1961–1980

Steel screw motorship
465.9′×60.2′×25.7′   3031 n   5764 g   9300 d
Built by Lithgows Ltd, Port Glasgow, Yard No 1142, for British & Burmese Steam Navigation Co Ltd (P. Henderson & Co, Managers). B & W oil engine 2 SCSA 4 cyl 750 mm–1500 mm (exhaust 500 mm) by J. G. Kincaid & Co Ltd, Greenock. 5850 bhp, 14 K.
1961 August, completed. Maiden voyage (Captain J. C. Gibson).
1964 Purchased by Elder Dempster Lines Ltd.
1966 Transferred to Guinea Gulf Line Ltd.
1972 Transferred to China Mutual Steam Navigation Co Ltd for one round trip to the Far East. Transferred to Elder Dempster Lines Ltd.
1975 Transferred to Guinea Gulf Line Ltd. 3031 n, 5764 g, 9449 d.
1980 28 October, sold for $1.4 million to Sidebank Investments Ltd, Isle of Man. Renamed **REGU**.
1981 Sold to Akrata Shipping Co Ltd, Cyprus. Renamed **JOELLE**. Registered Limassol.

367 FOURAH BAY

O.N. 303188   1961–1978

'Fourah Bay' class
Steel screw motorship
465.0′×62.3′×25.2′   4226 n   7704 g   8139 d
Built by Scotts' Shipbuilding & Engineering Co Ltd, Yard No 689, for Elder Dempster Lines Ltd. Registered Liverpool. Oil engine 2 SCSA 5 cyl 760 mm–1550 mm by Sulzer Bros Ltd, Winterthur. 7500 bhp, 16 K.
Passenger accommodation: 1 double-berth owner's suite.
1961 7 September, launched by Mrs J. Paine. 22 December, completed.
1962 Maiden voyage (Captain L. B. Sylvester).
1976 Fitted with telex for direct world-wide communication.
1978 5 January, sold to Xoces Ltd (The Mexican National Line), Bermuda (Ocean Transport & Trading Ltd, Managers). Renamed **MAGDA JOSEFINA**. Registered Hamilton (Bermuda flag).
1980 June, sold (with LEONOR MARIA, ex *FALABA*) for £555,000 to Faith Shipping Co (Commercial Shipping Corp, SA, Managers), Navarino Shipping & Transport Co SA, Greece. Renamed **ALEXANDER'S FAITH**. Registered Piraeus.

Above, **FOURAH BAY** *running trials* (Photo W. Ralston Ltd). *Below right,* **MAGDA JOSEFINA**, *formerly* **FOURAH BAY**, *at Brooklyn, New York, May 1980, and, left, at Philadelphia, June 1980* (Both photos M. Wild)

1982   13 August, laid up at Piraeus.
1983   5 October, sold to Lemina Maritime Co Ltd, Cyprus.
       Renamed **LEMINA**. Registered Limassol.
1984   Sold to Abdul Aziz Noor Mohammed & Co for demo-
       lition. 3 March, arrived Gadani Beach. 18 March, demo-
       lition commenced.

Ships of the 'Fourah Bay' class: FOURAH BAY (367), FALABA (368), FORCADOS (369), FULANI (370), FREE-TOWN (371), FIAN (372).

Fourah Bay is in Sierra Leone, now well known for its University. Appropriately, **FOURAH BAY** was Elder Dempster's first purpose-built Cadet Ship.

FALABA

FORCADOS (Photo Skyfotos)

368 FALABA (II)

O.N. 303200 1962–1978

'Fourah Bay' class
Steel screw motorship
465.0′×62.3′×25.2′ 4215 n 7703 g 8393 d
Built by Scotts' Shipbuilding & Engineering Co Ltd, Yard No 690, for Elder Dempster Lines Ltd. Registered Liverpool. Sulzer oil engine 2 SCSA 5 cyl 760 mm–1550 mm by the builders. 7500 bhp, 16 K.
Passenger accommodation: 1 double-berth owner's suite.

1962 9 January, launched by Miss Hilary Muirhead. 25 May, completed. 5 June, maiden voyage (Captain R. W. Philip).

1978 6 January, sold to Europa Ltd, (Mexican National Line), Hamilton (Ocean Fleets Ltd, Managers). Renamed **LEONOR MARIA**.

1980 June, sold (with *MAGDA JOSEFINA*, ex *FOURAH BAY*) for £597,000 to Trust Shipping Co (Commercial Shipping Corp SA), Greece. Renamed **ALEXANDER'S TRUST**. Registered Piraeus.

1983 Sold to Palmdale Navigation Co Ltd, Cyprus. Renamed **CITY OF ZUG**. Registered Limassol.

1984 26 September, sold for demolition at Chittagong by Nwuil Hague & Bros, 4 October, demolition commenced.

369 FORCADOS (IV)

O.N. 303893 1963–1975

'Fourah Bay' class
Steel screw motorship
465.0′×62.3′×25.5′ 4072 n 7689 g 8115 d
Built by Lithgows Ltd, Port Glasgow, Yard No 1146, for Elder Dempster Lines Ltd. Registered Liverpool. Sulzer oil engine 2 SCSA 5 cyl 760–1550 mm by Fairfield-Rowan Ltd, Glasgow. 7400 bhp, 16 K.
Passenger accommodation: 1 double-berth owner's suite.

1963 24 March, launched by Mrs F. L. Lane. 8 November, completed. Maiden voyage (Captain N. Taylor).

1973 Transferred to China Mutual Steam Navigation Co Ltd for one round voyage to the Far East. Transferred to Elder Dempster Lines Ltd.

1975 30 December, sold to Cameroun Shipping Lines, SA, Cameroun. Renamed **CAM AYOUS**. Registered Douala.

1981 March, sold to Clifton Shipping Co Ltd, Greece. Renamed **COPPER TRADER**. Registered Piraeus.

1983 October, laid up at Mombasa under arrest for debt until September 1984. Sold by the Admiralty Marshal to Greneco Maritime AB. Left Mombasa in tow for demolition at Karachi, arriving by 27 November. 28 November, demolition by J. K. Bros Pakistan Ltd, commenced.

FORCADOS, *from a painting, c.1963, by John Stobart (from* Sea *magazine)*

Above, **FULANI** *on trials* (Photo W. Ralston Ltd) *and, below, at Douala as* **CAM AZOBE** (Photo P. George)

Above, **COTTON TRADER**, *formerly* **FULANI**, *in the Gulf of Arabia in 1983, and below, another view of her as* **FULANI**

370 FULANI (III)

O.N. 303900   1964–1975

'Fourah Bay' class
Steel screw motorship
465.0′×62.3′×25.5′   4072 n   7689 g   8150 d
Built by Lithgows Ltd, Port Glasgow, Yard No 1147, for Elder
Dempster Lines Ltd. Registered Liverpool. Sulzer oil engine
2 SCSA 5 cyl 760 mm–1500 mm by Fairfield-Rowan Ltd, Glasgow. 7400 bhp, 16 K.
Passenger accommodation: 1 double-berth owner's suite.
1963   27 June, launched by Mrs T. Kennon.
1964   16 January, completed. Maiden voyage (Captain C. S. O'Sullivan).
1975   23 December, sold to Cameroun Shipping Lines SA, Cameroun. Renamed **CAM AZOBE**. Registered Douala.
1981   Sold to Chilton Navigation Ltd, Greece. Renamed **COTTON TRADER**. Registered Piraeus.
1983   12 July, explosion occurred in No 4 hold during voyage Dubai to Aden. Fire followed and crew abandoned ship. Aground in position 19°.02′N 57°.50′E. Subsequently taken in tow. 4 August, arrived off Fujairah.
1984   23 February, towed to Djoubiti and sold for demolition.
1985   Resold. 5 May arrived Gadani Beach. 13 May, demolition by Hamid Mahmood & Bros, commenced.

371 FREETOWN (II)

O.N. 306475   1964–1978

'Fourah Bay' class
Steel screw motorship
465.0′×62.3′×25.5′   4072 n   7689 g   8115 d
Built by Lithgows Ltd, Port Glasgow, Yard No 1149, for Elder
Dempster Lines Ltd. Registered Liverpool. Sulzer oil engine
2 SCSA 5 cyl 760 mm–1550 mm by Fairfield-Rowan Ltd, Glasgow. 7400 bhp, 16 K.
Passenger accommodation: 1 double-berth owner's suite.
1963   19 September, launched by Mrs R. H. Chalcroft.

FREETOWN (Photo Skyfotos)

1964   28 February, completed. Maiden voyage (Captain L. L. James).
1967   Transferred to Guinea Gulf Line Ltd.
1972   Transferred to Nederlandsche Stoomvaat Maatschappij 'Ocean' NV, Netherlands. Registered Amsterdam. 4002 n, 7537 g.
1978   6 May, sold to Chrysovalantou Shipping Corp, Greece, for £538,000. Renamed **PANSEPTOS**. Registered Piraeus.
1980   June, sold to Lion Shipping Co Pte Ltd, Singapore. Renamed **CHERRY RUBY**. Registered Singapore.
1981   14 April, Lloyd's List reports vessel on fire after mutiny and shooting. In tow of SMIT NEW YORK from off Penang to Singapore. 17 April, arrived West Jurong anchorage. Subsequently sold per Eckhardt & Co to Salem Steel Industries Ltd, Chittagong, for demolition.
1982   10 January, arrived Chittagong.

Note—This ship was intended for British & Burmese Steam Navigation Co Ltd service and was launched with 'GLASGOW' on the stern; this was altered to 'LIVERPOOL' before registration.

FREETOWN *in Guinea Gulf Line Ltd colours*

FIAN *running trials* (Photo W. Ralston Ltd)

326

370 FULANI (III)

O.N. 303900   1964–1975

'Fourah Bay' class
Steel screw motorship
465.0′×62.3′×25.5′   4072 n   7689 g   8150 d
Built by Lithgows Ltd, Port Glasgow, Yard No 1147, for Elder
Dempster Lines Ltd. Registered Liverpool. Sulzer oil engine
2 SCSA 5 cyl 760 mm–1500 mm by Fairfield-Rowan Ltd, Glasgow. 7400 bhp, 16 K.
Passenger accommodation: 1 double-berth owner's suite.

1963   27 June, launched by Mrs T. Kennon.
1964   16 January, completed. Maiden voyage (Captain C. S. O'Sullivan).
1975   23 December, sold to Cameroun Shipping Lines SA, Cameroun. Renamed **CAM AZOBE**. Registered Douala.
1981   Sold to Chilton Navigation Ltd, Greece. Renamed **COTTON TRADER**. Registered Piraeus.
1983   12 July, explosion occurred in No 4 hold during voyage Dubai to Aden. Fire followed and crew abandoned ship. Aground in position 19°.02′N 57°.50′E. Subsequently taken in tow. 4 August, arrived off Fujairah.
1984   23 February, towed to Djoubiti and sold for demolition.
1985   Resold. 5 May arrived Gadani Beach. 13 May, demolition by Hamid Mahmood & Bros, commenced.

371 FREETOWN (II)

O.N. 306475   1964–1978

'Fourah Bay' class
Steel screw motorship
465.0′×62.3′×25.5′   4072 n   7689 g   8115 d
Built by Lithgows Ltd, Port Glasgow, Yard No 1149, for Elder
Dempster Lines Ltd. Registered Liverpool. Sulzer oil engine
2 SCSA 5 cyl 760 mm–1550 mm by Fairfield-Rowan Ltd, Glasgow. 7400 bhp, 16 K.
Passenger accommodation: 1 double-berth owner's suite.
1963   19 September, launched by Mrs R. H. Chalcroft.

FREETOWN (Photo Skyfotos)

1964   28 February, completed. Maiden voyage (Captain L. L. James).
1967   Transferred to Guinea Gulf Line Ltd.
1972   Transferred to Nederlandsche Stoomvaat Maatschappij 'Ocean' NV, Netherlands. Registered Amsterdam. 4002 n, 7537 g.
1978   6 May, sold to Chrysovalantou Shipping Corp, Greece, for £538,000. Renamed **PANSEPTOS**. Registered Piraeus.
1980   June, sold to Lion Shipping Co Pte Ltd, Singapore. Renamed **CHERRY RUBY**. Registered Singapore.
1981   14 April, Lloyd's List reports vessel on fire after mutiny and shooting. In tow of SMIT NEW YORK from off Penang to Singapore. 17 April, arrived West Jurong anchorage. Subsequently sold per Eckhardt & Co to Salem Steel Industries Ltd, Chittagong, for demolition.
1982   10 January, arrived Chittagong.

Note—This ship was intended for British & Burmese Steam Navigation Co Ltd service and was launched with 'GLASGOW' on the stern; this was altered to 'LIVERPOOL' before registration.

FREETOWN in Guinea Gulf Line Ltd colours

FIAN running trials (Photo W. Ralston Ltd)

372 FIAN

O.N. 306477   1964–1975

'Fourah Bay' class
Steel screw motorship
465.0′×62.3′×25.5′   4072 n   7689 g   8150 d
Built by Lithgows Ltd, Port Glasgow, Yard No 1148, for Elder Dempster Lines Ltd. Registered Liverpool. Sulzer oil engine 2 SCSA 5 cyl 760 mm–1550 mm by Fairfield-Rowan Ltd, Glasgow. 7400 bhp, 16 K.
Passenger accommodation: 1 double-berth owner's suite.
1963   15 October, launched by Mrs J. C. Lucas.
1964   3 April, completed. Maiden voyage (Captain N. Pryce).
1975   9 September, sold to South East Asia Shipping Co Pte Ltd, India. Renamed **MAHAPRIYA**. Registered Bombay.
1982   Sold to Indian shipbreakers. 12 October, arrived Bombay and laid up at Darukhana.
1985   April, demolition commenced by A. Baddrun.
Note—**FIAN** was intended for the British & Burmese Steam Navigation Co Ltd service and was launched with 'GLASGOW' on the stern; this was altered to 'LIVERPOOL' before registration.

Fian is a town in north-east Ghana.

SUNJARV

373 SUNJARV

O.N. 304195   1964–1970

Steel screw motorship, bulk carrier. Engines aft
488.5′×62.2′×30.7′   5590 n   9993 g   15,050 d
Built by J. L. Thompson & Sons Ltd, Sunderland, Yard No 689, as **GJENDEFJELL**, for Aksjeselskap Falkefjell & Skibs A/S Dieseltank (Olsen & Ugelstad, Managers). Registered Oslo. Doxford oil engine, opposed pistons, 2 SCSA 4 cyl 670 mm–2320 mm by North Eastern Marine Engine Works, Wallsend. 4400 bhp, 14 K.
1958   Completed.
1964   Purchased by British & Burmese Steam Navigation Co Ltd for £425,000 and placed on long term time charter to Saguenay Terminals Ltd. First voyage (Captain D. Campbell). Renamed **SUNJARV**. Registered Glasgow. 4882 n, 10,179 g.
1970   31 July, sold for £335,000 to Corbridge Enterprises Ltd, Bermuda.
1971   Sold to Viaguardia Cia Nav SA, Greece. Registered Piraeus.
1972   Sold to Atrax Shipping Co Ltd, Cyprus. Renamed **AEGIS DUTY**. Registered Famagusta.
1973   5 December, foundered in position 38°.53′N 71°.47′W, voyage Turf Point to Savannah.
Note—British & Burmese Steam Navigation Co Ltd wished this ship to be named **SUNSALWEEN** but the charterers, who had the privilege of choosing, insisted on **SUNJARV**.

ELIZABETH HOLT

374 ELIZABETH HOLT

O.N. 185458   1965

'Elizabeth Holt' class
Steel screw steamer
448.9′×60.2′×24.0   2953 n   5579 g   8024 d
Built by Cammell Laird & Co Ltd, Birkenhead, Yard No 1226, for John Holt Line Ltd. Registered Liverpool. 2 steam turbines DR gearing by the builders. 5500 shp, 14½ K.
1952   7 October, launched by Mrs J. A. Holt.
1953   February, completed.
1954   11 January, transferred to Guinea Gulf Line Ltd on its formation.
1963   Placed under management of Thos & Jno Brocklebank Ltd.
1965   Acquired by Elder Dempster Lines Ltd with the purchase of Guinea Gulf Line Ltd, but did not enter the company's service. 11 May, sold to Transcargo Cia Mar SA, Greece. Renamed **ADMIRALTY CREST**, later **DESPINA N**. Registered Monrovia. 3048 n, 5493 g.
1968   Placed under management of Union Commercial Steamship Co.
1972   Sold to Acamar Navigation Corp, Greece. 3074 n, 5579 g.
1973   Renamed **LORAIN**. 21 October, arrived Kaohsiung for demolition by Chuan Yuan Steel Corp.
Ships of the 'Elizabeth Holt' class: ELIZABETH HOLT (374), FLORENCE HOLT (375)

375 FLORENCE HOLT

O.N. 185467   1965

'Elizabeth Holt' class
Steel screw steamer
448.9′×60.2′×24.0′   3052 n   5579 g   8024 d
Built by Cammell Laird & Co Ltd, Birkenhead, Yard No 1227, for John Holt Line Ltd. Registered Liverpool. 2 steam turbines DR gearing by the builders. 5500 shp, 14½ K.
1952   3 December, launched by Mrs J. C. Mather.
1953   May, completed.
1954   11 January, transferred to Guinea Gulf Line Ltd on its formation.
1963   Placed under management of Thos & Jno Brocklebank Ltd.
1965   Acquired by Elder Dempster Lines Ltd with the purchase of the Guinea Gulf Line Ltd, but did not enter the company's service. 11 May, sold to Diana Cia Mar SA, Greece. Renamed **ADMIRALTY FLYER**, later **TRIAS**. Registered Monrovia. 3047 n, 5493 g.

S.S. ROSE OF LANCASTER

Two of the ships acquired with the purchase of the Guinea Gulf Line Ltd in 1965. Above, **ROSE OF LANCASTER**, *and below,* **MARY HOLT**, *which, unlike the other three, made one voyage under Elder Dempster*

S.S. MARY HOLT

1971 Sold to Aldebaran Navigation Corp, Greece.
1973 29 January, laid up at Rotterdam.
1974 Sold by auction to Ardsley Shipping Corp, Greece. Renamed **DALTON**, later **MR. NORMAN**. 23 February, arrived Kaohsiung for demolition by Nan Yung Steel & Iron Co.

376 ROSE OF LANCASTER
O.N. 187174   1965

Steel screw steamer
440.9′×58.4′×23.0′   2670 n   5197 g   7000 d
Built by Wm Gray & Co Ltd, Hartlepool, Yard No 1290, for Red Rose Navigation Co Ltd, Bermuda (John Holt & Co (Liverpool) Ltd, Managers). Registered Liverpool. 2 steam turbines DR gearing by Central Marine Engine Works, Hartlepool. 4800 shp, 14 K.
1957 Launched by Mrs Bligh. December, completed.
1963 Placed under management of Thos & Jno Brocklebank Ltd.
1965 Acquired by Elder Dempster Lines Ltd with the purchase of Guinea Gulf Line Ltd, but did not enter the company's service. 11 May, sold to Splosna Plovba, Yugoslavia. Renamed **BOCNA**. Registered Koper (Yugoslavia flag). 2483 n, 4930 g, 7292 d. Passenger accommodation: 12.
1977 24 December, caught fire at Matadi, both boilers badly damaged.
1978 Sold to Brodospas for demolition and 23 March, arrived Split.

377 MARY HOLT
O.N. 301319   1965

Steel screw steamer
463.4′×60.0′×24.7′   3083 n   5577 g   8000 d
Built by Wm Gray & Co Ltd, Hartlepool, Yard No 1300, for Guinea Gulf Line Ltd (John Holt & Co (Liverpool) Ltd, Managers). Registered Liverpool. 2 steam turbines DR gearing by Central Marine Engine Works, Hartlepool. 4800 shp, 14 K.
1959 28 May, launched by Mrs J. N. M. Holt. October, completed.
1963 Transferred to the management of Thos & Jno Brocklebank Ltd.
1965 Acquired by Elder Dempster Lines Ltd with the purchase of the Guinea Gulf Line Ltd, and completed one round voyage London to West Africa (Captain E. Hansen). 27 September, sold to National Shipping Corp, Pakistan. Renamed **SIPSAH**. Registered Karachi.
1968 Tmk 2975 n, 5235 g. 4401 n, 7459 g.
1975 6 August, arrived Karachi. 22 November, sold to Hayden Steel Industries Ltd for demolition at Gadani Beach.

378 CARWAY
O.N. 308698   1967–1973

Steel screw motorship, vehicle carrier, side loader
290.5′×49.2′×12.5′
Tmk 402 n,   866 g   669 d   944 n,   1597 g   776 d
Built by Grangemouth Dockyard Co Ltd, Grangemouth, Yard No 538, for Elder Dempster Lines Ltd (Mountwood Shipping Co Ltd, Managers). Registered Liverpool. Oil engine 4 SCSA 8 cyl 15″–20″ by Mirrlees National Ltd, Stockport. 1864 bhp, 14 K.
1967 May, completed.
1973 10 July, sold for £420,000 to Spei Leasing S.P.A., Italy (Ignazio Messina & Cia, Manager). Renamed **JOLLY VERDE**. Registered Genoa. 943 n, 1596 g.
1985 August, reported laid up.

CARWAY

M.V. CARWAY IS AN EXPORT BOOSTER

A new addition to our Fleet, the 1,000 ton *Carway*, is playing her part in Britain's export drive.

Carway was built by the Grangemouth Dockyard Company Ltd. to the order of Elder Dempster Lines and is chartered to Seaway Car Transporters of Liverpool, an Elder Dempster subsidiary. She is managed by the Liverpool-based Mountwood Shipping Company and was the first British-designed drive-on vessel built specifically for exporting motor vehicles and caravans.

Carway's length is 290 feet overall, and she is now a familiar sight at Felixstowe, when she slips out of the harbour on a Friday *en route* to Copenhagen and Gothenburg. The round trip takes about six days.

The hull and superstructure are of mild steel and welded construction and the five car decks can carry around 400 family-sized cars. To accommodate caravans, one deck is 8 feet high— 2 feet higher than the other four decks. To prevent a build-up of exhaust fumes all the decks are serviced by a mechanical ventilation system.

Her breadth moulded is 48 feet and depth moulded to the main deck is 12 feet 3 inches. She is propelled by a Mirrlees diesel engine with a rating of 1,864 B.H.P., and was designed to serve the expanding Scandinavian market for British cars. In 1966 some 70,000 cars made the journey across the North Sea to customers in Denmark, Norway and Sweden, who now buy about 10% of our car exports.

Mountwood Shipping Company, *Carway's*

managers, have opened an office in Felixstowe beside a two-acre site, acquired as "parking space" for incoming and outgoing vehicles and caravans. From here, vehicles are driven to the quay and on to the ship, in single file, over integral ramps. In this way, *Carway* can load at the rate of 50 cars an hour. The four-ramp

1

2

1 *Triumph and BMC cars line up for embarkation for their journey to Scandinavian markets*

2 *The profile of* M.V. *Carway can be clearly seen in this aerial photograph taken at Felixstowe. The two integral ramps on the port side are in the closed position*

3

4

5

3 *Cars load in single file at a rate of 50 vehicles an hour. The adjustable ramps allow* Carwa *to operate over the tidal ranges she encounters on her journey*

4 *Safely stowed, these British cars will soon be showing their paces on Danish and Swedish highways*

5 *The well-equipped bridge on* Carway

normal tidal range in most of the ports she is likely to enter.

Access from one deck to another is by means of a fixed set of ramps arranged fore and aft on the ship's centreline and situated between the forward and after sets of embarkation doors.

Her design accentuates two export virtues—speed and damage-free delivery. Once vehicles are in position they are secured against movement in the worst weather of the North Sea. The four road wheels of loaded vehicles are harnessed in webbing attachments which are connected by snap hooks to steel chains which run athwartships on each deck.

As many as 390 vehicles have been carried on one voyage, no damage having been sustained to cargo on passage.

And it is not only the cargo that is well cared for. The 16 officers and men aboard are quartered in comfortable cabins fitted to the highest standards on forward and after deckhouses on the upper deck. Although *Carway* is not so sleek as some of her sisters in the Line she tackles her export role with workman-like efficiency.

Since the ship's large windage area and comparatively shallow draft would tend to make her less easy to handle than a conventional ship, a bow thrust unit of Pleuger manufacture and a Kort rudder have been fitted to improve manoeuvrability. There is a self-tensioning winch at each end of the ship to accommodate the rise and fall of the tide when she is moored alongside. A passive tank stabiliser, designed at the National Physical Laboratory, is located immediately below the wheelhouse.

An extensive system of bridge control is incorporated in duplicate bridge wing consoles. Each console provides direct control of the main engine bow thrust unit, and manual rudder and whistle controls.

The twin consoles also show engine speed, rudder angle, gyro compass course, control air and starting air pressures and have an engine room signalling device.

In the centre of the wheelhouse there is a combined telemotor steering/automatic pilot console incorporating the automatic pilot course settings and adjustments. Navigational aids include a Decca navigator, ships "head up" true motion radar, echo sounder and electric log.

All upper deck equipment is electric as is the galley and water heating. Two fibreglass lifeboats are fitted in McLachlan gravity davits and a 16-foot work boat is handled by a single arm slewing davit. Each deck house has its own ventilating system of the low velocity heating and forced ventilation type using a proportion of re-circulated air.

Carway is a welcome addition to the Fleet and, at a time when the emphasis is on export efficiency, has a useful contribution to make to the national economy.

From Sea *magazine*

system is one of *Carway's* several innovations. The ramps are hinged into recesses in the ship's sides and help to give her a speedy turn-round.

Winches on the top deck are arranged to raise or lower the hinged ramps to either of two embarkation deck levels. The winches also raise and lower the ramps between the working position on the quay and the vertical stowed positions in the recesses where the ramps give protection to the shell doors. The hinging of the ramps and the provision of the two embarkation levels enable the ship to operate over the

CLEARWAY, subsequently SPEEDWAY

379 CLEARWAY (I)/SPEEDWAY (II)

O.N. 335322   1969–1973

Steel twin screw motorship, vehicle carrier; side loader
301.9′×57.2′×15.6′   445 n   1207 g   1700 d
Built by Werft Nobiskrug GmbH, Rendsburg, Yard No 656, for Sealord Shipping Co Ltd, Great Yarmouth, as **SEALORD CHALLENGER**. Registered Great Yarmouth. 2× oil engines 4 SCSA 6 cyl 450 mm–550 mm by Atlas-Mak Maschinenbau GmbH, Kiel. 2800 bhp, 15 K.

1967   Completed.
1969   Acquired by Elder Dempster Lines Ltd (Mountwood Shipping Ltd, Managers).
1970   Renamed **CLEARWAY**. Registered Liverpool. 10 September, renamed **SPEEDWAY**.
1973   3 July, sold to Seaspeed Ferries Ltd, Cyprus. Renamed **SEASPEED FERRY**. Registered Famagusta.
1977   January, sold to Carlton Steamship Co Ltd (Burnett Chapman Ship Management, Managers), Newcastle. Renamed **FEDERAL BYBLOS**. Registered Newcastle. 436 n, 1204 g, 1522 d. 3 February, on fire at Almeria, considerable damage. Accommodation gutted, two

members of crew lost their lives. 19 March, arrived in the Tyne under tow. Repaired and lengthened at Swan Hunter Ship Repairers (Tyne) Ltd to 111.65 m (previously 92.0 m), 706 n, 1592 g, 2296 d.

1978   Sold to Federal Commerce & Navigation (1974) Ltd (Dalgleish Ship Management Ltd), Dartmouth, Nova Scotia. Renamed **FEDERAL TYNE**. Registered Newcastle.
1979   Sold to Fednav Ltd, Hong Kong. Renamed **FEDERAL HUMBER**. Registered St John's, Newfoundland.
1980   Sold to Carlton Steamship Co Ltd, Canada. Renamed **CARIBBEAN CLOUD**.
1981   Sold to Vicca Marine Corp, Panama. Renamed **KERRY EXPRESS**.
1984   Sold to Ogram Shipping Enterprises Inc, Panama. Registered Manila. Converted into livestock carrier.
1985   August, reported laid up.

380 SPEEDWAY (I)/CLEARWAY (II)

O.N. 339916   1970–1978

Steel twin screw motorship, vehicle carrier, side loader
300.2′×55.2′×12.8′   510 n   1160 g   1021 d
Built by Robb Caledon Shipbuilders Ltd, Leith, Yard No 507, for Seaway Car Transporters Ltd (Mountwood Shipping Ltd, Managers). Registered Liverpool. 2 × oil engines 4 SCSA 6 cyl vee 325 mm–370 mm by W. H. Allen, Sons & Co Ltd, Bedford. 3016 bhp, 14 K.

1970   Launched 18 February. May, completed. 10 September, acquired by Elder Dempster Lines Ltd. Renamed **CLEARWAY**.
1971   24 June, transferred from Felixstowe–Scandinavia service to United Kingdom–West Africa Conference Lines (UKWAL), Ro-Ro service from Poole to Lagos.
1978   6 June, sold for £378,000 to O'Shea (Dublin) Ltd. Renamed **O'SHEA EXPRESS**. Registered Liverpool.
1980   April, re-engined by Atlas-Mak Maschinenbau GmbH, Kiel. 2 × oil engines 4 SCSA 4 cyl 320 mm–420 mm, 3300 bhp.
1984   17 May, sold at auction to Y. A. Kabbani (Aspen Shipping and Trading, Managers). Registered Beirut.
1985   August in service.

SPEEDWAY, subsequently CLEARWAY

SKYWAY

TITAN (from a postcard issued by Ocean Transport & Trading Ltd)

381 SKYWAY
O.N. 339910   1970–1973

Steel screw motorship, vehicle carrier, side doors and stern ramp
301.9′×57.1′×15.5′   571 n   1175 g   1575 d
Built by Trosvik Verksted A/S, Brevik, Yard No 88, as **MANDEVILLE** for Universal Trading & Shipping Agency, Aksjeselskap (A. F. Klaveness & Co, Managers). Registered Oslo. 2× oil engines 4 SCSA 8 cyl 320 mm–450 mm geared to a single shaft by Atlas-Mak Maschinenbau GmbH, Kiel. 2800 bhp, 15 K.
Passenger accommodation: 12.
1968   Completed.
1970   Acquired by Elder Dempster Lines Ltd. Renamed **SKYWAY**. Registered Liverpool.
1971   Major refit at Middle Docks & Engineering Co Ltd, South Shields.
1973   23 March, sold to Seaspeed Trailerships Ltd, Cyprus. Renamed **SEASPEED TRAILER**. Registered Famagusta. 445 n, 1204 g, 1700 d.
1974   Sold to Federal Commercial Navigation Co Ltd, Montreal. Renamed **FEDERAL AVALON**. Registered Halifax. 521 n, 1279 g, 1568 d.
1981   Sold to Vicca Marine Corp, Panama. Renamed **AVALO**. Converted into a cattle carrier (capacity 1400 beasts). Registered Panama. 587 n, 1222 g.
1984   Renamed **MURRAY EXPRESS**. Registered Panama.
1985   August, in service.

382 TITAN
O.N. 339938   1971–1975

Steel screw steamer, very large crude carrier
1090.2′×149.7′×67.8′   90,609 n,   113,551 g   226,466 d
Built by Aktiebolag Gotaverken, Gothenburg, Yard No 847, for Elder Dempster Lines Ltd. Registered Liverpool. 2 steam turbines DR gearing by Stal-Laval Turbine Co and Aktiebolag Gotaverken, Finspong and Gothenburg. 32,450 shp, 15¾ K. Unattended machinery space equipment approved.
1970   21 December, launched by Mrs Maud Alexander.
1971   February, completed. Maiden voyage (Captain Pattison).
1975   October, sold to Mobil Shipping & Transportation Co Ltd, London. Renamed **MOBIL CONDOR**. Registered Monrovia.
1976   June, 91,140 n, 104,627 g, 230,099 d.
1982   29 May, arrived Pusan. 8 June, sold to Nissho Iwai Corporation for demolition by Dongkuk Steel Mill, Pusan.
Note—During Elder Dempster ownership **TITAN** wore the traditional flag and livery of A. Holt & Co's Blue Funnel Line. Titans were pre-Olympian gods, children of Mother Earth.

383 TALTHYBIUS
O.N. 301360   1971

Steel screw steamer, US VC-2 'Victory' class
455.2′×62.2′×28.5′   4555 n,   7607 g   10,750 d
Built by Permanente Metals Corporation (Shipbuilding Division), Yard No 1, Richmond, California, Yard No 546, for United States Maritime Commission as **SALINA VICTORY**. Registered San Francisco. 2 steam turbines DR gearing by Westinghouse Electrical & Manufacturing Co, Pittsburgh. 6000 shp, 15 K.
1944   December, completed.
1946   Sold, Nederlandsche Stoomvaart Maatschappij Oceaan, Holland. Renamed **POLYDORUS**. Registered Amsterdam. 4567 n, 7671 g.
1960   Transferred to Ocean Steam Ship Co Ltd (A. Holt & Co, Managers). Renamed **TALTHYBIUS**. Registered Liverpool. 4467 n, 7713 g.
1966   Tmk 2663 n, 5268 g, 8756 d. 4296 n, 7313 g, 10,750 d.
1969   Blue Funnel Line Ltd take over management.
1971   Transferred to Elder Dempster Lines Ltd and completed two round voyages to West Africa, after which laid up at Bromborough Dock. 4 December, sold to Nan Frong Steel Enterprise Co Ltd, Kaohsiung for demolition.
1972   10 January, demolition commenced.
Talthybius was a faithful squire and herald of Agamemnon.

TALTHYBIUS in Elder Dempster livery, 24 September 1971 (Photo K. P. Lewis)

384 CLYTONEUS
O.N. 182445   1971–1972

Blue Funnel 'A2' class
Steel screw motorship
487.0′×62.3′×28.3′   4838 n   8214 g   9240 d
Built by Caledon Shipbuilding and Engineering Co Ltd, Dundee, for Ocean Steam Ship Co Ltd (A. Holt & Co,

CLYTONEUS

Managers). Registered Liverpool. B & W oil engine 2 SCDA 8 cyl 550 mm–1200 mm (exhaust 400 mm) by J. G. Kincaid and Co Ltd, Greenock. 6800 bhp, 15½ K.

1948   9 April, launched by Mrs A. Powrie (Lady Provost of Dundee). August, completed. 7 September, maiden voyage from Birkenhead (Captain P. Elder, DSC).
1956   4434 n, 7620 g.
1967   Tmk 2554 n, 6484 d, 5753 g. 4127 n, 9240 d, 7436 g.
1969   Blue Funnel Line Ltd, take over management.
1971   December, transferred to Elder Dempster Lines Ltd.
1972   20 June, sold for US$283,191 to Dong Yung Steel & Iron Works, Kaohsiung, for demolition.

The Blue Funnel 'A2' class transferred to Elder Dempster Lines Ltd: CLYTONEUS (384), IDOMENEUS/LAERTES (388), AUTOLYCUS (399), ANTILOCHUS (400), AUTOMEDON/CYCLOPS (403).
Clytoneus was one of the sons of Alcinous, King of Phaeacia.

CALCHAS

385   CALCHAS
O.N. 181071   1971–1972

Blue Funnel 'A1' class
Steel screw motorship
487.0′×62.3′×28.3   4980 n   8298 g   9300 d
Built by Harland & Wolff Ltd, Belfast, Yard No 1310, for Ocean Steam Ship Co Ltd (A. Holt & Co, Managers). Registered Liverpool. B & W oil engine 2 SCDA 8 cyl 550 mm–1200 mm (exhaust 400 mm) by the builders. 7300 bhp, 15½ K.
1946   27 August, launched by Mrs L. D. Holt.
1947   Completed.
1957   December, transferred to Glen Line Ltd, London. Renamed GLENFINLAS. 4459 n, 7639 g.
1962   November, transferred to Ocean Steamship Co Ltd (A. Holt & Co, Managers). Renamed CALCHAS.

1967   Tmk 2554 n, 5753 g, 6570 d. 4129 n, 7436 g, 9300 d.
1971   22 December, transferred to Elder Dempster Lines Ltd.
1972   Transferred to China Mutual Steam Navigation Co Ltd.
1973   22 July, while loading at Port Kelang fire broke out causing heavy damage. Towed out of harbour and beached. 12 August, refloated and moored, damaged beyond repair. 27 August, left Port Kelang in tow for Singapore. 23 October, arrived Kaohsiung. 23 November, sold to Keun Hwa Iron & Steel Works and Enterprise Co Ltd for demolition.

The only Blue Funnel 'A1' class vessel transferred to Elder Dempster Lines Ltd.
Calchas was the chief soothsayer of the Greeks at Troy.
Glenfinlas was the Lady of the Lake.

386   POSTROVER
O.N. 357398   1972–1976

Steel screw motorship; products
Tanker   557.7′×79.3′×32.1′   10,277 n   15,144 g   24,293 d
Built by Astilleros Espanoles SA, Matagorda, Cadiz, Yard No 156, jointly for Elder Dempster Lines Ltd and Peninsular and Oriental Steam Navigation Co (Panocean Shipping and Terminals Ltd, Managers). Registered Liverpool. Sulzer oil engine 2 SCSA 6 cyl 760 mm–1500 mm by the builders (Bilbao works). 10,200 bhp, 16 K.
1972   January, completed. 13 April, inaugurated the opening of the new £1 million vegetable oil terminal of Panocean & Shipping Ltd, Eastham, Cheshire.
1976   Sold to New Product Shipping Corporation, Liberia. Renamed JUBILEE VENTURE. Registered Monrovia. 9748 n, 14,755 g.
1985   August, reported in service.

387   AKOSOMBO
O.N. 183798   1972–1973

Blue Funnel 'A3' class
Steel screw motorship
487.0′×62.3′×28.3′   4551 n   7692 g   9380 d
Built by Harland & Wolff Ltd, Belfast, Yard No 1416, as ASCANIUS for Ocean Steamship Co Ltd (A. Holt & Co, Managers). Registered Liverpool. B & W oil engine 2 SCSA 7 cyl 750 mm–1500 mm (exhaust 500 mm) by the builders. 7600 bhp, 16 K.
1950   15 June, launched by Miss Sarah Hobhouse. 21 November, delivered. 7 December, maiden voyage (Captain W. J. Eynon).
1954   4545 n, 7692 g.
1967   Tmk 2342 n, 5515 g, 6696 d. 4048 n, 7431 g, 9380 d.
1972   Transferred to Elder Dempster Lines Ltd. Renamed AKOSOMBO.
1973   Transferred to China Mutual Steam Navigation Co Ltd. Renamed ASCANIUS. Sold to Saudi Europe Line (Orri Navigation Lines), Saudi Arabia. Renamed MASTURA. Registered Jeddah. Tmk 2342 n, 5515 g, 6803 d. 4095 n, 7690 g, 9530 d.
1978   Sold for demolition to Hughes Bolckow Shipbreaking Co Ltd. 8 April, arrived Blyth.

The Blue Funnel 'A3' class transferred to Elder Dempster Lines Ltd: AKOSOMBO/ASCANIUS (387), BELLEROPHON (393), POLYDORUS (404), ATREUS (406).
Ascanius was a grandson of Anchises and a son of Aeneas.
Akosombo is a town on the Volta River, Ghana.

ASCANIUS, in Elder Dempster livery, but prior to being re-named **AKOSOMBO** (Photo J. Clarkson)

IDOMONEUS, *in Elder Dempster colours, in the Bonny River, Nigeria, 1975* (Photo M. Wild)

388 IDOMENEUS
O.N. 357440   1972, 1975–1976

Blue Funnel 'A2' class
Steel screw motorship
487.1′×62.3′×28.2′ 4945 n 8270 g 9430 d
Built by Vickers-Armstrong Ltd, Newcastle, Yard No 112,
as **LAERTES** for Nederlandsche Stoomvaart Maatschappij,
'Ocean' Naamlooze Vennootschap, Amsterdam. Registered
Amsterdam. B & W oil engine 2 SCDA 8 cyl 550 mm–1200 mm
(exhaust 400 mm) by J. G. Kincaid & Co Ltd, Greenock.
6800 bhp, 16 K.

1949 14 April, launched by Miss Ursula Rahusen. 19 Nov-
        ember, maiden voyage ex Amsterdam (Captain J. H.
        Jansen).
1953 4533 n, 7664 g.
1967 Tmk 2633 n, 5100 g, 6630 d. 4103 n, 7467 g, 9430 d.
1972 March, transferred to Elder Dempster Lines Ltd.
        August, transferred to China Mutual Steam Navigation
        Co Ltd (Blue Funnel Line Ltd). Renamed
        IDOMENEUS. Registered Liverpool.
1975 May, transferred to Elder Dempster Lines Ltd. Tmk
        2390 n, 5528 g, 6777 d. 4155 n, 7431 g, 9554 d.
1976 June, sold to Gulf Shipping Lines Ltd, Hong Kong.
        Renamed **GULF VOYAGER**. Registered Liverpool.
1978 Sold for demolition. 8 May, arrived Gadani Beach for
        demolition.

Laertes was the father of Odysseus.
Idomeneus was the valorous, if rather old, King of Crete who
fought with the Greeks in the Trojan War. On his homeward
voyage he made a vow to sacrifice to Poseidon (God of Water)
the first thing he would meet if he survived the storm. It turned
out to be his son, and he was later compelled to go into exile
as an expiation.

*This narrow gauge engine was brought from Freetown, Sierra Leone,
by **IDOMONEUS** in 1975, and is seen here on the quayside at
Liverpool ready for transporting to its present home at the Welsh
Railway Museum*

389 MANO (II)/OTI (II)
O.N. 187169 1972–1978

Blue Funnel 'M' class
Steel screw motorship
494.6′×65.3′×23.1′ 4894 n 8539 g 9660 d
Built by Caledon Shipbuilding and Engineering Co Ltd,
Dundee, Yard No 509, as **MENELAUS** for Ocean Steamship
Co Ltd (A. Holt & Co, Managers). Registered Liverpool. B &
W oil engine 2 SCSA 6 cyl 750 mm–1500 mm (exhaust 500 mm)
by Harland & Wolff Ltd, Belfast. 8500 bhp, 16½ K.
Passenger accommodation: 12.

1957 15 March, launched without ceremony owing to a shipyard strike. 18 October, maiden voyage (Captain J.
Simpson).
1962 Passenger accommodation removed.
1972 Transferred to Elder Dempster Lines Ltd. Renamed
MANO. Tmk 2754 n, 5541 g, 5900 d. 4501 n, 8216 g,
9600 d.
1977 August, renamed **OTI**.
1978 12 May, sold for £176,000 to Leon Rivera Lines Co Ltd,
Cyprus (Thenamaris Maritime Inc, Piraeus, Managers).
Renamed **EL STAR**. Registered Limassol.
1979 Sold for demolition. 1 March, work commenced by Dong
Kuk Steel Co Ltd at Busan, South Korea.

Ships of the Blue Funnel 'M' class (transferred to Elder
Dempster Lines Ltd and renamed): MANO/OTI (389),
OBUASI (407), ONITSHA (408), OPOBO (409), OWERRI
(410).

Mano is derived from the Mano River, Sierra Leone/Liberia
border.

Menelaus was the son of Atreus.

390 AGAMEMNON
O.N. 357439 1972–1977

OTT Bulk class
Steel screw motorship, bulk carrier
579.9′×75.2′×34.5′ 10,422 n 16,402 g 26,729 d
Built by Mitsui Shipbuilding & Engineering Co Ltd, Osaka,
Yard No 926, for Elder Dempster Lines Ltd. Registered Liver-
pool. B & W oil engine 2 SCSA 6 cyl 740 mm–1600 mm by
Mitsui Zosen, Tamano. 11,600 bhp, 15¼ K.

1972 April, launched by Mrs R. J. F. Taylor. Maiden voyage
(Captain M. Lees).
1977 Transferred to Blue Funnel Bulkships Ltd.
1978 14 June, sold for US$4.43 million to Protoporos Mari-
time Corp, Greece. Renamed **PROTOPOROS**. Registered Piraeus.
1984 May, sold to Placido Shipping Corp, Greece. Renamed
ALICIA. Sold to Black Sea Shipping Co Ltd, USSR.
Renamed **ANAPA**.
1985 August, in service.

Note—During the period of Elder Dempster ownership
AGAMEMNON wore the traditional flag and livery of A. Holt
& Co's Blue Funnel Line.

Five OTT bulkships ordered 1972–73 and allocated thus:
AGAMEMNON (390), ACHILLES (391), ANTENOR (392)
to Elder Dempster Lines Ltd; AJAX, ANCHISES to Ocean
Titan Ltd.

Agamemnon was King of Argos.

AGAMEMNON

ANTENOR

391 ANTENOR
O.N. 357447   1972–1978

OTT Bulk class
Steel screw motorship, bulk carrier
579.9′×75.2′×34.5′   10,420 n   16,406 g   26,729 d
Built by Mitsui Shipbuilding & Engineering Co Ltd, Osaka,
Yard No 927, for Elder Dempster Lines Ltd. Registered Liver-
pool. B & W oil engine 2 SCSA 6 cyl 740 mm–1600 mm by
Mitsui Zosen, Tamano. 11,600 bhp, 15¼ K.
1972   7 July, launched by Mrs A. C. Sparks. Trials 17.60 K.
       Maiden voyage (Captain T. Willows).
1978   16 March, sold to Mermaid Sea Carriers Corp, Liberia,
       for £1.88 million. Renamed **SIDERIS**. Registered
       Monrovia.
1985   August, in service.
Note—During the period of Elder Dempster ownership
ANTENOR wore the traditional flag and livery of A. Holt &
Co's Blue Funnel Line.
Antenor was a Trojan prince.

392 ACHILLES
O.N. 357456   1972–1978

OTT Bulk class
Steel screw motorship, bulk carrier
579.9′×75.2′×35.0′   10,420 n   16,406 g   26,729 d
Built by Mitsui Shipbuilding & Engineering Co Ltd, Fujinagata
Works, Osaka, Yard No 928, for Elder Dempster Lines Ltd.
Registered Liverpool. B & W oil engine 2 SCSA 6 cyl 740 mm–
1600 mm by Mitsui Zosen, Tamano. 11,600 bhp, 15¼ K.
1972   7 October, launched by Mrs R. Hobhouse. Trials
       17.667 K. Maiden voyage (Captain J. C. Morris).
1978   1 June, sold to Silverdale Shipping Co, Bermuda for
       £2.16 million (placed under management of Ocean
       Transport & Trading Ltd).

1982   Management transferred to owners.
1983   Sold to Flores Maritime Pte Ltd, Singapore.
1985   August, in service. Now managed by Transocean Mari-
       time Agencies, Monte Carlo.
Note—During the period of Elder Dempster ownership
ACHILLES wore the traditional flag and livery of A. Holt &
Co's Blue Funnel Line.
Achilles was the son of Perseus.

393 BELLEROPHON
O.N. 183793   1973–1976

Blue Funnel 'A3' class
Steel screw motorship
487.0′×62.3′×28.2′   4491 n   7707 g   9295 d
Built by Caledon Shipbuilding & Engineering Co Ltd, Dundee,
Yard No 437, for Ocean Steam Ship Co Ltd (A. Holt & Co,
Managers). Registered Liverpool. B & W oil engine 2 SCSA
7 cyl 750 mm–1500 mm (exhaust 500 mm) by J. G. Kincaid &
Co Ltd, Greenock. 7600 bhp, 16 K.
1950   2 May, launched by Miss D. Montgomery. September,
       completed. 14 October, maiden voyage (Captain H. C.
       Large).
1957   December, transferred to Glen Line Ltd, London.
       Renamed **CARDIGANSHIRE**. Registered Liverpool.
       4485 n, 7707 g.
1967   Tmk 2239 n, 5635 g, 8925 d. 4084 n, 7427 g, 9295 d.
1972   Transferred to China Mutual Steam Navigation Co Ltd
       (Blue Funnel Line Ltd, Managers). Renamed
       BELLEROPHON.
1973   October, transferred to Elder Dempster Lines Ltd.
1976   Transferred to China Mutual Steam Navigation Co Ltd.
       June, sold to Orri Navigation Lines, Greece. Renamed
       OBHOR. Registered Jeddah.
1978   23 September, arrived Karachi after sale to shipbreakers.
       November, demolition work began at Modern Com-
       mercial Corp, Gadani Beach.
Bellerophon was a son of Glaucus, King of Corinth. He changed
his name from Hipponous after killing Belerus.

BELLEROPHON (Photo K. Lewis)

'Belle(rophon)' stars in film

'Bellerophon's' stern showing her film name, port of registration and the Stars and Stripes.

OCEAN'S 'Bellerophon', stage name 'Belle', made her first appearance in front of the camera during the production of a full-length film in Dartmouth recently.

The film, called 'The Sailor', although the final title has not yet been decided, features Kris Kristofferson, Sarah Miles (of 'Ryan's Daughter' fame), and the young Jonathan Kahn.

Howarth Productions Ltd chartered the ship for 10 days, temporarily changing her name and port of registration to 'Belle' of Boston for her role as an American cargo liner.

Master of 'Bellerophon' while she was 'on location' was Captain William Griffith. Making sure things ran smoothly was retired Ocean Fleets master Captain William Moore, acting as liaison officer between the film and ship crews.

Everything went so well in fact that filming on the ship was completed a day ahead of schedule.

Second Engineer Geoffrey Atterton and Junior Engineer Phil Gorton made their own film debut. 'We were asked by the film crew to do a simple repair,' said Geoff, who comes from Perth, Australia, 'as this was the reason for the ship coming into Dartmouth.'

Helping out with technical advice on the film script was Chief Engineer Hugh Duncan. 'They wanted everything to be as authentic as possible', said Mr Duncan who lives in Aberdeen, 'right down to the make of the engine.' He added, 'We had to start the engines astern so the ship wouldn't move about too much while filming.'

Chief Officer of 'Bellerophon' Mr Philip Smith was in contact with the film crew on shore by walkie-talkie.

Chief Engineer Hugh Duncan (left) explains the 'repair work', standing next to him is Lau Wing (No 1) and Second Engineer Geoffrey Atterton.

Captain Moore (left) and Captain Griffith pictured on board 'Bellerophon' in Dartmouth.

Filming on the quay with 'Bellerophon' in the background.

From Ocean Mail

SHONGA

394 SHONGA (III)

O.N. 360166   1973–1984

'Shultz' class
Steel screw combo motorship
145.88 m×21.59 m×8.437 m
Tmk 2780 n, 5677 g, 8288 d. 5197 n, 9236 g, 11,618 d.
Built by Stocznia Szczecinska im A. Warskiego, Szczecin, Yard
No B430/02, for builder's own account. Purchased on completion by Montague Midland Airleasing Ltd. Mortgaged to
Elder Dempster Lines Ltd. Registered Liverpool. Sulzer oil
engine 2 SCSA 6 cyl 680 mm–1250 mm by H. Cegielski, Zaklady Przemyslu Metalowego, Poland. 9900 bhp (7385 Kw),
16½ K.
1973   Launched by Mrs G. J. Ellerton. Trials 18 K. Maiden
        voyage (Captain R. Wild).
1983   31 January, laid up in River Fal. May, recommissioned
        for service (United Kingdom to West Africa).
1984   10 April, sold to Hayden Inc, Monrovia. Renamed
        AROMA. Registered Monrovia. Renamed **DONA**

SHONGA at Tilbury (Photo M. Wild)

1985   August, in service.
Ships of the Shultz class: SHONGA (394), SHERBRO (395).
Note—Six of these 'Shultz' vessels were built, of which Elder
Dempster Lines Ltd acquired three intending to name the
third SOBO, but that ship was released to Nigerian National
Shipping Line and became RIVER HADEJA.

SHERBRO in Guinea Gulf Line Ltd colours

395 SHERBRO (III)

O.N. 364377   1974–1984

'Schultz' class
Steel screw combo motorship
145.68 m×21.52 m×8.383 m
Tmk 2780 n, 5677 g, 8128 d. 5197 n, 9239 g, 12,091 d.
Built by Stocznia Szczecinska im A. Warskiego, Szczecin, Yard

No B430/04, for builder's own account. Purchased on completion by Elder Dempster Lines Ltd. Registered Liverpool. Sulzer oil engine 2 SCSA 6 cyl 680 mm–1250 mm by H. Cegielski, Zaklady Przemyslu Metalowego, Poland. 9900 bhp (7385 Kw), 16 K.

1973 Launched by Mrs P. F. Earlam.
1974 Trials 18 K. Maiden voyage (Captain M. Johnson).
1984 Sold to Ring Maritime Inc, Liberia. Renamed **SHERRY**. Registered Monrovia. Sold to King Sea Maritime Inc, Liberia. Renamed **RITA**. Registered Liberia.
1985 August, in service.

ADRASTUS

396 ADRASTUS

O.N. 185477   1975–1978

Blue Funnel 'A4' class
Steel screw motorship
487.2′×62.4′×28.4′   4573 n   7859 g   9300 d
Built by Vickers Armstrongs Ltd, Newcastle, Yard No 134, for

Ocean Steam Ship Co Ltd (A. Holt & Co, Managers). Registered Liverpool. B & W oil engine 2 SCSA 7 cyl 750 mm–1500 mm (exhaust 500 mm) by Harland & Wolff Ltd, Glasgow. 7600 bhp, 16 K.

1953 22 July, launched by Mrs F. H. Boland. December, completed.
1954 8 January, sailed on maiden voyage from Amsterdam (Captain T. R. Phillips).
1961 January, transferred to Nederlandsche Stoomvaart Maatschappij 'Ocean', Naamlooze Vennootschap. Registered Amsterdam.
1967 Tmk 2701 n, 5299 g, 6615 d. 4171 n, 7572 g, 9300 d.
1975 22 January, transferred to Elder Dempster Lines Ltd. Registered Liverpool. Tmk 2629 n, 5873 g, 6721 d. 4213 n, 7583 g, 9449 d.
1978 23 February, sold to Rhodeswell Shipping Co SA, Cyprus. Renamed **ANASSA**. Registered Limassol.
1981 Sold 6 May, arrived at Gadani Beach for demolition by Gulf Trading Agency. 12 May, work commenced.

The Blue Funnel 'A4' class (transferred to Elder Dempster Lines Ltd): ADRASTUS (396), LYCAON (401), ELPENOR (405).

Adrastus was the King of Argos who led the ill-fated expedition known as 'the seven against Thebes'.

397 GLENLYON

O.N. 304336   1975

'Glenlyon' class
Steel screw motorship
543.8′×74.7′×30.1′   7002 n   11,918 g   10,550 d
Built by Nederlandsch Dok & Scheepsbouw Maatschappy, VOF, Amsterdam, Yard No 510, for Glen Line Ltd. Registered London. Oil engine 2 SCSA 9 cyl 900 mm–1550 mm by Sulzer Bros Ltd, Winterthur, Switzerland. 18,000 bhp, 20 K.
Passenger accommodation: 12.

1962 17 March, launched by Lady MacTier. October, completed. 26 November, Maiden voyage (Captain W. H. Hole).

GLENLYON (Photo Skyfotos)

1967   Tmk 4735 n, 9640 g, 10,255 d. 6774 n, 11,537 g, 11,355 d.
1975   31 January, transferred to Elder Dempster Lines Ltd. May, returned to Glen Line Ltd.
1978   Sold to Tarbord Shipping Co Ltd, Hong Kong. Renamed **EMERALD EXPRESS**. Registered Singapore.
1979   5 March, sold to Sie Youg Steel Wire Mill Co Ltd, Kaohsiung. 30 March, demolition commenced.

'Glenlyon' class vessels transferred to Elder Dempster Lines Ltd: GLENLYON (396), GLENFALLOCH (402).

Glenlyon is in Perthshire, north of Loch Tay. Fortingall, at the entrance to the glen, is reputed to be the birthplace of Pontius Pilate.

AUTOLYCUS

Built by Vickers-Armstrong Ltd, Newcastle, Yard No 107, for China Mutual Steam Navigation Co Ltd (A. Holt & Co, Managers). Registered Liverpool. B & W oil engine 2 SCDA 8 cyl 550 mm–1200 mm (exhaust 400 mm) by Harland & Wolff Ltd, Glasgow. 6800 bhp, 15½ K.
1949   Launched by Mrs A. McLellan. 8 June, maiden voyage from Birkenhead (Captain C. E. Broad).
1957   August, 4437 n, 7705 g.
1969   Blue Funnel Line Ltd, Managers. Tmk 2575 n, 5691 g, 6650 d. 4169 n, 7420 g, 9440 d.
1975   5 April, transferred to Elder Dempster Lines Ltd.
1976   16 February, sold to Gulf Shipping Lines Ltd, Hong Kong. Renamed **GULF TRADER**. Registered Liverpool.
1978   Sold to Taiwan shipbreakers. 29 April, arrived Kaohsiung for demolition. June, work by Non Feng Steel Enterprises Co Ltd commenced.

Autolycus was the maternal grandfather of Odysseus. When in disguise a scar on his thigh was recognised by his old nurse.

STENTOR (Photo World Ship Photo Library)

398 STENTOR
O.N. 181024   1975

Steel screw motorship
497.3′×64.3′×29.7′   6053 n   10,203 g   10,910 d
Built by Caledon Shipbuilding & Engineering Co Ltd, Dundee, Yard No 410, for Ocean Steam Ship Co Ltd (A. Holt & Co, Managers). Registered Liverpool. B & W oil engine 2 SCDA 8 cyl 500 mm–1200 mm by J. G. Kincaid & Co Ltd, Greenock. 6800 bhp, 14¾ K.
1946   Launched by Miss Olive Holt. June, completed.
1958   Transferred to Glen Line Ltd, London. Renamed **GLENSHIEL**. 6022 n, 10,195 g.
1963   Transferred to Ocean Steam Ship Co Ltd. Renamed **STENTOR**.
1969   Placed under Blue Funnel Line Ltd management. Tmk 3733 n, 6949 g, 9750 d. 5537 n, 9833 g, 10,910 d.
1975   Transferred to China Mutual Steam Navigation Co Ltd (Blue Funnel Line Ltd, Managers). Placed on Elder Dempster West African Trades. 5 March, sold to Taiwan shipbreakers. Renamed **TENTO** for delivery voyage. 6 April, arrived Kaohsiung for demolition by Nan Kwang Steel & Iron Works.

Stentor was Chief Herald of the Greeks.

Glenshiel is approached from Loch Ness by Invermoriston and Claunie Bridge, and it is awe-inspiring in its initial stages through the Pass of Strachel.

399 AUTOLYCUS
O.N. 182483   1975–1976

Blue Funnel 'A2' class
Steel screw motorship
487.0′×62.4′×28.3′   4852 n   8236 g   9440 d

400 ANTILOCHUS
O.N. 182486   1975–1976

Blue Funnel 'A2' class
Steel screw motorship
487.0′×62.3′×28.2′   4895 n   8238 g   9240 d
Built by Harland & Wolff Ltd, Belfast, Yard No 1372, for Ocean Steamship Co Ltd (A. Holt & Co, Managers). Registered Liverpool. B & W oil engine 2 SCDA 8 cyl 550 mm–1600 mm by the builders. 6800 bhp, 15½ K.
1948   2 November, launched by Lady F. Rebbeck.
1949   May, completed. 20 May, maiden voyage ex Birkenhead (Captain P. S. Atkins).
1951   4479 n, 7635 g.
1957   May, 4472 n, 7702 g.
1969   Blue Funnel Line Ltd, managers. Tmk 2485 n, 5591 g, 6460 d. 4140 n, 7378 g, 9240 d.
1973   Transferred to China Mutual Steam Navigation Co Ltd (Blue Funnel Line Ltd, Managers).
1975   22 May, transferred to Elder Dempster Lines Ltd.
1976   10 November, sold to Gulf (Shipowners) Ltd, Hong Kong for £242,500. Renamed **GULF ORIENT**. Registered Liverpool.
1978   Sold for demolition. 5 May, arrived at Gadani Beach for demolition. July, work by Al-Noor Steel Industries Ltd commenced.

Antilochus, the eldest son of Nestor, fought at the side of Agamemnon. He was killed by Memnon, King of the Ethiopians.

ANTILOCHUS (Photo J. Clarkson)

401 LYCAON (I)
O.N. 185489   1975–1976

Blue Funnel 'A4' class
Steel screw motorship
487.2′×62.3′×28.5′   4546 d   7859 g   9280 d
Built by Vickers-Armstrong Ltd, Newcastle, Yard No 138, for
China Mutual Steam Navigation Co Ltd (A. Holt & Co,
Managers). Registered Liverpool. B & W oil engine 2 SCSA
7 cyl 750 mm–1500 mm (exhaust 500 mm) by J. G. Kincaid &
Co Ltd, Greenock. 7600 bhp, 16 K.
1953   30 December, launched by Mrs T. M. Lawrie.
1954   June, completed. 12 July, maiden voyage (Captain J. P.
       Makepeace).
1960   Transferred to Nederlandsche Stoomvaart Maatsch-
       appij 'Ocean', Naamlooze Vennootschap. Registered
       Amsterdam.
1970   Tmk 2694 n, 5300 g, 6602 d. 4164 n, 7572 g, 9280 d.

1975   8 July, transferred to Elder Dempster Lines Ltd. Regis-
       tered Liverpool.
1976   December, transferred to China Mutual Steam Navi-
       gation Co Ltd (Blue Funnel Line Ltd, Managers).
       Renamed **GLAUCUS**.
1977   March, sold to Marlborough Maritime Inc, Panama.
       Renamed **UNITED VANGUARD**. Registered
       Panama.
1979   12 May, abandoned by crew 360 miles south-east of
       Madras in approximate position 10°.55′N 86°.25′E after
       developing engine trouble and leakages, voyage Sharjah
       to Bassein, Burma. Later reported afloat in position
       13°.20′N 88°.00′E. Ultimately wrecked on Buffalo Rock
       in position 16°.23′N 94°.13′E.

Lycaon was a son of Priam, King of Troy.
Glaucus was King of Corinth.

LYCAON (Photo J. Clarkson)

402 GLENFALLOCH
O.N. 304437   1975–1977

'Glenlyon' class
Steel screw motorship
543.8′×74.7′×30.1′   6966 n   11,918 g   11,445 d
Built by Fairfield Shipbuilding and Engineering Co Ltd, Govan,
Glasgow, Yard No 813, for Glen Line Ltd, London. Registered
London. Oil engine 2 SCSA 9 cyl 900 mm–1550 mm by Sulzer
Bros Ltd, Winterthur, Switzerland. 18,000 bhp, 20 K.
Passenger accommodation: 12.
1962   3 July, launched by Mrs H. B. Roper-Caldbeck.
1963   January, completed. 12 February, maiden voyage (Cap-
       tain T. R. Walker).

GLENFALLOCH (Photo Skyfotos)

1968   Tmk 4736 n, 9640 g, 10,353 d. 6774 n, 11,537 g, 11,445 d.
1975   24 August, transferred to Elder Dempster Lines Ltd.
1977   8 November, sold to China Ocean Shipping Co, Peking, for US$2.65 million. Renamed **QING HE CHENG**. Registered Shanghai.
1985   August, in service.
Glenfalloch is due north of Loch Lomond.

403   AUTOMEDON
O.N. 182456   1975–1977

Blue Funnel 'A2' class
Steel screw motorship
487.0′×62.3′×28.3′   4888 n   8231 g   9320 d
Built by Scotts' Shipbuilding & Engineering Co Ltd, Greenock, Yard No 639, for Ocean Steam Ship Co Ltd (A. Holt & Co, Managers) as **CYCLOPS**. Registered Liverpool. B & W oil engine 2 SCDA 8 cyl 550 mm–1200 mm by the builders. 6800 bhp, 15½ K.
1948   21 July, launched by Mrs W. Gavigan. 18 December, maiden voyage (Captain T. Bell).
1955   4476 n, 7632 g.
1967   Tmk 2397 n, 5520 g, 6550 d. 4160 n, 7416 g, 9320 d. Placed under Blue Funnel Line Ltd management.
1975   July, renamed **AUTOMEDON**. December, transferred to Elder Dempster Lines Ltd.
1977   Sold for demolition. 25 August, arrived Dalmuir for demolition by W. H. Arnott Young & Co Ltd.
The Cyclops were a tribe of lawless and godless shepherds in Sicily. Automedon was the charioteer of Achilles.

AUTOMEDON

POLYDORUS

404   POLYDORUS
O.N. 185428   1976–1978

Blue Funnel 'A3' class
Steel screw motorship
487.2′×62.3′×28.4′   4538 n   7799 g   9320 d
Built by Vickers-Armstrong Ltd, Newcastle, Yard No 126, for Ocean Steam Ship Co Ltd (A. Holt & Co, Managers) as **ALCINOUS**. Registered Liverpool. B & W oil engine 2 SCSA 7 cyl 750 mm–1500 mm (exhaust 500 mm) by J. G. Kincaid & Co Ltd, Greenock. 7600 bhp, 15½ K.
1951   27 November, launched by Mrs J. M. Ormston.
1952   Completed April. 28 April, maiden voyage (Captain A. F. Ffoulkes).
1960   Transferred to Nederlandsche Stoomvaart Maatschappij Oceaan, Naamlooze Vennootschap. Renamed **POLYDORUS**. Registered Amsterdam. 4557 n, 7785 g.
1973   November, transferred to China Mutual Steam Navigation Co Ltd (Blue Funnel Line Ltd). Registered Liverpool. Tmk 2663 n, 5762 g. 4190 n, 7540 g.
1976   April, operated in a joint venture Ocean Transport & Trading Ltd and S. H. Alatas & Co Ltd, Jeddah (managed by Ocean). Renamed **JOHARA**. Subsequently transferred to Elder Dempster Lines Ltd. Renamed **POLYDORUS**.
1978   Sold to Hesperus Navigation Corp, Panama. Renamed **MATINA**. Registered Panama. April, sold to Karachi shipbreakers. 5 July, demolition commenced.
Alcinous was King of Phaeicia.
Polydorus was a son of Priam, King of Troy.

405   ELPENOR
O.N. 185483   1976–1977

Blue Funnel 'A4' class
Steel screw motorship
487.0′×62.4′×28.2′   4509 n   7757 g   9100 d
Built by 1953 at Harland & Wolff Ltd, Belfast, Yard No 1477, for China Mutual Steam Navigation Co Ltd (A. Holt & Co, Managers). Registered Liverpool. B & W oil engine 2 SCSA 7 cyl 750 mm–1500 mm (exhaust 500 mm) by the builder. 7600 bhp, 16 K.
1953   11 November, launched by Lady Wakehurst.
1954   April, completed. 15 May, maiden voyage (Captain W. K. Hole).
1967   Tmk 2664 n, 5770 g, 6540 d. 4188 n, 7548 g, 9100 d.
1976   November, transferred to Elder Dempster Lines Ltd. Tmk 2680 n, 5713 g, 6553 d. 4152 n, 7425 g, 9246 d.
1977   24 June, sold for US$632,000 to Cremone Bay Shipping Co Ltd, Panama. Renamed **UNITED CONCORD**. Registered Panama.

ELPENOR (Photo J. Clarkson)

1979 Sold for demolition and 21 May, arrived Kaohsiung.
1980 19 August, demolition commenced by Chang Iron & Steel Works Co Ltd.

Elpenor was one of the followers of Odysseus who were temporarily turned into swine by Circé the sorceress. He was neither overbrave in war nor excelling in wisdom.

406 ATREUS
O.N. 183828   1977

Blue Funnel 'A3' class
Steel screw motorship
487.2'×52.3'×28.4'   4545 n   7800 g   9280 d
Built by Vickers-Armstrong Ltd, Newcastle, Yard No 125, for China Mutual Steam Navigation Co Ltd (A. Holt & Co, Managers). Registered Liverpool. B & W oil engine 2 SCSA 7 cyl 750 mm–1500 mm (exhaust 500 mm) by J. G. Kincaid & Co Ltd, Greenock. 7600 bhp, 15½ K.
1951 5 April, launched by Mrs E. G. Price. November, completed. 7 December, maiden voyage (Captain K. W. Kerr).
1972 Tmk 2664 n, 5770 g, 6589 d. 4188 n, 7548 g, 9280 d.
1973 Placed under Blue Funnel Line Ltd management.
1977 4 August, transferred to Elder Dempster Lines Ltd. October, sold to Sherwood Shipping Co Ltd, Hong Kong for US$430,000. Renamed **UNITED VALIANT**. Registered Singapore.
1979 Sold to Tung Ho Steel Enterprise Corp, Taiwan. 23 February, arrived Kaohsiung for demolition, commencing 13 March.

Atreus was the son of Pelops and Hippodamia and the father of Agamemnon and Menelaus.

ATREUS (Photo J. Clarkson)

407 OBUASI (III)
O.N. 301297   1977–1978

Blue Funnel 'M' class
Steel screw motorship
494.6'×65.3'×28.1'   4874 n   8530 g   9670 d
Built by Caledon Shipbuilding & Engineering Co Ltd, Dundee, Yard No 515, as **MACHAON** for Ocean Steam Ship Co Ltd (A. Holt & Co, Managers). Registered Liverpool. B & W engine 2 SCSA 6 cyl 750 mm–1500 mm (exhaust 500 mm) by J. G. Kincaid & Co Ltd, Greenock. 8500 bhp, 16½ K.
Passenger accommodation: 12.
1958 14 October, launched by Yang Teramat Hullia Tunku Maimunah.
1959 Completed April. Maiden voyage 6 May (Captain H. F. Readshaw).
1962 Passenger accommodation removed.
1968 Tmk 2665 n, 5336 g, 6024 d. 4421 n, 8246 g, 9825 d.
1975 Transferred to Nederlandsche Stoomvaart Maatschappi 'Ocean', Naamlooze Vennootschap. Registered Amsterdam.
1977 August, transferred to Elder Dempster Lines Ltd. Renamed **OBUASI**. Registered Liverpool.
1978 26 June, sold to Lenake Shipping Co Ltd, Cyprus (Thenamaris Maritime Inc, Managers) for £187,000. Renamed **EL SEA**. July, sold to Tartan Shipping Ltd, Greece. Renamed **MED ENDEAVOR**. Registered Piraeus.
1979 Sold for demolition. 26 February, demolition work began at Sing Cheng Yung Iron & Steel Co, Kaohsiung.

Machaon was the son of Aesculapius, the God of Health.

MENESTHEUS, subsequently **ONITSHA** (Photo J. Clarkson)

408 ONITSHA (III)
O.N. 187180   1977–1978

Blue Funnel 'M' class
Steel screw motorship
494.7'×65.3'×28.9'   4873 n   8510 g   9680 d
Built by Caledon Shipbuilding and Engineering Co Ltd, Dundee, Yard No 510, as **MENESTHEUS** for Ocean Steam Ship Co Ltd (A. Holt & Co, Managers). Registered Liverpool. B & W oil engine 2 SCSA 6 cyl 750 mm–1500 mm (exhaust 500 mm) by Harland & Wolff Ltd, Belfast. 8500 bhp, 16½ K.
Passenger accommodation: 12.
1957 26 August, launched by Mrs M. Hill.
1958 February, completed. 24 March, maiden voyage (Captain R. A. Hanney).
1962 Passenger accommodation removed.
1972 Transferred to China Mutual Steam Navigation Co Ltd (Blue Funnel Line Ltd, Managers). Tmk 2742 n, 5941 g, 5909 d. 4539 n, 8220 g, 9680 d.

1977 August, transferred to Elder Dempster Lines Ltd. Renamed **ONITSHA**.

1978 19 May, sold to Palermo Shipping Co Ltd, Greece for £148,000. Renamed **EL ISLAND**. Registered Limassol.

1979 Sold for demolition. 12 March arrived Kaohsiung. 12 April, work commenced at Lung Fa Steel and Iron Co Ltd, Kaohsiung.

Menestheus was the son of Perseus.

409 OPOBO (III)
O.N. 301346   1977–1978

Blue Funnel 'M' class
Steel screw motorship
494.7′×65.3′×28.9′   4880 n   8531 g   9670 d
Built by Caledon Shipbuilding and Engineering Co Ltd, Dundee, Yard No 520, for Ocean Steam Ship Co Ltd (A. Holt & Co, Managers) as **MARON**. Registered Liverpool. B & W oil engine 2 SCSA 6 cyl 750 mm–1500 mm (exhaust 500 mm) by J. G. Kincaid & Co Ltd, Greenock. 8500 bhp, 16½ K.
Passenger accommodation: 12.

1960 26 February, launched by Mrs R. S. MacTier. July, completed. 14 August, maiden voyage (Captain C. F. Lock).

1962 Passenger accommodation removed.

1973 Transferred to China Mutual Steam Navigation Co Ltd (Blue Funnel Line Ltd, Managers). Tmk 2833 n, 6044 g, 5929 d. 4531 n, 8252 g, 9670 d.

1975 Renamed **RHEXENOR**.

1977 July, transferred to Elder Dempster Lines Ltd. Renamed **OPOBO**.

1978 May, sold to Thenamaris Maritime Inc, Piraeus for £192,000. Renamed **EL FORTUNE**. Sold to Belton Shipping Corp, Greece. Renamed **EUROPE II**. Registered Piraeus.

1982 6 March, laid up at Piraeus.

1984 Sold to Trade Shipping Ltd, Malta GC. Registered Malta GC.

1985 August, reported laid up at Eleusis.

Maron was a priest of Apollo.

MARON, subsequently *OPOBO* (Photo J. Clarkson)

410 OWERRI (II)
O.N. 301299   1977–1978

Blue Funnel 'M' class
Steel screw motorship
494.5′×65.3′×28.9′   4873 n   8504 g   9770 d
Built by Vickers Armstrong (Shipbuilders) Ltd, Newcastle, Yard No 166, as **MEMNON** for China Mutual Steam Navigation Co Ltd (A. Holt & Co, Managers). Registered Liverpool. B & W oil engine 2 SCSA 6 cyl 750 mm–1500 mm (exhaust 500 mm) by Harland & Wolff Ltd, Belfast. 8500 bhp, 16½ K.
Passenger accommodation: 12.

1958 28 October, launched by Lady Jenkins.

1959 April, completed. 16 May, maiden voyage (Captain E. M. Robb).

1962 Passenger accommodation removed.

1967 Tmk 2781 n, 5541 g, 6030 d. 4524 n, 8222 g, 9770 d.

1975 April, renamed **STENTOR**.

STENTOR, subsequently *OWERRI*, in Elder Dempster colours (Photo J. Clarkson)

1977 April, transferred to Elder Dempster Lines Ltd. Renamed **OWERRI**.
1978 May, sold for £172,000 to Henlow Shipping Corp, Greece. Renamed **EUROPE**. Registered Piraeus.
1982 3 July, laid up at Stylis.
1985 August, reported still laid up at Stylis.
Memnon was King of Ethiopia, slain by Achilles.

411 SOKOTO (III)
O.N. 378030   1979–

'Sokoto' class
Steel screw Combo motorship
145.01 m×21.51 m×8.402 m
Tmk 3385 n, 5560 g, 8063 d. 5657 n, 9145 g, 11,644 d
Built by Stocznia Szczecinska im A, Warskiego, Szczecin, Poland, Yard No B430/07, for H. Schulat. Sulzer oil engine 2 SCSA 6 cyl 680 mm–1250 mm by H. Cegielski, Poznan. 9450 bhp (7050 Kw), 18 K.
1978 12 August, launched by Mrs P. H. D. Toosey, and acquired after completion by Midland Montagu Leasing (UK) Ltd, London.
1979 Leased to Elder Dempster Lines Ltd. Registered Liverpool. 2 April, maiden voyage (Captain S. A. McInnes).
1983 May, chartered by Nigerian Green Lines Ltd, Lagos. Renamed **BELLO FOLAWIYO**. Painted in charterer's livery.

1984 Reverted to Elder Dempster Lines Ltd. Renamed **SOKOTO**. In the present fleet.
Ships of the 'Sokoto' class: SOKOTO (411), SEKONDI (412).

Above, **BELLO FOLAWIYO**, *formerly and subsequently* **SOKOTO**, *in the Bonny River, August 1983. Below,* **SOKOTO** *at berth WS 3, Huskinson Dock, Liverpool, prior to her maiden voyage on 2 April 1979*

Above, **SEKONDI**, *as* **BELLO FOLAWIYO** (Photo Bob Bird).
Below, **SEKONDI**

Lines Ltd. Registered Liverpool. Sulzer oil engine 2 SCSA 6 cyl 660 mm–1250 mm by H. Cegielski, Poznan. 9450 bhp (7050 Kw), 18 K.
1978   2 December, launched by Mrs F. Roby.
1979   August, maiden voyage (Captain R. Mc. L. Munro).
1985   15 July, chartered to Nigerian Green Lines Ltd, Lagos. Renamed **BELLO FOLAWIYO**. December, reverted to Elder Dempster Lines Ltd. Renamed **SEKONDI**. In the present fleet.

413   SAPELE (IV)
O.N. 378104   1980–

Steel screw Combo motorship
145.88 m×21.59 m×8.44 m
Tmk 2747 n, 5657 g, 8159 d. 5167 n, 9240 g, 11,587 d.
Built by Stocznia Szczecinska im A, Szczecin, Poland, Yard No B430/11, for builder's account. Purchased by Midland Montagu Leasing (UK) Ltd, London, and leased to Elder Dempster Lines Ltd. Registered Liverpool. Sulzer oil engine 2 SCSA 6 cyl 680 mm–1250 mm by H. Cegielski, Poznan. 9990 bhp (7453 Kw), 18 K.
1979   7 September, launched by Mrs D. S. Sykes.
1980   January, completed. Maiden voyage (Captain A. J. Milmine).

412   SEKONDI (III)
O.N. 378095   1979–

'Sokoto' class
Steel screw Combo motorship
145.01 m×21.51 m×8.402 m
Tmk 2747 n, 5677 g, 8063 d. 5167 n, 9240 g, 11587 d.
Built by Stocznia Szczecinska im A, Warskiego, Szczecin, Poland, Yard No B430/07, and sold to Midland Montagu Leasing (UK) Ltd, London, and leased to Elder Dempster

SAPELE *loading at Middlesbrough*

349

1982 Chartered to Ministry of Defence for Falkland Islands duties. 14 June, arrived Falkland Islands. 5 November, returned to owners. 19 July, chartered to Ministry of Defence for Falkland Island duties.

1983 February, chartered to Curnow Shipping Ltd for voyage to Ascension Island. Thence chartered to Lamport & Holt Line Ltd for voyage South America to Europe, thereafter returned to owners.

1984 July, laid up in the Blackwater River. Subsequently re-commissioned.

1985 August, in the present fleet.

414 MARON
O.N. 378100   1980–1986

'Maron' class
Steel screw Combo motorship
164.57 m × 26.07 m × 10.672 m
Tmk 5864 n, 10,867 g, 15,418 d. 9192 n, 16,842 g, 21,310 d.
Built by Scotts' Shipbuilding & Engineering Co Ltd, Greenock, Yard No 749, for Ocean Transport & Trading Ltd. Registered Liverpool. Sulzer oil engine 2 SCSA 7 cyl 760 mm–1550 mm by the builders. 16,800 bhp (12,533 Kw), 18 K.

1979 26 April, launched by Lady Morse.
1980 Completed. Maiden voyage United Kingdom to West Africa (Captain D. MacLachlan).
1981 22 November, chartered to Overseas Containers Ltd. Renamed **STUDLAND BAY**. Painted in charterer's livery.
1982 Reverted to owners. Renamed **MARON**.
1986 20 January, sold to Nigerian Green Lines Ltd, Lagos (Ocean Fleets Ltd, Managers). Registered Bermuda. To be renamed **YINKA FOLAWIYO** and registered at Lagos. In service.

Ships of the 'Maron' class: MARON (414), MENTOR (415), MYRMIDON (416).

415 MENTOR
O.N. 389154   1980–1985

'Maron' class
Steel screw Combo motorship
164.57 m × 26.07 m × 10.653 m
Tmk 5544 n, 10,867 g, 15,479 d. 8872 n, 16,482 g, 21,180 d.
Built by Scotts' Shipbuilding & Engineering Co Ltd, Greenock, Yard No 750, for Ocean Fleets Ltd. Registered Liverpool. Sulzer

*Left, **MARON** at Liverpool when on charter to Hoegh Lines, Oslo. Below, after launching (Photo G. Young). Opposite, loading at Middlesbrough prior to her maiden voyage*

MARON

Above, **MENTOR** *after launching* (Photo G. Young), *and below, in drydock*

oil engine 2 SCSA 7 cyl 760 mm–1550 mm by the builders. 16,800 bhp (12,533 Kw), 18 K.

1979 8 August, launched by Lady Alexander.
1980 August, commenced maiden voyage, Glasgow (in ballast)–USA–Persian Gulf. Aramco charters (Captain S. A. McInnes). October, entered West African services of Elder Dempster Lines Ltd.
1981 5 December, chartered to Overseas Containers Ltd for a period of one year and livery changed to that of Ellerman Line. Renamed **CITY OF LONDON**.
1982 20 December, reverted to owners. Renamed **MENTOR** and laid up in River Fal.
1984 March recommissioned.
1985 April, sold to Hake Shipping Co, Cyprus. Renamed **NORMANNIA**. August, in service.

Mentor was a friend and counsellor of Odysseus.

416 MYRMIDON

O.N. 389162   1981–1986

'Maron' class
Steel screw Combo motorship
164.62 mm×26.07 mm×10.664 m
Tmk 5544 n, 10,867 g, 15,750 d. 8872 n, 16,482 g, 21,215 d.
Built by Scotts' Shipbuilding & Engineering Co, Greenock, Yard No 751, for Ocean Fleets Ltd. Registered Liverpool. Sulzer oil engine 2 SCSA 7 cyl 760 mm–1550 mm by the builders. 16,800 bhp (12,533 Kw), 18 K.

1980 19 February, launched by Mrs G. J. Ellerton. Maiden voyage chartered out to CGM, France (Captain H. K. Trimbell), one round voyage France to South Pacific.
1981 May, entered West African services of Elder Dempster Lines Ltd.

MYRMIDON *sliding down the ways into the Clyde* (Photo G. Young)

MYRMIDON *running trials* (Photo W. Ralston Ltd)

1982	22 June, chartered to the Ministry of Defence for Falklands Islands duties. 28 October, returned to owners.
1984	October, laid up in the Blackwater River. November, chartered to Maritime Associated Carriers, Hamburg, for one round voyage. Renamed **CAPE TOWN CARRIER**. Painted in charterer's livery during charter voyage.
1985	7 February, renamed **MYRMIDON** on reversion to owners.
1986	February, sold to Nigerian Green Lines Ltd, Lagos. Renamed **BELLO FOLAWIYO**. Registered Lagos. In service.

The Myrmidons were a Greek tribe led to Troy by Achilles.

Above, **MYRMIDON** *during her brief career as* **CAPE TOWN CARRIER***, and below,* **MENELAUS**

417 MENELAUS
O.N. 378032   1985–

'Menelaus' class
Steel screw Combo motorship
164.52 m × 26.07 m × 10.624 m
Tmk 5537 n, 10,443 g, 15,500 d. 8666 n, 16,031 g, 21,241 d.
Built by Mitsubishi Heavy Industries Ltd, Nagasaki, Yard No 1806, for Airlease International Nominees (Moorgate) Ltd, (Ocean Fleets Ltd, Managers). Registered Liverpool. Sulzer oil engine 2 SCSA 7 cyl 760 mm–1550 mm by the builders. 16,800 bhp (12,533 Kw), 18 K.

1977	16 April, launched by Mrs A. G. S. McCallum. Maiden voyage (Captain A. M. Blackburn).
1980	14 December, renamed **BARBER MENELAUS**.
1982	Transferred to Barber Menelaus Shipping Corp (Ocean Fleets Ltd, Managers), Panama. Registered Panama. Tmk 5244 n, 9436 g. 8685 n, 14,905 g.
1984	Transferred to Airlease International Nominees (Moorgate) Ltd (Ocean Fleets Ltd, Managers), London. Renamed **MENELAUS**. Registered Liverpool. Tmk 5586 n, 10,443 g. 8666 n, 16,030 g.
1985	8 February, allocated to Elder Dempster Lines Ltd, West African routes. In the present fleet.

Ships of the 'Menelaus' class: MENELAUS (417), MELAMPUS (418), MENESTHEUS (419), MEMNON (586) (see page 528).

418 MELAMPUS
O.N. 378039   1985–

'Menelaus' class
Steel screw Combo motorship
164.70 m × 26.07 m × 10.624 m
Tmk 5537 n, 10,443 g, 15,175 d. 8666 n, 16,031 g, 21,618 d.

MELAMPUS (Photo *Ocean Mail*)

356

Built by Mitsubishi Heavy Industries Ltd, Nagasaki Yard No 1808, for Airlease International Nominees (Moorgate) Ltd (Ocean Fleets Ltd, Managers). Registered Liverpool. Sulzer oil engine 2 SCSA 7 cyl 760 mm–1550 mm by the builders. 16,800 bhp (12,533 Kw), 18 K.

1977 Launched by Mrs W. Menzies-Wilson. Maiden voyage (Captain A. M. Blackburn).
1985 Allocated to Elder Dempster Lines Ltd, West African trade. In the present fleet.

Melampus understood the language of birds and with their help was to foretell the future.

419 MENESTHEUS
O.N. 378040   1985–

'Menelaus' class
Steel screw Combo motorship
164.60 m × 26.07 m × 10.623 m
Tmk 5537 n, 10,443 g, 15,087 d. 8666 n, 16,931 g, 21,618 d.

Built by Mitsubishi Heavy Industries Ltd, Nagasaki, Yard No 1809, for Airlease International Nominees (Moorgate) Ltd (Ocean Fleets Ltd, Managers). Registered Liverpool. Sulzer oil engine 2 SCSA 7 cyl 760 mm–1550 mm by the builders. 16,800 bhp (12,533 Kw), 18 K.

1977 27 August, launched by Mrs. O. Oladitan. Maiden voyage (Captain S. B. Gilliat).
1980 4 November, renamed **BARBER MENESTHEUS** at Kobe.
1982 5 November, transferred to Barber Menestheus Shipping Corp (Ocean Fleets Ltd, Managers). Registered Panama. Tmk 5244 n, 9463 g. 8685 n, 14,005 g.
1983 28 December, renamed **MENESTHEUS** at Port Everglades.
1984 18 April, registered Liverpool. 27 August, chartered to Lloyd Brasileiro. Renamed **LLOYD PARANA** at Rio de Janeiro.
1985 29 January, renamed **MENESTHEUS** at Santos. 26 March, arrived Liverpool and entered the West African service of Elder Dempster Lines Ltd.
1986 February, renamed **APAPA PALM**. In the present fleet.

Menestheus was a son of Perseus.
Apapa Palm was so named to retain the Palm Line Ltd presence in the West African trade.

MENESTHEUS (Photo Fotoflite)

M. S. "MENESTHEUS"

For AIRLEASE INTERNATIONAL NOMINEES
(MOORGATE) LIMITED
Naming : 30th November, 1977
Nagasaki, Japan

MENESTHEUS from a postcard published by Mitsubishi Heavy Industries Ltd

PART 2

Vessels engaged in the North Atlantic trade

Ship Nos 420–468

LAKE CHAMPLAIN (ship No. 458) (Photo McRoberts)

ALEXANDER ELDER

ASSAYE

420 ALEXANDER ELDER/MERRIMAC
O.N. 97770   1890–1899

Steel screw steamer, two decks
400.6′×45.2′×28.2′   2721 n   4173 g
Built by Harland & Wolff Ltd, Belfast, Yard No 223, for Elder, Dempster & Co. Registered Liverpool. T 3 cyl 25½″, 42″, 70″–51″ by the builders. 390 hp, 11 K.
1890   8 February, launched. April, completed.
1891   October, transferred to African Steamship Co.
1892   Renamed **MERRIMAC**. Registered London. 2696 n, 4177 g.
1891–1892   On charter to Atlantic Transport Co Ltd, employed on the London–Baltimore and London–Swansea–New York cargo services.
1894   First Elder Dempster vessel to maintain regular sailings on the North Atlantic. Operated on the cattle trade. On one trip carried 825 animals.
1895   30 January, ashore on Burbo Bank in the River Mersey when homeward bound from New Orleans.
1898   24 January, whilst bound from Liverpool to New Orleans, anchored and abandoned south-west coast Fayal. Crew saved. Tug JUPITER returned part crew to save vessel.
1899   15 July, stranded off Hearn Point signal station, Anticosta, voyage Bristol to Montreal. Towed off and repaired at Quebec. 25 October, departed Quebec for Belfast with cargo of timber and grain, disappeared without trace. Captain C. H. Davies and a crew of 35, lost their lives.

Alexander Elder was one of the founder members of Elder Dempster & Company. He was brother of John, the famous ship and engine builder.

The death of Captain Howell Williams a few weeks ago recalls a masterly piece of salvage work for which the late commander was responsible when serving as chief officer on our steamer *Merrimac* in 1895. The *Merrimac* was on a voyage from Liverpool to the United States and, when in mid-Atlantic, a ship was sighted lying-over on her beam ends and apparently on a point of sinking. When the *Merrimac* steamed up close to the sinking ship, it was observed that she had been abandoned. The ship appeared to be seaworthy, with the exception that her cargo of grain had shifted. Captain Morgan of the *Merrimac* decided to send a prize crew to board her, and Chief Officer Williams, together with the nine other members of the crew of the *Merrimac*, boarded the ship with instructions to trim her as much as possible and navigate her to Liverpool. The ship proved to be the large full-rigged Liverpool ship *Arno*, and marine insurance circles had entertained very little hope of her safety when news of her having been abandoned was first received. It took Captain Williams and his men close upon three weeks to navigate the *Arno* to Liverpool, where she was berthed in Salthouse Dock.
In the following year, 1896, Captain Williams received his first Elder, Dempster command, being appointed to the *Loango* but, unfortunately, failing health necessitated his retirement from the sea in 1907.

From Elder, Dempster House Magazine, June 1926

421 ASSAYE
O.N. 98949   1891–1897

Steel screw steamer, two decks.
401.0′×45.3′×28.1′   2797 n   4296 g
Laid down by Harland & Wolff Ltd, Belfast, Yard No 239, for Peninsular & Oriental Steam Navigation Co. Acquired on the stocks by African Steamship Co, Liverpool. Registered London. T 3 cyl 25½′, 42″, 70″–51″ by the builders. 390 hp, 11 K.
1891   9 May, launched. July, completed.
1897   5 April, (Captain R. Carruthers) wrecked on Blond Rock, Seal Island, Nova Scotia (43°.25′N 66°.00′W), voyage Liverpool to St John, New Brunswick. No loss of life.

MEMNON

422 PLASSEY/MEMNON (I)
O.N. 98125   1890–1917

'Memphis' class
Steel screw steamer, two decks
345.6′×40.9′×26.7′   2046 n   3176 g
Laid down as **TALAVERA** at Harland & Wolff Ltd, Belfast, Yard No 228, for T. & J. Brocklebank. Acquired on the stocks by African Steamship Co, and renamed **PLASSEY**. Registered London. T 3 cyl 22″, 36″, 60″–48″ by the builders. 300 hp, 10 K.
1890   22 May, launched. July, completed. Chartered for operation on the Indian trade by T. & J. Brocklebank.
1892   December, renamed **MEMNON**. Registered London.
1893   Chartered to Atlantic Transport Co Ltd. Employed on London to Baltimore and London to Philadelphia cargo services.
1904   Transferred to Elder Dempster Shipping Ltd. Registered Liverpool.

1917　12 March, torpedoed in a submerged attack without warning and sunk by German submarine UC66 (Oberleutnant zü See Herbert Pustkuchen) about 20 miles south-west of Portland Bill. Six lives lost.

Ships of the 'Memphis' class: PLASSEY (422), SOBRAON (423), MEMPHIS (424), ETOLIA (425), LYCIA (426).

Memnon was King of Ethiopia, son of Tithonus and the Goddess of the Dawn. He was slayed by Achilles.

MEMPHIS

MEXICO

423　SOBRAON/MEXICO
O.N. 98180　　　　　　　　　　　　　　1890–1895

'Memphis' class
Steel screw steamer, two decks
345.6′×40.9′×26.7′　2055 n　3185 g
Laid down as **BARROSA** by Harland & Wolff Ltd, Belfast, Yard No 232 for T. & J. Brocklebank. Acquired on the stocks by African Steamship Co and renamed **SOBRAON**. Registered London. T 3 cyl 22″, 36″, 60″–48″ by the builders. 300 hp, 10 K.
1890　17 September, launched. November, completed and chartered to T. & J. Brocklebank.
1891　Entered Liverpool to Baltimore trade.
1893　January, renamed **MEXICO**. Registered London. Chartered to Atlantic Transport Co Ltd. Employed on London to Baltimore and London to Philadelphia services.
1895　4 July, wrecked on Belle Isle, voyage Montreal to Bristol, cargo grain (Captain C. V. Daley).

424　MEMPHIS
O.N. 97827　　　　　　　　　　　　　　1890–1896

'Memphis' class
Steel screw schooner, two decks
345.6′×40.9′×26.7′　2053 n　3191 g
Built by Harland & Wolff Ltd, Belfast, Yard No 233, for Elder, Dempster and Co. Registered Liverpool. T 3 cyl 22″, 36″, 60″–48″ by the builders. 300 hp, 10 K.
1890　18 October, launched. November, completed and chartered to Atlantic Transport Co Ltd.
1891　August, transferred to African Steamship Co. Registered London.
1893　Entered London to New Orleans trade.
1896　17 November (Captain W. Williams), wrecked in dense fog at Mizen Head, Dunlough Bay, County Cork, voyage Montreal to Avonmouth, carrying cattle and general cargo. Nine lives lost.

425　ETOLIA
O.N. 93718　　　　　　　　　　　　　　1893–1906

'Memphis' class
Steel and iron screw schooner, two decks
345.6′×40.9′×26.7′　2108 n　3211 g
Built by Harland & Wolff Ltd, Belfast, Yard No 196, for City of Liverpool Steam Navigation Co Ltd (D. & C. MacIver, Managers), Liverpool. Registered Liverpool. T 3 cyl 24½″, 37″, 64″–48″ by the builders. 320 hp, 10½ K.
1887　8 January, launched.
1893　Acquired by African Steamship Co with the purchase of City of Liverpool Steam Navigation Co Ltd 2133 n, 3270 g.
1906　Transferred to Elder Dempster Shipping Ltd. 9 June, wrecked half mile south of Cape Sable Lighthouse, Nova Scotia, voyage St John, NB, to Barrow, cargo timber (Captain R. E. Jones). No loss of life.

ETOLIA

426　LYCIA
O.N. 93777　　　　　　　　　　　　　　1893–1904

'Memphis' class
Steel screw steamer, two decks
345.5′×40.9′×26.7′　2035 n　3135 g
Built by Harland & Wolff Ltd, Belfast, Yard No 198, for City of Liverpool Steam Navigation Co Ltd (D. & C. MacIver, Managers), Liverpool. Registered Liverpool. T 3 cyl 24½″, 37″, 64″–48″ by the builders. 320 hp, 10½ K.
1887　5 November, launched.
1888　May, completed.

1893 Acquired by African Steamship Co with the purchase of City of Liverpool Steam Navigation Co Ltd. 2117 n, 3282 g.
1895 Entered Avonmouth to Montreal trade.
1900 On charter to British Government for Boer War transport.
1901 Returned to Avonmouth–Montreal trade.
1904 Sold to Diederichen, Jebson & Co, Hamburg. Renamed **LAUSCHAN**. Registered Hamburg. 2056 n, 3190 g.
1909 Sold to Hugo Stinnes, Mulheim a/d Ruhr. Registered Mulheim.
1912 Hulked at Hamburg.

LYCIA

427 MOHAWK

O.N. 99066   1892–1896

'Mohawk' class
Steel twin screw steamer, three decks
445.0′×49.2′×30.0′   3646 n   5658 g
Launched by Harland & Wolff Ltd, Belfast Yard No 171, for Williams, Torrey & Field, London. Completed for African Steamship Co. Registered London. 2×T 3 cyl 22½″, 36½″, 60″–48″ by the builders. 600 hp, 12½″ K.
Passenger accommodation: 16 first class, 14 second.
1892 25 February, launched. May, completed and chartered to Atlantic Transport Co Ltd.
1896 October, sold to Atlantic Transport Co Ltd.
1898 Acquired by US Government for use as a transport during the Spanish-American War. Renamed **GRANT**.

1903 Transferred to Corps of Engineers for conversion to a hopper dredger of 4050 cubic yards capacity for the Columbia River project. Renamed **CHINOOK**.
1946 Scrapped.
Ships of the 'Mohawk' class: MOHAWK (427), MOBILE (428).
Note—Until 1937 **CHINOOK** was the largest and fastest hopper dredger in the United States of America.

MOBILE

428 MOBILE

O.N. 101966   1893–1896

'Mohawk' class
Steel twin screw steamer, three decks
445.0′×49.2′×30.0′   3725 n   5780 g
Launched by Harland & Wolff Ltd, Belfast Yard No 253, for Atlantic Transport Co (Williams, Torrey & Field Ltd, Managers), London. Acquired by African Steamship Co. Registered London. 2×T 3 cyl 22½″, 36½″, 60″–48″ by the builders. 600 hp, 12½ K.
Passenger accommodation: 80 first class, 1800 third.
1891 17 November, launched.
1893 March, completed and chartered to Atlantic Transport Co Ltd.
1896 Sold to Atlantic Transport Co Ltd.
1897 5 December, in collision with the Allan liner COREAN off the Newfoundland Banks, minor damage.
1898 Sold to US Government for use as transport in the Spanish-American War. Renamed **SHERMAN**.
During World War I engaged on troop movements between California and the Philippines.

CHINOOK, formerly MOHAWK

1918	Proceeded to Vladivostock to embark Czech prisoners of war (who had tramped across Siberia) for Trieste.
1923	Sold to Los Angeles Steamship Co Inc, Wilmington. Renamed **CALAWA II**. Registered Los Angeles. 4166 n, 7271 g. Fitted to burn oil fuel. Operated between Los Angeles and Honolulu.
1933	Sold for demolition at Osaka.

EUROPA

429 EUROPA

O.N. 84102   1893–1902

Iron screw barquentine, two decks
300.0′×36.0′×25.5′   1512 n   2308 g
Built by M. Pearse & Co, Stockton, Yard No 184, as **RAMLEH**, for Edward Bates & Sons, Liverpool. Registered Liverpool. C 2 cyl 36½″, 68″–42″ by Blair & Co, Stockton. 280 hp.

1881	March, launched.
1884	Sold to City of Liverpool Steam Navigation Co Ltd (D. & C. MacIver, Managers), Liverpool. Renamed **EUROPA**. Registered Liverpool. 1493 n, 2308 g.
1894	Sold to Ocean Transport Co Ltd (Elder, Dempster & Co, Managers), Liverpool. 1443 n, 2239 g.
1902	Sold to Pacific Ocean Steamship Line Energia, Russia. Renamed **WELIKIJ KNJAS ALEXANDER MICHILOWITSCH**. Registered Vladivostock. 1420 n, 2239 g.
1904	Sold to K. K. Utsunomiya, Tokio. Renamed **EUROPA**. Registered Tokio.
1906 and 1907	During this period the high pressure cylinder was bored out to 37″ and the low pressure cylinder bored out to 68 1/16″ diameter.
1908	Renamed **EUROPA MARU**. 1653 n, 2296 g.
1909	Sold to Goshi Shosen Kaisha Utsunomiya Kaisoten, Japan. Renamed **YOROPPA MARU**. Registered Yokohama.
1912	Sold to Inui Gomei Kaisha (Inui Shenei, Managers), Japan. Renamed **EUROPA MARU**. 1653 n, 2296 g. Registered Aioi.
1914	January, posted missing, voyage Port Arthur to Nagoya.

430 MARIPOSA

O.N. 99308   1892–1895

Steel twin screw steamer, two masts (a third was added later)
421.0′×48.0′×29.2   3428 n   5305 g
Built by Sir W. G. Armstrong, Mitchell & Co Ltd, Newcastle, as **RUTHENIA** for City of Liverpool Steam Navigation Co Ltd (D. & C. MacIver, Managers), Liverpool. Registered Liverpool. 2×T 3 cyl 24½″, 40″, 66″–45″ by R. W. Hawthorn Leslie & Co Ltd, Newcastle. 600 hp, 12 K.

1891	20 June, launched.
1892	4 November, acquired by Ocean Transport Co Ltd (Elder, Dempster & Co, Managers), with the purchase of the City of Liverpool Steam Navigation Co Ltd. Renamed **MARIPOSA**. Chartered to Atlantic Transport Co Ltd, London, for operation on their Liverpool–Canada service.
1895	27 September, (Captain W. Cave) wrecked in severe weather on Forteau Point, Labrador, voyage Montreal to Liverpool, cargo cattle and general.

Note—**MARIPOSA** had been sold to the Union Steamship Co Ltd, London, and it was intended to rename her **GASCON**. However, before the transfer took place she was lost.

MARIPOSA

ENGLISHMAN**, formerly **MONTEZUMA

431 MONTEZUMA (I)

O.N. 99359   1892–1898

Steel twin screw steamer, four masts, flush deck, three decks
430.0′×47.0′×22.4′   3574 n   5504 g
Built by Harland & Wolff Ltd, Belfast, Yard No 242, for City of Liverpool Steam Navigation Co Ltd (D. & C. MacIver, Managers), Liverpool, as **IONIA**. Registered Liverpool. 2×T 3 cyl 19″, 31″, 52″–42″ by Harland & Wolff Ltd, Belfast. 375 hp, 12 K.

1891	31 October, launched.
1892	20 October, acquired by Ocean Transport Co Ltd (Elder, Dempster & Co, Managers), with the purchase of the City of Liverpool Steam Navigation Co Ltd. Renamed **MONTEZUMA**. 4863 n, 6357 g. Chartered to Atlantic Transport Co Ltd.
1898	July, sold to Union Steamship Co Ltd, London. Renamed **SANDUSKY**. 4815 n, 6315 g. Registered Southampton.

1899 July, sold to Mississippi & Dominion Steam Ship Co (Richards, Mills & Co, Managers), Liverpool. Renamed **ENGLISHMAN**. Registered Liverpool.

1914 Sold to British & North Atlantic Steam Navigation Co Ltd (Dominion Line), Liverpool. 3345 n, 5257 g.

1916 24 March, torpedoed and sunk at noon by German submarine U43, in position 30 miles north-east of Malin Head, voyage Avonmouth to Portland, Maine. Sixty-eight survivors, including the Master, were rescued and taken to Oban. Ten crew lost.

432 NIAGARA
O.N. 87819   1892–1899

Iron screw brigantine, two decks
234.5′×40.0′×26.3′ 2044 n 3104 g
Built by M. Pearse & Co, Stockton, Yard No 210, for City of Liverpool Steam Navigation Co, Liverpool, as **ABANA**. Renamed **NIAGARA**. Registered Liverpool. C 2 cyl 40″, 75″–48″ by Blair & Co Ltd, Stockton. 300 hp, 10 K.

1883 March, launched.

1891 Placed under management of D. & C. MacIver, Liverpool.

1894 Management transferred to Elder, Dempster & Co.

1896 Sold to Ocean Transport Co Ltd (Elder, Dempster & Co, Managers), Liverpool. 1965 n, 3033 g.

1899 19 July, (Captain J. Coward) wrecked on Pipas Buceo Rocks, near Montevideo, voyage Cardiff via Boma to Buenos Aires, cargo coal and iron. Ship valued at £23,625, one-third un-insured.

SABINE, *formerly* **MARINO**

433 MARINO
O.N. 104458   1894–1898

Steel screw steamer, two decks
371.0′×43.2′×27.5′ 3002 n 3819 g
Built by Harland & Wolff Ltd, Belfast, Yard No 290, for Ocean Transport Co Ltd (Elder, Dempster & Co, Managers). Registered Liverpool. T 3 cyl 24″, 40″, 66″–42″ by Muir Houston, Glasgow. 268 nhp, 8½ K.

1894 10 November, launched.

1895 February, completed.

1898 Sold to Union Steamship Co Ltd, London. Renamed **SABINE**. Registered Southampton. 3008 n, 3827 g.

1900 Owners became the Union-Castle Mail Steamship Co Ltd (Donald Currie & Co, Managers), London.

1906 Employed carrying coal from Durban to Cape Colony.

1909 2992 n, 3805 g. From September to December 1909, chartered to the Australian Government to search for the WARATAH, missing off the South African coast since 26 July 1909. 7 December, returned to Cape Town without having found any trace of WARATAH.

1921 Sold to Bullard, King & Co Ltd, London. Renamed **UMZINTO**. Registered London.

1925 June, sold to Dutch shipbreakers. November, resold to Cantieri Navali ed Acciaiarce de Venezia and broken up in Italy.

QUEENSMORE

434 QUEENSMORE
O.N. 96394   1896–1898

Steel screw steamer, two decks
360.0′×46.0′×29.0′ 2488 n 3792 g
Built by Gourlay Bros & Co, Dundee, Yard No 138, for S. S. Queensmore Ltd (W. Johnson & Co Ltd, Managers), Liverpool. Registered Liverpool. T 3 cyl 29″, 45″, 74″–54″ by builders. 500 hp, 11½ K.

1889 26 June, launched. Damaged by fire whilst fitting out.

1890 January, completed.

1896 October, acquired by Elder, Dempster & Co. 2514 n, 3878 g.

1898 5 May, sold (together with *PARKMORE* for £60,000) to Manchester Liners Ltd (Furness Withy & Co Ltd, Managers), West Hartlepool. Renamed **MANCHESTER ENTERPRISE**. Registered Liverpool.

1899 Management transferred to owners. Registered Manchester. 1899 n, 3873 g.

1899 18 November, (Captain W. J. Wright) foundered in position 50°.25′N 42°.25′W, voyage Mersey to Montreal.

435 MONTPELIER
O.N. 106873   1897–1900

Steel screw steamer, two decks
344.0′×44.5′×25.9′ 2249 n 3483 g
Built by A. McMillan & Son Ltd, Dumbarton, Yard No 351, for African Steamship Co. Registered Liverpool. T 3 cyl 25″, 42″, 68″–45″ by D. Rowan & Son, Glasgow. 358 nhp, 11 K.

1897 29 June, launched. August, completed. 31 August, commenced maiden voyage, Greenock to New Orleans.

1899 Transferred to Elder Line Ltd.

1900 29 May, wrecked on Duck Island, Cape Ray, Newfoundland, voyage Las Palmas to Montreal, in ballast.

MILWAUKEE at completion (Photo McRoberts)

MILWAUKEE after her stranding in September 1898 (Photo McRoberts)

MILWAUKEE at Newcastle after completing repairs (Photo McRoberts)

436 MILWAUKEE
O.N. 106834   1897–1903

Steel screw steamer, two decks and shelter deck
470.0′×56.1′×31.9′ 4755 n 7317 g
Built by C. S. Swan & Hunter Ltd, Newcastle, Yard No 214, for Alfred Lewis Jones Esq (Elder, Dempster & Co, Managers). Registered Liverpool. T 3 cyl 28″, 46″, 75″–54″ by North Eastern Marine Engineering Co Ltd, Newcastle. 502 nhp, 12 K.

1897   16 January, commenced maiden voyage, Tyne to New Orleans, had engine breakdown, towed into Port Eades by ss BENGORE HEAD.

1898   Transferred to Elder, Dempster & Co. 16 September, stranded near Peterhead, Scotland (Captain J. Williams). Broken in two with explosives, 180′ of fore end left on the rocks, rest of ship towed to the Tyne.

1899   12 April, new fore part launched by builders. 24 June, repairs completed, sailed for Montreal. 4784 n, 7323 g. Transferred to Elder Line Ltd.

1900   21 February, commenced Boer War trooping duties. Transported General Cronje and 500 Boers to St Helena.

1903   Transferred to Canadian Pacific Railway Co with the sale of Elder, Dempster & Co's Beaver Line service.

1914   High pressure cylinder bored out to 28¾″ diameter.

1918   31 March, damaged by submarine in Irish Channel but made port. One man killed. 31 August, torpedoed and sunk 260 miles south-west Fastnet when U105 (Kapitänleutnant Friedrich Strackerjan) made a submerged attack on a group of unescorted outward-bound steamers.

U105 survived the war and surrendered at Harwich on 20 November 1918 under the terms of the Armistice. Allocated to France she was commissioned in the French navy as the JEAN AUTRIC. She was scrapped in 1937.

MILWAUKEE was the largest ship launched in England since the GREAT EASTERN. A model of her is held at Bristol Maritime Museum.

437 MOUNT ROYAL
O.N. 109498   1898–1903

Steel screw steamer, two decks
470.0′×56.0′×32.0′ 4559 n 7045 g
Built by C. S. Swan & Hunter Ltd, Newcastle, Yard No 230, for Elder, Dempster & Co. Registered Liverpool. T 3 cyl 28″, 46″, 75″–54″ by Central Marine Engine Works, West Hartlepool. 505 nhp, 12 K.

1898   17 August, launched. 30 November, commenced maiden voyage, Tyne to New Orleans.

1899   Boer War transport duties.

1900   Transferred to Elder Line Ltd. December, ran aground in River Weser, voyage New Orleans to Bremerhaven with cotton. Refloated without damage.

1903   6 April, transferred to Canadian Pacific Railway Co with the sale of Elder, Dempster & Co's Beaver Line service.

1908   Reboilered by Central Marine Engine Works, West Hartlepool, increasing number of boilers from three to four. 608 nhp 5926 n 7998 g. Passenger accommodation: 1500 third class.

1914   October, taken over by Admiralty and fitted out as a dummy battleship, representing HMS MARLBOROUGH.

1915   Converted into Naval oiler (circular tanks installed in holds). 5806 n, 8039 g. Renamed **RANGOL**.

1916   Purchased outright by Admiralty. 10 July, transferred to the management of Lane & MacAndrew Ltd, London. Renamed **MAPLELEAF**. Registered London.

1917   Transferred to the Shipping Controller, management unchanged.

1919   4 October, sold to British Tanker Co Ltd, London. Renamed **BRITISH MAPLE**. Registered London.

1922   6 June, in service as a bunker depot ship in Southampton Water.

1932   December, sold for £4000 to Metal Industries Ltd.

1933   25 January, demolition work commenced at Rosyth.

MOUNT ROYAL

MONARCH

MONTCALM

438 MONARCH
O.N. 106880   1897–1927

Steel screw steamer, two decks and shelter deck
470.0′×56.0′×31.9′   4770 n   7296 g
Built by C. S. Swan & Hunter Ltd, Newcastle, Yard No
224, for Furness Withy & Co Ltd (Elder, Dempster & Co,
Managers). Registered Liverpool. T 3 cyl 28½″, 46½″, 80″–54″ by
Wallsend Slipway Co Ltd, Newcastle. 548 nhp, 12 K.

1897 1 July, launched. 11 October, trials. On maiden voyage,
in collision with ss KINSALE (2412 g/built 1896) at
New Orleans.
1899 Acquired by Elder Dempster Shipping Ltd. 7120 n,
9041 g.
1905 At end of Russian–Japanese War, repatriated prisoners
of war from Japan to Vladivostock. 4776 n, 7355 g.
1912 Transferred to Elder Line Ltd.
1917 Taken over by Ministry of Shipping. Employed as a
collier.
1919 Returned to owner's normal service. 4842 n, 7466 g.
1927 Sold to SA di Nav Casmona, Genoa. Renamed
MONARCA. Registered Genoa. 4659 n, 7430 g
1931 August, sold for demolition.

MONARCH in Cape Town docks, while engaged on the Canada–
Cape service (Photo Ship Society of South Africa, Leendertz
collection)

439 MONTCALM
O.N. 106869   1897–1903

Steel screw steamer, two decks and shelter deck
445.0′×52.5′×27.6′   3458 n   5478 g

Built by Palmers Shipbuilding & Iron Co Ltd, Jarrow, Yard No
724, for African Steamship Co. Registered Liverpool.
T 3 cyl 30″, 50″, 81½″–54″ by the builders. 664 nhp, 12½ K.

1897 17 May, launched. 31 July, ran trials—achieved 13.34
knots. 3 September, commenced maiden voyage, Avonmouth to Montreal.
1900 Boer War transport duties.
1903 Transferred to the Canadian Pacific Railway Co with
the sale of Elder, Dempster & Co's Beaver Line service.
3508 n, 5505 g.
1913 Intermediate pressure cylinder bored out to 50$\frac{5}{16}$″.
1914 Requisitioned as a British Expeditionary Force transport. October, converted by Royal Navy to dummy
battleship to represent HMS AUDACIOUS.
1915 Disguise dismantled and became store ship.
1916 29 January, purchased by Admiralty (F. Leyland & Co
Ltd, Managers). Refitted as a tanker and sold October
to the Anglo Saxon Petroleum Co Ltd. Renamed
CRENELLA. Registered London. 3608 n, 5771 g. Fitted
for oil fuel.
1917 11 October, transferred to the Shipping Controller. 26
November, torpedoed off south-west coast of Ireland but
reached port.
1918 1 August, attacked by submarine off south-west Ireland,
torpedo missed.
1919 26 November, purchased by Anglo Saxon Petroleum Co
Ltd.
1920 19 October, sold to Velefa Steam Ship Co Ltd (Run-
ciman (London) Ltd, Managers), London
1923 20 June, sold to A/S Larvik Hvalfaugerselsk (Chr Niel-
sen & Co, A/S Managers), Larvik. Renamed **REY
ALFONSO**. Registered Larvik. 3480 n, 5938 g. Fitted
out as a whaling depot ship.
1925 Sold to H. M. Wrangell & Co A/S, Haugsund. Registered Haugesund.
1927 Sold to Anglo Norse Co Ltd (Hans Borge, Manager),
Tonsberg. Renamed **ANGLO NORSE**. Registered
Tonsberg. 4348 n, 7172 g.
1929 August, sold to Falkland Whaling Co Ltd, Jersey, CI.
Renamed **POLAR CHIEF**. Registered Jersey. 5512 n,
7166 g.
1941 2 July, acquired by Ministry of War Transport (Chr
Salvesen & Co, Managers). Renamed **EMPIRE
CHIEF**. 6279 n, 8040 g.
1946 3 August, sold to South Georgia Co Ltd (Chr Salvesen &
Co, Managers). Renamed **POLAR CHIEF**. Registered
Leith. 6334 n, 8091 g.
1952 29 April, arrived Dalmuir for demolition by W. H.
Arnott Young & Co Ltd, demolition being completed at
Troon.

Original name commemorates General the Marquis de
Montcalm (1712–1759).

MONTROSE

MONTEREY

440 MONTROSE

O.N. 108251   1897–1903

Steel screw steamer, two decks
444.3′×52.0′×27.5′   3457 n   5195 g
Built by Sir Raylton Dixon & Co Ltd, Middlesbrough, Yard No 441, for African Steamship Co, Liverpool. Registered London. T 3 cyl 30″, 50″, 82″–54″ by T. Richardson & Sons, Ltd, Hartlepool. 632 nhp, 12½ K.

- 1897   17 June, launched. 29 October, commenced maiden voyage, from Middlesbrough via Quebec to Montreal.
- 1900   14 March, commenced service as a Boer War Transport (No 93), eight round voyages, Liverpool to Cape Town.
- 1903   January, laid up at Liverpool. 6 April, transferred to the Canadian Pacific Railway Co with the sale of Elder, Dempster & Co's Beaver Line service. 5349 n, 7094 g. Passenger accommodation: 70 second class, 1800 third.
- 1914   August, towed *MONTREAL* from Antwerp to London. 5402 n, 7207 g. 28 October, purchased by Admiralty. 28 December, during preparation for use as a blockship at Dover harbour entrance, broke loose from her moorings, drifted out to sea in a gale and stranded one and a half miles north-east of the East Goodwin Light-vessel. **MONTROSE** broke in two and part of the wreck remained visible until 1963; her mast was used as a marker for Trinity House surveys.

Note—20 July 1910, during voyage Antwerp to Quebec, a radio message from **MONTROSE** led to the arrest of Dr Crippen, who had been detected amongst the passengers. This was the first occasion when ship's wireless was used in the detection of crime.

441 MONTEREY

O.N. 109427   1898–1903

Steel screw steamer, two decks
445.0′×52.2′×27.6′   3489 n   5455 g
Built by Palmers Shipbuilding & Iron Co Ltd, Jarrow, Yard No 728, for Elder, Dempster & Co. Registered Liverpool. T 3 cyl 30″, 50″, 81½″–54″ by the builder. 661 nhp, 12½ K.

- 1897   25 November, launched.
- 1898   25 May, trials. Speed 13.25 K.
- 1899   Transferred to Elder Line Ltd.
- 1900   16 March, commenced Boer War transport duties. Made one voyage Halifax to Cape Town and seven round voyages New Orleans to Cape Town, on one of which Lord Strathcona's Horse, constituting 500 Officers and Other Ranks, with horses and equipment were transported to Cape Town.
- 1903   6 April, transferred to Canadian Pacific Railway Co, London, with the sale of Elder, Dempster & Co's Beaver Line service. 15 July, wrecked on Plata Point, Miquelon Islands' (French territory), off the south coast of Newfoundland, voyage Montreal to Bristol with general cargo and cattle.

MONTEAGLE

442 MONTEAGLE

O.N. 110554   1899–1903

'Monteagle' class
Steel twin screw steamer, two decks
445.0′×52.2′×27.7′   3481 n   5468 g
Built by Palmers' Shipbuilding & Iron Co Ltd, Jarrow, Yard No 738, for Elder, Dempster & Co. Registered Liverpool. 2×T 3 cyl 26″, 43″, 70″–45″ by the builders. 738 nhp, 13 K.

- 1898   13 December, launched.

MONARCH, *in Dominion Line colours*

MONTEAGLE (Photo McRoberts)

1899	4 March, commenced maiden voyage—Tyne to New Orleans.
1900	2 February, commenced first voyage as Boer War Transport No 87 (Liverpool to Cape Town). 4487 n, 6955 g.
1902	24 May, resumed owner's Avonmouth to Montreal service. 12 July, stranded, but refloated. Captain W. L. D. Chapman's certificate suspended for three months for improper navigation. 8 November, stranded near Sispert Reef, Cape Rosier. Refloated, Master's certificate suspended for six months.
1903	6 March, transferred to Canadian Pacific Railway Co, with the sale of Elder, Dempster & Co's Beaver Line service. 3492 n, 5498 g.
1906	March, proceeded to Hong Kong via Tenerife and Durban. Placed on trans-Pacific service. 18 September, driven ashore during typhoon at Hong Kong. Stern post and rudder badly damaged.
1907	March, resumed normal service.
1914	September, requisitioned as Indian troopship.
1915	24 February, returned to trans-Pacific service. 3953 n, 6193 g.
1918	Registered Vancouver, BC (British flag). November, commenced first of three voyages to Vladivostock for the repatriation of prisoners of war.
1919	May, resumed normal service.
1921	April, rescued crew of French steamer HSIN TIEN off coast of China.
1922	22 September, loaded a cargo of timber at Vancouver for Montreal. 17 November, left Montreal for Avonmouth.
1923	29 January, arrived London after one North Atlantic voyage and laid-up. 3950 n, 6173 g. Renamed **BELTON**.
1924	Laid-up at Southend-on-Sea.
1926	15 April, sold to Hughes Bolckow Shipbreaking Co Ltd. 27 April, arrived Blyth in tow, for demolition.

Ships of the 'Monteagle' class: MONTEAGLE (442), MONTFORT (443).

Captain A. J. Hoskin was awarded the Medaille d'Honneur de Sauvetage de premiere classe by the French Government for the HSIN TIEN rescue.

Named to commemorate the memory of Lord Monteagle (1790–1866), Secretary of State for the Colonies.

MONTFORT

443 MONTFORT
O.N. 110568   1899–1903
'Monteagle' class
Steel twin screw steamer, two decks
445.0′×52.2′×27.8′   3492 n   5481 g
Built by Palmers' Shipbuilding & Iron Co Ltd, Jarrow, Yard No 739, for Elder Dempster Shipping Ltd. Registered Liverpool. 2×T 3 cyl 26″, 43″, 70″–45″ by the builders. 731 nhp, 13 K.

1899	13 February, launched. 26 April, commenced maiden voyage, Tyne–Quebec–Montreal. 11 November, commenced first voyage as Boer War transport, Liverpool to Cape Town.
1900	Transferred to Elder Line Ltd.
1901	July, aground off Isle of Wight when homeward from South Africa with 1000 troops on board. 4631 n, 7101 g.
1903	Transferred to Canadian Pacific Railway Co with the sale of Elder, Dempster & Co's Beaver Line service. 3550 n, 5519 g. Passenger accommodation: 30 second class, 1200 third.
1914	4126 n, 6578 g.
1918	1 October, torpedoed and sunk without warning, by German submarine U55, in position 170 miles west by south ¾ south from Bishop Rock, Scilly Isles. Five men lost, the Master among the survivors.

444 MONMOUTH (I)
O.N. 108337   1898
Steel twin screw steamer, two decks, spar deck and shelter deck
490.5′×56.3′×25.0′   6118 n   8001 g
Built by Harland & Wolff Ltd, Belfast, Yard No 327, for African Steamship Co, Liverpool. Registered London. 2×T 3 cyl, 19″, 31″, 52″–48″ by Fawcett, Preston & Co, Liverpool. 487 nhp, 12 K.

1897	23 December, launched.
1898	April, completed. Sold after only one voyage, to Mississippi & Dominion Line (British and North Atlantic Company Ltd), Liverpool. Renamed **IRISHMAN**. Registered Liverpool.
1902	Sold to National Line (A. S. Williams, Manager), London. Renamed **MICHIGAN**. Registered Liverpool.
1914	Sold to Atlantic Transport Co Ltd, London. 6280 n, 8162 g.
1926	Sold to Comm. E. Modiano, Italy. Renamed **CANDIDO**. Registered Trieste (Italian flag).
1927	Sold for demolition in Italy.

MONMOUTH (Photo J. Clarkson)

445 MONTCLAIR
O.N. 109407   1898–1901
Steel screw steamer, two decks
370.0′×46.0′×25.8′   2458 n   3806 g
Built by A. McMillan & Son Ltd, Dumbarton, Yard No 353, for Elder, Dempster & Co. Registered Liverpool. T 3 cyl 25″, 42″, 68″–45″ by D. Rowan & Son, Glasgow. 339 nhp, 10 K.

1898	April, completed.
1899	May, transferred to Elder Line Ltd.
1901	July, sold to A. Folch y Cia, Spain. Renamed **JOSE GALLART**. Registered Barcelona.

MONTCLAIR

Above, **MONTAUK,** *and, below, the wreck of* **MONTAUK** *in Chama Bay, January 1911*

1908   Sold to SA Nav Transatlantica, Spain. 2345 n, 3794 g.

1910   Sold to Pinillos, Izquierdos Soc en Commandite, Cadiz. Renamed **BALMES**. Registered Cadiz. High pressure cylinder rebored to $25\frac{7}{8}''$ diameter.

1925   Sold to Cia Transoceanica de Nav, Barcelona. Registered Barcelona.

1928   Sold to Hijo de Ramon A. Ramos (A. Ramos SA, Managers), Barcelona. Renamed **RAMON ALSONO R**.

1934   3020 n, 4017 g.

1936   Intermediate pressure cylinder rebored to $42\frac{5}{16}''$ diameter.

1942   Sold to R. Ramos Cordere, Barcelona.

1948   Sold to Hijo de Ramon A. Ramos, Sociedad Anonima, Barcelona.

1952   Scrapped after collision in River Scheldt.

446 MELROSE
O.N. 102690   1898–1899

'Melrose' class
Steel screw steamer, two decks
365.0′×47.0′×27.1′   2599 n   4038 g
Built by Wm Gray & Co Ltd, West Hartlepool, Yard No 480, for Burrell & Son, Glasgow, as **STRATHNAIRN**. Registered Glasgow. T 3 cyl 27″, 43″, 72″–45″ by Central Marine Engine Works, West Hartlepool. 404 nhp 10 K.

1894   8 April, launched. May, completed.

1898   Acquired by Elder, Dempster & Co, Liverpool. Renamed **MELROSE**. Registered Liverpool.

1899   November, sold to Aznar y Cia, Spain. Renamed **EREZA**. Registered Bilbao.

1902   Sold to Cia Belbaina de Navegacion (E. Aznar y Tutor, Managers), Spain.

1907   4 February, foundered off Cape Passaro, Sicily, voyage Greece to Barrow.

Ships of the 'Melrose' class: MELROSE (446), MONTAUK (447), MONMOUTH (448).

447 MONTAUK
O.N. 104590   1898–1911

'Melrose' class
Steel screw steamer, two decks
365.0′×47.0′×27.1′   2612 n   4040 g
Built by Wm Gray & Co Ltd, West Hartlepool, Yard No 486, for Burrell & Son, Glasgow, as **STRATHFILLAN**. Registered Glasgow. T 3 cyl 27″, 43″, 72″–45″ by Central Marine Engine Works, West Hartlepool. 404 nhp, 10 K.

1894   16 October, launched. 20 November, trials.

1898   December, acquired by Elder, Dempster & Co, Liverpool. Renamed **MONTAUK**. Registered Glasgow.

1901   Transferred to British & African Steam Navigation Co Ltd.

1911   14 January, wrecked in Chama Bay, Gold Coast, voyage Cardiff and Newport to West Africa, cargo coal and patent fuel.

448 MONMOUTH (II)
O.N. 105987   1898–1899

'Melrose' class
Steel screw steamer, two decks
365.0′×47.1′×27.0′   2627 n   4071 g
Built by Tyne Iron Shipbuilding Co Ltd, Newcastle, Yard No 108, for Burrell & Son, Glasgow, as **FITZPATRICK**. Registered Glasgow. T 3 cyl 27″, 43″, 72″–45″ by North Eastern Marine Engineering Co Ltd, Newcastle. 368 nhp, 10 K.

1896   March, completed.

1898   October, acquired by Elder, Dempster & Co. Renamed **MONMOUTH**. Registered Glasgow.

1899   Sold to Bucentaur Steam Ship Co (Bucknall Bros, Managers), London. Renamed **BUCRANIA**. Registered London.

1900   Owners absorbed into the Bucknall Steamship Lines.

1911   Sold to Kishimoto Kisen Kabieshiki Kaisha, Osaka. Renamed **SHINSEI MARU**. Registered Sumiyoshi. 3097 n, 4194 g.

1913   Registered Nishinomiya.

1915   Sold to M. Naruse, Kobe. 3108 n, 4205 g.

1916   23 March, sailed from Port Townsend, voyage Tacoma to Yokahama, and subsequently posted missing.

MANCHESTER TRADER, formerly PARKMORE

449 PARKMORE

O.N. 97829   1897–1898

Steel screw steamer, two decks
340.0′×42.7′×27.0′   2136 n   3318 g
Built by Charles J. Bigger, Foyle Yard, Londonderry, Yard No
17, for S. S. Parkmore Ltd (W. Johnston & Co Ltd, Managers),
Liverpool. Registered Liverpool. T 3 cyl 26″, 42″, 67″–51″ by
McIlwaine & McColl Ltd, Belfast. 300 hp, 12 K.
1890   16 August, launched. December, completed.
1897   January, acquired by Elder, Dempster & Co.
1898   May, sold (together with *QUEENSMORE* for £60,000)
       to Manchester Liners Ltd (Furness Withy & Co
       Ltd, Managers), West Hartlepool. Renamed
       MANCHESTER TRADER.
1899   Registered Manchester.
1903   27 August, struck breakwater entering Ayr harbour,
       holed port side and sank alongside quay. Refloated and
       repaired.
1912   Sold to Akties, Ferdinand Melsom (Johan Johanson
       & Co, Managers), Christiania (Oslo). Renamed
       FERDINAND MELSOM. Registered Christiania.
1914   Sold to H. Westfal Larsen, Bergen. Renamed
       KAUPANGER. Registered Bergen.
1915   Sold to Dampskipsintersssentskap Akties (H. Westfal
       Larsen, Manager), Norway. Registered Christiania.
       2104 n, 3345 g.
1916   13 December, torpedoed by German submarine U38
       (Kapitanleutnant Max Valentiner) off Cartagena,
       Spain, and sank in position 37°.18′N 0°.52′W, voyage
       Cardiff to Spezia, cargo coal.
U38 surrendered at Harwich on 23 February 1919 in accordance
with the Peace Treaty.

450 LAKE HURON

O.N. 84159   1899–1901

Iron screw steamer, two decks and spar deck
385.0′×42.8′×24.3′   2646 n   4040 g
Built by London & Glasgow Engineering & Shipbuilding Co
Ltd, Glasgow, Yard No 220, for Canada Shipping Co Ltd
(Beaver Line), Liverpool. Registered Liverpool. C 2 cyl 48″,
88″–60″ by builders. 467 nhp, 13 K.
Passenger accommodation: 70 first class, 50 second.
1881   10 September, launched.
1896   Transferred to H. E. Murray & G. Hyde (D. & C.
       MacIver, Managers), Liverpool.
1899   Transferred to Elder, Dempster & Co with the purchase
       of Beaver Line service. 15 July, commenced first voyage

LAKE HURON

under Elder Dempster flag, Liverpool–Quebec–Montreal.

1901   Stranded on Anticosti Island, later declared a constructive total loss. Wreck sold to G. Tardy, Genoa. Broken up in Italy.

Lake Huron is part of the Great Lakes system in Canada.

451   LAKE MEGANTIC/ PORT HENDERSON

O.N. 89953   1900–1912

Steel screw schooner, three decks
439.6′×46.3′×28.9′   3268 n   5100 d   5026 g
Built by W. Denny & Bros, Dumbarton (their largest to date), Yard No 282, for Shaw, Savill & Albion Co Ltd, London, as **ARAWA**. Registered London. T 4 cyl 37″, 61″ (2), 71″–60″ by the builders (this was the first two-crank triple expansion engine by Denny). 800 hp, 14 K.
Passenger accommodation: 95 first class, 60 second, 670 steerage.

1883   15 October, ordered. 16 November, keel laid.
1884   8 September, launched.
1885   2 January, completed (cost £122,956).
1893   Chartered to Huddart Parker & Co, operating between Sydney (Australia) and Vancouver.
1896   Sold to Cia Transatlantica, Cadiz. Renamed **COLON**. Registered Barcelona. 3935 n, 5044 g,
1899   Returned to Shaw, Savill & Albion Co Ltd, London. Renamed **ARAWA**. Registered London.
1900   Acquired by British & African Steam Navigation Co Ltd. Renamed **LAKE MEGANTIC**. Registered Glasgow. 3182 n, 5061 g. Requisitioned for Boer War trooping duties.
1901   Main mast removed and funnels heightened.

1905   Transferred to Imperial Direct West India Mail Service. Renamed **PORT HENDERSON**. Registered Liverpool. 3104 n, 5178 g. Operated on Avonmouth to West Indies service.
1906   May, reboilered. 1005 nhp.
1911   Transferred to British & African Steam Navigation Co Ltd.
1912   Sold to Wild & Lanz, Genoa. Renamed **ANAPO**. Registered Genoa.
1914   Sold to Soc Maritima Italiana, Genoa. Renamed **PORTO SAID**. 3110 n, 5301 g.
1915   10 December, sunk by U39 (Kapitänleutnant Walter Forstmann) with a torpedo after she had been forced to stop by gunfire. Position off coast of Cyrenaica, Mediterranean.

On 18 May 1918 U39, then under the command of Kapitänleutnant Heinrich Metzger, was attacked by two aircraft and so seriously damaged that she was forced to put into Cartagena, where she was interned until the end of hostilities, after which she was allocated to France and taken to Toulon, where in December 1923 she was broken up. Forstmann left U39 in December 1917 on his appointment as Senior Officer of the IIIrd U-Boat Flotilla, where he served until the end of the war.

452   LAKE ONTARIO

O.N. 93725   1899–1905

Steel screw steamer, three decks
374.5′×43.5′×29.5′   2923 n   4502 g
Built by J. Laing, Sunderland, Yard No 302, for the Canada Shipping Co Ltd (Beaver Line), Liverpool. Registered Liverpool. T 3 cyl 31″, 51″, 83″–54″ by G. Clark, Sunderland. 400 hp, 13 K.

PORT HENDERSON, *formerly* **LAKE MEGANTIC**, *when engaged on the West Indies service, from an old postcard*

LAKE ONTARIO

Passenger accommodation: 200 first class, 85 second.
1887 March, completed.
1890 Damage repairs.
1896 Lightly damaged in head-on collision with Dominion liner VANCOUVER (5141 g/built 1884). Transferred to: H. E. Murray & G. Hyde (D. & C. MacIver, Managers), Liverpool.
1899 Acquired by Elder, Dempster & Co with the purchase of Beaver Line service. 2741 n, 4289 g.
1905 Sold for demolition in Italy.
LAKE ONTARIO was the first British passenger vessel on the North Atlantic to have triple expansion engines, also the last vessel built for the Canada Shipping Co Ltd and the only one built with a clipper bow.
Lake Ontario is situated within the Great Lakes system in Canada.

LAKE ONTARIO

453 LAKE SUPERIOR
O.N. 91197   1899–1902

Iron screw steamer, two decks and spar deck
400.0′×44.2′×24.2′   2966 n   4562 g
Built by J. & G. Thomson, Glasgow, Yard No 222, for Canada Shipping Co Ltd, Liverpool. Registered Liverpool. C 2 cyl 48″, 90″–60″ by the builders. 430 hp, 13 K.
Passenger accommodation: 190 first class, 80 second.
1884 4 December, launched.
1896 Transferred to H. B. Murray & G. Hyde (D. & C. MacIver, Managers), Liverpool.

1899 Transferred to Elder, Dempster & Co with the purchase of Beaver Line service. 2880 n, 4562 g.
1902 31 March, stranded near St John, New Brunswick, Canada, whilst on passage to Liverpool. Declared a constructive total loss. Broken up where she lay.
Lake Superior, largest freshwater lake in the world, is one of the Great Lakes of North America.

Two views of **LAKE SUPERIOR**

454 MONTEZUMA (II)
O.N. 110604   1899–1903

Steel twin screw steamer, two decks and shelter deck
485.0′×59.0′×30.5′/26.5′   4734 n   7345 g
Built by A. Stephen & Sons Ltd, Glasgow, Yard No 383, for Elder, Dempster & Co. Registered Liverpool. 2×T 3 cyl 22½″, 38″, 61″–48″ by the builders. 660 nhp, 13 K.
1899 11 July, launched. September, maiden voyage Liverpool to New Orleans, followed by three round voyages New Orleans to South Africa carrying horses and mules.
1901 Transferred to British & African Steam Navigation Co Ltd.
1902 Placed on London–Canada service.
1903 6 April, transferred to Canadian Pacific Railway Co with the sale of Elder, Dempster & Co's Beaver Line service.
1914 October, requisitioned by Admiralty, fitted out as a dummy battleship representing HMS IRON DUKE.
1915 7 July, purchased outright by Admiralty and converted to an oiler. Renamed **ABADOL**. Registered Liverpool. 5385 n, 8360 g.
1917 7 February, sold to Lane & MacAndrew Ltd, London. Renamed **OAKLEAF**. Registered London. 5022 n, 8186 g. 25 July, torpedoed without warning and sunk by submarine UC41 in position 64 miles north west ¼ north from the Butt of Lewis. No loss of life.

MONTEZUMA (Photo McRoberts)

MONTEZUMA transformed in late 1914 to masquerade as HMS IRON DUKE (Photo Imperial War Museum)

MOUNT TEMPLE

MOUNT TEMPLE *alongside at Liverpool*

455   MOUNT TEMPLE

O.N. 113496   1901–1903

Steel twin screw steamer, two decks and shelter deck
485.0′×59.0′×30.4′   4989 n   7656 g.
Built by Sir W. G. Armstrong, Whitworth & Co Ltd, Newcastle,
Yard No 709, for Elder, Dempster & Co. Registered Liverpool.
2×T 3 cyl 22″, 37″, 61″–48″ by Wallsend Slipway Co Ltd,
Newcastle. 694 nhp, 13 K.
1901   18 June, launched. September, completed.
1903   6 April, transferred to Canadian Pacific Railway Co,
Liverpool (H. Mowatt, Manager) with the sale of Elder,
Dempster & Co's Beaver Line service. 4661 n, 7229 g.

1907   1 December, stranded on West Ironbound Island,
Lahave, Nova Scotia. Some 600 people rescued by a 200-
foot line and a basket rigged as a breeches buoy. All
spent the night on the island and next day taken to
Halifax by ss LAURIER.
1908   16 April, refloated. Later towed to Newport News by
the tug COVINGTON for repair.
1915   7556 n, 9792 g.
1916   6 December: captured by the German raider MOEWE,
three crew members killed. Master (Captain A. H.
Sergeant) and survivors taken prisoner. Boarding party
placed explosive charges. **MOUNT TEMPLE** was sunk
in position 620 miles west ½ south (true) from Fastnet.
Note—A half model of **MOUNT TEMPLE**, presented by Sir
Alfred Jones, is in the Committee room of Aigburth People's
Hall, Aigburth Vale, Liverpool.

LUSITANIA (Photo McRoberts)

380

LAKE ERIE (Photo McRoberts)

456 LUSITANIA
O.N. 65888   1900, 1901

Iron screw barque, three decks and awning deck
379.9′×41.3′×35.2′   2420 n   3825 g
Built by Laird Bros, Birkenhead, Yard No 381, for Pacific Steam Navigation Co. Registered Liverpool. C 2 cyl 60″, 104″–48″ by the builders. 550 hp, 13½ K.
Passenger accommodation: 70 first class, 85 second, and 700 third. Later reduced: 84 first, 200 second and 270 emigrant.

1871   20 June, launched. December, lost propeller a few hours after leaving Valparaiso. A caisson was built of timber and iron straps around the stern, inside which a new propeller was fitted. A remarkable feat for the time, so far away from dockyard facilities.
1877   Taken over by Orient Steam Navigation Co Ltd, London. 25 June, commenced first Orient sailing to Australia. 8 August, arrived Melbourne.
1879   Chartered by D. & C. MacIver for Canadian service.
1885   17 April, requisitioned for service as an Armed Merchant Cruiser during the 'Russian War scare'.
1886   New engines and boilers by T. Richardson & Sons, Hartlepool. T 3 cyl 36″, 60″, 96″–48″. 700 hp, 15 K. 2494 n, 3877 g.
1900   31 March, acquired by Elder, Dempster & Co. Registered Liverpool. 2518 n, 3912 g. July: sold to Pacific Steam Navigation Co.
1901   February, repurchased by Elder, Dempster & Co. 26 June, (Captain W. Mackay) wrecked three miles north of Cape Ballard, Seal Cove, Cape Race, Newfoundland voyage Liverpool to Montreal (on charter to Allan Line).

457 LAKE ERIE
O.N. 110631   1900–1903

Steel twin screw steamer, two decks and shelter deck
446.0′×52.0′×35.5′   4814 n   7550 g
Built by Barclay, Curle & Co Ltd, Glasgow, Yard No 420, for Elder, Dempster & Co. Registered Liverpool. 2×T 3 cyl 22″, 37½″, 60″–48″ by the builders. 660 nhp, 13 K.
Passenger accommodation: 100 first class, 80 second, 500 steerage.

1899   21 November, launched.
1900   January, completed. 30 January, commenced maiden voyage, Liverpool to the Cape as a Boer War transport. Made eight round voyages, then placed on Liverpool to Quebec and Montreal service.
1901   Transferred to British & African Steam Navigation Co Ltd.
1903   6 April, transferred to Canadian Pacific Railway Co. Canada with the sale of Elder, Dempster & Co's Beaver Line service.
1906   Passenger accommodation: 150 second class, 1000 steerage.
1910–13   On charter to Allan Line.
1913   29 March, renamed **TRYOLIA**. Registered Liverpool. Engaged on emigrant trade, Trieste to Canada.
1914   28 October, requisitioned as a British Expeditionary Force troop transport. Converted into a dummy battleship, representing HMS CENTURION. Later, when stripped of camouflage, used as a store ship.
1916   26 June, purchased outright by Admiralty. Circular tanks fitted for the carriage of oil. Renamed **SAXOL**. 7 October, placed under the management of Lane & MacAndrew Ltd, London. Renamed **ASPENLEAF**. Registered London. 3715 n, 6124 g. 30 December, mined in the English Channel—towed in.
1917   7 November, transferred to the Shipping Controller. Lane & MacAndrew retain management.

1919   12 September, sold to Anglo-Saxon Petroleum Co Ltd, London. Renamed **PRYGONA**.
1925   6 February, sold for demolition to Petersen & Albeck, Copenhagen.

Lake Erie is one of the Great Lakes of North America.

LAKE ERIE

458 LAKE CHAMPLAIN
O.N. 110650   1900–1903

Steel twin screw steamer, two decks and shelter deck
446.0′×52.0′×27.8′   4110 n   6546 g   7750 d
Built by Barclay, Curle & Co Ltd, Glasgow, Yard No 422, for British & African Steam Navigation Co Ltd. Registered Liverpool. 2×T 3 cyl 22″, 37½″, 60″–48″ by the builders. 660 nhp, 13 K.
Passenger accommodation: 100 first class, 80 second, 500 steerage.

1900   31 March, launched. 4 May, trials. 15 May, commenced maiden voyage, Liverpool to Montreal.
1901   25 May, left Liverpool and made history as the first ship on the North Atlantic to be fitted with wireless telegraphy. 4658 n, 7392 g.
1903   6 April, transferred to Canadian Pacific Railway Co with the sale of Elder, Dempster & Co's Beaver Line service. 14 April, departed Liverpool, inaugurating the Canadian Pacific Railway Co Atlantic service.
1906   Passenger accommodation: 90 second class, 1000 steerage.

LAKE CHAMPLAIN

1909 Engine and boiler modifications: port high pressure cylinder bored out to $22\frac{7}{16}''$ diameter; starboard high pressure cylinder bored out to $22\frac{1}{4}''$ diameter.

1911 Collision with iceberg, little damage, proceeded St John's, Nova Scotia.

1912 Further engine modifications: port high pressure cylinder bored out to $22\frac{5}{8}''$ diameter; port intermediate pressure cylinder bored out to $37\frac{3}{4}''$ diameter; starboard high pressure cylinder relined—22'' diameter; starboard intermediate pressure cylinder bored out to $37\frac{7}{8}''$ diameter.

1913 7 March, renamed **RUTHENIA**. Registered Liverpool. Engaged on the Trieste to Canada emigrant trade.

1914 August, requisitioned by the Admiralty for use as transport for the British Expeditionary Force. Renamed **REGINA**. Converted at Belfast into dummy battleship representing HMS *KING GEORGE V*. On completion stationed at Loch Etive and later at Scapa Flow.

1915 Stripped of camouflage, became store ship. Renamed **RUTHENIA**. 4846 n, 7208 g.

1916 29 January, bought outright by the Admiralty.

1918 Fitted with cylindrical tanks to carry 5000 tons oil. Registered London.

1919 Sailed for the China station. Winter seasons at Hong Kong. Summer seasons at Wei-Hai-Wei.

1922 4866 n, 7239 g.

1929 In use as a Naval storage hulk at Singapore.

1942 16 February, scuttled in the face of the Japanese invasion. Salvaged and repaired by the Japanese, tanks removed and primitive accommodation fitted. Renamed **CHORAN MARU**. Put into service as a troopship.

1945 Recovered by Royal Navy. Used to transport prisoners of war.

1946 30 October, stranded off Pladjoe, Moesi River. 12 November, refloated.

1949 Sold to British Iron & Steel Corp. 3 April, left Singapore in tow of tug ENGLISHMAN. 18 June, arrived Dalmuir. Allocated to W. H. Arnott Young & Co Ltd. Dismantled at Dalmuir. Towed to Troon for final demolition.

MONMOUTH

459 MONMOUTH (III)
O.N. 113379   1900–1903

Steel screw steamer, two decks and shelter deck
375.1'×48.1'×25.7'   2569 n   4078 g
Built by Sir Raylton Dixon & Co Ltd, Middlesbrough, Yard No 467, for British & African Steam Navigation Co Ltd, Liverpool. Registered Liverpool. T 3 cyl 25'', 41'', 69''–48'' by Sir C. Furness, Westgarth & Co Ltd, Middlesbrough. 363 nhp, 10 K.

1900 1 May, launched. 20 September, trials.

1903 6 April, transferred to Canadian Pacific Railway Co with the sale of Elder, Dempster & Co's Beaver Line service.

1916 17 November, damaged by mine off Cherbourg but towed in to port.

1918 7 September, beat off submarine attack by gunfire in the West Atlantic.

1919 31 December, sold to Imperial Oil Co Ltd, Sarnia, Ontario (C. O. Stillman, Managers). Registered Montreal.

1922 Sold to C. O. Stillman, Sarnia, Ontario.

1923 Sold to Kishimoto Kisen Kabushiki Kaisha (Kishmoto SS Co), Osaka. Japanese flag.

1924 Sold to Kishimoto Shokai Kabushiki Kaisha, Dairen, Manchuria. Renamed **SHINZAN MARU**. Registered Dairen under Japanese flag. 2558 n, 4248 g.

1929 Sold to Dalgosrybtrest, Vladivostok, Russia. Renamed **TRETIY KRABOLOV**. Registered Vladivostok. 2929 n, 5183 g.

1960 Broken up.

MONTREAL

460 MONTREAL
O.N. 113373   1899–1903

Steel twin screw steamer, two decks and shelter deck
469.5'×56.2'×31.9'   4430 n   6870 g
Built by C. S. Swan & Hunter Ltd, Newcastle, Yard No 252, for British & African Steam Navigation Co Ltd. Registered Liverpool. 2×T 3 cyl 22'', 37'', 61''–48'' by Wallsend Slipway Co Ltd, Newcastle. 702 nhp, 13 K.
Accommodation for 750 head of cattle.

1899 29 April, launched by Mrs Colmer.

1900 4 July, trials. October 1900 to May 1902, employed carrying horses and mules from New Orleans to South Africa, completed seven round voyages.

1903 6 April, transferred to Canadian Pacific Railway Co with the sale of Elder, Dempster & Co's Beaver Line service. 5552 n, 8644 g.

1914 August, at Antwerp, engine overhaul in progress, transferred her coal to *MONTROSE* and left in tow of two tugs for Flushing. *MONTROSE* took up the tow to the Thames just before the German army over-ran Belgium. Both carried refugees.

1915 1 April, requisitioned by British Government for service as a troop carrier. Later returned to owners and resumed Liverpool–Canada service.

1918 29 January, when outward bound for St John, New Brunswick, rammed by CEDRIC (21,040 g/built 1903) in Morecambe Bay, taken in tow towards Liverpool, but sank 30 January 27 miles from Liverpool N½W of Bar Lightship. Two lives lost.

GARTH CASTLE *in Castle Mail Packets Co Ltd colours*

461 GARTH CASTLE
O.N. 82849   1901

Iron screw brig, two decks
365.0' × 43.5' × 31.3'   2381 n   3705 g
Built by J. Elder & Co, Glasgow, Yard No 245, for Donald
Currie & Co, London. Registered London. C 2 cyl 51", 88"–57"
by the builders. 500 hp, 12½ K.
Passenger accommodation: 52 first class, 46 second.

1880   December, completed.
1888   New engines and boilers by Richardson & Son, West
       Hartlepool. T 3 cyl 33", 55", 88"–57". 600 hp, 13 K.
       2350 n, 3660 g.
1894   Transferred to Castle Mail Packets Co Ltd (Donald
       Currie & Co, Managers).
1900   Owners became Union Castle Mail Steamship Co Ltd
       (Donald Currie & Co, Managers).
1901   June, acquired by Elder, Dempster & Co for the Bristol/
       Jamaica service but employed on the North Atlantic
       service, making five round voyages.
1902   Sold to Khedivial Mail Steamship & Graving Dock Co
       Ltd, London. Renamed **ISMAILIA**. 2336 n. 3704 g.
1911   Lord E. Hamilton, Manager.
1921   Sold to Soc Armatrice Radivo-Frausin, Italy. Renamed
       BRUNETTE. Registered Trieste (Italian flag).
1923   Sold for demolition.
Garth, near Aberfeldy, Perthshire, was Sir Donald Currie's
estate.

LAKE SIMCOE

462 LAKE SIMCOE
O.N. 113488   1901–1905

Iron screw steamer, four decks
430.5' × 47.0' × 34.5   2893 n   5192 g
Built by J. Elder & Co, Glasgow, Yard No 284, as **EMS** for
Norddeutscher Lloyd. Registered Bremen. C 3 cyl 62" (2), 86"–
60" by the builders. 1000 hp, 17 K.
Passenger accommodation: 124 first class, 128 second.

1884   Completed.
1901   Acquired by Elder, Dempster & Co. Renamed **LAKE
       SIMCOE**. 2864 n, 4933 g. Registered Liverpool.
1902   Originated short sea cruises to Norwegian fjords.
1905   September, sold for £14,000 for demolition in Genoa.
Lake Simcoe is situated in Ontario Province, Canada.

TROJAN, subsequently **WASSAU,** *as a Boer War Hospital Ship*

463 WASSAU
O.N. 82404   1901–1902

Iron screw steamer, two decks and spar deck
364.5' × 42.6' × 28.6'   2258 n   3555 g
Built by J. & G. Thomson, Glasgow, Yard No 177, as **TROJAN**
for Union Steamship Co Ltd, London. Registered
Southampton. C 2 cyl 51", 88"–60" by James & Co, Glasgow.
600 hp, 13½ K.

1880   27 February, launched.
1887   New engines and boilers by T. Richardson & Sons,
       Hartlepool. T 3 cyl 34", 54", 89"–60", 600 hp, 2088 n,
       3471 g.
1896   Refrigerated compartments fitted.
1899   October, converted into hospital ship for Boer War
       duties.
1900   March, transferred to Union-Castle Mail Steamship Co
       Ltd (Donald Currie & Co, Managers), London.
       Acquired by Beaver Line (Elder, Dempster & Co, Man-
       agers). Renamed **WASSAU**. Registered Liverpool.
1901   29 January, commenced the first of four round voyages:
       Liverpool–Halifax–St John–New Brunswick. Converted
       into hospital ship for Boer War duties.
1902   Sold to J. Goutte, France. Renamed **ISLAM**. Registered
       Marseilles. 2224 n, 3662 g.
1904   Scrapped at Marseilles.
The Trojans were the inhabitants of Troy, a city state in Asia
Minor, which suffered a ten-year siege.

LAKE MANITOBA (Photo McRoberts)

464 LAKE MANITOBA

O.N. 113497   1901–1903

'Lake Manitoba' class
Steel twin screw steamer, two decks and shelter deck
469.5′×56.2′×31.9′   5705 n   8852 g
Built by C. S. Swan & Hunter Ltd, Newcastle, Yard No 263,
for Beaver Line (Elder, Dempster & Co. Managers). Registered
Liverpool. 2×T 3 cyl 23½″, 38″, 64″–45″ by Richardson,
Westgarth & Co Ltd, Hartlepool. 832 nhp, 13 K.
Passenger accommodation: 122 first class, 130 second, 500 third.
1901   6 June, launched. 24 September, commenced maiden
       voyage, Liverpool to Montreal.
1903   6 April, transferred to Canadian Pacific Railway Co with
       the sale of Elder, Dempster & Co's Beaver Line service.
       6275 n, 9674 g. 16 May, arrived Montreal on first C. P.
       crossing.
1909   Port intermediate pressure cylinder rebored to 38¼″ dia-
       meter. Passenger accommodation: 350 second class, 1200
       third.
1918   26 August, on fire at Montreal—scuttled, refloated fol-
       lowing month—8 October, sold by underwriters to
       Bishop Navigation Co Ltd, Montreal. Refitted at
       Halifax.
1920   Renamed **IVER HEATH**. Tonnage opening closed.
       5853 n, 9170 g. Registered Montreal under British flag.
1921   28 September, sold to Canada Steamship Lines,
       Montreal.
1923   25 July, sold to Stelp & Leighton Ltd (Crete Shipping
       Co), London.
1924   Broken up.
Ships of the 'Lake Manitoba' class: LAKE MANITOBA (464),
LAKE MICHIGAN (465).
Lake Manitoba is situated within the Great Lakes, Canada.

Above, **LAKE MANITOBA,** *and, below,* **LAKE MICHIGAN** *in
dock at Liverpool*

465 LAKE MICHIGAN

O.N. 115252   1901–1903

'Lake Manitoba' class
Steel twin screw steamer, two decks and shelter deck
469.5′×56.2′×31.9′   4538 n   7000 g
Built by C. S. Swan & Hunter Ltd, Newcastle, Yard No 264,
for Beaver Line (Elder, Dempster & Co, Managers). Registered
Liverpool. 2×T 3 cyl 23½″, 38″, 64″–45″ by Richardson,
Westgarth & Co Ltd, Hartlepool. 722 nhp, 13 K.
Passenger accommodation: 500 third class.
1901   28 September, launched.
1902   February, completed. 21 March, commenced maiden
       voyage United Kingdom to St John, New Brunswick.
       Made one trooping voyage to South Africa.
1903   6 April, transferred to Canadian Pacific Railway Co with
       the sale of Elder, Dempster & Co's Beaver Line service.
       6048 n, 9240 g.
1904   19 February, when on passage from St John, New Bruns-
       wick, towards London, in collision with barque
       MATTERHORN (1954 g/built 1882) (San Francisco
       for Antwerp) during strong gale force weather. Beached
       three and a half miles west of Dungeness with engine
       room and the stokehold flooded, headgear lost and bows
       damaged. Refloated four days later and towed to
       Gravesend for repair. Passenger accommodation: 2150
       third class.
1916   15 November, mined nine miles off Brest but able to
       reach port, under tow.
1918   16 April, torpedoed without warning and sunk by Ger-
       man submarine U100, 93 miles north-west from Eagle
       Island, County Mayo, Ireland. One life lost, that of the
       Master.
Lake Michigan is situated within the Great Lakes, Canada.

466 PANTHER

O.N. 89188   1902–1903

Iron screw sloop
105.2′×19.8′×10.7′   10 n   138 g
Built by Elliot & Jeffery, Cardiff, as **ELLIOT & JEFFERY**,
Yard No 1, to builder's own account. Registered Cardiff.
C 2 cyl 19″, 35″–20″ by the builders. 70 hp.
1884   Completed.
1901   New boiler fitted.
1902   Acquired by Mersey Towage and Lighterage Co (Elder,
       Dempster & Co, Managers). Renamed **PANTHER**.
       19 n, 150 g. Registered Liverpool.
1903   Transferred to Canadian Pacific Railway Co with the
       sale of Elder, Dempster & Co's Beaver Line service.
1921   Sold to Coulson Tug Co (John C. Coulson), South
       Shields.
1925   Sold to France, Fenwick & Co.
1926   Sold for demolition.

467 AFRICAN

O.N. 89213   1901–1903

Iron screw steam tug, two funnels
105.4′×19.8′×10.5′   2 n   145 g
Built by Elliot & Jeffery, Cardiff, Yard No 2, as **SIR W. T.
LEWIS**, to builder's own account. Registered Cardiff.
C 2 cyl 22″, 44″–24″ by builders. 80 hp.
1887   Completed.
1901   Acquired by Mersey Towage and Lighterage Co (Elder,
       Dempster & Co, Managers). Renamed **AFRICAN**.
       Registered Liverpool. 13 n, 159 g.
1903   Transferred to Canadian Pacific Railway Co with the
       sale of Elder, Dempster & Co's Beaver Line service.
1906   Major refit. New boiler and single funnel installed.
       Renamed **OTTER**.

ELLIOT & JEFFERY, *subsequently* ***PANTHER***, *lying ahead of* LAKE MANITOBA *at Liverpool* (Photo McRoberts)

OTTER, formerly **AFRICAN**

1922 Sold to Screw Towing & Lighterage Co (G. R. Nicholson). Renamed **MARSHCOCK**. 13 n, 165 g.
1946 27 May, sold to Rootledge & Co, Liverpool.
1948 Broken up at Bromborough after long lay-up in Albert Dock.

468 BEAVER
O.N. 105158   1901–1903
Screw steam tug, iron frames steel plated
106.3′ × 20.0′ × 11.2′   13 n   154 g
Built by Elliot & Jeffery, Cardiff, Yard No 4. Launched as

LADY LEWIS. Registered Cardiff. C 2 cyl 22″, 42″–24″ by the builders. 75 hp.
1897 May, completed.
1899 Renamed **POWERFUL**.
1901 Sold to Mersey Towage & Lighterage Co (Elder, Dempster & Co, Managers). Renamed **BEAVER**. Registered Liverpool.
1903 Transferred to Canadian Pacific Railway Co with the sale of Elder, Dempster & Co's Beaver Line service.
1922 Sold to J. Davis, Cardiff.
1932 Owners: J. Davis Towage & Salvage Co Ltd (J. Davis, Manager).
1938 Sold to Rees & Co for demolition at Llanelly.

BEAVER

PART 3

Vessels engaged in the Jamaica trade

Ship Nos 469–473

PORT ROYAL (Photo McRoberts)

469 PORT ROYAL
O.N. 111309   1901–1911

'Port Royal' class
Steel twin screw steamer, two decks and awning deck
370.2'×46.5'×22.0'   2487 n   4455 g
Built by Sir Raylton Dixon & Co Ltd, Middlesbrough, Yard
No 476, for Imperial Direct West India Mail Service Co Ltd,
Liverpool. Registered Liverpool. 2×T 3 cyl 24", 38", 64"–45" by
Richardson, Westgarth & Co Ltd, Middlesbrough. 799 nhp,
14 K.
Passenger accommodation: 100 first class, 50 second. Capacity
to carry 25,000 stems of bananas.
1900   8 November, launched.
1901   23 February, trials.
1911   April, sold to Hadji Ibrahim Mani Zada, Turkey. No
       port of registry but under Turkish flag.
1912   Transferred to Administration de Nav a Vapeur Otto-
       man. Renamed **MIDHAT PACHA**. Registered
       Constantinople.
1914   7 November, sunk by Russians near Eregli, Black Sea,
       about 200 miles east of the Bosporus.
Ships of the 'Port Royal' class: PORT ROYAL (469), PORT
ANTONIO (470).
Port Royal is situated on the south coast of Jamaica.

Above, **PORT ROYAL,** *below,* **PORT ANTONIO**

470 PORT ANTONIO
O.N. 111315   1901–1911

'Port Royal' class
Steel twin screw steamer, two decks and awning deck
370.0'×46.5'×22.0'   2482 n   4458 g
Built by Sir Raylton Dixon & Co Ltd, Middlesbrough, Yard
No 477, for Imperial Direct West India Mail Service Co Ltd.

Registered Bristol. 2×T 3 cyl 24", 38", 64"–45" by Richardson,
Westgarth & Co Ltd, Middlesbrough. 799 nhp, 14 K.
Passenger accommodation: 100 first class, 50 second.
1901   22 March, launched. July, completed.
1911   Sold to Hadji Ibrahim Mani Jade. Renamed **RECHID**
       PACHA. No port of registry but under Turkish flag.
1913   Sold to Administration de Nav a Vapeur Ottoman.
       Registered Constantinople.
1920   Transferred to Administration de Nav a Vapeur Turque.
1929   Sold to Turkiye Seyrisefain Idaresi, Turkey. Renamed
       RESITPASA. Registered Istanbul. 2482 n, 4458 g.
1934   Reputed to have been acquired by Turkish Navy and
       converted into a submarine depot ship.

471 PORT MARIA
O.N. 111310   1901–1910

'Port Maria' class
Steel screw steamer, two decks and awning deck
334.7'×40.2'×17.6'   1449 n   2910 g
Built by Ramage & Ferguson Ltd, Leith, Yard No 171, for
Elder, Dempster & Co. Registered Bristol. T 3 cyl 30", 50", 80"–
48" by the builders. 656 nhp, 14 K.
Passenger accommodation: 65 first class, 16 second.
1900   20 December, launched.
1901   March, completed. Transferred to Imperial Direct West
       India Mail Service Co Ltd.
1908   High pressure cylinder rebored to 31½" diameter.
1910   March, sold to Cie de Nav Mixte, France. Renamed
       MUSTAPHA. Registered Marseilles. After only one
       voyage (Marseilles to Algiers) offered for sale due to
       heavy coal consumption).
1913   March, sold to 'Sicilia' Soc di Nav, Genoa. Renamed
       TOCRA. Registered Palermo. 1471 n, 2901 g.
1924   Sold to Soc di Nav 'Italia', Genoa. 1320 n, 2932 g.
1927   Sold to Cia Italiana Transatlantica, Genoa. Registered
       Genoa.
1932   Sold to 'Tirrenia' (Flotte Riunite Florio-Citra), Italy.
       Registered Naples.
1933   Sold to Cantiere di Portovenere SA for demolition at La
       Spezia.
Ships of the 'Port Maria' class: PORT MARIA (471), PORT
MORANT (472).
Port Maria is situated at the eastern end of Jamaica island.

PORT MARIA

PORT ANTONIO (Photo McRoberts)

PORT MORANT (Photo McRoberts)

472 PORT MORANT

O.N. 111308   1901–1909

'Port Maria' class
Steel screw steamer, two decks and awning deck
329.6′×40.1′×17.6   1322 n   2831 g
Built by Alexander Stephen & Sons Ltd, Glasgow, Yard No
387, for Elder, Dempster & Co. Registered Bristol. T 3 cyl 30″,
50″, 80″–45″ by Alexander Stephen & Sons Ltd, Glasgow.
745 nhp, 14 K.
Passenger accommodation: 45 first class, 16 second.
1900   21 November, launched.
1901   February, completed.
1902   Transferred to Imperial Direct West India Mail Service
       Co Ltd.
1905   Transferred to Elder Line Ltd. Registered Liverpool.
1909   Sold to Cia Argentine de Nav (Nicolas Mihanovich
       Ltda, Managers), Argentina. Renamed **SARMIENTO**.
       Registered Buenos Aires. 1322 n, 2831 g.
1912   April, wrecked in the Magellan Straits.
Note—Prior to launch, vessel was cut in two and lengthened by
30 feet.
Name taken from Jamaica, Point Morant, Morant Cays.

473 PORT KINGSTON

O.N. 117715   1904–1911

Steel twin screw steamer, two decks and spar deck
460.0′×55.5′×24.4′   3814 n   7586 g
Built by Alexander Stephen & Sons Ltd, Glasgow, Yard No
403, for Imperial Direct West India Mail Service Co Ltd (Elder,
Dempster & Co, Managers). Registered Bristol. 2×T 3 cyl 30″,
50″, 80″–54″ by the builders. 1443 nhp, 17 K.
Passenger accommodation: 160 first class, 60 second class.
Fitted to carry 40,000 stems of bananas.
1904   19 April, launched. 12 July, trials. 18.53 K.
1905   16 January (Captain J. G. Parsons), storm damage,
       one life lost, on voyage from Avonmouth for Kingston,
       Jamaica, about 900 miles south-west of Lundy Island.
1906   29 December, Sir Alfred Jones and party sailed for
       Jamaica aboard **PORT KINGSTON** from Avonmouth.

1907   14 January, disastrous earthquake occurred in Jamaica.
       PORT KINGSTON lying at anchor at Kingston, driven
       ashore, later refloated with the assistance of *DELTA* and
       used as a hospital during the emergency.
1910   Laid up when service ceased.
1911   August, sold to Union Steam Ship Co of New Zealand
       Ltd, London. Renamed **TAHITI**. Registered London.
       4155 n, 7898 g. Passenger accommodation: 277 first
       class, 97 second, 141 third.
1914   Chartered by New Zealand Government as a transport.
       Carried troops to Gallipoli and France.
1916   12 September, attacked by submarine in the Medi-
       terranean, torpedo missed.
1917   20 February, chased by submarine in the English
       Channel, saved by gunfire.
1918   July, transferred to the British Transport Service. 3
       December, left Liverpool for Dunedin and eventual
       return to owners. Underwent extensive refit, converted
       to oil fuel.
1920   Two voyages on Vancouver service then placed on the
       San Francisco route.
1927   4 November, ran down the wooden harbour ferry GREY-
       CLIFFE in Willington Harbour, Sydney. Forty-two lives
       lost. Court of Inquiry allocated three-fifths of blame to
       GREYCLIFFE and two-fifths to **TAHITI**. The latter
       was steaming at ten knots in an area restricted to eight
       knots.
1930   15 August, 0430 hours when 460 miles south of
       Rarotonga, Cook Islands, the 18½″ diameter starboard
       propeller shaft fractured inboard of the stern tube and
       holed the hull plating. Assistance was summoned by
       wireless, VENTURA (5986 g/built 1900) and TOFUA
       (4345 g/built 1908) answered the call, stood by and took
       off passengers, mail, baggage, bullion and the crew.
       TAHITI sank in position 24°.40′S 166°.15′W, at 0442
       on 17 August.
Kingston is the capital of Jamaica.

Note—DELTA (149), LAKE MEGANTIC (451) and GARTH
CASTLE (461) were also involved in the West Indies trade.

PORT KINGSTON

PART 4

Vessels operating in West African coastal and inland waters

Ship Nos 474–526

Note—Further lists of small craft operated by Elder Dempster in 1949 and 1972 form Appendix I

KWAIBO (ship No. 506) at the builder's yard (Photo Clwyd Record Office)

474 OPOBO (I)
O.N. 77035   1877–1892

Iron screw ketch
120.2′×20.1′×8.7′   146 n   186 g
Built by Liverpool Forge Co, for African Steamship Co. Registered London. C 2 cyl 12″, 22″–20″ by the builders. 30 hp.
Designed for service in the Niger Delta.
1877   Completed and 3 December, left Liverpool on maiden voyage to Nigeria.
1878   1 January, arrived Lagos.
1882   Wrecked on Bonny Bar. No loss of life.
Opobo is a port on the Imo River (approximately 30 miles east of Bonny River).

475 RAMOS
O.N. 78639   1878–1885

Iron screw schooner, one deck
150.2′×21.1′×8.4′   136 n   233 g
Built by Cunliffe & Dunlop, Port Glasgow, for British & African Steam Navigation Co. Registered Glasgow. C 2 cyl 17″, 30″–20″ by the builders. 40 hp.
1878   July, completed.
1883   Transferred to African Steamship Co.
1885   3 October (Captain W. Hargraves), wrecked on Lagos Bar.
Ramos is one of the river-mouths of the Niger Delta.

476 DODO (I)
O.N. 80445   1879–1908

Iron screw brig, one deck
195.8′×25.2′×12.3′   326 n   531 g
Built by Cunliffe & Dunlop, Port Glasgow, Yard No 137, for British & African Steam Navigation Co. Registered Glasgow. C 2 cyl 24″, 42″–27″ by the builders. 80 hp.
Designed for service in the Niger Delta.
1879   March, completed.
1908   Declared unfit for further service and dismantled. 22 June, scuttled at Forcados, Nigeria.
Dodo is one of the river-mouths of the Niger Delta.

477 MARIA REGINA
O.N. 84054   1883–1886

Wooden brig
92.3′×28.9′×16.2   253 n   264 g
Built by unknown builders at unknown date.
1882–83   First mention in Register. Owner: J. Holt, Esq. Registered Liverpool.
1883–84   Sold to A. L. Jones, Esq.
1886–87   Not entered in *Lloyd's Register*.

478 MAAS
O.N. 87924   1887–1895

'Maas' class
Iron screw flat
125.5′×19.7′×7.1′   137 n   166 g
Built at Antwerp. Single cylinder engine 13″–12″. 20 hp.
1877   Completed.
1887   Acquired by British & African Steam Navigation Co Ltd. Registered Glasgow.
1895   Broken up.
Ships of the 'Maas' class: MAAS (478), SCHELDE (479).

479 SCHELDE
O.N. 87972   1889–1890

'Maas' class
Iron screw flat
125.5′×19.7′×7.1′   137 n   166 g
Built at Antwerp. Single cylinder engine 13″–12″. 20 hp.
1877   Completed.
1885   Sold to C. W. Pollexfen, Liverpool.
1887   Sold to T. M. Cracken, Liverpool.
1889   Acquired by Elder, Dempster & Co, Liverpool.
1890   Sold to Italian interests.
1896   Reported lost.

480 EARN
O.N. 89949   1890–1911

'Earn' class
Iron screw steamer, machinery aft, one deck (flush)
78.2′×22.0′×8.0′   74 n   109 g
Built by Blackwood & Gordon, Port Glasgow, Yard No 197, for W. Arrol & Co, Glasgow. Registered Glasgow. C 2 cyl by D. Gordon, Port Glasgow. 22 hp.
1884   Completed.
1887   New engines by White & Cooper, Dundee. C 2 cyl 11½″, 19¼″–16″. 25 hp.
1889   Lengthened by 35.6′ to 113.8′. 143 n, 181 g.
1890   Acquired by A. L. Jones, Esq (Elder, Dempster & Co, Managers).
1911   Sold to Cia de Embaracaciones Canarias, Las Palmas. Registered Las Palmas.
1924   Renamed **NUMERO 25**. 131 n, 164 g.
1935   Disappears from *Lloyd's Register*.
Ships of the 'Earn' class: EARN (480), ISLA (481).

481 ISLA
O.N. 90015   1890–1911

'Earn' class
Iron screw smack, machinery aft, one deck (flush)
78.4′×22.1′×8.1′   74 n   109 g
Built by Blackwood & Gordon, Port Glasgow, Yard No 201, for W. Arrol & Co, Glasgow. Registered Glasgow. C 2 cyl by D. Gordon, Port Glasgow. 22 hp.
1885   Completed.
1888   New engines by White & Cooper, Dundee. C 2 cyl 11½″, 19¼″–16″. 25 hp.
1890   Acquired by Elder, Dempster & Co.
1892   Registered Liverpool.
1911   Sold to Cia Embaracaciones Canarias, Las Palmas. Registered Las Palmas.
1924   Renamed **NUMERO 24**. 68 n, 105 g.
1931   Sold to Grand Canary Coaling Co Ltd, Las Palmas.
1935   Disappears from *Lloyd's Register*.

482 EKO
O.N. 64934   1899–1905

Steel screw steamer, one deck
130.7′×22.4′×11.2′   233 n   335 g
Built by Moller & Holberg, Stettin, Yard No 318, as **HOLLAND**, for Deutsche Kusten Dampfschiffahrts Gesellschaft, Hamburg. Registered Hamburg. C 2 cyl 17½″, 31½″–21½″ by Stettin Gesellschaft, Stettin. 38 hp.
1890   Completed.
1891   Sold to A. Hedman, Finland. Renamed **FREJ**. Registered Wasa (Russian flag).

1893 Sold to Witt & Busch, Hamburg. Renamed **EKO**. Registered Hamburg. 227 n, 337 g.
1899 Acquired by African Steamship Co. Registered Lagos (British flag).
1905 Sold to Lagos Government.
1907 Disappears from *Lloyd's Register*.
Eko was the former name of Lagos, the capital of Nigeria.

483 GARTH
O.N. 114861   1901–1904

'Garth' class
Steel screw steam barge, one deck, engines aft
107.3′×20.8′×7.6′   84 n   156 g
Built by G. K. Stothert & Co, Bristol, Yard No 244, for Bristol Lighterage Co Ltd, Bristol (Elder, Dempster & Co, Managers). Registered Bristol. C 2 cyl 12″, 24″–16″ by the builders. 28 hp.
1901 October, completed.
1904 Sold to Rea Transport Co Ltd (R. & J. H. Rea, Managers), Liverpool.
1908 Sold to Pioneer Tug & Lighter Co Ltd, Hull (J. E. Hewson, Manager).
1910 Sold to Gonzalez y Lavendera, Luarea, Spain. Renamed **MANOLO**. Registered Gijon. 60 n, 152 g.
1919 Disappears from *Lloyd's Register*.
Ships of the 'Garth' class: GARTH (483), MAESTEG (484).

484 MAESTEG
O.N. 111318   1901–1904

'Garth' class
Steel screw steam barge, one deck, machinery aft
107.3′×20.6′×8.0   88 n   160 g
Built by G. K. Stothert & Co, Bristol, Yard No 243, for Bristol Lighterage Co Ltd (Elder, Dempster & Co, Managers), Bristol. Registered Bristol. C 2 cyl 12″, 24″–16″ by the builders. 28 hp.
1901 October, completed.
1904 Sold to Rea Transport Co Ltd (R. & J. H. Rea, Managers), Liverpool.
1910 Sold to A. G. & V. Cosulich, Trieste, Austria. Renamed **NOGARO**. Registered Trieste (Austro-Hungarian flag).
1914 Owning company in liquidation, A. Hreglich, Manager.
1920 Returned to the ownership of A. G. & V. Cosulich, Trieste, Italy. Renamed **LOVCEN**. Registered Venice.
1921 Sold to SA Milanese Transporti Marittimi, Italy. Registered Venice.
1922 Sold to Alberto Gargiulp, Constantinople.
1924 Sold to Walter Grisete, Constantinople.
1925 Sold to Djemal Bey & Behie Hanoum, Constantinople. Renamed **DERIA**. Registered Constantinople.
1926 Sold to SA Turque du Monopole des Affaires du Port de Constantinople, Turkey. Renamed **SAKA**. 89 n, 154 g.
1931 Sold to Istanbul Liman Isleri Inhisari, TAS, Turkey.
1932 Disappears from *Lloyd's Register*.

TREDEGAR. *This photograph was taken at Bristol about 1933, and shows the collier owned by A. J. Smith, built by G. K. Stothert & Co, Bristol, in 1892 and powered by a single cylinder engine. Elder Dempster's* **GARTH** *and* **MAESTEG**, *although built nine years later, longer by 10 feet, and powered by compound engines, were undoubtedly similar in general layout and appearance (Photo Edwin Keen)*

485 RHYMNEY
O.N. 111314   1901–1905

'Rhymney' class
Steel schooner, one deck
100.3′×21.2′×8.7′   158 n   168 g
Built by Port Talbot Graving Dock & Shipbuilding Co Ltd, Port Talbot, for Bristol Lighterage Co Ltd (A. L. Jones, Managers). Registered Bristol.
1901   Completed.
1905   Sold to Rea & Co.
1908   Sank off Avonmouth.
Ships of the 'Rhymney' class: RHYMNEY (485), RHONDDA (486).

486 RHONDDA
O.N. 111321   1901–1905

'Rhymney' class
Steel schooner, one deck
100.0′×21.0′×8.7′   160 n   170 g
Built by Mordey Carney & Co Ltd, Newport, Yard No 64, for Bristol Lighterage Co Ltd (H. S. Flinn, Managers). Registered Bristol.
1901   Completed.
1902   Elder, Dempster & Co, Managers.
1903   20 August, (Captain C. Field) sank five miles SW Bell Buoy, River Usk, voyage Eley–Avonmouth with two passengers and cargo of coal. Both passengers and three crew lost. Subsequently raised.
1905   Disappears from *Lloyd's Register*.

487 KITTIWAKE
O.N. 108843   1903–1908

'Kittiwake' class
Steel screw cutter, one deck, engines aft
118.0′×22.0′×10.4′   110 n   241 g
Built by T. B. Seath & Co, Rutherglen, Yard No 308, for the Manchester & Liverpool Transport Co Ltd, London. Registered Manchester. C 2 cyl 16″, 33″–20″ by Fisher & Co, Paisley. 45 hp, 9 K.
1899   August, completed.
1903   Acquired by British & African Steam Navigation Co Ltd. Registered Liverpool. Operated on Lagos to Forcados branch service.
1908   24 April, stranded on Lagos Bar (Captain J. A. Owen). Declared a constructive total loss.
Kittiwake was a traditional name in the Manchester and Liverpool Transport Co Ltd fleet.
Ships of the 'Kittiwake' class: KITTIWAKE (487), PUFFIN (488), SEAGULL (489).

488 PUFFIN
O.N. 108848   1904–1911

'Kittiwake' class
Steel screw cutter, one deck, engines aft
118.0′×22.0′×10.4′   111 n   241 g
Built by T. B. Seath & Co, Rutherglen, Yard No 310, for the Manchester & Liverpool Transport Co Ltd, London. Registered Manchester. C 2 cyl 16″, 33″–20″ by Fisher & Co, Paisley. 45 hp, 9 K.
1899   December, completed.
1902   Sold to W. B. MacIver & Co. Ltd, Liverpool. Registered Liverpool.
1904   Acquired by British & African Steam Navigation Co Ltd. Employed on the West African coastal branch services, Lagos to Porto Novo and later Lagos to Forcados.

1911   Hulked at Lagos.
1912   Sank at Lagos.
Puffin was a traditional name in the Manchester & Liverpool Transport Co Ltd fleet.

489 SEAGULL
O.N. 108838   1905–1908, 1913–1919

'Kittiwake' class
Steel screw cutter, one deck, engines aft
118.0′×22.0′×10.4′   109 n   241 g
Built by T. B. Seath & Co, Rutherglen, Yard No 307, for the Manchester & Liverpool Transport Co Ltd, London. Registered Manchester. C 2 cyl 16″, 33″–20″ by Fisher & Co, Paisley. 45 hp, 9 K.
1899   August, completed.
1905   February, acquired by Elder, Dempster & Co. Registered Liverpool. Operated on Lagos branch service.
1906   Transferred to Cia de Vapor Correos Interinsulares Canarios, Las Palmas. Under Spanish flag.
1908   Sold to Vincente Diaz Llanos, Santa Cruz. Registered Tenerife.
1913   Acquired by Elder Line Ltd (Elder, Dempster & Co Ltd, Managers). Registered Lagos (British flag).
1914   Sold to Cia de Embarcaciones Canarios, Las Palmas. Renamed **YELWA**, later reverted to **SEAGULL**. Registered Tenerife. 110 n, 268 g. Placed under Elder Dempster management.
1919   Sold to B. Fernandez, Gijon. Renamed **GAVIOTA**. Registered Gijon.
1920   72 n, 243 g.
1921   Sold to E. Vigil-Escalera (Gregorio Vigil-Escalera, Manager), Spain. Registered Tenerife.
1926   160 n, 299 g.
1931   Sold to Heredos de Gregorio Vigil-Escalera y sa Esposa, Spain.
1933   Disappears from *Lloyd's Register*.
Seagull was a traditional name in the Manchester & Liverpool Transport Co Ltd fleet.

490 LAGOS (III)
O.N. 124054   1907–1924

'Lagos' class
Steel screw steamer
170.0′×26.0′×8.5′   187 n   392 g
Built by William Harkess & Son Ltd, Middlesbrough, Yard No 168, for Elder, Dempster & Co. Registered Liverpool. C 2 cyl 18½″, 40″–26″ by MacColl & Pollock Ltd, Sunderland. 65 hp, 11 K.
1907   Completed.
1908   Transferred to Elder Dempster Shipping Ltd.
1923   Transferred to Elder Line Ltd.
1924   4 October, sunk off Lagos after dismantling (hulk used as a naval target by HMS THISTLE).
Ships of the 'Lagos' class: LAGOS (490), FORCADOS (491).

491 FORCADOS (II)
O.N. 124063   1907–1925

'Lagos' class
Steel screw steamer
170.0′×26.0′×8.5′   191 n   397 g
Built by William Harkess & Sons Ltd, Middlesbrough, Yard No 169, for Elder, Dempster & Co. Registered Liverpool. C 2 cyl 18½″, 40″–26″ by MacColl & Pollock Ltd, Sunderland. 65 hp, 11 K.
1907   28 March, launched by Mrs W. Harkess.
1908   Transferred to Elder Line Ltd.
1925   8 February, dismantled at Lagos and scuttled.

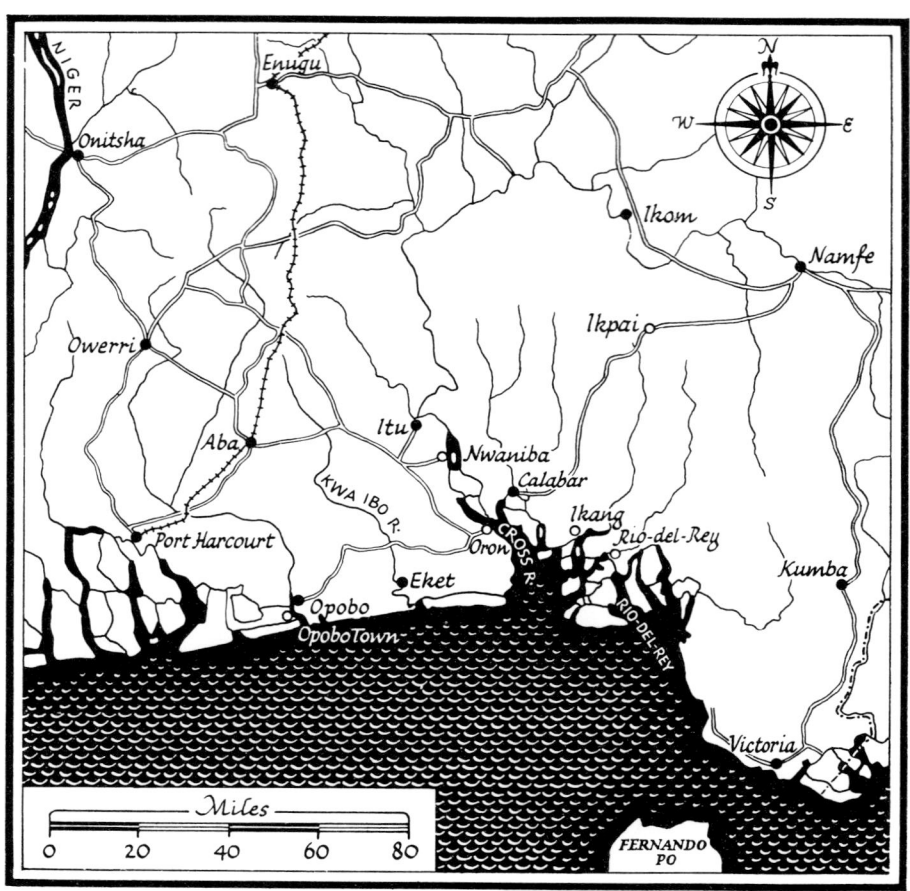

Calabar and the Cross River Trade

by G.H.AVEZATHE, C.M.G.

Mr G.H.Avezathe, C.M.G., who recently retired from the Board of Directors of Elder Dempster Lines, has very close personal knowledge of trade and shipping in West Africa. For ten years in the early part of his career he was the Company's agent in Calabar, where he built up the now important Cross River services. During the second world war as Ministry of War Transport representative at Lagos he controlled all merchant shipping from Senegal to South West Africa.

CALABAR (or Old Calabar as it was called when I first went there) is perhaps the most interesting of all our West Coast branches. Practically an island

surrounded by mangrove swamp at the commencement of the 300-mile Cross River, it offered ample opportunity for the development of Inland Water Transport, and it is in this sphere that I found so much pleasure in exploring the masses of creeks for possible trade.

In 1913 the station small craft consisted of the launches *Bansara, Cross, Onward* and a small wooden launch *Doris*. No regular services were run and the craft were employed mainly in the high river season for clearing produce for one firm on the upper river and another firm just beyond Itu, 50 miles from Calabar. Local lighterage was performed by the trading firms themselves by means of 10-ton wooden lighters propelled and steered from the stern by two Kroo boys taking advantage of the tides. Communication with the ships at anchor in the stream was by gigs paddled by six boys in brightly coloured loin-cloths, singlets and red woollen caps.

The Trading factories were named after the sailing vessels which became trading hulks and lay off the beaches before shore buildings were erected. Even in my time the Agent was always known by the African traders as "Captain". The factories still bear such names as Hope, Matilda and Parracca.

It was not until 1920 that any serious attempt was made to increase transport services on the river. Calabar, by reason of its position, was cut off from the rest of Nigeria, and the first attempt was a connection to the nearest mainland, Oron, 17 miles down river. An open lighter of ten tons capacity, fitted with long benches and roofed with canvas awnings, was towed alongside a ship's launch A daily ferry service leaving Calabar at 8.0 a.m. and Oron at 2.0 p.m. was thus started. At first the service was resented by canoe owners who plied this area, and they reduced their fares. But the extra comfort given to passengers, and the greater loads of foodstuffs and merchandise they could safely carry, appealed to the traveller. The service became popular, and it soon became obvious that a larger craft would be necessary. This could not be spared from our existing services on the Cross River, which we were busily expanding, so the *Oron* was commissioned. This twin-screw ferry capable of carrying 500 deck passengers, with first-class accommodation and ample space for a number of cars, went into service in July, 1938. But even this craft became too small for the growing trade and was followed by a larger and more luxurious vessel, the *Eket*, built to carry 1,050 passengers. The *Eket* has

Calabar River from Mission Hill.

The *Eket* alongside Elders pontoon at Calabar.

first- and second-class accommodation and a saloon for light refreshments. She arrived at Calabar early in 1950 and operated a daily service each way between Calabar and Oron; since March 1954 she operates a twice daily service and carries about 370,000 passengers annually.

Having established the Oron Ferry we turned to the further development of the Service and were naturally directed to nearby districts. Ikpa and Nwaniba seemed to be the best selected spots, tapping as they did the road to Eket – a district we could not at the time serve. A weekly service to those points was inaugurated, and several trading establishments took advantage of the transport services available. Then the Cross River itself, rather than its tributaries, came into the picture. Itu, with its road connections to the new town of Aba, on the rail line from Port Harcourt, was the obvious choice. Unfortunately, the river front of Itu offered little opportunity for further development. Okepedi, about three miles beyond in Enyong Creek, where a trading firm had been established for some years, appeared to be a likely spot, as it tapped the road to the new approach to Aba. With the guaranteed weekly River service, several firms opened up this district. The first firm to do so was given an opportunity in which we were able to give an unusual service. They opened a small retail shop, but as most of the trade was of the barter variety, whereby they exchanged goods for produce, they were not able to offer storage space for produce. We overcame the difficulty by sending by our weekly service an empty lighter. The lighter lay alongside their beach until the following week, by which time it was full, and the first 45 to 50 tons carriage of produce was thus assured for our weekly transport service.

As our transport became regular and reliable, passenger traffic increased. To give a better service we transferred two "Reo" lorries from Lagos. We issued a through ticket from Calabar to Itu by river, and by road from Itu to Aba, thus connecting Calabar by rail to all points.

To meet the increasing trade it again became necessary to implement our fleet. The *Inde*, specially designed for the service, was put into operation. The launch was fitted with a large upper deck, state-rooms, bathroom and conveniences. She also had electric light and fans – the first vessel for the Cross River so equipped. When I made the first trip in her I much regretted the electric light. When it was switched on all the flying insects of the river came to have a look!

Eventually we took over the Government service, and with it a large stern-wheeler, which we named *Ikom*, and a small shallow-draft launch *Mosquito*, which we re-engined. With these craft (whilst new vessels were being built for us), we started a fort-nightly timetabled service to all stations ending at Ikom, thus covering the whole of the river. We started a twice-daily ferry service with two house-boats and a ship's launch between Calabar and Creek Town.

The Cross River is not an easy one to navigate, owing to the constantly changing sandbanks, and the upper section presents draft problems. Sometimes little more than a foot of water finishes in deep small lakes, in which lurk hippo and crocodiles.

Our next problem was to supply a service to Eket. This meant going out to sea and crossing the six-foot Qua Ibo bar. Fortunately, we were able to borrow from Lagos the 300-ton seagoing vessel *Ila*, and start up a service. In the meantime we built the *Kwaibo*, a vessel of suitable design, with four state-rooms flanking a centre saloon. In addition to giving a service to Eket, she was used to connect the mail-boats (whose terminal port was then Calabar) with Victoria, so the state-rooms had great practical value.

The first shipment of palm oil in bulk was made from Calabar. Forty-inch casks weighing 17-cwt. each were lightered to the ship, and decanted into the ship's tank. The heads of the casks were stove-in and the oil then poured into the tank. "Poured" is perhaps the wong word. Calabar oil is not noted for its softness, and we had to use steam jets to liquefy it. I thought the tank would never fill, so many casks were needed. It was a messy job, sorting out the empty casks and returning them to their own beaches. I doubt if the right ones ever were returned! At the end of the operation we were well short of the required number. Perhaps they went into the tank with the palm oil. Only Liverpool can say what they found in the tank!

The United Africa Company soon solved the problem of bulk oil by building shore installations whereby the oil was gathered into tanks, and conveyed in a warm state by pipeline direct to ship's tanks.

In spite of all the discomfort and the primitive conditions involved in living and working in the Calabar area during this time of development I found it one of the most interesting periods of my life. The station had been full of interest and opportunity and when after ten years' service I was asked to take up a new appointment at Accra I left Calabar with real feelings of regret.

The *Eket* boarded up for her journey from the Mersey to Calabar.

From Sea *magazine*

BANSARA, from ED magazine

492 BANSARA
O.N. 131356   1911–1932

Steel twin screw ketch
105.0′×21.2′×6.7′   71 n   127 g
Built by Hepple & Co Ltd, South Shields, Yard No 613,
for West African Lighterage & Transport Co Ltd. Registered
Liverpool. 2×T 3 cyl 9″, 14″, 22″–12″ by Miller & Macfie Ltd,
Glasgow. 80 hp.
1911   Completed.
1934   12 January, deleted from United Kingdom registry.
Bansara is a ferry point in the Cross River, Eastern Nigeria.

Two scenes of village life in Liberia in the 1930's and 1940's

ATTENDANT

494 ILA
O.N. 135568   1914–1933

'Ila' class
Steel twin screw motor, machinery aft
135.0′×25.1′×9.1′   198 n   299 g   300 d
Built by Hawthorn & Co Ltd, Leith, Yard No 136, for British & African Steam Navigation Co Ltd. Registered Liverpool. 2 SCSA 4 cyl 15″–16⅛″ by J. & C. G. Bolinders & Co Ltd, Stockholm. 69 nhp, 8 K.
Operated on Lagos lagoon service. African master and crew.
1914   28 January, launched. Trial speed 11 K.
1933   April, transferred to Elder Dempster Lines Ltd.
1935   Dismantled. 17 September, scuttled in Badagry Creek, Lagos.
Ships of the 'Ila' class: ILA (494), IFE (495).

493 ATTENDANT
O.N. 135489   1913–1934

Steel twin screw cutter
124.7′×27.2′×10.8′   120 n   317 g
Built by Harland & Wolff Ltd, Govan, Yard No 447G, for Elder, Dempster & Co Ltd. Registered Liverpool. 2×T 3 cyl 10½″, 16½″, 26″–18″ by the builders. 91 hp.
1913   August, completed.
1915   Transferred to Elder Line Ltd.
1932   Transferred to Elder Dempster Lines.
1934   Sold to Malet Salvage Syndicate Ltd, London.
1950   25 September, sold to Lloyd's Albert Yard and Motor Packet Services (R. A. Beazley, Manager), Cork.

495 IFE
O.N. 136674   1914–1930

'Ila' class
Steel twin screw, machinery aft
134.9′×25.1′×9.1′   198 n   299 g   300 d
Built by Hawthorn & Co Ltd, Leith, Yard No 137, for African Steamship Co. Registered London. 2 SCSA 4 cyl 15″–16⅛″ by J. & C. G. Bolinders & Co Ltd, Stockholm. 69 nhp, 8¼ K.
Operated on Lagos lagoon service. African master and crew.
1914   12 March, launched. 28 May, trials.
1930   November, dismantled and scuttled.
Ife, 21 miles north of Aba, is a Divisional Headquarters town in the Oyo Province of Western Nigeria.

ILA

IFE

496 TOWYN
O.N. 140540   1919–1933

Steel screw tug
71.9′×18.2′×8.4′   63 g
Built at Montrose for Alexandra Towing Co Ltd, as
SALTHOUSE.
1917   Completed.
1919   Acquired by Elder, Dempster & Co Ltd for service in
West Africa. Renamed **TOWYN**.
1933   Dismantled and sunk off Lagos.

497 OTTA
O.N. 135441   1913–1936

Steel screw tug
121.5′×18.7′×6.8′   87 n   143 g
Built Papendrecht for British & African Steam Navigation Co
Ltd, Liverpool (John Craig, Manager). Registered Liverpool.
1913   Completed.
1936   1 May, deleted from United Kingdom registry, reported
unserviceable.
Otta is a village on Badagri Creek, near Lagos.

498 FREDA
O.N. 135576   1914–1933

Steel screw tug, one deck
70.5′×16.0′×6.6′   7 n   58 g
Built by Cox & Co (Engineers) Ltd, Falmouth, Yard No 151,
for Elder, Dempster & Co Ltd. Registered Liverpool. C 2 cyl
11″, 24″–16″ by the builders. 42 hp.
1914   April, completed.
1933   18 November, reported dismantled and scuttled.

499 FRESCO
O.N. 137433   1915

Steel screw tug, one deck
75.1′×17.1′×7.8′   74 g
Built by Scott & Sons, Bowling, Yard No 250, for Elder,
Dempster & Co Ltd. Registered Liverpool. C 2 cyl 13″, 28″–18″
by Gauldie, Gillespie & Co, Glasgow. 42 hp.
1915   March, completed. 5 October, sold to the Admiralty.
1926   26 November, sold to T. Round, Scarborough.
1928   25 June, sold to P. C. McLeod, Alloa.
1963   4 October, vessel reported broken up at Bo'ness.

500 ILESHA
O.N. 134704   1915

Steel, twin screw, engines aft
89.2′×17.0′×7.3′   52 n   109 g
Built by I. J. Abdela & Mitchell Ltd, Queensferry, Yard No
355, for Butler & Co, Bristol, as **KINGSHOLME**. Registered
Bristol for Bristol Channel service only. Oil engine 2 SCSA.
2 cyl by J. & C. G. Bolinders Co Ltd, Stockholm.
1914   Completed. Renamed **KINGSHOLM**.
1915   Acquired by Elder, Dempster & Co Ltd. Renamed
ILESHA. 8 August, stranded on Bardsey Island,
voyage Liverpool to West Africa. Refloated, sank later.
Ilesha is a town in Oyo Province, Nigeria, nearly 20 miles to
the south-east of Oshogbo.

501 WESTMERE
O.N. 145978   1924–1939

Steel screw tug, one deck
60.2′×16.1′×6.9′   44 g
Built by H. Robb Ltd, Leith, for Bromport Steam Ship Co Ltd
(H. R. Greenhalgh, Manager), Liverpool. Registered Liverpool.
C 2 cyl 13″, 26″–18″ by Gauldie, Gillespie & Co Ltd, Glasgow.
38 nhp.
1922   September, completed.
1924   Acquired by West African Lighterage & Transport Co
Ltd.
1939   16 February, United Kingdom registry closed, reported
unfit for further service.
Bromport named their ships after Cheshire villages ending in
mere.

502 INDE
O.N. 147270   1924–1959

Twin screw barge, one deck, machinery aft
105.1′×20.1′×6.4′   89 n   135 g
Built by J. Crichton & Co Ltd, Saltney, Chester, Yard No 396,
for Nigerian Transport Co Ltd. Registered Liverpool 2×oil
engines 2 SCSA 4 cyl 13″–13$\frac{5}{16}$″ by J. & C. G. Bolinders Co Ltd,
Stockholm. 119 nhp.
1924   Completed.
1932   Transferred to Elder Dempster Lines Ltd.
1957   Broken up.

503 KING TOM
O.N. 174239   1927–1953

Passenger ferry
54.1′×14.1′×4.7′
Built by Crichtons of Saltney and Connahs Quay, Yard No
442, for the West African Lighterage & Transport Co Ltd. 2
oil engines. 320 bhp.
1927   Completed.
1946   30 September, registered Freetown.
1953   Withdrawn from service following completion of the
Queen Elizabeth II Quay, Freetown.
1956   10 December, reported sunk.

504 SUBU
O.N. 144581   1928–1929

Steel screw barge, engines aft
105.5′×21.1′×7.1′   91 n   136 g
Built by W. Dobson & Co, Newcastle, for Hope Lighterage

Co Ltd, London (A. R. C. Johnson, Manager), as **EVELYN HOPE**. Registered London. Oil engine 2 SCSA 2 cyl by J. & C. G. Bolinders Co Ltd, Stockholm. 26 nhp.
1916 Completed.
1924 Sold to Prizeman & Co Ltd, London.
1925 Owners restyled Prizeman & Co (1925) Ltd.
1927 Acquired by Etna Stone & Shingle Co, Snettisham Ltd, London.
1928 Acquired by West African Lighterage & Transport Co Ltd. Renamed **SUBU**. Registered London.
1929 13 September, reported destroyed by fire and registry closed.

505 OKUNI
O.N. 149675   1928–

Steel twin screw lighter
71.1'×17.1'×6.4'   49 n   78 g
Built by J. S. Watson (Gainsborough) Ltd, Gainsborough, for Nigerian Transport Co Ltd, Liverpool. Registered Liverpool. 2×2 cyl oil engines 2 SCSA 10½"×11" by J. & C. G. Bolinders Co Ltd, Stockholm. 140 bhp, 10 K.
1928 Completed.
1934 Transferred to Elder Dempster Lines Ltd.
1959 2 June, transferred to West African Lighterage & Transport Co Ltd.
1985 31 August, on the United Kingdom register.

506 KWAIBO
O.N. 161061   1928–1941

Steel twin screw motor ferry
157.5'×26.1'×9.3'   223 n   396 g
Built by J. Crichton & Co Ltd, Saltney, Chester, Yard No 455, for Nigerian Transport Co Ltd. Registered Liverpool. 2×oil engines, 2 SCSA 4 cyl, 11¹³⁄₁₆"–12¹³⁄₁₆" by J. & C. G. Bolinders Co Ltd, Stockholm. 197 nhp, 9½ K.
Passenger accommodation: four state rooms.
1928 Completed.
1934 15 August, transferred to Elder Dempster Lines Ltd.
1941 1 August, stranded on Eket Bar. September, declared a constructive total loss.
Name derived from River Kwa Ibo that runs south into the Bight of Biafra, to the west of Imo River.

KWAIBO

507 SERABU
O.N. 144652   1928–1932

Steel motor barge for Channel and coasting service
105.5'×21.1'×7.3'   76 n   138 g
Built by W. Beardmore & Co Ltd, Glasgow, as **BEATRICE**

HOPE for Hope Lighterage & Co Ltd (A. R. C. Johnston, Managers), London. Registered London. Oil engines, 2 SCSA 2 cyl 10⅝"–11" by J. & C. G. Bolinders Co Ltd, Stockholm. 14 nhp.
1916 Completed.
1923 Sold to Prizeman & Co Ltd, London. 105 n, 142 g.
1927 Sold to Etna Stone & Shingle Co, Snettisham Ltd, Batley.
1928 Acquired by West African Lighterage & Transport Co Ltd. Renamed **SERABU**. 90 n, 137 g. Re-engined 2 SCSA 2 cyl Bolinder oil engine 11⅞"–12⁵⁄₁₆". 26 nhp.
1971 24 September, deleted from United Kingdom registry.

508 NAKWA
O.N. 161093   1929–1939

Steel steam tug
71.0'×16.1'×7.7'   10 n   79 g
Built by J. Crichton & Co Ltd, Saltney, Chester, Yard No 477, for West African Lighterage & Transport Co Ltd, Liverpool. Registered Liverpool. C 2 cyl by Plenty & Son, Newbury. 39 nhp.
1929 April, completed.
1939 22 February, sold to United Africa Co Ltd, London.
1956 17 April, broken up.
Name derived from Nakwa River, Ghana.

509 NORTHOP
O.N. 162412   1934–

Steel motor tug, one deck
72.1'×17.6'×5.8'   19 n   70 g
Built by Lytham Shipbuilding & Engineering Co Ltd, Lytham, Yard No 835, for Elder Dempster Lines Ltd. Registered Liverpool. Oil engine 2 SCSA 4 cyl 11½"–13½" by H. Widdop & Co Ltd, Keighley. 93 nhp.
1934 September, completed.
1985 31 August, on the United Kingdom registry.
Northop is a village in North Wales.

510 NEVERN
O.N. 162404   1934–1955

Steel steam tug, twin screw, one deck
75.8'×17.1'×7.1'   13 n   83 g
Built by W. J. Yarwood & Sons Ltd, Northwich, Yard No 453, for West African Lighterage & Transport Co Ltd. Registered Liverpool. 2×T 3 cyl 6½", 10", 16"–12" by MacKie & Baxter Ltd, Paisley. 33 nhp.
1934 June, completed.
1955 22 October, scuttled at Freetown.
Nevern is a village in North Wales.

511 NUNEATON
O.N. 164276   1935–1957

Steel motor tug, one deck
53.1'×14.1'×6.0'   2 n   42 g
Built by W. J. Yarwood & Sons Ltd, Northwich, Yard No 540, for Elder Dempster Lines Ltd. Registered Liverpool. Oil engine 2 SCSA 3 cyl 11½"–13½". 70 nhp.
1935 December, completed.
1957 8 February, sold to S. Hadi Ltd, Bathurst.
1985 31 August, on the United Kingdom register.

512 IKPA
O.N. 119820   1935–1959

Steel river steamer
105.0′×22.5′×4.5′   67 n   115 g
Built by Yarrow & Co Ltd, Scotstoun. C 2 cyl.
1925 Completed.
1935 Purchased by West African Lighterage & Transport Co Ltd, Liverpool.
1959 26 June, broken up.

513 NORTHWICH
O.N. 164330   1937–1956

Steel tug
72.3′×17.6′×5.9′   16 n   71 g
Built by Lytham Shipbuilding & Engineering Co Ltd, Lytham, Yard No 851, for West African Lighterage & Transport Co Ltd. Registered Liverpool. Oil engine 2 SCSA 4 cyl 11½″–13½″ by H. Widdop & Co Ltd, Keighley. 39 nhp.
1937 July, completed.
1956 Sold to H.M. Government of Sierra Leone.
1985 31 August, on the United Kingdom register.
Northwich is a town in Cheshire.

514 NEMBE (II)
O.N. 164338   1937–1964

Steel motor tug
72.3′×17.6′×5.9′   16 n   71 g
Built by Lytham Shipbuilding & Engineering Co Ltd, Lytham, Yard No 852, for Elder Dempster Lines Ltd, Liverpool. Oil engine 4 SCSA 4 cyl 11½″–13½″ by H. Widdop & Co Ltd, Keighley. 39 nhp.

1937 September, completed.
1964 10 December, broken up.

515 IFON
O.N. 172738   1938–1959

Steel twin screw motor barge for ferry services, engines aft
105.3′×26.1′×6.4′   105 n   155 g
Built by Ardrossan Dockyard Ltd, Ardrossan, Yard No 155, for Elder Dempster Lines Ltd. Registered Lagos (British flag). Oil engines 2 SCSA 5 cyl 8½″–12″ by H. Widdop & Co Ltd, Keighley.
1938 Completed.
1959 Disappears from register.
Ifon is a township 35 miles north of Benin in Nigeria.

516 ORON (II)
O.N. 166242   1938–1974

Steel screw ferry
131.5′×30.1′×8.2′   121 n   277 g
Built by Wm Denny & Bros Ltd, Dumbarton, Yard No 1328, for West African Lighterage & Transport Co Ltd. Registered Liverpool. 2×oil engines 2 SCSA 6 cyl 11½″–13½″ by H. Widdop & Co Ltd, Keighley. 600 bhp, 11½ K.
Passenger accommodation: 4 first class, 250 deck.
1938 18 February, keel laid. 2 June, launched by Mrs M. H. Smye. June, completed. Trials 11.699 K.
1974 1 October, sold to South Eastern State, Calabar (Government of Nigeria).
1984 Laid up at Calabar in derelict state.

ORON

407

ORON laid up adjacent to the former Elder Dempster office at Calabar, February 1984

ILARO (Photo Adenaike & Bros)

517 AUCHMACOY
O.N. 165252   1941–1950

Steel screw ferry
114.6′×23.1′×8.4′   119 n   255 g
Built by Hall Russell & Co Ltd, Aberdeen, Yard No 750, for Mitchell & Rae Ltd. Registered Aberdeen. Oil engine 2 SCSA 6 cyl 7$\frac{1}{16}$″–11$\frac{13}{16}$″ by British Auxiliaries Ltd, Glasgow. 52 nhp, 8$\frac{1}{2}$ K.
1939   November, completed.
1941   November, acquired by Elder Dempster Lines Ltd for branch service, Lagos and the Delta ports. Registered Liverpool.
1950   Engines removed for re-sale to former owners. Dismantled and scuttled 26 October off Lagos.

AUCHMACOY

518 ILARO (II)
O.N. 179677   1949–1964

Steel twin screw barge
107.0′×26.2′×6.6′   95 n   152 g
Built by Aldous (Successors) Ltd, Brightlingsea, for Elder Dempster Lines Ltd, Liverpool. Registered Lagos. 2×oil engines 2 SCSA 5 cyl 8$\frac{1}{2}$″–12$\frac{1}{2}$″ by H. Widdop & Co Ltd, Keighley. 150 bhp.
1949   November, completed.
1962   Transferred to West African Lighterage & Transport Co Ltd.
1964   Sold to A. Odunsi, Lagos.
1966   Sold to K. & K. Sea Trading Co, Lagos.

A CREEK JOURNEY ON THE 'ILARO'
by A. E. Williams

These are my impressions of my first voyage on Elder Dempster Agencies Limited tug *Ilaro* in the company of the Quartermaster Susu and others. We were bound for Okitipupa on the Oluwa creek, a distance of 200 miles from Lagos, and had two lighters fastened alongside, carrying a cargo of corrugated sheets required for the building of a hospital at our port of destination. We were required to load 100 tons of cocoa and sawn timber on our return journey, for shipment from Lagos to the United Kingdom.

We left Ebute-Ero Wharf, Lagos, at about 10.30 a.m. on December 1 and after a few minutes passed under Carter Bridge, joining Lagos to the mainland, and sailed into the Lagoon. I remember that we could just see land in the far distance and the difficulties of sea and river navigation were brought home to me for the first time.

After an hour or so we passed men fishing from a small canoe and shortly afterwards the port engine (this being a twin screw tug) developed a small fault which, however, the Engineer soon repaired. It was at about this time, midday, that the Lagos Port Authority launch *Rover* passed us carrying male for Lagos from Warri and the creek ports. At 1.30 p.m. we reached Palaba Island with the village of Ijede nearby and after steaming through thick bush on both sides of the creek for two hours or so we passed Ikosi, a new centre for the training of engineering students.

As the afternoon drew to a close we sailed close to Ejirin situated at a junction in the creeks and could see a large school building in course of erection. At 6.15 we arrived at Epe, quite a large township, where we anchored and settled down for the evening.

The following morning, December 2, we left Epe creek at 6.30 and after about 6 miles the water became quite choppy. These creeks are quite dangerous for a number of crocodiles were seen on the banks around Imina and Ise, the former being a large village boasting a Domestic Training Centre. Just before noon the Elder Dempster tug *Jebba* with two lighters alongside passed us homeward bound for Lagos and greetings were exchanged between the two quartermasters by hooter. This was near to the village of Odi, and shortly afterwards we met the G. L. Gaizer tug *Flotte* also towing two lighters. By lunch time we had reached Onigboroko, or Ebba, a town where the Public Works Department have built a Rest House for European Staff staying in the area.

Throughout this area thick bush or forest bordered the creeks on both sides and it was not until we reached Artijere that we saw a clearing of any sort; the sole occupation of this village is the collection and bundling of firewood for sale to other villages. Three-and-a-half miles from Artijere we passed Katha, a town where large flies, up to one-and-a-half inches in length, abound—these have a dangerous bite—and we were well pleased to moor at Aboto River Police Station some miles along the creek.

On the morning of December 3 we again sailed at 6.30 and at this early hour the air was misty with the dust blown down from the North by the Harmattan, but our Quartermaster Susu was experienced in these conditions and we steamed without incident to Adlala and Mamin, twin villages on opposite sides of the river. Only a short distance from these villages we passed Garugbo where the creek leading to Sapele joins the one along which we were sailing. A fishing village called Gbekebo, where the entire population, male and female, young and old, do nothing but fish all day, from the creek banks, heralded a fork in the river where we branched to the right and after two miles reached Aiyeka, one of our loading points. Here the Rowntree-Fry-Cadbury

Organization have warehouses and processing rooms for cocoa beans and we left one of our lighters at the jetty to be loaded and collected on our return journey.

Only another four miles up the river and we reached the termination of our journey, Okitipupa, at 3.30 p.m. After discharging our cargo of corrugated iron sheets, we loaded sawn timber, collected the other lighter, now loaded with cocoa, and commenced our journey back to Lagos.

from 'Sea' Magazine

IGBO (Photo Adenaike & Bros)

519 IGBO
O.N. 179679   1950–1964

Steel twin screw barge
107.0'×26.2'×6.6'   95 n   152 g
Built by Aldous (Successors) Ltd, Brightlingsea, for Elder Dempster Lines Ltd, Liverpool. Registered Lagos. 2×oil engines 2 SCSA 5 cyl 8½"–12½" by H. Widdop & Co Ltd, Keighley. 150 bhp.
1950   February, completed.
1959   17 April, transferred to West African Lighterage & Transport Co Ltd.
1964   27 November, sold to Niger Delta Development Board, Port Harcourt.
1966   Renamed **MINGI**.
Igbo is a sub-tribe of the Ilorin Emirate, Nigeria.

IBI at Calabar 22 October 1957 (Photo J. Powell)

520 IBI
O.N. 179682   1950–1966

Steel twin screw barge
107.0'×26.2'×6.6'   95 n   152 g
Built by Aldous (Successors) Ltd, Brightlingsea, for Elder

Dempster Lines Ltd, Liverpool. Registered Lagos. Oil engines 2 SCSA 5 cyl 8½"–12½" by H. Widdop & Co Ltd, Keighley. 150 bhp.
1950   May, completed.
1960   13 May, transferred to West African Lighterage & Transport Co Ltd.
1966   Renamed **PEPPLE**.
Ibi is a town on the south bank of Benue River, Nigeria, about 100 miles above Makurdi. Pepple is the terminal loading port for iron ore, 14 miles above Freetown, Sierra Leone.

521 NESTON
O.N. 180440   1949–1959

Steel steam tug, war TID type
65.0'×17.0'×7.4'   53 n   54 g
Built by R. Dunston Ltd, Thorne, Doncaster, Yard No 571, for Ministry of War Transport, as **TID 150**. Registered London. C 2 cyl 12½", 26"–18" by North East Marine Engine Co (1938) Ltd. 220 ihp, 8½ K. Folding funnel fitted. Also, fitted with permanent awning for tropical use.
1945   4 May, launched. 16 July, completed.
1947   Sold to Harris Barges, Liverpool. Renamed **CRAGDALE**.
1949   7 July, acquired by Elder Dempster Lines Ltd, Liverpool. Renamed **NESTON**. Registered Liverpool. Exported to Lagos, Nigeria as deck cargo per *MARY KINGSLEY*.
1959   9 October, broken up.
Neston is the name of a Cheshire village.

522 NUBIA (II)
O.N. 180268   1950–1959

Steel steam tug, war TID type
65.0'×17.0'×7.4   53 n   54 g
Built by R. Dunston Ltd, Thorne, Doncaster, Yard No 502, for Ministry of War Transport, as **TID 93**. Registered London. C 2 cyl 12½", 26"–18" by North East Marine Engine Co (1938) Ltd, Sunderland. 220 ihp, 8½ K.
1944   25 May, launched. August, completed.
1950   7 July, acquired by Elder Dempster Lines Ltd, Liverpool. Renamed **NUBIA**.
1959   9 October, broken up.

EKET coming alongside at Calabar, 1983

500,000
a year

By Andrew Bell—EDA Lagos

If you told anyone that Elder Dempster carries over half a million passengers a year, they would think of *Aureol*, but *Eket* and *Oron*, on the Calabar to Oron ferry service, carry more passengers in a week than *Aureol* does in a year.

For over 50 years, EDL has provided Calabar's link with the mainland. Calabar is geographically isolated on a finger of land which thrusts into the Cross River delta. Recently Calabar has become the capital of the South Eastern State and the ferry service is the link between the two main ports of the state. The route runs for 16 miles southwards down the Calabar River estuary and then turns north at Parrot Island, up the Cross River to the small town of Oron.

Dependent on the state of the tide, the journey takes just over an hour and a half. It calls for a high degree of skill not only in shiphandling, for the terminal at Oron allows only portside berthing, whatever the tide is doing, but also navigation. Rain, morning mist and a hot dry wind at various times restrict visibility.

Skills

The ferries have always been officered and crewed by Nigerians. The skills that they develop, varying from ship-handling to stowing the ferries' car decks, reach the highest degree of quiet efficiency.

It is impressive to see *Eket* come sweeping into Oron's landing stage, a miniature liner in an improbable tropical setting. The Rivermasters of the ferries are as famous in their own social setting as the clipper captains of a century ago were in Liverpool.

Their names are known in every local household and compound. Thomas Amafrey, who was awarded the BEM in 1954 before he retired; Josiah Anozie, long in command of *Eket* and who

retired in 1970; E. E. Odo, the youngest and most promising of his generation, who tragically died in March 1971; and today, E. O. Bassey and T. A. Ekong.

Father

The founding father of the ferry service was G. H. Avezathe, who arrived at Calabar in 1913 and, after a long and distinguished career, retired in 1954, having achieved a CMG and an Elder Dempster Lines directorship. His is a name still admired and respected in Nigeria.

In 1920, Avezathe as the Calabar agent risked the wrath and witchcraft of the local canoe owners and put a 10-ton lighter, towed by a launch, on to a daily run between Calabar and Oron. To the lighter was added benches and an awning.

Local traders soon found they could not only travel in comfort and safety but also carry many more goods. To this day these cargoes are incredibly varied and are a cross-section of everything that can be found in an African market.

Avezathe proved the trade was there and, in July 1938, the specially built *Oron*, capable of carrying 500 passengers and two vehicles, went into service. Built by the now defunct Dyenn organisation of Dumbarton, she is still in service today, a magnificent monument to her designer, builders and successive engineers-in-charge at Calabar. With minor alterations, *Oron* is as she was built. In the 50's she was extensively replated and what was an area for two lorries can now be used by six cars. It is difficult to believe that when her consort joined the service in 1950, it was intended to lay *Oron* up.

Design

In the post-war building boom *Eket* was at the other end of the scale from *Aureol*. Her design is as evergreen. *Eket* was more than a scaled-up version of *Oron*. She has a capacity of 1,000 passengers and as many as 14 vehicles; no mean feat of design on a hull 179 ft long and 30 ft wide.

From J. Samuel White's yard at Cowes on the Isle of Wight, this unusual ship had an unusual sponsor. Miss Constance M. Pickard, in her 41-year career with Elder Dempster's, rose higher than any woman before or since, to the position of assistant secretary. In 1962, during a trip to Africa, Miss Pickard had the very obvious pleasure of seeing her ship in service. Prepared for the delivery voyage in Southampton, *Eket* was well boarded up and made the voyage to Calabar in 22 days with only one stop in Las Palmas. She was crewed by a group of the Company's cadets whose conditions were rugged. One of the survivors of this group is Ocean Fleets' Captain J. O. Jones.

Success

Eket was an immediate success. By 1954 there were two sailings a day and the annual number of passengers carried had risen to 370,000. *Eket's* success spawned the building by Yarrow's of the much smaller *Itu*. She was built for a twice weekly service from Calabar to Creektown, Ikoneto, Ikot Offiong, Eteheten, Afia Ison and Itu up the

Above:
'Oron' alongside at Calabar

Left:
Captain L. O. Bassey on the bridge with Rivermaster A. E. Cobham at the wheel.

Facing page:
'Eket'— Disembarkation at Calabar.

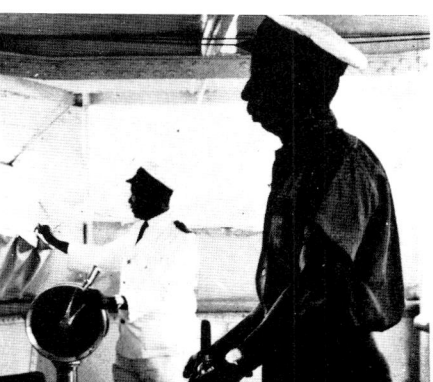

Cross River. As the rapid development of roads killed off river transport and lighterage, *Itu* never reached her full potential. Her light scantlings enabled her to operate fully laden at the unbelievable draft of 2 ft 6 in. In 1960 she was withdrawn from the Itu service and used to back up *Eket* and *Oron* on the main line ferry service. Although useful for off-peak sailings, she could carry no cars, and alternative employment was actively sought for her elsewhere and, for a short while between Calabar and neighbouring Creektown. *Itu* was in the final stages of being broken up in 1967 when the Nigerian civil war swept over Calabar.

Luckily for all, *Eket* and *Oron* survived the civil war and the awakening within the South Eastern State has seen a resurgence of Calabar. The ferry service is working hard to meet the increasing demands upon it and whatever the future holds for this pair of hard working ships, they will go down in Elder Dempster's history as being deservedly famous.

From Sea *magazine*

411

ITU

523 EKET
O.N. 119841   1950–1972

Steel twin screw ferry
173.1′×30.1′×8.2′   169 n   394 g
Built by J. Samuel White & Co Ltd, Cowes, Isle of Wight, Yard
No 1963, for West African Lighterage & Transport Co Ltd.
Registered Calabar (British flag). 2×oil engines 2 SCSA 6 cyl
11½″–13½″ by H. Widdop & Co Ltd, Keighley. 600 bhp, 11½ K.
Passenger accommodation: four cabin class and 1050 deckers.

1949   25 October, launched by Miss C. M. Pickard. Maiden
       voyage. Departed from Southampton to Calabar via
       Las Palmas commanded by Captain A. H. Perkins and
       crewed by Company Cadets.
1962   Registered Lagos (British flag).
1965   Registered under Nigerian flag.
1972   1 October, sold to the Government of Nigeria (South
       Eastern State).
1984   Laid up at Calabar.

Eket is a small town near the mouth of the Kwa Ibo River in
the Calabar Province of Eastern Nigeria.

524 NUPE
O.N. 180295   1953–1956

Steel steam tug, war TID type
65.0′×17.0′×7.4′   53 n   54 g
Built by R. Dunston Ltd, Thorne, Doncaster, Yard No 527, for
Ministry of War Transport, as **TID 106**. Registered London.
C 2 cyl 12½″, 26″–18″ by North East Marine Engine Co (1938)
Ltd, Sunderland. 220 ihp, 8½ K.

1944   14 August, launched. 1 November, completed.
1949   20 December, sold to Dashwood & Partners Ltd, London
       (C. G. Sandell, Manager). Renamed **TIDTUG**.

1953   9 April, acquired by Elder Dempster Lines Ltd, Liver-
       pool. Renamed **NUPE**. Registered Liverpool.
1956   17 October, sold to HM Government of Sierra Leone.

Nupe is a major tribe of Nigeria; they inhabit the Ilorin–Jebba–
Bida–Baro area.

525 NUTTALL
O.N. 180288   1954–1960

Steel steam tug, war TID type
65.0′×17.0′×7.4′   53 n   54 g
Built by R. Dunston Ltd, Thorne, Doncaster, Yard No 523, for
Ministry of War Transport, as **TID 102**. Registered London.
C 2 cyl 12½″, 26″–18″ by North East Marine Engine Co (1938)
Ltd, Sunderland. 220 ihp, 8½ K.

1944   17 July, launched. 7 October, completed.
1948   20 December, sold to Edmund Nuttall & Co (London)
       Ltd, London. Renamed **NUTTALL**. Registered
       Liverpool.
1954   27 September, acquired by West African Lighterage &
       Transport Co Ltd, Liverpool. Registered Lagos.
1960   19 December, broken up.

526 ITU
O.N. 196686   1954–1967

Steel twin screw ferry for service on Cross and Calabar rivers
110.5′×21.0′×2.7′   64 n   129 g   46 d
Built by Yarrow & Co Ltd, Glasgow, Yard No 2071, for West
African Lighterage & Transport Co Ltd. Registered Lagos
(British flag).

2×oil engines 2 SCSA 4 cyl 215 mm–305 mm by H. Widdop & Co Ltd, Keighley. 240 bhp, 9½ K.

1954 July, completed. Shipped in two sections to Lagos by *ONITSHA*. Re-assembled at Wilmot Point dockyard and proceeded through the creeks of the Niger Delta to Port Harcourt, thence under tow of *SAPELE* to Calabar.

1966 Registered Lagos (Nigerian flag).

1967 January, broken up.

Itu is a Divisional Headquarters town on the Cross River, 40 miles above Oron, Calabar Province, Eastern Nigeria.

Two views of Freetown during World War Two; above, a convoy at anchor, seen from Tower Hill, below, a cable ship lies quietly at anchor

The Motor Ferry *Itu* on her trials in the Gareloch

Built for Elder Dempster by Yarrow and Company on the River Clyde for service on the Calabar-Itu run calling at Creek Town, Ikoneto, Ikot Offiong, Etehetem and Afia Isong, the Itu *carried out her trials on the Gareloch on June 25, 1954.*

Afterwards she was 'cut' in two and shipped on the deck of the M.V. Onitsha *to Lagos.*

The Itu *is a twin-screw tunnel type vessel of some 64 tons register, 110 feet in length, 22 ft. 6 in. in the beam and with a loaded draught of 2 ft. 6 in.*

In this article Captain Smith (Nautical Adviser) describes the hazards of the voyage when he took the M.V. Itu *from Lagos to Calabar up the Niger River and through the creeks.*

'Through the Creeks...'

by CAPTAIN A. SMITH

THE River Niger and its tributaries, chiefly the Benue River, have, during long ages, brought seaward with them vast quantities of sand and silt, pushing the sea back and forming an immense delta. The piled-up sand has formed a barrier extending along the coast. Inside this barrier the waters divide to form channels. The land between the channels is bound together by mangroves with the result that over a wide region there are now innumerable creeks, wide or narrow, deep or shallow, but all connected one to the other and forming one of the most remarkable natural waterways in the world. Some at the mouths of the Escravos, Forcados and Bonny Rivers are regularly used by our ocean-going vessels. There are many others, some of which have entered into the history of Western Africa before falling into disuse . . . forgotten by all but the earliest 'Coasters'. This great waterway extends from Lagos in the west to Opobo

in the east. The land rises only a few feet above water level. On its banks grow the mangrove and the screw pine, and behind, on the more solid ground, the typical palms of West Africa. Occasionally the scene of swamp and bush and jungle is broken by a little fishing village, built on stilts; high water mark comes within a few inches of the floors of the dwellings; the children learn to swim and to paddle canoes before they learn to walk. . . . .

I had seen the M.V. *Itu* on her trials on the Gareloch. I knew the Coast well. I first went there in 1917 when the normal voyage from Lagos to Calabar was over Lagos Bar and thence direct by sea to Calabar Fairway Buoy and up river to Calabar itself. It was common knowledge at that time that the mail from Lagos to the Benin ports went 'inland through the creeks'—a phrase always accompanied by a gesture which was intended to indicate knowledge but barely served to conceal utter ignorance. When I was asked to take the *Itu* from Lagos to Calabar 'through the creeks' I had little idea of what to expect or what an experience it was to prove.

On August 7, 1954, the two sections of the *Itu* were hauled up the Nigerian Marine Slipway at their Apapa Dockyard. The slipping was in the hands of our Wilmot Point Engineering Company, with Mr Young of Yarrows as Technical Adviser. Whilst this work was going on I was busy arranging storing, surveying and interviewing possible pilots. Everything had to be laid on in advance and nothing forgotten, or we would go without. There were no wayside emporiums where we could replenish stocks. Our biggest headache was fresh water, for the *Itu* carried only one ton, which, for the voyage before us, was not overmuch considering that it was for every purpose. Niger River water is what the Africans call 'sweet', but, although they drink it unfiltered, Europeans consider it quite unfit even for washing. We partially overcame the shortage of fresh water by carrying six 45-gallon drums aft which were filled immediately before leaving Lagos. They served also as ballast in increasing the after-draught, which I needed for better steaming purposes. Before we had been long on our passage I discovered that even our one ton of water was unpalatable. We fell back, at mealtimes, on Coca-Cola.

As crew I had two quartermasters, three deckhands, a cook/steward, two engineers, together with the Chief Engineer of our Lagos motor craft *Ilaro*, Mr Rufus Oni, who was to prove his worth a dozen times over. Also with me, as 'Guarantee Chief', was Mr Woodhead, our Launch Engineer from Wilmot Point. Mr

A scene during the joining of the two sections at Lagos

Woodhead is by way of being an expert in Widdop engines, with which the *Itu* is installed, so I did not expect any trouble from that quarter. A Yorkshireman, with lots of grit and good humour, he was to prove invaluable, not only as an engineer, but as a man who most willingly turned his hand to anything when I was tied to the bridge.

On Monday, August 16, the operation of joining the *Itu* having been completed, she again took the water for the final finishing touches before beginning her voyage. It was necessary to proceed under Carter Bridge before the funnel and mast could be stepped, and so we took her to Tinubu Wharf until the Wednesday following when a suitable berth would be available. Many and varied were the heights between low water and the under part of the bridge offered to me, so to make sure I went with a lead line and measured it. Mr Young had given me the maximum height of our highest part above the water line and I found that there would be ample clearance for us if we went at the particular time we had decided upon. Accordingly, we proceeded as arranged, escorted by one of the Lagos tugs, to the U.A.C.* Wharf at Iddo, where facilities were placed at our disposal for the completion of the job in hand. The *Itu* then was moved over to P.Z.'s Wharf at Idemagbo the same evening as a precaution against the weather.

After many trials and tribulations and much exhortation we finally left this berth at 3.15 p.m. the following afternoon, Thursday. I had with me as pilot for the first stage of the journey one of the Nigerian Marine Senior Rivermasters, by name Jumbo Mbolo, who amply proved his unsurpassed knowledge of the

* *United Africa Company.*

Lifting the fore-section from the M.V. *Onitsha* at Lagos
Photograph by J. A. Adesanya

415

rivers and creeks. Old Coasters will remember him, perhaps, as Commander Trinick's orderly.

Jumbo had given 3 p.m. that day as deadline for leaving as he said that it was unsafe to anchor in Lagos Lagoon on account of tornadoes. As we had only 15 fathoms of cable on each anchor I felt he was right. We thought we should do well enough if we reached Ejinrin on the first day. We were not to know how the *Itu* would steam and in any case we should have to go easily for a day or so until we were assured that everything was all right. The current was against us, but in spite of all this we made our goal at 8 p.m., finding the wharf and berthing alongside it with the aid of the searchlight.

We cast off next morning when there was only enough light to see. Soon we were passing the rather large town of Epe, and then about an hour later we entered the Narrows leading to the Lekki Flats. Here the water is very shallow and we had to reduce speed considerably as we proceeded through the buoyed channel. As we were passing one of the buoys the *Itu* took a sudden sheer to port and would not steer. We immediately stopped the engines and searched for the cause, without result; as Jumbo said the place was full of sunken logs it was thought that it might have been one of these that had caught on the rudder. On re-starting the engines she behaved perfectly so we proceeded on our way. The gear had been put through so many tests before we sailed and there was no apparent reason why it should misbehave now.

We entered a narrow creek and met with the first of the sudd which sometimes blocks these waters.

Sudd is a water plant very like a small polyanthus with long trailing roots in the water and, so closely packed it can be most troublesome if it fouls the propeller.

Soon after lunch we passed the large town of Aboto, which has a doubtful claim to notoriety. Its inhabitants are reputed to be specialists in gathering 'tombo'. It is a native gin obtained from the palm trees. Almost every other tree was gashed near the fronds and from this wound there oozed into a calabash the raw material of 'tombo'. It would seem that this eventually kills the tree, and judging from the number of dead palm trees the inhabitants of Aboto had been in the 'tombo' business for quite a long time. Suddenly I heard what was once a familiar cry. Looking up I saw a flock of parrots flying overhead.

The creek became narrower, winding and more hazardous. Rounding one of the bad bends, we suddenly came upon the Nigerian Mail launch from Sapele, the *Rover*, with a large lighter on his starboard side coming down towards us. He surely must have heard our whistle, which we had been blowing frequently, but he gave no response, and it was only by the barest of margins that we cleared him. On sight of us the captain seemed to lose his head. From the whistles he blew it was impossible to know what he intended to do. I think he was just hoping for the best. We had no time to take a breath after this excitement when we came upon a strange sight. . . . There, right in the middle of the mangrove swamp was an area of hard ground composed of hard white sand. On it was a small village. Right through it a canal had been cut

Passing an African village on a creek in the Niger Delta

416

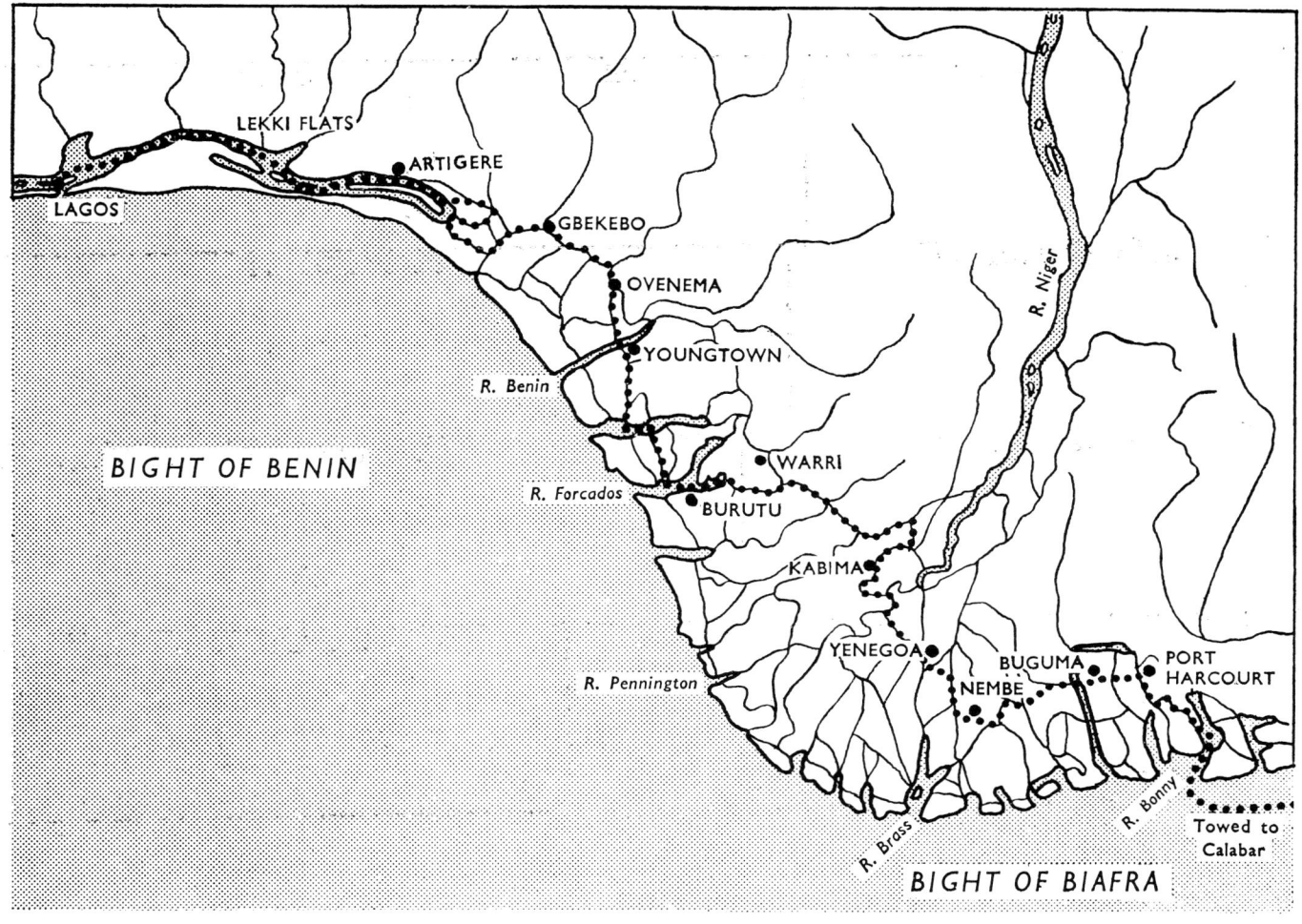

The way taken by the *Itu* from Lagos to Port Harcourt

to join another creek which ran in an entirely oppo-site direction from the one we were then in. As we approached the village we could see that the creek was almost completely blocked with sudd and grass and it would have been impossible to pass through. The canal, however, by-passed the long loop ahead and we were saved several miles on the journey by being able to use it. We proceeded slowly through the canal, being paced on the bank by large numbers of the villagers. They were almost at arm's length. With a right-angled turn to starboard we left the canal to find ourselves in a wide creek whose water was overgrown with grass for more than two-thirds of its width. We were left with a winding canal of about 120 feet wide in which to carry on our journey. We were proceeding merrily down this channel when, after turning one of the bends, the steering gear failed and before we could take any countering action the *Itu* ran three parts of her length on to this grass. Obviously something had gone wrong. All the Q.M. could say was, 'Massa, she no 'teer'. I was now be-

ginning to associate the Lekki Flats incident with this, so as she was lying quite comfortably on the grass we made a thorough investigation to ascertain the cause of the trouble. We were some time before it was found, as it was one of those things which only occur periodically. Once found, we soon remedied the defect, and then came the task of getting the *Itu* off the grass into the navigable channel. The grass itself was grow-ing in about twenty feet of water, so that the ship was partially waterborne, but we had two attempts at backing off before she consented to move. Once she did she gently slid into the water. Mr Woodhead's fears that we might have to go back to Lagos by canoe were not realized. When we were ready to resume our passage the *Itu*, which had been drifting down the creek, was heading the wrong way. In turning her round we had only about five feet at either end as we were athwart the river.

These delays had cost us some time and so, for the night, we tied up alongside a lighter at the U.A.C. Wharf at Gbekebo. The inhabitants of Gbekebo were noted in former days for a mild form of blackmail which they apparently practised. Any canoe passing either up or down the creek was mulcted in a toll which, from what Jumbo informed me, it was advisable to pay . . . or else.

Our night at Gbekebo was the second since we left Lagos and we had settled down to the mode of life we were now leading. Jackson, our cook/steward, was producing some quite passable meals out of tins. Our only 'fresh meat', some kippers, had been 'disposed of'. Our kerosene fridge proved to be very temperamental and would only work at night when we were stopped. Drinking water was our worst problem. It proved to be most unpalatable. To add to our discomfort we found, when we unpacked it, that the water filter was broken. Fortunately we still had a supply of Coca-Cola and we rationed it out at two bottles a head each day. Our 'dining room' was a table for two in the after part of the sun deck. I had had a large mosquito net made in Lagos for the purpose of dining on this deck after sunset, and also in the daytime when the mango flies were around.

This net was strung across the deck on wires which I rigged up, and although it looked a trifle 'Heath Robinson', it certainly proved very effective. Jackson became quite adept at ducking under it with a plate of soup. For washing we overcame the danger of river water by lacing it liberally with Dettol.

After our night at Gbekebo we resumed our journey in heavy incessant rain. Large grass islands which boys of the Nigerian Marine were cutting from huge tracts of grass, were floating down the creek and to avoid trouble we were constantly dodging them. At two places we found boys of the Marine with a rope on floats drawn right across our path, trying, and succeeding in, diverting these islands down the unused creeks. They had to draw the ropes clear for us to

Jumbo Mbolo . . . 'unsurpassed knowledge of the creeks'

pass. Soon after leaving Gbekebo, still in heavy rain, we began to pass a never ending stream of canoes, all 'manned' by women on their way to market.

About nine that morning we passed the large town of Arogbo. We were becoming used to the warm welcomes of the villagers. Shortly after Arogbo the starboard engine slowed up. Something was round the propeller. It was here that I learned that one of the deckhands had been picked for his capacity to deal with such an emergency. He was an excellent skin diver, but his services as such were not required as, by opening up the starboard side of the 'after peak' and taking off the manhole door the propeller was exposed to view directly underneath. A huge palm frond had wound itself round the propeller and stripped itself in the process, leaving us with a fibrous mass wound tightly round the propeller and shaft. While we were clearing it Jumbo came rushing along calling for all hands to come along. We left the job in hand and found that we were drifting on to a large tree trunk which was lying right across the river. It caught us by the after house and slightly bent one of the rails. We then entered the 'snake bends'. In these bends the current ran strongly with us and to make matters worse we were beset by whirlpools of considerable size. Although we were never out of control the *Itu* was flung about from side to side most alarmingly. When, finally, we emerged from them, quite unscathed, into a broad creek, we sighed with sheer relief.

Soon after noon we passed the town of Ovenema,

The *Itu* ran three parts of her length on the grass

418

Captain Smith and the Chief Engineer, H. Woodhead

and once again the creek narrowed considerably. We were again compelled to round the bends, backing and filling with the engines, which lessened our control of the vessel, but again we got through to the Gwato creek without harm. Here I was getting into familiar waters and very soon we were in the Benin River where we could relax a little from the tension of the previous hours. We passed Youngtown at a most favourable time as far as the tide was concerned and, with the exception of a short run in the Escravos River, we carried the water with us all the way to Forcados, where we made fast for the night to the dredger *Queen Mary* alongside the Government Wharf.

Sunday was the next day and the fourth day of the journey. After a night of torrential rain we left at 6.30 a.m. on the long drag against the current up the Niger River. We passed Burutu where there were no signs of activity, due no doubt to the still heavily falling rain. It was now mangroves all the way, which, with the rain, made matters even more depressing. The voyage now had taken on quite a different complexion. This was the main river where, after Gana Gana, the banks were hard ground.

Soon after Gana Gana, after we had left all the mangroves behind, we began to pass quite a number of large villages, looking extremely clean and orderly and most of them possessing a football pitch with quite professionally made goalposts. We were loudly cheered as we passed. From one came the sound and the smoke of a gun being fired . . . three times. We were not quite sure whether this was in salute or whether they were taking a pot shot at us.

By 5.30 p.m. that afternoon we had reached Sagbama, the point where we turned downstream towards the delta again. The current was now with us and we literally flew down and did so well that we reached Kabima, where we decided to stay the night.

On approaching this place we rounded upstream and, having sighted a suitable tree for our moorings, we crept towards the bank. The water was quite deep, but we had to go warily in case there were any snags under water which we could not see. The village turned out *en masse* to greet us and were very co-operative in taking our moorings and passing them round the tree and back on board. A few ship's biscuits in return made us very popular. The villagers were augmented by the inhabitants of a smaller village a mile or so farther up the creek, or river, as it was at this time, and they had all assembled on the bank which was only a few feet away from, and on the same level as, the sun deck. They were most friendly in their welcome and a little while after our arrival I received the following letter:

Captain on Board   Kabima Village
   the Screws   22.8.54.
           Happy Welcome Sir.
Gentlemen,
           For your information.
The ladies and gents of this town are cordially inviting you all to our new Dance.
        Awaiting for your answer.
The purpose of this dance is to welcome your arrival to our village.
          Greetings.
          Yours obediently,
          Councillor S. B. Akardah,
          22.8.54.

A pleasant gesture indeed, and one we greatly appreciated.

Our dinner that night was taken as usual under the mosquito net, and we had good cause for blessing it too. Immediately darkness fell, the vessel was invaded by a swarm of large flying ants which almost blacked out the lights. Jackson had his work cut out that evening to keep them out of the soup. Next morning the decks were covered with fallen wings.

We left very early while the villagers slept in the African dawn. We were now entering our fifth day since leaving Lagos. It was during this day that I completely lost my bearings. The only reliable chart of the area we were now entering is one which I now learn is published for their own use by a private enterprise. It is based on an aerial survey. Jumbo seemed quite unperturbed, however. His knowledge of these creeks is quite uncanny, so I had the fullest confidence in him. I believe the last of our vessels which passed over the same route was completely lost for a whole day and I can quite understand it. We headed this way and that way, none of which seemed to make sense, but eventually we came out at Sabagreia, a town which is marked on the chart. It was here we joined that part of the Niger which flows to the Nun entrance. It was up this river that Lieut. Glover made his way in that celebrated voyage of the *Dayspring*, which was later to be wrecked up river. One can still see part of her engines on the platform of Jebba Station.

After turning at Sabagreia we proceeded without incident towards the place where we were to change our pilots. The relief for Jumbo had been arranged at Lagos to be waiting for us at Yenegoa, but on our arrival we were informed that he had been and gone back. Here we were, miles from anywhere, thirty miles from the nearest telegraph station. What should we do? Wait until we managed to send a wire? Even Jumbo was not sure of the way. The U.A.C. Agent suggested the name of a youth who had taken one of their launches through to Port Harcourt and had also been through several times with rafts of logs. We managed to contact him and he assured me that he did know the way quite well. His manner convinced me that he did. When I told him that the draught was 'so much', indicating it by the height of my hand above the deck, he smiled as though to say 'how simple!' About ships he knew nothing, but we could supply that side of the business. As long as he knew the way and where the banks were we were quite happy, so off we started. We were steaming through what had now begun to be wide creeks until late in the afternoon with nothing to see except a native village here and there among the endless mangroves. Thousands of parrots flew over us on their way back from the feeding grounds to their nests. This was the only sign of either bird or animal life that we saw, for, although the places were reputed to be swarming with crocodiles we did not see a single one.

After a night of torrential rain we hove up at daybreak and resumed our passage. We were now entering our sixth day and, judging by our surroundings, mangroves, mangroves and still more mangroves, with nothing else to break the monotony, we were right in the depth of the delta. The creeks were exceedingly narrow now, some of them no wider than 50 to 60 feet, and the bends were becoming more difficult to negotiate. The foliage of the trees extended over the creeks from side to side, making in places a veritable tunnel with light penetrating through the ceiling in varying degrees. I was assured that this was the correct route, and friend Jumbo seemed to know a little more of this route than he would admit, so I felt reassured that we should not become lost, as had one or two other craft I had heard of. The engines were getting more than a fair share of manoeuvres as it was utterly impossible to get round the bends without backing and filling each time. Eventually, to our great relief, we 'burst out' into a fairly broad creek and noticed the familiar line of salt water meeting fresh. By this I assumed we were

In one of the narrow creeks

not very far from the sea, and the creeks became tidal instead of the one way current we had experienced so far. A little after 8 a.m. we were passing over the Nembe Flats, where the water was very shallow and I was now expecting at any moment the narrowest part of the journey. The P.M.O.* at Apapa had warned me of this narrow creek, which is known as Mammy Creek, and surely enough half an hour later we entered it. When the pilot warned me we were coming to it I could not see the entrance and slowed down. It proved to be an eight-point turn to port through an archway of trees, but it took two 'goes' before we made it. Then followed a series of breathtaking experiences before we finally emerged at the other end. The corners were most acute and the tide had hold of us at most of them. We were flung sideways into the bush on more than one occasion, tree branches, fortunately very pliable, swept along the upper deck, leaving us covered in black ants and large red spiders, and leaving also a carpet of leaves on the sun deck. On one bend, as we were sweeping round in the tide, I heard a crack and then shouts. The engines were stopped in case of the propellers striking snags, but she still had headway on her, and then a splash was heard. It was our deckhand diver who had dived overside to rescue the flagpole which had been snapped off. He, at least, was not going on without the flag. I had already taken in the forward pole, but had to replace it as it was the only thing to guide the helmsman in his steering. To see which way the *Itu* was swinging it was better to look aft as the bridge was so far forward, and a small deck canopy forward of the bridge prevented a sight of the stem. The flag and pole having been duly rescued we proceeded on our way. With great relief we entered a broad river, which from what Jumbo told me, I made out to be the St Bartholomew River. I now had finished the narrow creeks with two

* *Principal Marine Officer, Nigerian Marine.*

420

bent rails, one slightly bent stanchion and one flag-pole snapped off but easily scarfed. Not too bad, considering where we had been.

We were steaming up the broad river heading northwards and as we passed a narrow creek entrance which was pointed out to me as a short cut, we saw the N.M. Launch *Delia* coming out. The crew hailed us, so we stopped the engines as Jumbo had the idea that the pilot who should have met us at Yenegoa was on board. His belief proved correct. He took over from our young African, swung her round and proceeded towards the entrance to the small creek. Whatever the young African had done, he had certainly kept us in deep water, but the first effort the N.M. pilot made was to put us on the bank. Fortunately with our shallow draught we managed to slide over it. It was not soft mud of which I was afraid, but the snags that might be on the soft mud. However we came to no harm and off we went hoping to make Port Harcourt that same evening. Except for a bent bridge awning on the port side and another bent rail we came through unscathed and we found ourselves in the Sombrero River about five miles below the entrance to Billee Creek. Here I was in familiar waters again and we carried on at full speed through the Buguma Channel, round by the Bakana Bank and up river towards Hutton Creek. We turned into this creek just on dark and then into Kathleen Creek through which we went in complete darkness, and then out into the main Port Harcourt river. There we were in the lighted buoy channel, and then on to Port Harcourt itself. At 8.20 p.m. we were safely moored alongside one of our lighters at the northern steps and the journey through the creeks was ended.

After all business had been attended to I paid a visit to the Harbour Master, who informed me that in view of the prevailing weather conditions and certain physical aspects of the *Itu's* construction he recommended strongly that she should be towed on the sea passage from Port Harcourt to Calabar. This was something in the nature of a bombshell, but there was nothing we could do, so we set about preparing for the tow. I had taken with me from Lagos a length of $2\frac{3}{4}$ wire, just in case it was needed for anchoring or pulling her off banks, etc., and this now became a bridle which I fixed forward ready to connect to our towing vessel. The s.s. *Sapele* had been appointed to escort us over the Bar and down to Calabar, but instead of escort, she now became the tug. The engine room doors of the *Itu* were completely sealed up—we had sealed up the side casings of the engine room itself to five feet in Lagos. Ventilators into the engine room were sealed and then she was ready. Our 'tug' had come up to Port Harcourt on the morning of Saturday, August 28, where she was to load some cargo, so we gave her our cases of spares and one or two other items which we had lashed on deck, and at 1.30 p.m. the same day we steamed out of Port Harcourt on the last stage of our journey. Steaming slowly down the river we awaited the sight of our consort, and then followed her down the river. It was here that I found that the Q.M.s were not bad on the steering if they could see something to guide them, but in the wide open spaces of Bonny River they were hopeless. So I now became helmsman and had to take her most of the way down. After the *Sapele* anchored below Bonny we proceeded alongside her and connected up the tow. All that now remained was to await the most favourable time to commence the journey. I had decided that the best time to cross the Bar was on the night lee tide, and as it was estimated that this would begin to run soon after 1 a.m. this time became our deadline. The *Itu's* crew boarded the *Sapele*, I lit the side lights, the tow was slipped and the *Sapele* hove up her anchor. We commenced the journey about 2 a.m. towing at six knots and giving all buoys a wide berth in case of any yawing. Instead the *Itu* followed on quite meekly, keeping station dead astern without the slightest attempt at deviating from a straight course. By 5.30 a.m. we were safely over the Bar, which could not have been better for our purpose, and we set a course for Calabar Fairway Buoy. After an uneventful passage, during which, fortunately, the weather was as good as I have seen it in these areas, we made Calabar Buoy, turned up river and finally came to an anchor between 6 and 7 buoys at 7.30 p.m.

As we were now in quiet waters the *Itu* was hove alongside, we jumped aboard and in two minutes Mr Woodhead had the generator going and we began slipping our gear. This done, we lay alongside the *Sapele* for the remainder of the night. We were off on the final leg of the journey by 5.30 next morning, Monday, August 30, and arrived at our destination at 7.40 a.m. The Oron Ferry, the *Eket*, was leaving on the first of her daily journeys at 8 a.m. so we awaited her departure and took her place at the Company's Wharf. Quite a gathering of the clans was there to greet us and as I looked upon her from the office window as she lay at the wharf I thought of that first day I had seen her in such vastly different surroundings. Built on a river, she will ply her trade on a river. Thousands of miles lie between them to say nothing of creeks and mangrove swamps and whirlpools. Having escorted her from her first trials in the Firth of Clyde to the turgid tropical waters of West Africa I felt a peculiar pride in her . . . and in the Company which at such cost—not so much of money but of imagination and courage—had provided this new ferry service in this period when West Africa and her people are coming of age.

From Sea *magazine*

This stern-wheeler was photographed in the Warri river in the 1950s (Photo J. Holt)

PART 5

Vessels managed by Elder Dempster during the two World Wars

Ship Nos 527–562

*The memorial cairn at Halifax, Nova Scotia, to those lost in the sinking of **POINT PLEASANT PARK** (ship No. 555)*

LUCIA

HANS WOERMANN, subsequently GOLD COAST

527 LUCIA
O.N. 136789   1915

Steel screw steamer
352.0′×45.0′×26.0′   2414 n   3899 g
Built by Furness Withy & Co Ltd, West Hartlepool, Yard No 307, for Hamburg Amerikanische Packetfahrt AG, Hamburg, as **SPREEWALD**. Registered Hamburg. T 3 cyl 25½″, 43″, 72″–48″ by Richardson, Westgarth & Co Ltd, West Hartlepool. 359 nhp, 12 K.
1907   Completed.
1914   September, captured as war prize by HMS BERWICK. Requisitioned by the Admiralty. Registered London.
1915   Management allocated to Elder, Dempster & Co Ltd. Renamed **LUCIA**.
1916   Converted for service as Submarine Depot Ship.
1946   4 September, sold to Cia Maritime Geojunior, Panama. Renamed **SINAI**.
1951   Sold to Italian shipbreakers at Spezia.

528 HUNSDON
O.N. 139058   1915–1918

Steel screw steamer, longitudinal framing
335.2′×48.1′×21.1′   1744 n   2899 g
Built by AG 'Wesser', Bremen, Yard No 176, as **ARNFRIED**, for Hamburg Bremer Africa Linie. Registered Bremen. T 3 cyl 23¹³⁄₁₆″, 39³⁄₁₆″, 63³¹⁄₃₂″–43⁵⁄₁₆″ by the builders. 364 nhp, 12 K.
1911   2 April, launched. 10 May, completed.
1914   27 September, captured at Duala, by HMS CUMBERLAND.
1915   Requisitioned for HM Government Service. Placed under management of Elder, Dempster & Co Ltd. Renamed **HUNSDON**.
1918   21 March, chased by submarine in English Channel, saved by gunfire. 18 October, torpedoed without warning by submarine UB92, and sunk one mile south from Strangford light-buoy. One life lost.

529 GOLD COAST
O.N. 137489   1915–1917

Steel screw steamer
341.8′×44.3′×26.7′   2596 n   4059 g
Built by D. J. Dunlop & Co, Port Glasgow, Yard No 247, for Woermann Linie KG, Hamburg, as **HANS WOERMANN**. Registered Hamburg. T 3 cyl 24″, 38″, 63″–42″ by the builders. 257 nhp, 9 K.
1900   Completed.
1914   Captured in the Cameroon River during World War I.

1915   25 November, management allocated to Elder Line Ltd. Renamed **GOLD COAST**. Registered Liverpool. 2714 n, 4255 g.
1917   19 April, torpedoed and sunk in a surface attack by UC47 (Oberleutnant zur See Paul Hundius) 14 miles south of Minehead Light, voyage West Africa to Liverpool, general cargo. Captain E. E. Allen and all his crew survived.

UC47, then under the command of Oberleutnant zur See Günther Wigankow, was sunk with all hands on 18 November 1917 when she was rammed and depth-charged by the patrol boat P57 in 54°.01′N 00°.22′E. Hundius, then a Kapitänleutnant, was killed sometime in September 1918, when UB103 under his command was lost with all hands between Flanders and her patrol area off the west coast of France. It is thought she may have been mined in the Dover Strait. After the German U-boat arm was resurrected in 1935, initially with only one flotilla, the flotillas were given the names of distinguished U-boat captains of the First World War. When the 6th Flotilla was formed in 1938, it took the name Hundius Flotilla.

Gold Coast was the pre-independence name of Ghana.

THE LAST VOYAGES OF THE S.S. "GOLD COAST"
W. T. Swannell

The "Gold Coast" was the re-named "Hans Woermann", a passenger ship which had carried—I think—35 to 50 passengers. When taken over by us, her passenger accommodation had been taken out, and was mostly used as bunker space. She made four voyages down the Coast, and I was aboard the third and fourth. I remember that when I first joined her in Toxteth Dock, she had been bunkering in Herculaneum and we were told dockers had walked off when she heeled over—she was very tender. We sailed on Voyage 3, it must have been in September 1916, Captain E. E. Allen, Chief Officer D. Clarke and a stranger to Elders as 2nd Officer—no 3rd Officer. There was very little cargo in No.2 Hatch—we carried a lot of bunkers, and I was highly honoured to try to run No.1 as Mr. Clarke spent most of his time aft.

HANS WOERMANN

On one of these voyages, having successfully rounded the "Fork", we ran aground coming into the Benin River as we were rounding the buoy at Youngtown. We had no wireless, but Lagos got to know, and I think it was the Branch Boat "Bassa" which came to our aid. She came alongside, I suppose we off-loaded some cargo into her, and we came off the bank, heeled over on to the "Bassa", broke her bridge but with no serious consequence. I was on the high side of the after deck, sitting on the tafrail which ran from amidships right aft.

On Voyage No.4 we sailed from Liverpool 29th December 1916, vessel sunk 19.4.17, Liverpool 21.4.17, as per my Discharge Book. It happened soon after I had turned in my watch below 8–12 p.m. We kept a gun watch on the poop deck, beside a wooden gun, four on—four off. I think it was an imitation gun on this occasion, we were later to have a twelve pounder on the ships and finally we were delighted to have a 4 inch, in those days a very good gun.

However, I had just got off to sleep, when a large explosion awoke me. I had trousers on, pulled on some more clothes and went to the boat deck. We had listed badly over to starboard. My boat was by this time almost in the water—I had been up to the gun on the poop—so I decided to go down to a boat on the port side as the Jacob's ladder was against the ship's side. All four boats got away safely and we pulled off. Two submarines surfaced, one of which told the 2nd Mate—Mr. Reynolds—to pull back and get some instruments from the Chart Room. However, the "Gold Coast" went down before he could get there. We heard some rifle shots and as it was getting dark we lay quietly on our oars. We heard later that the second submarine told another boat's crew in which direction to steer for Queenstown. We were sighted next morning by the "Myosotis", I think she was a sloop. She came up full speed, full astern, rope ladders hanging over the side and we clambered up. Three boats' crews were taken aboard, but there was no sign of the 2nd Mate's boat. We were landed at Queenstown, had a very good, meal, some clean clothes and put on the train for Kingstown. Another good meal of fresh salmon etc. We looked around Kingstown the next morning and then went aboard a cross channel boat to Holyhead, thence by train to Liverpool.

When I returned to Liverpool after 4 weeks holiday, I learned that the 2nd Mate's boat had been taken in tow by an old tramp doing 8 knots, taken to Liverpool to prove that rifle shots had been fired at it and holed it. I was told one Engineer had been wounded and two African firemen, none seriously but badly enough.

From Elders of Elders October 1980

POLLADERN

530 POLLADERN
O.N. 137499   1916–1917

Steel screw steamer
419.8′×54.5′×28.2′   3440 n   5514 g
Built by Bremer Vulkan, Vegesack, Yard No 542, for Deutsche Ost Afrika Linie, as **EMIR**. Registered Hamburg. Q 4 cyl 24″, 34$\frac{11}{16}$″, 50$\frac{13}{32}$″ and 72$\frac{13}{16}$″–53$\frac{3}{16}$″ by builders. 601 nhp, 12 K.
1911   Completed.
1914   5 August, captured near Gibraltar by HMS CORMORANT.
1916   Requisitioned by HM Government and management allocated to Elder, Dempster & Co Ltd. Renamed **POLLADERN**. Registered Liverpool.
1917   Management transferred to J. Herron & Co, Liverpool.
1922   Sold to Sun Shipping Co Ltd (Mitchell, Cotts & Co, Managers), London. Renamed **SUNHEATH**. Registered London. 3825 n, 5932 g.

*Launch of **PINDOS**, subsequently **HUNTSCAPE** (Photo Bank Line Ltd)*

1927 Sold to Norddeutscher Lloyd, Bremen. Renamed **ILMAR**. Registered Bremen.
1936 Sold to Hamburg-Bremen Afrika Linie, GmBH (Woermann Linie AG—Deutsche Ost Afrika Linie).
1941 4 March, renamed **HAMBURG** and used as a Fish Factory vessel at Vaags Fjoid. Attacked and sunk by HMS OFFA off Lofoten Islands, Norway.

531 HUNTSCAPE
O.N. 136795   1916–1919

Steel screw steamer
338.8′×48.2′×20.5′   1778 n   2933 g
Built by Bremer Vulkan, Vegesack, Yard No 2935, as **PINDOS** for Deutsche Levante Linie, Hamburg. Registered Hamburg. T 3 cyl 23⅝″, 38³⁄₁₆″, 61¹³⁄₁₆″–43⁵⁄₁₆″ by the builders. 245 nhp, 10 K.
1911 Completed.
1914 Captured and requisitioned by the Admiralty.
1915 Management allocated to Andrew Weir & Co, London. Renamed **HUNTSCAPE**. Registered London.
1916 Management transferred to Elder, Dempster & Co Ltd.
1919 Management transferred to W. Robertson, Glasgow.
1920 Sold to Det Selmerske Rederi, Trondheim. Renamed **WILFRED**. Registered Trondheim.
1929 Sold to Aksjeselskap Norasiatic Coal Transports, Oslo. Registered Nedaros (Norwegian flag).
1932 Registered Trondheim.
1935 Sold to N. E. A. Moller (Moller & Co, Managers), Shanghai. Renamed **DAISY MOLLER**. Registered Shanghai (British flag). 3062 n, 4087 g.
1938 Sold to Moller Line Ltd, Shanghai.
1943 13 December, torpedoed and sunk by Japanese submarine R0110 (Captain Ebato) in position 16°.21′N, 82°.13′E.

532 ITAJAHY
O.N. 143082   1918–1922

Steel screw steamer, two decks
361.6′×51.2′×25.7′   2535 n   4155 g
Built by Reiherstieg Schiffswerfte & Maschinenfabrik, Hamburg, for Hamburg-Sudamerikanischen Dampfschiffahrts GS, Hamburg. T 3 cyl 24⅞″, 40¼″, 66⅛″–47³⁄₁₆″ by the builders. 300 nhp, 10 K.
1915 Completed.
1918 Acquired by The Shipping Controller as War prize, placed under the management of Elder, Dempster & Co Ltd. Registered London.
1922 Sold to British & South American Steam Navigation Co Ltd (R. P. Houston, Managers), Liverpool. Renamed **HESIONE**. Registered Liverpool. 2516 n, 4125 g.

1932 Transferred to Houston Line (London) Ltd.
1937 Sold to Stanhope Steamship Co Ltd (J. A. Billmeir & Co Ltd, Managers), London. Renamed **STANWOOD**. Registered London. 2499 n, 4185 g.
1939 10 December, voyage Leith to Dakar, cargo coal. Caught fire at Falmouth whilst in dock and towed out to anchor near the North Bank. It was decided to flood her holds in an attempt to put out the fire but either it was overdone or mismanaged for she sank so suddenly that the tugs FAIRNILEE and NORTHGATE SCOT, tied up alongside, had to cut their mooring lines and firehoses to avoid being dragged down. Even then the suction of the sinking dragged drew both tugs across her decks, one ramming the bridge, the other, the ship's foremast. All the crew of the **STANWOOD** escaped except for the radio operator who was drowned in his bunk. As **STANWOOD** went down, she slipped off the shallow edge of the bank into deep water and sank in about 90 feet on the Mylor side of the Trefusis. Extensive salvage was carried out on the wreck over the years but a quantity of wreckage remains.

533 RODA
O.N. 143087   1918–1919

Steel twin screw steamer
441.2′×52.9′×29.7′   4639 n   7266 g
Built by Reiherstieg Schiffswerfte & Maschinenfabrik, Hamburg, Yard No 423, for Deutsche Dampfschiffahrts Gesellschaft, Kosmos, Hamburg. Registered Hamburg. 2×T 3 cyl 22¹⁄₁₆″, 39⅜″, 63¹³⁄₁₆″–42⅛″ by the builders. 532 nhp, 12 K.
1908 Completed.
1918 Acquired by The Shipping Controller as war prize, placed in the management of Elder, Dempster & Co Ltd. Registered London.
1919 Sold to The City Line Ltd (W. S. Workman, Manager). Renamed **CITY OF VALENCIA**. Registered Glasgow. December, collided with PORT CAROLINE at Middlesbrough.
1922 September, answered an SOS call from the HAMMONIA (Hamburg-Amerika Line), sinking off the coast of Portugal. Seven survivors were taken off and 4th Engineer MacKenzie, of the **CITY OF VALENCIA** was seriously injured when his leg was crushed between the ship's side and a lifeboat when helping to rescue the survivors. The owners of the HAMMONIA presented the Master of the **CITY OF VALENCIA**, Captain Williamson, with a dining-room clock, the Officers with binoculars and the crew (including two Asians) with silver watches. Captain Williamson was also presented with Lloyds' Silver Medal. Lloyd's also presented a brass plate to be fixed on board the vessel in recognition of the heroic services by the Master, Officers and crew of the **CITY OF VALENCIA**.

HESIONE, fomerly ITAJAHY

CITY OF VALENCIA, formerly RODA

1926 4539 n 7329 g.
1929 December, collided with ROKER.
1934 Sold for breaking-up by Hughes Bolckow & Co Ltd, Blyth.

534 ESTRELLA
O.N. 124300   1917–1918
Steel screw steamer
280.5′×42.2′×16.6′   881 n   1740 g
Built by Clyde Shipbuilding & Engineering Co Ltd, Port Glasgow, Yard No 300, for Sanwarine Steamship Co Ltd (R. A. Sanderson & Co, Manchester, Managers), as **SANWARINE**. Registered Manchester. T 3 cyl 22″, 35″, 59″–39″ by the builders. 217 nhp, 10 K.
1912 Completed.
1914 Sold to Bergenske Dampskibsselskab, Norway. Renamed **ESTRELLA**. 892 n, 1757 g. Registered Bergen.
1917 Placed under the management of Elder, Dempster & Co Ltd by The Shipping Controller. Registered London.
1918 5 March, mined and sunk five miles south ½ west of Shipwash light vessel off Harwich. Twenty lives lost.

UHENFELS, subsequently **EMPIRE ABILITY**
(Photo Hansa Line)

535 EMPIRE ABILITY
O.N. 167423   1940–1941
Steel screw steamer
503.9′×62.2′×27.7′   4507 n   7603 g   10,340 d
Built by Deutsche Schiff & Maschinenbau AG 'Weser', Bremen, Yard No 886, as **UHENFELS**, for 'Hansa', Deutsche Dampfschiff-fahrts Gesellschaft, Bremen. Registered Bremen. T 3 cyl 30¾″, 49¼″, 78¾″–55⅛″ by the builders. 672 nhp, 12 K.
1931 Completed.
1939 5 November, captured at Crete by HMS HEREWARD.
1940 Acquired by Ministry of War Transport and placed under the management of Elder Dempster Lines Ltd. Renamed **EMPIRE ABILITY**. 23 October, damaged by aircraft bombs in Gareloch.
1941 27 June, torpedoed and sunk by U69 (Kapitänleutnant Jost Metzler), position 23°.50′N, 21°.10′W, voyage Mauritius to United Kingdom, cargo sugar and rum, with the loss of two lives. **EMPIRE ABILITY** (Captain W. Flowerdew) was sunk in U69's third attack on the convoy (SL78). The first had been unsuccessful, the second had resulted in the sinking of the RIVER LUGAR, the third came at 0237 (British Double Summer Time), when Metzler in a surface night attack fired one torpedo at a large steamer at a range of 650 metres. The target was hit amidships, caught fire and sank within 21 minutes. Metzler describes his victim as a modern ship with a cruiser stern, a noticeably heavy derrick on her forward mast, two masts and two pole masts, six hatches and

two lifeboats. He also remarks that she was armed with two stern guns and was similar in type to the CLAN ROBERTSON and of about 8000 grt. (There is no doubt that the ship torpedoed in that attack was the **EMPIRE ABILITY**.)

U69's fate was described in connection with the *SANGARA* (291).

KELTIER, subsequently **KATANGA**

536 KATANGA
O.N. Not allocated   1940–1945
Steel screw steamer War 'A' type, one deck
400.2′×52.3′×28.4′   3216 n   5199 g   8200 d
Built by Swan Hunter & Wigham Richardson Ltd, Wallsend, Newcastle, Yard No 1038, as **WAR DAFFODIL**, for the Shipping Controller (Geo. Pyman & Co, Managers). Registered London. T 3 cyl 27″, 44″, 73″–48″ by R. & W. Hawthorn Leslie & Co Ltd, Hebburn. 518 nhp, 11 K.
1917 December, completed.
1918 Collier and food supply vessel from South America to the East.
1919 Sold to Lloyd Royal Belge SA, Belgium. Renamed **KELTIER**. Registered Antwerp.
1927 Sold to Africaine de Nav SA. Renamed **KATANGA**. 3088 n, 5052 g.
1931 Sold to Cie Maritime Belge (Lloyd Royal) SA, Belgium.
1940 Managed by Elder Dempster Lines Ltd. 25 October, damaged by mine. 28 October, beached. Refloated, towed to Liverpool for repair.
1945 Reverted to owners.
1949 Sold to E. Szabodos, Italy. Renamed **PAOLO II**. Registered Venice. 3158 n, 5205 g.
1955 Sold to Angelo di Enrico Ravano, Italy. Renamed **VARENNA**. Registered Genoa.
1958 7 September, arrived at Spezia for demolition by SA Cant. Nav. 'Santa Maria'.
Katanga is a large province of Zaire.

537 DE LA SALLE
O.N. Not allocated   1940–1943
Twin screw steamer, three decks
440.0′×56.7′×34.6′   5124 n   8400 g
Built by Barclay, Curle & Co Ltd, Glasgow, Yard No 582, for Cie Generale Transatlantique, Paris. Registered Havre. 2×T 3 cyl 21½″, 37″, 64″–48″ by the builders. 568 nhp, 14 K.
1921 9 February, launched. 8 October, commenced maiden voyage St Nazaire to New Orleans.
1940 Under management of Elder Dempster Lines Ltd.
1943 9 July, (Captain J. LeManchec) torpedoed and sunk by U508 (Kapitanleutnant George Staats) in position 05°.50′N 02°.22′E, voyage Liverpool to East London,

428

Kapitanleutnant Staats (Photo Bundesarchiv)

altered towards his intended targets and while still swinging fired, at 0243 (British Double Summer Time), a spread salvo of three torpedoes at a range of 1000 metres at the cargo liner and an overlapping iron-ore freighter, despite an obtuse angle on the bow. A minute later U508 crash dived to 160 metres. Two torpedo explosions, 1 minute 55 seconds and 3 minutes after firing, were heard. Then, at 0249, an ineffectual counter-attack was carried out by the escort, during which eight depth-charges were dropped. That was followed by an equally ineffectual hunt, in which the escort clearly failed to obtain a contact (none of this is surprising, as the escort vessel in question, the Free French corvette COMMANDANT DETROYAT, had no asdics or radio direction-finder). At 0355 U508 surfaced again to clarify the situation before twilight. Staats saw several lights and on closing them caught sight of the two torpedoed ships, both being stopped and surrounded by about 15 lifeboats and many liferafts, all very full. At 0425 he fired a torpedo to finish off the iron-ore ship, which sank by the stern at 0432 (she was the *MANCHESTER CITIZEN*). Staats then turned his attention to the two-funnelled cargo liner, which he estimated at 12,000 grt, and fired one stern tube at 0452. The **DE LA SALLE** was hit a second time and sank at 0458. Unable to position U508 for an attack on the constantly circling escort vessel Staats withdrew to the southward to reload. Eight crew and two passengers lost their lives.

general cargo. U508, travelling at the slowest speed possible, owing to phosphorescence, was attempting to slip between a large cargo liner (which was the **DE LA SALLE**) and the starboard escort when the escort saw the boat and turned towards. As a result, Staats quickly

I left Freetown in convoy on the 3rd July, 1943, for South Africa. We had on board about 2150 tons of general cargo and 100 passengers, of which 2100 tons and 99 passengers were from England and 50 tons and one passenger from Freetown. Fine weather during the passage, light breeze from the south, sea slight swell. On the 8th July at 00.43. being some 60 miles from Lagos we got a torpedo in the starboard boiler room. This compartment was immediately flooded, also the two adjacent oil tanks, engine room and No. 3 hold. The ship took a list from 8/10° to starboard. Great quantities of oil were thrown in the air, probably through the after escape from the boiler room, drenching the decks which became very slippery. A heavy swell caused us to roll to starboard. The engines stopped causing the electric light to fail. Order to abandon

DE LA SALLE (Photo M. Bar)

ship was given. This was difficult under the conditions ruling. It was, however, well carried out despite some serious accidents. Two lifeboats were quickly put out of action and a third was making a lot of water. Of 238 persons taken off, including 138 crew and 100 passengers (65 men and 35 women) there was only loss of life of two persons, both passengers, who fell off the rope ladders. They were a Rev. Dutch Father and a Mr. Simpson, British Subject. This was a very good abandonment due to the calmness, the authority and the efficiency of the Chief Officer.

I told the boats to stay near the ship but taken by the swell and the wind and being not easily managed, they got rather too far away. With the Chief Officer I made a round of the whole ship. On the deck we found the 3rd Engineer and three members of the crew. These four could not tell my why they had not followed the others. I found at the bottom of the hold of hatch 3, a man with a broken arm, lying on one of the boards in the hold in a bath of oil. It was the Chief Pantry Steward, Charles Tesson. With great difficulty we got him on to the deck to get him away as soon as possible. The three men who were in the boiler room must have been killed on the spot. A fourth, sick in the starboard hospital, suffered the same fate. Immediately after the explosion this place was flooded with hot oil. Three other men, who were also there, were able to escape with difficulty, one of whom, the Hospital Steward, being badly burnt about the legs. As no boats came back alongside and being too far to call them we looked for some means of escape for these last remaining members of the crew. We were seven. On the poop to port there was a raft which had not come out of its guides. We put all our strength to push it over without success. We were working on this when a second torpedo caught us in the No. 4 hold starboard. It must have been about 02.00 hrs. The ship was shaken violently, but being already water-logged the shock was a great deal less than the first one. This was the ship's death blow. It was immediately obvious that she was sinking fast. The emergency lighting went out and it was pitch black. I saw the water swirl round No. 5 hatch going over the coamings. There was nothing for it but to jump in the water. I was myself in the water level with the poop when the "DE LA SALLE" disappeared completely. She sank only a few minutes after the second explosion. Fortunately there were no violent surgings and no suction as might have been feared. The ship sank in the same positions as she was 8/10° list to starboard, slanting a little forward. No noise, no explosion, no surging. A quite death without resistance.

We were seven of us swimming in a sea of oil, no boat in sight. Besides it was dark and a strong swell made things very difficult, putting us under quite often. We soon found ourselves isolated one from the other. After looking around and exhausting efforts which seemed to me a very long time, I had the unexpected luck of seeing the good old raft which we had not been able to launch. I used my last strength in climbing on with great difficulty. I called the others but one voice only answered. It was the 3rd Engineer, who came towards me, I helped him to get on to the raft with me. The Chief Officer must have disappeared some 10 metres or so from me, also the three men mentioned above, impossible to give them help. The fourth managed to stretch himself on a hatch cover. He stayed there more than four complete days before being picked up by a coastal steamer, the "CALABAR" arriving at Lagos. He was an Annamite Dao Van Ho. This man displayed a remarkable resistance staying thus without moving for four days and four nights, without eating or drinking, surrounded by huge fish and sharks.

From our raft, where we were black from oil, we were picked up at daybreak by one of our boats and during the morning a Corvette took us on board. The eight lost of the crew are four men killed on the spot, including three in the boiler room: Joseph Hamon, Fireman, Georges Agnes, Fireman, and one sick in the hospital Aya Ali Mohamed, Trimmer. The four others who disappeared after the sinking of the ship are the Chief Officer Henri Sciaud, the Assistant Steward Le Ruz Andre, the Assistant Grocer Julien Hiriart, and last Chief Pantry Steward Charles Tesson, who was injured.

All the survivors arrived at Lagos towards 15.50 hrs. We were taken at once on to a steamer where we were well looked after and received emergency clothing. On the 11th July we were taken to camps in the town. I got into touch with the British Authorities and we got through all the British formalities and crew questions, money questions, clothing and repatriation. It was decided that those embarked at Liverpool would be repatriated to England and all the others to Casablanca. However, the first were allowed to choose which they would prefer, of these eight men only one chose Casablanca.

Captain J. Le Manchec

U508 was sunk with all hands in the Bay of Biscay on 12 November 1943 by US Liberator 'C' of 103 Squadron.

538 MACON
O.N. 166308   1941

Steel screw steamer, two decks
379.7′×53.1′×26.7′ 3895 n 5141 g
Built by Todd Dry Dock & Construction Co, Tacoma, Washington, for United States Shipping Board as **DELIGHT**. Registered Seattle. T 3 cyl 24″, 40″, 70″–48″ by Seattle Construction & Dry Dock Co, Seattle. 339 nhp, 10 K.
1919 Completed.
1929 Sold to James Griffiths & Sons Inc, Seattle. Registered Wilmington.
1930 Sold to Great Southern Lumber, Co, New Orleans. Registered New Orleans.
1931 Sold to Swayne & Hoyt Ltd, San Francisco. Registered San Francisco. Renamed **POINT ANCHA**.
1933 Sold to Gulf Pacific Mail Line Ltd (Inc), San Francisco. 2978 n, 4727 g.
1937 Re-engined by Seattle Construction & Dry Dock Co. T 3 cyl 25⅛″, 41¹³⁄₁₆″, 72″–48″ and DR steam turbine 358 nhp.
1940 Sold to Diana de Vapore SA. Registered Panama.
1941 Acquired by Ministry of War Transport and placed under the management of Elder Dempster Lines Ltd. Renamed **MACON**. Registered Liverpool. 3267 n, 5135 g. 24 July, torpedoed by Italian submarine BARBARIGO (Capitano di Corvetta Francesco Murzi) and sunk in position 32°.48′N 26°.12′W, voyage Porta Delgade to Freetown, general cargo, with the loss of four lives.

MACON underwent lengthy repairs during 1940 to render her seaworthy, before leaving Liverpool (Captain J. 'Eye-brow' Williams) late in that year. The voyage was terminated some days later when water seeped into the fuel oil system. On 27 January 1941, **MACON**, now commanded by Captain A. English, seconded from A. Holt & Co, sailed from Liverpool for Freetown. After experiencing engine trouble she put into the Azores on 18 February, when the boilers failed. She remained there until 22 July to effect repairs, after which she resumed the voyage. The torpedo struck at 2230 on the port side by way of No. 3 hold and the engine room, blowing the covers off No. 3 hatch and wrecking the two port side lifeboats. The ship was abandoned and the survivors pulled some 250 feet away. Meanwhile the submarine surfaced, fired a warning shot at No. 3 boat which was returning to **MACON**, and then shelled the wreck, which exploded and sank after a hit in the magazine.

Captain English decided to head north for the Azores, about 350 miles away, in fair weather with a steady north-east wind. The two boats soon parted and continued independently. No. 1 boat, with Captain English aboard, sighted a vessel at 0130 on 3 August. This proved to be HMS LONDONDERRY, which came alongside and took the survivors, 17, aboard. The Chief Steward and Chief Engineer had died during the eight-day ordeal.

No. 3 lifeboat experienced very hot weather, and Second Officer Butler soon found it necessary to ration the water supply, despite an ingenious attempt to distil sea water by converting a galvanised bucket into a brazier, boiling sea water in an empty oil can and allowing the vapour to drop through tubing improvised from a rubber tourniquet into an empty water beaker. The resultant liquid proved drinkable, albeit with a slightly oily flavour. Coincidentally, on 3 August they, too, sighted a ship, CLAN MACPHERSON, which took them aboard. Captain C. M. O'Byrne afterwards admitted that he approached the lifeboat with great caution as he suspected a decoy, owing to the "strange looking contraption" hanging from the mast (Mr Butler's ersatz water purifier).

Captain O'Byrne was presented with a silver cigarette case by the survivors as a token of their appreciation, and HMS LONDONDERRY was presented with a bugle for use aboard her and her successors in name.

BARBARIGO (Tenente di vascello Umberto De Julio) was returning from Batavia carrying rubber and tin when she was lost in the Eastern Atlantic. Almost certainly she was sunk by aircraft in mid June, either off the Azores or in the Bay of Biscay. Macon is a town in France, north of Lyons.

DEDICATION AGREEMENT - H.M.S. LONDONDERRY

(1)   The gift of a bugle which forms the subject of this Agreement is presented by Messrs. Elder Dempster Lines Ltd. to H.M.S. LONDONDERRY in appreciation of services rendered and kindness shown to the survivors of S.S. MACON.

(2)   When H.M.S. LONDONDERRY is in Commission the gift is to be kept on board in such place as the Commanding Officer may select, and when she is not in Commission is to be deposited with, and kept in the custody of, the Commodore of the Royal Naval Barracks at the Port to which she may be attached.

(3)   It is intended that the gift shall be an ornament of H.M.S. LONDONDERRY so long as she remains in the Royal Navy, and shall descend to her successors of the same name. If at any time there shall be no ship in the Royal Navy bearing the name of LONDONDERRY the gift shall be held in the custody of the Commodore of the Royal Naval Barracks at which it was deposited on the ship being paid off or it may be lent (with the special permission of the Admiralty on each occasion) to ships other than the one named.

DATED this *twentyfourth* day of *February* 1942.

W.H. Cripps

Chairman

ELDER DEMPSTER LINES, LIMITED.

Approved

A.V. Alexander

FIRST LORD OF THE ADMIRALTY.

From : Commander I.C. Bailey-Willmot, Royal Navy

Commanding Officer
HMS LONDONDERRY
BFPO Ships

603

J E Cowden Esq
Assistant Secretary
UK/West Africa Lines Joint Service
Room 323 India Buildings
Water Street
Liverpool L2 OQD

19 November 1982

Dear Mr Cowden

GIFT OF BUGLE TO HMS LONDONDERRY

Thank you for your letter JEC/VH of 3 November 1982 concerning the bugle presented by Elder Dempster Lines to the first HMS LONDONDERRY. I am very pleased to be able to tell you that the bugle to which you refer is still held onboard HMS LONDONDERRY under the terms of the Dedication Agreement.

The present HMS LONDONDERRY is a Type 12 Frigate of the ROTHESAY Class. Since her last refit, when her armament was removed, she has been used as a trials and training ship. I enclose a recent photograph, which I hope you will find of some interest.

Yours sincerely

Ian Bailey Willmot

AKINITY, formerly EMPIRE RUBY (Photo Skyfotos)

539 EMPIRE RUBY
O.N. 168971   1941–1946

Steel motor tanker, War 'Chant' type, one deck
176.7′×30.7′×11.6′   312 n   667 g   800 d
Built by G. Brown & Co (Marine) Ltd, Greenock, for Ministry
of War Transport (Elder Dempster Lines Ltd, Managers).
Registered Greenock. Oil engine 2 SCSA 6 cyl 12⅝″–16¾″ by
Newbury Diesel Co Ltd, Newbury. 600 bhp, 10 K.
1941   Completed November.
1944   6 March, rescued 32 survivors from ss JOHN HOLT,
       torpedoed and sunk by U66 (Kapitanleutnant Gerhard
       Seehausen), voyage Douala to Lagos.
1946   Sold to Athel Line Ltd, London.
1947   Renamed **ATHELRUBY**.
1952   Sold to F. T. Everard & Sons Ltd, London. Renamed
       AKINITY. Registered London.
1965   3 April, arrived Bruges for demolition by Van Heijghen
       Freres.

540 TOMBOUCTOU
O.N. 142488   1941–1943

Steel screw steamer, War 'B' type, two decks
400.4′×52.3′×28.4′   3167 n   5179 g   8200 d
Built by Workman, Clark & Co Ltd, Belfast, Yard No 442, as
WAR PEEWIT for the Shipping Controller. Registered Belfast
T 3 cyl 27″, 44″, 73″–48″ by the builders. 517 nhp, 11 K.
1919   31 May, launched. Sold to Ulster Steam Ship Co Ltd,
       Belfast, and completed June as **BALLYGALLY HEAD**.
1924   Sold to West Hartlepool Steam Navigation Co Ltd, West
       Hartlepool. Renamed **KEPWICKHALL**. Registered
       West Hartlepool.
1930   Sold to Cie Marseilles de Nav a Vapeur (Cie Fraissinet),

Marseilles. Renamed **TOMBOUCTOU**. Registered
Marseilles. 3253 n, 5302 g.
1940   8 September, seized at Point Noire. Acquired by Min-
       istry of War Transport, Elder Dempster Lines Ltd,
       appointed Managers. Registered Liverpool. 3538 n,
       5636 g.
1943   Moxey Saxon & Co Ltd, London, appointed Managers.
1944   Cie Maritime Francaise, London, appointed Managers.
1946   Returned to pre-war owners. Registered Marseilles.
1948   Sold to Cia Maritime Atychides SA. Renamed
       ISPAHAN. Registered Genoa.
1950   Registered Panama.
1951   Sold to Seereederei Adolf Wiards. Renamed **MONIKA
       WIARDS**. Registered Bremen. 3186 n, 5181 g.
1952   Ownership transferred to Adolf Wiards, Hamburg.
       3328 n, 5532 g.
1959   Sold for breaking up. Renamed **RHODA** for delivery to
       breakers. 8 August, arrived Osaka for demolition by
       Oku Shoji KK. 14 August, work commenced.

TOMBOUCTOU (Photo M. Bar)

541 CAP EL HANK
O.N. 166309   1941–1945

Steel screw steamer, two decks
300.6′×43.7′×22.7′   1422 n   2340 g
Built by Burntisland Shipbuilding Co Ltd, Burntisland, Firth of Forth, Yard No 104, as **NELLY LASRY**, for Joseph Lasry, Paris. Registered Oran. T 3 cyl 22″, 36″, 59″–39″ by Cooper & Greig Ltd, Dundee. 286 nhp, 10 K.
1920   July, completed.
1933   Renamed **ARDENNES**. 1406 n, 2275 g.
1936   Sold to Cie Generale Transatlantique, Paris.
1938   Sold to SA de Gerance et d'Armement, Paris. Renamed **CAP EL HANK**. Registered Dunkirk. 1393 n, 2307 g.
1941   Acquired by Ministry of War Transport (Elder Dempster Lines Ltd, Managers). Registered Liverpool. 1473 n, 2578 g.
1945   Returned to former owners.
1950   Registered Rouen.
1951   Registered Dunkirk. Sold to Society Franco Chinoise de Transports Maritime and Fluviaux, SARL, Saigon, Viet-Nam, Indo-China. Renamed **TAI SEUN HENG**. Registered Saigon (French flag).
1954   Sold to George Gremble & Co Ltd, Hong Kong. Registered Hong Kong (British flag). O.N. 196120.
1958   Sold to Shun Cheong Steam Navigation Co Ltd, Hong Kong.
1963   Sold to Chip Hua Manufacturing Co (1947) Ltd for demolition at Hong Kong.

STARLING

542 STARLING
O.N. 162483   1941–1945

Steel screw steamer
246.0′×40.2′×12.8′   628 n   1320 g
Built by Ailsa Shipbuilding Co Ltd, Troon, Yard No 416, for General Steam Navigation Co. Registered London. T 3 cyl 18″, 29″, 48″–36″ by the builders. 201 nhp.
1930   October, completed.
1941–45   Operated on West African coastal services under the Elder Dempster flag and partially manned by Elder Dempster Lines Ltd.
1950   December, fitted for oil fuel.
1951   573 n, 1356 g.
1960   10 August, arrived Grays for demolition by T. W. Ward & Co Ltd.

General Steam Navigation Co applied the names of birds to their ships.

OUED GROU (Photo G. Mercier)

543 OUED GROU
O.N. 168263   1942

Steel screw steamer
194.2′×31.3′×12.7′   456 n   797 g
Built by D. W. Kremer & Sohn, Elmshorn, Yard No 489, as **PETER** for Aug. Bolton Wm. Miller's, Machfolger. Registered Hamburg. T 3 cyl 14½″, 23⅘″, 37⅖″–25½″ by Steen & Kaufmann, Elmshorn. 72 nhp.
1921   Completed.
1925   Sold to Cie de Navigation Paquet, Marseilles. Renamed **OUED GROU**. Registered Marseilles.
1942   Acquired by the Ministry of War Transport, placed under the management of Elder Dempster Lines Ltd. Registered London. 4 November, torpedoed and sunk

Kapitanleutnant Bauer (Photo Bundesarchiv)

by U126 (Kapitanleutnant Ernst A. Bauer) in Bight of Benin, position 04°.53′N 04°.49E, on a coastal voyage from Lagos, general cargo. Extract from U-boat Commander's Log Book:

0643 Smoke bearing 290. Turn towards and hove ahead.
0815 Dive.
0940 Fire tube 2—hit.
Speed of target 8½ knots, speed of torpedo 30 knots, range 315 metres, running time 21 seconds, depth setting 2 metres. Steamer's name is Oued Grou (792 tons), home port Marseille.
0945 Surface. Steamer has sunk. I try to find the Chief Engineer and the Master. According to statements by survivors both went down with ship.
Resume passage.

Both the Master (Captain S. Dodgshon) and Chief Engineer survived, but five lives were lost.

MALAKAL at Tasso Island, Upper Reaches, Freetown in 1943
(Photo Captain E. Whitehead)

544 LIKOMBA/MALAKAL
O.N. Not allocated   1942–1948
Steel motorship
118.6×22.2×7.5   96 n   199 g
Built by G. Renck, Junr, Hamburg, for Afrikenische Frucht AG (Resderei F. Laeisz, GmbH, Managers), Hamburg. Registered Tiko (German flag). Oil engine 2 SCSA 3 cyl 11¹³⁄₁₆″–16³⁄₁₆″ by Manseat Motoren GmbH, Hamburg-Bergedort. 74 nhp.
1939 Completed.
1942 Captured by British at Fernando Po. Placed under the management of Elder Dempster Lines Ltd. Renamed **MALAKAL**.
1948 Sold to Liberian Government.
1965 Disappears from *Lloyd's Register*.

545 LAFONIA
O.N. 131348   1942–1943
Steel screw steamer
283.3′×36.1′×19.0′   1091 n   1872 g
Built by Greenock & Grangemouth Dockyard Co, Grangemouth, Yard No 330, for Samuel Hough Ltd, as **DOROTHY HOUGH**. Registered Liverpool. T 3 cyl 21″, 35″, 57″–39″ by J. G. Kincaid & Co Ltd, Greenock. 249 nhp, 10 K.
1911 Completed.
1915 Sold to Coast Lines Ltd. Renamed **SOUTHERN COAST**.
1936 Fitted for oil fuel. Sold to Falkland Islands Co Ltd. Renamed **LAFONIA**. 1228 n, 1961 g. High pressure cylinder rebored to 21¹³⁄₁₆″.

1942 Acquired by Ministry of War Transport and placed under the Management of Elder Dempster Lines Ltd.
1943 26 March, North Sea convoys moving in opposite directions met and resulted in the sinking of **LAFONIA** after collision with ss *COMO* (Ellerman Wilson Line 1222 g/ built 1910) in position 55°.21′N 01°.22′W

On the 24th March 1943, the "Lafonia" left the Thames bound for the Tail of the Bank. She was proceeding in convoy, consisting of a number of vessels made up in two columns line ahead. The commodore ship, "Empire Unity", was leading the port column, while the vice-commodore was the "Windsor Queen", leading the starboard column. We were steaming in ballast, our draft being 15 ft 3 ins forward and 18 ft 5 ins aft, and third ship in the starboard column, the "Garforth" being immediately ahead of us, between the Vice-Commodore and the "Lafonia", and there being a vessel flying the flag No. 17 proceeding immediately astern of us, whose name I do not know, but which I believe had joined the convoy from Harwich. Astern of the No. 17 was the "Monkstone", No. 19. The columns were to be three cables apart and the vessels in the columns to be two cables astern of their next ahead.

At the outset, the vessels were to sail without lights, but after passing Flamborough Head we were permitted to exhibit dimmed navigation lights. The speed of the convoy was officially seven knots, but speed had on occasion to be varied to maintain our position in the convoy. We in fact were working our engines by reference to engine revolutions, in order to maintain our proper station and at the material time, the engines were being worked to 54 revolutions to give a speed of seven and a quarter knots.

I was on the bridge keeping an eye on things from time to time as we proceeded. I had been advised that we were to meet a Southbound convoy in the vicinity of Buoy 20 D, and when at 11.18 buoy 20 D was reported to be abeam I returned to the bridge and took charge, remaining there in charge until the collision with the "Como" occurred, it being my intention to remain until we had passed the Southbound convoy.

At midnight we had the buoy 20 E abeam on our port hand at a distance of about three to four cables from us. We had originally sighted the buoy bearing about four points on our port bow. We were at that time steering a course of North 5 West by the standard and steering compasses to make a course of 345 degrees true. There was no deviation on the compasses, the only error being in respect of the 10 degrees Westerly deviation. The course we were steering was to take us up safely past buoy 20 T.

The weather at this time was overcast and dark with some haze, and there appeared to be a tendency for fog to develop, which it later did. The wind was about North by East, a moderate breeze, with a moderate sea and heavy swell, so that the vessel was pitching slightly, but not uncomfortably. The tide was setting in the direction of 350° true at the rate of about one knot.

We at that time had our navigation lights exhibited and burning dimly. These consisted of single mast head light, port and starboard side lights and a fixed blue stern light.

At midnight, the Chief and Third Officers arrived on the bridge and relieved the two Second Officers, but I still remained in charge of the bridge. The Chief Officer was afterwards on the port side of the bridge, while I and the Third Officer were in the centre of the bridge. A lookout man was also posted on the port wing of the bridge, but he was a native, and it was rather cold, and I expect he would be sheltering behind the gun. In any event, we were not really relying on him to keep a lookout as the two officers and myself were doing so. No lookouts were posted forward because of the fact that we were spraying forward. Another native was at the wheel in the enclosed wheelhouse in the centre of the bridge. The officers checked that he was actually steering the course of North 5 West after he had taken over the wheel.

In addition, we had a gunner stationed by the gun on the starboard wing of the bridge, two gunners at the guns, one on either side of the boat deck about amidships, and a further gunner standing by the gun aft, in each case there being a native assistant with the gunner.

At about 0006 on the 26th March, when we were proceeding on the course of North 5 West, making 7¼ knots, I heard signals of one long blast for fog sounded by vessels ahead of us, to port of us and on our quarter, which I judged to be sounded by other vessels proceeding in the same convoy as we were. By that time visibility had been reduced to about three cables. I therefore instructed the Chief Officer to sound our whistle a long blast for fog and to keep it sounding regularly. I also advised him to instruct all the gunners in the gun nests to report instantly to the bridge if they saw or heard anything unusual. At the same time I had the navigation lights switched on at their full power.

DOROTHY HOUGH, *subsequently* **LAFONIA**

At this time, the stern light of the vessel ahead of us in the convoy was only visible occasionally, from which I judged that she was ahead of her proper station and keeping in position just about the limit of visibility, possibly about 3 cables or more distant from us.

At about 0018 I again was in a position to see the stern light of the vessel next ahead of us, when it appeared to be about three cables distant from us and bearing right ahead. The stern light was only in view momentarily before it again disappeared from view. Shortly afterwards I heard the signal "Q" sounded in the morse code on a ship's whistle, and know such signal to be the appropriate signal for the commodore of a Southbound convoy. I also heard the commodore of our convoy reply by sounding the signal "C" in the morse code, that being the appropriate signal for the commodore of a Northbound convoy.

At 0025 by my watch, which was checked with the Third Officer's watch, I sighted the mast head and port light of what I assumed to be the commodore ship of the Southbound convoy, bearing practically dead abeam on our port hand and as near as I can judge about three to four cables distant from us. Almost immediately afterwards I made out the mast head and red light of another vessel following astern of the one I had first sighted, both vessels then being in sight at one and the same time. I gauged the distance as being three to four cables by reference to the distance at which I had last sighted my next ahead. I could still hear the signals of one long blast sounded by vessels ahead of us, and judged that there were other vessels in the Southbound convoy to come on and pass us. When, therefore the two vessels I have mentioned had both got abaft our beam, I took no further notice of them, but continued to watch ahead and to port in the expectation of sighting further vessels.

At 0030 by my watch I decided as a precautionary measure to order the engines to stand by, so as to be sure that the engineers were prepared to take prompt action if such was required. At 0032 I heard a long blast sounded by a vessel which appeared to me to be very close to us, and bearing somewhere from about ahead to fine on the port bow. I did not know whether the vessel sounding the signal was one of the Southbound convoy, or whether it was our next ahead which had reduced speed and was falling back so I rang the telegraph to stop and our whistle was sounded a further signal of one long blast in reply. In fact, it had been sounded a long blast in the course of being sounded regularly at short intervals just before I heard the signal sounded close ahead of us.

Very shortly afterwards, certainly not more than a minute after I heard the signal, I sighted the masthead light and port sidelight of a vessel which subsequently proved to be the "Como" looming up out of the fog bearing practically dead ahead of us and approximately two to three cables distant as near as I can judge. Our speed at this time as near as I can judge would be about four to five knots through the water, with the engines stopped and we were still steering the course of North 5 West magnetic.

I immediately ordered the wheel hard astarboard and ordered the Third Officer to sound a signal of one short blast to which the "Como" immediately replied with one short blast.

The Chief Officer rushed into the wheel house to see that the wheel in fact was put hard to starboard and found that the native at the wheel had properly carried out the order. As a result of this action, the lights of the "Como" began to open out on our port bow until they were bearing about a point on the port bow, at which time I suddenly observed the "Como" open her green light and I realised that she was swinging to port, and not to starboard as she had signalled. I therefore immediately ordered the telegraph full speed astern and personally sounded a signal of three short blasts on our whistle to which the "Como" replied with three short blasts. The Chief Officer actually rang the telegraph full speed astern as I was sounding the whistle. The Third Officer at about this time exclaimed that she was turning the wrong way and very shortly afterwards, within a matter of seconds, her red light was shut out from view. Very shortly afterwards the vessels collided. Apparently the stem of the "Como" struck us on our port side forward about in the way of the break of the forecastle head a heavy blow, causing us to heel over the starboard and accentuating our swing to starboard. The vessels went clear of one another fairly quickly, with our head swinging to starboard and presumably assisted by the fact that the engines of both vessels were going astern and I rang the telegraph to full ahead and ordered the wheel amidships to prevent our quarter from swinging round into contact with the "Como" and smashing our lifeboats, which were swung outboard. I looked at the compass on giving these orders, and noticed that our head had swung round to E.S.E. The Third Officer noted the time when the engines were put full ahead as 0035. The lights of no other vessels were visible at the time the contact took place.

After checking our swing to starboard I stopped the engines and sounded the letter "F" in the morse code on the ship's whistle to indicate we were disabled, and requesting vessels to stand by us and at the same time had the "not under command" lights exhibited.

We then switched on our emergency lighting, and floodlit the boat deck to assist in getting the boats away. Whilst the emergency lighting was switched on the "Monkstone" came up on our port quarter and remained standing by. When it became evident that the vessel's position was somewhat precarious, we sent away all the crew in the ship's boats, with the exception of two of the deck officers, the carpenter, three engineers and myself. The crew, with the exception of those I have mentioned, went across to the "Monkstone" at about 0050 to 0055. The others of us remained on the ship until about 0230, by which time the vessel had developed a list of about thirty degrees to starboard and the water had risen until No. 1 hold was flooded while water was in the No. 2 hold, the stokehold and the engine room, and there were signs that the bulkhead between Nos. 1 and 2 holds was liable to give way at any time.

436

The vessel was rolling sluggishly in the sea, and gradually settling and it was therefore decided to leave the ship until daylight and we proceeded across to the "Monkstone" on one of the rafts. The "Monkstone" remained in the vicinity until daylight, but we last saw the "Lafonia" at about 0300 after which she was lost from view.

At daylight, we commenced to search for the "Lafonia" but without seeing anything of her beyond traces of wreckage and fuel oil, and eventually we were approached by a destroyer, the Commanding Officer of which advised us that the "Lafonia" had sunk, and that he had seen her balloon floating on the water.

The place of collision was approximately Latitude 55° 19 mins 30 secs N. and Longitude 1° 19 mins 48 secs West, that is in the Northbound swept channel between buoys 20E and 20T and about two miles short of a position abeam of 20T buoy.

I blame the "Como" for being out of her station in her convoy and for being in the Northbound swept channel. I also blame her for altering course to port towards us, so making a collision inevitable, which action was contrary to the signal of one short blast sounded by her. In fact, had she kept her original course and speed I consider that we would have just about gone clear of her by the action which we had taken.

We made efforts to preserve the logs and records. On taking to the raft to cross to the "Monkstone" the Third Officer in fact had with him the deck scrap log as well as a piece of paper on which he had made a note, but in the course of proceeding across to the "Monkstone" the scrap log was unfortunately lost. One of the engineers had the engine movement book which, with the piece of paper I have referred to, are still in existence, together with the chart which was being used. Since the accident I personally have made out a note of the times and the various incidents, in order that I could make a verbal report to my owners of what had occurred, and which note I now produce.

A native named Jim Brown who was on articles as quartermaster was apparently sleeping in his bunk which was in the forecastle right forward and up against the port side of the ship where the impact took place. When the crew were mustered after the impact he was not found, and on enquiries being made his room mate stated that Brown was in his bunk when the crash took place, but was not seen immediately afterwards. It can therefore only be presumed that he must have fallen through the hole in the ship's side in the way of his bunk, presumably after he had been killed by the actual impact. I myself went forward and made a search, but was unable to get into the man's room and could find no trace of him.

Statement taken at
Liverpool, 30th March 1943   Captain M. O. V. Whitfield

546   HAI HING
O.N. Not allocated   1940–1942
Steel twin screw motorship
287.2′×45.1′×17.0′   1445 n   2561 g
Built by Gotaverken Aksjeselkap, Gothenburg, Yard No 427, for Bruusgaard, Kiosteruds Skibsaksjeselskapet (Bruusgaard, Kiosteruds & Co, Managers). Registered Drammen (Norwegian flag). 2×oil engines 4 SCSA 6 cyl $21\frac{5}{8}''$–$39\frac{3}{8}''$ by the builders. 543 nhp.
1929   Completed.
1940   Acquired by Ministry of War Transport and placed under the management of Elder Dempster Lines Ltd.
1942   4 November, torpedoed and sunk by U178 (Kapitan zur See Hans Ibbeken) in position 25°.55′S 33°.10′E, voyage Durban to Bombay, general cargo. U178 was patrolling submerged off Lourenço Marques, and Ibekken had just observed a freighter leave harbour, which to his annoyance remained in territorial waters while heading south, when just after 0900 (Central European Time) he saw what he describes as a cargo liner of some 4000 g approaching from seaward. In a snap attack Ibbeken fired one torpedo, which on striking the target produced a heavy explosion on board her, possibly due to ammunition or depth-charges being detonated. The ship broke in two, the forward section assuming a vertical position before sinking with incredible rapidity. The whole ship was gone within two minutes and only a few survivors were seen clinging to wreckage. As U178 surfaced to find out the victim's name, the freighter sighted earlier opened fire, so U178 dived again and withdrew before resurfacing. Meanwhile, the freighter was reporting the sinking and heading back to Lourenço Marques. In the belief that now no other ship would leave territorial waters U178 made off.

U178, then under the command of Kapitänleutnant Spahr, was scuttled by her crew in Bordeaux on 20 August 1944. Ibekken survived the war.

HAI HING

BOURBONNAIS at Mombasa c. 1931 (Photo L. Dunn)

BOURBONNAIS (Photo M. Bar)

547 BOURBONNAIS II
O.N. 136268   1942–1947

Steel screw steamer
375.5′×52.2′×25.7′ 2831 n 4411 g
Built by Greenock & Grangemouth Dockyard Co Ltd, Greenock, Yard No 348, for A. Mackay & Co, Glasgow, as **SAINT
KENTIGERN**. Registered Glasgow. T 3 cyl 25″, 41″, 68″–48″
by Rankin & Blackmore, Greenock. 320 nhp.
1914   Completed.
1917   Sold to The Bay Steam Ship Co Ltd, London. Renamed
        BAYTIGERN. Registered London. Employed as a
        munitions carrier to North Russia.
1922   Sold to Cie Maritime des Transports Coloniaux, Paris.
        Renamed **BOURBONNAIS**. Registered Marseilles.
        2836 n, 4484 g.
1933   Sold to Nouville Cie Havraise Peninsulaire de
        Navigation, Paris.
1942   Acquired by Ministry of War Transport. Placed under
        management of Elder Dempster Lines Ltd. Renamed
        BOURBONNAIS II. Registered London.
1947   Returned to former owners—Nouvelle Cie Havraise Pen-

insulaire de Navigation. Renamed **BOURBONNAIS**.
Registered Havre.
1952   Sold for breaking up by Hughes, Bolckow Ltd, Blyth.

548 BANFORA
O.N. 168804   1942–1946

Steel screw steamer
480.0′×57.2′×34.9′ 5949 n 9615 g 6413 d
Built by Koninklijke Maatschappij 'De Scheld', Flushing, Yard
No 150, as **INSULINDE**, for Rotterdamsche Lloyd (W. Ruys
& Zonen, Managers). Registered Rotterdam. 2×T 3 cyl 29″,
47″, 81″–52″ by the builders. 942 nhp.
1913   31 October, launched.
1932   5868 n, 9496 g.
1934   Sold to Cie Generale de Navigation a Vapeur (Fabre
        Line), Marseilles. Renamed **BANFORA**. Registered
        Marseilles. 478.4′×57.1′×26.3′, 5577 n, 9347 g.

BANFORA in Fabre Line colours (Photo L. Dunn)

1942 Acquired by Ministry of War Transport (Elder Dempster Lines Ltd, Managers). Registered Liverpool.
1946 Returned to former owners. Registered Marseilles.
1955 5577 n, 9347 g.
1957 Sold to Shipbreakers. Renamed **BANFORA MARU**. November, arrived Kawasaki for demolition by Amakashi Sangyo KK.

549 HAI LEE
O.N. Not allocated   1942

Steel twin screw motorship
337.7′×49.0′×26.1′   2160 n   3616 g   4300 d
Built by Akers Mekaniskeverksted, Aktieselsk, Oslo, Yard No 463, for Bruusgaard Kiosteruds Dampskipsaksjeselskap. Registered Drammen (Norwegian flag). 2×oil engines 4 SCSA 8 cyl 21⅝″–39⅜″ by Aksjeselskap Akers Mekanisk Verkstad, Oslo. 742 nhp, 15 K.
Passenger accommodation: 12.
1934 July, completed.
1942 Managed and partially manned by Elder Dempster Lines Ltd.
1951 April, 2160 n, 3616 g.
1967 Sold to Lorinda Shipping SA, Hong Kong. Renamed **REBECCA**. Registered Panama.
1972 Sold to Blue Marine (Far East) Ltd, Hong Kong. Renamed **SELINA**. Registered Panama.
1973 March, sold to Tyler Navigation Co, Panama. April, sold to Tung Ho Steel Enterprises Co Ltd for demolition at Kaohsiung. 26 August, work commenced.

NEW NORTHLAND at Cemeau, Canada, c. 1938–9, with GASPESIA in background (Photo K. C. Griffin)

550 NEW NORTHLAND
O.N. 149409   1942–1946

Steel screw steamer, strengthened for navigation in ice
287.7′×47.2′×22.3′   2029 n   3445 g
Built by Swan Hunter & Wigham Richardson Ltd, Wallsend, Newcastle, Yard No 1214, as **NORTHLAND**, for Eastern Shipping Co Ltd, Quebec. Registered Newcastle. T 3 cyl 23½″, 38″, 62″–42″ by the builders. 393 nhp.
Passenger accommodation: 142 first class, 76 third.
1926 April, completed.
1927 Renamed **NEW NORTHLAND**.
1928 Transferred to Clarke Steamship Co, Quebec. Registered Quebec (British flag).
1940 Requisitioned by Canadian Government.
1942 Acquired by British Ministry of War Transport (Elder Dempster Lines Ltd, Managers). Refitted at Smith's

HAI LEE

439

Above, **NEW NORTHLAND** *leaving Lagos at the end of the war,*
left, as **NUEVO DOMINICA**

Dock, South Shields, to troopship standards, accommodation for 660.

1946 Returned to owners.

1947 Sold to Seaway Steamship Line Ltd, Windsor, Ontario. 1885 n, 3502 g. Sold to Government of the Dominican Republic. Renamed **NUEVO DOMINICANO**. Registered Ciudad Trujillo. 2029 n, 3445 g.

1953 27 November, foundered off North coast of Cuba.

551 TOUAREG

O.N. 168812   1942–1943

Steel screw steamer, two decks

390.3′×50.2′×25.7′   3123 n   5135 g

Built by SA Chantier et Ateliers de Provence, Port de Bouc, for Cie Marseillaise de Navigation a Vapeur (Cie Fraissinet), Marseilles. Registered Marseilles T 3 cyl 29$\frac{1}{16}$″, 46″, 75″–45″ by the builders. 376 nhp, 13 K.

1924 Completed.

1936 Registered owners: Cie de Navigation Fraissinet, Marseilles.

1940 16 September, captured in the Gulf of Guinea by Royal Navy and escorted into Takoradi and interned.

TOUAREG (Photo M. Bar)

440

1942 January, requisitioned by Ministry of War Transport and placed under management of Elder Dempster Lines Ltd for service as a training ship for merchant seamen. 9 March, registered Liverpool.
1943 21 April, under the management of Moxey, Saxon & Co Ltd, London. 20 December, under the management of Cie Maritime Francaise (London).
1944 February 26, under the management of the Union Castle Mail Steamship Co Ltd, London.
1945 26 October, returned to owners.
1947 Broken up at Ghent, by van Heyghen Freres.
Touareg are a nomadic tribe of the Sahara.

VILLE DE TAMATAVE

552 VILLE DE TAMATAVE
O.N. 168806   1942–1943
Steel screw steamer, two decks and shelter deck
392.9′×53.5′×24.8′   2983 n   4993 g
Built by Ateliers et Chantiers de la Seine Maritime, Worms et Cie, Seine Inferieure, Yard No 59, for Cie Havraise Peninsulaire de Navigation a Vapeur, Paris. Registered Havre. T 3 cyl 26$\frac{15}{16}$″, 44″, 75″–48$\frac{1}{16}$″ by the builder. 370 nhp, 12 K.
1931 Completed.
1938 Registered owners: Nouvelle Cie Havraise.

1941 30 June, intercepted by HMS DUNEDIN off Ascension Island.
1942 Acquired by Ministry of War Transport and placed under the management of Elder Dempster Lines Ltd. Registered Liverpool.
1943 Alfred Holt & Co appointed managers. 12 January, sailed outward bound in convoy ONS 160, serving as Commodore ship. 24 January, convoy scattered by gales and in a position about 500 miles east of Cape Race VILLE DE TAMATAVE (Captain G. Dault) was sighted on her beam ends. Prevailing weather conditions made rescue work impossible. Later in the day it was confirmed she had foundered with 'all hands', including the convoy commodore, Admiral Sir H. J. S. Brownrigg, KBE, CB, DSO, who was the most senior naval officer, on either side, to be killed on active service.

553 BERGA
O.N. 174325   1942–1949
Steel screw steamer, well deck, machinery aft
186.7′×30.2′×12.1′   523 n   804 g
Built by Astilleros del Mediterraneo SA, Barcelona, Yard No 110, for SA Nav Espanola, Valencia (Manuel Garcia del Moral, Managers). Registered Barcelona. T 3 cyl 12″, 20″, 32″–24″ by Alexander Bros, Barcelona. 84 nhp.
1921 January, completed.
1923 Sold to Edwin G. Tyerman, Middlesbrough. Renamed BARFLO. Registered Middlesbrough. 420 n, 751 g.
1927 Sold to Hejos de Romulo Bosele Soc en Commandite, Barcelona. Renamed BERGA. Registered Barcelona.
1942 Acquired by Ministry of War Transport and placed under the management of Elder Dempster Lines Ltd, Liverpool. Registered Gibraltar. 460 n, 840 g.
1949 Sold to Varano Steam Ship Co Ltd (Fred V. Andlaw, Manager), Gibraltar.
1955 Sold to Mario Dominguis Marques, Rio de Janeiro. Registered Rio de Janeiro.
1956 5 January, struck a reef off Maranhao and sank, voyage Sao Luiz to Rio de Janeiro, cargo vegetable oil, babassu and rice.

ALIWAL, formerly EMPIRE LIDDELL, laid up at Durban

554 EMPIRE LIDDELL
O.N. 142873   1943–1947

Steel screw steamer, War 'C6' type
235.4′×36.1′×15.7′   784   1425 g
Laid down by Wm Harkess & Son Ltd, Middlesbrough, Yard
No 229, for the Shipping Controller as **WAR BURE**. T 3 cyl
18″, 30″, 50″–33″ by Richardson, Westgarth & Co Ltd,
Middlesbrough. 500 ihp, 9½ K.

1920 17 April, launched. Sold to the Government of Nigeria
      and completed as **ENUGU**. Registered Lagos (British
      flag).
1943 Purchased by Ministry of War Transport and placed
      under the management of Elder Dempster Lines Ltd.
      Renamed **EMPIRE LIDDELL**. Registered London.
1947 Sold to Arden Hall Steamship Co (Pty) Ltd, Cape Town.
      Renamed **HOEVELD**. Registered Cape Town (British
      flag).
1949 Returned to Durban from Mombasa following serious
      fire damage. Refitted at Maydon Wharf, Durban.
1950 Sold to South African National Steamship Co (Pty),
      (Van Riebeeck Lines (Pty) Ltd, Managers), Cape Town.
      Renamed **ALIWAL**. Registered Cape Town.
1953 Registered Panama.
1957 Sold to Aliwal Steamship Co (Pty) Ltd, Durban.
1958 March, following 25 months laid up, towed across Dur-
      ban harbour by tug A. M. CAMPBELL to Salisbury
      Island.
1961 Broken up at Isipingo Iron Works, Durban, by McWil-
      law Iron & Steel Foundary (Pty) Ltd.

555 POINT PLEASANT PARK
O.N. 174814   1943–1945

Steel screw steamer, War 'Park' type
424.6′×57.2′×34.9′   4244 n   7136 g   10,000 d
Built by Davie Ship Building & Repairing Co Ltd, Lauzon,
Province of Quebec, Yard No 548, for the Canadian Government (Parks Steam Ship Co Ltd, Managers). Registered Montreal (British flag). T 3 cyl 24½″, 37″, 70″–48″ by Dominion
Engineering Works Ltd, Montreal. 2500 ihp, 10 K.

1943 8 November, completed and chartered by Ministry of
      War Transport and placed under the management of
      Elder Dempster Lines Ltd. Registered London.
1945 23 February, U510 (Oberleutnant Alfred Eick) on the
      surface intercepted the steamer, opened fire then dis-
      charged a torpedo which sank **POINT PLEASANT
      PARK** in position 29°.42′S 09°.58′E, voyage Canada to
      Cape Town, with the loss of nine lives. The submarine
      was returning from East Asia having left Jakarta 6
      January and eventually arrived St Nazaire 24 April.

Point Pleasant Park is situated at the extreme south end of the
City of Halifax, Canada, where it commands an unobstructed
view of Halifax Harbour.

REPORT OF LOSS OF POINT PLEASANT PARK BY ENEMY
ACTION

Officers of Watch and Lookouts:
    R. S. Taylor, 2nd Officer⎫
    B. Aichison, Cadet   ⎬ on Bridge.

Lookouts–At station at L.A. Gun:
    Campbell, Deck Hand.

on Flying Bridge:
    Rigby, Deck Hand.

Engineer on Watch:
    A. Devonshire, 3rd Engineer.

        Times are G.M.T.+1 hour.

Feb. 23rd Ship steering=136° speed 10.5 knots wind S.E. force 3, sea
slight, mod. swell, in position 2940 S 0958 E, was struck by torpedo
(Accoustic) about 25 feet forward of stern Frame at 14.00 Hrs.
Explosion of torpedo caused stern part of vessel to collapse and water
to rush into No.5 hold and through tunnel into engine room, engine
room bulkhead having been damaged by the blast coming through the
tunnel.

The propellor having been blown off the engines began to race and
machinery was stopped by 3rd Engineer, Mr. Devonshire. All auxiliary
pumps were started in an effort to keep the water down in engine room
but could not cope with the inrush of water.

Starboard side crew accommodation was totally destroyed, eight men
being presumed killed outright, as no sign of them was seen. Five men
were injured and as all ladders had been destroyed, these men had to
be drawn up through the skylight, special mention being made of A.B's
Slade & Procter, who entered the flooded compartment and assisted in
the rescue of these men. All injured men were given attention by
Chief Steward Roberts and 2nd Steward Laing before being placed in
lifeboats.

Water was found to be making in all after hatches and ship was
gradually sinking by the stern.

At 14.10 dynamo had to be shut off due to water reaching above the
bedplate, emergency wireless transmitter brought into operation but
no signals could be sent due to some defect (to some defect) which
could not be ascertained. Owing to Main aerial being down, signals
from main transmitter were doubtful as no reply was received. It was
afterwards found that some of these signals had been received by two
shore stations but on a wave band of 666 metres instead of 600.

At 14.20 orders were given to abandon ship in view of possibility of
further action by enemy if this was delayed. At 14.25 ship abandoned
and boats pulled away to safe distance, all confidential books having
been placed in the tin recently thrown overboard and observed to sink.

14.30 enemy submarine surfaced off port bow about 700 yds away
circled the ship twice and after second time opened fire on ship with
40 m.m. gun firing about twelve rounds into No.3 & 2 holds, she then
layed-off ship, returning later and firing further shots into ship.

With the sub. on the surface it was impossible to make any attempt
to reboard the ship until 16.00 hrs. when sub. made off to westward.
The motor was started and proceeded towards the ship, but before
reaching her she upended and sank quickly, the time being 16.15.

A roll call was taken of each boat and the aforesaid eight men found
to be missing. Three boats made fast and motor boat began to tow on
a E×S course. Weather was gradually deteriorating and at 18.00 tow
line fouled the propellor of No.3 boat and it was decided, after futile
attempt to clear propellor to lay to sea anchor all night.

A heavy sea ran all night, wind S.E. force 4, all hands very seasick,
boats shipping heavy water requiring constant baling.
24th Wind S.E. force 4 07.00 all boats set sail, steering E×S (Mag.)
to make E×N true, which with Nly. drift we hoped to make a course
good of about E.N.E.

All boats kept in company throughout day; No.2 boat being slower
the other reduced sail to make this possible, boats continually shipping
water due to cross sea and heavy swell. Estimated run until noon on
this day 10 miles. Death in No.3 boat of Munro (Greaser) reported at
08.00, the men, dying during the previous night.
25th Continued sailing throughout night, boats keeping in contact by
means of torch flashes. At 07.00 No.2 boat being so far astern, decided
to return, started motor and coming up with her took her in tow and
rejoined No.3 boat, which made fast astern of No.2. Owing to heavy
sea and swell tow rope parted and all boats then resumed sailing
independently, distress messages being transmitted by No.2 boat every
2 hours. At 18.00 No.2 being well astern returned and took in tow,
catching up with No.3 boat at 23.00 hrs. very heavy weather, all boats
shipping water; all hands extremely uncomfortable. Estimated distance
covered 40 miles on same course.
26th Contact with No.3 boat ceased during night although a search,
using motor opened up, was made, three or four sweeps being made
over area. At 05.00 motor gave out, No.2 & 4 boats then proceeded to
sail independently keeping in close company a sharp lookout being kept
for No.3. Estimated distance this day was 54 miles on same course. 3
men taken from N.2 owing to her being overloaded.
27th Wind sly. force 3 sea moderate, heavy cross swell, very little
sunshine, sky being 9/10 overcast, no sign No.3 boat, distress calls
being sent out by No.2 at frequent intervals. Weather deteriorated
towards dark and water was continually being shipped. Estimated
distance covered 60 miles.
28th Weather conditions same, boats keeping in close company. At
15.30 motor started and No.2 boat made fast, motor kept at slow speed
and boats used all sails throughout the night. Estimated distance this

Oberleutnant Eick (Photo Bundesarchiv)

day 60 miles. Wireless transmitter out of order due to generator, no further signals possible.

1st March At 03.30 motor broke down completely and both boats proceeded independently keeping in company, weather conditions remained very poor and both crews extremely uncomfortable. Estimated distance the day 54 miles.

2nd Wind S×W force 2 freshening to force 5 at night. Sea and swell gradually increasing. At noon No.2 boat which was now sailing faster, due to being able to use jib (this not possible while aerial was up) was last seen 1 mile ahead and well to windward. No further contact made this day. Weather conditions very bad after dark, boats being practically unmanageable. Estimated distance 54 miles.

3rd Weather conditions improved towards dawn but temperature fell rather low, everybody suffering from damp and cold. No sign of No.2 boat. Estimated distance 30 miles.

4th Wind fell to light airs during night and boats layed-too. At 06.00 land observed ahead and on both bows. No.2 boat observed 1 mile to northward, wind having died out oars were shipped and both boats closed land to investigate possibilities, estimated position in region of Conception Bay. 07.00 engines of aircraft heart, signals made (smoke) but not observed by aircraft. 16.00 boats closed for consultation when smoke was observed to westward, signals immediately made, but not observed from ship, use then made of Heliograph in both boats which was observed and the ship altered her course to investigate. 17.20 No.2 boat crew picked up. 17.30 No.4 boat crew picked up by H.M.S.A.S. AFRICANA which had been sent out to search. No. 3 boat having been picked up 36 hours previously and taken to Luderitz Bay, AFRICANA proceeded to Walvis Bay, arriving with both boats in tow at 17.30 hours on 5th March.

NO.3 LIFEBOAT
All times are G.M.T.+1 hour.

Feb. 23rd 1945
14.00 Torpedoed.
14.25 Abandoned ship. Twenty-one men were embarked in this boat, which was the last to leave; boat was rowed away from ship and closed the other boats. The Captain and two men were transferred to No.5 boat.

R. Munroe, Greaser, who was evidently seriously injured, though not visibly, was made as comfortable as possible. He complained of back pains and could not use his legs. Morin and Roberts were also treated for injuries.

14.30 approx. Submarine surfaced and shelled ship; after circling vessel two or three times he finally made off in a westerly direction at 16.00.

16.10 Vessel sank. Boats were then towed by No.4 boat which had motor. Towrope broke twice.

18.00 approx. Towrope fouled No.4 propellor. Everyone very seasick by this time. No.3. cast off towrope and boats lay together throughout night. Cold wind, occasionally shipping spray. Rudder unshipped by towrope.

Feb. 24th
02.00 R. Munroe died.
06.00 Body placed over side.
07.00 Shipped rudder, hoisted sail and proceeded to steer E×N (approx.). Impossible to obtain latitude at noon owing to violent motion of boat. Boats still together at dusk. Watches were set, four hours on, twelve off. Boats kept in touch by flashing torch at intervals.

Feb. 25th Proceeding under full sail moderate breeze.
15.30 Wind freshened, shipped some water and spray, Everyone wet and cold. Nos. 2 and 4 boats well astern. Noon position 20-40S 10-21E.

Feb. 26th
00.30 Nos 2 & 4 boats came up. Jacobson, who was steering during middle watch reported no sign of other boats at 03.30, last seen on our port beam. Could see no sign of them at daylight so carried on. Shipping spray and water all night. Noon Pos. 28-13S 11-00E.

Feb. 27th Mainly overcast all day, unable to dry our clothes. Noticed water turning greener in the afternoon so judged we were in soundings. Spent a very wet and uncomfortable night. Noon latitude 17-19S.

Feb. 28th Fine and clear during day. Spent day drying clothes. Wind freshened later and swell increased. Noon pos. 26-49S 11-47E.

March 1st Cloudy and clear but cold, swell moderated. Towards midnight wind and sea increased, sea becoming more confused, heavy swell, shipping spray and water continually.

March 2nd Decided soon after midnight that it was too dangerous to carry on under full sail so lowered mainsail and kept on under the jibsail only. Made a cover with the mainsail so that most of the men were protected from spray. At about 05.00 gave everyone half a mug of water, which revived us considerably.

08.45 Sighted land but continued on under jib.
12.00 Close enough to land to make out a bay so decided to investigate. Hoisted mainsail, swell decreasing. As we approached the land we could make out the masts of schooners inside the bay behind Mercury Island. As we rounded the northerly point of Mercury Is. we were approached by the fishing vessels Radiance and Boy Russell. Radiance passed us a line but it fouled his propeller so we took a line from Boy Russell and were pulled alongside and taken aboard. Everyone given bread and jam and water, and later soup and coffee.

Capt. Veer of the Boy Russell decided to take us down to Luderitz as soon as swell decreased.

We left Mercury Is. anchorage at 02.00 and arrived Luderitz 15.30 on March 3rd. Our treatment on board the Boy Russell was excellent. We were treated with the utmost kindness and consideration. Should like to recommend that Capt. of the Boy Russell be compensated for the fuel used in taking us to Luderitz. On arrival at Luderitz we were examined by a doctor and Morin, Turbide and Roberts sent to hospital for further treatment. The remainder were taken to hotels.

We were cared for by the Navy League (Chairman Mr. Weiss) and later entertained by the S.A.W.A.S. (President Mrs. Hofmeyer). Recommend that these two bodies be thanked for their kindness and generosity.

Lifeboat provisions were adequate though only three men ate pemmican. We could also have used more blankets and suggest that the weather cloth be made to run the whole length of the boat from the canopy for'd to right aft. as the man at the tiller was continuously exposed to spray. Discipline was excellent the whole time.

After the explosion on the vessel Mr. Rosendale, 4th Engineer states that 2 firemen and 2 greasers were trapped in Greasers' room and that he chopped screen away from skylight and helped them out. The men trapped were R. Munroe, W. Helms, E. Bourque and E. Turbide.

R. S. Taylor	2nd. Officer	W. Jones	Ord. Seamen
R. Livingstone	2nd. Engineer	R. Morin	Ord. Seamen
F. Rosendale	4th Engineer	D. Bedford	Ch. Cook
O. Robinson	5th. Engineer	V. Froude	2nd. Cook
M. Hull	Cadet	W. Helms	Fireman
O. Jacobsen	Bosun	E. Borque	Fireman
M. Roberts	A.B.	E. Turbide	Fireman
		W. Chatterton	Gunner (D.E.M.S.)

R. S. Taylor
2nd. Officer

(Sgd) O. OWENS
Master

CHATEAUROUX

556 AMSTELKERK

O.N. Not allocated   1943–1945

Steel screw steamer
368.7′×53.2′×22.0′   2314 n   4338 g
Built by Nuscke & Co, Aktiengesellschaft, Grabow, near Stettin, Yard No 286, for Vereenigde Nederlandsche, Scheepvaart-maats, Holland. Registered at The Hague. 2 DR gearing steam turbines by Escher Wyss Engineering Works, Zurich. 3000 shp.
1929   February, completed.
1934   Placed under the management of Holland West-Afrika Linjie. 2347 n, 4340 g.
1940   2453 n, 4457 g.
1943   Operated on the United Kingdom–West Africa trade, partially manned by Elder Dempster personnel.
1945   Returned to Holland West-Afrika Linjie.
1953   11 October, arrived Antwerp for demolition by SA Cinda, Liege.

557 CHATEAUROUX

O.N. 166318   1944–1945

Steel screw steamer, well deck
364.1′×52.8′×24.5′   2778 n   4736 g
Built by Tyne Iron Shipbuilding Co Ltd, Newcastle, Yard No 221, for Soc Maritime Auxiliaire de Transports, Nantes. Registered Nantes. T 3 cyl 23½″, 38″, 64″–42″ by Armstrong Whitworth & Co Ltd, Newcastle. 347 nhp.
1921   February, completed.
1928   Sold to Cie Francaise des Chemins de Fer de Paris, Orleans (Soc Maritime Auxiliaire de Transports, Managers). 2546 n, 4185 g.
1932   Sold to Cie Delmas Freres & Vieljeux, La Rochelle. Registered La Rochelle.

AMSTELKERK

1937	Transferred to Cie 'Delmas Vieljeux.
1943	4 March, damaged by aircraft bombs in position 41°.10'N 15°.10'W.
1944	Acquired by Ministry of War Transport, Elder Dempster Lines Ltd appointed managers. Registered Liverpool. 2783 n, 4765 g.
1945	11 July, arrived at Preston for demolition by T. W. Ward Ltd.

558 EMPIRE MAYLAND
O.N. 169387   1945–1948

Steel screw steamer, War 'C' (shelter deck) type, engines aft
144.0'×27.1'×8.0'   123 n   394 g   300 d
Built by C. Hill & Sons Ltd, Bristol, for Ministry of War Transport (Elder Dempster Lines Ltd, Managers). Registered Bristol. T 3 cyl 9", 16", 26"–18" by White's Marine Engineering Co Ltd, Newcastle. 375 ihp, 9 k.

1945	February, completed.
1948	Sold to Ho Hong Steamship Co (1932) Ltd, Singapore. Renamed **HONG SOON**. Registered Singapore (British flag). For service in Indonesian Archipelago and Timor.
1955	Sold to Government of Portuguese Timor. Renamed **D. ALEIXO**. Registered Dili-Timor (Portuguese flag).
1965	Sold to Tat Pin Shipping & Trading Co, Malaysia. No port of registry but under British flag.
1966	Deleted from *Lloyd's Register of Shipping* due to lack of current information.

ESSO TIOGA, *formerly* ***EMPIRE WRESTLER***
(Photo J. Powell)

559 EMPIRE WRESTLER
O.N. 169100   1946–1947

Steel screw tanker, War 'Chant' type, one deck
193.0'×30.7'×14.1'   380 n   797 g   850 d
Built by Grangemouth Dockyard Co Ltd, Grangemouth, for Ministry of War Transport (F. T. Everard & Sons Ltd, Managers). Registered Grangemouth. T 3 cyl 15", 25½", 41"–30" by Aitchison-Blair Ltd, Clydebank. 710 ihp, 9 k.

1943	Completed.
1946	Placed under management of Elder Dempster Lines Ltd.
1947	Sold to Anglo American Oil Co Ltd, London. Renamed **ESSO TIOGA**.
1949	Transferred to Esso Petroleum Co Ltd.
1963	350 n, 769 g. Sold for demolition at St. Davids. Subsequently re-allocated.
1964	7 January, demolition commenced at Inverkeithing by T. W. Ward & Son Ltd.

560 STANLEY PARK
O.N. 174799   1946–1947

Steel screw steamer, War 'Park' type
424.7'×57.2'×34.9'   4243 n   7145 g   10,000 d
Built by Marine Industries Ltd, Sorel, Province of Quebec, for Canadian Government, (Parks Steamship Co Ltd, Managers.) Registered Montreal. T 3 cyl 24½", 37", 70"–48" by Dominion Engineering Works Ltd, Montreal. 2500 ihp, 10 K.

1943	August, completed.
1946	Management transferred to Elder Dempster Lines (Canada) Ltd.
1947	On bare boat charter from Dominion of Canada to Ministry of Transport. Managers: Dalhousie Steam & Motor Ship Co Ltd. Registered London.
1948	Sold to Acadia Overseas Freighters, Halifax, Ltd. Renamed **HALIGONIAN DUCHESS**. Registered Halifax NS.
1950	Transferred to the management of Counties Ship Management Co Ltd. Renamed **MALDEN HILL**. Registered London. 4345 n, 7168 g.
1964	Sold to Trafalgar Steam Ship Co Ltd (Tsavliris (Shipping) Co Ltd, Managers), London. Renamed **NEWMOOR**.

MALDEN HALL,
formerly ***STANLEY PARK***
(Photo M. Cassar)

1968 Sold to Kantara Shipping Ltd (Tsavliris (Shipping) Co Ltd, Managers), Cyprus. Registered Famagusta. July 21, arrived Spezia in tow. Demolition by Contieri Navali del Golfo commenced December.

561 HELUAN

O.N. 43086   1919–1920

Steel twin screw steamer
441.2'×52.9'×29.8'   4517 n   7262 g
Built by Reiherstieg Schiffswerfte und Maschinenfabrik, Hamburg, for Deutsche Dampfschiffahrts GS Kosmos, Hamburg. Registered Hamburg. 2×T 3 cyl 22", 39½", 64¼"–42". 750 nhp, 11½ K.
Passenger accommodation: 69 first class, 22 second.
1908   Completed.
1919   Acquired by The Shipping Controller as a War prize and management allocated to Elder, Dempster & Co Ltd.
1920   Sold to City of Oran Steam Ship Co Ltd (City Line Ltd, Managers). Renamed **CITY OF LUCKNOW**. Registered Glasgow.

HELUAN

1923   Sold to Deutsche Dampfschiffahrts GS Kosmos, Hamburg. Renamed **HELUAN**. Registered Hamburg.
1926   24 November, transferred to Hamburg Amerika Packetfahrt AG, Hamburg.
1931   November, broken up at Osaka.

562 EMPIRE BURE

O.N. 181651   1947

Steel twin screw steamer
439.1'×57.0'×34.1'   5172 n   8178 g   4420 d
Built by SA John Cockerill, Hoboken, Belgium, Yard No 562, as **ELIZABETHVILLE**, for Cie Belge Maritime du Congo SA, Antwerp. Registered Antwerp. 2×Q 4 cyl 23", 33", 47", 67"–48" by the builders. 5000 ihp, 13 K.
1921   November, completed.
1931   Placed under management of Agenci Maritime Internationale, Antwerp. 4802 n, 8351 g.
1934   4869 n.
1947   Acquired by Ministry of Transport (Lamport & Holt Line Ltd, Managers). Renamed **EMPIRE BURE**. Registered London. 4591 n, 8502 g. 5 June to 11 October, chartered and partially manned by Elder Dempster Lines Ltd, completed two round voyages, Liverpool to West Africa.
1950   Sold to Charlton Steam Shipping Co (Chandris (England) Ltd, Managers), London. Renamed **CHARLTON STAR**. Registered London. 8396 g.
1958   Sold to Maristrella Navigation SA, Liberia. Renamed **MARISTRELLA**. Registered Monrovia.
1960   19 January, arrived Osaka. Sold to Jida Co Ltd, 28 January delivered. 12 February, demolition commenced at Sakai City.
Elizabethville is a large provincial town in Zaire.
Note—EGBA (221), ZINI (308) and ZUNGERU (309) were also under Elder Dempster management during World War Two.

ELIZABETHVILLE, *subsequently* **EMPIRE BURE**

PART 6

Non-operational vessels, hulks, floating dock, etc

Ship Nos 563–581

SHACKAMAXON (*ship No. 577*) (Photo Merseyside County Museums)

DARRO

563 DARRO
O.N. 132026   1912–1916

RMSP 'D' class
Steel twin screw steamer
500.7'×62.3'×40.2' 7291 n 11,484 g
Built by Harland & Wolff Ltd, Belfast, Yard No 427, to the
order of Royal Mail Steam Packet Co for Imperial Direct West
India Line Ltd. Registered Belfast. 2×Q 4 cyl 23″, 34″, 48″,
69″–51″ by the builders. 680 nhp, 14½ K.
Passenger accommodation: 90 first class, 40 second, 860
steerage.
1912   15 May, launched. 30 October, trials.
1916   Sold to Royal Mail Steam Packet Co.
1917   21 February, collided with and sank troopship *MENDI*
       off St Catherine's Point.
1918   13 October, attacked by submarine in Irish Channel,
       torpedo missed.
1933   December, sold for demolition at Osaka.
RMSP 'D' class: DARRO (264), DRINA (265), and three not
owned by Elder Dempster companies, DEMERARA, DESNA
and DESEADO.

564 DRINA
O.N. 132027   1913–1916

RMSP 'D' class
Steel twin screw steamer
500.7'×62.3'×40.2' 7288 n 11,483 g
Built by Harland & Wolff Ltd, Belfast, Yard No 428, to the
order of Royal Mail Steam Packet Co. Registered Belfast.
2×Q 4 cyl 23″, 34″, 48″, 69″–51″ by the builders. 680 nhp, 14½ K.
Passenger accommodation: 90 first class, 40 second, 860
steerage.

1912   29 June, launched.
1913   January, completed for Elder Line Ltd.
1914   Hospital ship.
1915   February, returned to owners.
1916   Sold to Royal Mail Steam Packet Co.
1917   1 March, torpedoed without warning and sunk two
       miles west of Skokholm Iskand (Pembrokeshire coast) by
       German submarine UC65 with the loss of 15 lives.

DRINA

565 STATIRA
O.N. Not traced   1858

Schooner, part iron bolts
77 n 97 g
Built at Newport. Registered Newport.
1839   Completed for Mr Hughes.
1851   Owned by a Mr Buckingham.
1852   Engaged on coastal trade from Newport.
1858   Purchased by African Steamship Co. Hulked in Sierra
       Leone.

566 HELENA
O.N. Not traced   1858

630 g
Built 1838 at Liverpool.
1848   Owned by Hargreaves & Locketts, Liverpool. Registered Liverpool.
1849   Sold to Mr Locketts.
1858   Acquired by African Steamship Co and hulked at Fernando Po.

567 DEE
O.N. Not traced   1862–1863

Wooden paddle three-mast barquentine
213.9′×33.4′×30.0′   1019 n   1848 g
Built by John Scott & Sons, Greenock, for the Royal Mail Steam Packet Co. Registered London. 2 cyl side lever paddle engines by Scott, Sinclair & Co, Greenock. 400 hp, 9 K.
1841   July 10, launched.
1842   Maiden voyage January 14.
1862   12 December, sold to African Steamship Co for use as a coaling hulk at Freetown.
1863   2 September, disabled off Portuguese coast in severe weather, abandoned, and subsequently foundered.

568 WILLIAM MONEY
O.N. not traced   1859–1866

Ship, teak, saul and oak, part iron bolts, sheathed felt and yellow metal
835 tons
1820   built at Calcutta.
1839   Major repairs carried out.
1849   Owners, Green & Co. Registered Bristol. Engaged on the Bristol–Calcutta trade.
1855   Owners, Gibbs & Co, Liverpool. Registered Liverpool. Engaged on the Liverpool to Australia trade.
1859   8 June, purchased by African Steamship Co for use as hulk in West Africa.
1866   13 June, sank at Fernando Po.

569 EARL BALCARRAS
O.N. 24963   1866–1871

Ship, teak, sheathed felt and yellow metal, 26 guns
174.8′×43.8′×5.9′   1485 g
Built by the Honourable East India Co yard, Bombay, as **EARL OF BALCARRAS**, for the United Company of Merchants of England, trading to the East Indies.
1815   Completed.
1835   February, sold to John Hine, London.
1837   June, sold to Remington & Co and Jamsetjee Jeyebhoy, Bombay.
1847   May, sold to Jeyebhoy, Bombay.
1848   September, sold to J. Somes, London.
1851   Owner now styled Somes Bros.
1862   2 December, acquired by African Steamship Co for voyage to Sierra Leone and subsequent use as a coal hulk at Bonny. Renamed **EARL BALCARRAS**.
1871   Beached and broken up at Bonny.
In her early days she carried a crew of 130, consisting of her commander, six mates, surgeon and assistant surgeon, six midshipmen, purser, bo'sun, gunner, carpenter, master-at-arms, armourer, butcher, baker, poulterer, caulker, cooper, two stewards, two cooks, two bo'sun's mates, two carpenter's mates, one cooper's mate, one caulker's mate, six Quartermasters, one sailmaker, seven officers' servants and 78 seamen. She was built like a frigate, her double row of ports being precisely like two-decked line of battle ships.

She had been an unusually fast ship of her type, making, in 1836, a passage to Bombay of 79 days, from England. As speed was far from being the first consideration of her builders, and sail was always reduced at night, it was an exceptionally fine performance for a ship well past her prime.

Joseph Somes, who bought the ship, was formerly on the East India Company's payroll as a ship's husband. On the demise of the old 'John Company', he commenced business on his own, and before long had his own ships trading to every part of the world. His houseflag only differed from the White Ensign in the canton, by having an anchor instead of the Union Jack.

570 ANNA
O.N. 51940   1866

Brig, fir and spruce timbers, sheathed felt and yellow metal, part iron bolts. One deck, two masts, square stern. The figurehead was that of a female.
111.08′×25.04′×13.08′   258 n   258 g
Built by Bell at West Cape, Prince Edward Island for J. C. Pope. Registered Prince Edward Island.
1865   10 July, completed for service Prince Edward Island to Liverpool. 10 August, sold to James Duncan and James Malcolm.
1866   5 June, sold to James Stillwell and John McKee. 13 June, acquired by African Steamship Co. Registered London. Sailed from Liverpool to Lagos and hulked.

571 INKERMAN
O.N. Not traced   1867

100 tons
1867   7 June, acquired by African Steamship Co. Intended to be hulked at Cameroun to receive cargo at town of Greepatch to Anchorage. 11 December, wrecked in the River Mun. The pilot made an error, having mistaken the river for the River Brass, where a part cargo was to be delivered. Vessel plundered by local natives.

572 MARQUIS
O.N. Not traced   1867–1871

100 tons
1867   11 December, acquired by African Steamship Co as a replacement for *INKERMAN* for use as a 'receiving ship' in West Africa. Despatched to West Africa under tow of steamer.
1871   13 December, sold.

573 TERRIER
O.N. Not traced   1869–1871

100 tons
1869   Acquired by African Steamship Co and hulked in West Africa.
1871   13 December, withdrawn from service.

EARL OF BALCARRAS

451

574 COCKATOO
O.N. 42596   1869

650 tons
1869 Acquired by the Company of African Merchants (recorded in the Minutes of the African Steamship Co) and hulked in West Africa.

575 ADRIATIC
O.N. 29762   1873–1885

Wood, side paddle steamer, two funnels
343.8' × 50.0' × 24.1'   2389 n   3650 g
Breadth over paddleboxes 79.0'
Built by George and James Steers, New York, for the New York and Liverpool United States Mail Steam Ship Co (Collins Line). Registered New York. Two oscillating engines by Stillman & Allen, Novelty Ironworks, New York. 1300 hp, 13 K.
Passenger accommodation: 316 first class, 60 second.
1856 8 April, launched. Completion delayed by subsequent alterations.
1857 Completed late autumn. 23 November, commenced maiden voyage, New York to Liverpool. Made one voyage only. Coal consumption 145 tons per day.
1858 Sold at creditors' auction to Brown Bros & Co.
1859 Sold to North Atlantic Steamship Co, together with ATLANTIC and BALTIC for US$50,000. Made five round voyages, New York–Cowes–Havre, then laid up for three years.
1861 April, sold to Wm Malcolmson, London. December, sold to Atlantic Royal Mail Steam Navigation Co.
1864 Laid up at Birkenhead following an engine room explosion.
1869 October, sold to E. Bates & Co, Liverpool, and converted to sailing ship for services in the Pacific.
1873 Purchased by African Steamship Co for use as a hulk at Bonny.
1885 Beached and broken up.
1980 **ADRIATIC** featured on Australian ten dollar postage stamp. She was the last and largest wooden paddle steamer to be built for the North Atlantic passenger and mail service.

576 KENT
O.N. 74   1875

Clipper ship
170.0' × 29.8' × 20.8'   927 g
Built by Money Wigram, Blackwall, for own account. Registered London.
1852 Completed.
1853 27 January, sailed on her maiden voyage London to Port Phillip, arriving 20 April (83 days). 26 October, sailed London to Melbourne.
1854 12 January, arrived Melbourne (78 days).
1874 Owner: R. S. Cunliffe of Glasgow.
1875 Acquired by British & African Steamship Co for service as a hulk in the Niger Delta. In this year her mate was accused of murdering the Master by pushing him overboard in the Bonny River. Mate repatriated to England per BONNY (Liverpool Daily Post 1875).
1921 Writing in 'The Blackwall Frigates', Basil Lubbock stated that he believed **KENT** remained afloat, as a hulk, on the West African coast.
KENT had an enviable record for speed amongst the Australian clippers, regularly making 83-day passages to Australia. In 1862 she came upon the becalmed tea fleet in approximately 01°N in the Atlantic and beat them to Dungeness.

Of the many changes that have taken place on the West Coast of Africa during the past fifty years, few have been more striking than those which time has wrought in that part of Nigeria known as the Oil Rivers.

Bonny in the '70's consisted of a native village situated on an island swamp and a row of hulks moored in "line ahead", as near to the beach as possible. There was no Government, an occasional visit from a British Consul, who resided at Fernando Po, sufficing to meet the demands of administration. There were no European houses, none, or very little "cash money," no post office and (does it necessarily follow?) no postage stamps. To-day, there are all these proofs of civilization, whilst Bonny is a central transmitting station for both submarine and land cables. The trading hulks—ugly word this, suggestive of the days of transportation and Botany Bay—whilst not perhaps things of beauty, were nevertheless very comfortable to live in. As there must be many "Coasters" of to-day, who have never seen one, a description of the conversion of a sailing ship into a hulk may not be misplaced.

A vessel not exceeding 1,000 tons and preferably with a full poop was chosen, and after being extra sheathed and extra coppered and loaded with a suitable trading cargo, of which bags of salt formed the major portion, was despatched to the Coast. On arrival at her destination she was brought as close in shore as the depth of water would permit, always allowing, of course, sufficient distance to enable her to swing to her anchors at change of tide. Two anchors, coupled with a length of cable to form a "bridle," were then "let go," and the hulk's chain shackled to the ring in the "bridle"; with this, the mooring arrangements were complete. All sails, yards, masts, and rigging, were then sent down, leaving nothing more than the lower masts standing. These were cut down to the required height and a ridge pole, running fore and aft, laid upon them. The pole, together with suitable scantlings, formed the frame-work for galvanized sheet iron roof which then followed. After the cabin under the poop had been stripped of all fittings and shelves fitted on the bulkheads, and a counter erected, the "shop" was ready for stocking. Spirits were stored in the "'tween" decks below the shop, bale goods and cases in the main hatch, whilst salt, shooks, and other rought goods, were placed in the fore part. The offices and bedrooms were erected on the poop on both sides of an alleyway which ran aft to a spacious dining room.

The galvanized roof was somewhat steep, sloping down to within three feet of the bulwarks over which it projected for a distance of about six feet. These hulks were thus completely protected from the elements and as they swung to the tide every six hours, were consequently healthy and sanitary abodes.

In the '70's, there were several trading hulks at Bonny. Commencing from the North, was the *Charles Horsfall*, a fine vessel with "painted ports," owned by Messrs. Horsfall Brothers. This particular firm suffered heavily during an epidemic of yellow fever in 1873, losing a member of the family, agents and assistants. About this time, Messrs. Horsfall Brothers, owned two steamers, namely, the *Palm* and *Plantain*. The former vessel traded to the Rivers, whilst the latter carried the Horsfall flag to other parts of the world. Some few years later this firm retired from the West African trade, the *Charles Horsfall* being sold and subsequently transferred to Benin by her new owners. Next in line came the *Victoria* (Messrs. Stuart & Douglas) with Mr. Sturdey as agent, followed by the *Benledi* (Messrs. Hatton and Cookson) with Mr. R. Knight as agent. Next followed the *Indian Queen* (Mr. S. Cheetham), the next hulk in line being the *Onward* (Messrs. Irvine & Woodward) the then agent being happily still with us, and, in his retirement, honoured and respected by all who know him. This line of hulks was headed by the *Arabian* (Messrs. Continental & African Co.) with Mr. David Hopkins in charge. Mr. Hopkins deputised for the British Consul at Fernando Po, when the latter gentleman was on leave. Subsequently, Mr. Hopkins was appointed British Consul for Angola (S.W. Africa) and resided at St. Paul de Loanda. On his death, a memorial stone was erected in the churchyard at Bonny.

Each hulk had opposite to it, on the river bank, a "beach," on which a galvanized shed was erected. This was the cooperage where Accra men set up the casks which were sent on board the hulk to be filled with palm oil, as required.

In addition to the trading hulks already mentioned, the British & African Steam Navigation Company had the *Kent*, an old Australian liner owned by Messrs. Money Wigram and Co., of London, and the *Shackmaxon*, an American-built ship. The African Steam Ship Company owned the *Adriatic*, formerly a paddle-wheel steamer belonging to the now defunct Collins Line which traded between Galway and New York.

This completes the list of "live" hulks, and among the "dead" ones were the remains of the old man-of-war, *Isis*, the *Erin-go-bragh*, and the *Ben-ma-Chree*, the latter two vessels well known in their day as cross-channel packets in the Irish and Manx services respectively. *Ichabod!*

It was under the tropical heavens of Western Africa that the fates willed it that all these ships should end their days. Like many good and true men, they ended their days whilst still in "harness."

From the *Elder Dempster Magazine* March 1922

577 SHAKAMAXON
O.N. 1293   1879
Clipper ship, copper fastened and sheathed with yellow metal
170.8′×36.2′×21.4′   990 g
Built at Philadelphia, USA, for Cope Line, USA.
1851   Completed.
1854   7 December, sold for £28,000 by Tonge, Curry & Co, Liverpool, at Public Auction to R. Curwin for service between Liverpool and Australia.
1859   Owners: James Heap.
1878   Owner: R. S. Cunliffe, Cardiff.
1879   Purchased by British & African Steam Navigation Co for service as a hulk in the Niger Delta.

578 BULLDOG
O.N. Not traced   1892–1896
Tug
58 g
21 hp
1892   Acquired by African Steamship Co.
1896   3 March, sold.

579 BELGIAN KING
O.N. 94663   1898–1899
Iron screw steamer, one deck, three masts
365.5′×41.0′×29.5′   2167 n   3354 g
Built by Sunderland Shipbuilding & Engineering Co, Sunderland, Yard No 107, as **CHATEAU LEOVILLE** for Cie Bordelaise de Navigation a Vapeur, Bordeaux. Registered Bordeaux. C 2 cyl 44″, 83″–48″ by North Eastern Marine Engineering Co Ltd, Sunderland. 400 hp
1881   June, launched.
1890   Sold to R. M. Hudson, Sunderland. Renamed **CONNEMARA.** Registered Sunderland.

1895   Sold to G. B. Hunter (T. Ronaldson & Co, Managers). Renamed **BELGIAN KING.** Registered Newcastle. Re-engined by Wallsend Slipway Co Ltd, Newcastle. T 3 cyl 24″, 40″, 64″–45″. 303 nhp.
1898   Elder, Dempster & Co appointed Managers.
1899   Management reverted to owner.
1914   Placed under the management of M. Gumuchdjian, Constantinople.
1914   20 September, foundered near Cape Kureli on passage from Tribijonde, to Constantinople with passengers and a cargo of sheep and oxen.

580 FARADAY
O.N. 68535   1922
Iron twin screw steamer, three masts
360.4′×52.3′×34.7′   3125 n   4908 g
Built by Mitchell, Newcastle, for Siemens Bros & Co. C 4 cyl 30″(2), 68″(2)–48″ by T. Clark & Co, Newcastle. 500 hp.
1874   Completed.
1922   Acquired by the Sierra Leone Coaling Co. Used as a coaling hulk at Freetown. Subsequently reported to be serving in Algiers.
FARADAY was one of the first specially designed cable-laying vessels to be built, and during her career covered most of the world. During World War I, she was employed in the North Atlantic, the Arctic, and in Japanese waters.

581 SIR ALFRED
O.N. Not allocated   1905–1938
Floating dock
Extreme length   218.0′
Breadth at entrance   75.0′
Depth of sill at high water   36.0′
Lifting power   2700 tons
Built by Swan & Hunter Ltd, Newcastle, for the Nigerian Dry Dock & Engineering Co Ltd.
1905   Completed, towed to West Africa and based at Forcados.
1919   Based at Lagos.
1938   Disappears from *Lloyd's Register of Shipping.*

SIR ALFRED, *from an old postcard*

LANZAROTE (*ship No. 210*) (Photo World Ship Photo Library)

454

ADDENDA
Ship Nos 582–585

582 PREMIER
O.N. Not traced   −1888

Brig   219 g
1863, completed.
1888   26 March, owner A. L. Jones Esq, Liverpool. Registered Llanelly. Reported stranded at Saffi, Morocco, whilst loading beans.

583 WILLIAM
O.N. Not traced   −1898

Wooden lighter
60 g
Built 1828
1898   Owned by Elder, Dempster & Co, Bristol. In collision with ss NIGEL (825 g/built 1882) off Black Rock, river Avon.

584 LYCAON (II)
O.N. 364438   1982–1985

'Lycaon' class
Steel screw motorship, two decks
162.31 m×22.20 m×9.170 m   5948 n   11,760 g   13,449 d
Built by Kherson Shipyard, Kherson, Ukraine, USSR, Yard No 2008, for China Mutual Steam Navigation Co Ltd. Registered Liverpool. B & W oil engine 2 SCSA 6 cyl 740 mm–1600 mm by Bryansk Engine Works, Bryansk, USSR. 10,600 bhp (7908 Kw), 18 K.
1976   Completed.
1977   7 January, arrived Liverpool for delivery.
1979   6285 n, 11,804 g, 13,447 d.
1982   Tmk 3783 n, 7712 g, 6285 n, 11,803 g, 13,447 d. 14 June, arrived San Carlos Water, having been chartered by the Ministry of Defence for service in the Falkland Islands campaign whilst engaged on charter to UKWAL.
1983   Returned to owners.

1985   Transferred to Blue Funnel Bulkships Ltd (Ocean Fleets Ltd, Managers). August, sold to Mercury Transport Inc, Panama.
Renamed **CHRYSOVALANDOU FAITH**. In service.
Ships of the 'Lycaon' class: LYCAON (584), LAERTES (585).

585 LAERTES
O.N. 364439   1982–1983

'Lycaon' class
Steel screw motorship, two decks
162.31 m×22.02 m×9.17 m   5948 n   11,750 g   13,449 d
Built by Kherson Shipyard, Kherson, Ukraine, USSR, Yard No 2009 for China Mutual Steam Navigation Co Ltd. Registered Liverpool. B & W oil engine 2 SCSA 6 cyl 740 mm–1600 mm by Bryansk Engine Works, Bryansk, USSR. 10,600 bhp (7908 Kw), 18 K.
1976   Completed
1977   7 January, arrived Liverpool for delivery.
1979   6285 n, 11,804 g, 13,447 d.
1981   Tmk 3783 n, 7713 g, 6285 n, 11,804 g, 13,447 d.
1982   Chartered by the Ministry of Defence for service in the Falkland Islands campaign.
1983   Sold to Dimskai Shipping Company SA (Attica Navigation & Management Corporation, Managers), Athens. Renamed **EVIA LUCK**. Registered Panama. Tmk 3892 n, 7065 g. 6755 n, 11,321 g, 16,120 d.
1985   31 August, in service.

NOTE

Various vessels, including some owned by Ocean Transport and Trading plc, were chartered for occasional voyages to West Africa, under UKWAL, and painted in Elder Dempster colours although not specifically allocated to Elder Dempster.

Clearly, to list all of these would be impossible. However, as a matter of recent historic interest, two of these, LYCAON and LAERTES, are included in a feature from *Sea* magazine in 1983 covering the Company's involvement in the Falklands war, (see page 456).

*This photograph of a Chinese flag vessel was taken at Hong Kong in 1982. The name is not identifiable, but the ship appears to be the 'Sherbro' class, possibly **SALAGA** (ship No. 313), which was delivered to Hsinkiang for demolition in March 1973* (Photo Captain E. Whitehead)

ELDER DEMPSTER SHIPS IN THE FALKLANDS

THREE yellow-funnelled cargo liners took on a new route this summer to the South Atlantic, as part of the British task force in the Falkland Islands.

Elder Dempster's 'Lycaon', 'Myrmidon' and 'Sapele' sailed from the warmer climes of British summer 8,000 miles to the freezing winter and heavy seas of the Southern Atlantic.

'Lycaon' was the first E.D. ship to be called up by the British Ministry of Defence, but she was quickly followed by 'Myrmidon' and 'Sapele', carrying cargoes of land rovers, tractors, trailers, fork-lift trucks, generators, aircraft engines, propellors, pre-fabricated accommodation, mattresses, pillows and much besides.

First to arrive in the war zone was 'Lycaon', sailing into San Carlos water on June 14th, the day before the surrender of the Argentine forces and the cessation of hostilities.

'Lycaon' is the one ship, at time of writing, that remains in the Falkland Islands. 'Myrmidon' returned to London at the end of October and 'Sapele' followed, arriving in Hull on November 5th. Both have now rejoined the Elder Dempster fleet as part of the United Kingdom/West Africa Lines Joint Service.

'Sapele' – a helicopter accidentally severed her aerial mast.

'Lycaon' lies at anchor off Port Stanley. She arrived the day before the conflict ended.

The debris of war – a crashed Harrier jet. 'Myrmidon' can be seen lying at anchor in the background.

From Sea *magazine January 1983*

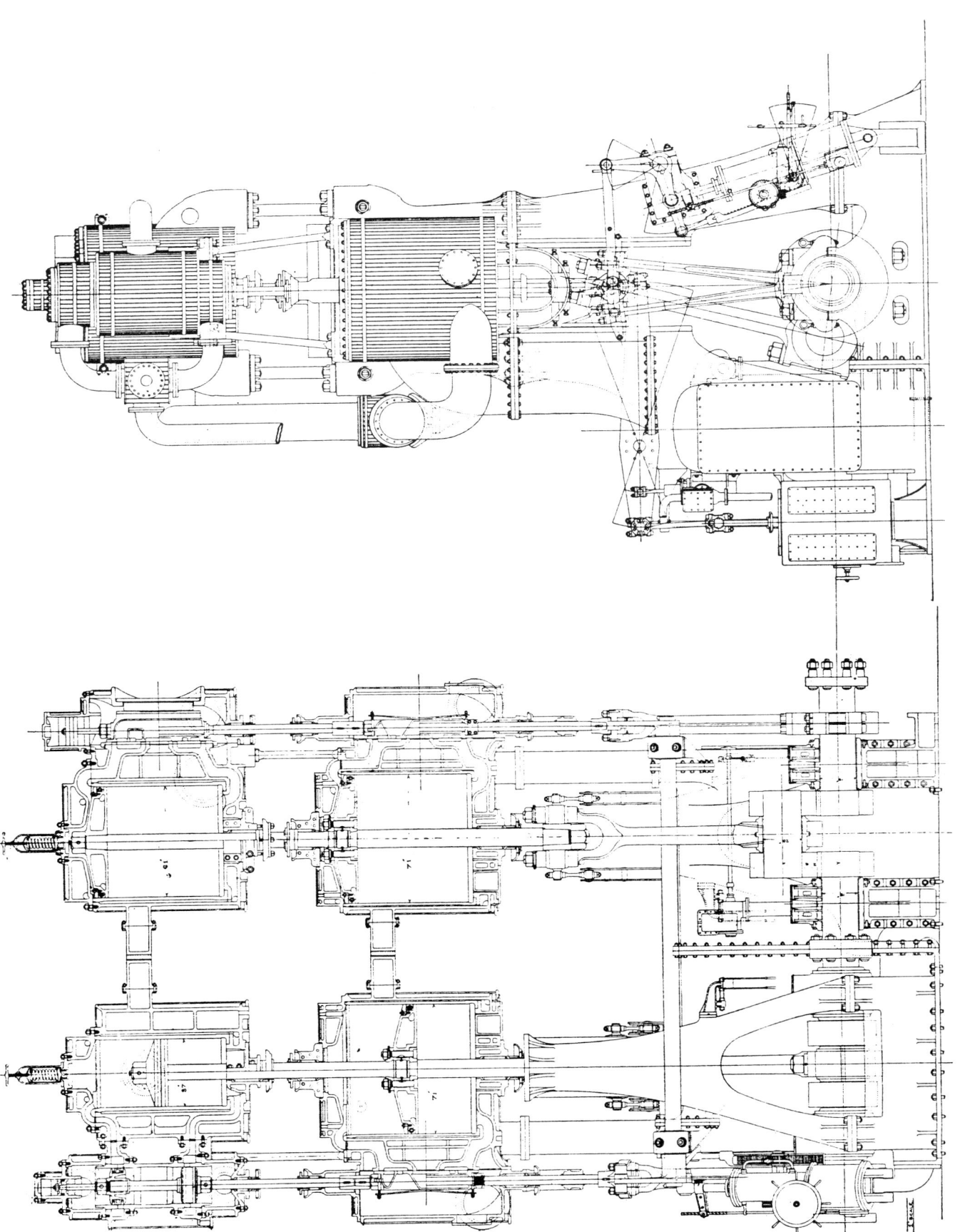

*Engine drawing of **ARAWA**, subsequently **LAKE MEGANTIC** and **PORT HENDERSON** (ship No. 451), the first ever two-crank triple expansion engine*

APPENDIX I

Elder Dempster, in addition to their Main and Branch Line service, operated also, numerous Passenger Launches, Tugs and Lighters other than those already listed.

Small craft fleet 1949

Official No.	Name	Built	Date	Owner
119816	MAMFE		1934	EDL
147316	TAFFO		1918	EDL
161220	KOMBO		1929	EDL
161127	OKO		1929	WALT
174416	ABAK	Northwich	1948	EDL
168809	ABOH	Northwich	1941	WALT
182444	ADAISO	Northwich	1948	WALT
119823	ADUN	Northwich	1926	WALT
181076	AFIKPO	Northwich	1946	WALT
163631	DEMOISELLE	Gosport	1930	EDL
166275	EDIBA	Northwich	1939	WALT
161094	ESSENE	Northwich	1929	EDL
172611	GWILLIAN	Wallasey	1937	WALT
166298	GWYNETH	Glasgow	1940	WALT
161079	IDOMO	Glasgow	1928	EDL
119837	IDUA	Northwich	1924	WALT
162338	IJEBU	Northwich	1931	EDL
162333	IKOYI	Northwich	1931	EDL
162331	ITORI	Northwich	1930	EDL
174239	KING TOM		1942	WALT
119835	LM 84	Northwich	1926	WALT
119836	LM 93	Northwich	1929	WALT
166283	LM 99	Northwich	1939	WALT
167326	MABELLA	Rowhedge	1939	SLCC
172734	MALLARD	Northwich	1934	EDL
161101	OGULA	Lytham	1920	EDL
164333	OKPOHA	Northwich	1937	WALT
119840	SL 7	Northwich	1945	WALT
174402	SL 8	Northwich	1945	WALT
166253	THROSLE	Northwich	1938	WALT
137205	DURGAN	Falmouth	1919	WALT
144677	IKANG	Falmouth	1916	EDL
119815	IKOTANA	Glasgow	1930	EDL
119820	IKPA	Scotstoun	1925	WALT
142879	OGENI	Govern	1931	EDL
167202	SEADON	Neder Hardinveld Holland	1938	SLCC
175871	BENDU	Faversham	1936	SLCC
164285	CBR 4	Northwich	1936	WALT
164290	CBR 5	Northwich	1936	WALT
164291	CBR 7	Northwich	1936	WALT
166232	CBR 11	Northwich	1938	WALT
168035	CARNARVON	Gainsborough	1923	SLCC
161138	DU 3	Northwich	1929	EDL
161121	DU 4	Lytham	1929	EDL
119838	ED 1	Northwich	1928	WALT
119824	ED 2	Northwich	1927	WALT
119825	ED 6	Northwich	1927	WALT
119818	ED 8	Govan	1925	WALT
118919	ED 9	Govan	1925	WALT
119826	ED 10	Northwich	1926	WALT
119821	ED 12	Scotstoun	1929	WALT
119839	ED 13	Northwich	1925	WALT
119822	ED 14	Scotstoun	1929	WALT
119827	ED 15	Northwich	1915	WALT
119828	ED 17	Northwich	1925	WALT
119829	ED 18	Northwich	1920	WALT
119830	ED 19	Northwich	1920	WALT

Official No.	Name	Built	Date	Owner
119831	ED 20	Northwich	1921	WALT
119832	ED 21	Northwich	1921	WALT
119833	ED 22	Northwich	1924	WALT
119834	ED 23	Northwich	1924	WALT
119817	ED 25	N. Woolwich	1928	WALT
119813	ED 26	Lagos	1929	WALT
119814	ED 27	Lagos	1929	EDL
174411	ED 32	Lagos	1947	WALT
174412	ED 33	Lagos	1947	WALT
172748	EDL 2	Lagos		EDL
174418	EDL 8	Groningen	1948	EDL
172740	EDL 16	Wiltmot Point	1939	WALT
172736	EDL 27	Northwich	1927	EDL
172741	EDL 31	Wiltmot Point	1939	WALT
168036	GRAND FLEET	Lekker, Holland	1934	SLCC
172629	KISSY	England	1939	SLCC
172628	KRUTO	England	1940	SLCC
174245	KUKUNA	Faversham	1936	SLCC
171206	Lighter EDL 1	Lagos	1936	EDL
171207	Lighter EDL 5	Lagos	1936	EDL
171208	Lighter EDL 6	Lagos	1936	EDL
171209	Lighter EDL 7	Rebuilt Lagos	1933	EDL
171210	Lighter EDL 9	Rebuilt Lagos	1933	EDL
171291	Lighter EDL 10	Lagos	1936	EDL
171292	Lighter EDL 11	Lagos	1936	EDL
171293	Lighter EDL 16	Lagos	1936	EDL
171294	Lighter EDL 17	Lagos	1933	EDL
171295	Lighter EDL 18	Lagos	1933	EDL
171296	Lighter EDL 19	Lagos	1933	EDL
171297	Lighter EDL 20	Lagos	1933	EDL
171298	Lighter EDL 21	Lagos	1935	EDL
171299	Lighter EDL 22	Lagos	1935	EDL
171300	Lighter EDL 23	Lagos	1935	EDL
171341	Lighter EDL 24	Lagos	1934	EDL
171342	Lighter EDL 25	Lagos	1934	EDL
171343	Lighter EDL 26	Lagos	1934	EDL
171344	Lighter EDL 28	Lagos	1936	EDL
171345	Lighter EDL 29	Lagos	1936	EDL
171346	Lighter EDL 30	Lagos	1936	EDL
171347	Lighter EDL 31	Lagos	1936	EDL
171348	Lighter EDL 32	Lagos	1936	EDL
171349	Lighter EDL 33	Lagos	1936	EDL
171351	EDL E26	Lagos	1938	EDL
171352	EDL 1	Lagos	1938	WALT
171353	EDL 2	Lagos	1938	WALT
171350	EDL F25	Lagos	1938	EDL
172739	EDL F27	Lagos	1939	WALT
171203	F 22	Lagos	1937	WALT
171204	F 23	Lagos	1937	WALT
171205	F 24	Lagos	1937	WALT
142880	Lighter No 1	Lagos	1931	EDL
142881	Lighter No 2	Lagos	1931	EDL
172733	Lighter No 3	Lagos	1927	WALT
171359	Lighter TS	Lagos	1933	WALT

Official No.	Name	Built	Date	Owner
171201	Lighter F 17	Lagos	1935	WALT
171202	Lighter F 21	Lagos	1935	WALT
157518	MABEKKI	King Tom	1935	EDL
137709	MABOLE	Freetown	1929	WALT
157524	MABUM	King Tom	1936	WALT
157516	MADONKE	King Tom	1934	EDL
157517	MAFILE	King Tom	1934	EDL
157531	MAGBURKA	King Tom	1937	WALT
157520	MAKOBO	King Tom	1935	WALT
157512	MAKRIE	King Tom	1933	EDL
157523	MAKUMP	King Tom	1936	WALT
1726177	MANANKON	King Tom	1939	WALT
157535	MANDO	King Tom	1937	WALT
168038	MANGUARD	Lekker, Holland	1934	SLCC
174232	MANJAMA	King Tom	1942	WALT
172615	MANOWA	King Tom	1939	WALT
174230	MANWA	King Tom	1941	WALT
157534	MARA	Freetown	1937	WALT
157529	MARAMPA	King Tom	1937	WALT
172620	MASADUGU	King Tom	1940	WALT
157527	MASANKI	King Tom	1936	WALT
172624	MASAYMA	King Tom	1940	WALT
157515	MATAM	King Tom	1934	EDL
157521	MATERI	King Tom	1935	WALT
157519	MATINDI	King Tom	1930	WALT
172612	MATTRO	Freetown	1938	WALT
174240	MIN I			WALT
174241	MIN II			WALT

Official No.	Name	Built	Date	Owner
174242	MIN VII			WALT
172613	MOBIL	King Tom	1938	WALT
174231	MOHERA	King Tom	1941	WALT
172625	MUSAIA	King Tom	1940	EDL
172143	OPOBO No 1	Lagos	1940	EDL
172744	OPOBO No 2	Lagos	1940	EDL
162351	PB 1	Northwich	1931	EDL
162352	PB 2	Northwich	1931	EDL
174226	PENDEMBU	Holland	1935	SLCC
172626	RONIETTA	England	1939	SLCC
174227	ROKELL	Holland	1935	SLCC
172750	T 1	Lagos	1942	WALT
174401	T 2	Lagos	1942	WALT
157544	T 3	King Tom	1929	WALT
157545	T 4	King Tom	1929	WALT
175875	T 6	King Tom	1948	WALT
157525	T 9	King Tom	1936	WALT
157526	T 10	King Tom	1936	WALT
157528	T 11	King Tom	1936	WALT
172614	T 12	King Tom	1939	WALT
172616	T 13	King Tom	1939	WALT
172618	T 14	King Tom	1939	WALT
172619	T 15	Freetown	1940	WALT
172745	T 16	Lagos	1940	WALT
172746	T 17	Lagos	1940	WALT
172747	T 18	Lagos	1941	WALT
174415	T 19	Freetown	1947	WALT
164271	W 10	Lytham	1935	WALT
172627	WALMA	England	1940	SLCC

This bell is now in Calabar museum

The former Elder Dempster Office at Calabar, photographed in 1983

Launches Tugs and Lighters

Recent additions to our Small Craft Fleet

M.T. *Ashaka*, built in 1955 by Botje Ensing and Co., Groningen, Holland, is a 90 b.h.p. Widdop-engined tug stationed at Sapele

by George Hunter, B.Sc.Hons., M.I.N.A.
Naval Architect, Elder Dempster Lines

LAST year an extensive small craft replacement programme was completed. In the first six or seven years after the Second World War, building went on almost continuously to provide replacements and additions to our West African river and harbour fleet, which, of necessity, had been allowed to de-

teriorate to the limit of its endurance. In 1953 we embarked on a more ambitious programme of building with a view to improving lighterage, towage and other harbour services. This reached its climax in 1954 when we took delivery of one passenger tender, ten tugs and nineteen lighters. We now have about one hundred

M.T. *Nempe* is a Lagos tug, constructed in 1954 by Shipyard 'De Hoop', Hardinxveld, Holland. Her twin screws are driven by two 120 b.h.p. Widdop engines

M.T. *Jakpa* was built in Groningen, Holland, by Botje Ensing and Co. in 1954. Four tugs of this type were constructed for service at Lagos, *Jekri* and *Jakpa* having 120 b.h.p. and *Jos* and *Jebba* 150 b.h.p. Widdop engines

M.V. *Iju*, a passenger tender originally stationed at Lagos and now at Freetown, was built in 1954 by Shipyard 'Alphen', P. de Vries Lentsch, Alphen a/d Rijn, Holland. Seating is provided for 26 passengers, and a 185 b.h.p. Crossley engine gives her a speed of 10 knots

and thirty-five craft less than ten years old. About seventy of these, representing roughly one-third of our entire small craft fleet, have been built in the last four years.

The thirty different classes of launches, tugs and lighters constructed since the war have been designed to meet our special requirements. They have been built in numerous shipyards in the United Kingdom and the Netherlands and also in our own establishments at King Tom, Freetown, and Wilmot Point, Lagos. All the power craft are fitted with oil engines supplied by various British engine builders.

A noteworthy feature has been the introduction to our fleet of a type of small tug designed exclusively for towing duties. Formerly most of our towing units had been open launches of 30 to 90 brake horse-power suitable for passenger carrying as an alternative to towing. Since 1953 nineteen tugs of various designs with engines of 60 to 150 brake horse-power and one of 240 brake horse-power have been built.

Another development has been the use of light alloys. The demand for higher speeds led to the adoption of aluminium alloy for the hulls of three launches, this material being lighter than steel and

M.L. *Falaba* is a 13-knot 16-passenger launch stationed at Takoradi. She was constructed entirely of light alloy by Grimston Astor Ltd (now Universal Launches Ltd), Bideford, in 1952, and has a 102 b.h.p. Foden engine. M.L. *Ikeja* is similar, and is a familiar sight in Lagos harbour

461

M.L. *Iddo,* originally named *Yaba,* is a 10-knot light alloy staff launch at Lagos, built in 1953 by Brooke Marine Ltd. Lowestoft, fitted with a 43 b.h.p. Perkins engine and seating 10 passengers

A Lagos swim-ended lighter and a Warri-Sapele moulded lighter are representative of many which Botje Ensing and Co. have built at Groningen for our service in various ports

more durable than wood. We have also used it extensively in the superstructures and funnels of tugs, with consequent saving of weight and increased stability.

The difficulty of obtaining adequate towrope pulls from tugs of restricted draft with correspondingly small propellers led to the fitting of Kort nozzles on

M.T. *Panpo* is stationed at Sapele, and her sister *Ikasa,* formerly *Panya,* at Calabar. These tugs were built in 1954 by James Pollock, Sons and Co. Ltd. Faversham, and have 90 b.h.p. Widdop machinery

five tugs. A Kort nozzle takes the form of a ring of hydrofoil section fitted round the propeller. This increases propeller efficiency and also provides an additional thrust which is roughly analogous to the lift obtained from the aerofoil shape of aircraft wings.

These and other developments, such as spraying steel decks with zinc to protect them from corrosion, have been to some extent experimental and have been introduced in response to the continual demand for improvements. They are now being proved generally successful in practice.

From Sea *magazine*

Motor Launch **ABAK,** *1948*

O. N.	Name	Built	Date	Owner
	KONO	Lagos	1963	EDL
	OLOMA	Lagos	1965	EDL
	KURRA FALLS	Lagos	1966	EDL
	JAMATA	Lagos	1956	EDL
	IKOM	Lagos	1954	EDL
	KWA (Lifeboat ex ITU)			EDL
	CALABAR	Lagos	1966	EDL
	BABADORI	Freetown	1963	EDL
	DEIDO	Freetown	1963	EDL
	IJU (Launch)	Freetown	1954	EDL
	BADAGRY	Lagos	1965	EDL
	IGBOBI	Lagos	1960	EDL
	OWO	Lagos	1957	EDL
	PANPO	Lagos	1954	EDL
	JUASA	Lagos	1956	EDL
	JUKWA	Lagos	1956	EDL
	JEMA	Lagos	1956	EDL
	IKASA	Lagos	1954	EDL
	ABORI	Lagos	1959	EDL
	ASAFO	Lagos	1959	EDL
	NEMPE	Lagos	1954	EDL
321545	TB 1		1935	EDL
321564	TB 2		1939	EDL
321513	TB 3		1964	EDL
321553	TB 4		1965	EDL
169664	THORN		1939	EDL
321537	CALABAR		1966	EDL
199246	ED 51		1954	EDL
196690	ED 57		1954	EDL
196676	L 50		1950	EDL
196697	ED 60		1955	EDL
196702	362		1955	EDL
196703	363		1955	EDL
196696	ED 59		1955	EDL
171353	EDL 2		1946	EDL
315553	ASHAKA		1955	EDL
199234	JAKPA		1955	EDL
199236	JEBBA		1955	EDL
	ETHIOPE		1970	EDL
	AWOSO	Lagos	1959	EDL
	ASEBU	Lagos	1959	EDL
	AKUSE	Lagos	1960	EDL
	ATIEKU	Lagos	1961	EDL
	JEDUA	Lagos	1956	EDL
	IKPAN	Lagos	1954	EDL
	AXIM	Liverpool	1957	EDL
	CAPE THREE POINTS	Liverpool	1958	EDL
	DU 4 (W 3)	Liverpool	1935	EDL
	F 38	Lagos	1950	EDL
	F 44	Lagos	1951	EDL
	F 45	Lagos	1951	EDL
	351	Lagos	1955	EDL
	352	Lagos	1955	EDL
	362	Lagos	1955	EDL
	363	Lagos	1955	EDL
	EDL 15	Lagos	1949	EDL
	EDL 44	Lagos	1953	EDL
	EDL 50	Lagos	1950	EDL
	S 1	Lagos	1956	EDL
	T 9	Lagos	1956	EDL
	ED 59	Lagos	1955	EDL
	ED 60	Lagos	1955	EDL
	EDL 2	Lagos	1946	EDL
	P 8	Liverpool	1961	EDL
	EDL 58	Lagos	1955	EDL

O. N.	Name	Built	Date	Owner
	BR 4	Lagos	1955	EDL
	TIKO 1—Oil Barge, on charter to CDC, EDL colours			
	T 31	Lagos	1954	EDL
	T 32	Lagos	1953	EDL
	T 34	Lagos	1954	EDL
	T 35	Lagos	1954	EDL
	T 36	Lagos	1956	EDL
	T 37	Lagos	1956	EDL
	T 38	Lagos	1956	EDL
	T 39	Lagos	1956	EDL
	T 40	Liverpool	1961	EDL
	T 41	Liverpool	1961	EDL
	T 42	Liverpool	1961	EDL
	F 41	Lagos	1951	EDL
	EDL 51	Lagos	1951	EDL
	P 1	Lagos	1956	EDL
	P 2	Lagos	1956	EDL
	P 3	Liverpool	1960	EDL
	P 4	Liverpool	1960	EDL
	P 5	Liverpool	1961	EDL
	P 6	Liverpool	1961	EDL
	P 7	Liverpool	1961	EDL
	IKOYI		1971	EDL
	FALABA	Takoradi	1952	EDL
	IJEKA	Lagos	1952	EDL
	KURAMO		1969	EDL
315512	IKOMETO		1954	EDL
315516	IKANG		1954	EDL
315515	IKOM		1954	EDL
315513	IKURU		1954	EDL
199245	ED 44		1954	EDL
196700	ED 45		1955	EDL
196701	ED 46		1955	EDL
196682	ED 50		1953	EDL
199247	ED 52		1954	EDL
199248	ED 53		1954	EDL
199249	ED 54		1954	EDL
159250	ED 55		1954	EDL
196689	ED 56		1954	EDL
196691	ED 58		1954	EDL
164285	CBR 4		1936	EDL

SL9, November 1947

463

APPENDIX II

This is the story of a great fleet of ships. Behind them is a great body of men and women, without whom the ships would have counted for nothing. We draw upon archival and family records to present a few facts about some of the many whose life's work it has been to make the ELDER DEMPSTER story.

Above left, Alexander Elder, and, right, John Dempster
Below left, The inscription on the statue of Sir Alfred Jones, right, the statue on Liverpool's waterfront.

IN MEMORY OF
SIR ALFRED LEWIS JONES K.C.M.G.
A SHIPOWNER STRENUOUS IN BUSINESS HE EN-
LARGED THE COMMERCE OF HIS COUNTRY BY HIS
MERCANTILE ENTERPRISE AND AS FOUNDER OF
THE LIVERPOOL SCHOOL OF TROPICAL MEDICINE MADE
SCIENCE TRIBUTARY TO CIVILIZATION IN WESTERN
AFRICA AND THE COLONIES OF THE BRITISH EMPIRE

Alfred L. Jones.
(Elder Dempster & Co.)

Telegrams:- FANTEE, LIVERPOOL.
FANTEE, LONDON.

London Address:-
13, Stratton Street,
Piccadilly, W.

Colonial House,
Water Street,
Liverpool.

24th May, 1907.

My dear Yardley,

I am very sorry I shall not be able to see you before you go away. You have got a fine ship and I am glad to see the passengers spoke very well of your attention and kindness to them on the voyage home. I am sure you will do all you can to make the ship comfortable this ~~xxxx~~ voyage and popular with all the people. Take care to wire the day before to where you are going to next day and arrange your speed every afternoon with the Chief Engineer with a view to economising in coal. Write us fully from all points anything that you think will interest us and which we ought to know.

I will make another voyage with you as soon as I can.

Best wishes for the voyage and that you may be as successful as you wish,

Yours faithfully,

Captain Yardley,
s.s. "Karina". (Ship No. 169)

465

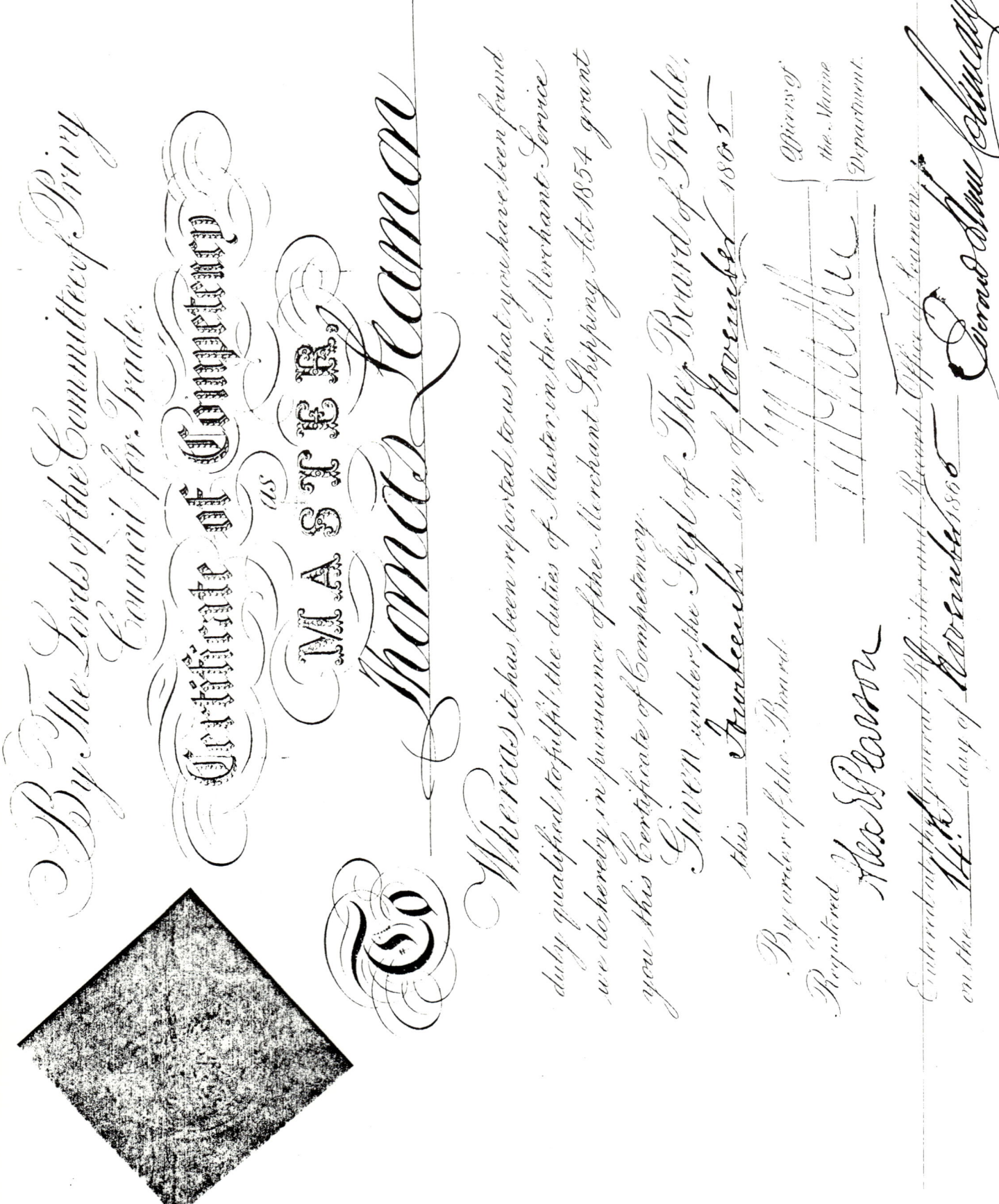

Cert of Certificate

No. 1,200 Renewed

Address of Bearer Wellesley Virk Jarrow L Dunn

Date and Place of Birth 1635 Milton Abbt. Devon

No. of Register Ticket 475,796

Signature Samuel Stephens

This Certificate is given upon an Ordinary Examination passed at London on the Sixth day of January 1864.

Every person who makes, or procures to be made, or assists in making any false Representation for the purpose of obtaining for himself or for any other person a Certificate either of Competency or Service, or who forges, assists in forging or procures to be forged or fraudulently alters, assists in fraudulently altering, or procures to be fraudulently altered, any such Certificate or any Official Copy of any such Certificate or who fraudulently makes use of any such Certificate or any Copy of any such Certificate which is forged altered, cancelled, suspended, or to which he is not justly entitled, or who fraudulently lends his Certificate to or allows the same to be used by any other person shall for each offence be deemed guilty of a Misdemean or, and may be summarily punished by imprisonment with or without hard labour for a period not exceeding Six months or by a penalty not exceeding £100, and any Master or Mate who fails to deliver up a Certificate which has been cancelled or suspended is liable to a penalty not exceeding £50.

Issued at the PORT of London on the 15ᵗʰ day of March 1865

Stove

ELDER DEMPSTER LINES, LIMITED.

3 LINNET LANE, LIVERPOOL, 17.

Ref:—STEAMSHIP.

MIDSHIPMEN—CONDITIONS OF SERVICE.

APPLICANTS if without previous nautical training, should have had a good Secondary Education of not less than four years' duration and be able to produce satisfactory references. They should be between 16 and 18 years of age, and preferably still at school. They should have attained the educational standard of School Certificate. A good mathematical knowledge (including Trigonometry) is essential.

PERIOD OF SERVICE—Boys still at school will be indentured for four years. Boys holding Passing-Out Certificates from H.M.S. "Conway," H.M.S. "Worcester" or The Nautical College, Pangbourne, will be indentured for three years. Applicants who have alternative technical training to offer will be considered on their merits. No appointment will be made without a personal interview.

MEDICAL—Applicants should be of good physique and are required to submit a doctor's certificate of fitness and freedom from organic disorder. A Board of Trade eyesight certificate is essential. Candidates are advised also to submit to an eye specialist's examination, to ensure freedom from any latent defect of eyesight which might subsequently develop. Teeth must also be in good order.

PREMIUM.—No premium is required.

WAGES.—£9 will be paid for first, £12 for second, £15 for third, and £24 for fourth years. Boys from the training establishments above will commence as second year boys.

ACCOMMODATION.—Four boys are usually berthed together in their own quarters. Meals are taken in the saloon. All bedding, towels, etc., are found by the Company.

LEAVE.—Leave of absence will be granted at the discretion of the Master abroad and the Owners at home. It is usually granted at the conclusion of each voyage.

APPOINTMENT.—The first year is to be regarded by both parties as probationary, and either party is at liberty during that period to cancel the indentures without reason assigned.

UNIFORM.—The Company's uniform will be worn. Particulars are set out in the kit list to be forwarded on appointment.

ROYAL NAVAL RESERVE.—If desired, and subject to the exigencies of the service, midshipmen may be allowed to do their training as probationary midshipmen R.N.R. during their apprenticeship.

BOOKS & INSTRUMENTS. It is compulsory for each boy to have before sailing, a copy of Brown's Signalling, Dictionary, First Aid to the injured, Gregory & Hadley's Classbook of Physics, Burton's Nautical Tables or Norie's Nautical Tables, Nicholl's Guide Vol.1, Nicholl's Seamanship and Nautical Knowledge, Reed's Seamanship & Nautical Knowledge: after first year he must add Sextant, and Binoculars. The Nautical Almanac (Abridged) for the current year must be obtained yearly.

Every candidate will be required to give an honourable undertaking that the Company will, at their option, have the first call on his services as a seagoing officer at the conclusion of his apprenticeship.

For the Guidance of Parents or Guardians of Midshipmen desirous of entering the Elder Dempster Line

The Company carries midshipmen—that is, apprentices being trained to become officers—aboard of its vessels except those in the West African coast trade. Boys who have served one of two years on a sailing ship or two years on the training ships *Conway* or *Worcester* are the most suitable, but all well educated boys of sufficient physique who are willing to work hard are eligible. It is very desirable that boys should be able to handle a boat and swim before joining the service. The boys are berthed apart from the crew, as far as possible having special rooms allotted to them—usually two in a room. As a vacant berth occurs a voyage on trial is given to the candidate next on turn. At the end of the voyage, if the candidate's conduct is satisfactory to the Company, indentures will be issued. In order to sit for a second mate's examination the candidate must prove four years' apprenticeship, four years actually at sea, or two years on the *Conway* or *Worcester* and three years at sea. Travelling expenses to join the first ship are paid by the boys, and subsequently, except when on holiday leave, by the Company. No premium is required and no salary is given. A nominal gratuity of £4 is given at the end of a satisfactory apprenticeship, and the Company gives what assistance it can by means of employment to midshipmen who have served a satisfactory apprenticeship to enable them to qualify for high grade certificates. The main difficulty in becoming an officer arises in getting employment as a junior officer to qualify for a higher certificate after apprenticeship in the mercantile marine. The Company makes a rule of retaining and promoting as far as possible the midshipmen trained in the service where they are suitable. Captains and officers are encouraged to take an interest in the midshipmen. The Company pays for the laundrying of midshipmen's underclothes. Parents and guardians are requested to be sparing in their allowance of pocket money to the boys, and it is recommended that money be paid to the boys through the captain. Money will only be advanced by the captains if previously remitted to them or the head office, Water Street, Liverpool. It is very desirable that the candidates' eyesight should be tested by the Board of Trade previous to the voyage on trial. This will be done at the cost of 1s. The voyage on trial will count towards the four years' apprenticeship provided the boy gets a certificate of service from the captain. After twelve months' service boys are required to possess a sextant. The Company has now on its steamers a number of time-expired midshipmen as officers, whose training has been found quite satisfactory.

MIDSHIPMEN are expected to make themselves conversant with the following during their apprenticeship:

Names and parts of the ship.
Arrangement and use of masts, guys, standing and running gear.
Rule of the road at sea.
Method of changing from hand to steam gear.
Method of oiling and cleaning steering gear.
Use of the hand and machine sounders.
Steering.
Compass and methods of adjustment, deviation, variation, etc.
Effect of right- and left-handed propeller when going ahead and astern.

Signalling by flag and semaphore.
The handling of boats with oars and sails.
Knotting and splicing.
The handling and qualities of ropes.
The methods of mixing oils and paints.
Keeping the ship clear of rust.
Duties of junior officer at sea and at anchor.
Dunnaging of hold and stowing of cargo.
Handling of ballast tanks.
Pipe arrangement and principle of tanks.

System of sounding tanks and bilges.
Loading and discharging cargo.
Handling heavy weights.
Treatment of iron and steel, prevention of rust.
Qualities of oil and paints.
Method of taking the sun and stars.
Method of raising and securing the anchor.
Laying course on chart.
Keeping a log book.
Tallying cargo.
Securing ports, cargo and hatches.

CLOTHES.

No special stipulation is made regarding the clothing of midshipmen, except that they be respectably dressed in navy blue and wear peak caps and Company's buttons and badge, and that uniform is only to be used on board the ship. When at sea, dungarees or old tweeds or serges should be worn. The following is reasonably necessary as a minimum:

	Cost About £ s. d.			Cost About £ s. d.			Cost About £ s. d.
Navy blue worsted twill suit, complete ...	2 5 0	Sou' Westers ... from	0 1 6	Cotton socks ... from	0 0 7½
Or West of England cloth (which is recommended as more economical) ...	2 10 0	Suit oilskins ... ,,	0 8 6	Drawers ... ,,	0 2 6
		Boots ... ... ,,	0 5 6	Singlets ... ,,	0 2 6
Dungaree suit ...	0 5 6	Cap with badge and chin strap	0 6 6	Shirts, woollen ,,	0 3 0
		Woollen socks from	0 0 10	Pith helmet or large soft straw hat for use in Tropics.	

This Indenture, made the....22nd....d
born the † ..28th....day of..March....

residing at ....8 Windsor Road, Southport

in the county of Lancaster, of the second part,
of *.........8 Windsor Rd Sou

WITNESSETH, That the said..CHARLES..ERNES[

ELDER DEMPSTER LINES, LIMITED, and the

hereby covenants that, during such time, the said

commands, and keep their secrets, and will, when req

charge, or come into the hands, of the said Apprentic

Masters, or their Assigns, nor will he consent to any

thereof; and will not embezzle or waste the Goods of

absent himself from their service without leave; n

And it is further agreed that if the Apprentice is co

injury which continuously disables him from performi

at their discretion terminate this Agreement by writ

side shall thereupon cease.

IN CONSIDERATION WHEREOF, the said Masters hereby

Assigns, will and shall use all proper means to teach

applies himself diligently thereto, of a ship's officer,[2]

and the Masters also agree to provide the said Appr

Medical and Surgical Assistance, and pay to the sai

£75. for the first year £90 for the se

† Date of Birth.

*Full Address.

[1] If there is a Surety his name is to be inserted here; but a Surety is not essential. If there is not one, the part relating to him should be struck out.

[2] This space is available for additional stipulations.

the said Apprentice providing for himself all wearing

said Masters): AND IT IS HEREBY AGREED, tha

apparel for the said Apprentice, they may deduct any

Apprentice as aforesaid: and for the performance of t

and ELDER DEMPSTER LINES, LIMITED, dot

Executors, Administrators, and Assigns, in Honour;

the said CHARLES ERNEST WOODWARD

ELDER DEMPSTER LINES, LIMITED, and the

In witness whereof, the said parties have heret

Signed, sealed, and delivered, in the presence o

Witness to Signature of Masters:

Name........R. M. William

Occupation........Clerk

Address....73, Heyville Rd Beb

Witness to Signature of Apprentice:

Name....Leonard Snowe

Occupation........Clerk

Address....73 Richland Rd Le

Witness to Signature of Surety:

Name....Leonard Snow

Occupation........Clerk

Address....73 Richland Rd

MERCANTILE MARINE OFFICE
22 MAR 1949
LIVERPOOL

Registered at the port of ....LIVERPOOL

this....22ND....day of....MARCH...., 194.9.

Signed....

NOTE.—This Indenture must be executed in duplicate, and the
either to the Registrar-General of Shipping and Seamen, T
One Indenture duly endorsed will be returned to the Maste
The Merchant Shipping Act, 1894, further requires the Masters t

Sch. 6. Form N 8A.

TICE'S INDENTURE.

March .... 194.9... between. CHARLES ERNEST WOODWARD.
.... 1931... in Liverpool .... in the county of.. Lancaster. .... now
.... of the first part, ELDER DEMPSTER LINES LIMITED, of Liverpool,

Charles Ernest Woodward

........, in the county of.. *Lancaster* .... of the third part.

..RD .... hereby voluntarily binds himself Apprentice unto the said
.. for the term of.... Four .... years from the date hereof: And the said Apprentice
.. e will faithfully serve his said Masters, and their Assigns, and obey their lawful
.. e to them true accounts of their goods and money which may be committed to the
.. at the said Apprentice will not, during the said term, do any damage to his said
.. ge being done by others, but will, if possible, prevent the same, and give warning
.. rs, or their Assigns, nor give or lend the same to others without their licence; nor
.. t Taverns or Alehouses, unless upon their business; nor play at unlawful games:
.. any offence under the Merchant Shipping Acts, or if he suffers from any sickness or
.. enants on his part herein contained for a period exceeding six months, the Masters may
.. to the Apprentice or his Surety at any time, and all obligations hereunder on either

.. with the said Apprentice, that during the said term they, the said Masters, and their
.. pprentice or cause him to be taught the business of a Seaman, and so long as he

.. h sufficient Meat, Drink, Lodging, and, except in Great Britain, with Medicine and
.. ice the sum of £.390 .... , in the manner following; (that is to say,)
.. ar £105 for the third year and £120 for the fourth and last year

.. d necessaries (except such as are herein-before specially agreed to be provided by the
.. y time, during the said term, the said Masters, or their Assigns, provide any necessary
.. perly expended thereon by them from the sums so agreed to be paid to the said
.. nts herein contained, each of them, the said.. CHARLES ERNEST WOODWARD .... ,
.. bind himself, his Heirs, Executors, and Administrators, unto the other of them, their
.. e performance of the covenants on the part of the said Apprentice herein contained,
.. ety, doth hereby bind himself, his Heirs, Executors, and Administrators unto the said
.. s, in Honour.

.. eir hands and seals, the day and year above written.

For ELDER DEMPSTER LINES LIMITED

Place of Seal.

John H. Joyce .... (Masters)
Director.

Place of Seal.

Charles Ernest Woodward .... (Apprentice)

Place of Seal.

Charles Ernest Woodward .... (Surety)

.. om the Apprentice is bound must, within seven days of the execution of the Indenture, take or transmit
.. London, E.C.3, or to the Superintendent of a Mercantile Marine Office, both Indentures to be recorded.
.. prentice.
.. above, any assignment or cancellation of the Indenture, or the death or desertion of the Apprentice.

(G.J.P. 3/47—750)

Reprinted from

The Journal of Commerce
AND
Shipping Telegraph.

SATURDAY, JANUARY 14TH, 1928.

RETIREMENT of a LIVERPOOL CAPTAIN.

PRESENTATIONS BY BROTHER SHIPMASTERS.

ACTION WHICH SAVED MONROVIA.

RECENTLY two of the commanders in the Elder Dempster Line, Captain H. A. Yardley, D.S.C., who had 35 years' service with the company, and Captain James Tyrer, who had 32 years with the company, retired, and a very interesting ceremony took place in the offices of the company at Liverpool, when both these gentlemen were made presentations by their brother shipmasters employed by the Elder Dempster Line. The presentations took the form of an inlaid mahogany grandmother chiming clock to Captain Yardley, and to Captain Tyrer a mahogany drawing-room time piece, and a canteen of cutlery, both suitably inscribed. The presentations were made by Captain G. A. Cotterell (marine superintendent), and there were also present Mr. Fred N. Harrop (office manager), Captains Johnston Hughes, J. M. Draper, T. E. Williams, P. Sola, D.S.C., J. McDowell, W. C. Baxter, and Mr. G. H. Willis (manager of the Customs Department), who acted as secretary of the fund.

Captain Cotterell said he had been requested to perform that pleasing task on behalf of their old colleagues and contemporaries in Elder Dempster and Co., and to ask them to accept the presents as a token of their sincere regard and good wishes on their retirement from active service in the company's steamers. The ceremony was mixed with a certain amount of regret for him, because he could not help but feel, in his position, that as each one retired he was losing the loyal co-operation and support which he had always had from the older and wiser masters of the firm. Those men, through mature knowledge and experience had safely and successfully run their ships for years, and had done so much to place the reputation of the masters of the firm on a high standard of efficiency, and to which Captains Yardley and Tyrer had contributed their fair share. (Hear, hear.) The company had not lost a single steamer since the war through careless or inefficient navigation, and it was a record to be proud of, and one which he hoped they would continue to maintain. (Hear, hear.) After the years they had been at sea and the many watches they had kept, Captain Yardley, when he heard the clock strike eight bells in the middle watch would have the satisfaction of knowing that it was some other fellow who had to turn out and, as far as he was concerned, he had both anchors down and his ropes coiled up.

Captain Yardley, in responding, said of the presentations made to him on retiring, he would value none greater than the one coming from his own cloth. He chose the clock in preference to a piece of plate, which very often was stowed away in green baize, and only produced on special occasions. The clock would stand out and welcome those who called upon him, and in the days to come, when it chimed, tender memories would go back to those who were following on at sea, wishing them good luck, freedom from trouble, and, eventually, a happy issue to the smoother waters of retired life. (Hear, hear.)

Captain Tyrer also suitably responded, and thanked his colleagues for their very pleasing gift.

Captain Johnston Hughes, of the Apapa, and Captain T. E. Williams, of the Aba, associated themselves with all that Captain Cotterell had said with regard to their colleagues, wishing them a long and happy retirement. They also desired to thank Mr. Willis for arranging the presentation.

Capt. Yardley is a native of Birmingham, serving his apprenticeship with Messrs. Henry Ellis and Sons, of London, in their sailing ships White Rose, Suffolk, and Oneida, in which he made voyages to South African ports and the East Indies. On securing his second mate's ticket, Capt. Yardley was appointed second officer of the Glasgow wooden barque Ringdove, in which he made one voyage to the Brazils, then to Colombo, and back home to London. She was an old vessel, and it was a case of either manning the pumps and keeping them going or the ship sinking under their feet. He then joined the Liverpool-owned barque Astracana, in which he made a voyage to Portland, Oregon, but, unfortunately, during the homeward voyage disaster overtook the vessel, as she struck a coral reef in the South Pacific. Capt. Yardley was then acting as mate of the ship, and the crew had to take to the two boats, the master taking charge of one boat and Capt. Yardley the other. For seven and a half days and nights they were drifting in the South Pacific, during which time they suffered great privations from exposure, thirst, and hunger, both boats reaching the island of Tahiti within 24 hours of each other. On arrival at the island, the shipwrecked crew were very hospitably received and treated by the natives, and also by some Frenchmen who were in residence on the island. Capt. Yardley then proceeded from the island to San Francisco as a D.B.S., and came home overland to Liverpool. He then joined the Aberdeen ship Yallarol as second officer, in which he made one voyage, and then joined Messrs. C. T. Bowring and Co., of Liverpool, the principal at the present time being the ex-Lord Mayor of Liverpool (Sir F. C. Bowring), with whom he remained for about three years, serving in their barque Viola and also in their steamers.

Capt. Yardley passed for master in September, 1888, and for extra master in May, 1889, when only 27 years of age, without any tuition, never having attended a navigation school for any of his examinations. It was in June, 1892, that Capt. Yardley joined the Elder Dempster Line as second officer of the steamer Boma, and was appointed to command in May, 1898, since when he has commanded many of the Elder Dempster steamers. He holds the Distinguished Service Cross, Lloyd's Silver Medal, the Liverpool Shipwreck and

THIRTY-FIVE YEARS IN THE WEST AFRICAN TRADE.

CAPT. H. A. YARDLEY, D.S.C.

Humane Society's Medal and Diploma, and a silver cigarette case presented by the Lords Commissioners of the Admiralty as a memento of services rendered during the war 1914-1918, in the conveyance of confidential mails overseas. He is also a Knight Official of the Liberian Humane Order of African Redemption, most of these having been awarded to him in recognition of the fight he put up against a German submarine off Monrovia, Liberia, during the war, when in command of the Burutu.

RESCUE OF WEST AFRICAN NATIVES.

Captain Yardley was the recipient of a life-saving certificate on vellum, presented to him by the Liverpool Shipwreck and Humane Society, in recognition of his meritorious and humane services in rescuing four West African natives from their overturned canoe, which had capsized in a heavy tornado on the 8th May, 1925. The presentation took place at the offices of the Mercantile Marine Service Association, Tower-building, Liverpool.

The story of the rescue for which the award was made is as follows:—When the steamer Appam was nearing Sierra Leone, four West African natives were discovered drifting on the bottom of an overturned canoe. The canoe had left Sierra Leone with the four men and a woman as its occupants, and at ten o'clock at night, during a heavy tornado, the canoe capsized, and the woman was drowned. The four men scrambled on the top, and were drifting about until 1 30 the following afternoon, which was Saturday, May 9th, when they were sighted by the Appam, and their signals of distress responded to.

Captain Yardley navigated his vessel with consummate skill, running right up alongside the canoe, and taking the men off with life lines. They were in a thoroughly exhausted condition, as they had been adrift for $15\frac{1}{2}$ hours, under a strong tropical sun, and would undoubtedly have lost their lives but for the timely appearance of the Appam.

Captain Yardley is a very old and valued member of the Mercantile Marine Service Association.

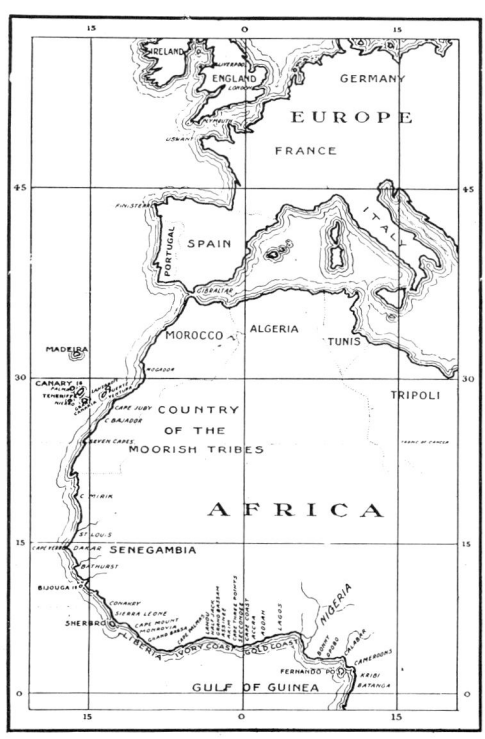

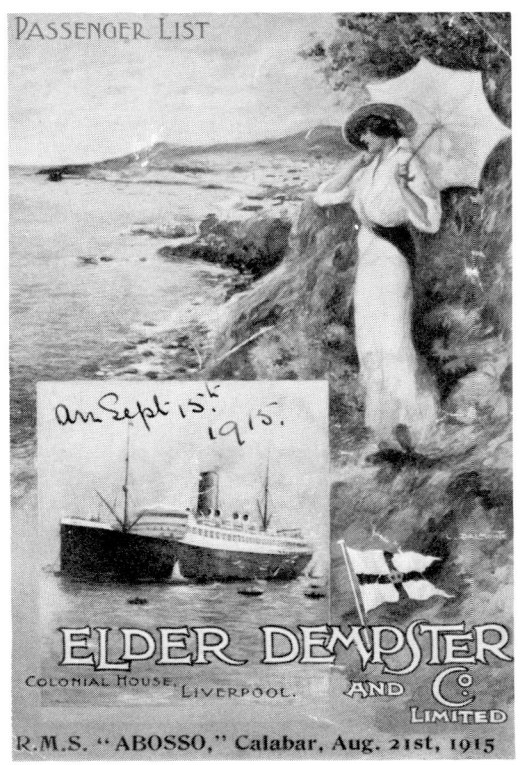

Cover of an ABOSSO (ship No. 213) passenger list, of August 1915, when Captain Yardley commanded her

473

The Hughes Family

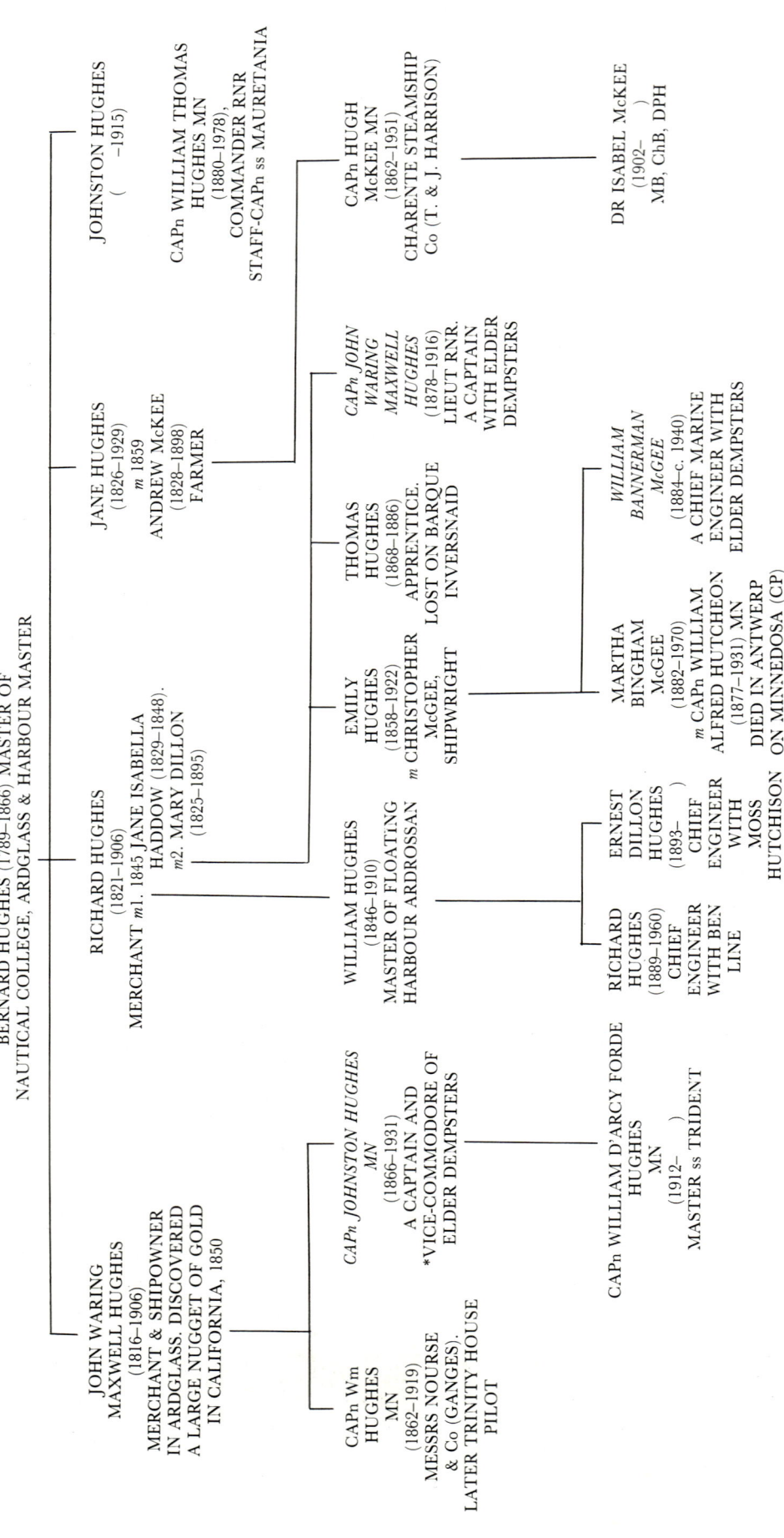

BERNARD HUGHES (1789–1866) MASTER OF
NAUTICAL COLLEGE, ARDGLASS & HARBOUR MASTER

JOHN WARING
MAXWELL HUGHES
(1816–1906)
MERCHANT & SHIPOWNER
IN ARDGLASS. DISCOVERED
A LARGE NUGGET OF GOLD
IN CALIFORNIA, 1850

RICHARD HUGHES
(1821–1906)
MERCHANT m1. 1845 JANE ISABELLA
HADDOW (1829–1848).
m2. MARY DILLON
(1825–1895)

JANE HUGHES
(1826–1929)
m 1859
ANDREW McKEE
(1828–1898)
FARMER

JOHNSTON HUGHES
(–1915)

CAPn WILLIAM THOMAS
HUGHES MN
(1880–1978),
COMMANDER RNR
STAFF-CAPn ss MAURETANIA

CAPn Wm
HUGHES
MN
(1862–1919)
MESSRS NOURSE
& Co (GANGES).
LATER TRINITY HOUSE
PILOT

CAPn JOHNSTON HUGHES
MN
(1866–1931)
A CAPTAIN AND
*VICE-COMMODORE OF
ELDER DEMPSTERS

WILLIAM HUGHES
(1846–1910)
MASTER OF FLOATING
HARBOUR ARDROSSAN

EMILY
HUGHES
(1858–1922)
m CHRISTOPHER
McGEE,
SHIPWRIGHT

THOMAS
HUGHES
(1868–1886)
APPRENTICE.
LOST ON BARQUE
INVERSNAID

CAPn JOHN
WARING
MAXWELL
HUGHES
(1878–1916)
LIEUT RNR.
A CAPTAIN
WITH ELDER
DEMPSTERS

CAPn HUGH
McKEE MN
(1862–1951)
CHARENTE STEAMSHIP
Co (T. & J. HARRISON)

CAPn WILLIAM D'ARCY FORDE
HUGHES
MN
(1912–)
MASTER ss TRIDENT

RICHARD
HUGHES
(1889–1960)
CHIEF
ENGINEER
WITH BEN
LINE

ERNEST
DILLON
HUGHES
(1893–)
CHIEF
ENGINEER
WITH MOSS
HUTCHISON

MARTHA
BINGHAM
McGEE
(1882–1970)
m CAPn WILLIAM
ALFRED HUTCHEON
(1877–1931) MN
DIED IN ANTWERP
ON MINNEDOSA (CP)

WILLIAM
BANNERMAN
McGEE
(1884–c. 1940)
A CHIEF MARINE
ENGINEER WITH
ELDER DEMPSTERS

DR ISABEL McKEE
(1902–)
MB, ChB, DPH

*Note—The title of Commodore was not officially instituted until 1948
(see page 476). Captain Johnston Hughes was therefore second senior
Captain in the fleet.

Prepared by Martin J. Crossley Evans, BA,
grandson of Dr Isabel McKee

474

JOHNSTON HUGHES (1866–1931)

Master Mariners Certificate 018762 (Liverpool 1892)

VOLTA	15 voyages	1893–1896
AXIM	3 voyages	1896–1897

1st Command

ss TENERIFFE	6 voyages	1897–1899
ss AXIM	1 voyage	1894
ss BOMA	1 voyage	1894
ss ROQUELLE	1 voyage	1894
ss BONNY	1 voyage	1900
ss ACCRA	7 voyages	1900–1902
ss BANANA	1 voyage	1902
ss ACCRA	8 voyages	1902–1904
ss BATANGA	1 voyage	1905
ss MURAJI	1 voyage	1905
ss AKABO	5 voyages	1905–1906
ss NIGERIA	4 voyages	1907–1909
ss ARO	2 voyages	1908
ss NIGERIA	3 voyages	1908–1909
ss MENDI	16 voyages	1909–1912
ss MANDINGO	1 voyage	1912
ss ELMINA	39 voyages	1912–1920
ss ZARIA	1 voyage	1921
ss ABA	31 voyages	1921–1926
ss APAPA	18 voyages	1927–1930

John Waring Maxwell Hughes (1878–1916)

Master Mariner's Certificate 03537 (Liverpool)

1st Command

COALING	9 voyages	1906–1910
MONTENEGRO	8 voyages	1911–1913
BENIN	2 voyages	1914

Full time service in RNR from December 1914. Killed in action.

Captain Johnston Hughes on the bridge of **ELMINA** *(ship No. 206), 1912 (Photo M. J. Crossley Evans)*

Captain J. W. M. Hughes in 1912 (Photo M. J. Crossley Evans)

Captain J. W. M. Hughes and Officers of **COALING** *(ship No. 177)*

Commodore J. J. Smith

JIM COWDEN (left) outlines the careers of the six Masters who held the title 'Commodore of the Fleet' between 1948, when the rank was instituted, and 1966, when it lapsed with the amalgamation of Elder Dempster and Blue Funnel fleets.

IRISH-BORN Captain John Joseph Smith was the first to hold the title 'Commodore of the Fleet' when he raised his flag on board the mail ship 'Apapa' in 1948.

He first went to sea before the mast in a three-masted full-rigged ship, 'Barcore', and then in a four-masted barque, 'Balasore'. After a spell with the Irish Fishery Cruiser Patrol he sailed as Second Officer in 'City of Cadiz', trading between Ireland and the Continent.

He joined Elder Dempster in 1914 as Third Officer of 'Obuasi' sailing for West Africa. When war broke out, 'Obuasi' was commandeered as a transport ship. She carried troops from Accra to Keta and Lome – which had been captured by the British – and then she brought German

158th American Brigade to take part in the attack on North Africa.

Later, Commodore Smith recalled:

"The Americans were all from the Middle West – and none of them had seen a ship before.

"Suddenly my cabin door burst open and the American C.O. appeared, looking wildly excited. 'Say, Cap.,' he shouted, 'one of my boys has just told

COMMODORES

prisoners to Southampton.

In 1917 J. J. Smith was an officer in 'Abura' when she was torpedoed by a German submarine off Ireland. He and the other survivors spent a week in the lifeboats before they finally landed at Larne.

His promotion to Master came in 1934 when he was appointed to command 'Appam'. Later he took over 'Calabar' from the builders.

The Second World War brought J. J. Smith even more experience of submarine warfare – at the receiving end. He was on board the old 'Accra' when she was torpedoed off the Irish coast.

During the war he was in command of 'Sobo' in a convoy which carried the

me he has seen a big shark passing by. What the hell are you going to do about it?'

"Not thinking, I said: 'One? – there are lots of them around here. Why worry?' This seemed really to un-nerve him.

"He replied: 'Well, I can tell you brother, if we're hit none of your boys will see the lifeboats – you fellows can have the landing barges.'

"Apparently he thought it would take a day to get the lashings off the barges. I had to show him how quickly they could be freed by touching a stern hawse slip.

"At that he felt obviously relieved and said: 'Well, I take my hat off to you

Commodore W. Munt

'Aureol' (14,800 tons gross), the handsomest ship ever to wear Elder's colours, was commanded by four of the Commodores.

Cargo/passenger liner 'Tarkwa' which twice flew the Commodore's flag.

OF THE FLEET

dog-gone Limeys'.

"The thought had evidently not occurred to him that if a torpedo hit us there would have been no question of taking to the boats. The cargo of high octane fuel, barrels of oil, bombs and ammunition needed but a spark for the 'Sobo' to disintegrate.

"On the day fixed for the attack, an enemy plane did drop a torpedo. But with the helm hard a-port 'Sobo' turned so quickly the torpedo shot alongside about ten feet off.

Bombing

"We landed our troops 15 miles from Algiers and not a single shot was fired from shore. The following day we went to Algiers which had been captured by our forces. That first night in the anchorage was a bad one with the German and Italian air forces coming over in hundreds, bombing and blasting.

"But 'Sobo' kept clear of everything – though some bombs fell very close – and we did not lose even a light bulb." In fact, the ship survived until 1963, when she was sold for breaking up.

Commodore Smith's last command was to the Company's new flagship, the mail ship 'Aureol'. After 46 years' seafaring he retired in 1954.

His successor as Commodore was **Captain William Munt,** a Yorkshireman, who had joined Elder Dempster in 1909 at the age of 16.

During the First World War he joined

Commodore C. H. Sweeny

the RNR and volunteered for special service in Q-boats.

Q-boat work was generally reckoned one of the most dangerous services. Merchant ships were fitted with concealed guns; and their crews were dressed as ordinary merchant seamen.

The job of a Q-boat was to ply along trade routes looking as peaceful as possible while keeping a sharp look-out for enemy submarines. As soon as a U-boat was sighted the bulwarks were let down and the guns came up.

Q-boats played no small part in preventing Britain from being blockaded and the people from running short of supplies.

During William Munt's service in the Q-boat HMS 'Saros', the ship claimed a total of seven U-boats sunk and six other

enemy vessels severely crippled.

He did not go through the war entirely unscathed for he was torpedoed in the Straits of Messina in 1916.

When the war ended he rejoined Elder Dempster in the hospital ship 'Ebani', taking South African troops home and returning to Rotterdam with German prisoners-of-war. His first command was 'Egori' in 1936.

Commodore Munt retired in 1959. When he sailed out of Takoradi harbour on his last voyage home in command of 'Aureol', the Ghana Railway and Harbours Authority arranged for impressive farewell ceremonies in his honour.

All ships in port sounded their sirens and the fleet of tugs operating in the harbour formed an escort as the vessel left. A Ghana Naval Detachment was stationed at the harbour entrance and buglers of the Ghana Regiment sounded farewell.

The next Commodore was **Captain Charles Herbert Sweeny.** He had joined Elder Dempster in 1919 as Fourth Officer in 'Gaboon'. His first command was 'Daru' in 1940.

Two of his other wartime commands were sunk by enemy action – 'Mattawin' off the American East Coast in 1942 and 'Mary Slessor' which struck a mine the following year while in convoy from Gibraltar to UK.

After Commodore Sweeny's retirement in 1960 the title 'Commodore of the Fleet' passed to **Captain Ernest Kingan,** Master of the cargo/passenger ship

'Tarkwa', operating on the Liverpool/Port Harcourt express service.

With 46 years' Elder Dempster service already under his belt, he preferred to raise the Commodore's flag on board 'Tarkwa' rather than transfer to the Company's mail ships.

Ernie Kingan had joined Elder Dempster in 1914 as an office boy in the timetable department. He transferred to the sea-going staff in 1919 when he was appointed an apprentice in 'Roda' which was originally a German-owned ship taken by Britain as a 'prize of war'.

In 1945 came his first command, 'Bourbonnais', a French vessel placed under the management of Elder Dempster Lines during the war years. Two years later he took command of 'Calumet', in which he had served as Chief Officer from 1935. He retired in 1962.

Looking back on his career, Commodore Kingan recalled that refrigeration in some ships in the 1920s was limited to ice-boxes.

"It was a great occasion when the ship was stopped on the homeward voyage in the middle of the Cape Blanco fishing fleet," he said.

Bartering

"The bartering of various ship's stores for fresh fish gave the ship's company the finest meal of the voyage."

Recalling the days before air-conditioned ships, he said: "The shutting down of the generators (and fans) at 10 pm in port, especially in the Creeks was not conducive to a good nights' rest".

'Tarkwa' was again to fly the Commodore's flag when Liverpool-born **Captain William Rowlands** was appointed Commodore in January, 1963.

He joined the Company from T. & J. Harrison as Fourth Officer of the motorship 'Aba'. Later he was engaged for about eight years on the company's Canadian services.

His first command was 'David Livingstone' in 1940. He was Master of 'Daru' when she was bombed and sunk off the south-east coast of Ireland. All the crew were rescued by escorting destroyers. Commodore Rowlands retired in 1964 after 32 years with Elder Dempster.

His successor – and the last to hold the title Commodore – was Merseysider **Captain T. E. M. Jenkins.** He was the first Commodore not to have served in junior ranks with the Company.

He had joined Elder Dempster Lines (Canada) as Master in 1945 from the Jamaica Direct Fruit Line. He was Master of the latter Company's 'Jamaica Pioneer'

Commodore E. Kingan

Commodore W. Rowlands

Commodore T. E. M. Jenkins

when she was torpedoed and sunk in the North Atlantic in 1940.

In 1962 he was Master of 'Aureol' when she carried President and Mrs. Tubman back to Liberia following their State Visit to Britain.

Commodore Jenkins' retirement in 1966 co-incided with the amalgamation of the Elder Dempster and Blue Funnel fleets and thus the title 'Commodore of the Fleet' lapsed.

Of the six Commodores, only one survives – Commodore Sweeny who lives on the Wirral and actively supports Elder Dempster Pensioner Association events.

Captain Munt
Commodore of the Fleet

COMMODORE WILLIAM MUNT was born on August 2, 1893, in the city of York. His father, a doctor, served in the R.A.M.C. and was lost in the South African War in 1899.

Although he did not come from seafaring people, the call of the sea was in him as long as he can remember and he was only sixteen when in January 1909 he joined Elder Dempster. Apart from war service he has been with the Company ever since. He took his Second Mate's certificate in July 1913 and was appointed Third Officer of R.M.S. *Kavina*. Later he served in the s.s. *Egba* and the s.s. *Eloby*. In these ships he got to know the West African trade which has been the scene of his life work ever since.

He was twenty-one when the First World War broke out and at once joined the R.N.R. Having taken his First Mate's certificate he was appointed to the rank of Lieutenant, and joined H.M.S. *Crescent* for prize crew duties. Early in 1915 he volunteered for special service on the Q-boats. While he was serving aboard H.M.S. *Saros*, under the command of Commander R. C. Smart, R.N., his ship was responsible for sinking seven German U-boats. He took part in six other engagements when the enemy vessels were severely crippled. Q-boat service was generally reckoned the most dangerous service in the First World War. Merchant ships were fitted with concealed guns. Their crews were dressed as ordinary merchant seamen, and the business of the Q-boats was to ply along the trade routes looking as peaceful as possible while keeping a sharp look-out for enemy submarines. As soon as a German U-boat was sighted the bulwarks were let down and the guns came up. They played no small part in the First World War in keeping the approaches to Britain free for merchant traffic and preventing the British Isles from being blockaded and the British people from starving.

Commodore Munt often took part in a novel method of attack when they would tow a British submarine under the ship's bottom on a chain cable bridle. The submarine could be slipped from the bridle instantaneously to attack an enemy submarine. 'Any young officer looking for excitement,' says Commodore Munt, 'got it in the Q-boat service.'

He did not go through the First World War entirely unscathed for he was torpedoed in the Straits of Messina in June 1916. He returned to service aboard H.M.S. *Excellent*.

After attending gunnery school for further extensive training and passing his Master's certificate, Commodore Munt was appointed to another Q-boat, H.M.S. *Hareldo*, the ship on which he was to remain until the end of the war. There he was able to do excellent work, in the Mediterranean particularly, shadowing convoys and picking up survivors.

When the war came to an end he could have stayed on in the Royal Navy but preferred to rejoin Elder Dempster. His first appointment was to the hospital ship s.s. *Ebani*, taking South African troops home and bringing back German prisoners to Rotterdam.

He was later appointed Chief Officer on the s.s. *Bathurst* under the command of Captain A. E. Webster. He recalls that in October 1919 during a passage out to West Africa they towed an American vessel, the s.s. *Atlantic City*, into Funchal, Madeira. The s.s. *Atlantic City* had developed engine trouble.

During his time as Chief Officer in the s.s. *Boma* he towed the s.s. *Bendu*, which had lost her propeller, a long way up to Las Palmas.

In November 1936 he was appointed Master in s.s. *Egori*, and subsequently served on the M.V.'s. *Daru, Deido, Sobo, Henry Stanley, Tamele*, and later on the Royal Mail ships, M.V. *Apapa* and M.V. *Accra*. On September 15, 1954, he was appointed to the command of the M.V. *Aureol*, and on April 14, 1955, he became Commodore of the Elder Dempster fleet.

From Sea *Magazine*

Profile

The late

Captain Herbert Flowerdew

IT came as a great shock to his many friends when they learned that Captain Herbert Flowerdew, Commander of the M.V. *Apapa*, had died with such tragic suddenness in the early hours of June 28 when the ship was approaching Takoradi.

Captain Flowerdew began his long career with the Company when he joined the s.s. *Konakry* as Apprentice in 1912. He completed his apprenticeship in the *Monarch*, *Kwarra* and *Kaduna* on the Canada-Cape service. Soon after he obtained his Second Mate's Certificate he was appointed Third Officer of the s.s. *Salagd*. He remained in this capacity in the same ship until the latter part of 1916, when he joined the R.N.R. as a Sub-Lieutenant and saw active service in several spheres of the First World War.

At the end of the war he returned to the Company's service and was appointed Second Officer of the s.s. *Itajahy*, and subsequently in this capacity and later as Chief Officer he served in many ships of the Company's fleet. While he was serving as Chief Officer of the *Adda* he received his first command, and joined s.s. *Eboe* as Master. Captain Flowerdew later saw service as Master in many Elder Dempster ships, and when in command of the s.s. *Calumet* on government duties he was awarded the O.B.E. for meritorious services.

Bert Flowerdew, as he was affectionately known to all his contemporaries, had, by his quiet, retiring and unassuming manner and kindly nature, drawn around him a host of friends, both ashore and afloat, and he will always be remembered by them for his high integrity and sterling character. He had been a fine seaman and shipmate during his forty years' service.

Messages from His Excellency the Governor of the Gold Coast and Captain J. E. S. de Graft Hayford, Chairman of the Gold Coast Cocoa Marketing Board, were among the many expressions of sympathy received on Captain Flowerdew's death.

Captain Flowerdew was a Member of the Honourable Company of Master Mariners and a Younger Brother of Trinity House. He always took a warm interest in the training of the Company's midshipmen, and we are grateful to record that Captain Flowerdew's sister, his nearest relation, has presented all his nautical instruments and equipment to the Company's Cadet ship *Obuasi* for the use of the midshipmen serving in her, and as a permanent memorial to her brother.

From Sea *Magazine*

Commodore H. R. Lane

Marine Superintendent,
Elder Dempster Lines Limited

(Photograph by James Bacon)

AFTER leaving Liverpool Collegiate School, H. R. Lane joined H.M.S. *Conway* as Cadet in 1914. He was aboard when the *Conway* broke from her moorings off Rock Ferry and had to be towed into Birkenhead Dock. In 1916 young Lane obtained his Extra Certificate and left the *Conway* (he was then Senior Cadet Captain) and joined the Royal Navy as Midshipman, R.N.R. He saw service with the 10th Cruiser Squadron in the North Atlantic and on Arctic Patrol in H.M.S. *Moldavia*. He was also in H.M.S. *Kildary*, one of the famous 'Kil' ships, on a roving commission from the Mediterranean to Murmansk in Northern Russia.

After demobilization in 1919, Mr Lane obtained his Second Mate's Certificate and joined Messrs J. Chambers & Company as Third Officer. Two years later, after passing his Mate's Certificate, he was promoted to Second Officer and sailed in Chambers's Eastern Service from New York round the world and back to New York.

Returning home early in 1923 Mr Lane obtained his Master's Certificate and then joined the Cunard Steam Ship Company as Third Officer, serving in R.M.S. *Carmania*, *Laconia* and *Carinthia*. These ships were employed mainly on holiday cruises. During this period Mr Lane was promoted Lieutenant R.N.R. and rejoined the Royal Navy for 18 months, serving in destroyers and in the submarines H.43, M.3 and L.26.

In 1928 Mr Lane joined Elder Dempster & Company, Ltd., and sailed as Second Officer in the *Gambia*, *Patani* and *Aba*. After being promoted to Chief Officer, he served in the *Bompata*, *Eboe*, *Egba*, *Mattawin*, *Swedru*, *Aba*, *Adda* and *Abosso*.

A few days before war was declared in 1939, Commander Lane, R.N.R., as he then was (having been promoted in January, 1938), sailed in the *Abosso* (commanded by Captain P. Sola, D.S.O.). It was an exciting departure from Liverpool, as the *Abosso* was full to capacity with men ordered to return to their posts on the Coast. The ship was blacked out and carried a 4-inch A.A. gun and a 6-inch gun aft with Royal Marine gunners. As the ship left Madeira, war was declared and all hands and many passengers were employed painting the ship grey overall.

Commander Lane left the *Abosso* to relieve the late Captain Harding in the *Bodnant* on a coastal voyage. He was called up for active service with the Royal Navy in August, 1940, but after an appeal from the Company he did not join the Royal Navy until October, 1940, when he was appointed to H.M.S. *Spartitate* for duty as Commodore of Coastal Convoys (Glasgow to Methil Northern Route).

In March, 1941, Commander Lane was appointed to H.M.S. *Zaza* (Liverpool Outer Defences) and after this ship was paid off in September of the same year, he was appointed to H.M.S. *President IV* for East Coast Convoy duty (Southend to Methil). After being lent to the Admiralty in the spring of 1943 for the North Africa Invasion, Commander Lane was appointed to H.M.S. *Dinosaur* for 'Combined Operations' for command of L.C.T.s. In June, 1943, he was awarded the O.B.E. (Military Division) for his services in East Coast Convoys and was promoted to Captain, R.N.R. He was appointed to H.M.S. *Eaglet* soon afterwards, and promoted to Commodore R.N.R. for Ocean Convoys. In June, 1944, Commodore Lane took part in the invasion of Normandy with the American Forces, and afterwards returned to Ocean Convoys. As Commodore he had charge of one of the largest convoys (172 ships) to sail from the U.K. to U.S.A.

From Sea *Magazine*

LOOKING BACK—A LIFETIME AT SEA

by
Commodore E. Kingan

COMMODORE Ernest Kingan retired from Elder Dempster Lines Limited on December 31, 1962, after nearly 49 years' service with the Company. He began his sea-going career in 1919. It is only in retrospect, he writes, that the great changes in the Fleet can be realized

Commodore Kingan aboard M.V. Tarkwa, *whose officers and crew presented him with a cocktail set to mark his retirement*

THE transition was a slow one from the triple expansion coal-burners of my early days to the modern diesel vessels with air-conditioning, swimming baths, refrigeration and modern navigational aids. The refrigeration in some of the ships in which I sailed as an apprentice was limited to ice-boxes; and it was a great occasion, homeward bound, when the ship was stopped in the middle of the Cape Blanco fishing fleet and the bartering of various ship's stores for fresh fish gave the ship's company the finest meal of the voyage. Air-conditioning was still very much in the future, and the shutting down of the generators at 10 p.m. in port, especially in the Creeks, was not conducive to a good night's rest.

The training of apprentices was a somewhat hit-or-miss affair, instruction depending substantially on whatever free time the Officers could afford. The opening of River House and the building of the Cadet ship *Fourah Bay* marked a new epoch.

From its earliest days Elder Dempster has played no small part in the development of West Africa; and the great changes in the ports, from rickety traders' jetties to modern quays with cargo-handling facilities, are well within my memory. Our vessels carried (and still carry) most of the constructional material, and it called for considerable ingenuity on the part of the ship's Officers, particularly with heavy lifts necessitating the rigging of a spar by the ship, to land the material ashore with the ship lying yards from the beach, against a mudbank. Our present vessels' up-to-date cargo gear has greatly simplified these operations.

Before the establishment of the Government Hydrographic Departments the lifting and re-laying of navigational buoys was carried out by the Company's vessels. I recall being left perched on the top of the St. Ann's Shoals buoy when, after replacing it, I left the *Egori* in a surf-boat to light the new buoy. There was a change of tide and the ship began to swing dangerously near. Captain H. Watson decided to heave up and get clear. It was with very mixed feelings that I saw the *Egori* apparently steaming away and leaving me like the man in the Bovril advertisement, except that the sinking feeling was uppermost.

The development and prosperity of West Africa will continue and I am certain that Elder Dempster Lines, not only as a shipping company but also as a medium for the training of Africans, will play its part ably for many years to come.

THE YEARS BETWEEN

COMMODORE Kingan joined the Company as office boy in 1914 in the old Time-table Department.

In 1919 he was aboard the Roda *as an apprentice and was appointed 4th officer of the* Appam *in 1922.*

Two years later he became 3rd Officer of the Biafra *and in another two years 2nd Officer of the* Benin.

In 1935 he joined the Calumet *as Chief Officer, and his first command was the ammunition ship* Bourbonnais *based at Freetown, Sierra Leone, in 1945.*

From 1947, when he returned to the Calumet *as Master, he has commanded many of the Elder Dempster Lines' ships, the last one being the* Tarkwa, *which he first joined in 1958.*

When appointed Commodore of the Line in November, 1960, he chose to remain in the Tarkwa *in preference to the larger passenger liners.*

Born in 1900, Commodore Kingan lives in Queen's Avenue, Meols, Wirral. He has a wife and a son.

From Sea *Magazine*

Mr F. Killick

FORTY-TWO years with Elder Dempster Lines is the distinguished record of service of Mr Fred Killick, Chief Steward of our Cadet ship, the M.V. *Obuasi*.

In the course of these forty-two years Fred Killick was shipwrecked three times. In 1928, when he was Chief Steward of the *Bonny*, the ship was wrecked off Cape Palmas, Liberia. Eventually she became a total loss. The stand-by ship had only an ice box and no refrigerator and therefore it was impossible to store the foodstuffs from the wreck. Mr Killick recalls with a chuckle how, for three weeks, the crew dined like City Liverymen off the salvaged food and he himself had the time of his life producing menus which would have done credit to the maitre d'hotel in a first class restaurant.

In September 1939 Mr Killick was on board the *Mattawin* on the Canada–Cape run. The *Mattawin* was torpedoed by the enemy. Some three years later he experienced his third shipwreck, when the *New Columbia* was also torpedoed.

Fred Killick's first voyage was as a cabin boy at a salary of £2 a month on the s.s. *Kish*, owned by the Clyde Shipping Company. Every other voyage he has made has been under the Elder Dempster Lines' flag.

His first job with us was as assistant cook on the *Batanga*. On his arrival in West Africa he caught malaria. He vowed he had had enough and would never go back to the Coast again. Early in 1919, however, he sailed as second cook on the *Akabo*, and was soon promoted to Chief Cook. In rapid succession he was appointed to the *Bathurst*, the *Bata*, the *Onitsha*, the *Gaboon*, the *Boma*, and the *Benin*, and eventually sailed as Chief Steward on the *Warri* in 1924. After being shipwrecked in the *Bonny*, he returned to Liverpool to join the *Bereby* and remained with her until she was laid up in 1931. He saw further service in the *Dagomba*, the *Macgregor Laird* and the *Dixcove*.

Apart from his two personal experiences of submarine warfare, Mr Killick spent most of the war on board the *Calgary*. After the war he saw further service on the *Cochrane* and the *Sulima*. In 1952 he was appointed to his present position on board the Cadet ship.

If seafarers in general have a nice taste in food as well as healthy appetites, the appetites of the cadets are gargantuan. The proof of his success is the fact that there is no one on board the *Obuasi* more popular with the midshipmen than the Chief Steward. Last year the cadets were so thrilled with their Christmas dinner, that when—at last!—the meal was over, the cadets attempted to chair Mr Killick and to carry him round the deck in triumphant procession. The attempt had to be abandoned because Mr Killick is no bantam weight, but the cheers of the cadets for the Chief Steward rang out across the water and must still ring pleasantly in his ears.

Mr Killick is an amateur painter of more than a little merit. We reproduce here a photograph of one of his paintings of a charming corner in Positano, Italy. Most of his paintings he gives away, either to his fellow seafarers or to friends he has made during his long service.

From Sea Magazine

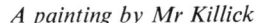

A painting by Mr Killick

Capt. Alec Smith

CAPTAIN ALEC SMITH, nautical adviser to Elder Dempster Lines, retired in September 1959 after forty-three years' continuous service. His story, like that of many, begins on the Clyde. He served his apprenticeship with Gow Harrison and Company. They owned tramps, and it was on tramps that young Alec Smith went to sea and, indeed, became Third Officer.

In those days, just before the first world war, every tramp voyage was a kind of saga, an adventure into the unknown. They covered the seven seas, greeting each port as it came to them, never knowing the destination of the next cargo they would pick up and, what was worse, never knowing when the ship would take on a cargo homeward bound.

August 4, 1914, found the ship on which young Alec Smith was serving in the Indian Ocean, running the Easting down, bound for Auckland, New Zealand. It was only when they arrived there that the crew learned that the Great War had at last broken the uneasy peace in Europe, and that the trampling, drilling German foolery had spilled across the Belgian frontier. She unloaded her cargo of oil at Dunedin, and the ship was requisitioned by the New Zealand Government and converted into a troopship which sailed from Wellington, just before Christmas 1914. She carried with her a company of the New Zealand Light Horse, and eight hundred horses on deck and in the 'tween decks. At Albany, Western Australia, they made a rendezvous with Australian troops, and, escorted by the submarine E.2, began a voyage to an unknown destination.

A few weeks of anxious watchfulness were to pass before she reached Alexandria—although the *Emden* which had clearly established itself as the terror of the Indian and Pacific Oceans had already been despatched by the Australian light cruiser *Sydney*.

The ship came on to London, and young Smith was to see at first hand the disastrous landing at the Dardanelles before he was appointed Third Officer of the *Vienna* and the *Vancouver*.

In January 1917 Smith had had enough tramping, and presented himself to the Marine Superintendent of Elder Dempster and Company, asking for an appointment as an officer. He had already taken his Second Mate's certificate. He joined the s.s. *Warri* as Third Officer, and fourteen months later joined the *Kaduna* in the Gulf of Mexico trade.

After four voyages he obtained his Mate's certificate, and was appointed Second Officer of the s.s. *Melville*, trading between Canada and the Cape. After service on the s.s. *Monarch* and the s.s. *Egba* he was transferred to the M.V. *Aba* as Second Officer. The *Aba* was the first motor passenger-liner in the history of shipping, and it was while serving on her that he received promotion to the rank of Chief Officer.

He served on the old *Benin*, on the *Biafra* for eight years, enjoyed temporary command of the *Edward Blyden*, and then on the *Aba* and the *Abosso*. Captain Smith pays many tributes to the Commander of the *Abosso*, Captain J. C. Shooter, and it was while serving under him that he received his first regular command on board the M.V. *Alfred Jones* in February 1937. Successively he served on the *Calabar*, the *Mary Slessor*, and took over the *Sangara* from Scott's of Greenock, and was again transferred to the *Abosso*.

But once again the peaceful trade of the merchant mariner, the peaceful service of the people's need, was overshadowed by war. Elder Dempster's *Edward Blyden* was taken over by the Admiralty and converted

New Elder Dempster Offices at Ibadan

Mr K. H. Postance of Ibadan sent us the two photographs reproduced above showing the exterior of the Elder Dempster Agencies office at Ibadan, and (above, left) a corner of one of the pleasantly furnished administrative offices

PROFILE—*Concluded*

into an A.S.I.S. with Captain Smith in command. Her destination was, for security reasons, a secret, so that even the Company had no idea of her whereabouts, until the Admiralty reluctantly confided that she was in Loch Sween in the West of Scotland. Marauding enemy submarines became more and more daring, and she was removed to Loch Goil where she remained until she was ordered to proceed to the Near East.

Captain Smith's next appointment was to the *Sobo* and then to the *Sansu*, before he took command of the *Banfora*, a French ship 'borrowed' from the Vichy French and managed by Elder Dempster for the Ministry of War Transport. It was an arduous time, and in twelve months he took trips to Iceland, to and from Canada, to the Suez Canal via the Cape of Good Hope, and returning from Suez to the Clyde by way of India, Kenya, the Cape, Brazil, the West Indies and New York. It seems scarcely credible in peace time, but such were the detours of war.

Captain Smith had earned the gratitude of his country, and it was especially tragic that on his return to the United Kingdom 'they brought him bitter news to hear, and bitter tears to shed'. His son was on board the *Henry Stanley* which was torpedoed with the loss of all hands, except for the Master, Captain Jones, who was taken prisoner on board the enemy submarine.

Captain Smith was seconded to the Ocean Salvage and Towage Company as Salvage Officer, and went out to Freetown to recover ingots from the Dutch vessel *Springfontein*. This he accomplished with characteristic skill, and in between he managed to salvage a lot of copper from the *Mokambo*.

Growing tired of salvage, Captain Smith returned to the Company's service in command of the *Mary Kingsley*, took over the *Salaga* from Hawthorn Leslie's yard, became Staff Captain of the *Accra* and finally Captain. It was while serving as Captain of the *Accra* that he was appointed to the position of Nautical Adviser to the Company, from which position he has just retired after nearly twelve years' service.

Captain Smith can tell many a tale of the old days, of the hardships of those days when there was no air-conditioning; when refrigerators were unheard of; when, on a single voyage, a cargo-ship would call at as many as thirty West African ports, and crews worked from daylight to dark in the surf ports; when ships' navigational equipment consisted of two compasses and a sounding machine. There was no such thing as radar, echo-sounders, or direction-finders. When taking cargo on board—'a kind of Carter Paterson service' says Captain Smith—there were no regular meal times. Instead, there was 'five minute chop', and twenty minutes was considered a long lunch hour.

And yet he has the old coaster's affection for the West African trade of that epoch. 'The Masters,' he says, 'were hard taskmasters, but good fellows.' He remembers with affection surviving old colleagues such as Harry Pantin, Freddie Clarke and 'Pop' Shooter.

He has retired to Martlesham in Suffolk. We hope he will have many pleasant years as certainly he has many lively memories.

From Sea *Magazine*

Kroomen from Freetown

Chipping Gang. Photographed by
Captain Simpson, O.B.E., M.V. *Tarkwa.*

THE African "Chipping gang" shown in the photograph are additional temporary members of the ship's complement usually embarked either at Freetown or Takoradi. This particular group is from Freetown.

They are mostly members of the Kroo tribe indigenous to what was formerly known as the Grain Coast, now Liberia. They have been associated with shipping for some generations and their ancestors colonised near Freetown for the purpose of employment as sea-going workers.

Their primary duty on board ship is the handling of cargo both out of and into the ship. They become very competent workers under proper supervision. In between ports when there is no cargo work they are employed in assisting in the maintenance of the ship, especially the scaling (commonly known as "chipping") of steel work which requires constant attention in the humid climate of West Africa.

The Kroomen carried in this type of ship number 75, i.e. five gangs of fifteen each including winch drivers, gangwaymen and labourers. They are in the charge of a Headman and 2nd Headman and work to the requirements of the ship's Officers. To work the ship to full capacity in the main ports the ship's "boys" are augmented by further gangs. These are supplied locally if available.

Carrying labour in the ship has many advantages. In the first place an adequate supply of labour is assured. When approaching a port everything can be made ready for discharging or loading on arrival. When loading, the final touches can be applied without holding the ship in port. In addition the Headmen and Key men know their particular ship and a great deal of maintenance can be done between ports.

Without intending any disparagement to other African workers, the Kroomen from Freetown and the Berebys from Takoradi are best equipped for this type of work.

Captain G.D.SIMPSON, O.B.E., M.V. *Tarkwa.*

From Sea *Magazine*

M.V. Obuasi

as Cadet Training Ship : Elder Dempster's novel experiment

IDSHIPMEN in the ranks of the Elder Dempster Line will "learn by doing" on board the M.V. *Obuasi* which in August sailed from Liverpool for West Africa – via the Continent – on her first voyage as the company's cadet training ship.

This experiment has attracted the attention of the general public as well as officers of the Ministry of Transport and people in shipping circles generally.

Under the command of Captain Robert Arthur Roberts, the *Obuasi's* entire deck crew – with the exception of the bosun and the carpenter – consisted of fourteen midshipmen. This is the normal deck crew. The ship also carried – as is normal in the other new ships of the Elder Dempster Fleet – four other midshipmen, carrying out the usual duties of midshipmen.

The fourteen cadets were accommodated in spacious two-berth cabins with well-appointed recreation and mess rooms. The senior midshipman, who acted as bosun's mate, holds an E.D.H. Certificate, equivalent to an A.B.'s qualification. So, too, did nine others. Those who had not had sufficient time to qualify for this certificate carried out the duties of junior deck

Launching of the Obuasi by Mrs Malcolm Bruce Glasier on 24 June, 1952.

ratings. Nearly all the boys hold the Life Boat Certificate.

Throughout the voyage they carried out all the work normally required of a deck crew. They were given their turn at watch-keeping on the bridge, and

The Obuasi anchored in Funchal Bay.   *Photo by courtesy of Messrs Perestrelles*

OFFICERS AND CREW OF THE CADET TRAINING SHIP M.V. OBUASI

Back row : *left to right :* A.G.Maxwell, J.Jones, P.J.Bowman, R.K.Prakel, P.Burden, J.H.T.Menson, R.S.Hayton, G.H.Ryan, N.Richardson.

Middle row : A.A.Munro, J.F.Forster, D.H.Koker, J.F.Reilly, J.Miles, C.Wood, C.Milner, T.L.Parry, S.D.Chapman, Radio Officer R.S.Moss.

Front row : J.K.Crone (Third Officer), G.H.Kendrick (Third Officer), X.Fisher (Second Officer), M.Murphy (Chief Officer), R.A.Roberts (Master), J.P.McConnell (Chief Engineer), F.J.Henighan (Second Engineer), P.FitzPatrick (Third Engineer), F.A.Killick (Chief Steward).

opportunities were afforded to enable them to keep abreast of their theoretical work. Arrangements were also made for their leisure time. The ship carried a comprehensive library and opportunities were given to them at ports overseas to take part in games and in sightseeing tours.

When the *Obuasi* called at Hamburg, the cadets were taken on an instructional tour of the docks and then on a tour of the city. In the evening they went to a theatre as the guests of the British Sailor's Society. At Rotterdam, the midshipmen also toured the harbour and then went across to Amsterdam where the Elder Dempster agents, Messrs Meyer and Company, took them on a conducted tour and enabled them to see a demonstration of cargo handling gear.

Captain Roberts says that the conduct of the midshipmen on the voyage was "exemplary" and that without exception the boys were capable of carrying out the duties of able seamen to his complete satisfaction.

The Company's intention is that every midshipman in their service should do at least two voyages in this ship during the period of their apprenticeship.

It is believed that this practical experiment will make Elder Dempster's future officers first-class seamen. It is also believed that the cadets will develop an increased loyalty to the Company and a sense of belonging to the same team when finally the time comes for them to take up duty, in smaller groups, on board the Company's various ships.

The midshipmen themselves have expressed their appreciation of the Company's experiment. In a letter to the management, Midshipman John Miles, writing on behalf of all the midshipmen on board, says: "We hope to show our appreciation by making the M.V. *Obuasi* the finest vessel in the Company."

From Sea *Magazine*

J. H. Tachie-Menson

The first Ghanaian to gain a Master Mariner's Certificate

Mr J. H. Tachie-Menson, Master Mariner, replying to the speeches of tribute at the reception given in his honour

OUR warmest congratulations go to Mr J. H. Tachie-Menson on his being the first Ghanaian to obtain his Master Mariner's Certificate. The event was celebrated when Mr Tachie-Menson arrived at Takoradi on Tuesday, March 1, 1960, on the Elder Dempster flagship, the M.V. *Aureol*. The occasion was marked by the Company with a little ceremony on board the *Aureol* held a few hours after the liner berthed.

Captain T. E. M. Jenkins presented Mr Tachie-Menson with a pair of binoculars to mark the distinction he had achieved, and to mark, too, the fact that he is leaving the service of Elder Dempster Lines to take up an appointment with the Ghana Government Harbour Service.

'Elder Dempsters,' said Mr W. J. Joyce, our Takoradi Agent, 'are pleased and proud to have trained Mr Tachie-Menson. Our good wishes go with him, for he has gained the affection of all the Masters and Officers with whom he has sailed.'

Mr Tachie-Menson's family have all contributed to the advance of their country, and it was particularly pleasant that his father, Mr Charles Tachie-Menson, who was an Elder Dempster Agent in Cape Coast, was able to be present.

Born in Cape Coast in 1928, and educated at Adisadel College, Mr Tachie-Menson joined the Elder Dempster Lines in 1951. He has since spent most of his time at sea, successfully gaining his Second and First Mate's certificates, and finally his Master's certificate.

Also present at the ceremony were the General Manager of Ghana Railways and Harbours, Mr H. F. P. Plumridge, and the District Commissioner for Ahanta, Mr K. E. Assaam.

James Tachie-Menson served as Chief Officer aboard **BENIN**, *his only appointment as such with Elder Dempster. Here* **BENIN** *is seen, after sale, as* **YORKWOOD**. (Photo K. C. Griffin). *Mr Tachie-Menson subsequently joined Black Star Line.*

TRAINING FOR SERVICE AT SEA IN OUR FLEET

M.V. *Fourah Bay*, above, our specially built Cadet ship on her trials. She was launched at Scotts' Yard, Greenock, last September, by Mrs. G. Paine, daughter of Mr. J. H. Joyce, our Chairman, and went into service last December under the command of Captain L. B. Silvester.

★

TUCKED away among the Company records is the Log Book of the s.s. *Charity*—the ship on our cover—which shows that in 1853 two Midshipmen and a Boy Fiddler signed on for service on the High Seas. The Log is an historic and remarkable document in two respects: it may have been the first occasion that the term 'midshipmen' was used in the Merchant Navy—it was certainly one of the earliest—and whereas seamen nowadays use guitars and tape recorders to provide music in their leisure hours, a hundred years ago it seems the Company signed on musicians for the purpose.

As the equipment on Deck or in the Engine-room becomes more complex, the training of the Navigating Officers and Engineer Officers of the future becomes of

greater importance to the Company. In 1950, when only 52 Midshipmen were under training, the Company was involved in a considerable programme of building new ships to replace ships lost in the War and, foreseeing the increased number of qualified officers that would be required once the rebuilding programme got into its stride, decided to increase the number of Midshipmen's berths in the Fleet to 120. In 1951 a new Midshipmen's Department was formed responsible for recruiting and training.

Every Midshipman on joining the Company who has not attended a pre-sea training college goes to either the Aberdovey or Moray Outward Bound Sea School for a month.

As Dr. Kurt Hahn, late Headmaster of Gordonstoun

490

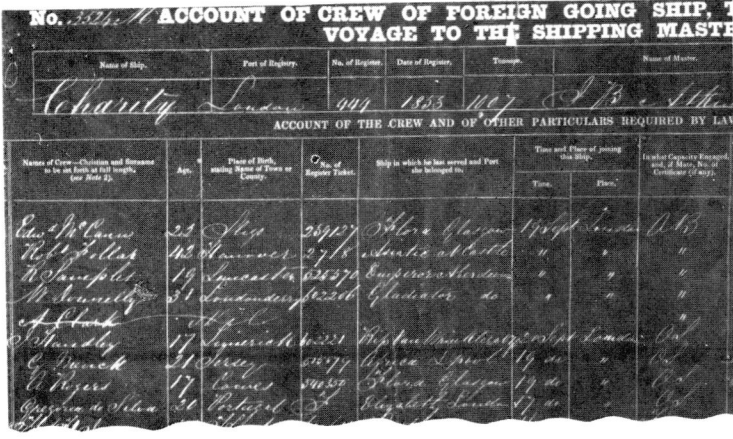

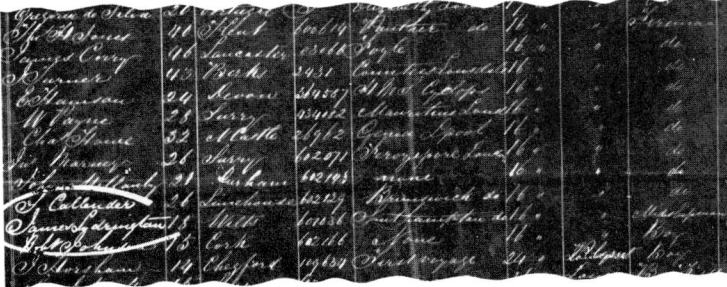

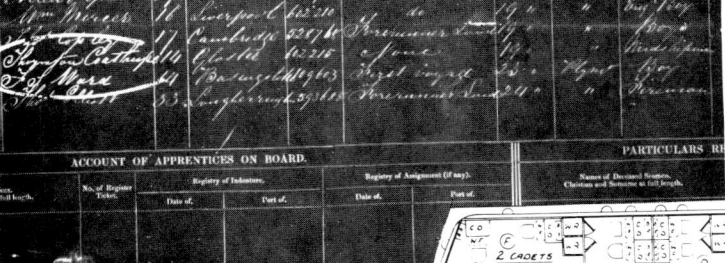

TRAINING . . .

School, once said, "It is wrong to coerce people into opinions, but it is our duty to impel them into experience." And so on the threshold of his career a Midshipman is given the opportunity, through the challenging surroundings of the hills and sea in Wales and Scotland, to learn to lead; to be a true member of his community; to gather a store of unforgettable memories and of shared experience.

An officer should be capable of carrying out every order which he gives. This is the criterion of leadership and is essential for obtaining willing obedience. The Company, therefore, started its own training vessel which would be manned on deck throughout by Midshipmen, and in August, 1953, the M.V. *Obuasi* sailed on her second voyage under the Command of Captain R. A. Roberts on a new and exciting venture. For seven years 'Bosun George' guided the Midshipmen in running the ship's daily routine and passing on to them his knowledge of the art of true seamanship. The Company is grateful to him for all he did to make this venture a success.

The Midshipmen had their own cine projector aboard, dinghies to sail, ample time to study, sextants with which to take 'sights' and educational tours arranged for them when in ports. There is no doubt that the nine to twelve months of the apprenticeship spent in this ship did good morally and physically,

M.V. *FOURAH BAY*, 1961

Accommodation for sixteen Cadets is arranged on the upper deck. There are three additional two-berth cabins on the boat deck.

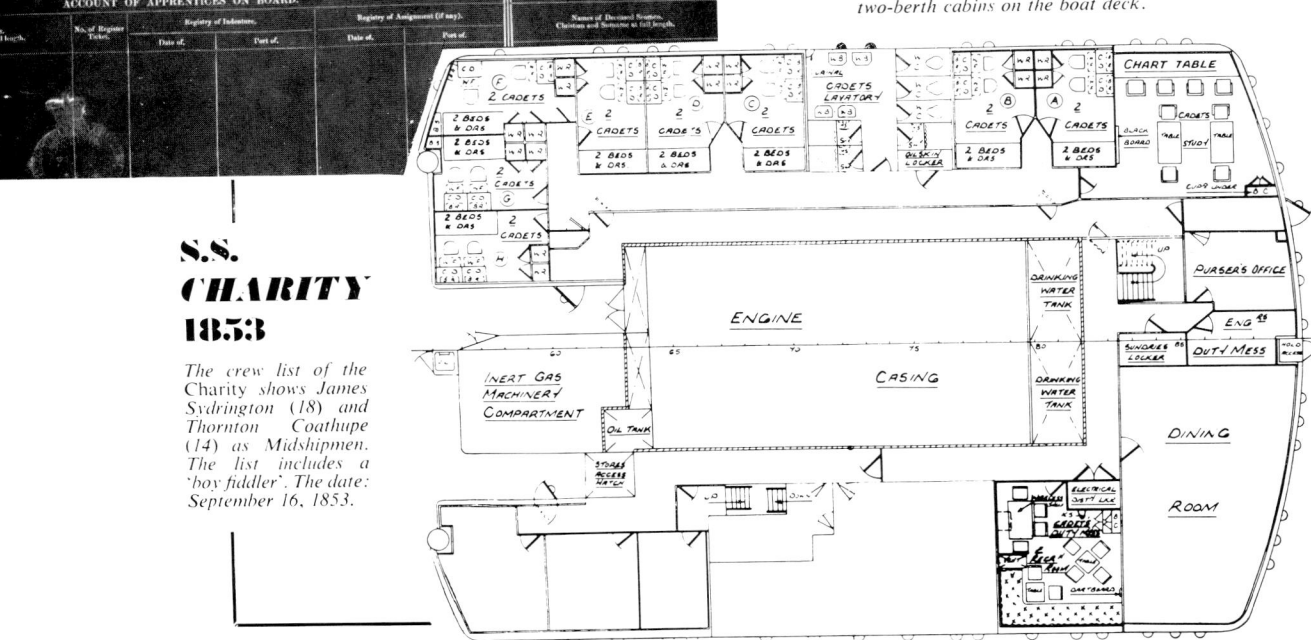

S.S. CHARITY 1853

The crew list of the Charity shows James Sydrington (18) and Thornton Coathupe (14) as Midshipmen. The list includes a 'boy fiddler'. The date: September 16, 1853.

instilled seamanlike qualities into future officers and built an esprit de corps within the Company. Young men are bound to have high spirits at times, and there were occasions when an excess of youthful enterprise led some of the Midshipmen into some high-spirited adventures; some of the consequences of these were not always foreseen in the planning stages! But on balance the Midshipmen who sailed in the *Obuasi* gained sound knowledge and were good ambassadors for the Company on the sports field.

Ships age, and changes have to be made if training is to keep abreast of technical knowledge. On completion of her voyage in July, 1961, under the command of Captain J. W. Hutchinson, the M.V. *Obuasi*

★

They trained on the OBUASI

★

Some of the officers and Midshipmen of the Company's first training ship M.V. Obuasi *taken nearly ten years ago. In the back row (fifth from left) is J. H. Tachie-Menson, who became the first Ghanaian to gain a Master Mariner's Certificate. Captain Tachie-Menson seen in the picture above replying to tributes at a reception given in his honour by Elder Dempster, trained under Captain R. A. Roberts. He has since been appointed to command the* M.V. Nasia River *of the Black Star Line.*

reverted to normal crew manning on deck and the Midshipmen were appointed to the Company's specially built Cadet Ship, the M.V. *Fourah Bay*, in December, 1961.

In the West African Trade it is imperative that the Navigating Officers should be men of practical ability, able to use initiative and ingenuity in their day-to-day duties.

For this reason, the training given aboard the *Fourah Bay* is essentially practical as well as academic.

A Midshipman has three Ministry of Transport examinations to pass before he obtains his Master's Certificate. To ensure that he has the necessary academic background to make the best of the correspondence course which lasts throughout his apprenticeship, he should have at least three passes (preferably in Mathematics, Science and English) in the G.C.E. examination, or their equivalent in his passing-out examination if he has attended a pre-sea training college, such as the King Edward VII Nautical College, Plymouth School of Navigation or H.M.S. *Conway*. Prizes are awarded by the Company for the best papers submitted by Midshipmen in the annual Merchant Navy Training Board Examinations. In 1958 the Captain Flowerdew Memorial Award, sponsored by Mrs. E. McCulloch, the late Captain H. Flowerdew's sister, was inaugurated in memory of his many years' service with the Company. A pair of binoculars is presented by the Honourable Company of Master Mariners, of which Captain Flowerdew was a Liveryman, to the best all-round Midshipman each year.

Up to the end of the Second World War the customary method of training Engineer Officers was by an apprenticeship served in a shore engineering establishment, generally a shipyard. This method was never wholly satisfactory in that many apprentices were left very much to their own devices and at times received

Captain R. A. Roberts at his desk on the Obuasi *which, in August, 1953, became the Company's first training vessel manned throughout by Midshipmen. The* Obuasi *has now returned to normal crew manning.*

little practical instruction, and gained little real understanding of the best traditions of the Merchant Navy. Certain liner companies took up the question of training with the Ministry of Transport, and the Alternative Training Scheme for Apprentice Marine Engineers came into being. It was inaugurated in 1952, since when the Elder Dempster Lines have progressively increased their intake of apprentices and it is now hoped to engage 24 apprentices each year.

The age of entry is between 16 and 17½ years. Boys

must be up to their G.C.E. 'O' Level standard in at least Mathematics and Physics. Applications are considered between January and March and successful applicants begin training in early September.

The training given covers a period of four and a half years and is designed to contain as much practical and theoretical work as possible, and is divided into three phases:

Phase I: Two years' full-time study at Riversdale Technical College, Liverpool, for the Ordinary National Diploma in Mechanical Engineering. This is the qualification which should be gained by every apprentice on the completion of his first two years.

Phase II: Eighteen months' sea time as Cadet Engineers to gain practical experience at sea. The Company arrange and pay for a correspondence course to enable Cadets to study for their endorsements to the Ordinary National Diploma in Electro-technology, Naval Architecture and Marine Engineering Knowledge.

Phase III: Twelve months' training in practical work in a local workshop or ship repair yard, during which time the apprentices attend a technical college for one full day each week, completing study for their endorsements.

On completion of the apprenticeship the Cadet becomes a Junior Engineer Officer. Once he has completed fifteen months' service at sea he becomes eligible to sit for the Ministry of Transport 2nd

RIVER HOUSE, the Company's new residential training establishment at Liverpool which is expected to be ready for occupation by October, 1962. Midshipmen and Cadets attending courses at the Riversdale Technical College will have their own cabins in the north and south blocks. Linking them will be dining and recreation rooms. With the provision of the new establishment, the 'boarding out' system will no longer be necessary. The architects are Messrs. Weightman and Bullen, Liverpool.

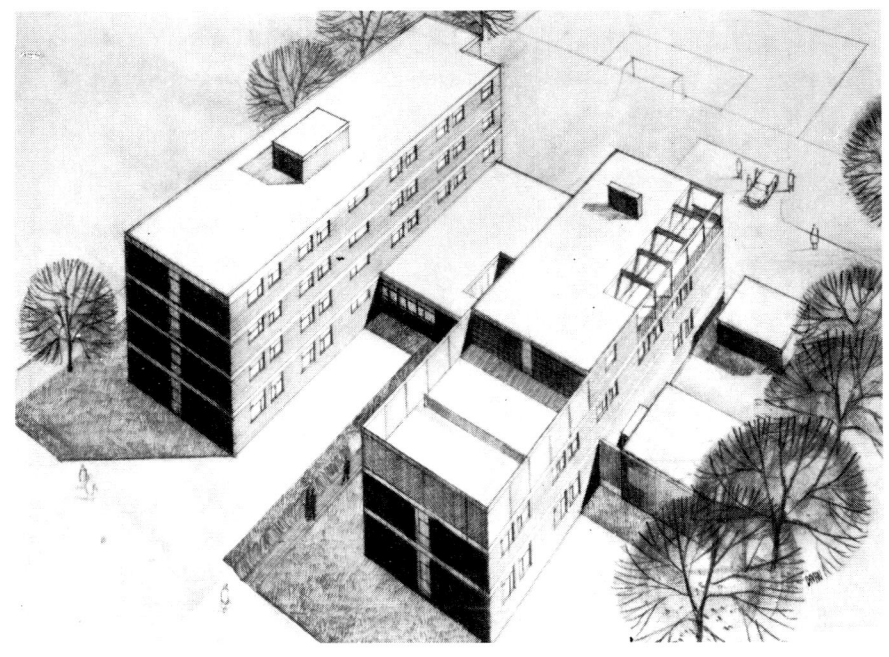

Class Certificate of Competency and provided he obtains his Ordinary National Diploma and endorsements during his apprenticeship, has only one subject to pass—Engineering Knowledge. Within three years of completing his apprenticeship, it is possible for him to obtain a First Class Ministry of Transport Certificate of Competency and hold the rank of 2nd Engineer Officer.

For several years now it has become more and more apparent to the Shipowner that if his Masters, Navigating and Engineer Officers are going to be able to keep pace with future developments in the Industry, they must have a good academic background and a thorough technical training. In order to attract into the industry not only the G.C.E. 'O' Level but the Sixth former who has passed his 'A' Level examinations, it has recently been agreed with the Ministry of Transport that navigating apprentices with passes in at least five subjects in the G.C.E. Examination, of which two, including either Mathematics or Physics, must be at 'A' Level, will be entitled to nine months' remission of sea service. The remission granted by obtaining any appropriate 'A' Level passes can be counted together with the remission for attending a Mid-Apprenticeship Course and any pre-sea remission obtained, provided the total remission does not exceed eighteen months.

In past years many Midshipmen have gained high marks in their Correspondence Course and Merchant Navy Training Board Examinations, but there have been some who have lacked the self-discipline needed to apply themselves to their studies. It has become more and more apparent that the shipping industry is appreciating the value of Mid-Apprenticeship residential course of six months at an approved Nautical College to encourage a Midshipman to keep up to date with his theoretical work, as well as to enable him to broaden his knowledge of other subjects.

The Mid-Apprenticeship Course is now recognized by the Ministry of Transport, and in future all Company Midshipmen will spend six months of their apprenticeship attending a residential course at the Liverpool Nautical College. This six-month period will count as full sea time. In order that full advantage of this new scheme can be taken, the Company has

Training put to the test . . .

'An officer should be capable of carrying out every order which he gives. It is the criterion of a leader and essential for obtaining willing obedience, as well as knowing how long it really does take . . .' A practical demonstration is given here by a second Officer as he supervises the loading of deck cargo on the M.V. Donga.

decided to build its own residential establishment in Riversdale Road to be known as River House. River House will accommodate 90 Midshipmen and Engineering Cadets while they attend courses at the Riversdale Technical College, while taking E.D.H. certificates, attending Lifeboat School, or in Liverpool for their voyage interviews. With the help of our good friends at Merchant Navy House the present system of boarding-out has worked well for many years. It will come to an end, however in October, 1962, when River House should be ready for use. Accommodation will be provided for the principal and his wife, and for an assistant housekeeper. The Midshipmen and Cadets will have single 'cabins' in two blocks connected by a Dining Hall and Recreation rooms. A hobbies room, football field and other opportunities for recreation and sports will be provided.

It is the Company's hope that by living together as a purposeful community, our Midshipmen and Engineer Cadets will acquire a deep appreciation of their future careers as maritime officers and develop esprit de corps which will stand the Officers concerned and the Company in good stead in the years to come.

From Sea Magazine

APPENDIX III

A NAUTICAL MISCELLANY

WEST COAST OF AFRICA.
ARRIVAL OF THE ARMENIAN.

The royal mail steamship Armenian, Captain Leamon, arrived in the Mersey yesterday morning with the West African mails, 50 passengers, 1000 bales African cotton, 1308 ounces gold dust, 9029 dollars, 1900 francs, and 2472 sovereigns. Her dates are—Benin, Dec. 7; Fernando Po, Dec. 2; Brass River, Dec. 4; New Calabar, Dec. 6; Bonny, Dec. 7; Lagos, Dec. 10; Accra, Dec. 11; Cape Coast Castle, Dec. 14; Sierra Leone, Dec. 21; Bathurst, Dec. 25; Teneriffe, Dec. 31; and Madeira, Jan. 2. The Armenian brings 27 passengers in the cabin, and 25 distressed seamen, being portions of the crews of the wrecked vessels Laughing Water, Governor Elias, and Bagdad Packet.

Trade was brisk at Fernando Po, notwithstanding that smallpox still prevailed to a great extent among the native population.

The screw-steamer St. Patrick, with convicts on board for the south coast, had put into Fernando Po in a disabled condition, her machinery being damaged. The vessel would be detained at least a month for repairs.

There is nothing of importance to report from the Cameroons. The river was healthy, but business was at a complete standstill.

A slight improvement had occurred in trade at Old Calabar since the sailing of the last steamer. The ship Moultan sailed for Glasgow on the 28th November. When off the bar her commander, Captain Kiddie, committed suicide by jumping overboard. His body came up alongside the vessel the next day. The chief officer of the ship Golden Age was put in charge of the vessel, which sailed from the bar on the 30th. The Navigator arrived from Glasgow on the 28th November.

Trade had much improved at Bonny during the month of December, oil being freely brought down from the interior. The ship Flora M'Ivor arrived on the 27th November, and the Rattler on the same day. The Elizabeth Latham entered the Bonny River on the 2nd December. The captain and part of the crew of the ship Laughing Water, wrecked on Bonny Bar, came home in the Armenian.

Brass was healthy, but there was very little business doing in oil.

Trade at Benin still stopped, in consequence of the fine imposed by Commodore Wilmot on the natives for outrages committed on Dr. Henry's establishment not being paid. There is a balance of 30 puncheons of oil owing, which the traders were in hopes would be settled during the month of January.

Trade very brisk at Lagos since the roads from Abeokuta had been opened. A great quantity of cotton was daily arriving. There were at least 4500 bales in the town when the Armenian sailed. She brought 1200 bales.

There were 1500 slaves in irons at Whydah ready for shipment. Her Majesty's ship Zebra was stationed off the port, and had her boats cruising in search of the vessel, which is said to be a large steamer, the same that has made several voyages with large cargoes so successfully, and the one that has given our cruisers upon more than one occasion such annoyance. The schooner Commodore, from London to Lagos, passed Addah on the 11th December.

At Accra trade had slightly improved, and several lots of cotton had arrived from the Volta. The brig Governor Elias was totally wrecked on the 27th December. The crew were saved and landed at Accra.

An average amount of business was done at Cape Coast Castle during December, and a good trade is looked for the coming season. Her Majesty's ship Gladiator was to sail on the 16th for Lagos.

The mail steamer Macgregor Laird, arrived from England, sailed for the leeward on the 16th of December. The barque Manners Sutton passed the Cape on the 15th.

Business was very dull at Sierra Leone. Great preparations were being made for the races and the exhibition. Lieutenant Hawkins, of H.M.S. Pandora, died on the 24th of November; and Captain Merritt, overlooker for Messrs. Evans, on the 30th.

There is not much of importance to report from Bathurst. Several small lots of cotton of a very superior staple had arrived from the interior. The brigantine Monarch, laden with cotton, had been towed in by the steamer Saxon to Teneriffe, dismasted, and the mate washed overboard.

The mail steamer Calabar arrived from England on the 30th ultimo, and sailed same day for Teneriffe. The steamer Bagdad Packet, from Liverpool for Matamoras, put into Madeira, was surveyed and condemned, and the crew sent home in the Armenian.

No fewer than eight blockade runners had arrived en route for Bermuda from England during one week.

VALUABLE PRIZE PICKED UP AT SEA.

On the afternoon of the 6th of January the Armenian fell in with the new ship Phryne, abandoned at sea. The ship is 1300 tons register, and was bound from St. John's, N.B., to Liverpool, with a cargo of timber, and valued at about £50,000. The Phryne was abandoned about the 10th of December, off the Portuguese coast, with loss of rudder, and the insurance effected by her owners in Liverpool amounted on last Monday to about £20,000. Captain Leamon, of the Armenian, sent a boat alongside the derelict, which on examination proved to be perfectly tight and seaworthy, as she had only 19 inches of water in her hold. He at once put on board a volunteer crew, under the command of Captain M'Kenzie, who was returning on leave of absence from the coast, where he commanded the African Company's ship William Money. Capt. M'Kenzie, after receiving a supply of provisions, water, ropes, and some sails, was directed to steer north, as the weather was fine and the wind fresh from the south-west. When boarded, the Phryne's hull was in very good order, as were also her masts and yards. She had four sails bent, but beyond this the ship was stripped of all her running gear. From the weather the Armenian subsequently experienced, there is little doubt the Phryne will be heard of in a day or two.

DEATH OF DR. BAIKIE, THE AFRICAN TRAVELLER.

By this arrival we learn with regret the death of the well-known African traveller Dr. Baikie, who expired, after a very short attack of fever and dysentery, at Sierra Leone, on the 30th November last. By the previous mail we announced that Dr. Baikie, after travelling for six years in the interior of Africa, and after having established a native colony some distance from the confluence of the Niger, returned to Lagos on the 21st October in her Majesty's ship Investigator, which had been up the Niger 400 miles on a cruise. We believe Dr. Baikie intended returning to Liverpool by the last mail, but in consequence of being obliged to assort and re-arrange the accumulations of over six years' travel in an uncivilised country he was compelled to stay on the coast until the next homeward mail. The deceased gentleman was, we understand, born at Arbroath, Scotland, and was educated for the medical profession in Edinburgh. He would at the time of his death be about 40 years of age. So with Dr. Livingstone in England, Dr. Baikie and Bishop Mackenzie dead, and Captain Burton removed, Western Africa is at present without a traveller of note.

List of Passengers.—From Fernando Po: Captain Cutajar, Captain M'Kenzie, P. Elkman, and F. Prune. From Old Calabar: D. Henderson and J. Janse. From Bonny: Captain Bell, Captain James, Captain Bennett, W. Murphy, and six men from the wreck of the Laughing Water. From Lagos: D. M'Kenzie. From Accra: Captain Heffmann, G. T. H. Lyall, Captain Hoare, E. R. Reeks, and eight men from the wreck of the brig Governor Elias. From Cape Coast Castle: F. Dogerty, Lieutenant Osborne, Mr. Leslie, Mrs. Leslie, W. Barnes, and Captain Blakesley. From Sierra Leone: J. Smith, Captain Wilkinson, and J. Lynch. From Madeira: Mr. Halloway, A. Peterson, D. Dickson, and nine seamen belonging to the Bagdad Packet (&c.

THE BRITISH  AND AFRICAN
STEAM NAVIGATION Co Ltd
ELDER DEMPSTER AND Co LIMITED,
MANAGERS.

CHRISTMAS DAY 1928.
DINER
S/s. "BURUTU"

Hors d'Oeuvres Varies.

Porée de Tomate

Consommé Célestine

Lobster Kedgeree.

Chicken a la Mekango.

Asparagus Riché

ROAST TURKEY

SAVOURY STUFFING.

Braised York Ham.

BAKED & BOILED POTATOES.

FRENCH BEANS

Yuletide Pudding.

NOËL SAUCE

PEAR FLORENTINE.

COFFEE   FRUIT.   WINES

BOTTLED BEER. MINERALS.

*Christmas 1928 style—**BURUTU***

497

Elder Dempster Lines

Menu

Christmas Day

1957

m.v. "Tarkwa"

Christmas 1957 style—TARKWA

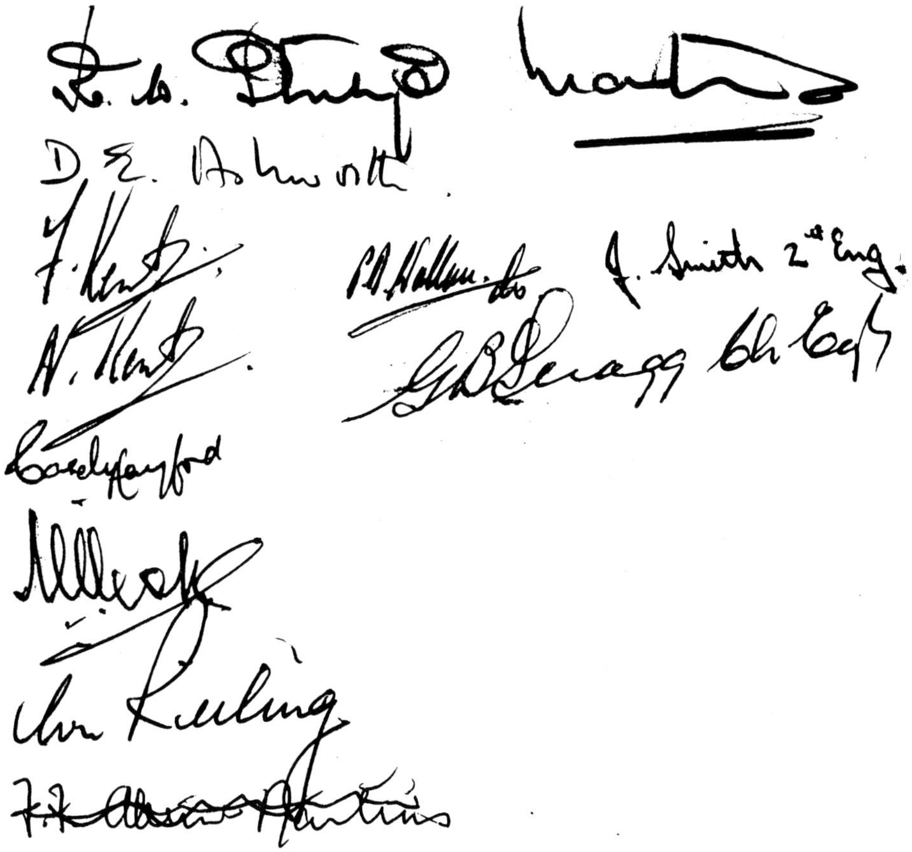

Christmas Dinner

Hors d'œuvres varies

Consommé Royal   Potage American

•

Fried Fillet of Plaice, Tartare Sauce

Poached Hake, Fillet of Egg Sauce

•

Noisettes of Lamb, Printaniere

Asparagus Tips, Butter Sauce

•

Roast Sirloin Beef, Horseradish Sauce

Braised York Ham, Madere

Roast Norfork Turkey, Chipolata

Brussels Sprouts   Garden Peas

Roast and Boiled Potatoes

Cold Cuts:

•

Ox Tongue   Pressed Beef   Salad in Season

•

Plum Pudding, Brandy Sauce

Jelly and Cream   Strawberry Ice Cream

Yule Logs   Christmas Cake   Mince Pies

Dessert   Nuts

Coffee

Christmas 1957 style—TARKWA

499

"NIGERIAN INDEPENDENCE DAY". Sat. 1/10/60
DINNER.

Grapefruit Juice.   Pineapple Juice.

Smoked Norwegian Salmon with Prawns.

Consomme Prince De Galles. Cream Bourdaloue.

Fresh River Trout, Meuniere Style.

Beef Tournedos, Africaine.

Roast Stuffed Norfolk Turkey, Nivernaise.
Cranberry Sauce.

Chicken Pepper Soup, African Style.

Roast. Boiled and Garfield Potatoes.

Minted Garden Peas.   Christmas Cabbage,
Valencienne.

COLD BUFFET.

Obeche Logs, Melba Sauce.

Boiled York Ham.   Salami Sausage.

Roast Leg of Lamb, Mint Sauce. Spiced Beef.

Lettuce. Tomatoes. Radishes. Cole Slaw.
Spring Onions.

Mayonnaise and French Dressings.

Coupe Nigeria.   Lagoon Pudding,
Custard Sauce.

Plain and Creme De Menthe Ice Cream.

Ye Olde English Trifle.

Free and Easies.   Ibadan Gateau.
Independence Cake.

Cheese Platter.   Biscuits.

Dessert.   Assorted Nuts.
Coffee.

Nigerian Independence Day—CALABAR menu

ELDER DEMPSTER LINES

LIVERPOOL

*Nigerian Independence Day—**AUREOL** menu cover*

August 1963—AUREOL menu

Dinner

★ ★ ★

Appetisers:

Juices: Pineapple, Prune, Orange
Grapefruit Maraschino

Soups

Consomme Mimosa   Cream Andalouse

Fish:

Supremes of Halibut, Normande

Farinaceous:

Rissotto Italienne

TO ORDER - 10 minutes

Eggs: Princess

Vegetarian:

Dutch Potato Mould

Entrée:

Fried Calves Sweetbreads, Sauce Robert

Chicken a la King

Roast:

Quarters of Canterbury Lamb and Mint Sauce

Vegetables:

Garden Peas   Puree Cultivature

Boiled, Browned, Creamed & Pont Neuf Potatoes

Sweets:

St. Jean Pudding   Orange Table Creams

Peach Dame Blanche

Banana & Vanilla Ice Cream

Savoury

Sardine Sur Croute

Fruit Bowl   Assorted Nuts   Coffee

We are pleased to serve RED or WHITE WINE
by the glass at 1/6

★ ★ ★

Cold Buffet

Jellied Beef Bouillon   Vichysoise

Soused Halibut   Tuna Fish Salad

Spiced Beef   Liverwurst
Roulade of Veal   Gammon Ham   Ox Tongue

Salads

Lettuce   Tomato   Beetroot   Cucumber

Fedora

Dressings

Mayonnaise   French

Thousand Island   Creme Crue

Iced Coffee

★ ★ ★

Coffee and Liqueurs will be served as Passengers desire,
either in the First Class Lounge or in the Dining Saloon.

It is our aim to satisfy.   Passengers wishing to discuss Food or Service
are kindly requested to ask for the Head Waiter.

Captain: W. E. HUMPHREYS
Chief Steward: H. E. Dunn
Chef de Cuisine: P Brindley, M.C.F.A

502

R.M.V. "ACCRA" Final Voyage Northb'nd First Class Captain: C?? O'Sullivan Purser: J.E. Cowden

PROGRAMME OF EVENTS

Tuesday Sept 26 Noon Sailed from Lagos, Nigeria

Wednesday „ 27
a.m. / p.m. Arrive/Depart TAKORADI, Ghana.
9-15 p.m. LIGHT MUSIC in the Lounge
9-15 p.m. Music for Dancing in the Smokeroom

Thursday „ 28
4-15 p.m. CRICKET MATCH on the Prom. Deck Passengers v Crew
9-00 p.m. CINEMA in the Restaurant
"THE MAGNIFICENT TWO"
Featuring: Morcambe and Wise
Cartoon: Second Chance
9-15 p.m. SCRABBLE COMPETITION in the Cardroom

Friday „ 29
9-30 a.m. ADULT SCAVENGER HUNT Starts at the Bureau
7-30 p.m. DINNER DANCE in the Restaurant

Saturday „ 30
10-00 a.m. SPORTS and DECK GAMES commence
4-15 p.m. AQUATIC SPORTS at the Pool
9-15 p.m. BINGO and TAKE YOUR PICK in the Smokeroom followed by Dancing in the Smokeroom

Sunday Oct 1
NIGERIA INDEPENDENCE DAY
11-00 a.m. MORNING SERVICE in the Lounge
Hymn Numbers:- 303; 257; 202. 219;
1st. Lesson: 2. Samuel 12 Verses 1 to 23
2nd. Lesson: Colossians 1 Verses 1 to 12
5-15 p.m. CHILDREN'S GAMES and BUFFET PARTY in the restaurant
9-00 p.m. A Selection of MUSIC FROM THE SHOWS
9-15 p.m. Bridge in the Cardroom
9-15 p.m. Music for Dancing in the Smokeroom

Monday „ 2
9-30 a.m. ADULT TREASURE HUNT starts at the Bureau
9-30 a.m. CHILDREN'S SPORTS on the Prom. Deck
7-30 p.m. FANCY DRESS GALA EVENING:
Passengers are requested to wear Fancy Dress during Dinner whenever possible. The Parade will take place at 9-00 p.m.
Dancing after dinner; Spot Waltz, Paul Jones, etc.

Tuesday Oct 3
9-30 a.m. CHILDRENS SCAVENGER HUNT Starts at the Bureau
p.m. Arrive / Depart LAS PALMAS, Grand Canary
9-15 p.m. LIGHT MUSIC in the Lounge

Wednesday „ 4
9-00 p.m. CINEMA in the Restaurant
"TRIPLE CROSS"
Featuring: Christopher Plummer, Yul Brynner
Cartoon: To Beep or Not to Beep
9-15 p.m. CHESS TOURNAMENT in the Cardroom
9-15 p.m. LIGHT MUSIC in the Lounge

Thursday „ 5
10-00 a.m. FINALS of all Deck Games
4-15 p.m. CHILDREN'S FILM MATINEE in the Smokeroom
5-15 p.m CHILDREN'S FANCY DRESS PARADE, Restaurant
9-15 p.m. RACE MEETING at the Akratrak, Smokeroom, followed by Music for Dancing
9-15 p.m. WHIST DRIVE in the Cardroom

Friday „ 6
9-30 a.m. CHILDREN'S TREASURE HUNT Starts at the Bureau
4-15p.m. CRICKET MATCH on the Prom. Deck Passengers v Crew
9-00 p.m. CINEMA in the Restaurant
"RAMPAGE AT APACHE WELLS"
Featuring: Stewart Grainger
Cartoon: Animal Cracker Circus
9-15 p.m. Music for Dancing in the Smokeroom

Saturday „ 7
a.m. TOTE on the CESAREWITCH
7-30 p.m. FAREWELL DINNER DANCE in the Restaurant
Presentation of SPORTS PRIZES during dinner

Sunday „ 8
11-00 a.m. SERVICE in the Lounge
Hymn Numbers:- 640, 261; 299; 300.
1st. Lesson. 2 Samuel 18 Verses 1 to 16
2nd Lesson: Colossians 2 Verses 6 to 15
9-00 p.m. A Selection of MUSIC FROM THE SHOWS

Monday „ 9
a.m. Arriving at LIVERPOOL, England

ACCRA—final voyage programme

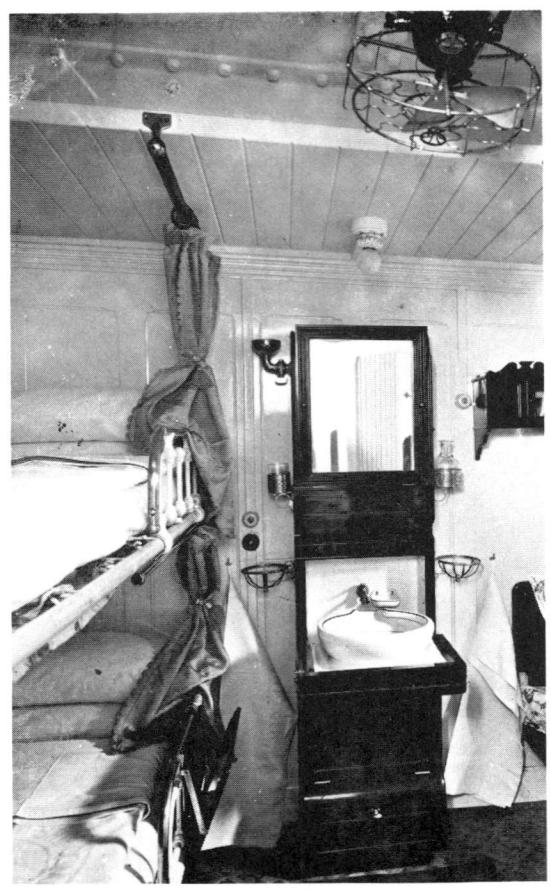

1 *Heavy linen and damask reflect the pre-1914 respect for quality in this two-berth cabin on the s.s. Abosso*

2 *Undertones of the "art nouveau" period in the first-class smokeroom of the s.s. Appam*

3 *A gymnasium on one of the steamers— not a medieval torture chamber*

TWILIGHT OF THE WEST AFRICAN STEAMERS

Ship designers at the turn of the century followed a curious fashion. They tried to make the passenger forget that he was in a ship at all and sought inspiration for their interiors in the stately homes of England—as these photographs show. They are the last of the steam-engined mailboats designed for Elder Dempster's West Africa run.

It is unlikely that anyone concerned with their construction 50 years ago could have imagined that they were the last of the line and that the diesel engine was soon to supplant the steam engine which, with various refinements, had served the West African mailboat faithfully for 60 years.

Interior pictures of ships tend to disappear into some mysterious void and we are lucky to have a collection, fading slightly but showing clearly what the public rooms and cabins of the old *Abosso* and *Appam* looked like. Only one of these was destined for long life.

The *Abosso* was launched in August, 1912, and completed in December of the same year. She was built by Harland & Wolff Limited, as were her sisters *Appam* and *Apapa*, completed in 1913 and 1914 respectively. These ships were smaller versions of *Darro* and *Drina* of the Royal Mail Steam Packet Company.

Gross tonnage was about 7,800 in each case and quadruple expansion engines and twin screws gave a speed of 13/14 knots. Originally

5

5 *Cane and bamboo, current craze of fashionable decorators, furnished the first-class lounges in both the* Appam *and the* Abosso

4 *The* Appam *sailing from Liverpool*

4

some 400 first- and second-class passengers were catered for but numbers were reduced later. The cabin plan of *Appam* in the 1920s showed berths for about 140 first-class passengers.

Both the *Abosso* and the *Apapa* fell victim to enemy action in the first World War. The *Abosso* was torpedoed in April, 1917, with the loss of 65 lives, and the *Apapa* in November, 1917, close to Point Lynas, with the loss of 77 lives.

The *Appam*, perhaps, was lucky to survive. Captured in January, 1915, by the German raider *Moewe*, she was taken to Newport News, U.S.A., and interned. After a long legal battle she was returned to her owners in April, 1917. No doubt the vengeance of the Germans was feared for she was renamed *Mandingo*, not reverting to her old name until after the war.

Mr. Daniel Bacon, the Company's Agent at New York who had done so much to secure the *Appam*'s release, was presented with a silver model of the ship by her grateful owners in 1922.

The *Appam*, which went to the shipbreakers in 1936, was managed by Elder Dempster & Co. and owned by the British & African Steam Navigation Co. (her sisters belonged to the African Steam Ship Co.). She must have been one of the last mailboats of that Company with a black funnel. Some time after the 1914–18 war her funnel colour was changed to yellow, although the British and African cargo steamers kept their black funnels.

6

6 *Nothing made of plastic here*

7

7 *Boat deck of the* Abosso

From Sea *Magazine*

ITINERARY.

SOUTHBOUND		M.S. ACCRA	M.S. ADDA	M.S. APAPA	M.S. ABOSSO	M.S. ACCRA	M.S. ADDA	M.S. APAPA	M.S. ABOSSO	M.S. ACCRA	M.S. ADDA	M.S. APAPA
LIVERPOOL	Depart	1 Nov.	8 Nov.	22 Nov.	6 Dec.	20 Dec.	27 Dec.	10 Jan.	24 Jan.	7 Feb.	14 Feb.	28 Feb.
MADEIRA	Arrive	5 ,,	13 ,,	26 ,,	10 ,,	24 ,,	1 Jan.	14 ,,	28 ,,	11 ,,	19 ,,	3 Mar.
LAS PALMAS	,,	6 ,,	—	27 ,,	11 ,,	25 ,,	—	15 ,,	29 ,,	12 ,,	—	4 ,,
BATHURST	,,	9 ,,	—	30 ,,	—	28 ,,	—	18 ,,	—	15 ,,	—	7 ,,
FREETOWN	,,	11 ,,	18 Nov.	2 Dec.	16 Dec.	30 ,,	6 Jan.	20 ,,	3 Feb.	17 ,,	24 Feb.	9 ,,
MONROVIA	,,	—	19 ,,	—	17 ,,	—	7 ,,	—	4 ,,	—	25 ,,	—
TAKORADI	,,	14 Nov.	21 ,,	5 Dec.	19 ,,	2 Jan.	9 ,,	23 Jan.	6 ,,	20 Feb.	27 ,,	12 Mar.
ACCRA	,,	15 ,,	22 ,,	6 ,,	20 ,,	3 ,,	10 ,,	24 ,,	7 ,,	21 ,,	28 ,,	13 ,,
LAGOS	,,	16 ,,	23 ,,	7 ,,	21 ,,	4 ,,	11 ,,	25 ,,	8 ,,	22 ,,	29 ,,	14 ,,
PORT HARCOURT	,,	19 Nov.	—	10 Dec.	—	7 Jan.	—	28 Jan.	—	25 Feb.	—	17 Mar.
SUELLABA (for Duala) VICTORIA CALABAR	,,	—	26/29 Nov.	—	24/27 Dec.	—	14/17 Jan.	—	11/14 Feb.	—	3/6 Mar.	—

NORTHBOUND		M.S. ACCRA	M.S. ADDA	M.S. APAPA	M.S. ABOSSO	M.S. ACCRA	M.S. ADDA	M.S. APAPA	M.S. ABOSSO	M.S. ACCRA	M.S. ADDA	M.S. APAPA
CALABAR	Depart	—	28/29 Nov.	—	26/27 Dec.	—	16/17 Jan.	—	13/14 Feb.	—	5/6 Mar.	—
PORT HARCOURT	,,	22 Nov.	—	13 Dec.	—	10 Jan.	—	31 Jan.	—	28 Feb.	—	20 Mar.
LAGOS	,,	25 ,,	2 Dec.	16 ,,	30 Dec.	13 ,,	20 Jan.	3 Feb.	17 Feb.	2 Mar.	9 Mar.	23 ,,
ACCRA	,,	26 ,,	3 ,,	17 ,,	31 ,,	14 ,,	21 ,,	4 ,,	18 ,,	3 ,,	10 ,,	24 ,,
TAKORADI	,,	27 ,,	4 ,,	18 ,,	1 Jan.	15 ,,	22 ,,	5 ,,	19 ,,	4 ,,	11 ,,	25 ,,
MONROVIA	,,	29 ,,	—	20 ,,	—	17 ,,	—	7 ,,	—	6 ,,	—	27 ,,
FREETOWN	,,	30 ,,	7 Dec.	21 ,,	4 Jan.	18 ,,	25 Jan.	8 ,,	22 Feb.	7 ,,	14 Mar.	28 ,,
BATHURST	,,	1 Dec.	—	22 ,,	—	19 ,,	—	9 ,,	—	8 ,,	—	29 ,,
LAS PALMAS	,,	4 ,,	12 Dec.	25 ,,	8 Jan.	22 ,,	30 Jan.	12 ,,	26 Feb.	11 ,,	19 Mar.	1 Apl.
MADEIRA	,,	5 ,,	13 ,,	26 ,,	9 ,,	23 ,,	31 ,,	13 ,,	27 ,,	12 ,,	20 ,,	2 ,,
PLYMOUTH	Arrive	9 ,,	17 ,,	30 ,,	13 ,,	27 ,,	4 Feb.	17 ,,	2 Mar.	16 ,,	24 ,,	6 ,,
LIVERPOOL	Arrive	10 Dec.	18 Dec.	31 Dec.	14 Jan.	28 Jan.	5 Feb.	18 Feb.	3 Mar.	17 Mar.	25 Mar.	7 Apl.

Royal Mail sailings c. 1937

ITINERARY.

SOUTHBOUND		M.S. ADDA	M.S. APAPA	M.S. ABOSSO	M.S. ACCRA	M.S. ADDA	M.S. APAPA	M.S. ABOSSO
LIVERPOOL	Depart	14 June	28 June	12 July	26 July	2 Aug.	16 Aug.	30 Aug.
MADEIRA	Arrive	19 ,,	2 July	16 ,,	30 ,,	7 ,,	20 ,,	3 Sep.
LAS PALMAS	,,	—	3 ,,	17 ,,	31 ,,	—	21 ,,	4 ,,
BATHURST	,,	—	6 ,,	—	3 Aug.	—	24 ,,	—
FREETOWN	,,	24 June	8 ,,	22 July	5 ,,	12 Aug.	26 ,,	9 Sep.
MONROVIA	,,	25 ,,	—	23 ,,	—	13 ,,	—	10 ,,
TAKORADI	,,	27 ,,	11 ,,	25 ,,	8 Aug.	15 ,,	29 Aug.	12 ,,
ACCRA	,,	28 ,,	12 ,,	26 ,,	9 ,,	16 ,,	30 ,,	13 ,,
LAGOS	,,	29 ,,	13 ,,	27 ,,	10 ,,	17 ,,	31 ,,	14 ,,
PORT HARCOURT	,,	—	16 July	—	13 Aug.	—	3 Sep.	—
SUELLABA (for Duala) VICTORIA CALABAR	,,	2/5 July	—	30 July 2 Aug.	—	20/23 Aug.	—	17/20 Sep.

NORTHBOUND		M.S. ADDA	M.S. APAPA	M.S. ABOSSO	M.S. ACCRA	M.S. ADDA	M.S. APAPA	M.S. ABOSSO
CALABAR	Depart	4/5 July	—	1/2 Aug.	—	22/23 Aug.	—	19/20 Sep.
PORT HARCOURT	,,	—	19 July	—	16 Aug.	—	6 Sep.	—
LAGOS	,,	8 July	22 ,,	5 Aug.	19 ,,	26 Aug.	9 ,,	23 Sep.
ACCRA	,,	9 ,,	23 ,,	6 ,,	20 ,,	27 ,,	10 ,,	24 ,,
TAKORADI	,,	9 ,,	23 ,,	6 ,,	20 ,,	27 ,,	10 ,,	24 ,,
MONROVIA	,,	—	25 ,,	—	22 ,,	—	12 ,,	—
FREETOWN	,,	12 July	26 ,,	9 Aug.	23 ,,	30 Aug.	13 ,,	27 Sep.
BATHURST	,,	—	27 ,,	—	24 ,,	—	14 ,,	—
LAS PALMAS	,,	17 July	30 ,,	13 Aug.	27 ,,	4 Sep.	17 ,,	1 Oct.
MADEIRA	,,	18 ,,	31 ,,	14 ,,	28 ,,	5 ,,	18 ,,	2 ,,
PLYMOUTH	Arrive	22 ,,	4 Aug.	18 ,,	1 Sep.	9 ,,	22 ,,	6 ,,
LIVERPOOL	Arrive	23 July	5 Aug.	19 Aug.	2 Sep.	10 Sep.	23 Sep.	7 Oct.

Royal Mail sailings c. 1937

ELDER DEMPSTER LINES, LIMITED

Printed in England.

WEST AFRICAN MAIL AND PASSENGER SERVICE.

Subject to cancellation and/or alteration without notice.

SOUTHBOUND		M.V. ABOSSO	M.V. ACCRA	M.V. ADDA	M.V. APAPA	M.V. ABOSSO	M.V. ACCRA	M.V. ADDA	M.V. APAPA	M.V. ABOSSO	M.V. ACCRA	M.V. ADDA	M.V. APAPA	M.V. ABOSSO	M.V. ACCRA	M.V. ADDA
LIVERPOOL ...	Depart	13 Apl.	27 Apl.	4 May	18 May	1 June	15 June	29 June	13 July	27 July	10 Aug.	17 Aug.	31 Aug.	14 Sept.	28 Sept.	5 Oct.
MADEIRA ...	Arrive	17 ,,	1 May	9 ,,	22 ,,	5 ,,	19 ,,	4 July	17 ,,	31 ,,	14 ,,	22 ,,	4 Sept.	18 ,,	2 Oct.	10 ,,
LAS PALMAS	,,	18 ,,	2 ,,	—	23 ,,	6 ,,	20 ,,	—	18 ,,	1 Aug.	15 ,,	—	5 ,,	19 ,,	3 ,,	—
BATHURST ...	,,	—	5 ,,	—	26 ,,	—	23 ,,	—	21 ,,	—	18 ,,	—	8 ,,	—	6 ,,	—
FREETOWN ...	,,	23 Apl.	7 ,,	14 May	28 ,,	10 June	25 ,,	9 July	23 ,,	6 Aug.	20 ,,	27 Aug.	10 ,,	24 Sept.	8 ,,	15 Oct.
MONROVIA ...	,,	24 ,,	—	15 ,,	—	11 ,,	—	10 ,,	—	7 ,,	—	28 ,,	—	25 ,,	—	16 ,,
TAKORADI ...	,,	26 ,,	10 May	17 ,,	31 May	13 ,,	28 June	12 ,,	26 July	9 ,,	23 Aug.	30 ,,	13 Sept.	27 ,,	11 Oct.	18 ,,
ACCRA ...	,,	27 ,,	11 ,,	18 ,,	1 June	14 ,,	29 ,,	13 ,,	27 ,,	10 ,,	24 ,,	31 ,,	14 ,,	28 ,,	12 ,,	19 ,,
LAGOS ...	,,	28 ,,	12 ,,	19 ,,	2 ,,	15 ,,	30 ,,	14 ,,	28 ,,	11 ,,	25 ,,	1 Sept.	15 ,,	29 ,,	13 ,,	20 ,,
PORT HARCOURT ...	,,	1 May	—	22 May	—	20 June	3 July	—	31 July	—	28 Aug.	—	18 Sept.	—	16 Oct.	—
SUELLABA (for Duala) VICTORIA CALABAR	,,	—	15/18 May	—	5/8 June	† 18/19 June	—	17/20 July	—	14/17 Aug.	—	4/7 Sept.	—	2/5 Oct.	—	23/26 Oct.

SOUTHBOUND		M.V. ABA	M.V. APAPA	M.V. ABOSSO	M.V. ACCRA	M.V. ADDA	M.V. APAPA	M.V. ABOSSO	M.V. ACCRA	M.V. ADDA	M.V. APAPA	M.V. ABOSSO	M.V. ACCRA	M.V. ADDA	M.V. APAPA	M.V. ABOSSO
LIVERPOOL ...	Depart	12 Oct.	19 Oct.	2 Nov.	16 Nov.	23 Nov.	7 Dec.	21 Dec.	4 Jan.	11 Jan.	25 Jan.	8 Feb.	22 Feb.	1 Mar.	15 Mar.	29 Mar.
MADEIRA ...	Arrive	16	23 ,,	6 ,,	20 ,,	28 ,,	11 ,,	26 ,,	8 ,,	16 ,,	29 ,,	12 ,,	26 ,,	6 ,,	19 ,,	2 Apl.
LAS PALMAS	,,	—	24 ,,	7 ,,	21 ,,	—	12 ,,	26 ,,	9 ,,	—	30 ,,	13 ,,	27 ,,	—	20 ,,	3 ,,
BATHURST ...	,,	—	27 ,,	10 ,,	—	—	15 ,,	—	12 ,,	—	2 Feb.	—	2 Mar.	—	23 ,,	—
FREETOWN ...	,,	22 Oct.	29 ,,	12 ,,	25 Nov.	3 Dec.	17 ,,	31 Dec.	14 ,,	21 Jan.	4 ,,	18 Feb.	4 ,,	11 Mar.	25 ,,	8 Apl.
MONROVIA ...	,,	—	—	13 ,,	—	4 ,,	—	1 Jan.	—	22 ,,	—	19 ,,	—	12 ,,	—	9 ,,
TAKORADI ...	,,	25 Oct.	1 Nov.	15 ,,	28 Nov.	6 ,,	20 Dec.	3 ,,	17 Jan.	24 ,,	7 Feb.	21 ,,	7 Mar.	14 ,,	28 Mar.	11 ,,
ACCRA ...	,,	26 ,,	2 ,,	16 ,,	29 ,,	7 ,,	21 ,,	4 ,,	18 ,,	25 ,,	8 ,,	22 ,,	8 ,,	15 ,,	29 ,	12 ,,
LAGOS ...	,,	27 Oct.	3 ,,	17 ,,	30 ,,	8	22 ,,	5 ,,	19 ,,	26 ,,	9 ,,	23 ,,	9 ,,	16 ,,	30 ,,	13 ,,
PORT HARCOURT ...	,,	—	6 Nov.	—	3 Dec.	—	25 Dec.	—	22 Jan.	—	12 Feb.	—	12 Mar.	—	2 Apl.	—
SUELLABA (for Duala) VICTORIA CALABAR	,,	—	—	20/23 Nov	—	11/14 Dec	—	8/11 Jan.	—	29 Jan. 1 Feb.	—	26 Feb. 1 Mar.	—	19/22 Mar.	—	16/19 Apl.

† DOES NOT CALL SUELLABA (FOR DUALA) AND VICTORIA.

NORTHBOUND		M.V. ABOSSO	M.V. ACCRA	M.V. ADDA	M.V. APAPA	M.V. ABOSSO	M.V. ACCRA	M.V. ADDA	M.V. APAPA	M.V. ABOSSO	M.V. ACCRA	M.V. ADDA	M.V. APAPA	M.V. ABOSSO	M.V. ACCRA	M.V. ADDA
CALABAR ...	Depart	—	17/18 May	—	7/8 June	—	—	19/20 July	—	16/17 Aug.	—	6/7 Sept.	—	4/5 Oct.	—	25/26 Oct.
PORT HARCOURT	,,	4 May	—	25 May	—	22 June	6 July	—	3 Aug.	—	31 Aug.	—	21 Sept.	—	19 Oct	—
LAGOS ...	,,	7 ,,	21 May	28 ,,	11 June	25 ,,	9 ,,	23 ,,	6 ,,	20 Aug.	3 Sept.	10 Sept.	24 ,,	8 Oct.	22 ,,	29 Oct.
ACCRA ...	,,	8 ,,	22 ,,	29 ,,	12 ,,	26 ,,	10 ,,	24 ,,	7 ,,	21 ,,	4 ,,	11 ,,	25 ,,	9 ,,	23 ,,	30 ,,
TAKORADI ...	,,	8 ,,	22 ,,	29 ,,	12 ,,	26 ,,	10 ,,	24 ,,	7 ,,	21 ,,	4 ,,	11 ,,	25 ,,	10 ,,	24 ,,	31 ,,
MONROVIA ...	,,	—	24 ,,	—	14 ,,	—	12 ,,	—	9 ,,	—	6 ,,	—	27 ,,	—	26 ,,	—
FREETOWN ...	,,	11 May	25 ,,	1 June	15 ,,	29 June	13 ,,	27 July	10 ,,	24 Aug.	7 ,,	14 Sept.	28 ,,	13 Oct.	27 ,,	3 Nov.
BATHURST ...	,,	—	26 ,,	—	16 ,,	—	14 ,,	—	11 ,,	—	8 ,,	—	29 ,,	—	28 ,,	—
LAS PALMAS	,,	15 May	29 ,,	6 June	19 ,,	3 July	17 ,,	1 Aug.	14 .	28 Aug.	11 ,,	19 Sept	2 Oct.	17 Oct.	31 ,,	8 Nov.
MADEIRA ...	,,	16 ,,	30 ,,	7 ,,	20 ,,	4 ,,	18 ,,	2 ,,	15 ,,	29 ,,	12 ,,	20 ,,	3 ,,	18 ,,	1 Nov.	9 ,,
PLYMOUTH ...	Arrive	20 ,,	3 June	11 ,,	24 ,,	8 ,,	22 ,,	6 ,,	19 ,,	2 Sept.	16 ,,	24 ,,	7 ,,	22 ,,	5 ,,	13 ,,
LIVERPOOL ...	,,	21 May	4 June	12 June	25 June	9 July	23 July	7 Aug.	20 Aug.	3 Sept.	17 Sept.	25 Sept.	8 Oct.	23 Oct.	6 Nov.	14 Nov.

NORTHBOUND		M.V. ABA	M.V. APAPA	M.V. ABOSSO	M.V. ACCRA	M.V. ADDA	M.V. APAPA	M.V. ABOSSO	M.V. ACCRA	M.V. ADDA	M.V. APAPA	M.V. ABOSSO	M.V. ACCRA	M.V. ADDA	M.V. APAPA	M.V. ABOSSO
CALABAR ...	Depart	—	—	22/23 Nov.	—	13/14 Dec.	—	10/11 Jan.	—	31 Jan. 1 Feb.	—	28 Feb. 1 Mar.	—	21/22 Mar.	—	18/19 Apl.
PORT HARCOURT	,,	—	9 Nov.	—	6 Dec.	—	28 Dec.	—	25 Jan.	—	15 Feb.	—	15 Mar.	—	5 Apl.	—
LAGOS ...	,,	3 Nov.	12 ,,	26 Nov.	8 ,,	17 Dec.	31 ,,	14 Jan.	28 ,,	4 Feb.	18 ,,	4 Mar.	18 ,,	27 Mar	8 ,,	22 Apl.
ACCRA ...	,,	4 ,,	13 ,,	27 ,,	9 ,,	18 ,,	1 Jan.	15 ,,	29 ,,	5 ,,	19 ,,	5 ,,	19 ,,	28 ,,	9 ,,	23 ,,
TAKORADI ...	,,	4 ,,	14 ,,	28 ,,	10 ,,	19 ,,	2 ,,	16 ,,	30	6 ,,	20 ,,	6 ,,	20 ,,	29 ,,	9 ,,	23 ,,
MONROVIA ...	,,	—	16 ,,	—	12 ,,	—	4 ,,	—	1 Feb.	—	22 ,,	—	22 ,,	—	11 ,,	—
FREETOWN ...	,,	8 Nov.	17 ,,	1 Dec.	13 ,,	22 Dec.	5 ,	19 Jan.	2 ,,	9 Feb.	23 ,,	9 Mar.	23 ,,	1 Apl.	12 ,,	26 Apl.
BATHURST ...	,,	—	18 ,,	—	14 ,,	—	6 ,,	—	3 ,,	—	24 ,,	—	24 ,,	—	13 ,,	—
LAS PALMAS	,,	12 Nov.	21 ,,	5 Dec.	17 ,,	27 Dec.	9 ,,	23 Jan.	6 .	14 Feb.	27 ,,	13 Mar.	27 ,,	6 Apl.	16 ,,	30 Apl.
MADEIRA ...	,,	—	22 ,,	6 ,,	18 ,,	28 ,,	10 ,,	24 ,,	7 ,,	15 ,,	28 ,,	14 ,,	28 ,,	7 ,,	17 ,,	1 May
PLYMOUTH ...	Arrive	—	26 ,,	10 ,,	22 ,,	1 Jan.	14 ,,	28 ,,	11 ,,	19 ,,	4 Mar.	18 ,,	1 Apl.	11 ,,	21 ,,	5 ,,
LIVERPOOL ...	,,	17 Nov.	27 Nov.	11 Dec.	23 Dec.	2 Jan.	15 Jan.	29 Jan.	12 Feb	20 Feb	5 Mar.	19 Mar.	2 Apl	12 Apl.	22 Apl.	6 May

Inter-coastal connecting Services to Forcados, Warri, Port Harcourt, Calabar, Victoria and *Fernando Po are maintained by the M V "CALABAR" Passengers from the Mail Ships transfer at Lagos.
*If circumstances warrant.

Above: Royal Mail sailings 1938–9

Alongside: Sailing schedule 1962

9th January, 1962

SHIP	CAPTAIN	VOYAGE	LATEST REPORT		DESTINATION PORTS
LIVERPOOL - WEST AFRICA					
EXPRESS MAIL, PASSENGER AND CARGO SERVICE					
ACCRA	Lightbody, W. R. M.	122	Due LIVERPOOL	9th Jan.	Liverpool
APAPA	Ralston, P. M.	120	Left LIVERPOOL	4th Jan.	Bathurst, Freetown, Takoradi (E.T.A. 16th January), Apapa
AUREOL	Jenkins, T. E. M.	89	Leaving APAPA	9th Jan.	Liverpool (E.T.A. 22nd January)
EXPRESS CARGO AND PASSENGER SERVICE					
OWERRI	Weller, F.	25	Arrived BROMBOROUGH	7th Jan.	Liverpool
TAMELE	Cleator, J. A.	78	Leaving LIVERPOOL	13th Jan.	Freetown, Lagos, Victoria, Port Harcourt
TARKWA	Kingan, E.	81	Due FREETOWN	9th Jan.	Bromborough (E.T.A. 22nd January), Liverpool
LONDON - WEST AFRICA					
EXPRESS PASSENGER AND CARGO SERVICE					
CALABAR	Webber, F. St. H.	29	Left MADEIRA	7th Jan.	London (E.T.A. 12th January)
WINNEBA	Humphreys, W. E.	30	Leaving FREETOWN	9th Jan.	Takoradi (E.T.A. 12th January), Apapa
U.K./CONTINENT - WEST AFRICA					
SOUTHBOUND					
BHAMO	Sheridan, M.	14	Leaving LIVERPOOL	11th Jan.	Dakar, Bathurst, Conakry, Abidjan, Takoradi, Tema, Cotonou, Apapa, Sapele
DALLA	Brown, J. W.	3	Left DAKAR	7th Jan.	Bathurst, Freetown, Lower Buchanan (E.T.A. 12th Jan.), Abidjan, Takoradi, Accra, Tema, Lome, Apapa, Burutu, Warri, Sapele
DARU	Ness, A.	13	Left ROTTERDAM	7th Jan.	Conakry, Freetown, Takoradi, Lagos, Apapa, Port Harcourt, Douala, Victoria, Tiko, Santa Isabel, Calabar
DUMBAIA	Dunne, R. E.	4	Leaving CONAKRY	13th Jan.	Takoradi, Accra
EBANI	Bryan, W. B. R.	39	Leaving APAPA	10th Jan.	Port Harcourt
EBOE	Laddie, W.	39	Left LONDON	6th Jan.	Dakar, Apapa, Port Harcourt
EGORI	Hutchinson, J. W.	21	Leaving LONDON for R'dam	20th Jan.	Freetown, Lagos, Port Harcourt, Port Gentil, Matadi, Lobito
FOURAH BAY	Silvester, L. B.	1	Left MILFORD HAVEN	6th Jan.	Freetown, Takoradi (E.T.A. 18th Jan.), Lome, Cotonou, Apapa, Douala, Calabar, Pointe Noire, Matadi
KABALA	Laing, I. L.	11	Leaving LOWER BUCHANAN	8th Jan.	Takoradi, Lagos (E.T.A. 12th Jan.), Apapa, Port Harcourt
KEPWICKHALL	Strickland, H. G.	1	Leaving TAKORADI	7th Jan.	Burutu, Warri, Sapele
KINDAT	Hamilton, S. B.	37	Left LONDON	6th Jan.	Freetown, Takoradi, Accra, Tema, Burutu, Warri, Sapele
KOHIMA	Aitken, R. W. H.	29	Arrived MONROVIA	6th Jan.	Lower Buchanan, Grand Bassa, Sinoe, Cape Palmas
ONITSHA	James, L. L.	39	Leaving ROTTERDAM	10th Jan.	Freetown, Lagos, Apapa, Port Harcourt, Matadi, Lobito
SHERBRO	Nicholls, J.	55	Left LONDON	30th Dec.	Freetown, Abidjan, Takoradi (E.T.A. 15th Jan.), Douala, Victoria, Tiko, Calabar
SULIMA	Owen, S.	50	Leaving LIVERPOOL for Milford Haven	18th Jan.	Madeira, Las Palmas, Takoradi, Cape Coast, Winneba, Accra, Lome, Lagos, Burutu, Warri, Sapele
TRANSEUROPA	Barlag, Wilhelm	1	Due CONAKRY	8th Jan.	Abidjan, Accra (E.T.A. 17th Jan.), Tema, Lome, Cotonou, Warri, Burutu, Sapele
WOLFGANG RUSS	Gottfried Stolzenburg	1	Due FREETOWN	8th Jan.	Lagos, Apapa, Port Harcourt, Port Gentil, Matadi
WOOLWICH	Mudd R. T.	3	Due TAKORADI	9th Jan.	Winneba, Accra, Tema, Lagos (E.T.A. 15th Jan.), Apapa, Port Harcourt, Victoria, Calabar
NORTHBOUND					
DEGEMA	McWilliam, R.	10	Arrived AMSTERDAM	5th Jan.	Rotterdam
DEIDO	Coughlan, D. H.	3	Leaving LAGOS	10th Jan.	Holland (E.T.A. 27th January), London
DUMURRA	Rowlands, W.	2	Leaving MONROVIA	10th Jan.	Dublin (E.T.A. 19th January), Liverpool
DUNKWA	Brooke, J. A.	6	Leaving MONROVIA	7th Jan.	Hull (E.T.A. 19th January), London
KADEIK	McInnes, S. A.	31	Due SAPELE	10th Jan.	Dublin (E.T.A. 14th Feb.), Manchester, Liverpool
KADUNA	Wilkie, J.	19	Due ROTTERDAM	8th Jan.	London
KALADAN	Fox, S.	34	Arrived AVONMOUTH	8th Jan.	Liverpool
KALEWA	Armstrong, G. A.	44	Leaving SANTA ISABEL	9th Jan.	Amsterdam (E.T.A. 19th February), Bremen, Hamburg
KANBE	Coogans, J.	40	Leaving POINTE NOIRE	11th Jan.	Avonmouth (E.T.A. 17th February), Manchester, Liverpool
KANDAW	MacLeod, A.	24	Leaving SAPELE	15th Jan.	Belfast (E.T.A. 11th February), Manchester, Liverpool
KATHA	Hamilton, S. B.	41	Repairs North Shields		
KOYAN	Johnston, J. M.	31	Arrived ROTTERDAM	6th Jan.	Rotterdam
KENTUNG	Fair, M. F. M.	27	Leaving WARRI	8th Jan.	London (E.T.A. 15th February)
KUMBA	Grassick, J. S.	10	Arrived GREENOCK	6th Jan.	Glasgow, Liverpool
OBUASI	Bellamy, W. E.	35	Leaving CALABAR	9th Jan.	Manchester (E.T.A. 2nd February), Liverpool
PATANI	Jones, R. I.	25	Leaving LAGOS	11th Jan.	Aarhus (E.T.A. 7th Feb.), Copenhagen, Hamburg, Bremen
PEGU	Gibson, J. C.	2	Leaving LAGOS	9th Jan.	Rotterdam (E.T.A. 24th January), London
PERANG	Bentley, J.	24	Arrived ROTTERDAM	5th Jan.	Rotterdam
SHONGA	Woods, R. T. E.	55	Leaving ABONEMA	8th Jan.	Glasgow (E.T.A. 9th February), Liverpool
SOBO	Wild, R.	89	Arrived HULL	6th Jan.	Hamburg
SWEDRU	McCulloch, H.	50	Leaving LAGOS	12th Jan.	Bromborough (E.T.A. 29th January), Liverpool
MEDITERRANEAN - WEST AFRICA					
OTI	Pryce, N.	21	Due LAGOS	8th Jan.	Genoa (E.T.A. 8th February)
PRAHSU	Robinson, P.	10	Due ACCRA	9th Jan.	Tema, Lome, Lagos, Apapa, Port Harcourt
U.S.A. - WEST AFRICA					
DIXCOVE	Griffith, W.	10	Due TAKORADI	8th Jan.	Norfolk (E.T.A. 28th Jan.), Baltimore, Philadelphia, Boston, New York, Halifax N.S.
DONGA	Davies, A. G.	5	Due NORFOLK	10th Jan.	Baltimore, Philadelphia, Boston, New York, Halifax N.S.
PINEMORE	Saunders, I. R. C.	1	Due DOUALA	8th Jan.	U.S.A.
SALAGA	Hansen, E. R.	54	Leaving BALTIMORE	8th Jan.	Philadelphia, New York, Halifax N.S.
SEKONDI	Thomas, A. A.	52	Due TAKORADI	7th Jan.	Accra, Tema, Lagos (E.T.A. 12th Jan.), Apapa, Port Harcourt
CALCUTTA/EAST PAKISTAN-WEST AFRICA					
CLOVERBANK	Brant, R.		Leaving CALCUTTA for East Pakistan, Rangoon, Madras, Tuticorin	early Jan.	Luanda, Matadi, Douala, Apapa, Lagos, Cotonou, Lome, Tema, Accra, Takoradi, Abidjan, Freetown, Conakry, Bathurst
ISIPINGO			Due FREETOWN	9th Jan.	Bathurst
MINCHBANK	Carver, H. A.		Due ACCRA	4th Jan.	Takoradi, Abidjan, Freetown, Dakar
SHIRRABANK	Wigham, L.		Ready CALCUTTA	end Feb.	West Africa
WEST AFRICAN COASTAL SERVICE					
EKET	Anozie, J. S.		Oron Ferry Service		
FORCADOS	Wallace, P. D.		Nigerian Intercoastal Service		
ITU	Ekong, T. A.		Oron Ferry Service		
ORON	Bassey, L. O.		Oron Ferry Service		
SAPELE	Greenwood, R.		Freetown/Monrovia Service, Arrived MONROVIA	5th Jan.	

BUILDING

VESSEL	8,000 tons d/w at Greenock
VESSEL	8,000 tons d/w at Port Glasgow
VESSEL	8,000 tons d/w at Port Glasgow
VESSEL	8,000 tons d/w at Port Glasgow
VESSEL	8,000 tons d/w at Port Glasgow

Our Fleet at strength again

Rebuilding since 1946 – Wartime casualties made good – Elder Dempster ships since the War

WAR always produces a grim balance sheet. The Second World War produced the grimmest balance sheet in man's heroic, tortured history.

The losses in men and ships suffered by Britain's Merchant Navy provide the substance of one of the heaviest entries in Britain's accounts and the material for a saga of endurance, fortitude, bravery not surpassed in the most splendid pages of history.

So it was, too, with Elder Dempster. In the summer of 1938 the Elder Dempster flag was flown by no fewer than forty-two sea-going vessels. Of these twenty-six were claimed as victims of the war at sea: only sixteen survived. Only a fraction of these lossses could be replaced during the war, but five ships were added to the fleet, bringing the strength to twenty-one on V.E. day. Pre-war tonnage was 213,000 tons gross: at the end of the war it was 108,000 tons gross.

These were the hard facts that the Board of Management of Elder Dempsters had to face. Of the mail boats, the *Aba* was the sole survivor of the war. She had been fitted out as a hospital ship, and, as such, she had performed magnificent service. But, she, too, after the war was deemed to be too old to merit the cost of refitting and was sold.

Added to the difficulties caused by the drastic reduction in the fleet and the high cost of rebuilding, the Managers had also to weigh problems which were novel and difficult to resolve. There was the whole question of the future of the trade with West Africa.

This trade had been seriously dislocated by the war and to attempt to estimate its future and its requirements was almost impossible for the Managers.

There was also the question of air transport. No one knew and no one could guess with any accuracy the effect of air travel on the demand for sea passages. During the war immense advances had been made in aviation and these, transferred to civil aviation, constituted a new factor which had to be taken into account. The Board found some consolation in their long experience of the Coast. If there were unknown factors to be reckoned with, at least they had some satisfaction in the knowledge that no company had such a complete understanding of the known factors.

They therefore faced the future with confidence and without undue lamentation for the heavy toll of war, they bent themselves to the task of replacement and rebuilding.

* * *

Reference is made elsewhere in this issue to the achievement of salving the *Sangara*, torpedoed off the West African coast in 1941, and towed to the United Kingdom for repairs and refit in 1946. One of the first casualties became one of the first replacements of depleted strength.

* * *

1946 As an immediate step towards bringing the fleet up to strength the Company purchased from the Canadian Government five standard cargo ships.

s.s. *Zini.*

M.V. *Shonga.*

After the war, Canadian opinion was in favour of the establishment of a Canadian Merchant Navy. It was required that the vessels should be registered in Canada and the crews should be composed of Canadian seamen. To this end, a new company, Elder Dempster Lines (Canada) Limited, was incorporated, and the vessels were registered in Montreal.

The service to South Africa was carried on for about four years, but in 1950 it became impractical to continue it. There were many reasons for this. The restriction of import into South Africa was one: the dollar shortage was another. Clearly the volume of cargo from Canada to the Cape had seriously declined. Nor was the dream of establishing a Canadian Merchant Navy exactly happy in its fulfilment. It produced constant problems both for the Canadian owners and for the Canadian Government. The general high level of wages in Canada made competition with other nations extremely difficult: finally a protracted seamen's strike settled the fate of Canada's Merchant Navy. Elder Dempster concluded arrangements whereby the five vessels were transferred to United Kingdom Registry and manned by British crews. The trade between Canada and the Cape was carried on, on behalf of Elder Dempster, by the Union Castle Mail Steamship Company Limited. The "C" class ships which had not been sailing fully loaded were now put to better use in the United Kingdom-West Africa and other services.

* * *

In 1946 the Company decided to buy two standard coasters which it had already been operating for the Government in West Africa. Steamers of one thousand tons, they were renamed the *Sapele* and the *Warri*. They had been designed for service in the Far East but their shallow draught and other features made them completely suitable for tropical service, for the shallows of the West Africa coast and for running to the creeks. Based on Lagos, the coasters proved a great success and another vessel of this type, the *Forcados*, was acquired three years later.

The names of these ships in part reflect the growing industrial development of West Africa since the war, development due in part to the exertions of the great private companies such as the United Africa Company, and partly to the money made available through Colonial Development and Welfare. Before the war Sapele was a mere bush market town on the edge of the jungle, but also happily placed on the bend of the river. It was chosen by the United Africa Company as the site of a great lumber development. In the jungle great trees, most of them over one hundred years old, are felled and floated downstream to Sapele. There, at one of the world's most up-to-date plywood factories, they are sawn, rolled, milled and pressed; and now Sapele plywood is known all over the world. A similar development has taken place at Samreboi in the Gold

M.V. *Benin*.

Coast. Today, in addition to plywood, some of the finest furnishing woods reach the world markets from West Africa. Elder Dempster ships play their full part in this transportation.

* * *

1947 Two liberty ships which had been under the Company's management were purchased in 1947. The Company had adopted the practice of giving to the ships in each class of vessel names beginning with the same initial letter. As this class was likely to be small, the letter "Z" was selected as a means towards the more economical use of the alphabet. The two ships were re-named the *Zini* and the *Zungeru*. A little later, a third ship of this class was purchased. To her was given the name *Zungon*.

1947 saw the Company's rebuilding programme begin to produce substantial results. That year saw the completion and the coming into service of the first of the new "S" class ships. Built to the Company's own design, it was a development of the popular and efficient pre-war "S" class which in itself had represented a great advance in the design for the West African trade.

Into the design and building of these ships went all those features which a century's experience of the trade and the latest technical knowledge made possible. Approximately 4,800 tons gross, and with a speed of twelve and a half knots, these motor vessels are of a size which allows them to navigate and load in areas where larger vessels are hampered by the West African shallows. In each, twelve passengers can be accom-

M.V. *Onitsha*.

510

modated in eight single and two double-berth cabins, and the ships have proved most popular with those passengers who prefer a leisurely voyage between strenuous tours, or who wish to sail direct to or from ports not normally served by the mail boats. The ships are named the *Salaga*, the *Sekondi*, the *Sherbro*, the *Shonga*, the *Sulima* and the *Swedru*.

After a lapse of several years, during which large numbers of passengers had been compelled, *faut de mieux*, to travel by troopship, the mail boat re-entered the U.K.-West Africa scene in 1947. The R.M.V. *Accra*

M.V. *Eboe*.

represented a development of the *Abosso*, the flagship, which was lost in 1942. The R.M.V. *Accra* and the R.M.V. *Apapa* (which was completed in 1948) bear the names of the earlier mail boats which were lost in 1940. Of 11,600 tons gross, each of these ships has a speed of sixteen knots. They carry a complement of 245 first and 24 third class passengers and have 142 cabins. Originally they maintained a three-weekly service between Liverpool, Las Palmas, Freetown, Takoradi and Apapa. Their comfort and cuisine are freely acknowledged: they brought to West Africa a welcome symbol of the skill of the North Country. On leaves, they provide for those who have willingly subjected themselves to the strains, as well as the satisfactions, of life on the Coast, a touch of luxury which is not unwelcome to those who serve West Africa, often enough in lonely stations far from the amenities of twentieth century living.

1948 saw the completion of the immediate post-war building programme.

*   *   *

1950 In 1950, the collier *Baro* and the coaster *Benin* joined the fleet. Both these ships are steamers, the first to be built to the order of Elder Dempster since 1924 – a striking commentary on the popularity of the diesel engine. The *Baro* (1,500 tons gross) is normally employed in the coal trade from Port Harcourt while the *Benin* (2,483 tons gross) is on the West Africa-South Africa service or on West African coastal work. The seven thousand ton steamer *Avisbay*, which had been on charter, was purchased by the Company in 1950 and renamed *Prah*. She is a steamer with a history: she started life as a naval auxiliary and was extensively

altered by her first commercial owners before joining the Elder Dempster fleet.

In the meantime, it had been possible to make a judgment on the effect – actual and probable – of civilian airline competition on the passenger trade to and from West Africa. The number of passengers to West Africa was perceptibly increasing. Long waiting lists for passengers showed that the competition from the air was not quite so formidable as there had been at one time some reason to imagine. The mail boats sailed regularly with scarcely a vacant berth.

*   *   *

1951 It was therefore with confidence, as well as some legitimate pride, that the flagship *Aureol* was brought into the service in 1951: the advent of the flagship enabled the Company to announce fortnightly sailings to and from West Africa.

The *Aureol* is by any standard an outstanding vessel. Of 14,800 tons gross she is by far the largest ship ever owned by Elder Dempster Line or by our predecessors. She is, too, quite certainly the most handsome ship to sail under Elder Dempster colours since the beautiful West Indies ships of half a century ago.

Five hundred feet long, the *Aureol* is a motor vessel with a speed of sixteen knots. She carries 269 first-class and 76 cabin class passengers who are able to enjoy the amenities of a ship on which time, labour, money and infinite thought were spent.

*   *   *

1952 Two rather unusual cargo ships were added to the Fleet in 1952 – the *Eboe* and the *Ebani*. Each of 9,000 tons gross and with a speed of sixteen knots, these motor ships constitute the first class specially designed and built for the United States – West Africa service. Twelve passengers are carried in most comfortable accommodation, each cabin having its own bathroom. As in all the post-war ships, too, the crew accommodation is excellent, and in these ships each member of the crew enjoys a cabin to himself. The *Ebani* and the *Eboe* are the third and fourth Elder Dempster ships to bear these names and they meet the demand for a direct service between New York and the Congo.

1952 also saw a notable addition to the ships available to the Company's fleet when the Holdings Company obtained control of the British and Burmese Steam Navigation Company Limited. Managed by P. Henderson & Company – and better known as "the Henderson Line" – this company had built since the war a number of motor ships, many of which had been chartered by Elder Dempster. Bearing Burmese place names, these "K" class ships have proved most suitable for the West African trade, and the control of the owning Company ensures their constant availability. Three ships now under construction will bring this class up to a total of eleven ships, averaging 5,500 tons gross.

The *Onitsha* and the *Obuasi* were also completed in 1952. Cargo ships of 5,800 tons gross and with a speed of 12½ knots, they represent an enlarged version of the "S" class. The *Onitsha* is equipped with a 150-ton derrick which makes her the heavy-weight ship of the fleet, supplementing the duties carried out for so long by the *Mary Kingsley*.

* * *

1953 Three ships (in addition to the "K" class vessels already mentioned) are now being built for Elder Dempster. One is the *Owerri*, a sister ship to the *Onitsha* and the *Obuasi*, and two vessels which are to be named the *Patani* and the *Perang*. The new "P" class ships will be about 6,000 tons gross and have a speed of 11½ knots.

There is, of course, a corollary to the building up of the Fleet – the disposal of ships which have become redundant or are too old for the particular service. At the end of the war, the *Aba* was the sole survivor of the mail boats: she had been fitted out as a hospital ship and as such she had given magnificent service throughout the war. On her return to civilian life she was considered not to be worth the cost of reconversion, and was sold. The *Biafra*, the sole survivor of the biggest class – of fourteen ships – ever owned by Elder Dempster, was sold in 1951: she is still in service and has since visited the West Africa coast under her new name, *George*. The *Macgregor Laird* was sold recently to the Anglo-Saxon Petroleum Company Limited, who have converted her into a depot ship for service in connection with the search for underwater oil. The Company particularly regretted parting with the *Calabar* which was also sold this year. Built in 1935, she clearly had many useful years of service before her. During the war, and after, she maintained the passenger service between West Africa and Capetown which she herself had instituted. Circumstances made it impossible to continue the *Calabar* on this run

and she became redundant as a member of the Elder Dempster Fleet.

The curtailing of one or two services has had its compensation in the initiation of new services. Regular sailings outward are now being made from Glasgow. Homeward calls have been made at ports not usually served – to the West Hartlepools with timber, for loading at Middlesbrough and, most unusually, at Ipswich. Our ships have made several calls at Scandinavian ports since the war and even sail sometimes beyond the Iron Curtain with cargoes of cocoa for Gdynia.

* * *

Cargoes, too, change. Timber has already been mentioned. There is an increased tendency for oil to be carried in bulk. The United Kingdom finds in the raw materials of West Africa a constantly increasing source of supply to replace traditional markets now closed for currency or other reasons. The outward trade has been stimulated by the increased spending power of the West African population and the great programme of development: the construction of the Takoradi Harbour, the extensions to which were formally opened earlier this year; the projected Volta Dam power scheme; the works initiated by Colonial Development and Welfare; and projects put in hand by the Nigerian and Gold Coast Governments themselves; all contribute to a rapidly expanding economy.

In point of number of vessels and of carrying capacity, the Elder Dempster Fleet will be maintained at such a strength as will enable it to meet all the demands caused by these new developments.

* * *

Always there is a touch of poetry in this linking of these thrusting, emerging nations of West Africa with the Mother Country which has played such an important part in their development. "Out of Africa always something new ..." Much will emerge in the years ahead that is new and vital – not only for this great awakening Continent but for the older civilizations of the West. We believe our long experience of the Coast, our long friendship with the peoples of West Africa, our dedication to the needs of those who serve West Africa, either on the Coast or in the United Kingdom, will continue to be of value. We provide the ships and the men to man them, and it is a pleasant thing that here, too, Africa and Britain meet and that the young men now being trained include not only the descendants of those who have sailed the seas for a thousand years, but also keen, alert young West African midshipmen who are showing themselves eager to acquire a knowledge of navigation and to submit to that discipline which is the making of a good ship's company, a good fleet, a good *service*.

Loading Nigerian timber into Tamele's hold.

From Sea *Magazine*

A Master looks back on 30 years of change in W. African shipping

by Captain Robin Munro

Captain Robin McLeod Munro reflects on 30 years' service with the Company between 1952-82, a period embracing tremendous changes in the West African trades. His first command was a conventional cargo liner, 'Maradi' in 1965. His last ship before retirement was 'combo' containership 'Sekondi'.

I JOINED Elder Dempster's s.s. 'Cabano' in London docks on a dull winter's day in October, 1952, an apprehensive young officer since my previous sea-going career had been spent mostly in the Far East or, just prior to joining Elders, on the Australian and New Zealand services of another shipping company.

On those services stevedoring and cargo handling had been the business of shore establishments, ships' officers having purely a watching and supervising brief. The ports were sophisticated and there was plenty of spare time and opportunity for a young man to make the most of the visits.

But now I was entering a completely different world where ships' officers had to work long hours overseeing the discharge and loading of cargo on the West African coast. This required actual physical supervision; knowledge was not enough. A young officer personally had to sling heavy or awkward lifts as well as ensuring that cargo was not damaged or overcarried.

It was also his personal responsibility to rig the derricks and prepare his section for cargo working – the Third Officer on the fore-deck and the Second Officer on the after-deck. An officer was on duty throughout the time his section was working, quite possibly from daylight to late at night. This could then be followed by an overnight run to the next discharging port.

So the work continued from the time a ship arrived on the West African coast until she left the last port on the homeward voyage. I remember it as a time of being perpetually tired and dirty; of looking forward to work ceasing so that one could have a shower and a little relaxation before resting in preparation for the next day.

However, in retrospect it was a

'Creek navigation was more exacting in the early years . . .' (From a painting, circa 1963, by John Stobart).

rewarding time. For a young officer was able to put into practice aspects of his training which were not needed on runs to more advanced parts of the world. It was a time of continual learning, not only for young officers but also for many of those who now hold senior positions in Elder Dempster and in the governments and harbour authorities of the West African countries which were shortly to gain their independence.

Although I did not know it at the time, I made my first voyage with Elder Dempster at the start of a period of many changes. Some ports I visited I was seldom if ever to see again. Places such as Cape Coast, Winneba, Abonema and latterly Victoria were phased out and the surf ports of Accra, Lome and Cotonou were replaced by man-made harbours.

Ports continued to change over the years – and are still changing! Some disappeared altogether, some were replaced by new ones while others like Abidjan and Lagos prospered and grew to unimagined size. Yet others fell into decline, to be rejuvenated latterly as government money is made available to expand hard-pressed and antiquated ports and facilities.

It has been a period in which Kroo labour for working cargo at the various ports was phased out as local stevedoring firms were set up, employing indigenous labour. During the early days of the newly-formed stevedoring companies one often met – and it was a pleasure to do so – people one had worked with previously on board ship, as likely as not in a physical or labouring capacity. Because of what we had all learnt together they were now in the forefront of the exacting business of employing and training labour which in the majority of cases had never seen or worked in a ship before.

African staff

Changes were also occurring in the various shipping agencies on the Coast. A nucleus of expatriates devoted a large percentage of their time to training African staff to become the agents and managers of the future and eventually take over the running of the agencies.

Little did any of us at that time envisage how far-reaching all the changes would be. But friends were made in a way which earned mutual respect for varying points of view and it was largely due to these friendships that the transition during the past 30 years has been made with every one endeavouring to make a success of each

'The skill of the Takoradi log gangs is legendary . . .'

new innovation and change.

Elder Dempster was always to the fore in this period of change, not least regarding ships and crews. It was the Company's farsightedness (although not always appreciated by sea staff at the time) which led to the introduction of West African cadets on board ED ships and to the setting up of training facilities for West African crews.

In later years – when I had become a Master – many pilots, harbourmasters and senior officials boarded my ships and took delight in announcing that they were Elder Dempster-trained. That early training, as with our own staff, has paid dividends. At the formation of the Nigerian National Shipping Company and Black Star Line the co-operation between sea-going staff could only be matched by that between the agency staffs as the 'fledglings' spread their wings.

Cargo has been changing throughout my years in the West African trade, from the early days of break-bulk to the present time when all I can envisage for the future is the full use of containerisation, roll-on/roll-off and bulk shipping. Whatever the future holds I feel that the more exciting days of the West African trade are over (although one can never be sure). So much has changed in a

relatively short space of time that it is hard to believe that another transformation could come about in the next 30 years.

When I first arrived on the West African scene every ship sailed home full. Space was at a premium. Sawn timber was stowed plank by plank to utilise every inch of space. Logs were bulldozed into position above and below decks by means of bullropes.

Takoradi log gangs

The skill of the Takoradi log gangs is legendary, especially when one remembers that in those days ships were ordinary shelter and 'tween deckers, not specifically designed for such cargoes, as vessels are now. It was a joy to watch and work with a good timber gang under, for example, Willie Joe as they chased their logs and slid them into seemingly impossible positions.

Today, daily tonnages of logs loaded are more than double those of Willie Joe's day. However, were it possible to arrange a competition between one of the old log-loading gangs and one from the present day my money would be on the old gang and on their stowing more tonnage in a given space!

Very little produce is now being

exported from West African countries –
with the notable exceptions of the Ivory
Coast and Cameroon – but it is to be
hoped that this trend will change and
that once again ships will sail home fully
laden. This could only be beneficial to
both exporting and importing
countries.

Changes usually came later in the
West African trade than elsewhere, due
to the nature of the trade itself and also
to the lack of facilities in West African
ports. As the benefits of palletisation,
mechanical handling and finally containerisation became evident in other
trades Elder Dempster was in the forefront of their introduction into West
African trades.

But these moves produced their own
problems as the majority of ports were
just not equipped to handle modern
stowage, nor were the stevedoring
companies up to the new ideas. When
one looks back it really was very much a
case of improvisation, for, cargoes
loaded with mechanical equipment
could be the very devil to discharge
without.

Frequently chaos reigned but progress could not be denied. I doubt
whether some of the earlier shipments
were a success, financially or otherwise,
but it was a beginning of the move
which forced a change in thinking both
on board ship and in West African
ports.

These days ships' officers and port
authorities in West Africa are far more
aware of the advantages of modern
mechanical equipment, stowage and
handling methods – especially of the
costs involved when a ship is delayed
awaiting shoreside transport.

For various reasons not all goods can
be discharged direct on to the wharf. A
large amount of cargo has to be discharged straight into a consignee's
transport and this can cause serious
problems.

An efficient ship's officer on the West
African coast is not now concerned
purely with the safe stowage of cargo
and optimum port rotation. A third
element has crept in – the ability to
continue work should a consignee fail to
turn up to take delivery of his cargo.

This is an area which can and does
cause frustration. Fortunately, relations between ship and consignee are
usually very good, born of an understanding over the years of each other's
problems. Each needs to realise that in
the long run, close co-operation well in
advance will help to avoid the frustra-
tions of the non-arrival of consignees'
transport or equally those of a consignee kept waiting while other cargo is
worked because his transport was not
available when requested.

Post-war fleet

There have been big changes, too, in
ships in the past 30 years. In the 1950s
Elder Dempster's fleet included wartime-built ships such as the 'Z' Class
(American 'Liberty' ships) and the 'C'
Class (of which the 'Cabano' was one,
built in Canada for the British Government and sold to shipping companies
after the war). There were also the new
class of 'S' boats built after the war for
the trade, and the new mail boats were
in service in a flourishing passenger
trade. The wartime-built ships were
functional but were not really suited to
the West African trade. They were a
stop gap while a new fleet designed for
the trade was built up.

The new fleet was designed, above all,
to lift from the Creek ports the
maximum amount of cargo on the
minimum draught. Ships had more and
heavier cargo-handling derricks and
also deep tanks for carrying palm oil,
then a large export commodity from
West Africa, and also latex from
Monrovia. But it was the Creeks which
governed the ships and their design and
which made the trade unique.

A ship entering the Creeks – and most
were programmed to do so – had to be
self-sufficient in every way and yet had
to ensure it was carrying only the
minimum in fuel and water to allow the
maximum lift of cargo. One hundred
tons of fresh water earned nothing
whereas 100 tons of cargo did – and
there was invariably cargo available.

Stowage and the distribution of cargo
was critical. These had to be worked out
and checked several times a day towards
the end of loading to ensure that under-
declaration of log weights and water
content of the logs were both taken into
consideration so that the ship would be
trimmed correctly in the end.

'Sekondi'... 'My last ship... her sophisticated equipment has simplified the workload...'

In addition to trim, allowance had, and still has, to be made for the difference in the density of the river water at, say, Sapele and of the sea water at the bar. This could be worth an extra several hundred tons of cargo – and it was always a matter of pride to load your ship to the maximum.

Over the years there was many an irate shipper whose cargo had been shut out from a particular ship. But they understood the problems, one of the main causes being under-declaration of weights or because logs had been in water for a long time. Every effort was made to load to the maximum draught, trusting on occasions to that little bit of extra water which experience has taught us is there when leaving the Creeks. The latter is yet another example of lessons learnt over the years, all of which can be critical – and judged only by the man on the spot.

Knowledge of anticipated conditions at various times of the year is still passed on from Master to Mate and makes the trade that bit unusual. But it is personal experience that counts in the end. Shortly before I retired the Creek pilots were on strike. But because of my experience we carried on to our destination – followed by four ships that were strangers to the Creeks.

Creek navigation

Creek navigation was more exacting in the early years since the ships, although designed with large-area rudders, did not have the manoeuvrability of today's vessels. Fortunately the Creeks are mangrove swamp areas with soft mud, and so running into the bank was no problem.

Indeed, in such places as the 'fork' on the way up to Sapele it was policy to clip the inner bank to help erode it and in course of time make a larger turning area. Nowadays it is the exception to run into the bank since over the years the bend has become enlarged and less acute.

Little did one suspect in the early years that dredging would clear and straighten the sharper bends and deepen the channels through shoal water. Ships now load far deeper, and the days of 'bumping' over the bar are behind us.

The 'F' Class were the last Elder Dempster ships designed and built specifically for the West African trade. Indeed, in my opinion they were the last of the Company's vessels which could be termed 'ships' – as opposed to the cargo carriers operated today.

Present-day designs with accommodation and engine room situated aft, now becoming common practice, do not, it seems to me, look like ships. However, these new designs have been evolving a long time and do make maximum use of carrying capacity, which when all is said and done is the main objective.

I sailed as Master of 'Fourah Bay' for several years and this was a most interesting period since the ship was not only one of the last of the Company's conventional vessels but she was also used to experiment with new ideas.

Originally a full cadet ship, 'Fourah Bay' was latterly involved in various developments in automation including bridge control of the engine, a method then in its infancy. She also inaugurated the Apapa Express Service, which was designed to speed up the flow of cargo from Liverpool to Apapa, replacing the scheduled mail boat service, the latter ships having outlived their usefulness.

Containerisation

Containerisation began and alterations were made to 'Fourah Bay' to improve her container capacity and cargo handling, thus ensuring the quick turnrounds required by the new schedule. From this developed the present-day system of UK/West Africa Lines' scheduled express services to and from mainline ports, augmented by 'sweeper' services covering the smaller ports where priority berthing cannot be guaranteed nor schedules maintained with any degree of accuracy.

My last ship was 'Sekondi'. She is one of the new breed of 'combo' carriers with a capacity for both containers and break-bulk cargo, designed for worldwide trading. With increased cargo-handling capabilities in West Africa, she is ideal for the trade. Not too large, she is also eminently suitable for the Creeks.

Her sophisticated equipment, both navigational and cargo-handling, has simplified the workload. However, modern aids also bring new and additional problems, especially on the engineering side. But training and experience, plus a dedicated and efficient staff such as I was fortunate to have in 'Sekondi', made my last few years in the West African trade easier.

Changes continue and traditional shore jobs such as budgeting and repairs are the norm for seafarers as ships become more self-supporting units. Now, having retired and had time to reflect, I believe I was fortunate to have been involved in this period of change and expansion of the West African trade and with the proud name of Elder Dempster.

From
Sea *Magazine*

A Railway Engine named 'Elder Dempster'

'Elder Dempster Lines' was one of the 'Merchant Navy' Class Locomotives first introduced in 1941 by the Southern Railway. Each of the locomotives bore the name of a well-known shipping company and many technical features, new at the time, were introduced in their construction. In 1956 British Railways re-designed this 'Merchant Navy' Class and the re-designed 'Elder Dempster Lines' locomotive emerged in 1958 from British Railway's Eastleigh works. The photograph shows the locomotive in its rebuilt form, it was withdrawn from service in July, 1967, with the introduction of electrified services on the Bournemouth Line.

ACKNOWLEDGEMENTS

The authors wish to record their thanks to the undermentioned for information, recollections, and assistance given, and in particular they which to record their appreciation of the support and encouragement of Ocean Transport and Trading plc, without which this work would have been impossible.

Lloyd's Register of Shipping
The Public Records Office, Kew
The Guildhall Library, London
The Merseyside County and Maritime Museums, Liverpool
The Registrar General of Shipping and Seamen, Cardiff
Strathclyde Regional Archives
Archive and Record Centre, Dundee
The staff and former staff of Elder Dempster Lines Limited
The Elders of Elders—The Elder Dempster Pensioners Association
The Ex-Pursers' Circle (EPC)
The Central Record team of the World Ship Society
Cammell Laird plc, Birkenhead
Compagnie Maritime Belge du Congo, Antwerp
Hapag-Lloyd, Hamburg
Ministry of Defence, Naval Historical Branch, London
Woermann Linie, Hamburg
J. Cook
Commander I. C. Bailey-Wilmot, RN, HMS Londonderry
M. J. Crossley Evans
D. Keen
W. Bramford Hallam
G. Mercier
L. Norbury-Williams
K. C. Griffin
Professor A. E. Rodin, MA (Wright State University, Dayton, Ohio)
J. Allen

Many others not individually mentioned have contributed freely of their time and recollections. We are very grateful to them all.

The following works were consulted during the course of our researches, and in certain cases we are obliged to the editors for permission to reproduce copyright material. Wherever possible copyright holders have been approached for permission; if any have inadvertently been overlooked we can only offer our humble apologies.

Cape Times, Cape Town
Elder Dempster House Magazine 1922–1926
Sea—The Elder Dempster House Magazine 1953–1984
Fairplay Shipping Weekly
The Irish Times
Liverpool Courier
Liverpool Daily Post
The Liverpool Echo
The Journal of Commerce
Lloyd's Daily Index
Lloyd's Law Reports
Lloyd's List
Lloyd's Lists of Missing Ships
Marine News (Journal of the World Ship Society)
Mercantile Navy List
Mercantile Marine Magazine 1857
Profile Warships—Kriegsmarine U107 (Dr Jurgen Rohwer)
Sea Breezes
Ships Monthly
The Times

African Steamship Company Minute Books
Blohm und Voss (Hans Georg Prager)
British Merchant Vessels Lost at Sea 1914–1918 (HMSO)
British Merchant Vessels Lost at Sea 1939–1945 (HMSO)
Canadian Pacific Steamship Company (George Musk)
Compagnie Maritime Belge, Antwerp 1895–1945 (Lloyd Royal)
Dictionary of Disasters at Sea (Charles Hocking)
Die U Boot Erfolge der Achsenmachte 1939–1945 (Dr Jurgen Rohwer)
The Elder Dempster Fleet in the War 1914–1918 (R. J. Paul)
A History of the United Molasses Company Limited 1926–1975 (W. A. Meneight, MBE)
The Hopper Dredger (Its History, Development, and Operation (F. C. Schefiauer)
The Legend behind the Name (K. St Johnston, N. C. F. Barber and T. J. Bond)
The Lion and the Unicorn (F. Pedler)
A Merchant Fleet at War (Capt. S. W. Roskill, RN)
The Merchant Navy (Archibald Hurd)
North Atlantic Seaway (N. R. P. Bonsor)
The Overseas Pensioner
The Passage Makers (M. Stammers)
The Price of Peace—Elder Dempster 1939–1945 (J. E. Cowden)
Ships and South Africa (Marischal Murray)
A Short History of the ships of John Holt & Company (Liverpool) Limited and the Guinea Gulf Line Limited
Sir Alfred L. Jones—Shipping Entrepreneur par Excellence (Dr P. N. Davies)
Song of the Clyde (F. M. Walker)
The Trade Makers—Elder Dempster in West Africa 1852–1972 (Dr P. N. Davies)
Trading in West Africa (Dr P. N. Davies, MA, PhD, PRSA)
The Tides of War and the Port of Bristol 1914–1918 (W. G. Neale)
U-Boats in the Atlantic (P. Beaver)
Victoria Cross Battles of the Second World War (C. E. Lucas-Phillips)
The White Ships (R. M. Parsons)
Victims of Yalta (Count Nikolai Tolstoy)
Yes, we have some—The story of Elders & Fyffes (P. Beaver)

The authors and publishers wish to add their thanks and appreciation to the printers, Page Bros (Norwich) Ltd, and in particular to John Hutchinson, for their skill in translating this work into volume form and for their sound advice and encouragement.

ILLUSTRATIONS

Photographs are acknowledged *in situ*, other than those supplied from the Departments of Archives and Public Relations of Ocean Transport and Trading plc, and/or the authors' collections. We are grateful to all those who supplied photographs. Every effort has been made to identify copyright holders but in the case of certain photographs this has not been possible. If, therefore, we have unintentionally infringed we wish to apologise. Every endeavour has been made to faithfully reproduce material, some of which is archival material, and some of which has suffered the ravages of time.

INDEX TO FLEET LIST

*Launch of **SHONGA** (ship No. 312), showing her name painted on the white half-rounds* (Photo J. Hall)

STOP PRESS

586 MEMNON (II)

O.N. 378037   1986–

'Menelaus' class
Steel screw motorship
164.520 m×26.070 m×10.630 m
Tmk 5537 n, 10,443 g, 17,000 d, 8666 n, 16,031 g, 21,242 d.
Built by Mitsubishi Heavy Industries Ltd, Nagasaki, Yard
No 1807, for Airlease International Nominees (Moorgate) Ltd
(Ocean Fleets Ltd, Managers). Registered Liverpool. Sulzer
oil engine 2 SCSA 8 cyl 760 mm–1550 mm by the builders.
16,800 bhp (12,357 Kw). 18 K.
1977   Launched by Mrs P. Walters. August, completed.
1980   Transferred to Barber Menelaus Shipping Corp

(Ocean Fleets Ltd, Managers). Renamed **BARBER MEMNON**. Registered Monrovia. Tmk 5244 n, 9436 g, 15,293 d. 8685 n, 14,905 g, 21,287 d.
1983   Transferred to Airlease International Nominees (Moorgate) Ltd (Ocean Fleets Ltd, Managers). Renamed **MEMNON**. Registered Liverpool.
1984   Chartered to Lloyd Brasileiro, Brazil. Renamed **LLOYD SAN FRANCISCO**.
1985   Tmk 5536 n, 10,442 g, 15,293 d, 8666 n, 16,030 g, 21,287 d.
1986   January, returned to owners and renamed **MEMNON**. March, allocated to West African service of Elder Dempster Lines Ltd. In the present fleet.

528

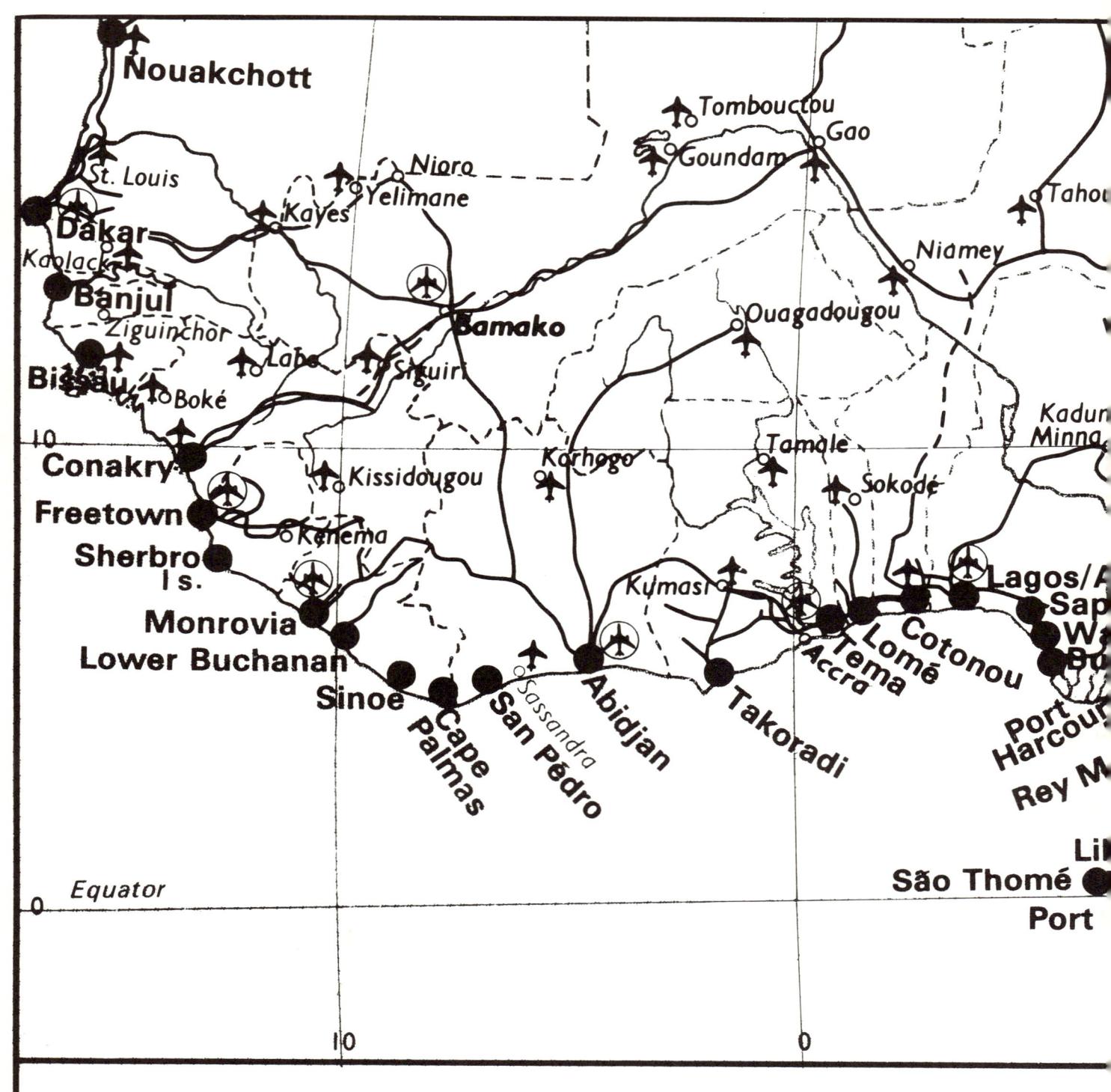

APPROXIMATE DISTANCES TO LONDON BY SEA

Name	Nautical Miles	Name	Nautic
Nouakchott	2397	Cotonou	4
Dakar	2534	Lagos/Apapa	4
Banjul	2620	Port Harcourt	4
Bissau	2725	Douala	4
Conakry	2935	Rey Malabo	4
Freetown	3008	Bata	4
Monrovia	3187	Libreville	4
Abidjan	3642	Pointe Noire	4
Tema	3875	Matadi	4
Lomé	3985	Luanda	4

© 1975   George Philip & Son Limited

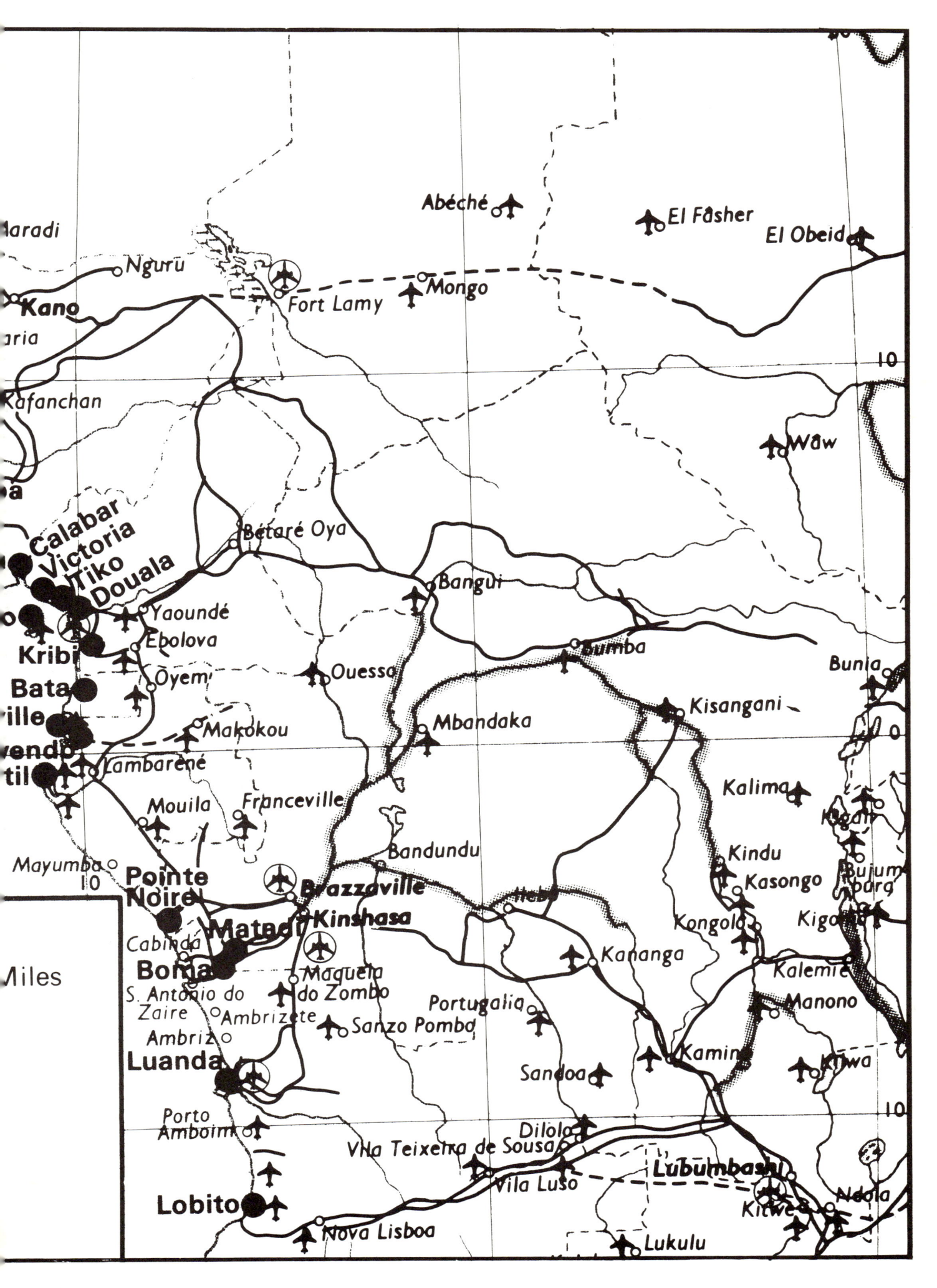